I0902545

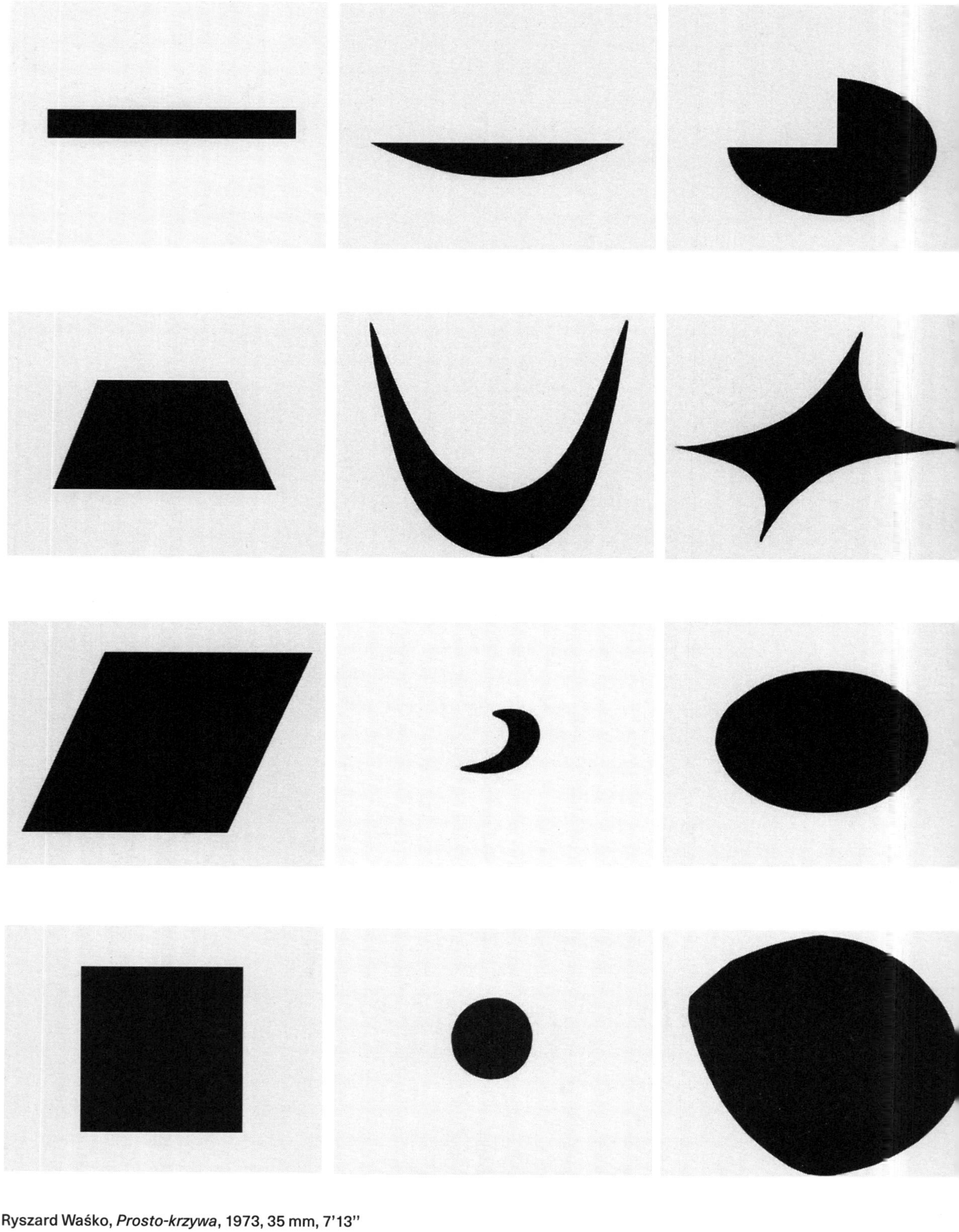

Ryszard Waśko, *Prosto-krzywa*, 1973, 35 mm, 7’13’’
Ryszard Waśko, *The Straight Curve*, 1973, 35 mm, 7’13’’

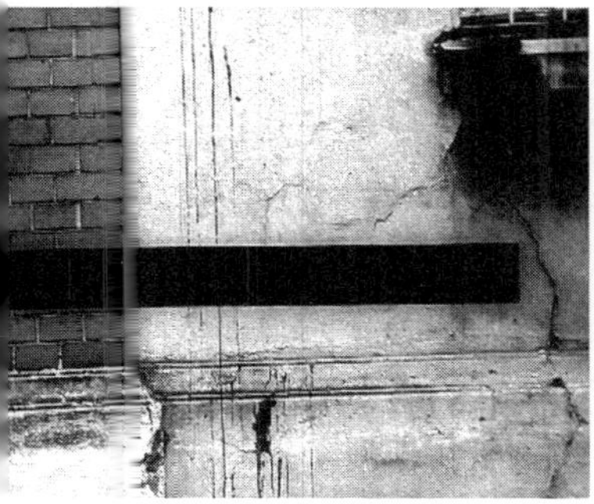
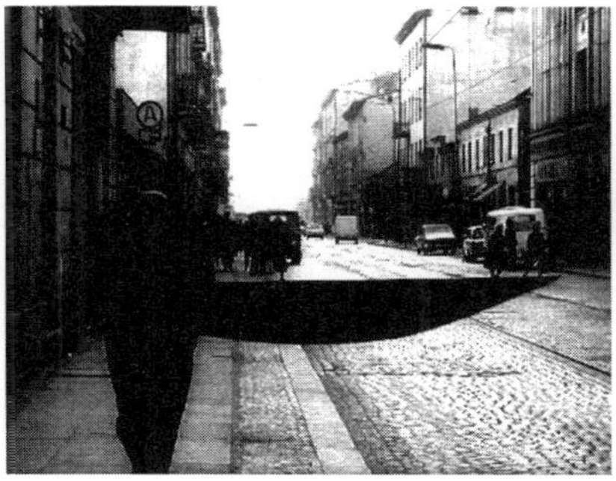
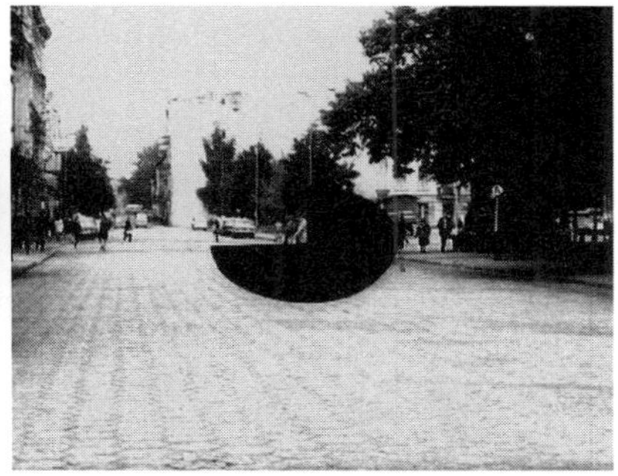
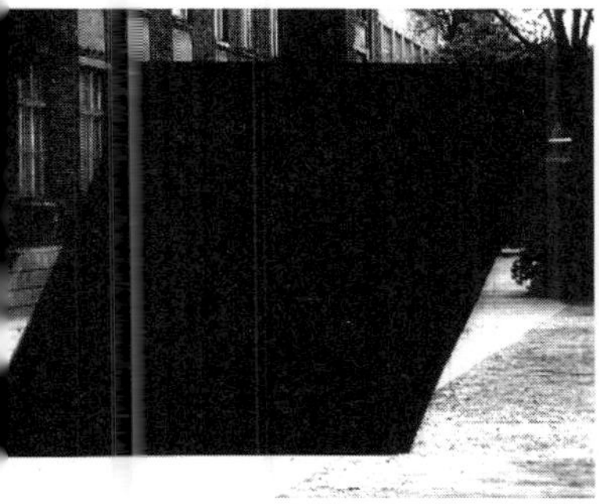
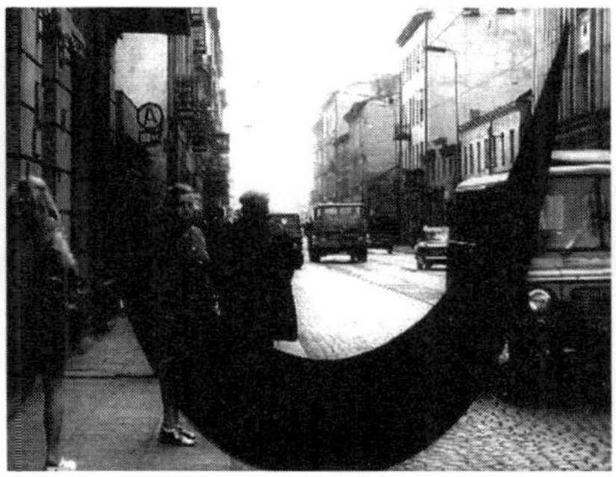
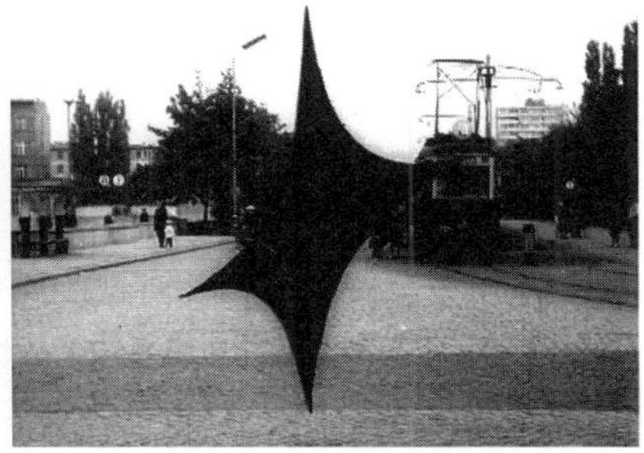
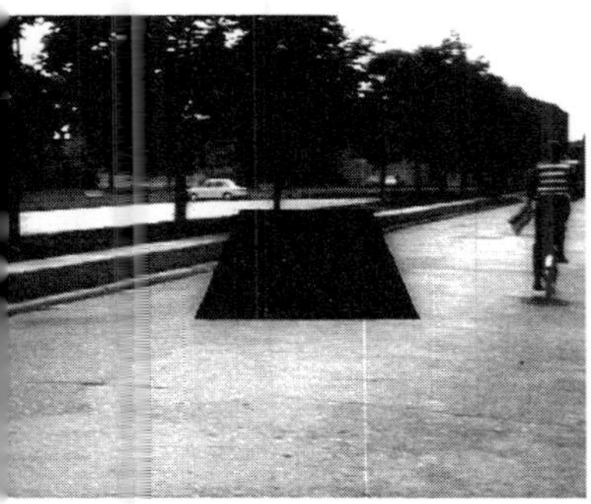
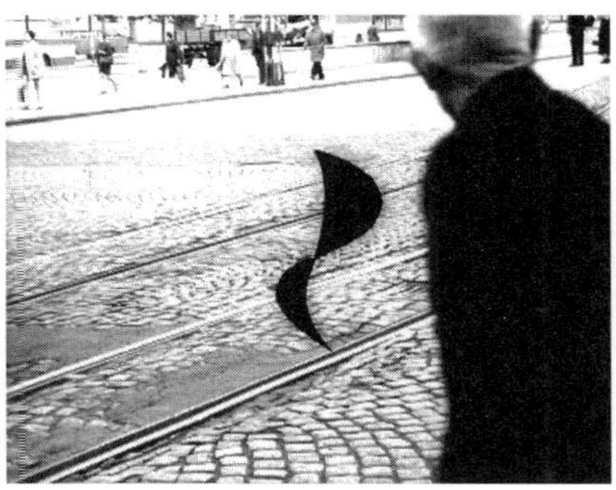
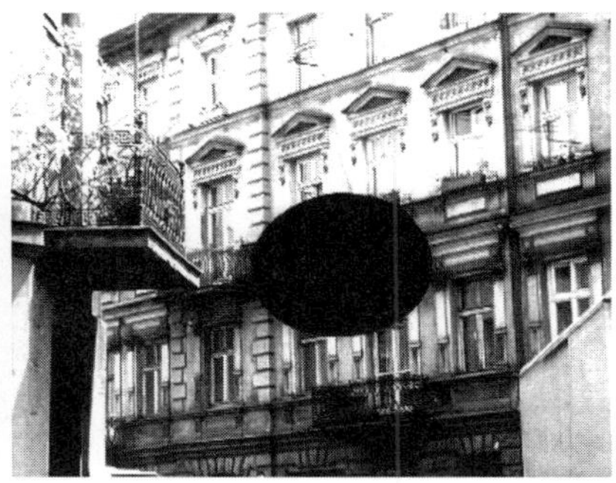
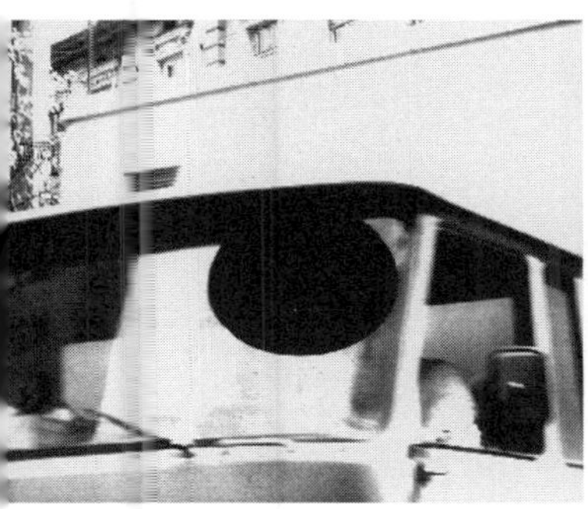
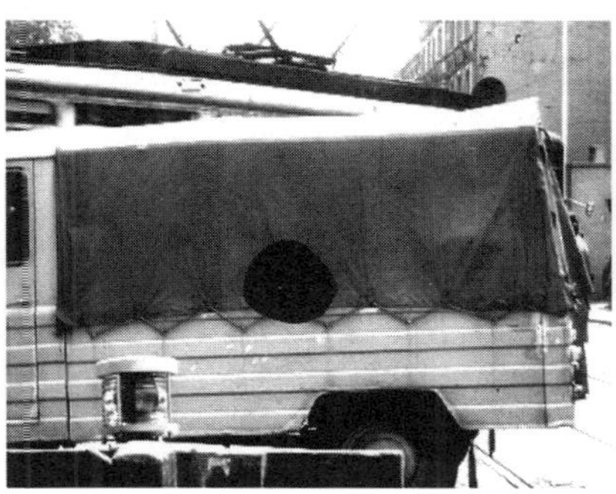
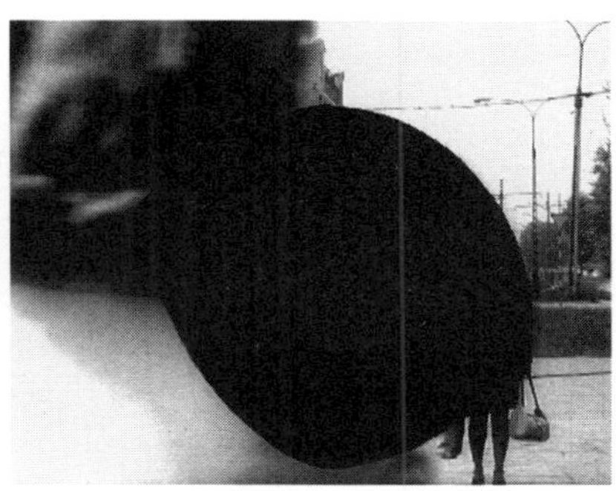

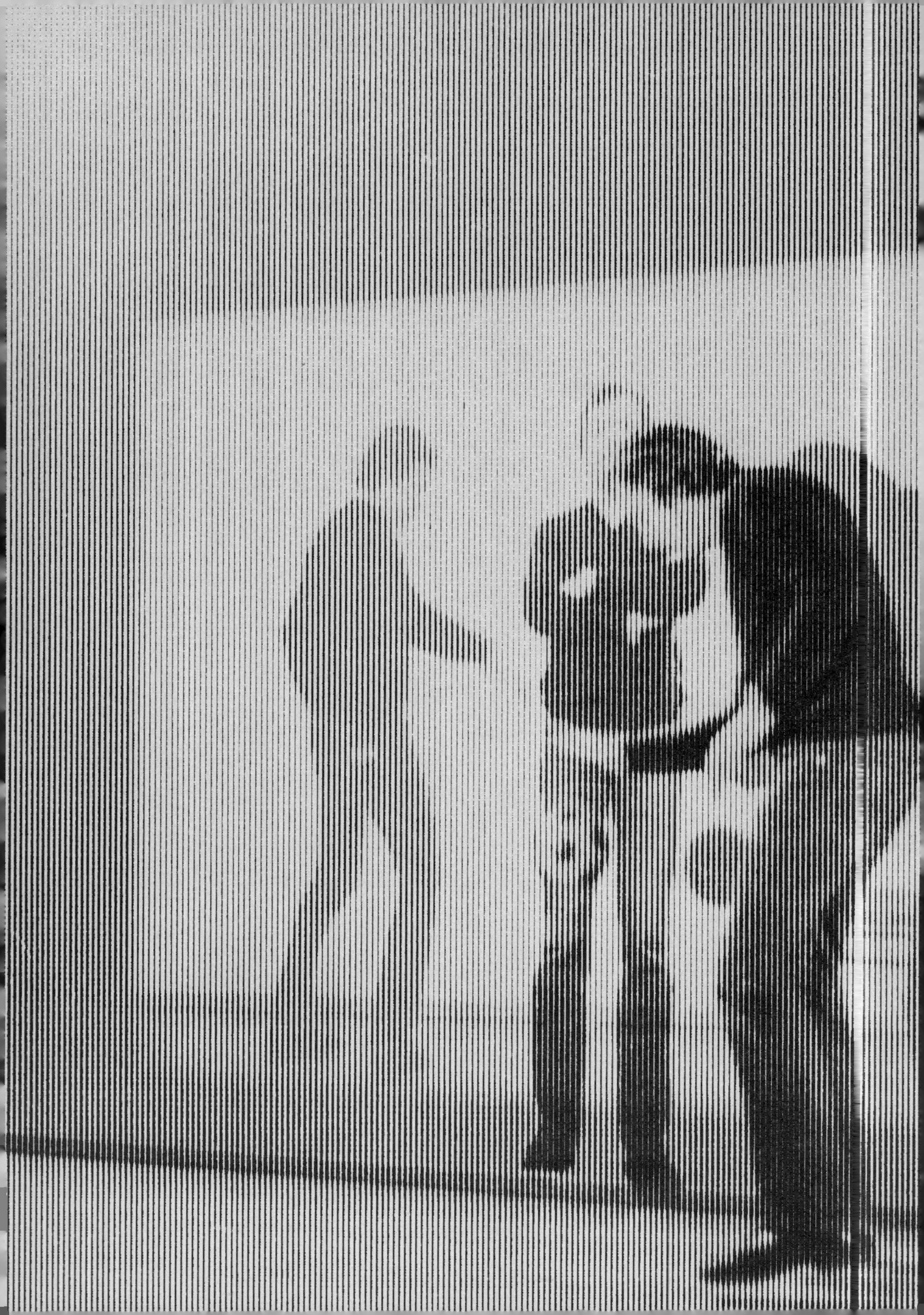

WORKSHOP OF THE FILM FORM

WARSZTAT FORMY FILMOWEJ

Edited by / Redakcja:
Marika Kuźmicz
Łukasz Ronduda

Contents

10 Works

145 Marika Kuźmicz
Workshop of the Film Form

193 Mike Sperlinger
Tautological Cinema: Some Notes on Self-evidence in the Workshop of the Film Form

201 Maeve Connolly
'The place of our dreams':
Łódź Film School and the Workshop of the Film Form

215 Łukasz Ronduda
Workshop of the Film Form
or the Coalition of Art Workers in a Workers' State

223 George Clark
Contact with the Polish Avant-garde Guaranteed:
Modes of Exchange in the Workshop of the Film Form

233 Jan Verwoert
Gestures Towards a New Life:
The Avant-Garde as a Historical Provocation

341 Biographies

Spis treści

10 Prace

243 Marika Kuźmicz
Warsztat Formy Filmowej

289 Mike Sperlinger
Tautologiczne kino: kilka uwag na temat oczywistości w działach twórców Warsztatu Formy Filmowej

299 Maeve Connolly
„To jest miejsce naszych snów". Działalność Warsztatu Formy Filmowej w Szkole Filmowej w Łodzi

313 Łukasz Ronduda
Warsztat Formy Filmowej czyli koalicja robotników sztuki w robotniczym państwie

321 George Clark
Zapewniamy kontakt z polską awangardą artystyczną: tryby wymiany w Warsztacie Formy Filmowej

333 Jan Verwoert
Gesty na Rzecz Nowego Życia: Awangarda jako historyczna prowokacja

369 Biogramy

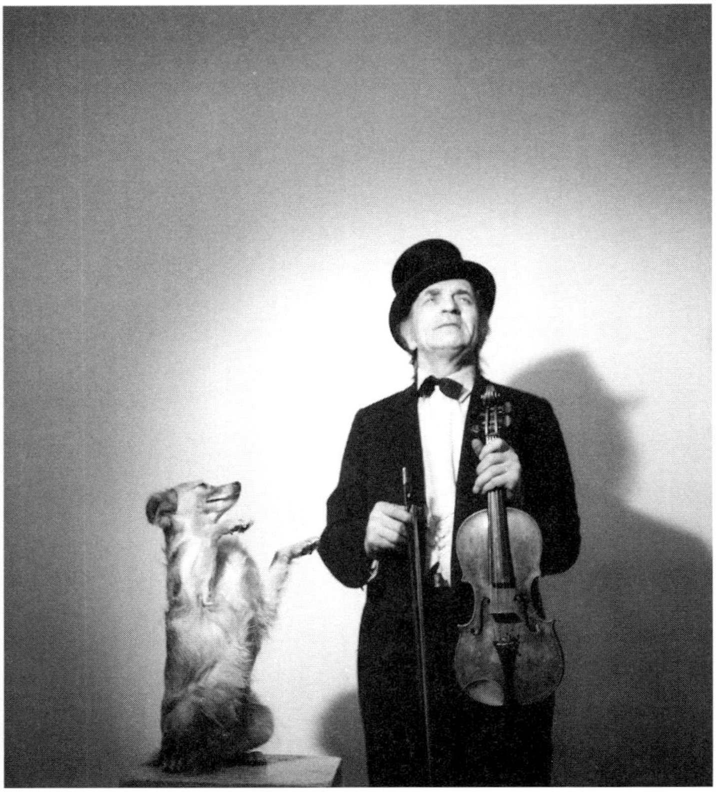

Pan Wacław Antczak, Łódź, 1972
Mr. Wacław Antczak, Łódź, 1972

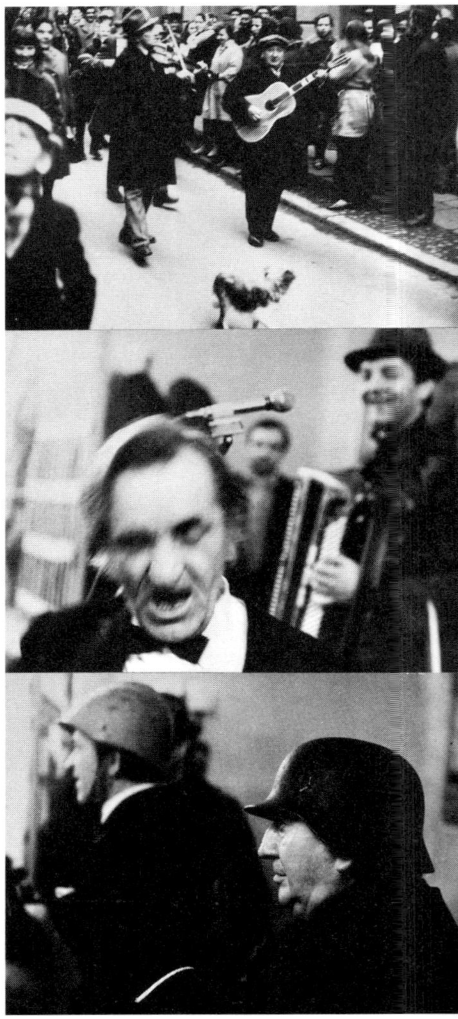

Jak? Jakby lepiej, 1972, 35 mm, 10'
Film A. Różyckiego poświęcony W. Antczakowi

How Is It? As if It's Getting Better..., 1972, 35 mm, 10'
A film by A. Różycki devoted to W. Antczak

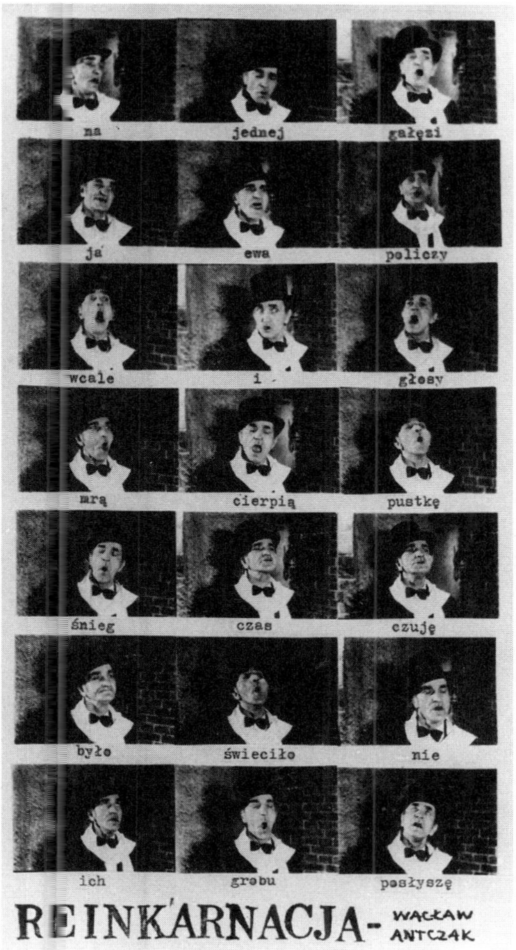

Reinkarnacja, stopklatki z filmu (Pan Wacław recytuje swój wiersz), 1974
Reincarnation, stills (Mr. Wacław reciting his poem), 1974

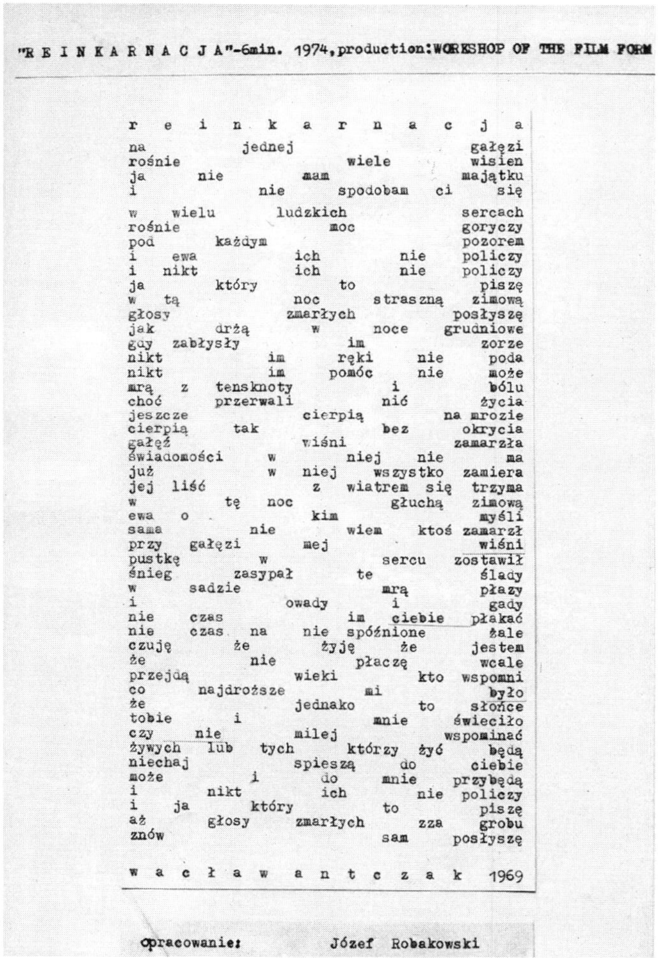

"R E I N K A R N A C J A"-6min. 1974,production:WORKSHOP OF THE FILM FORM

r e i n k a r n a c j a

na jednej gałęzi
rośnie wiele wisien
ja nie mam majątku
i nie spodobam ci się

w wielu ludzkich sercach
rośnie moc goryczy
pod każdym pozorem
i ewa ich nie policzy
i nikt ich nie policzy
ja który to piszę
w tą noc straszną zimową
głosy zmarłych posłyszę
jak drżą w noce grudniowe
gdy zabłysły im zorze
nikt im ręki nie poda
nikt im pomóc nie może
mrą z tensknoty i bólu
choć przerwali nić życia
jeszcze cierpią na mrozie
cierpią tak bez okrycia
gałęź wiśni zamarzła
świadomości w niej nie ma
już w niej wszystko zamiera
jej liść z wiatrem się trzyma
w tę noc głuchą zimową
ewa o kim myśli
sama nie wiem ktoś zamarzł
przy gałęzi mej wiśni
pustkę w sercu zostawił
śnieg zasypał te ślady
w sadzie mrą płazy
i owady i gady
nie czas im ciebie płakać
nie czas na nie spóźnione żale
czuję że żyję że jestem
że nie płaczę wcale
przejdą wieki kto wspomni
co najdroższe mi było
że jednako to słońce
tobie i mnie świeciło
czy nie milej wspominać
żywych lub tych którzy żyć będą
niechaj spieszą do ciebie
może i do mnie przybędą
i nikt ich nie policzy
i ja który to piszę
aż głosy zmarłych zza grobu
znów sam posłyszę

w a c ł a w a n t c z a k 1969

opracowanie: Józef Robakowski

Reinkarnacja, zapis poematu Wacława Antczaka, 1969 (opracował Józef Robakowski)
Reincarnation, typescript of the poem by Wacław Antczak, 1969 (edited by Józef Robakowski)

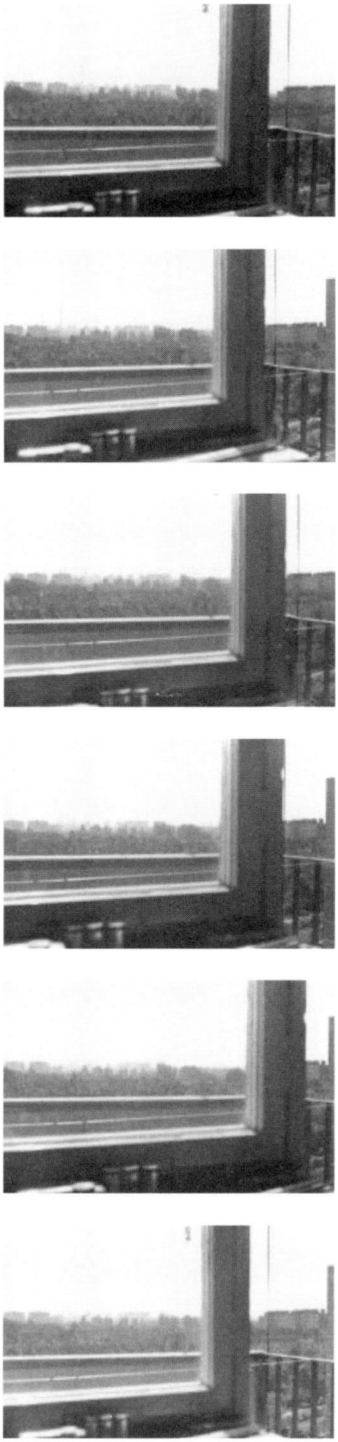

Tomasz Konart, *Fotografia i pamięć*, 1978, fot. cz.-b.
Tomasz Konart, *Photography and Memory*, 1978, B&W photograph

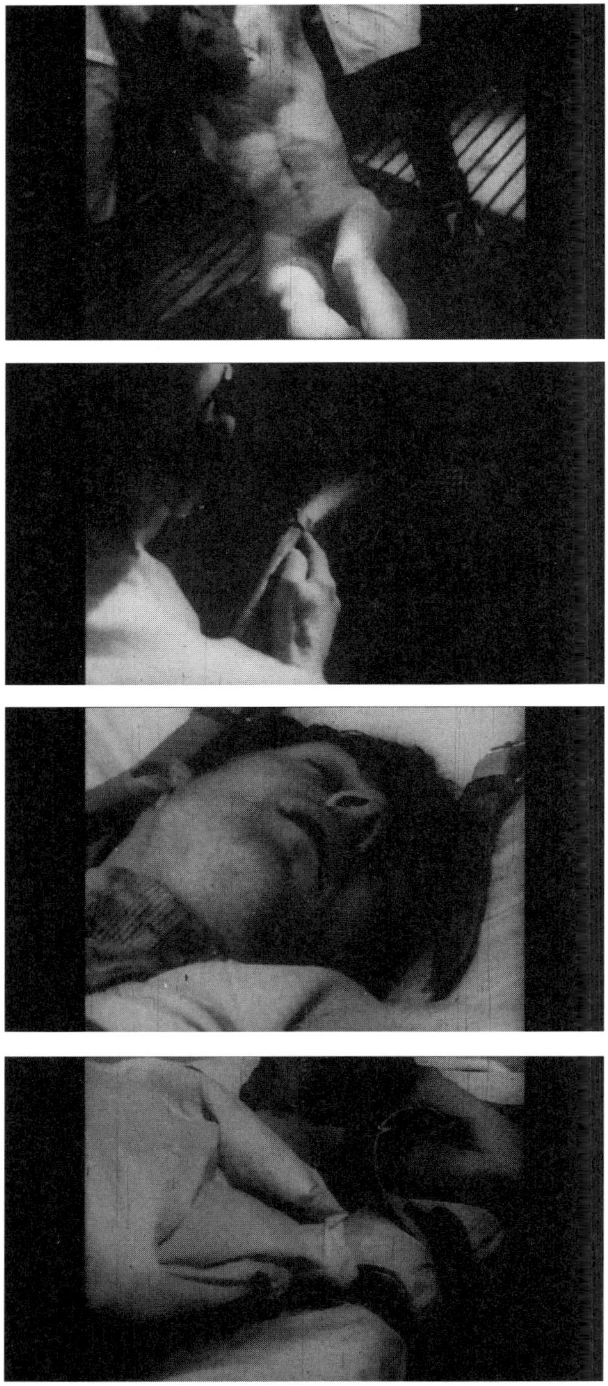

Marek Koterski, *Ech*, 1972, 35 mm, 10'47"
Marek Koterski, *Ah*, 1972, 35 mm, 10'47"

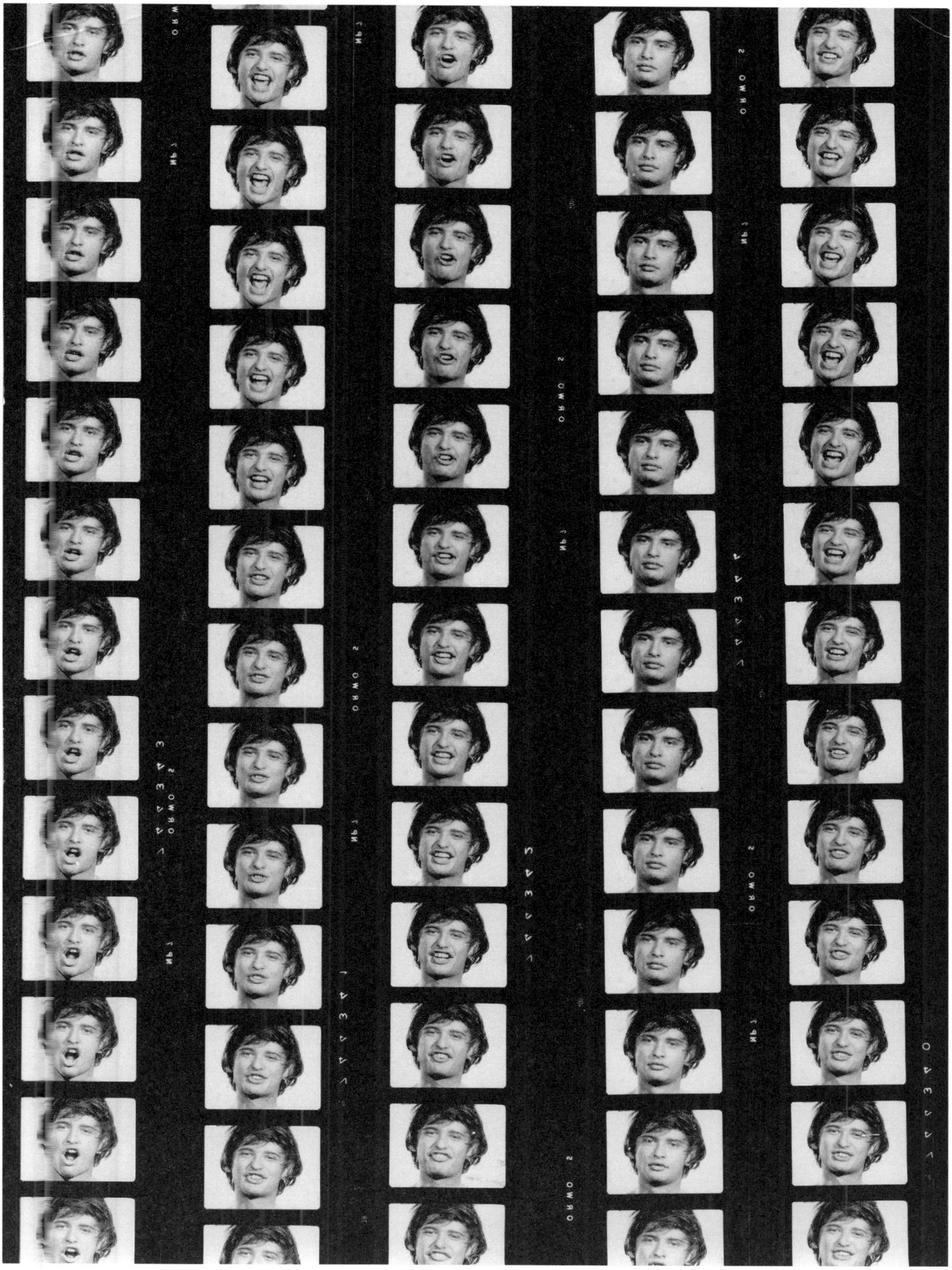

Paweł Kwiek, Jacek Łomnicki, *Twarz*, 1971, 35 mm (niezachowany)
Paweł Kwiek, Jacek Łomnicki, *Face*, 1971, 35 mm (unpreserved)

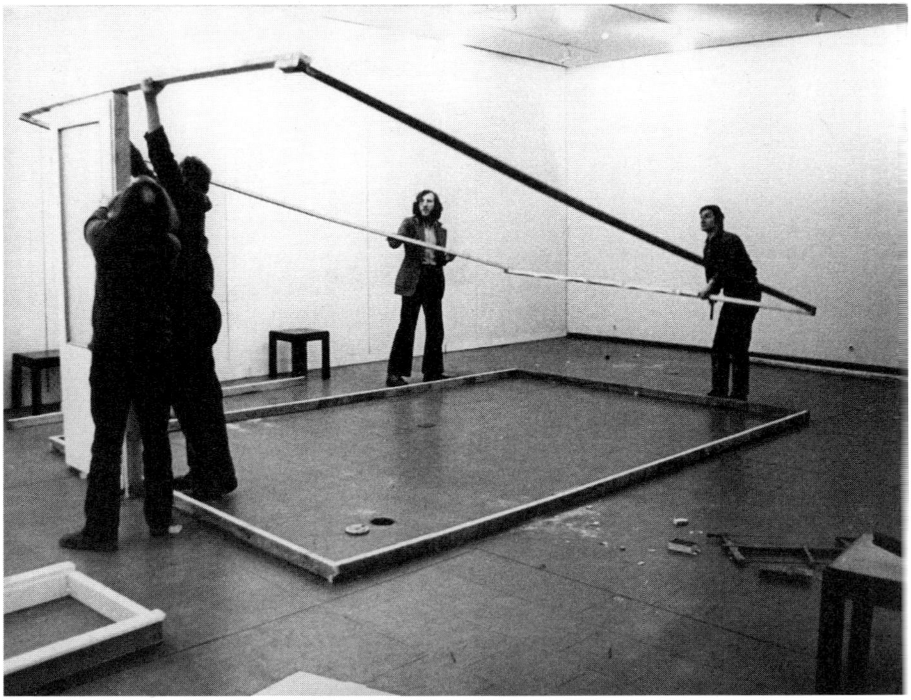

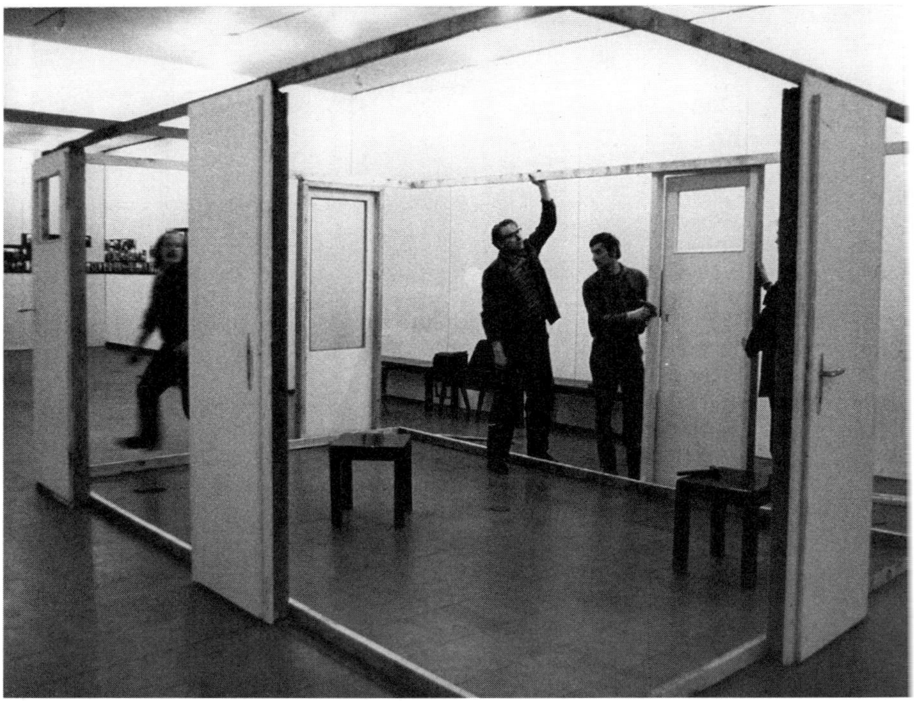

Antoni Mikołajczyk, *Konstrukcja* (Akcja Warsztat, Muzeum Sztuki), 1973, instalacja
Antoni Mikołajczyk, *Constuction* (Action Workshop, Muzeum Sztuki, Łódź), 1973, installation

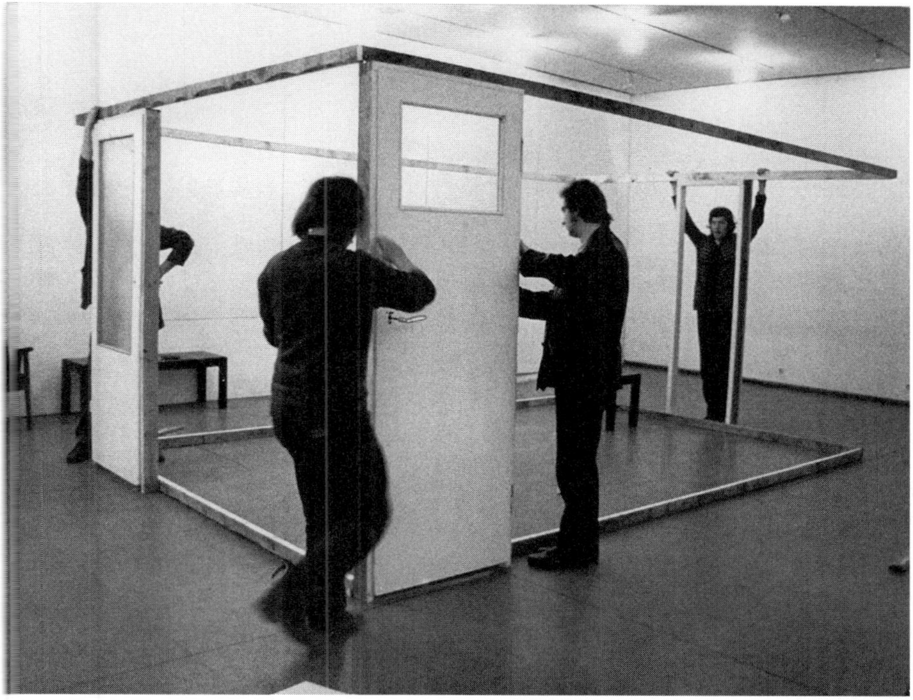

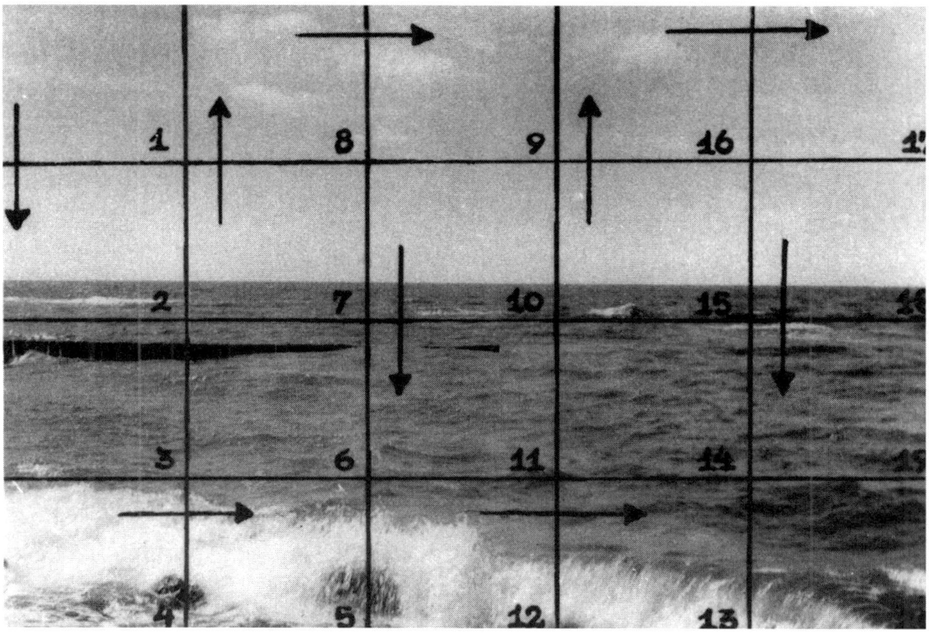

Antoni Mikołajczyk, *Anatomia*, 1974, fot. cz.-b.
Antoni Mikołajczyk, *Anatomy*, 1974, B&W photograph

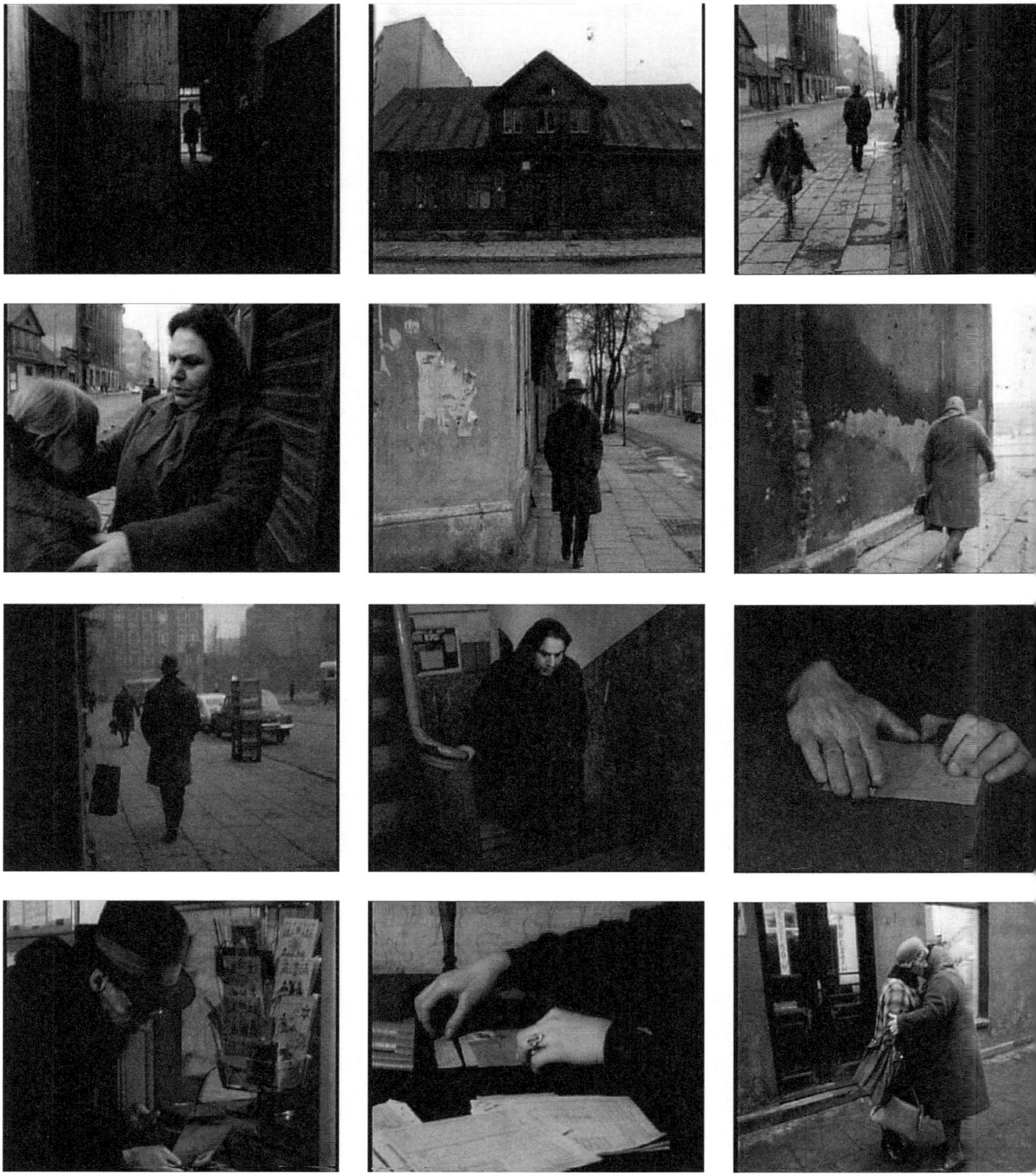

Andrzej Barański, *Kręte ścieżki*, 1970, 35 mm, 6'11"
Andrzej Barański, *Winding Paths*, 1970, 35 mm, 6'11"

Zbigniew Rybczyński, *Kwadrat*, 1972, 35 mm, 3’30’’
Zbigniew Rybczyński, *The Square*, 1972, 35 mm, 3’30’’

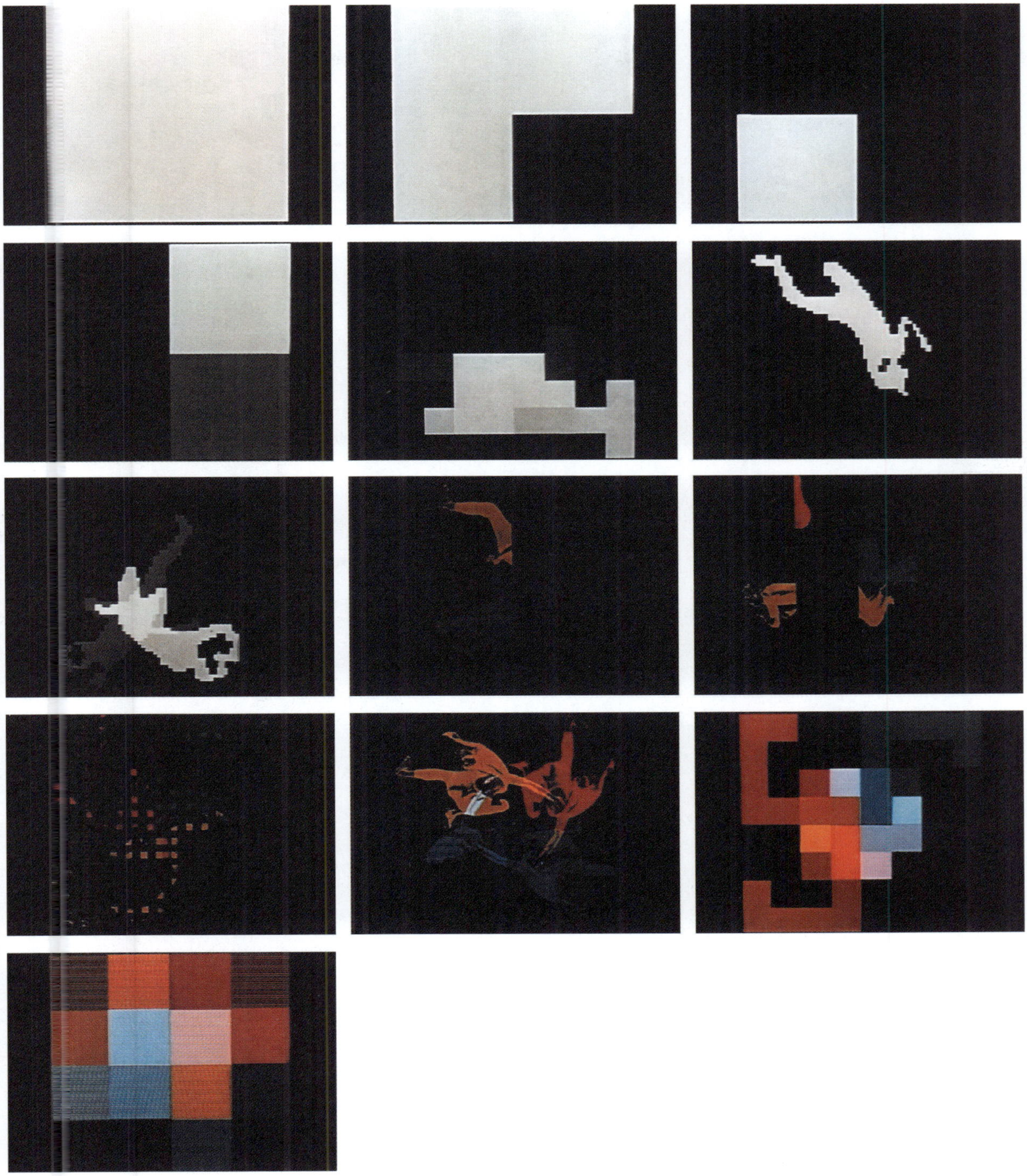

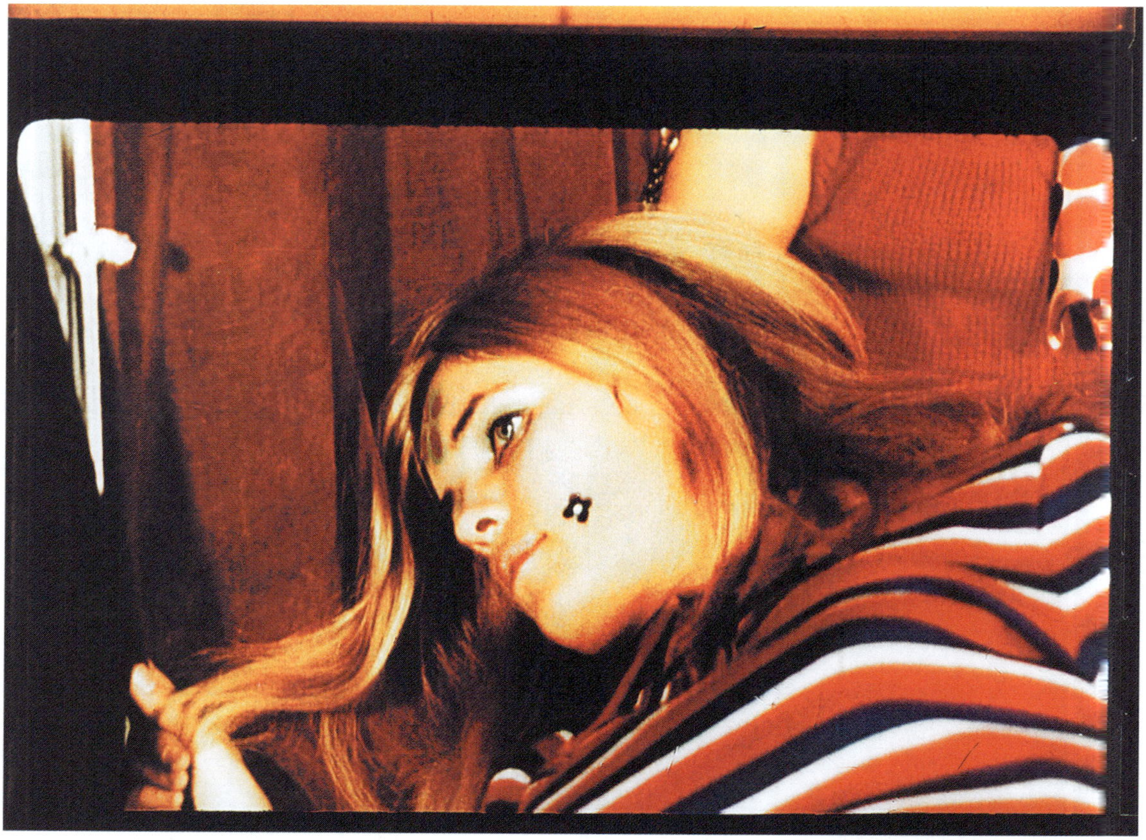

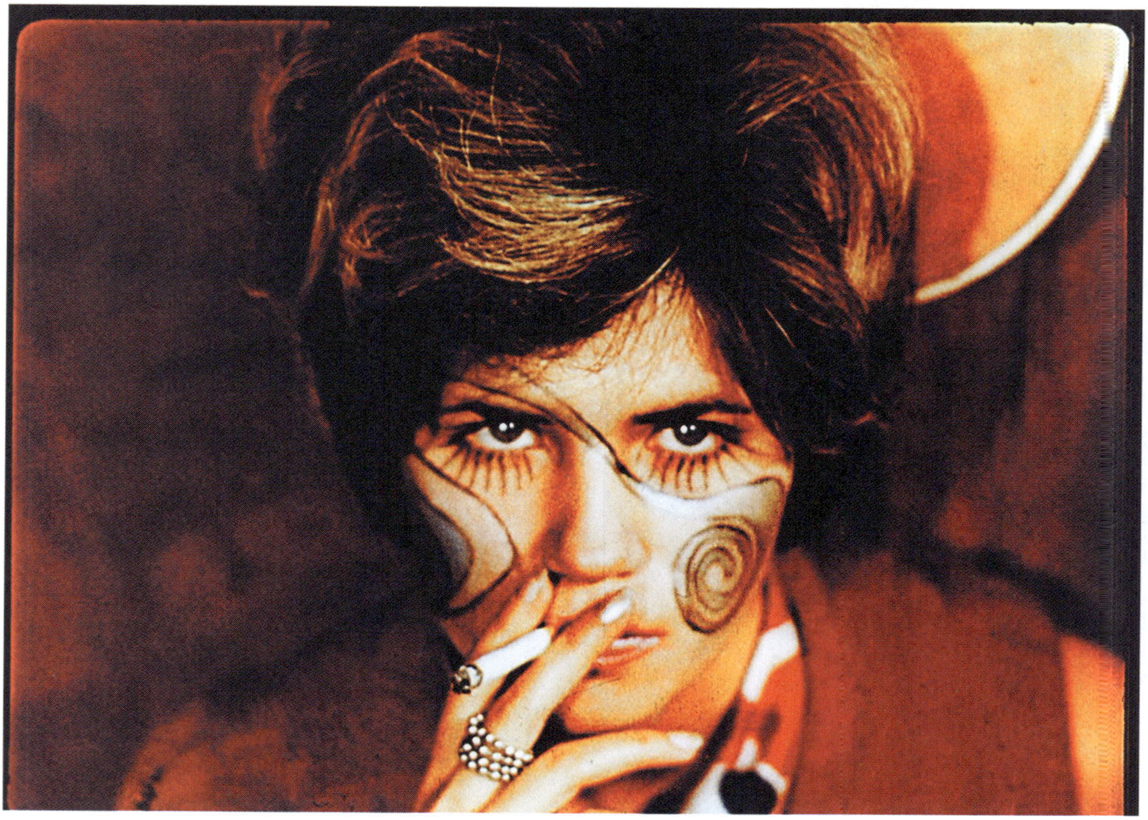

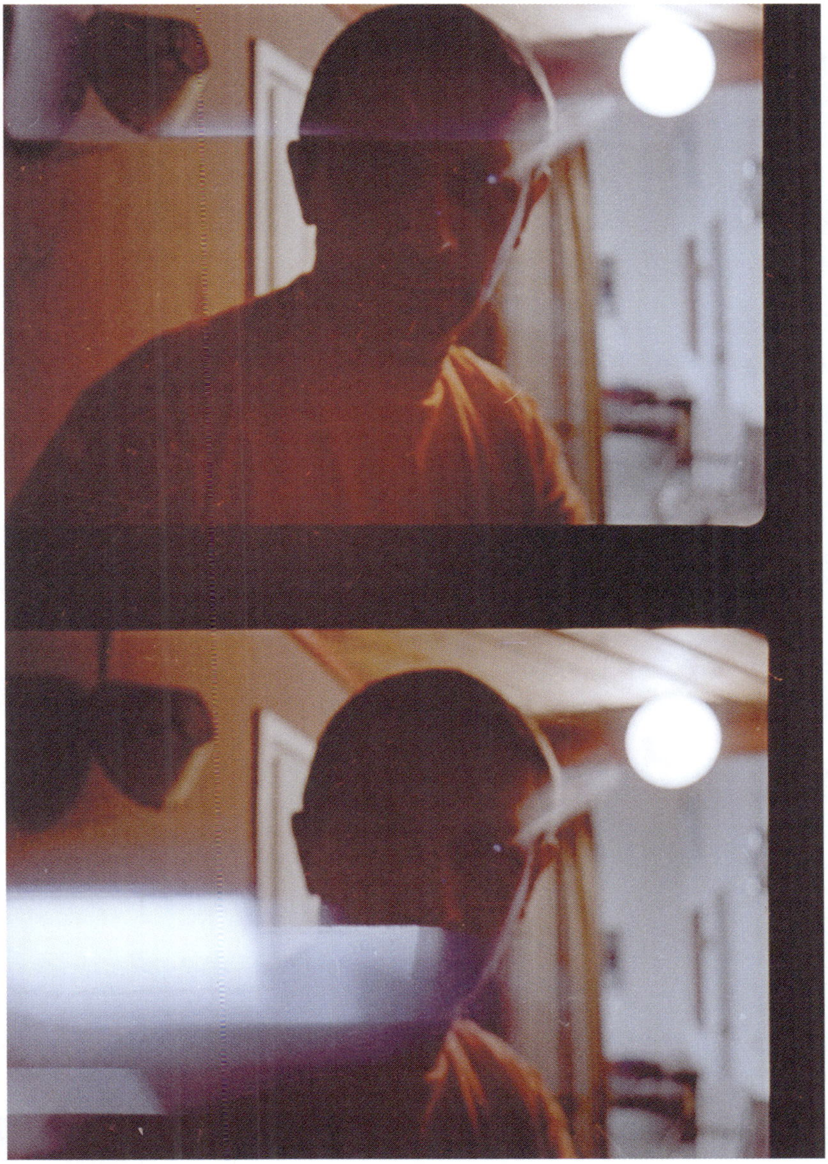

Ryszard Gajewski, *Pierzgalski*, 1970, 35 mm, 2'50''
Ryszard Gajewski, *Pierzgalski*, 1970, 35 mm, 2'50''

Ryszard Gajewski, *Hippie*, 1970, 35 mm (film niezachowany)
Ryszard Gajewski, *Hippie*, 1970, 35 mm (unpreserved)

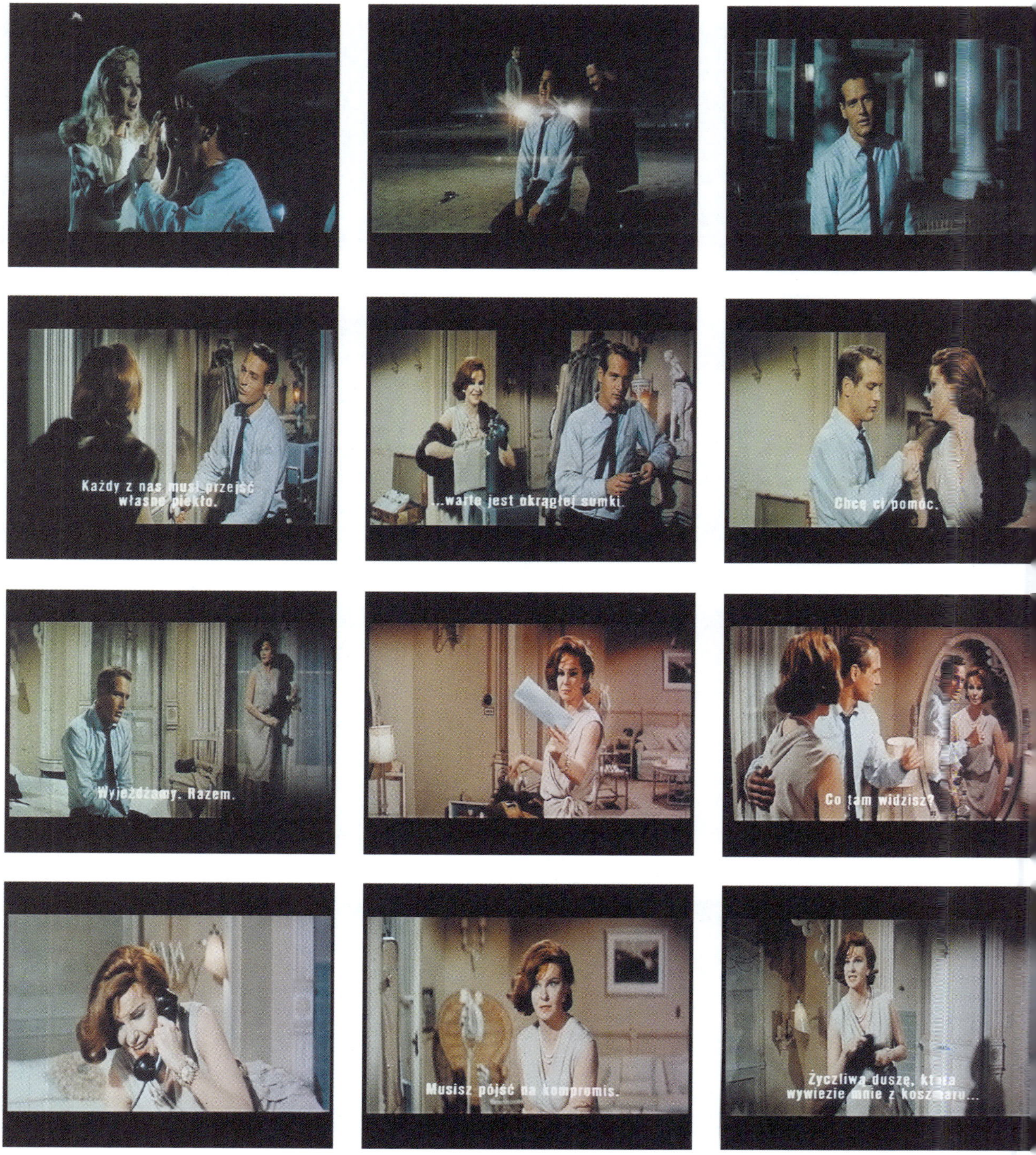

Tadeusz Junak, *Epizod*, 1973, 35 mm, 15'27''
Tadeusz Junak, *Episode*, 1973, 35 mm, 15'27''

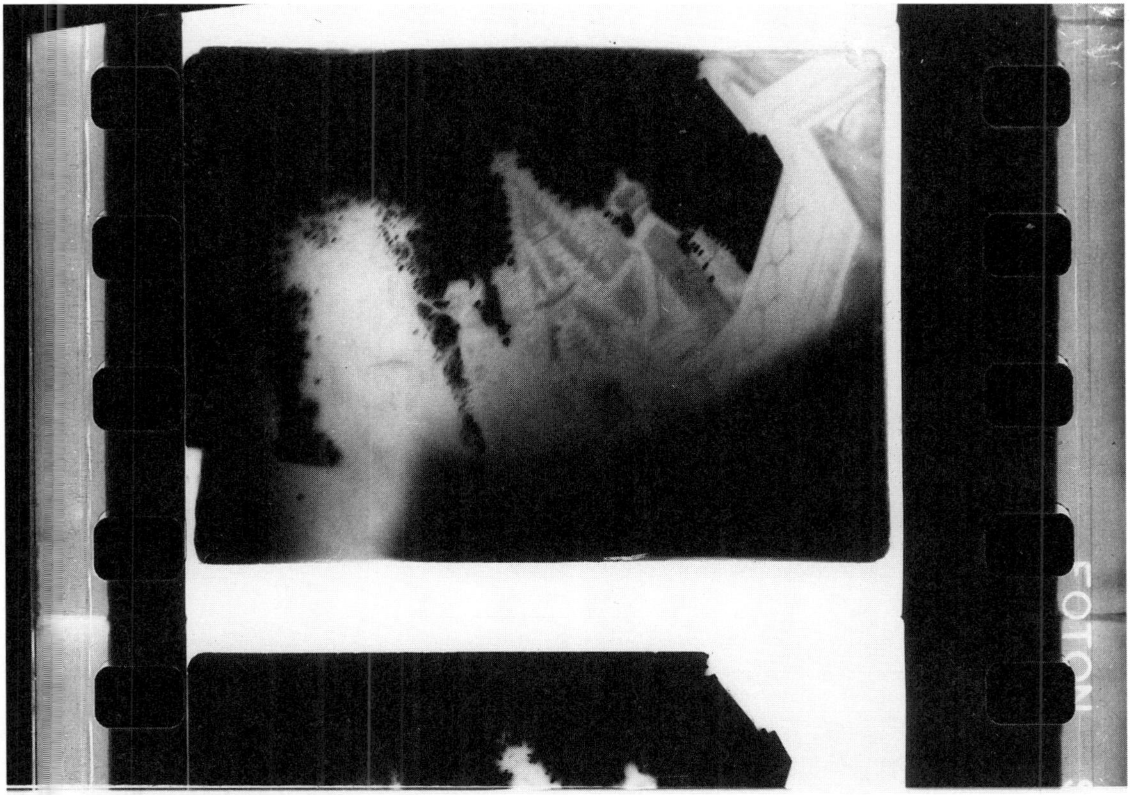

Ryszard Gajewski, *Wirówka*, 1970/72, 35 mm, 2'50''
Ryszard Gajewski, *Centrifuge*, 1970/72, 35 mm, 2'50''

OBRAZ POZORNY

Video-instalacja. Galeria "Dom Środowisk Twórczych" - Łódź, listopad 1976

APPARENT IMAGE - Video installation

Gallery Dom Srodowisk Twórczych - Łódź, November 1976

Kamera video umieszczona jest w galerii przed tarczą zegara. Mikrofon wzmacnia dźwięk zegara, monitor obok zegara przekazuje jego obraz. Obraz ten jednak jest transmitowany z ukrytej kamery, która przekazuje nieruchomy obraz zdjęcia fotograficznego tego samego zegara.

Na początku rzeczywistość i jej obraz pozostają identyczne. Po pewnym czasie następuje niezgodność między godziną zegara a godziną obrazu na monitorze. Ta niezgodność daje się zauważyć dopiero jednak po dłuższym upływie czasu. Okazuje się, że identyfikacja rzeczywistości i jej obrazu zakłóca dokładną percepcję obydwu.

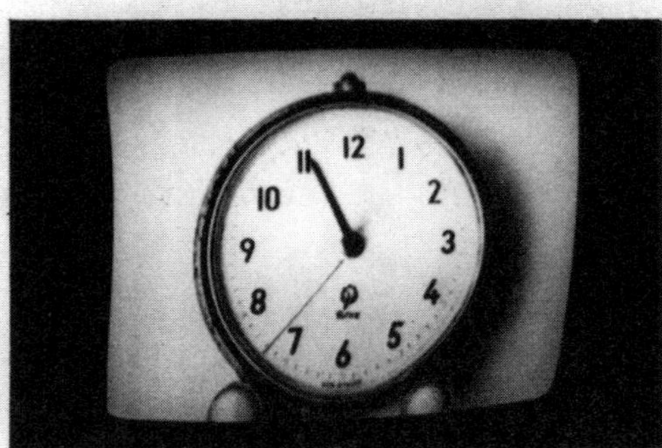

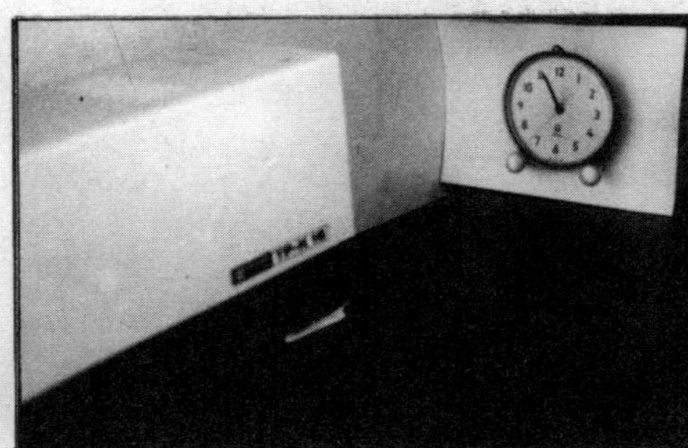

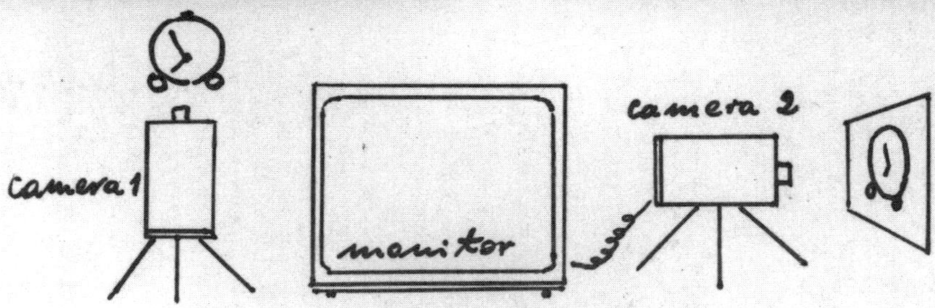

A video camera was placed in the gallery facing clock. A microphone amplfied it's ticking. The monitor in the room showed an image of the clock. This image, however was transmitted from hidden camera which was transmitting a still photograph of the clock.

At the begining, reality and image were identical. After some time a dischord appeared between the two. This dischord was perceived only after a long time, which proved to me that the identification of reality and it's recorded image prevents accurate perception of either.

Antoni Mikołajczyk, *Obraz pozorny*, 1976, instalacja wideo
Antoni Mikołajczyk, *Apparent Image*, 1976, video installation

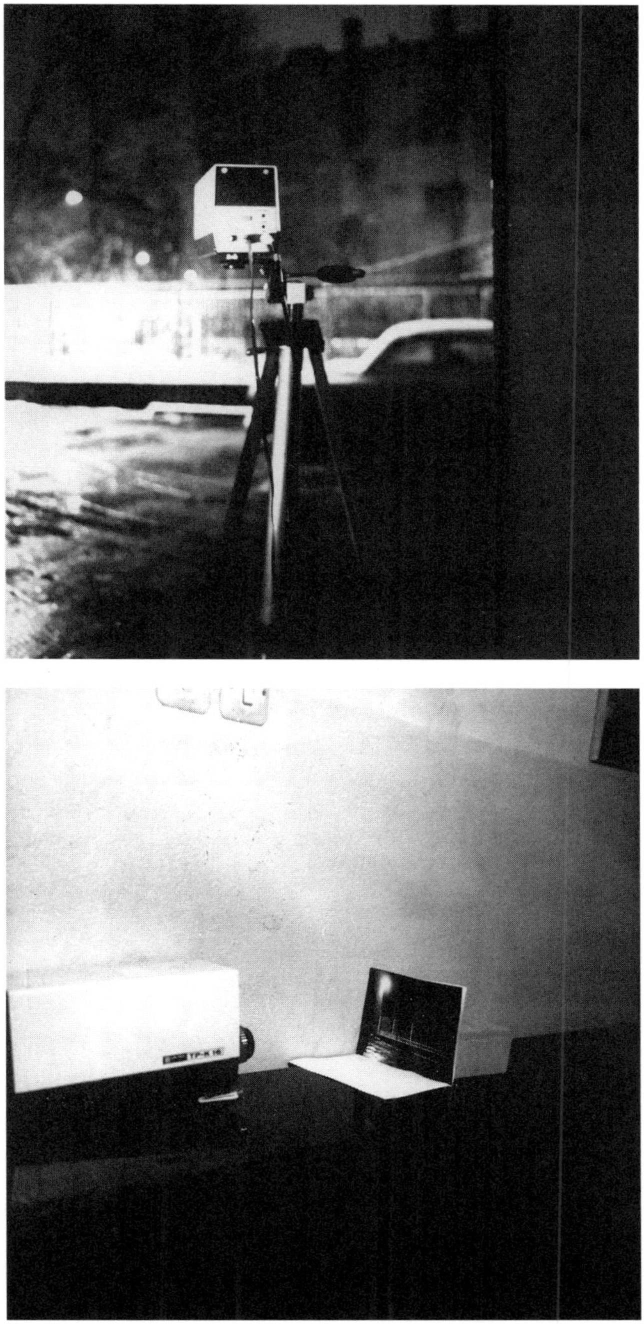

Antoni Mikołajczyk, *Rzeczywistość – obraz rzeczywistości*, 1976, instalacja wideo
Antoni Mikołajczyk, *Reality – Image of the Reality*, 1976, video installation

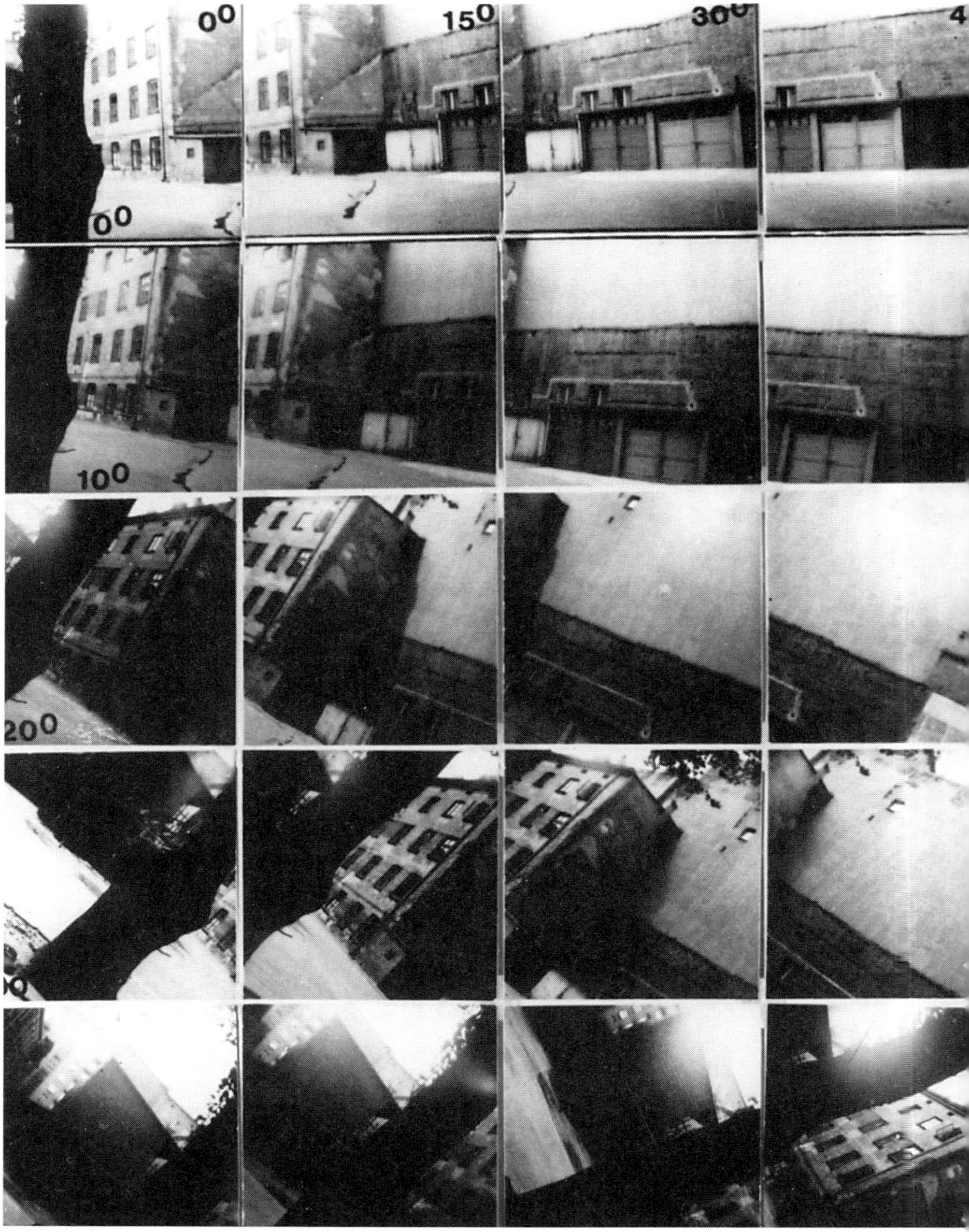

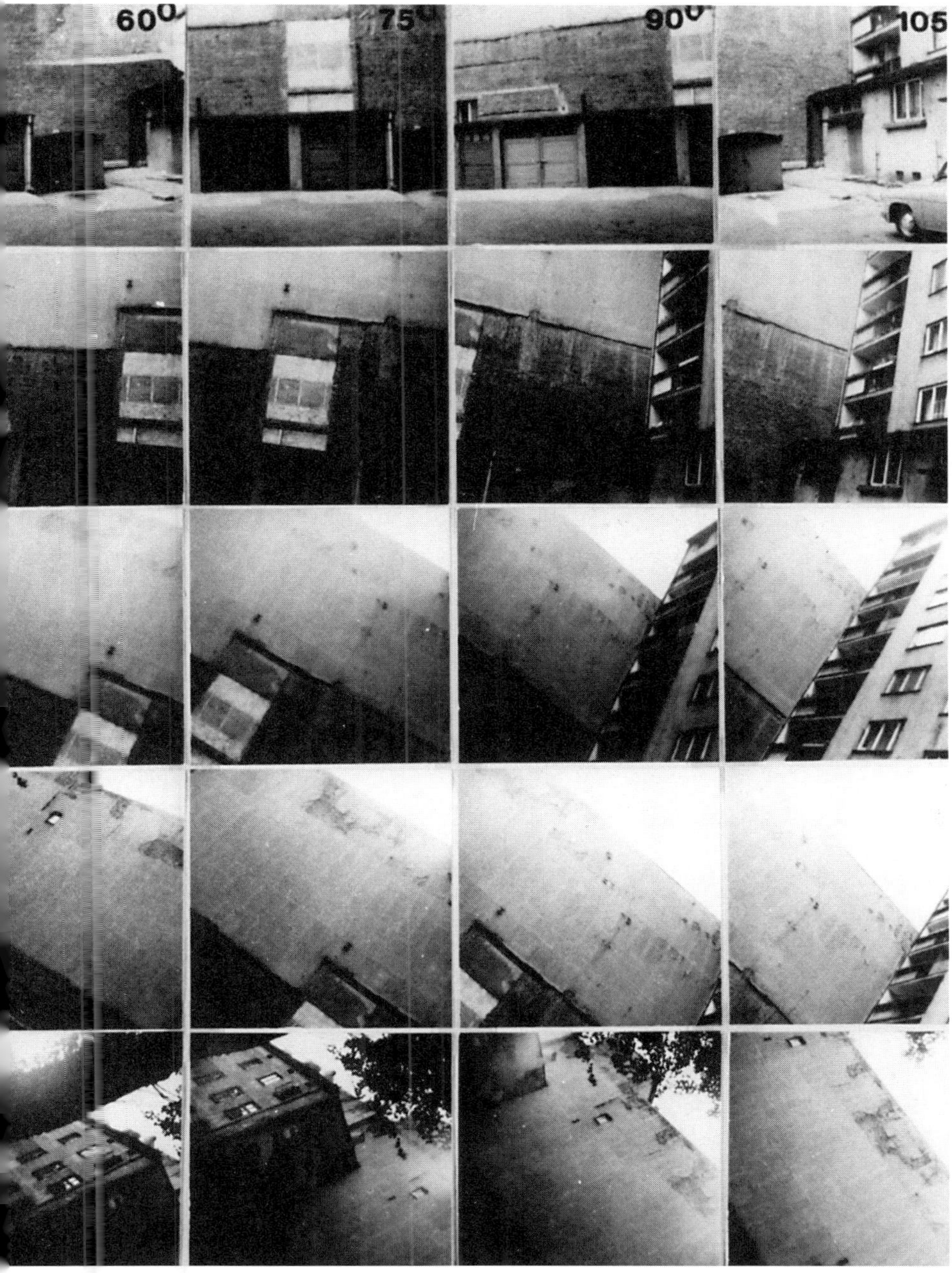

Antoni Mikołajczyk, *Rejestracja totalna*, 1974, fotografia cz.-b.
Antoni Mikołajczyk, *Total Registration*, 1974, B&W photograph

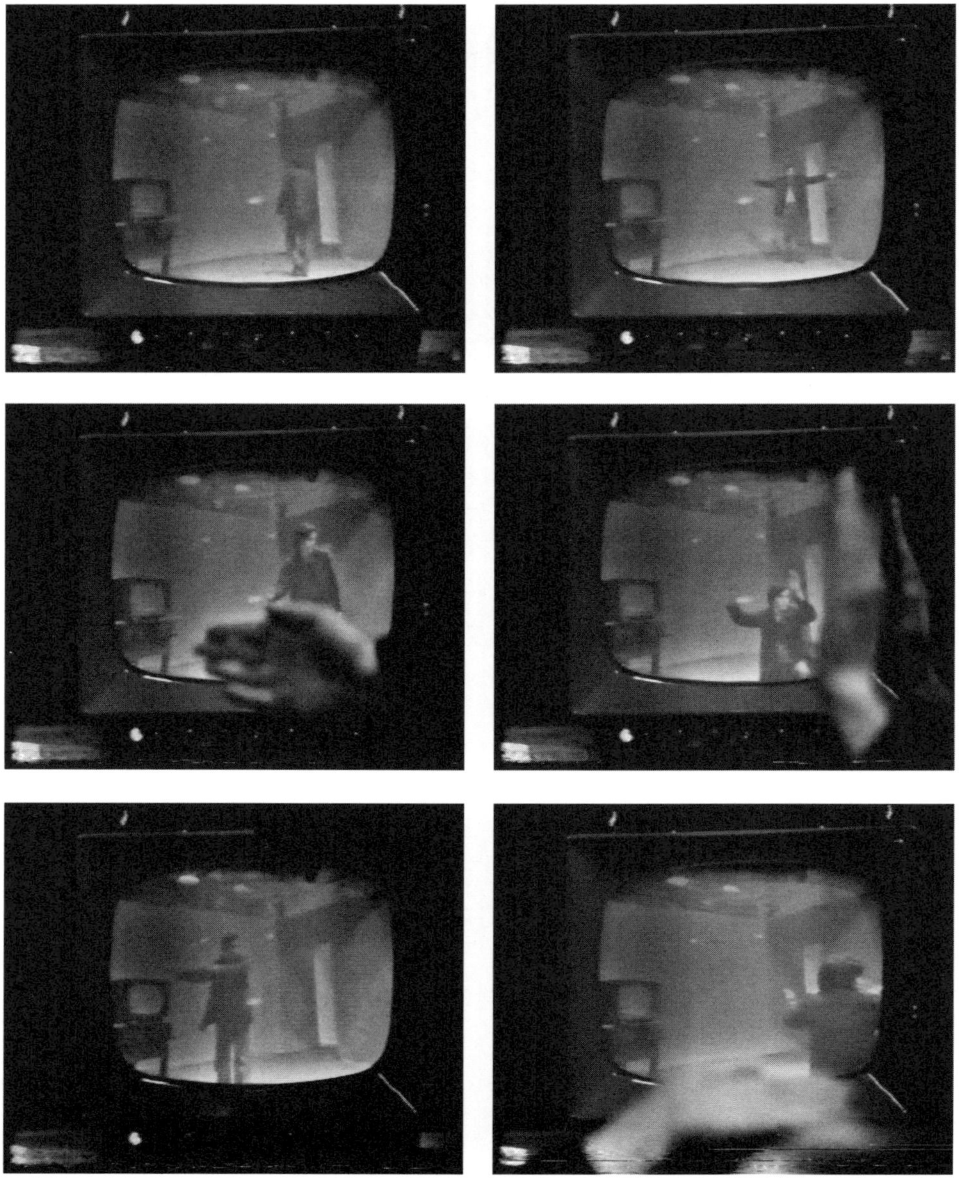

Andrzej Paruzel, *Sytuacje wideofotograficzne*, 1976, instalacja wideo
Andrzej Paruzel, *Videophotographic Situations*, 1976, video installation

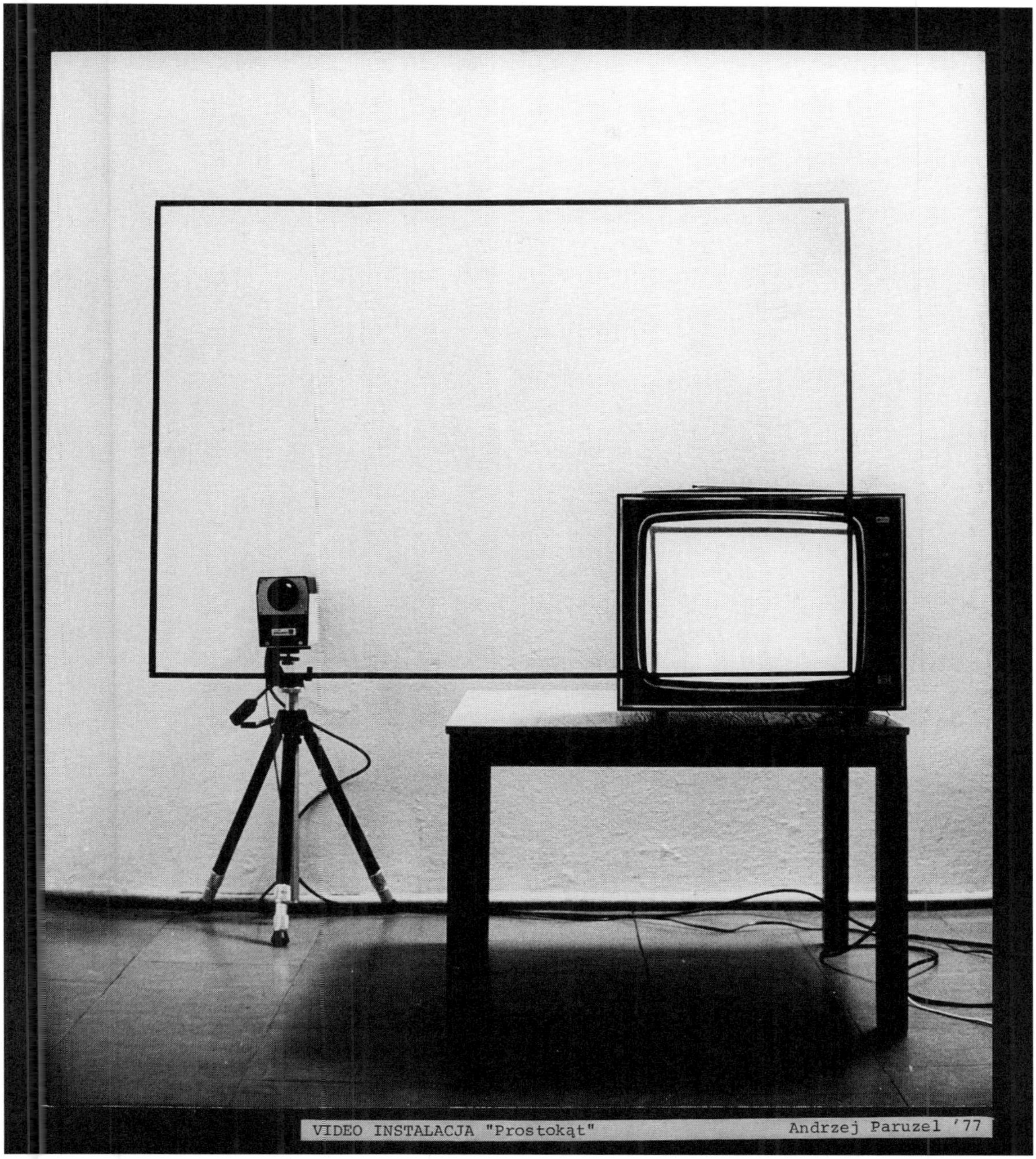

Andrzej Paruzel, *Prostokąt – sytuacje wideofotograficzne*, 1977, instalacja wideo
Andrzej Paruzel, *Rectangle – Videophotographic Situations*, 1977, video installation

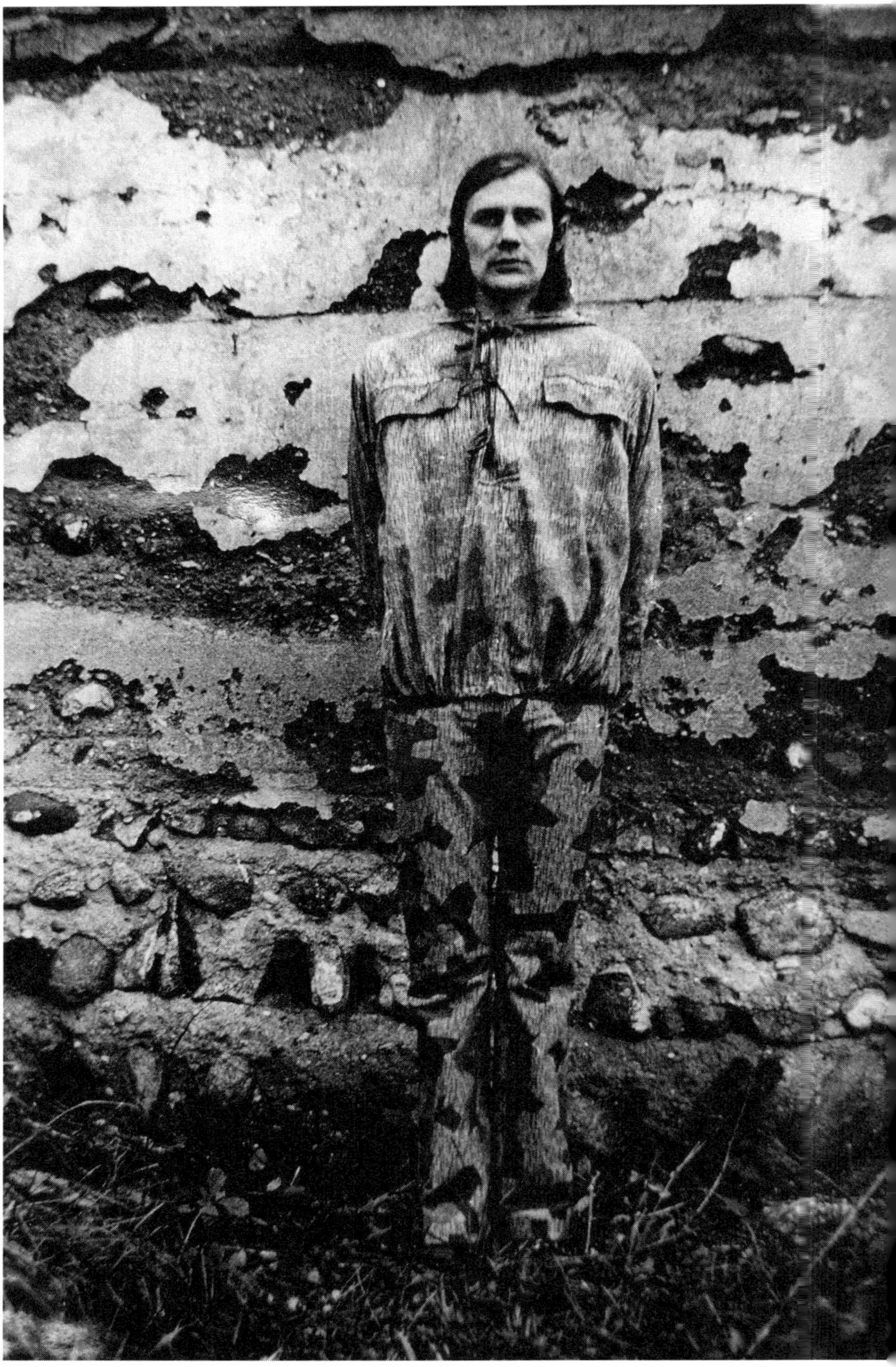

Janusz Połom, *Kamuflaż*, 1972, fot. cz.-b.
Janusz Połom, *Camouflage*, 1972, B&W photograph

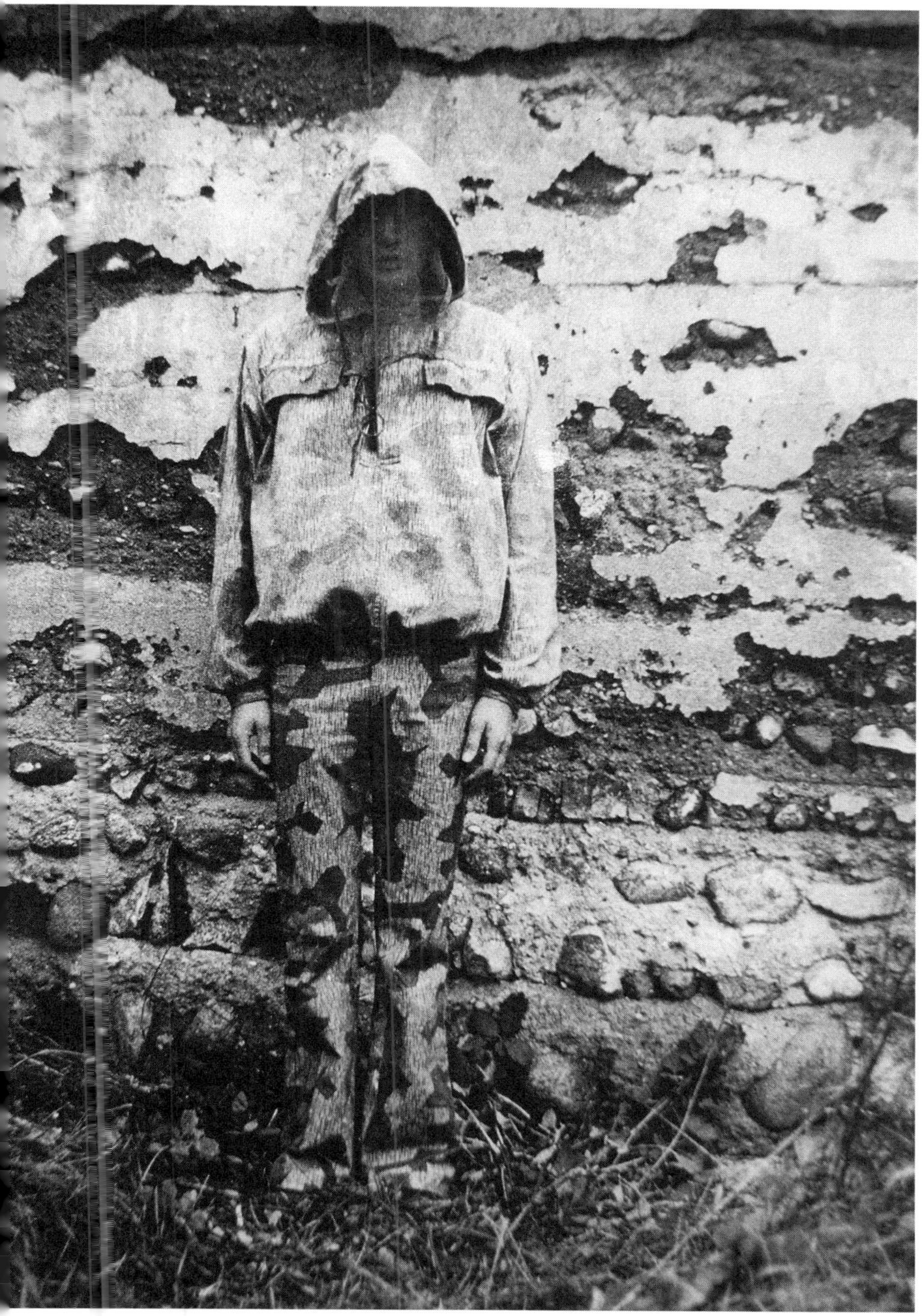

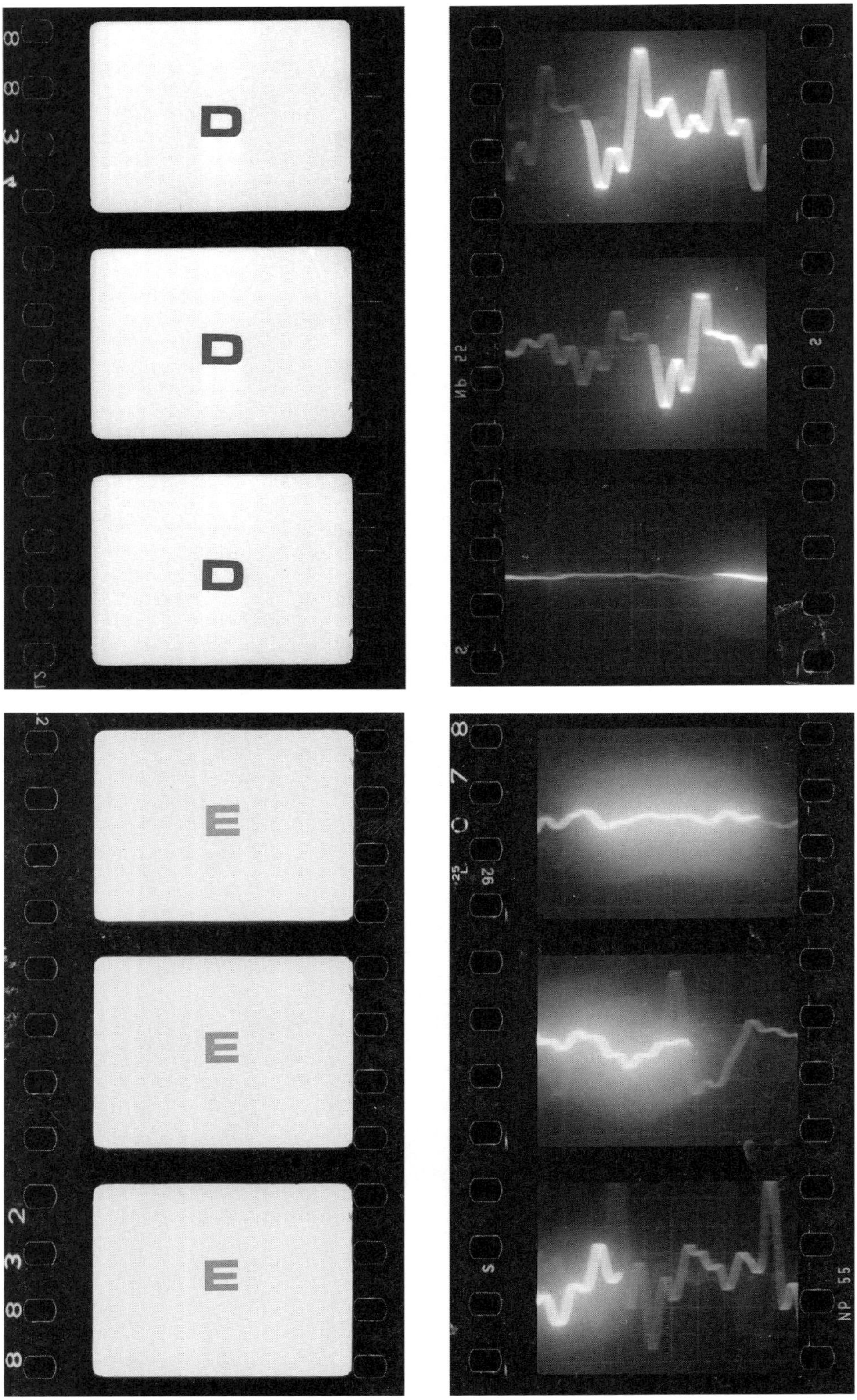

Janusz Połom, *Alfabet*, 1974, 35 mm, 2'13''
Janusz Połom, *Alphabet*, 1974, 35 mm, 2'13''

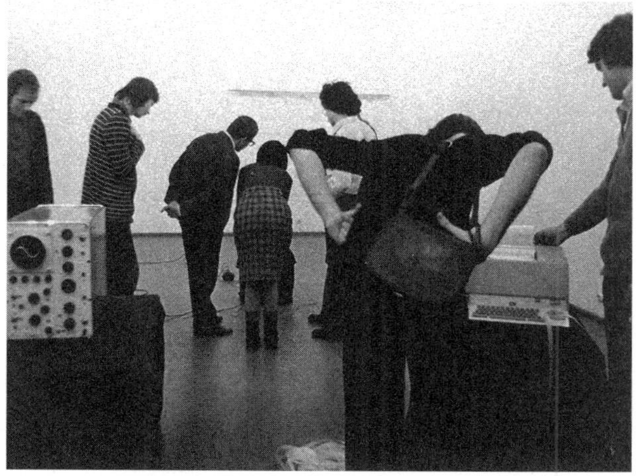

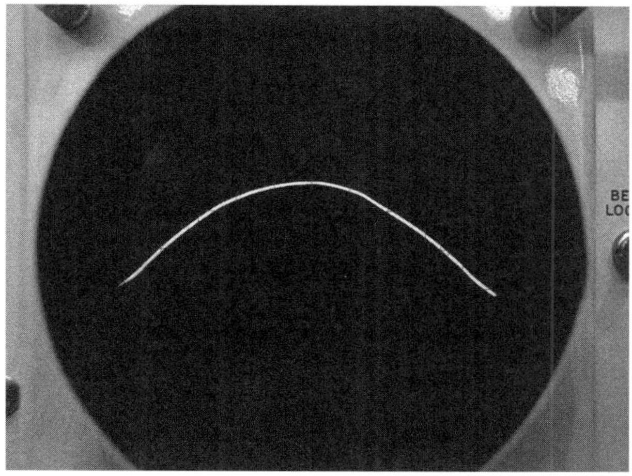

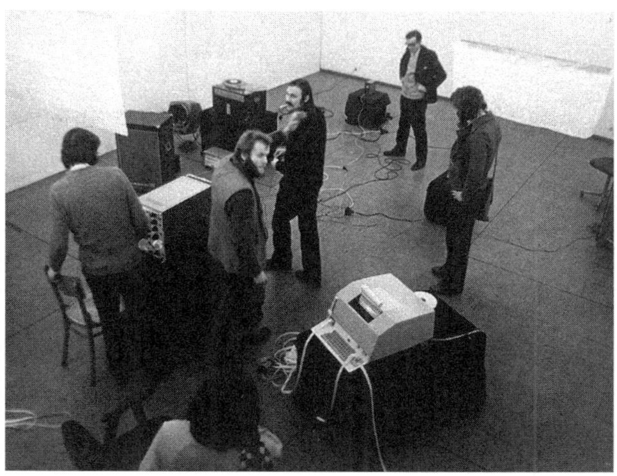

Janusz Połom, *Elektroniczne antynomie*, Akcja Warsztat, Muzeum Sztuki w Łodzi, 1973
Janusz Połom, *Electrical Antinomies* (Action Workshop, Muzeum Sztuki, Łódź), 1973

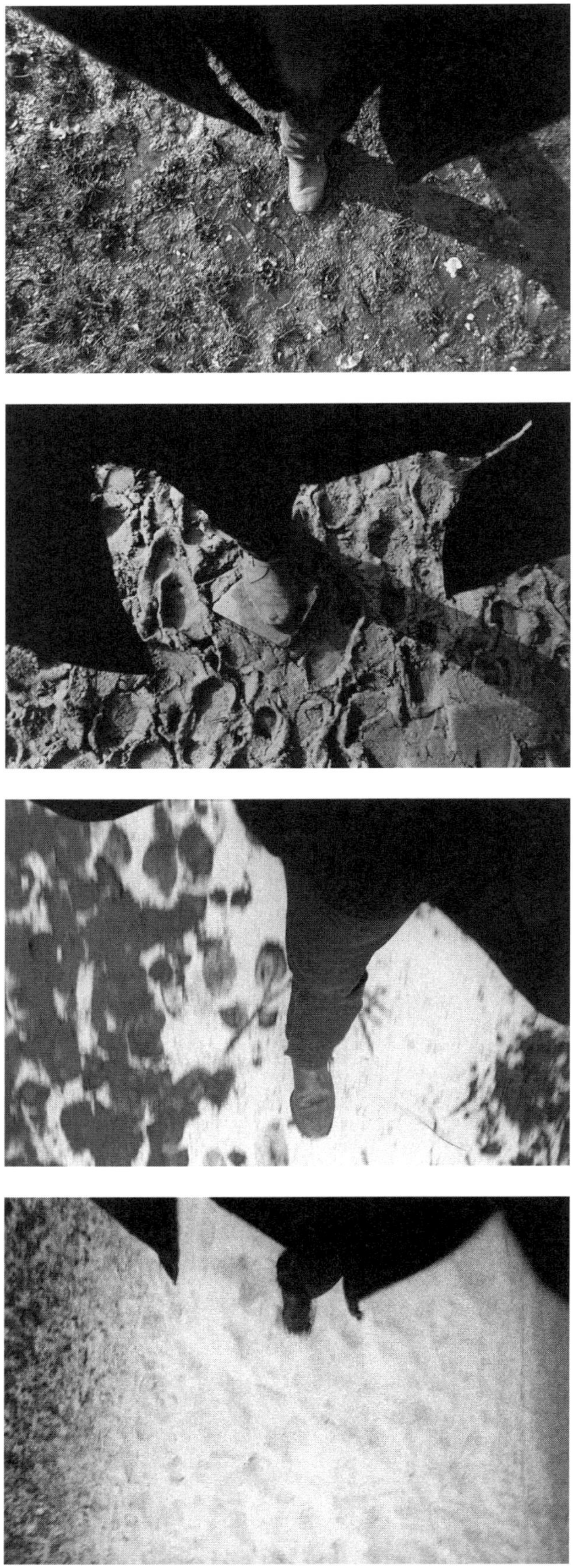

Janusz Połom, *Ku wiośnie*, 1972, fot. b.-cz.
Janusz Połom, *Towards Spring*, 1972,
B&W photograph

Janusz Połom, *Obrazy dźwiękowe*, 1975, fot. cz.-b.
Janusz Połom, *Sound Pictures*, 1975, B&W photograph

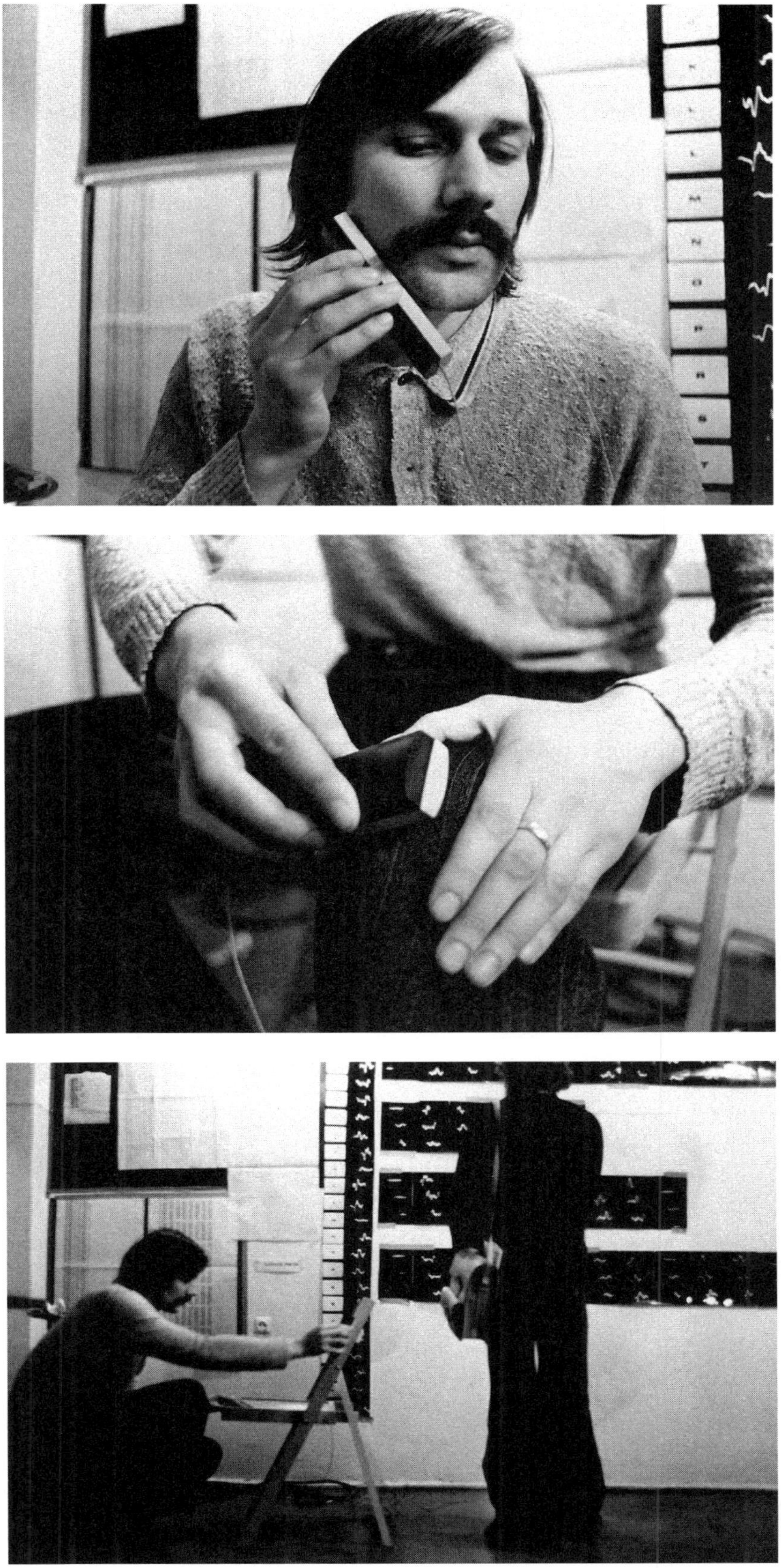

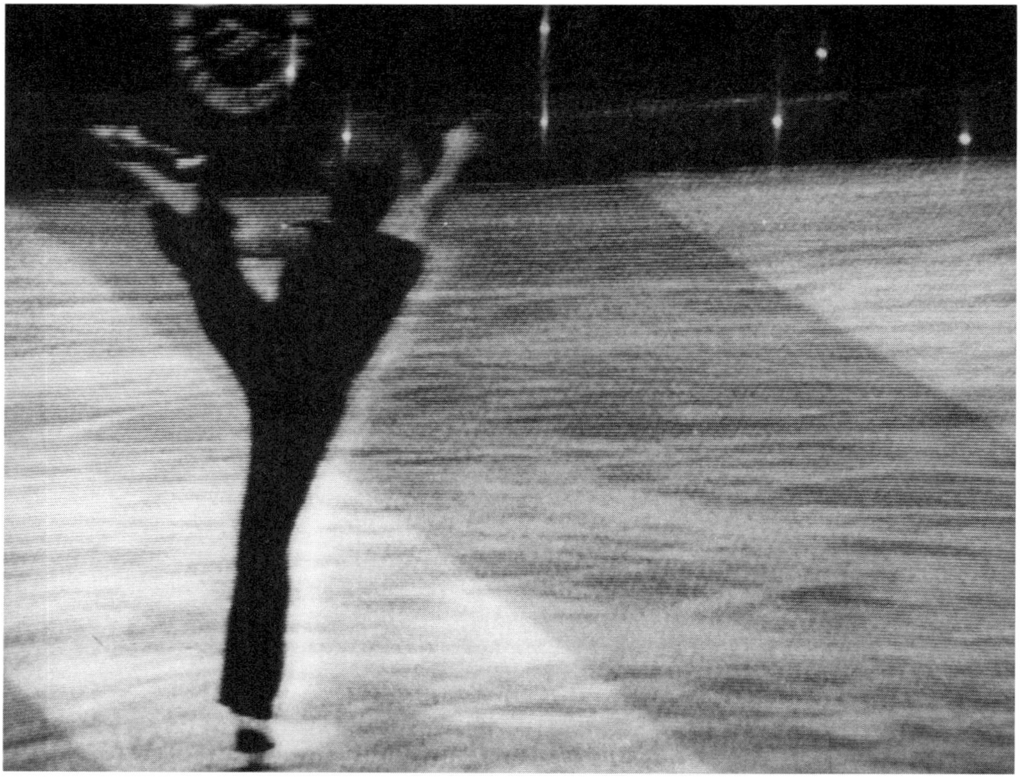

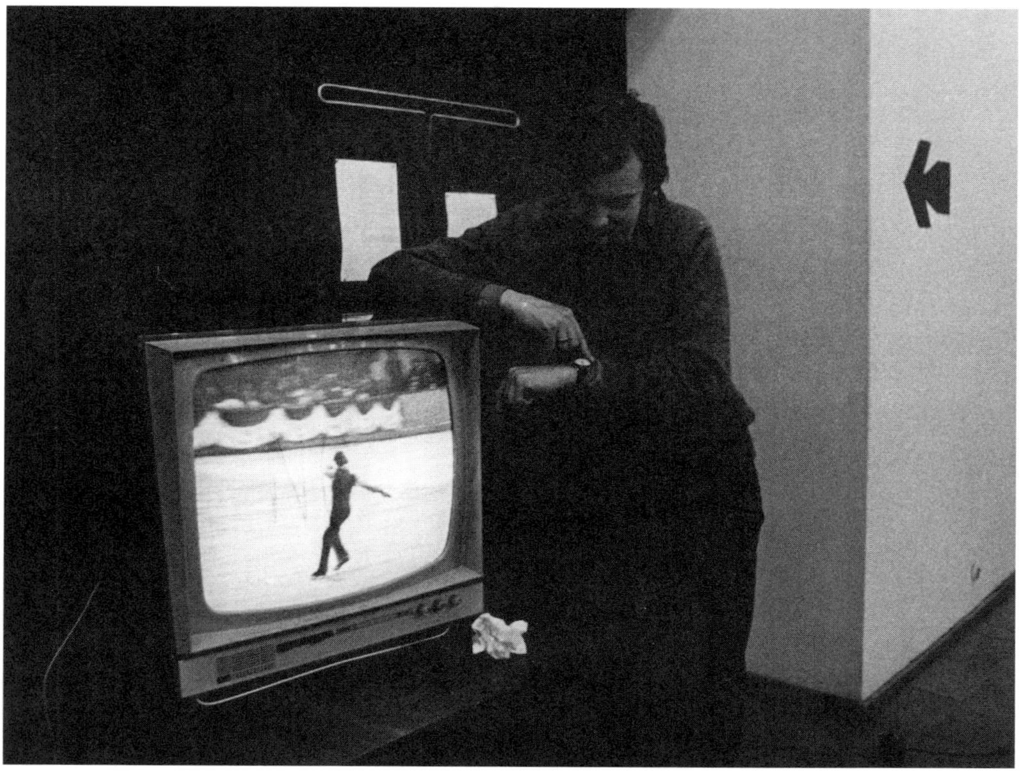

Andrzej Różycki, *Seans telewizyjny,* Akcja Warsztat, Muzeum Sztuki w Łodzi, 1973
Andrzej Różycki, *TV-Broadcast,* (Action Workshop, Muzeum Sztuki, Łódź), 1973

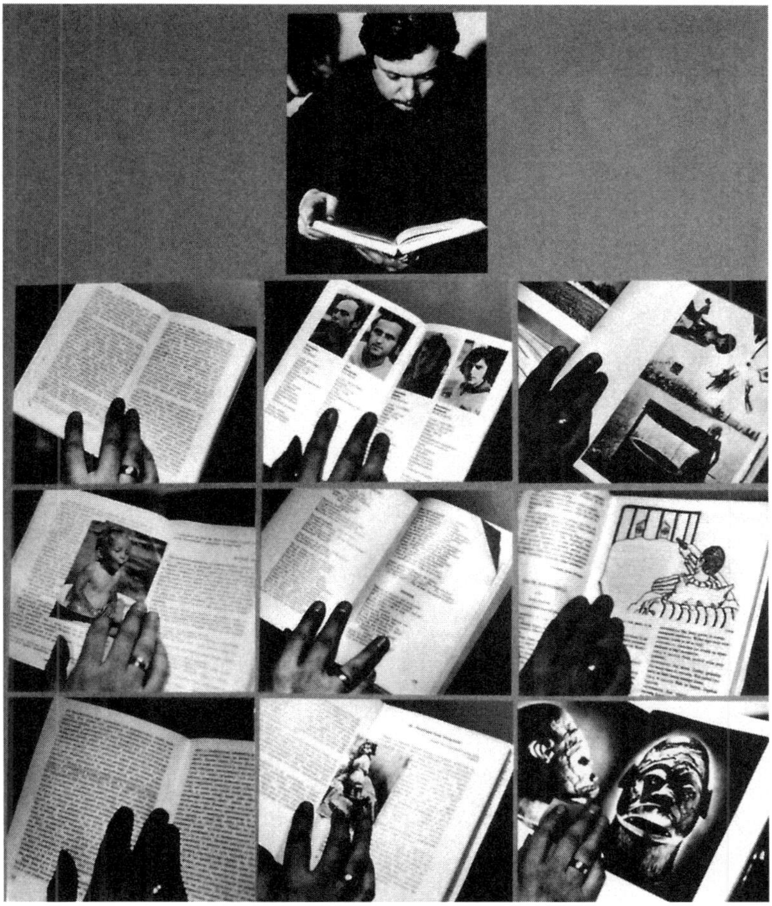

Andrzej Różycki, *Fotografia warunkowa*, 1973, fot. cz.-b.
Andrzej Różycki, *Conditional Photograph*, 1973, B&W photograph

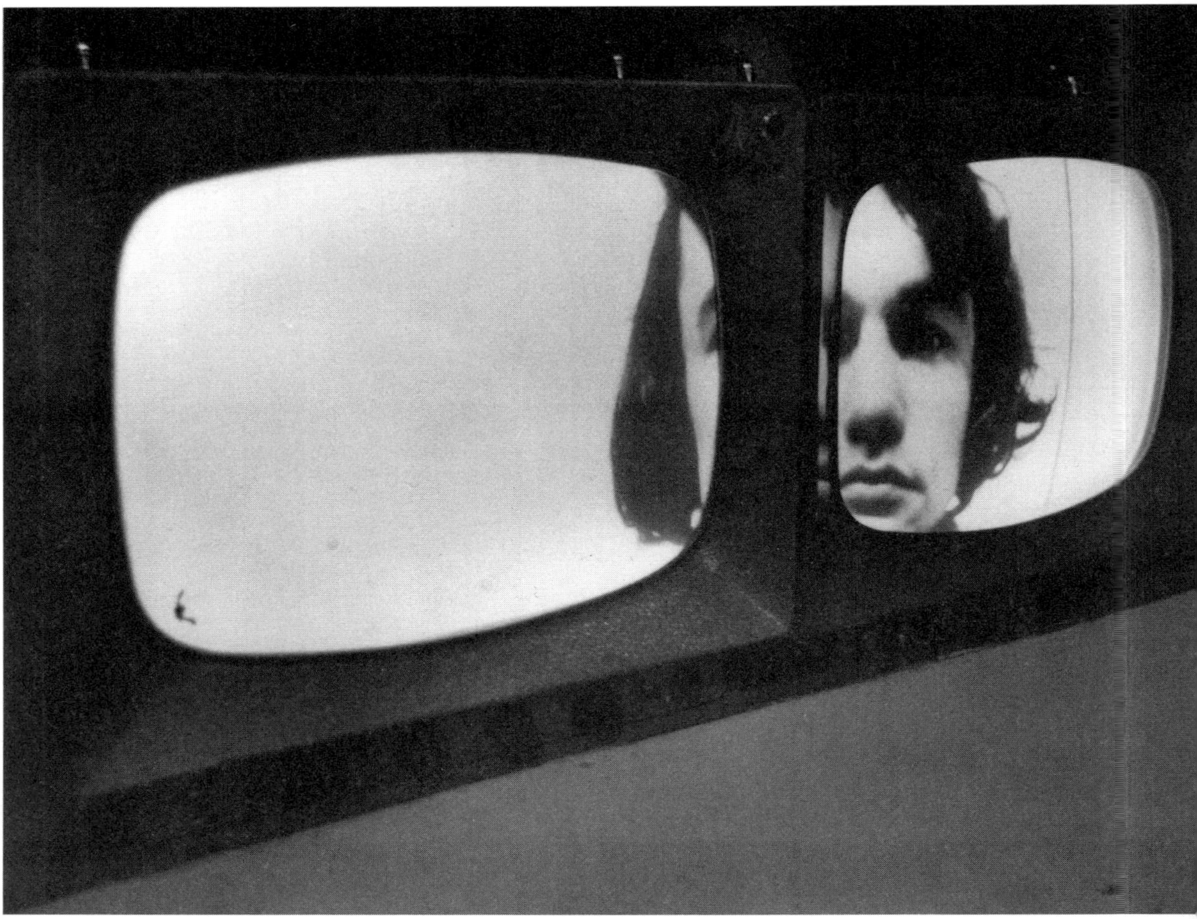

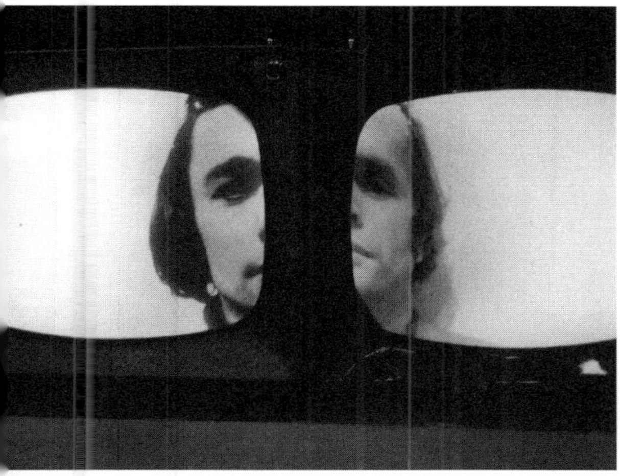
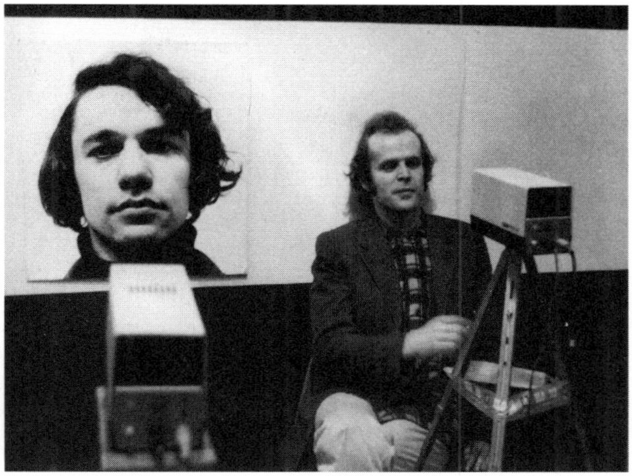
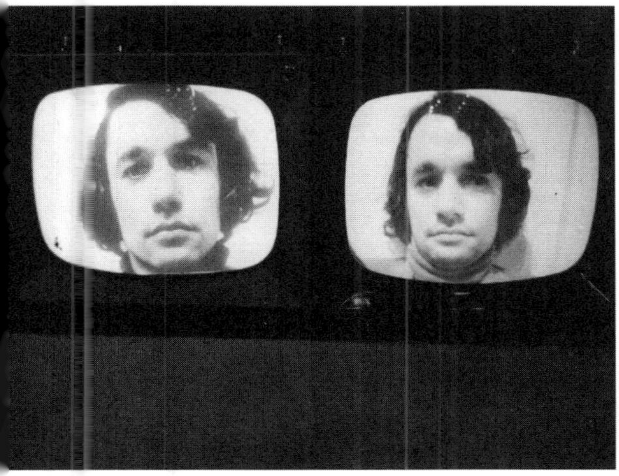
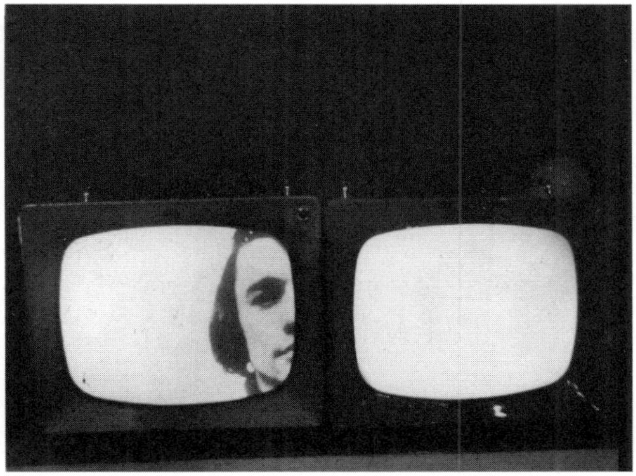
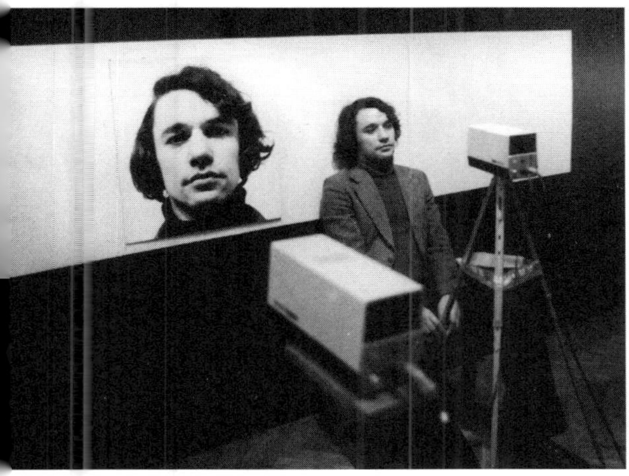
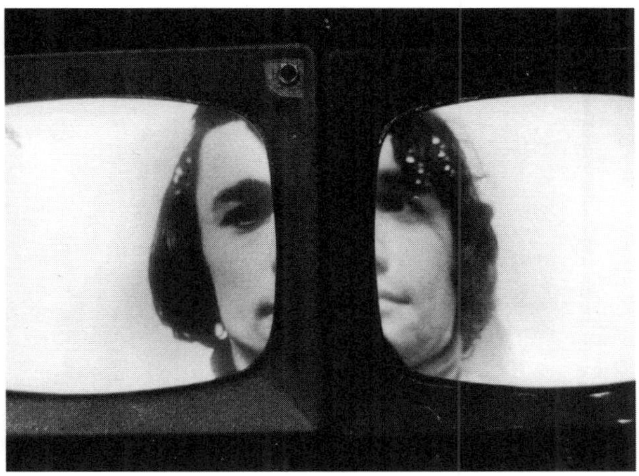

Andrzej Różycki, *Video-Duo*, 1975
Andrzej Różycki, *Video-Duo*, 1975

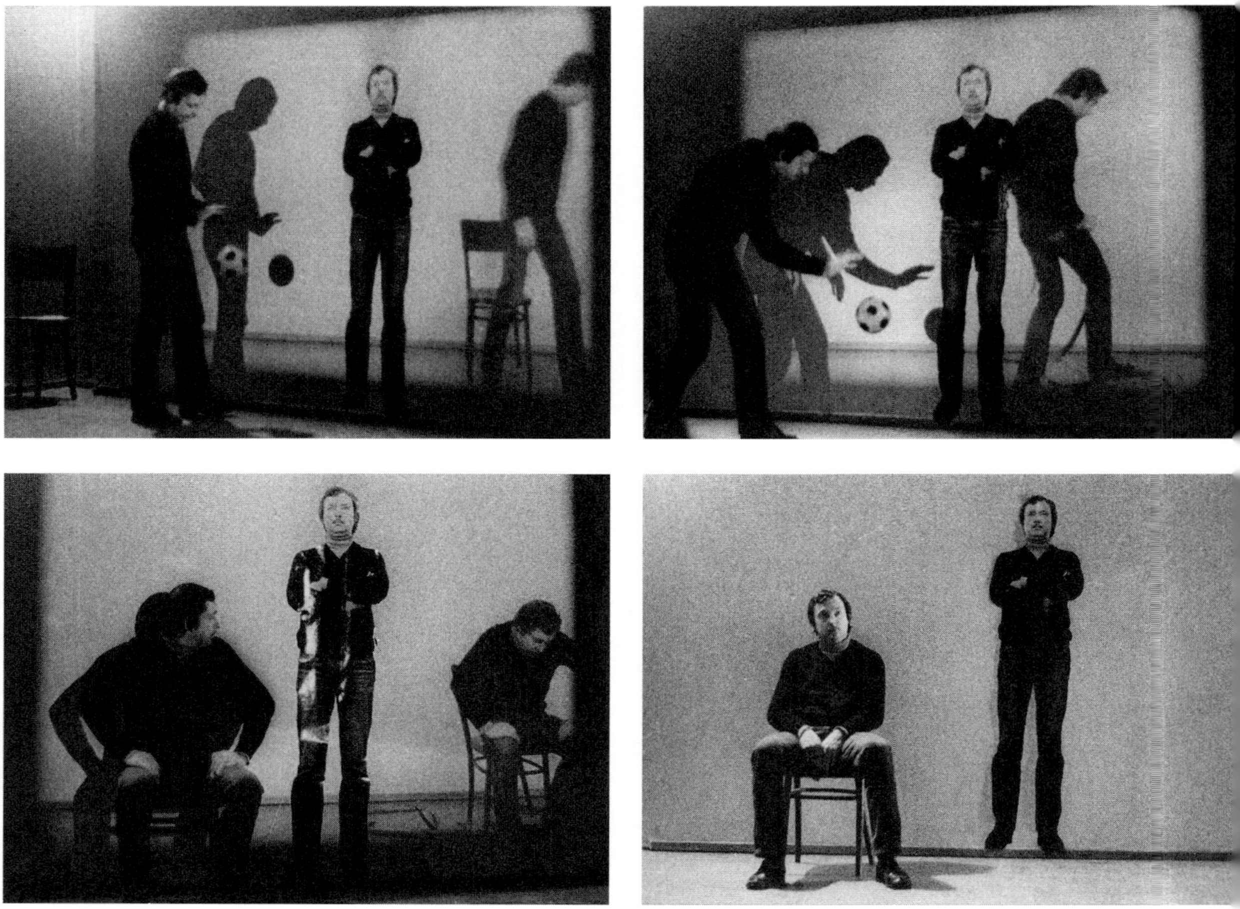

Andrzej Różycki, *Identyfikacja pozorna*, 1975, fot. cz.-b.
Andrzej Różycki, *Seeming Identification*, 1975, B&W photograph

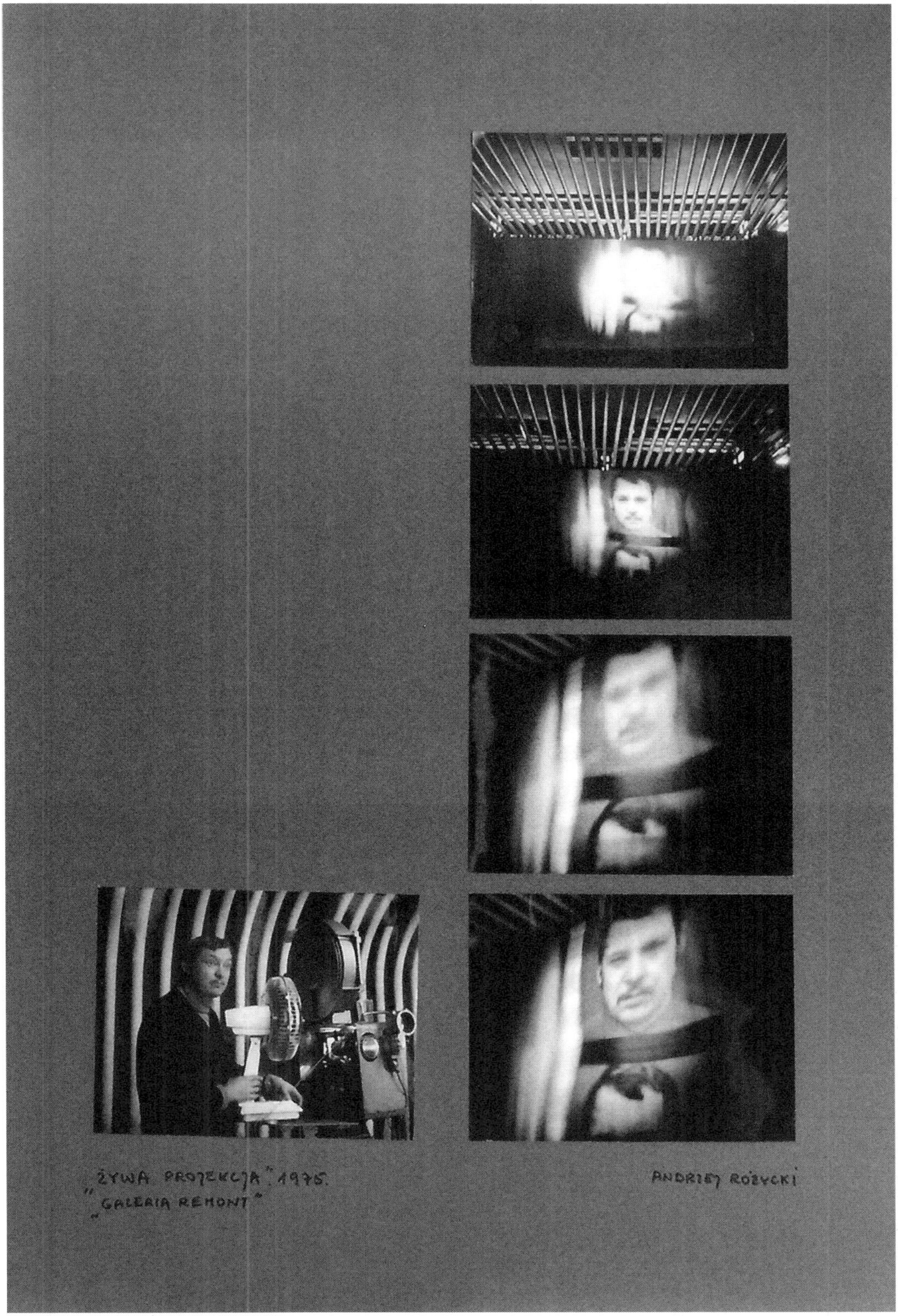

Andrzej Różycki, *Żywa projekcja* (Galeria Remont w Warszawie), 1975, fot. cz.-b.
Andrzej Różycki, *Live Projection* (Remont Gallery, Warsaw), 1975, B&W photograph

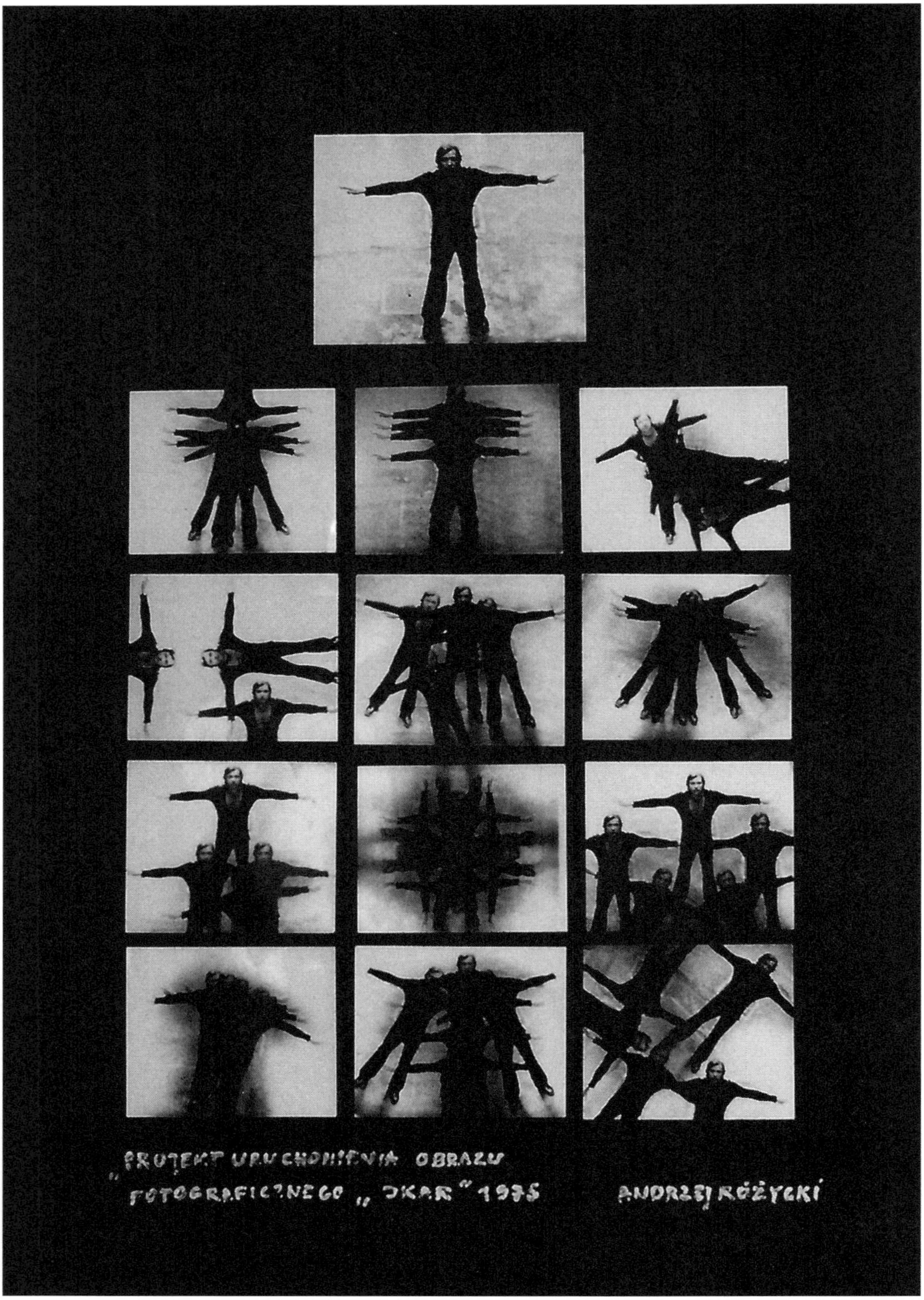

Andrzej Różycki, *Ikar – zdjęciowy projekt ożywienia obrazu*, 1975, fot. cz.-b.
Andrzej Różycki, *Ikar – photographic project of reviving of image*, 1975, B&W photograph

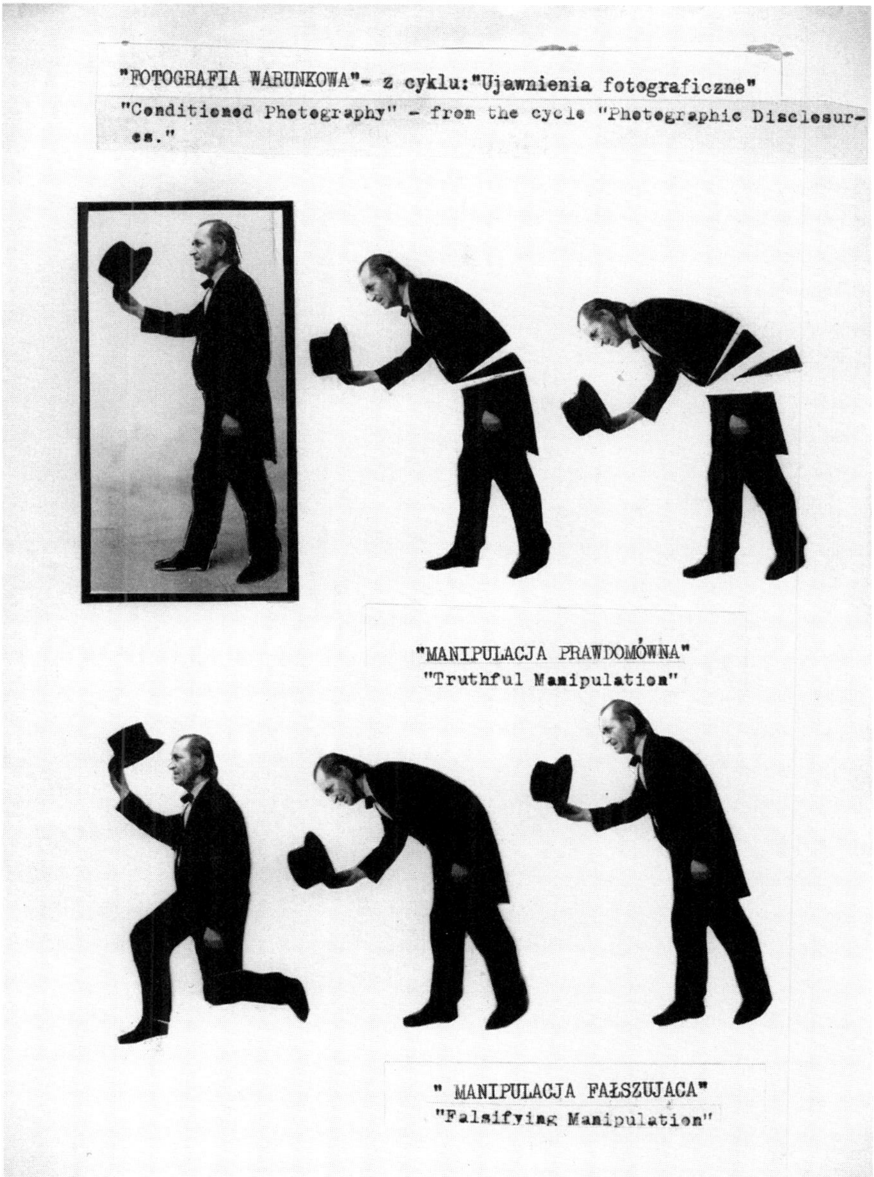

Andrzej Różycki, *Fotografia warunkowa*, 1972/73, fot. cz.-b.
Andrzej Różycki, *Conditional Photograph*, 1972/73, B&W photograph

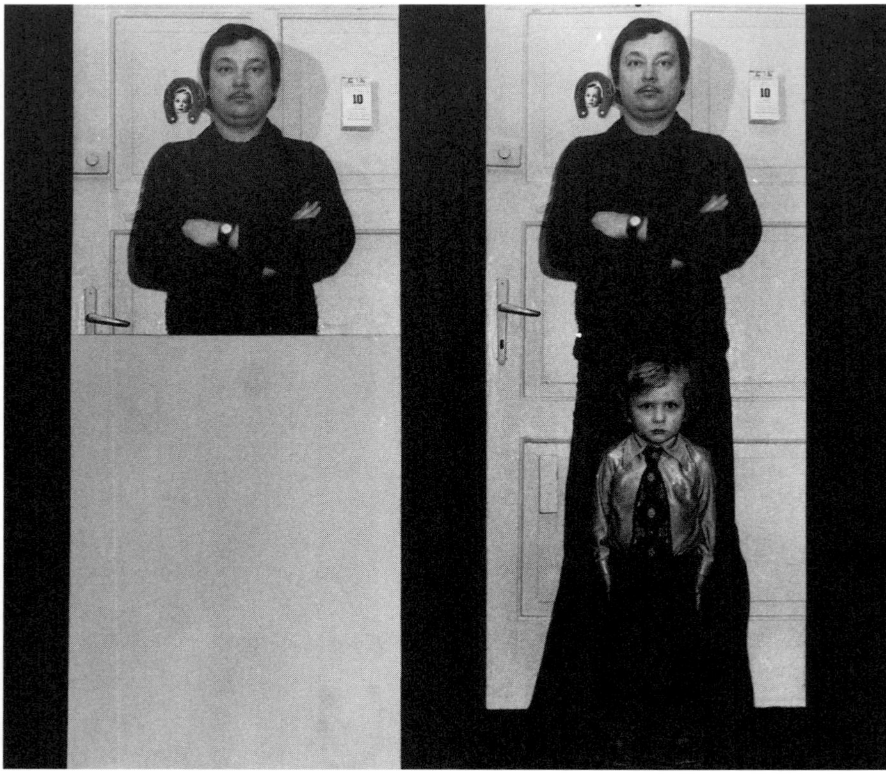

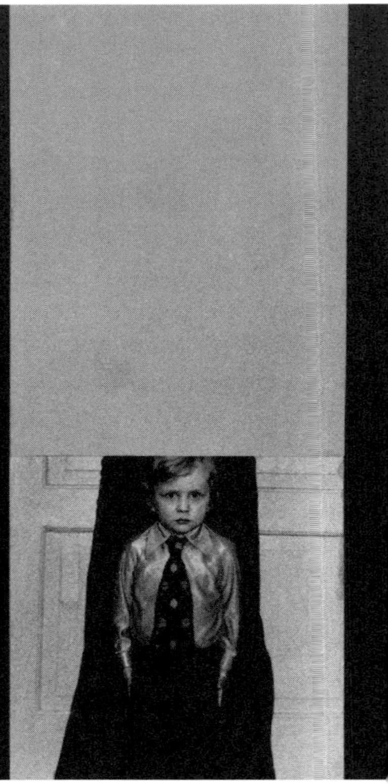

Andrzej Różycki, *Bez tytułu (Borys)*, 1973, fot. cz.-b.
Andrzej Różycki, *Untitled (Borys)*, 1973, B&W photograph

Andrzej Różycki, *Fotografia warunkowa (Okno)*, 1975, fot. cz.-b
Andrzej Różycki, *Conditional Photograph (Window)*, 1975,
B&W photograph

Andrzej Różycki, *Fotografia warunkowa*, 1975, fot. cz.-b.
Andrzej Różycki, *Conditional Photograph*, 1975, B&W photograph

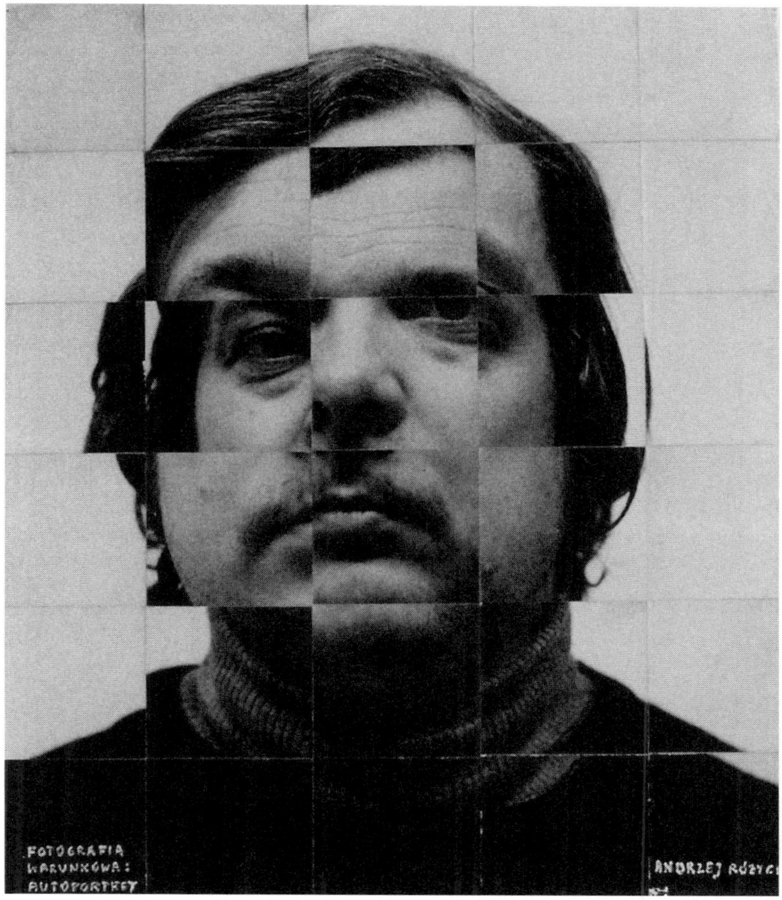

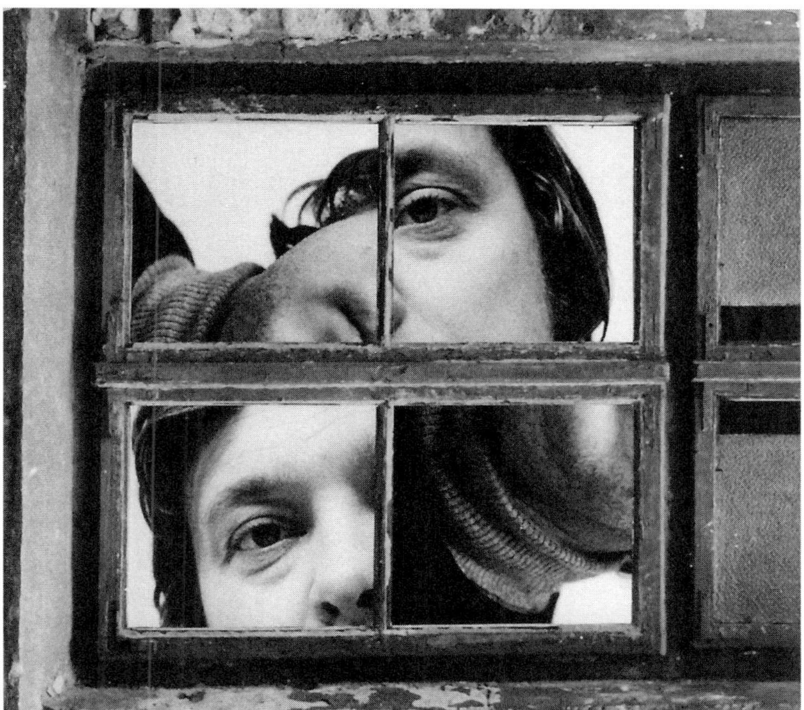

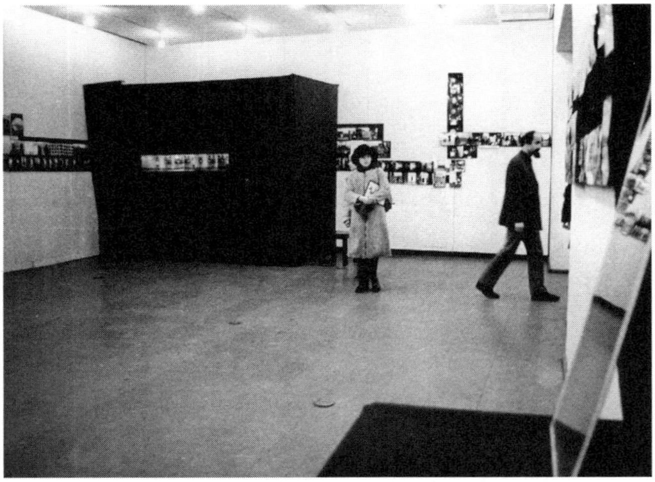

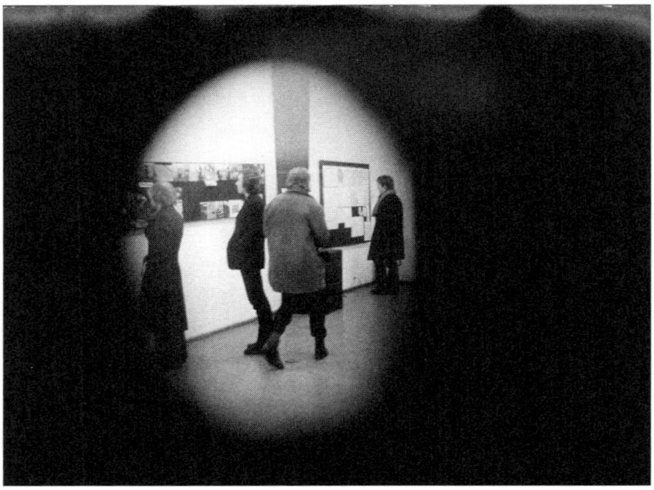

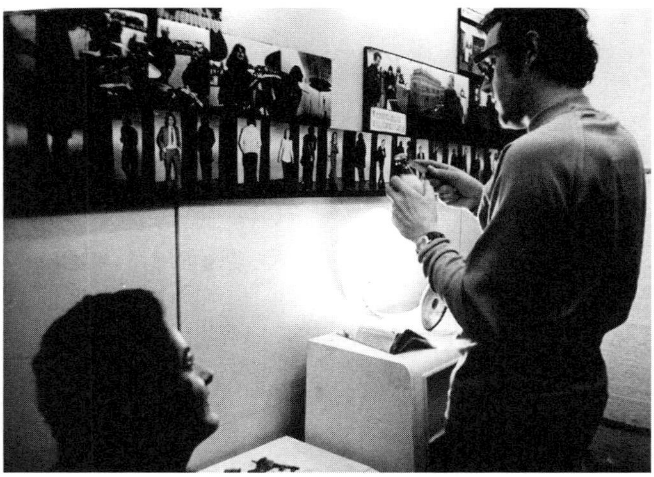

Kazimierz Bendkowski, Akcja Warsztat, Muzeum Sztuki, Łodź, 1973
Kazimierz Bendkowski, Action Workshop, Muzeum Sztuki, Łodź, 1973

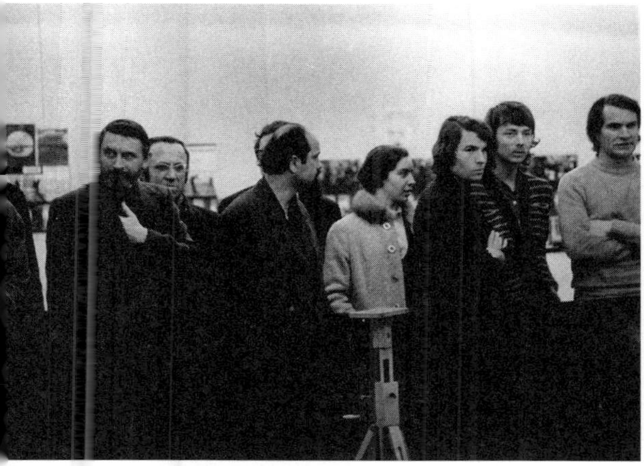

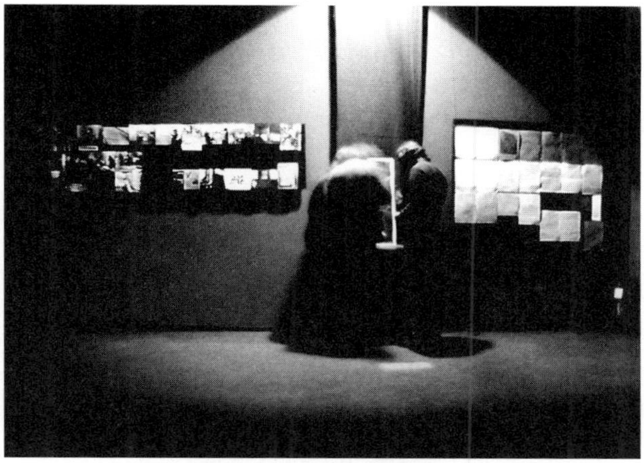

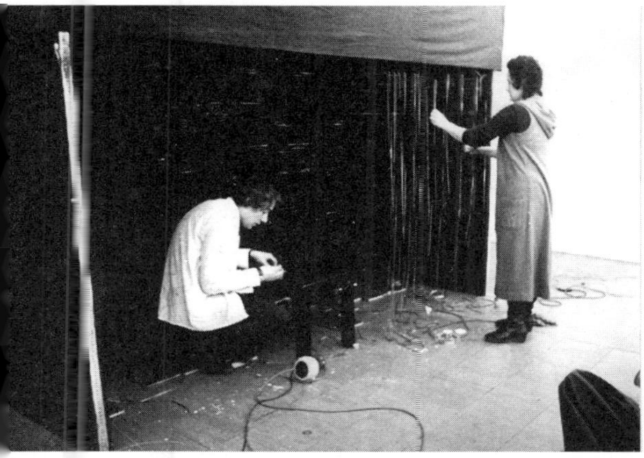

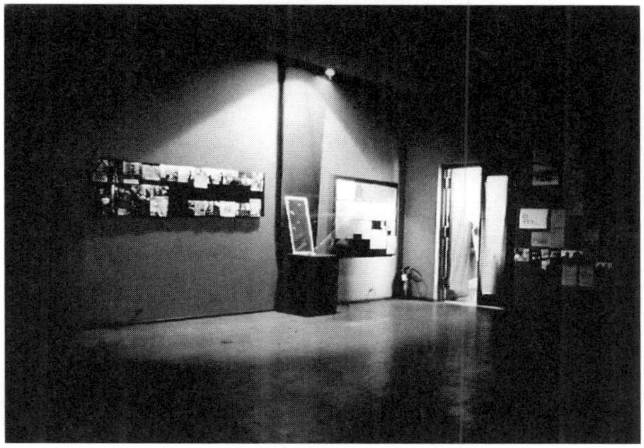

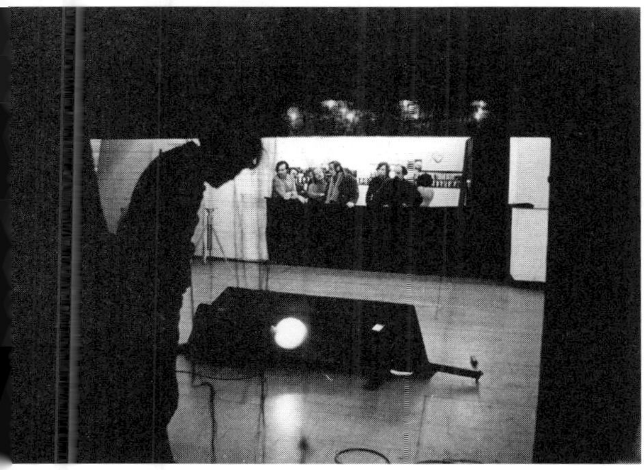

azimierz Bendkowski, *Obiekt w czerni* (Akcja Warsztat, Muzeum
ztuki w Łodzi), 1973
azimierz Bendkowski, *Object in Black* (The Action Workshop,
luzeum Sztuki in Łodź), 1973

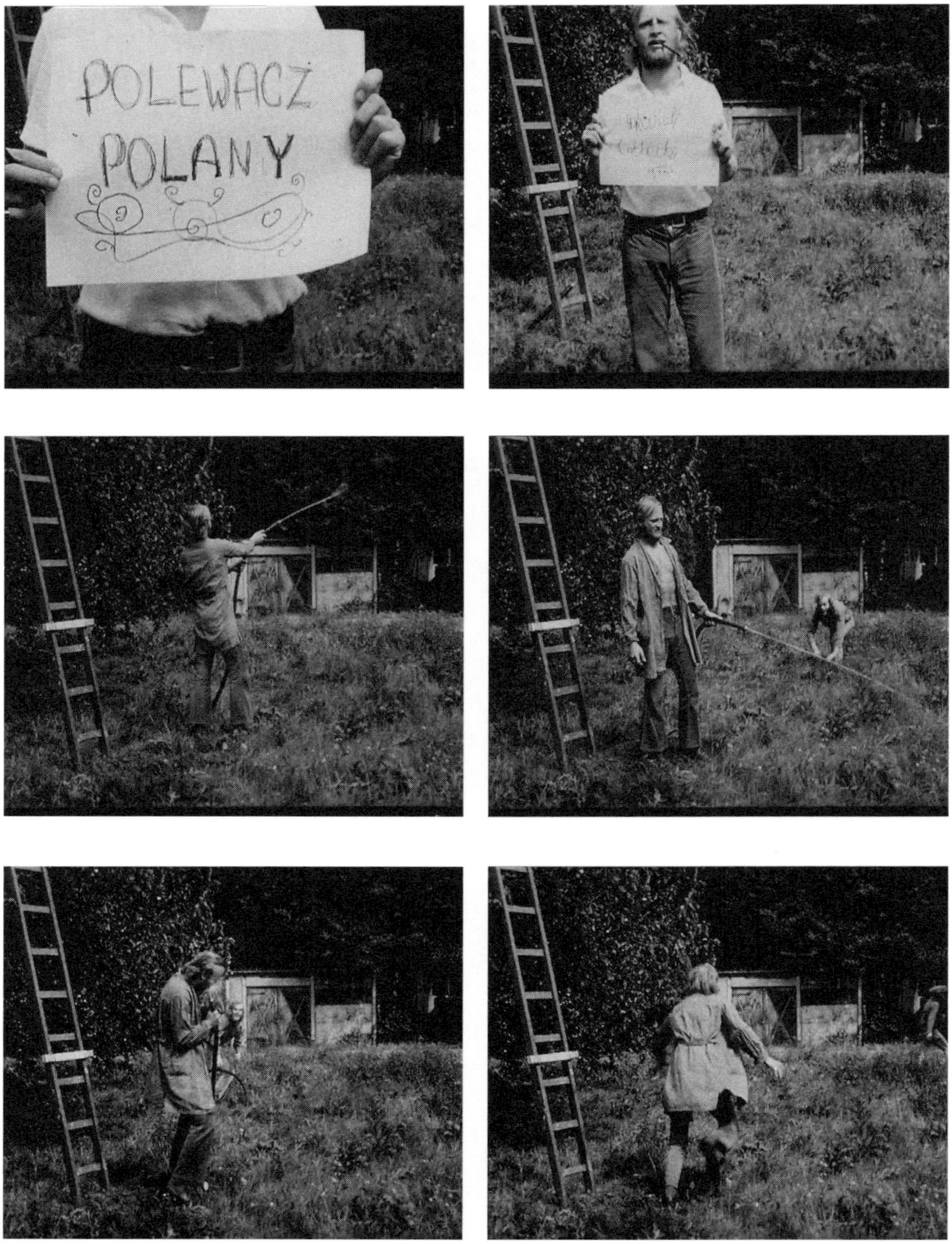

Paweł Kwiek, *Kinolaboratorium*, 1973, 35 mm, 13'20''
Paweł Kwiek, *Cinelaboratory,* 1973, 35 mm, 13'20''

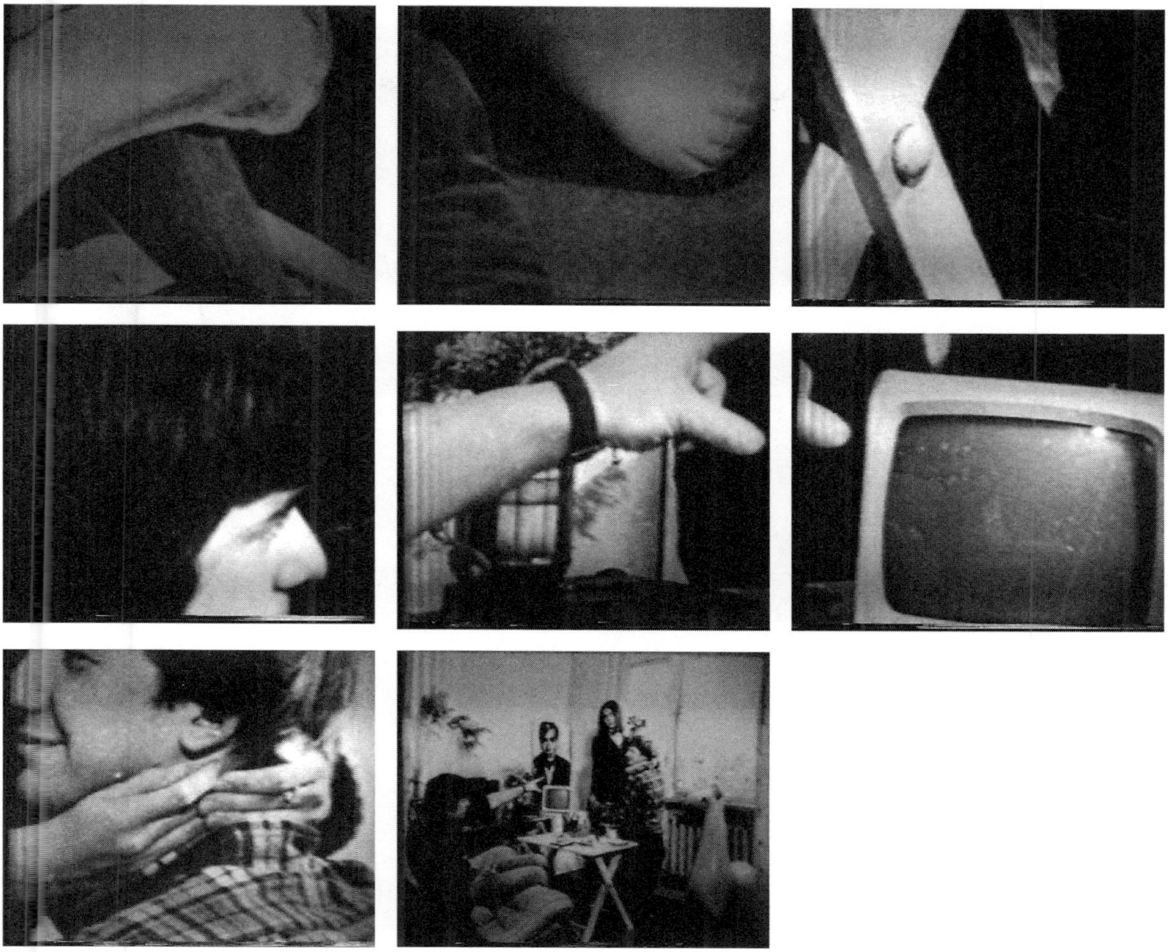

Janusz Szczerek, *Analiza*, 1979, wideo, 12’40”
Janusz Szczerek, *Analysis*, 1979, video 12’40”

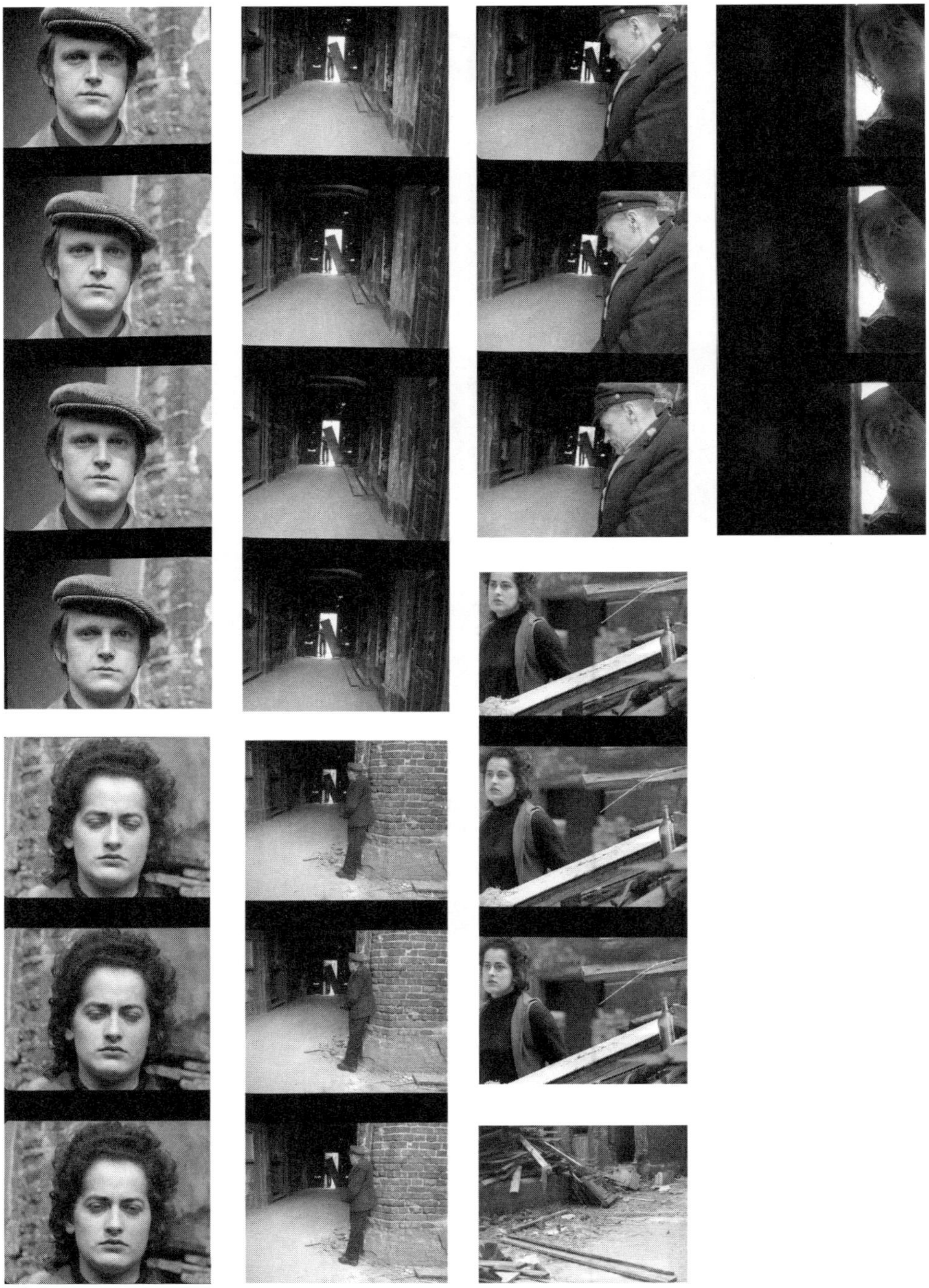

Kazimierz Bendkowski, *Obszar*, 1973, 35 mm, 5'20"
Kazimierz Bendkowski, *An Area*, 1973, 35 mm, 5'20"

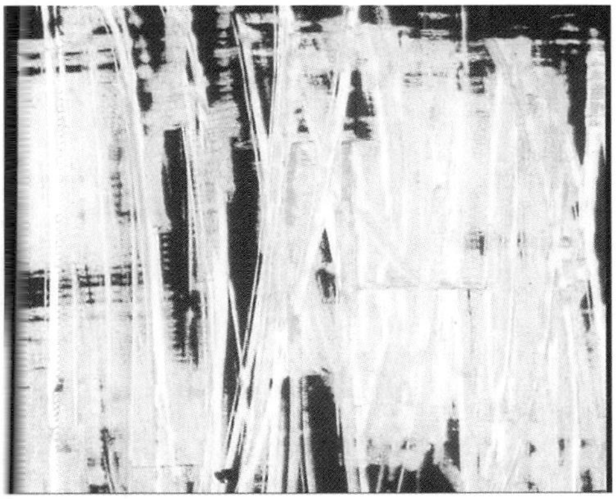
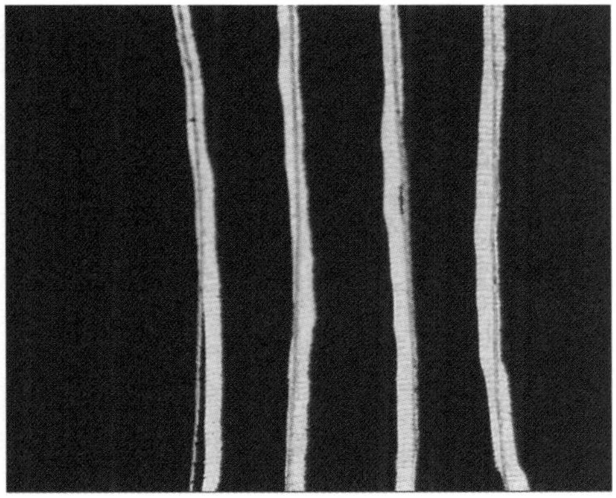
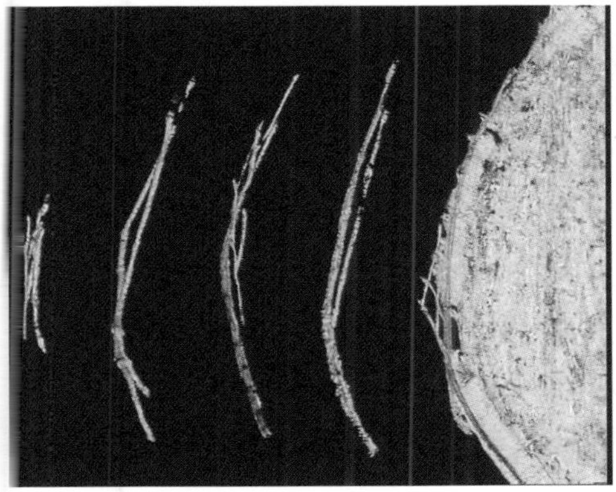
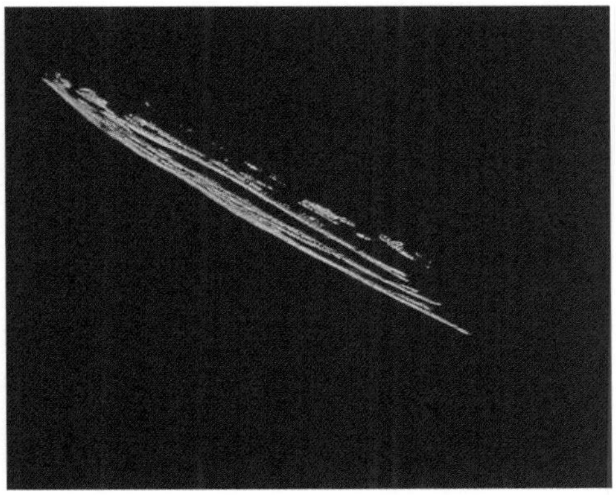
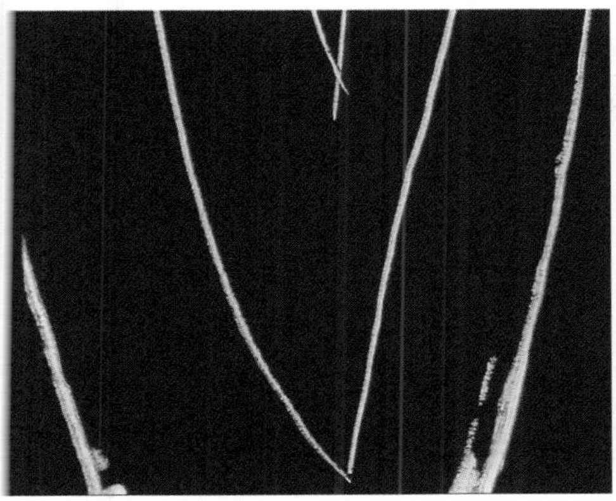
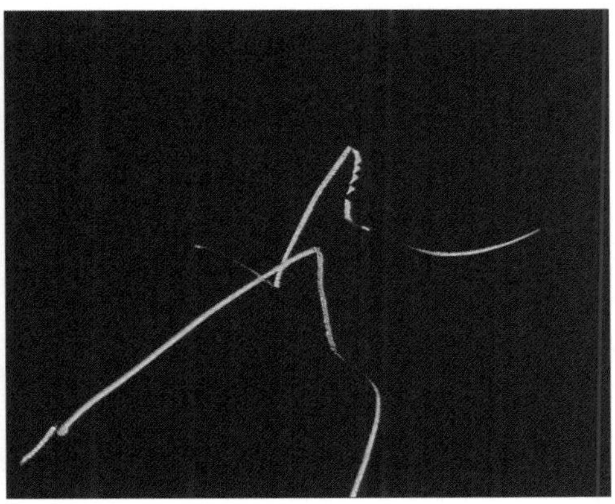
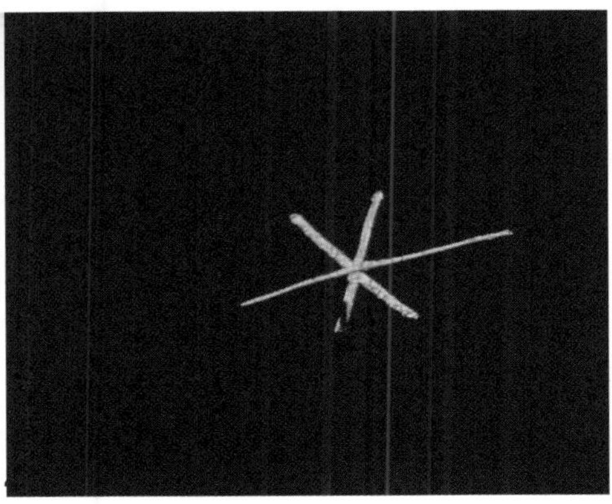

Józef Robakowski, *22x*, 1971, 35 mm, 5'24''
Józef Robakowski, *22x*, 1971, 35 mm, 5'24''

Józef Robakowski, *Próba II*, 1971, 35 mm, 1'58''
Józef Robakowski, *Trial II*, 1971, 35 mm, 1'58''

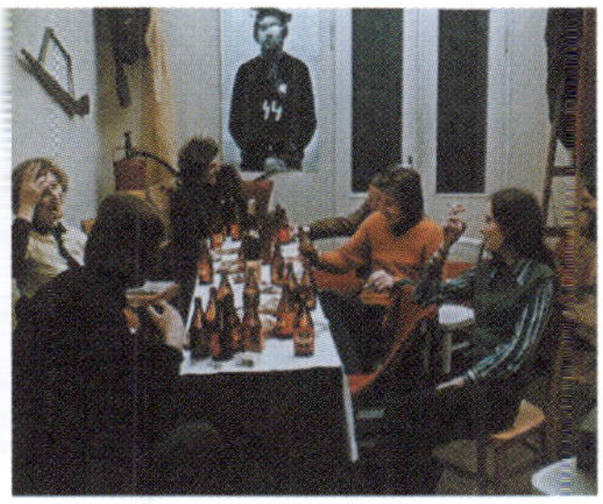
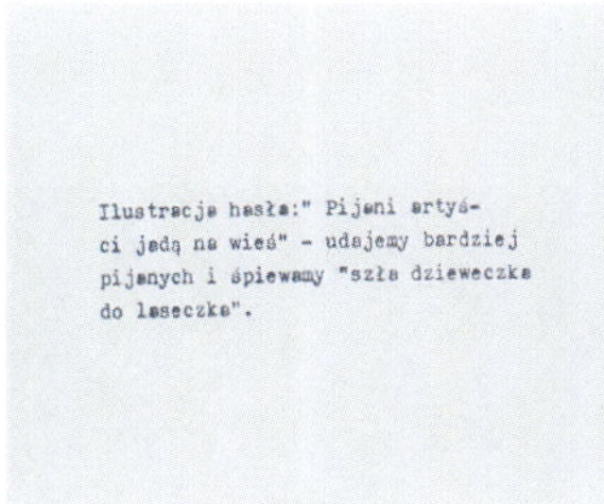
Ilustracja hasła:" Pijani artyści jadą na wieś" - udajemy bardziej pijanych i śpiewamy "szła dzieweczka do laseczka".
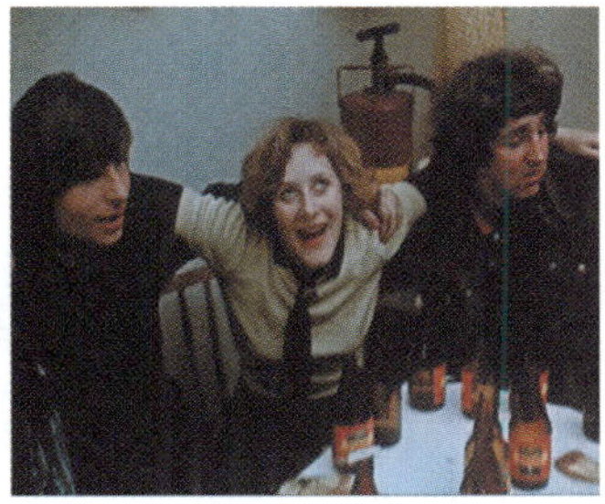
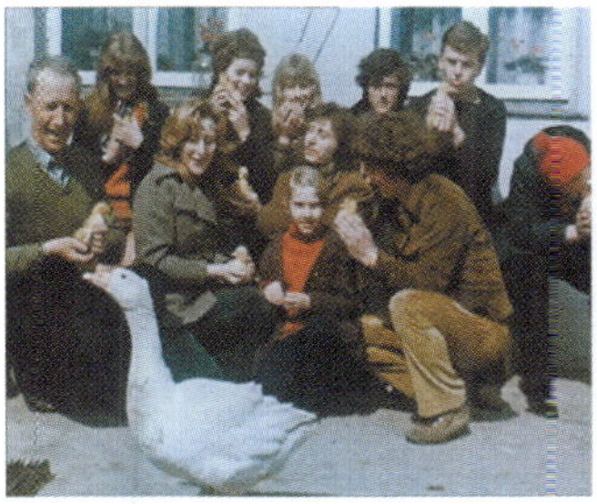
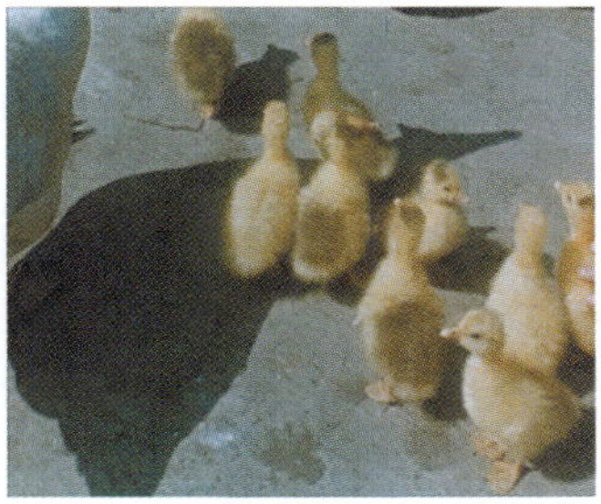
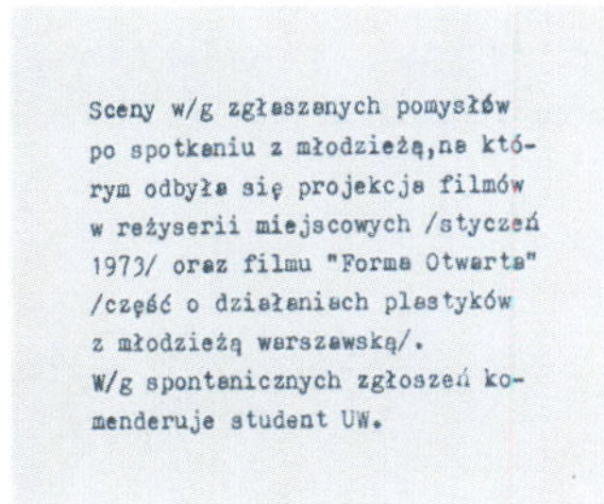
Sceny w/g zgłaszanych pomysłów po spotkaniu z młodzieżą,na którym odbyła się projekcja filmów w reżyserii miejscowych /styczeń 1973/ oraz filmu "Forma Otwarta" /część o działaniach plastyków z młodzieżą warszawską/.
W/g spontanicznych zgłoszeń komenderuje student UW.
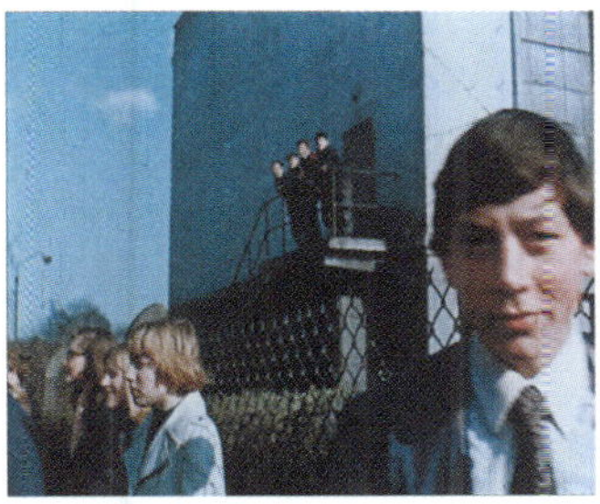
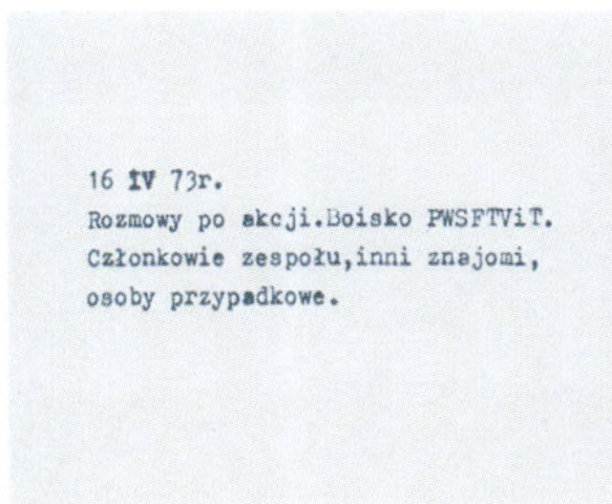
16 IV 73r.
Rozmowy po akcji.Boisko PWSFTViT.
Członkowie zespołu,inni znajomi,
osoby przypadkowe.
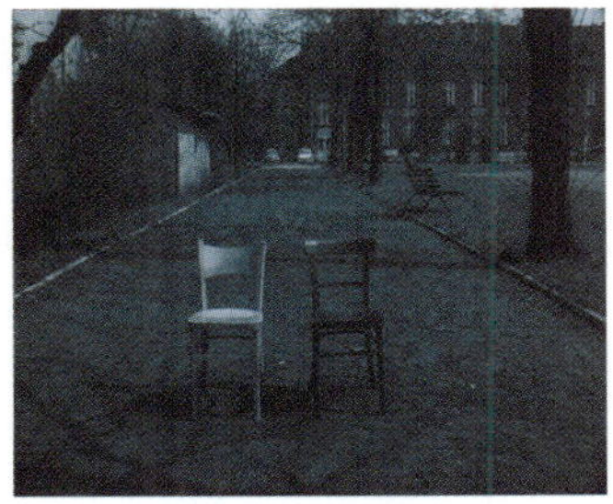
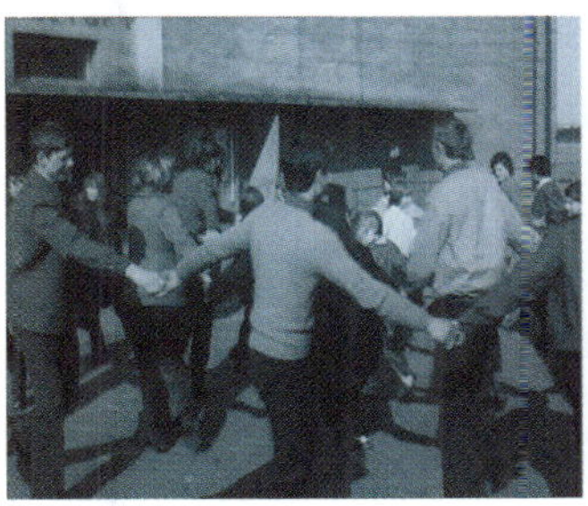
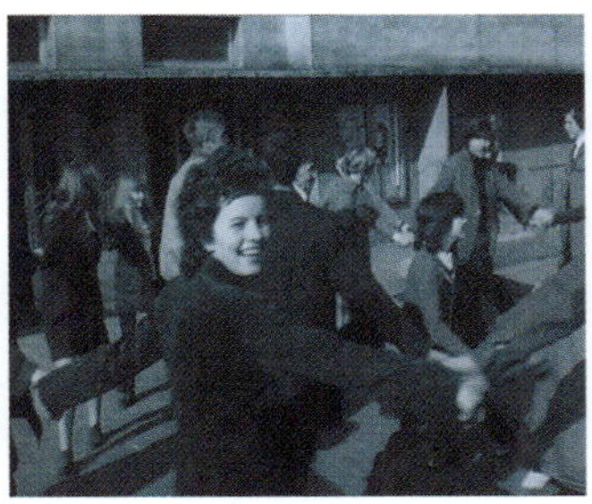
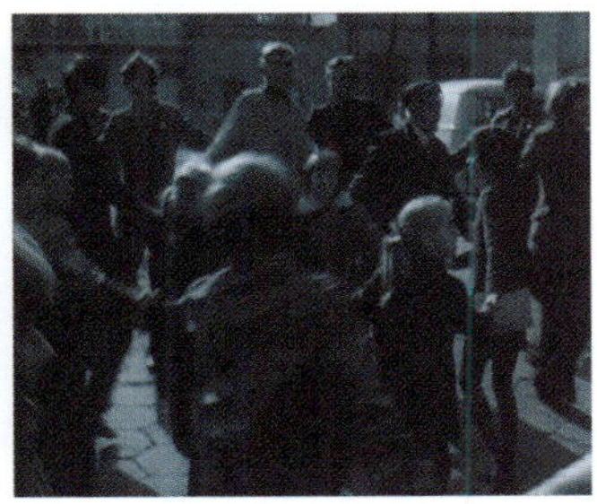
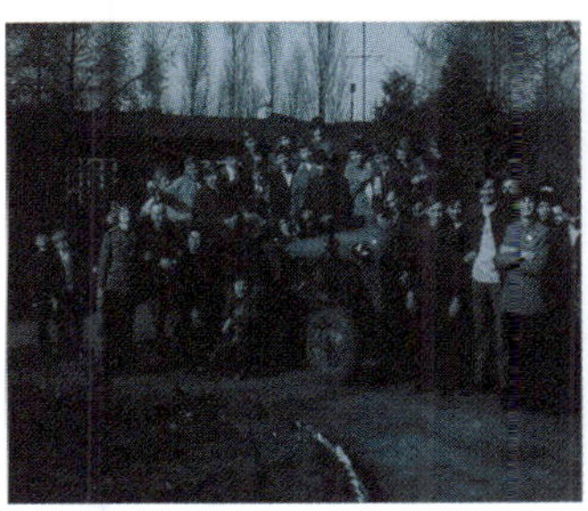
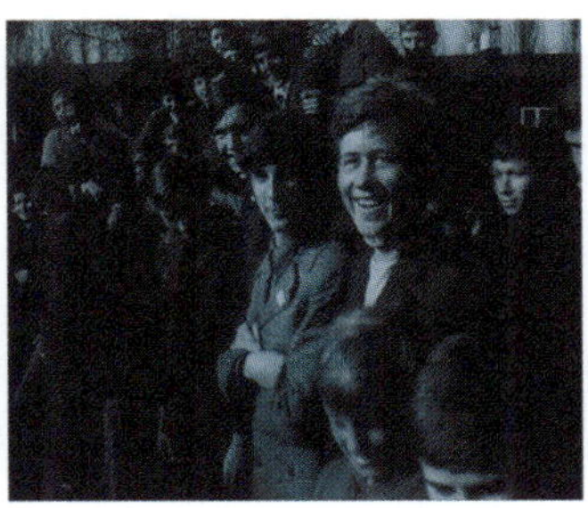
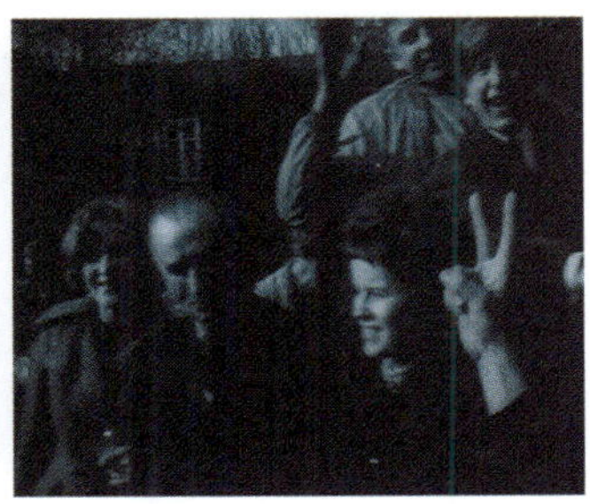

Paweł Kwiek, *Niechcice*, 1973, 35 mm, 5'01"
Paweł Kwiek, *Niechcice*, 1973, 35 mm, 5'01"

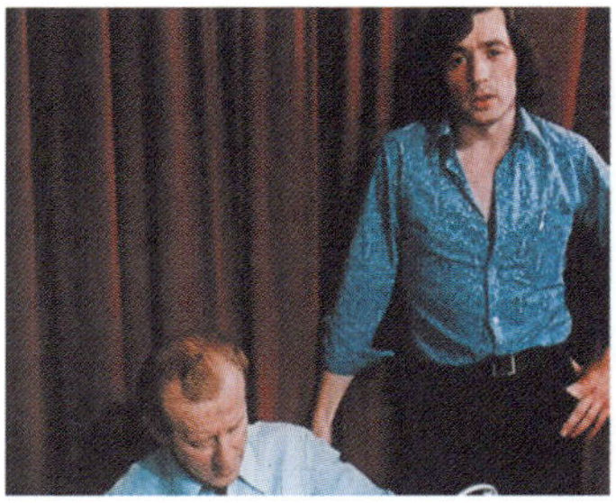

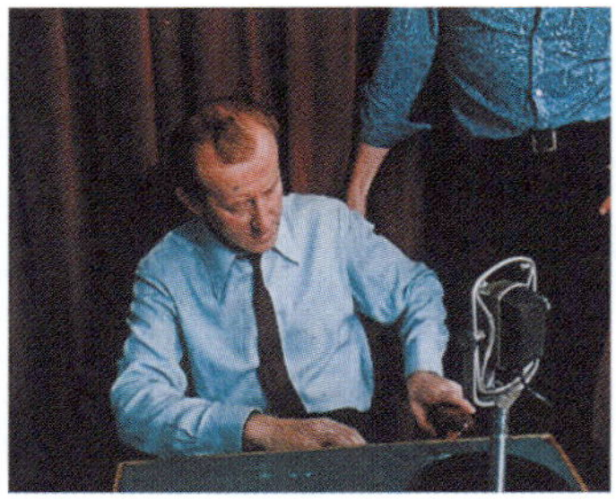

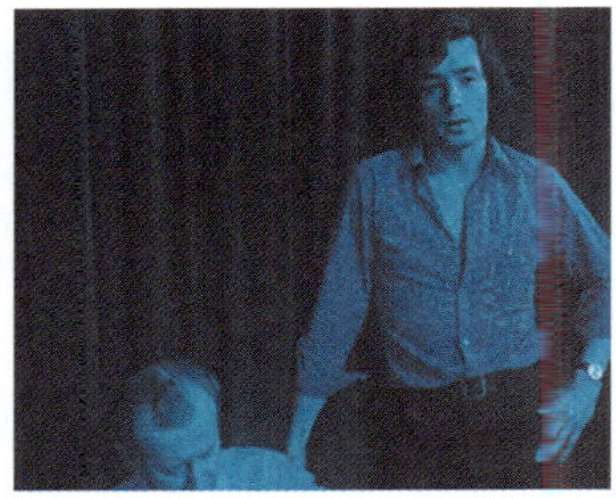

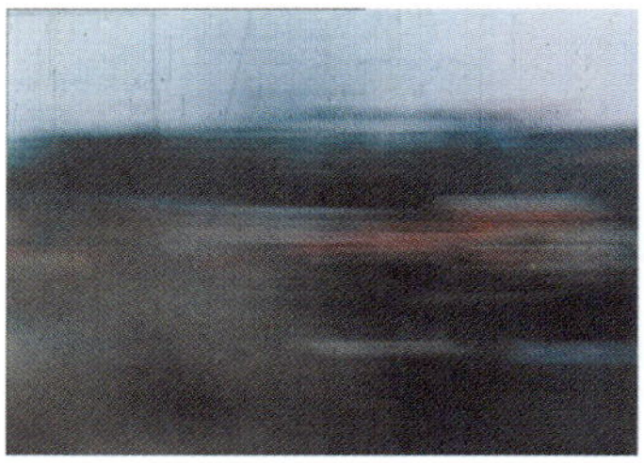

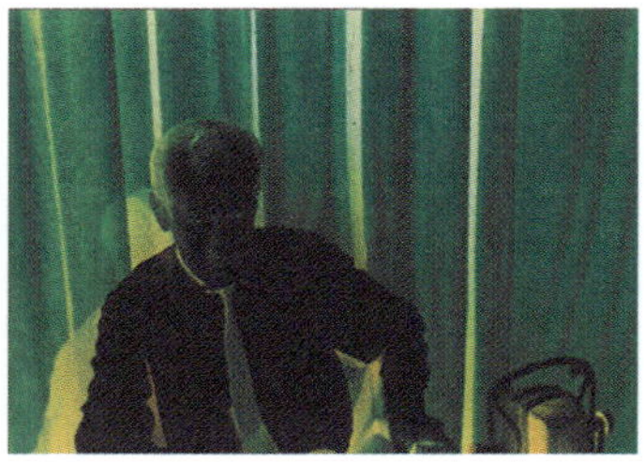

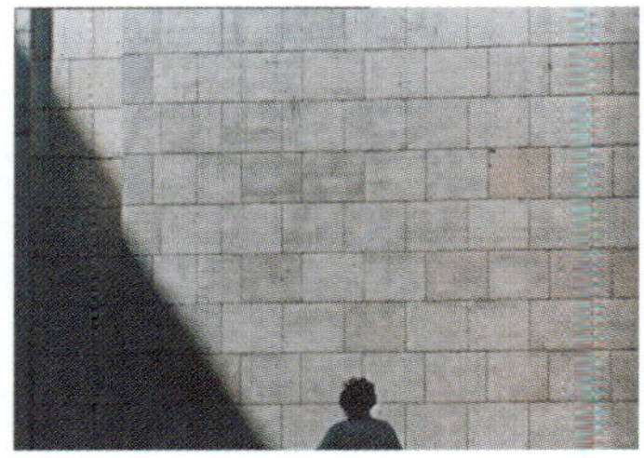

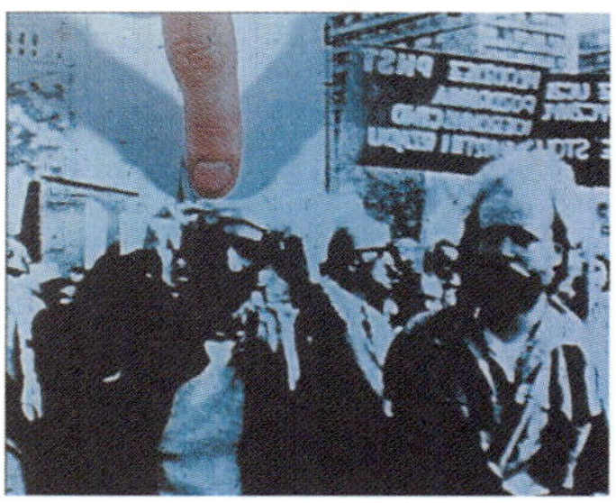

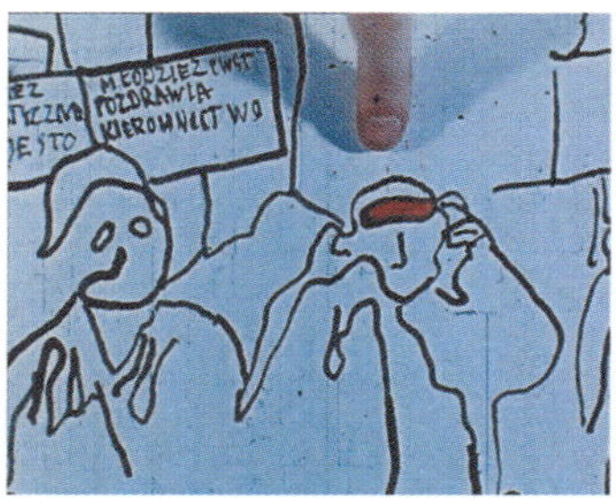
MŁODZIEŻ PWST
POZDRAWIA
KIEROMNICTWO

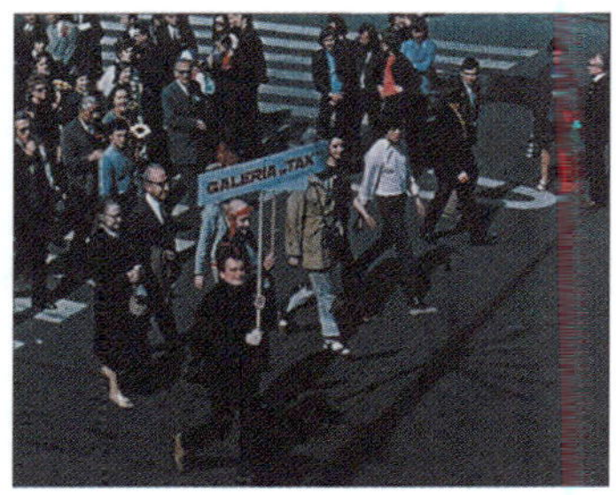

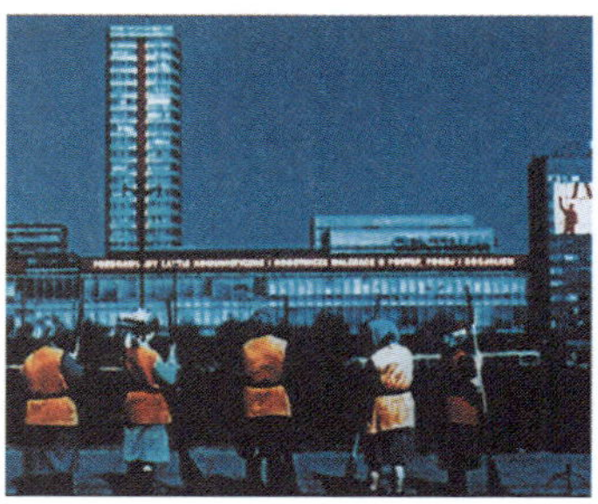

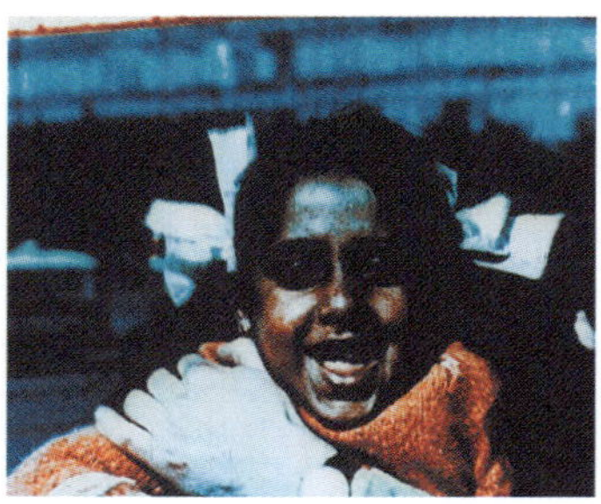

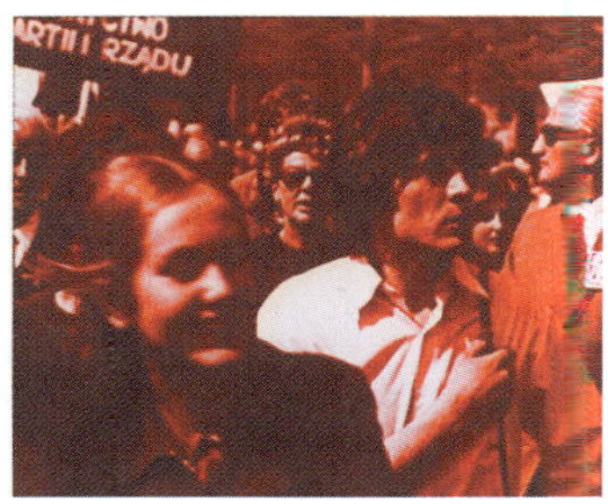
ARTII RZADU

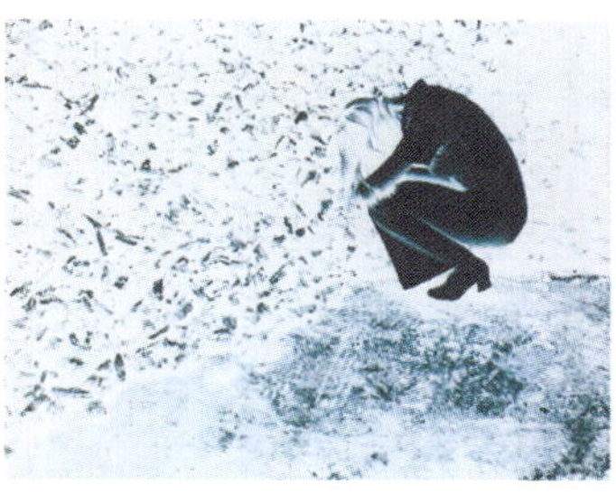

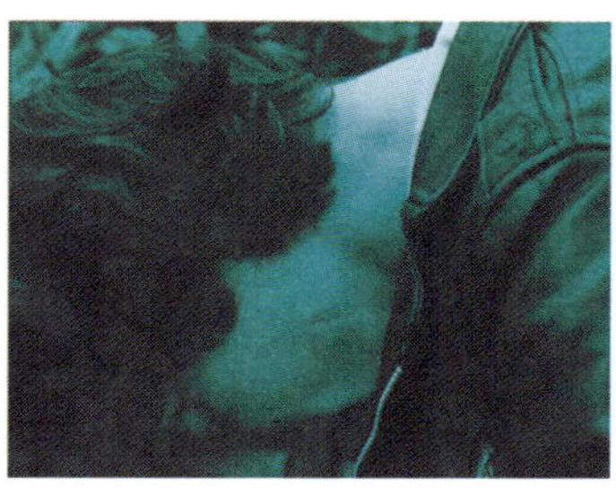

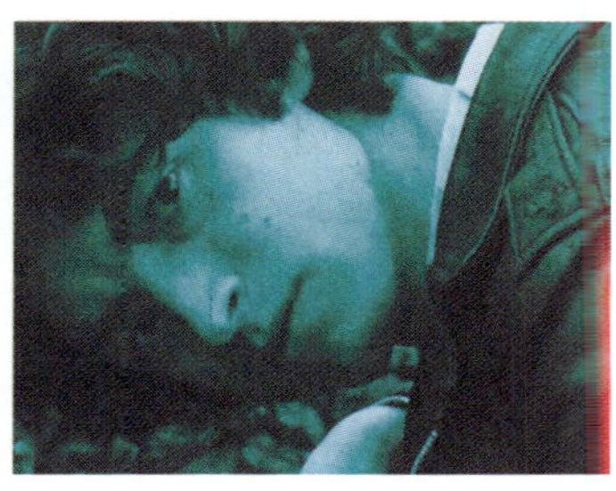

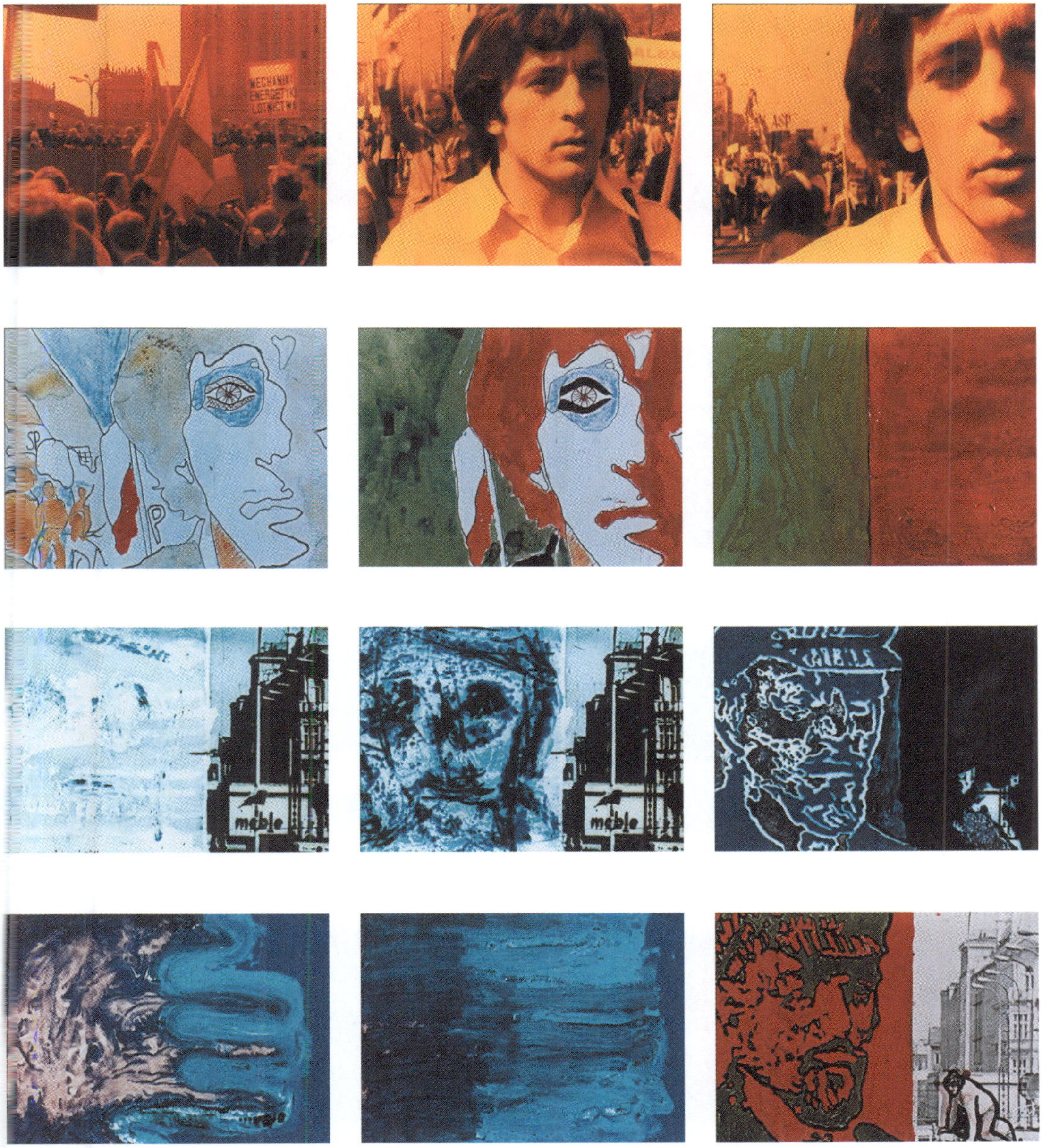

Paweł Kwiek, *1,2,3... Ćwiczenia operatorskie*, 1972, 35 mm, 8'10''
Paweł Kwiek, *1,2,3... Cinematographer's Exercise*, 1972, 35 mm, 8'10''

Paweł Kwiek, *Osieki*, 1974, 35 mm, 15’29’’

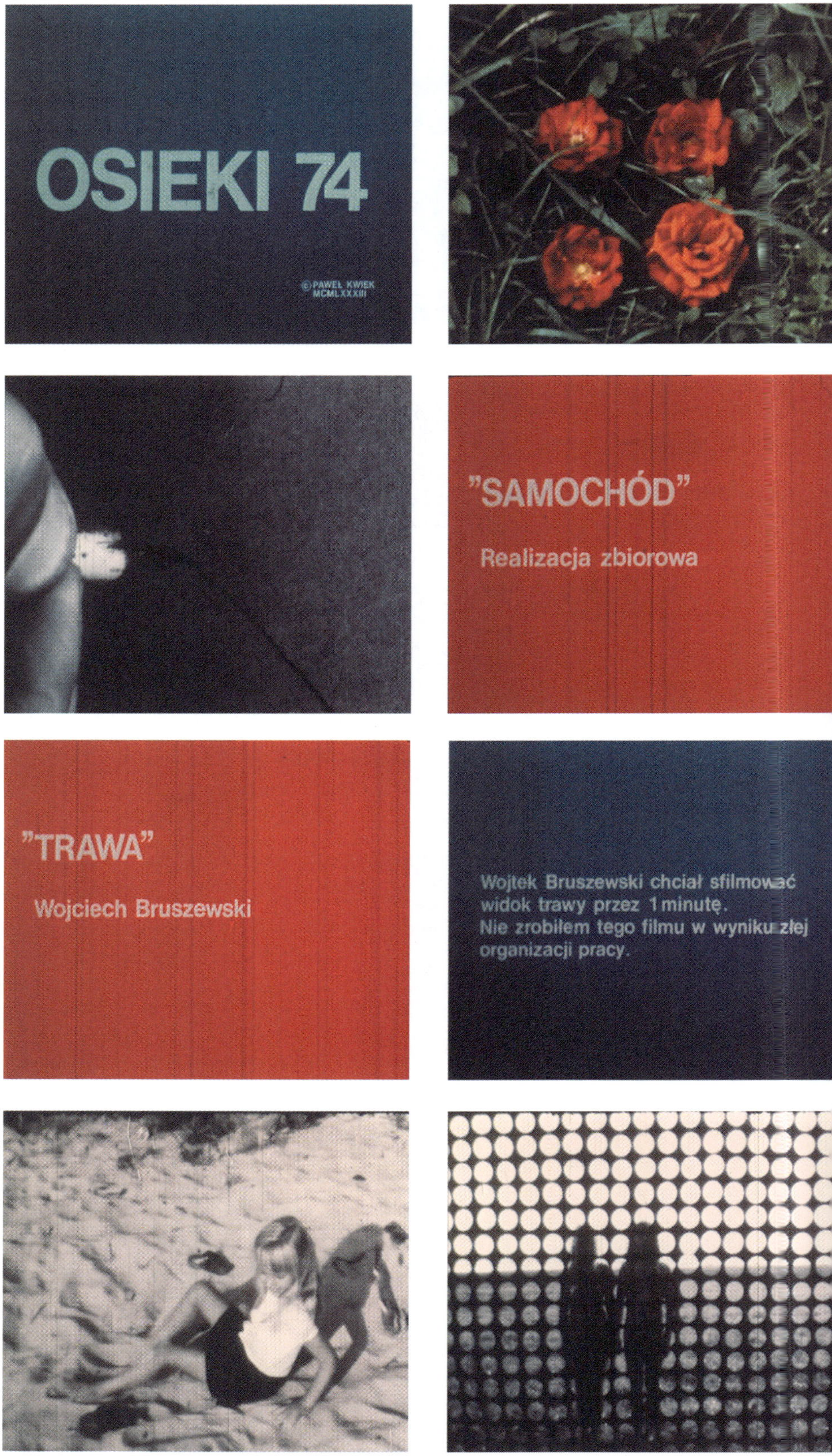

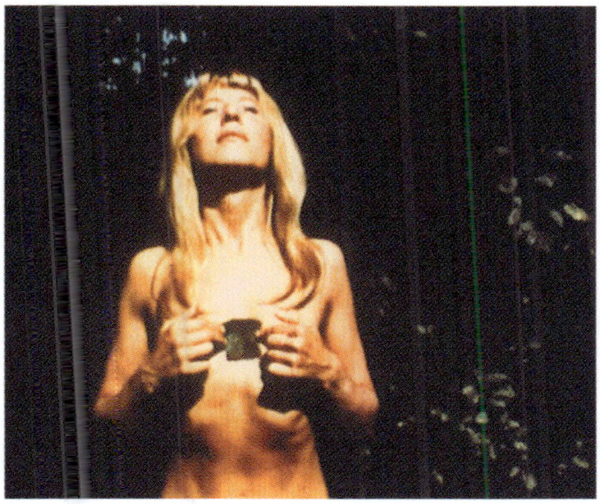

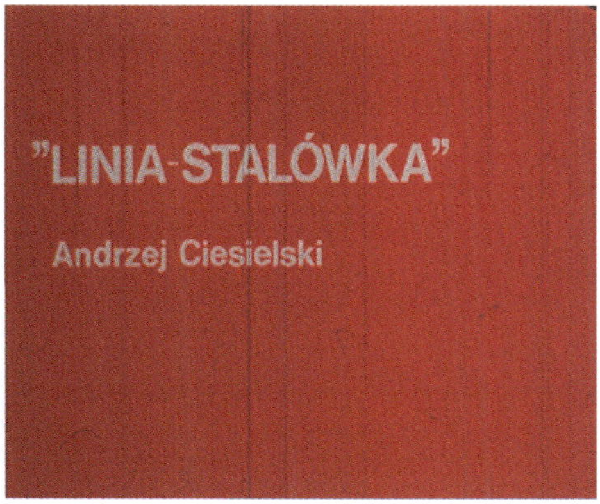
"LINIA-STALÓWKA"
Andrzej Ciesielski

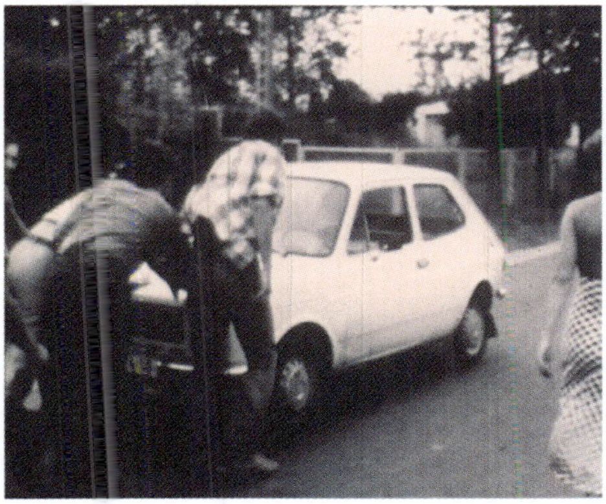

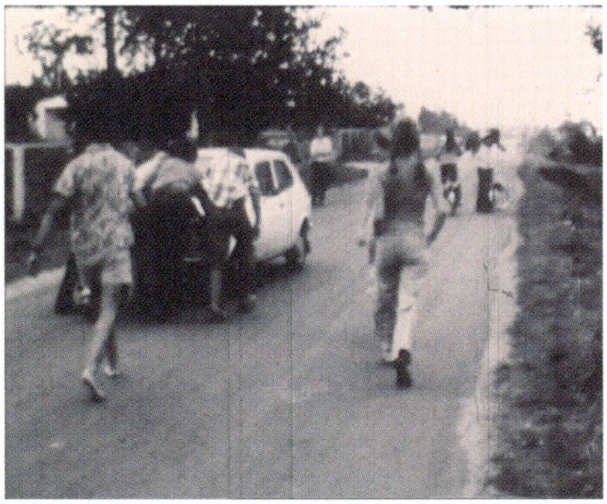

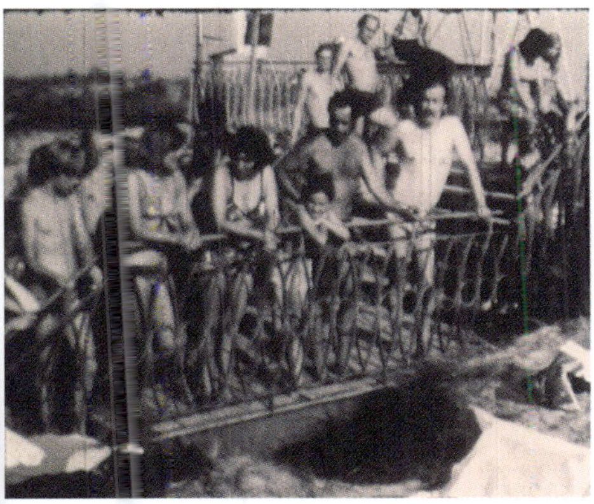

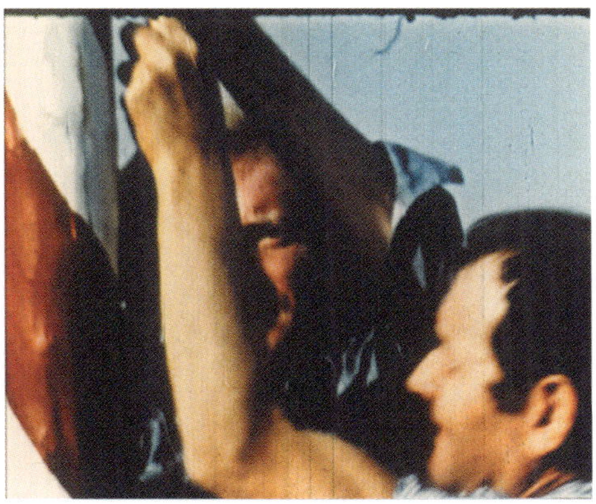

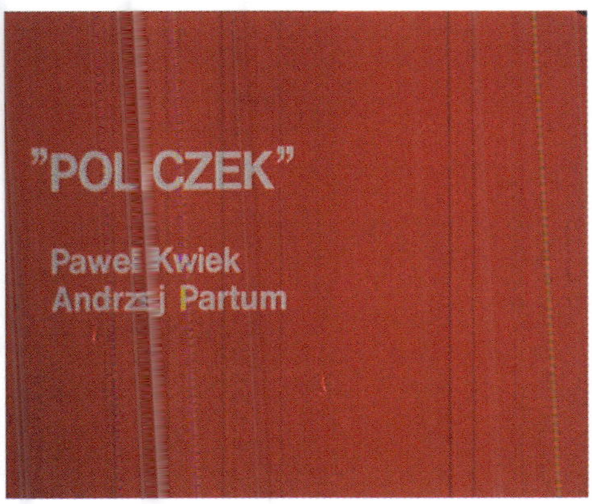
"POLICZEK"
Paweł Kwiek
Andrzej Partum

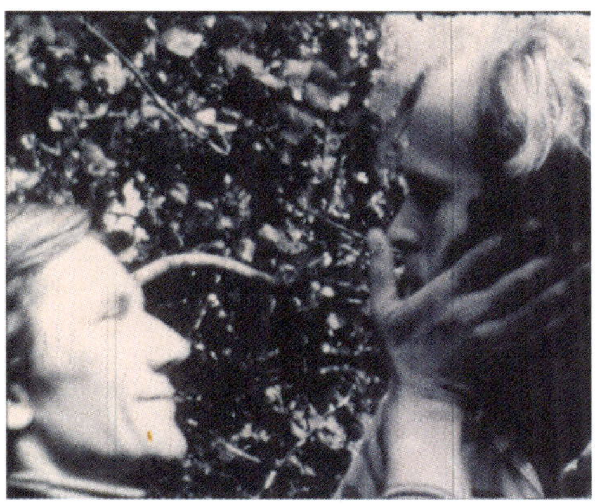

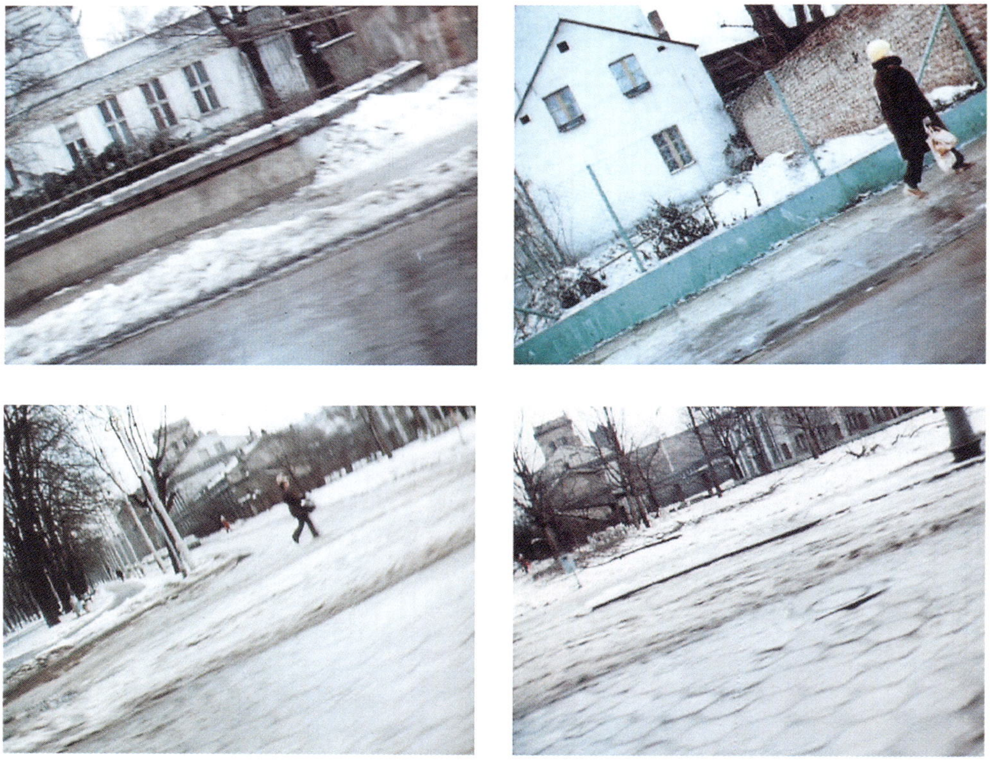

Ryszard Waśko, *Podroż Pana Antczaka do kiosku przy ul. Długiej,* 1973, 35 mm, 4'32''
Ryszard Waśko, *The Journey of Wacław Antczak to the Kiosk in Główna Street*, 1973, 35 mm, 4'32''

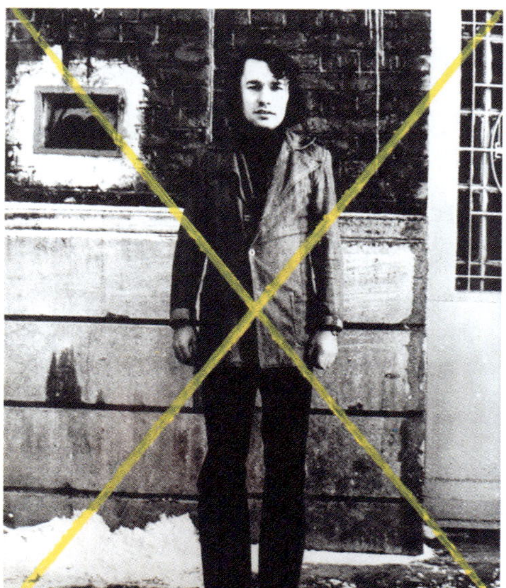

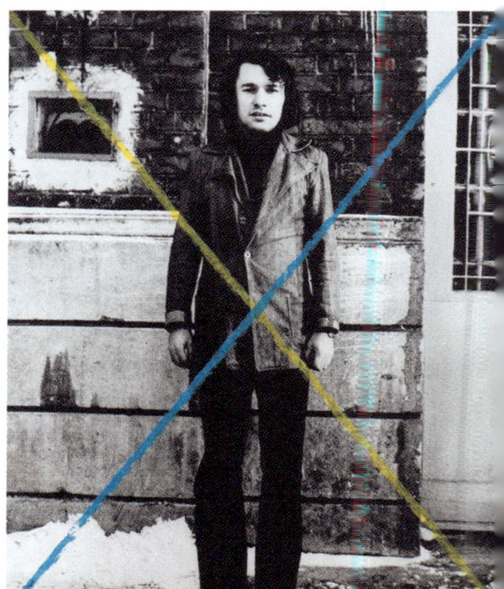

Ryszard Waśko, *Układ I-IV*, 1972, 35 mm, 2'52''
Ryszard Waśko, *Configuration I-IV*, 1972, 35 mm, 2'52''

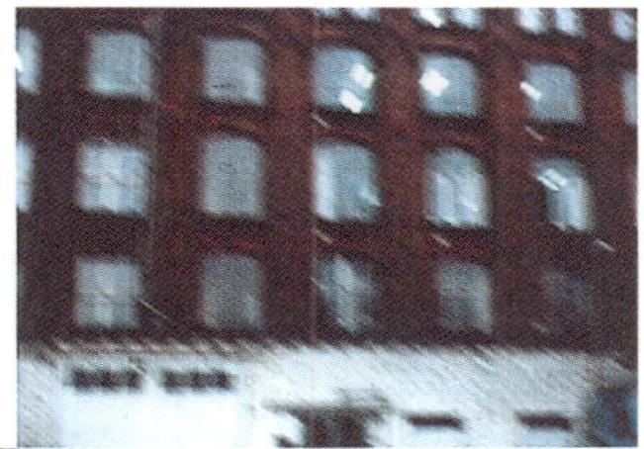
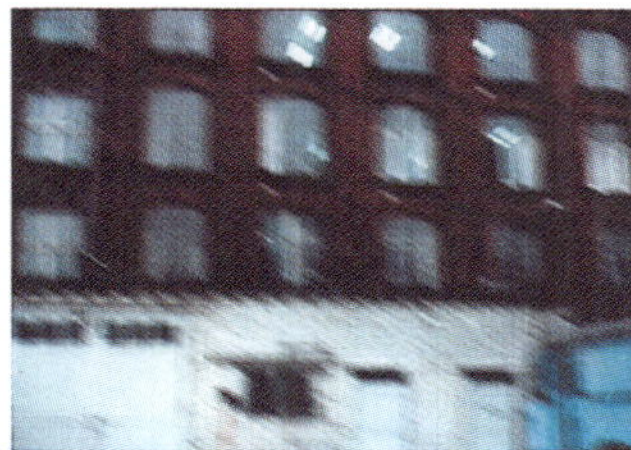
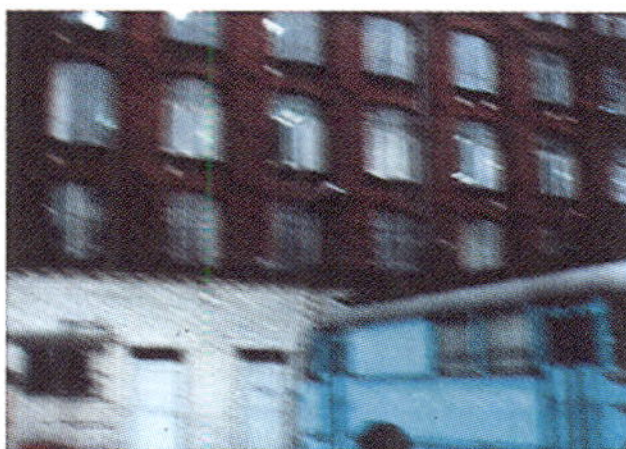
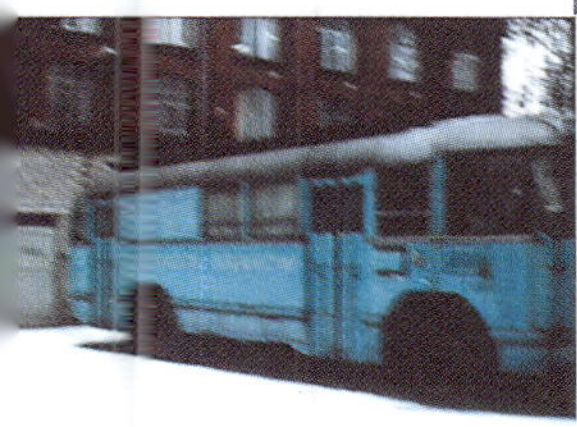

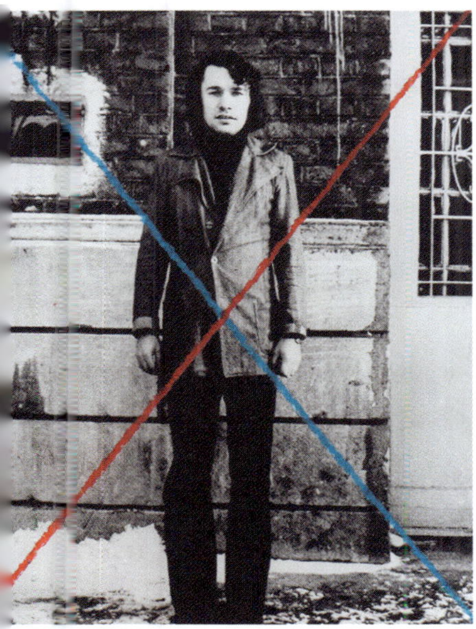
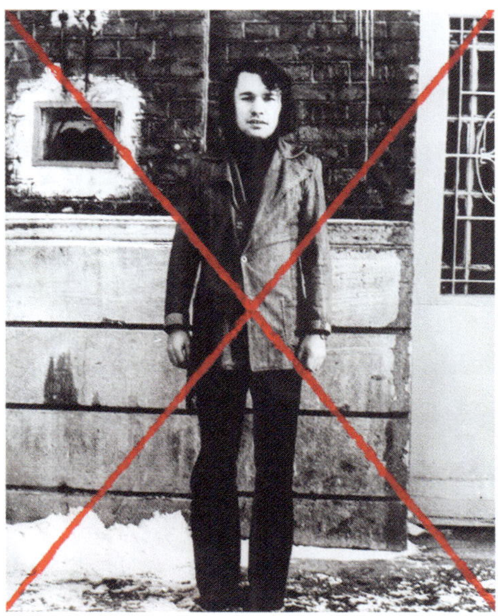

Ryszard Waśko, *Autoportret z linią*, 1975, fot. cz.-b., kreda
Ryszard Waśko, *Self-portrait with the Line*, 1975, B&W photograph, chalk

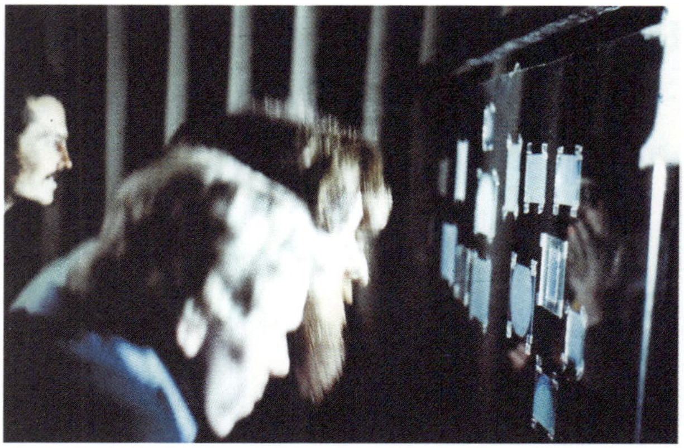
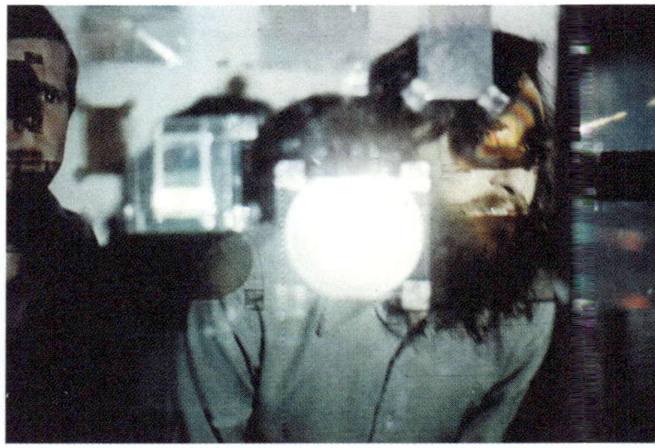
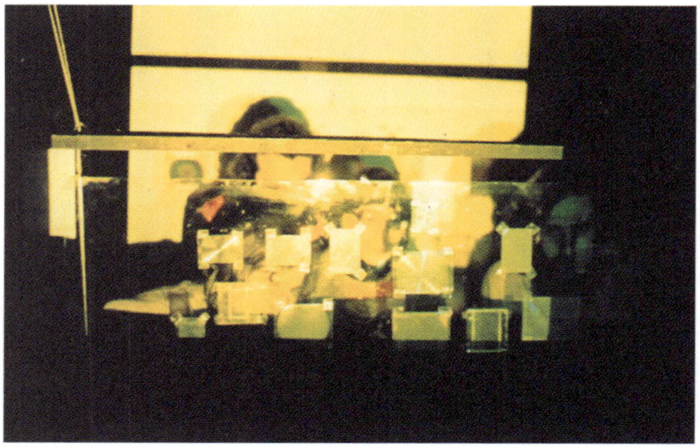
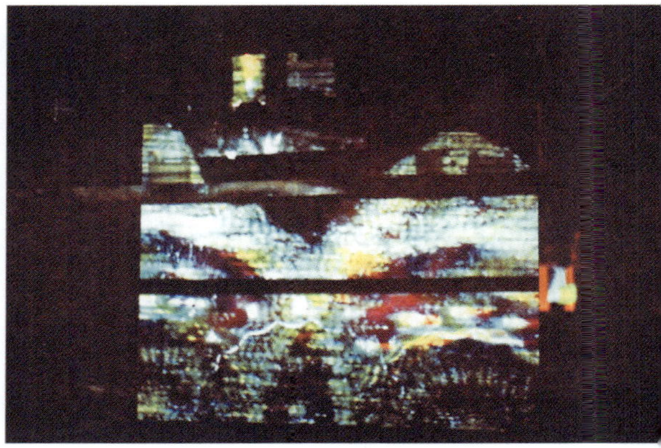
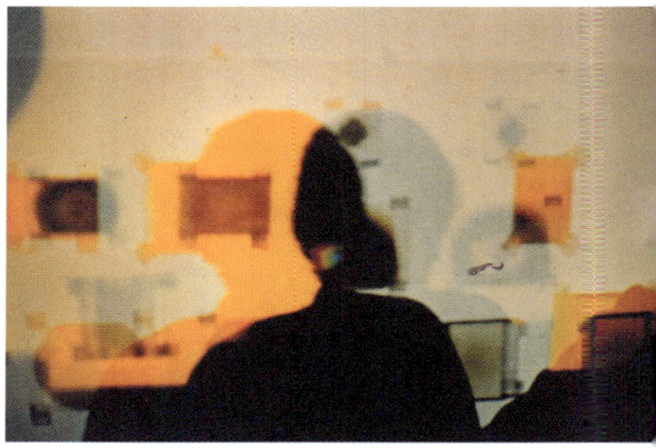
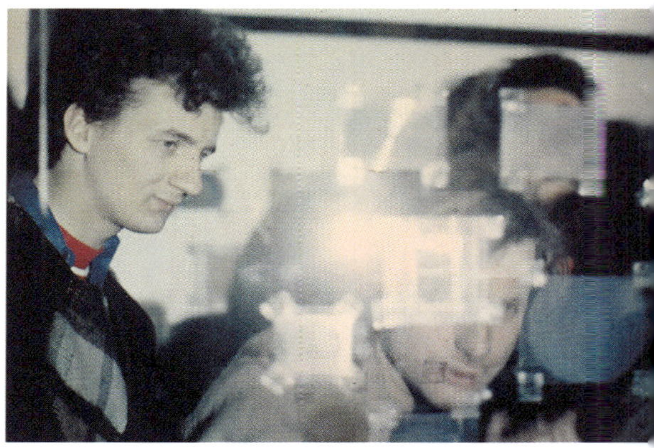

Kazimierz Bendkowski, *Mechaniczny zapis obrazu* (widoki wystawy w Galerii Remont w Warszawie), 1973
Kazimierz Bendkowski, *Mechanical Recording of the Image* (view of the exhibition, Remont Gallery, Warsaw), 1973

Kazimierz Bendkowski, *Centrum*, 1973, 35 mm, 5’22’’
Kazimierz Bendkowski, *Centre*, 1973, 35 mm, 5’22’’

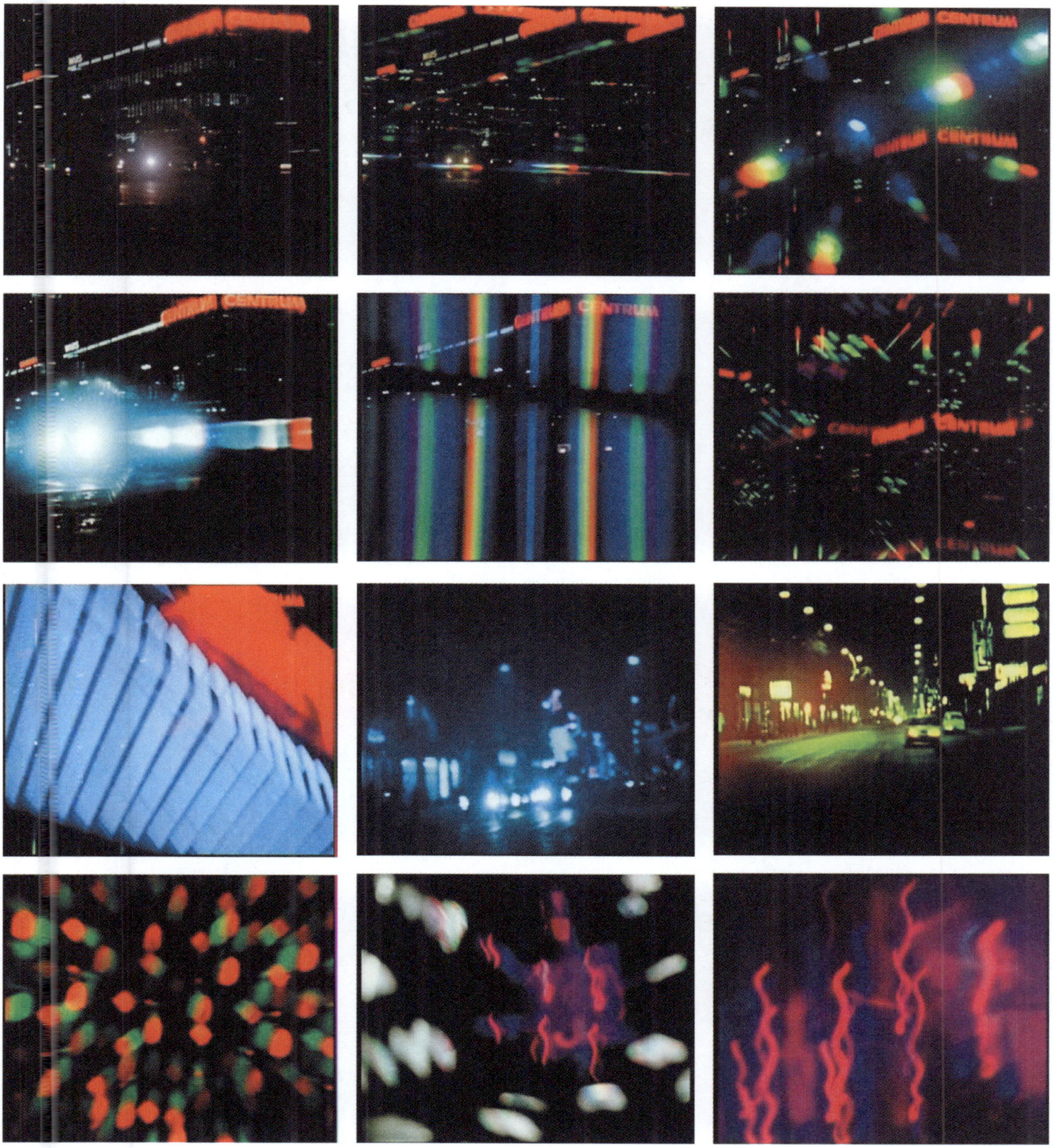

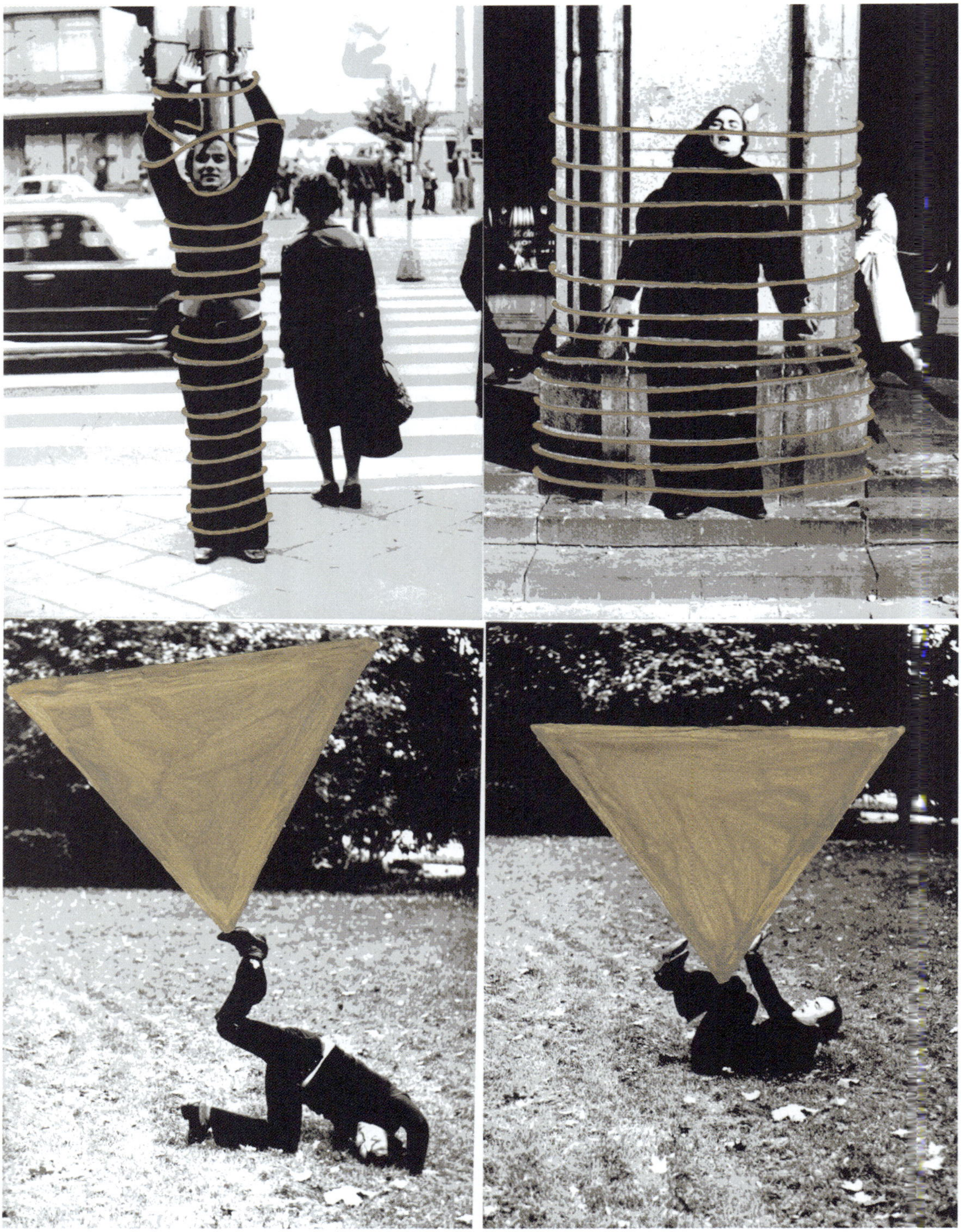

Kazimierz Bendkowski, *Gold*, 1972-77, fot. cz.-b., flamaster
Kazimierz Bendkowski, *Gold*, 1972-77, B&W photograph, marker

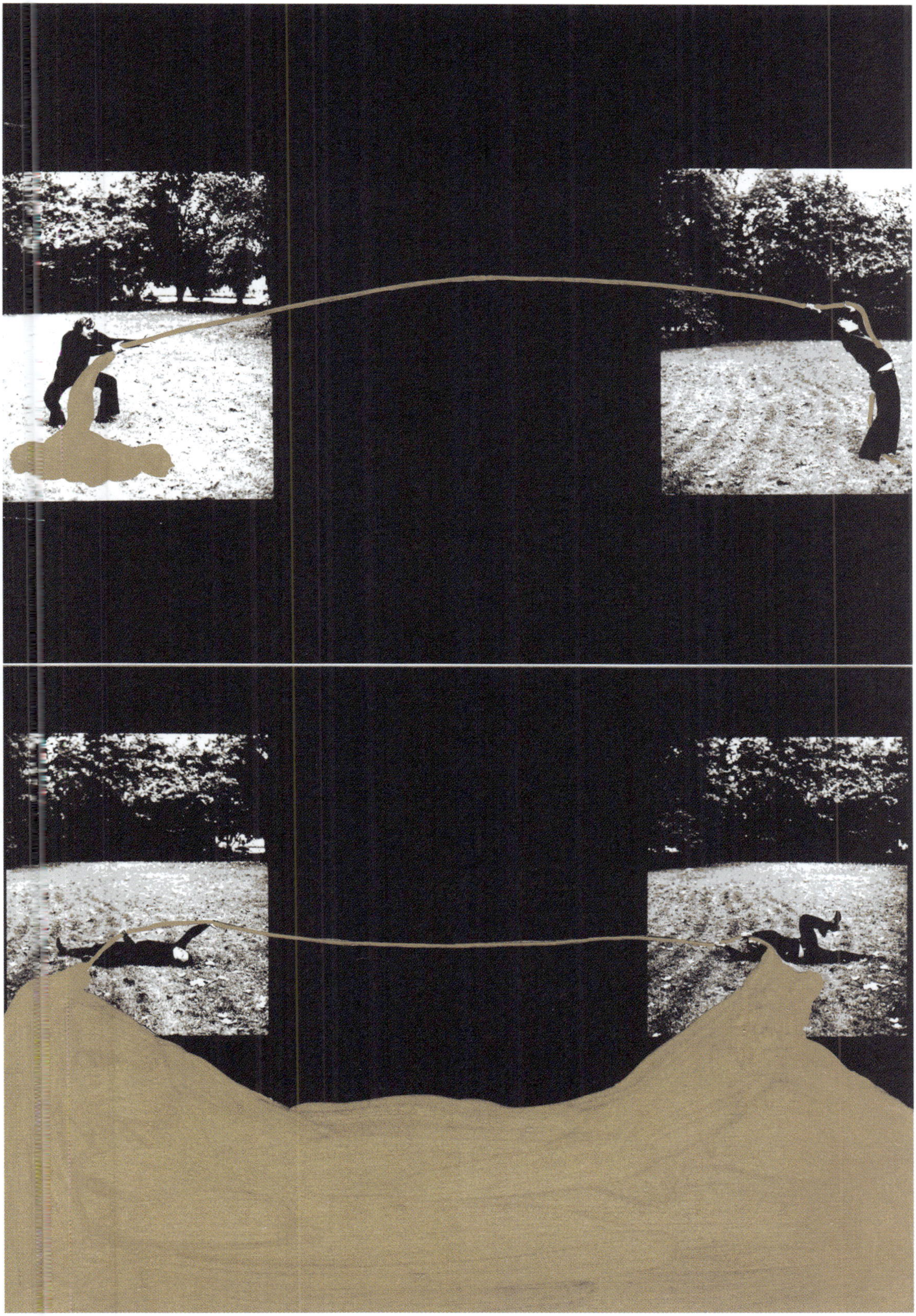

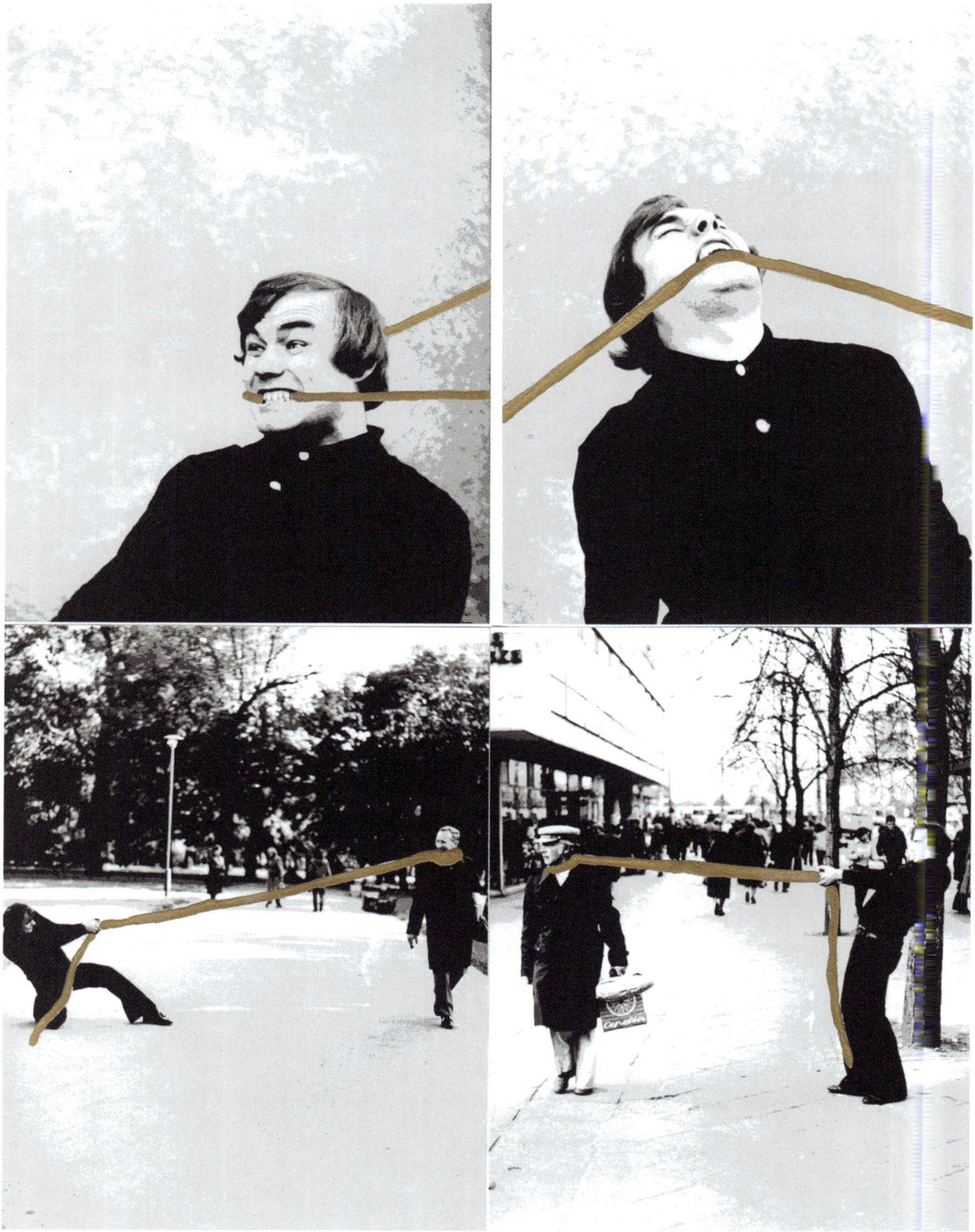

Kazimierz Bendkowski, *Gold*, 1972-77, fot. cz.-b., flamaster
Kazimierz Bendkowski, *Gold*, 1972-77, B&W photograph, marker

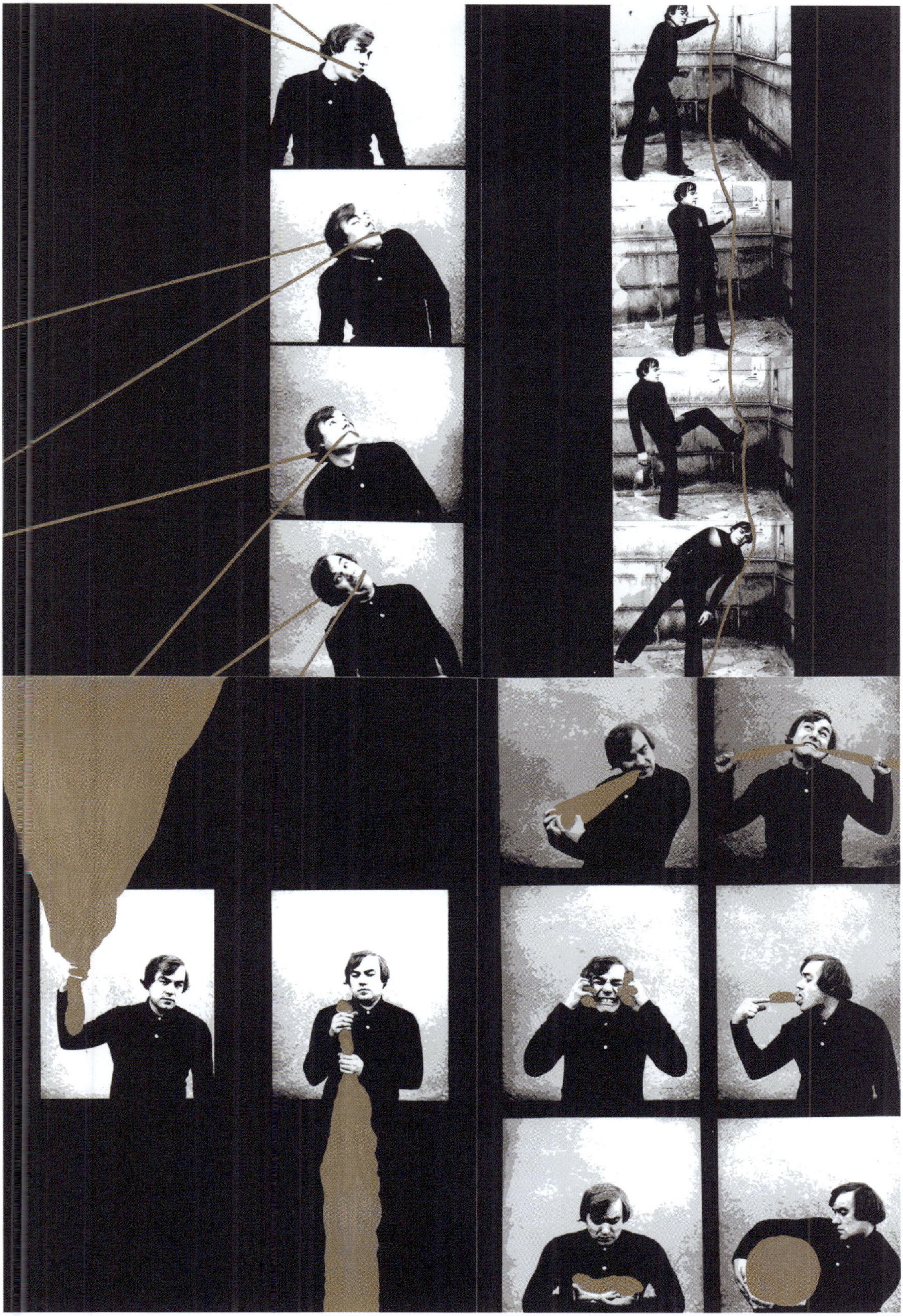

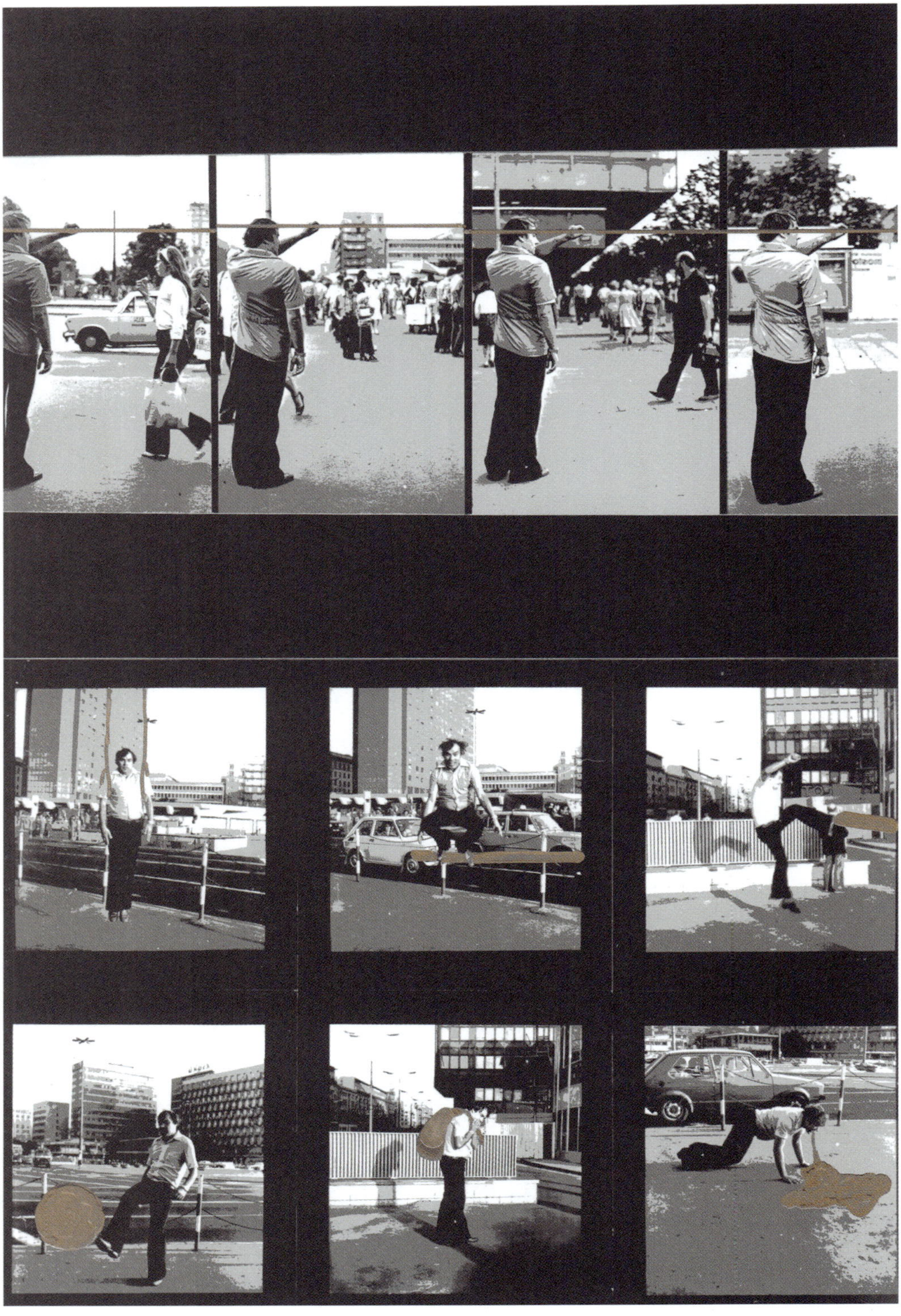

Kazimierz Bendkowski, *Gold*, 1972-77, fot. cz.-b., flamaster
Kazimierz Bendkowski, *Gold*, 1972-77, B&W photograph, marker

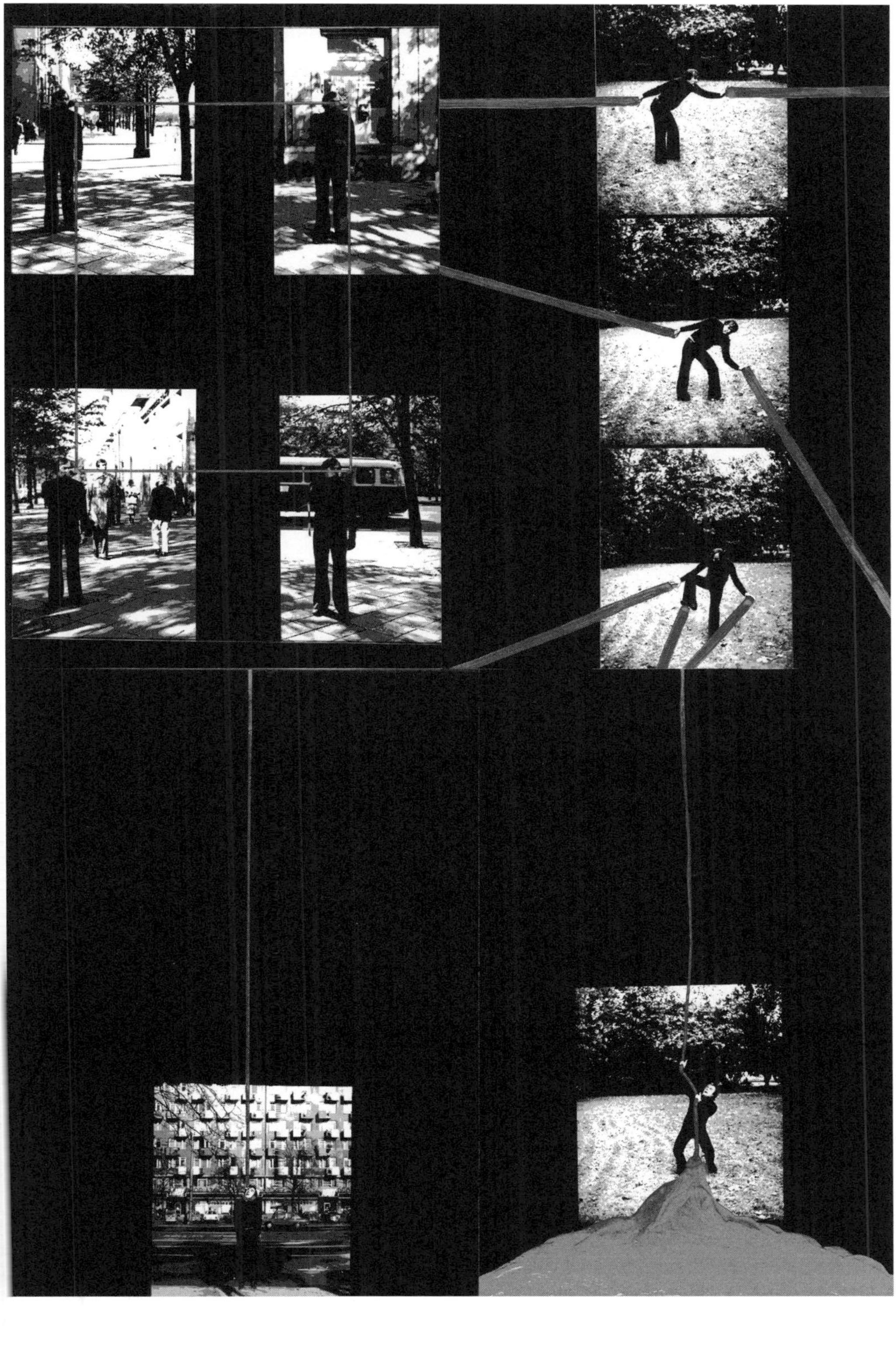

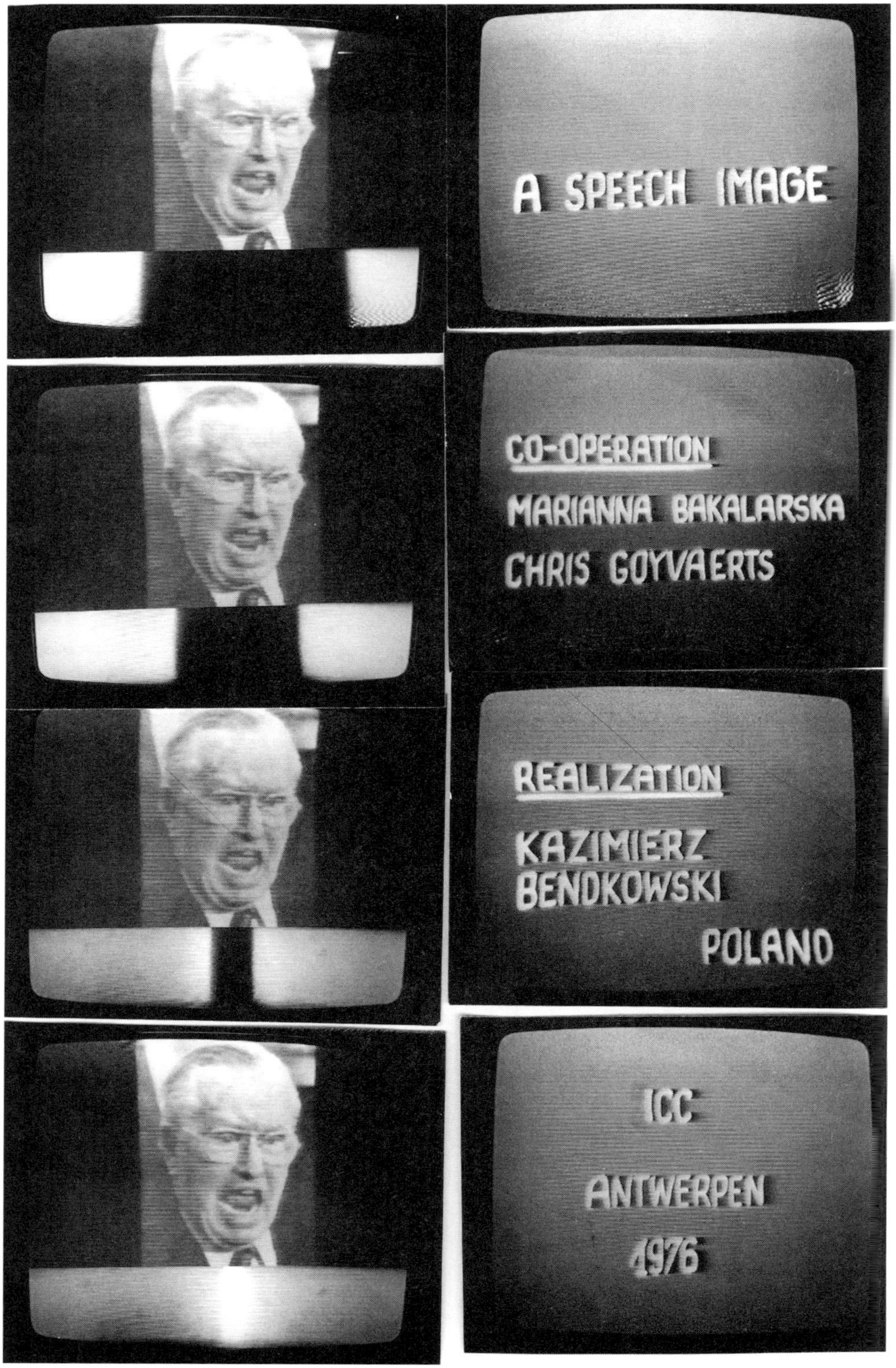

Kazimierz Bendkowski, *Obraz mowy*, 1976, wideo
Kazimierz Bendkowski, *A Speech Image*, 1976, video

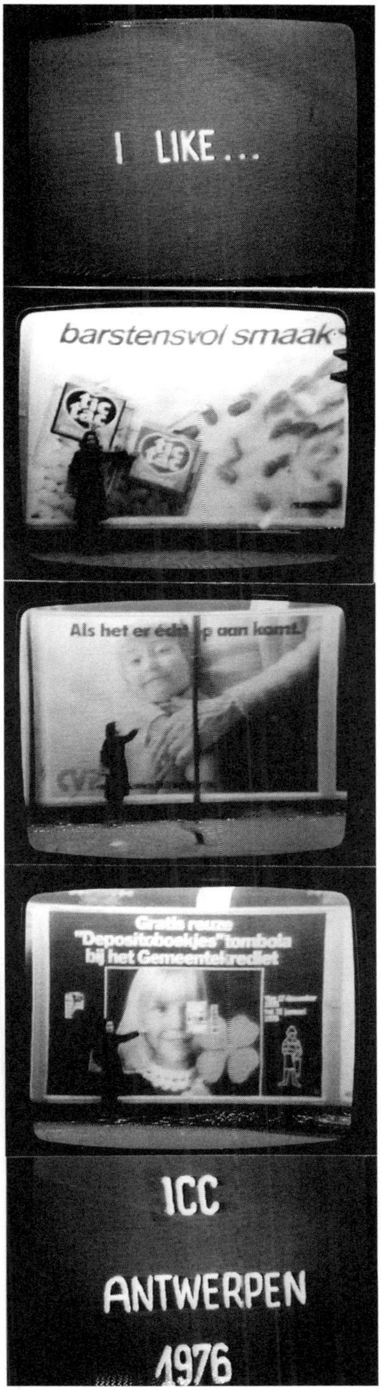

Kazimierz Bendkowski, *Lubię...*, 1976, wideo
Kazimierz Bendkowski, *I like...*, 1976, video

Kazimierz Bendkowski, *Moje...*, 1976, wideo
Kazimierz Bendkowski, *My...*, 1976, video

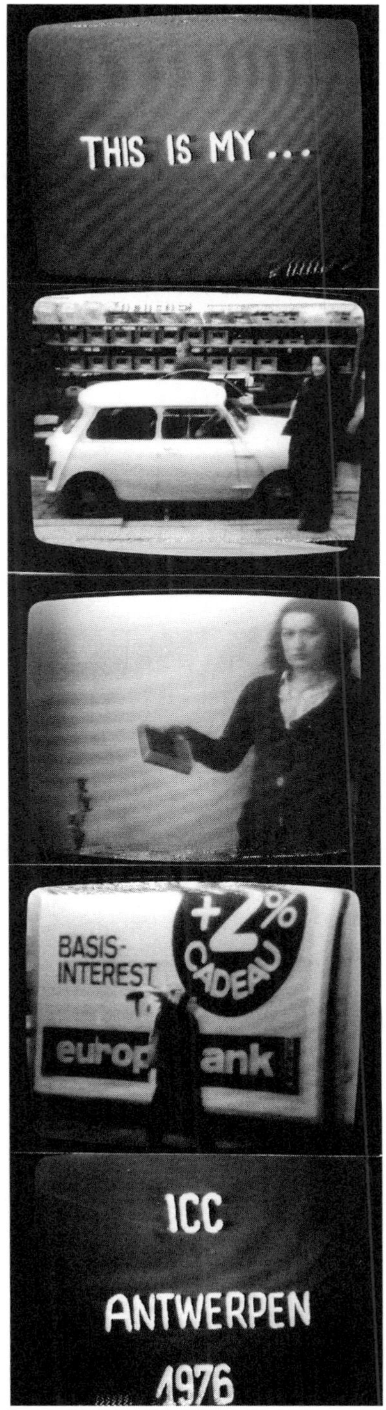

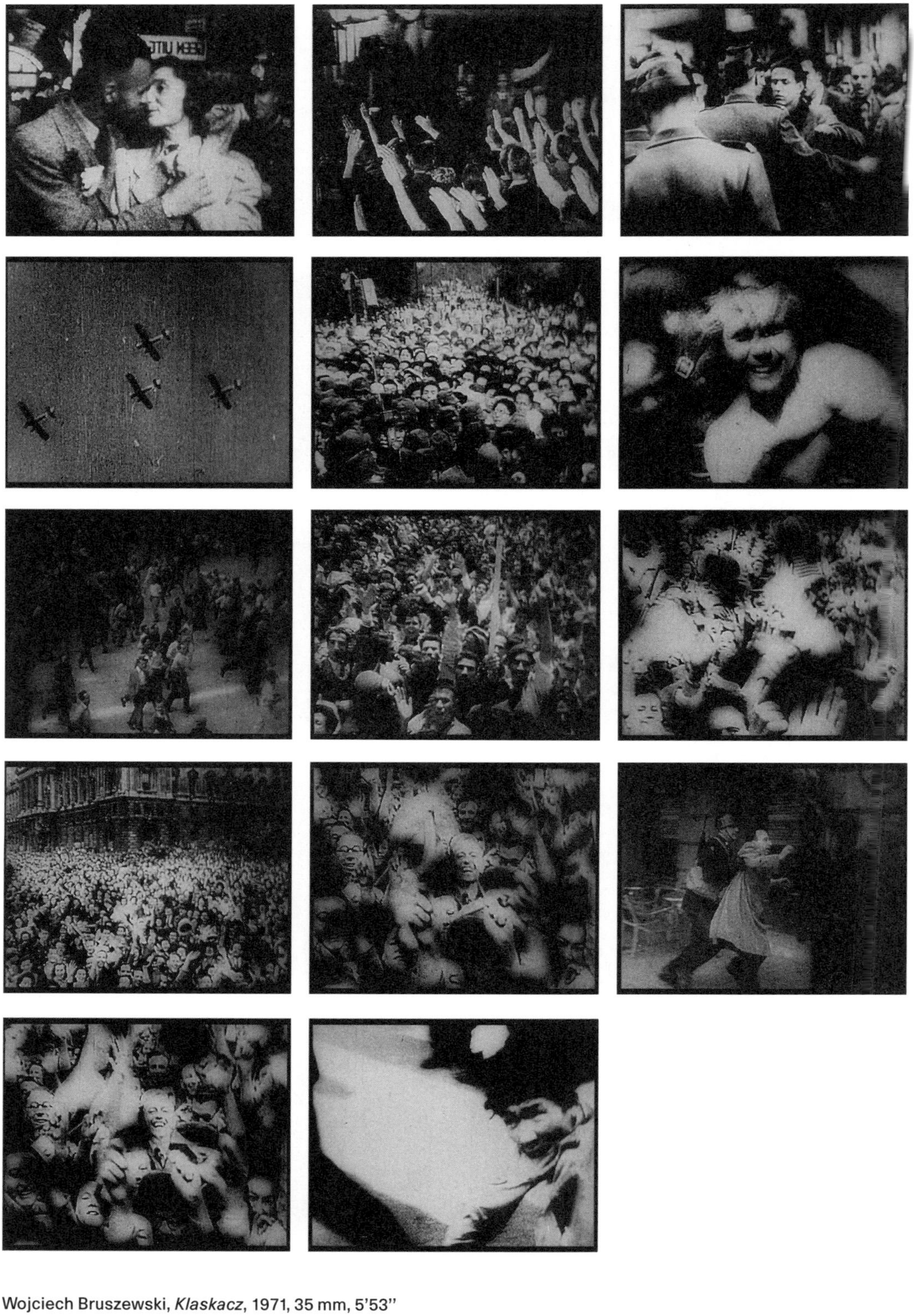

Wojciech Bruszewski, *Klaskacz*, 1971, 35 mm, 5'53''
Wojciech Bruszewski, *The Clapper*, 1971, 35 mm, 5'53''

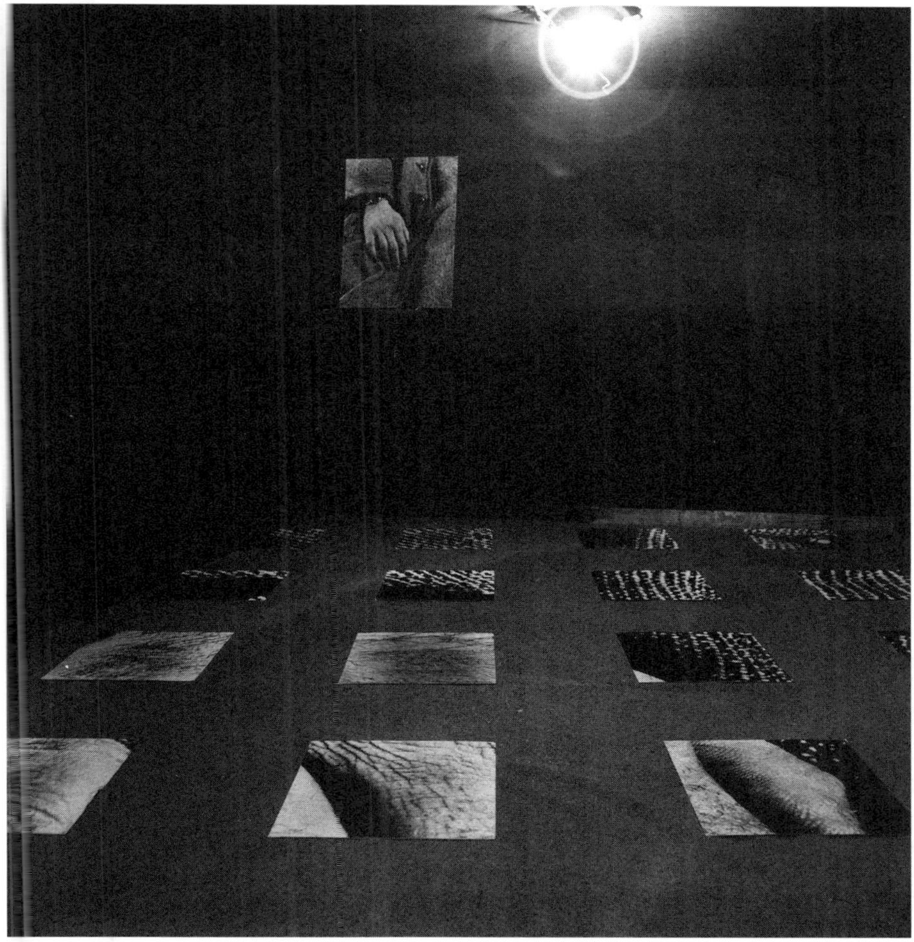

Wojciech Bruszewski, *Ciąg dalszy – ręka*, 1971, fot. cz.-b.
Wojciech Bruszewski, *Continued – Hand*, 1971, B&W photograph

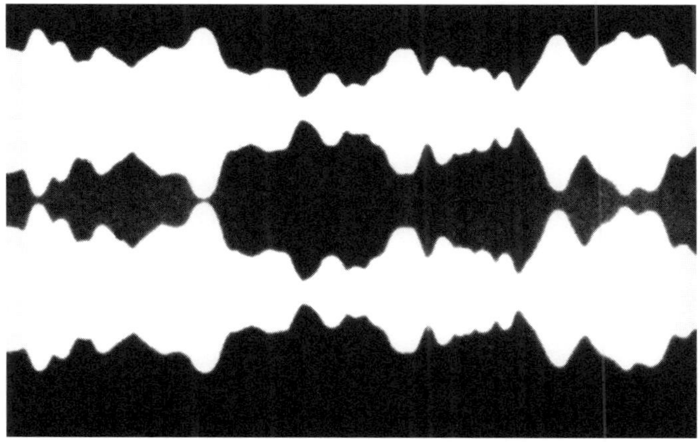

Wojciech Bruszewski, *Fotografia dźwięku*, 1971, fot. cz.-b.
Wojciech Bruszewski, *Photograph of Sounds*, 1971, B&W photograph

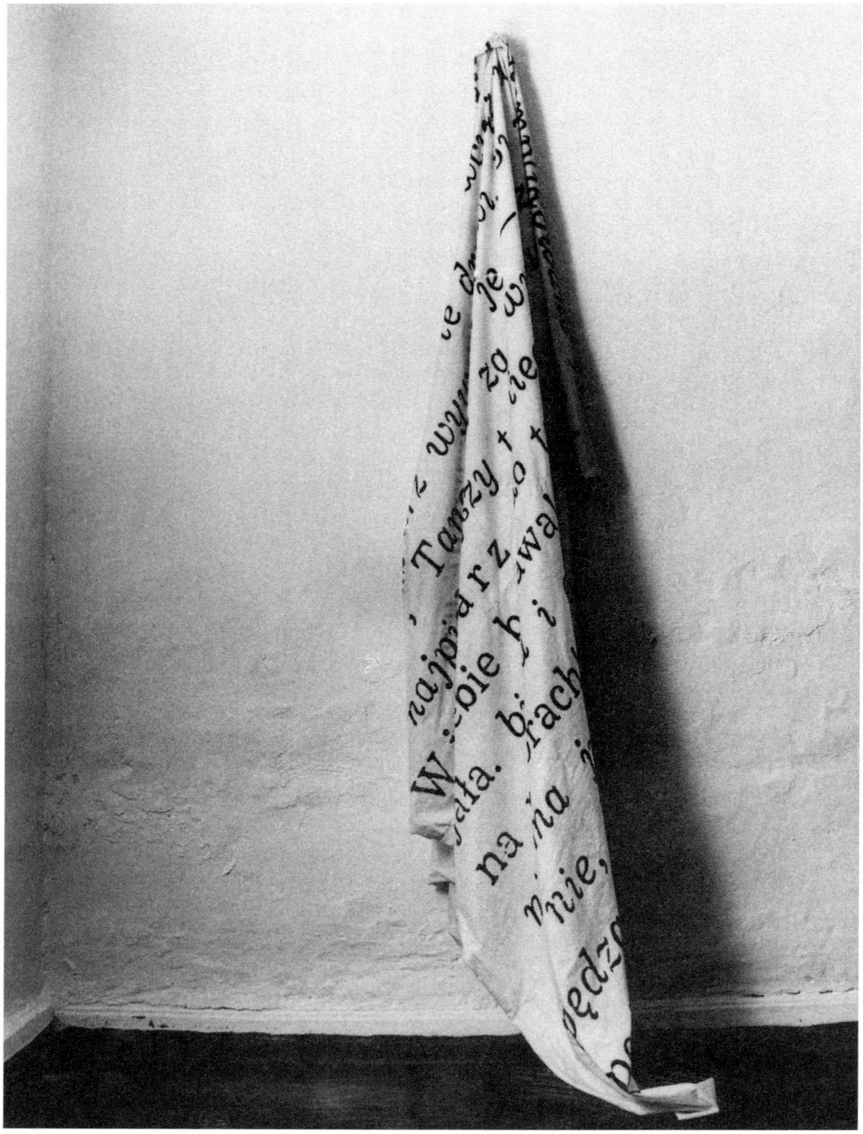

Wojciech Bruszewski, *Tekst*, 1970, obiekt
Wojciech Bruszewski, *Text*, 1970, object

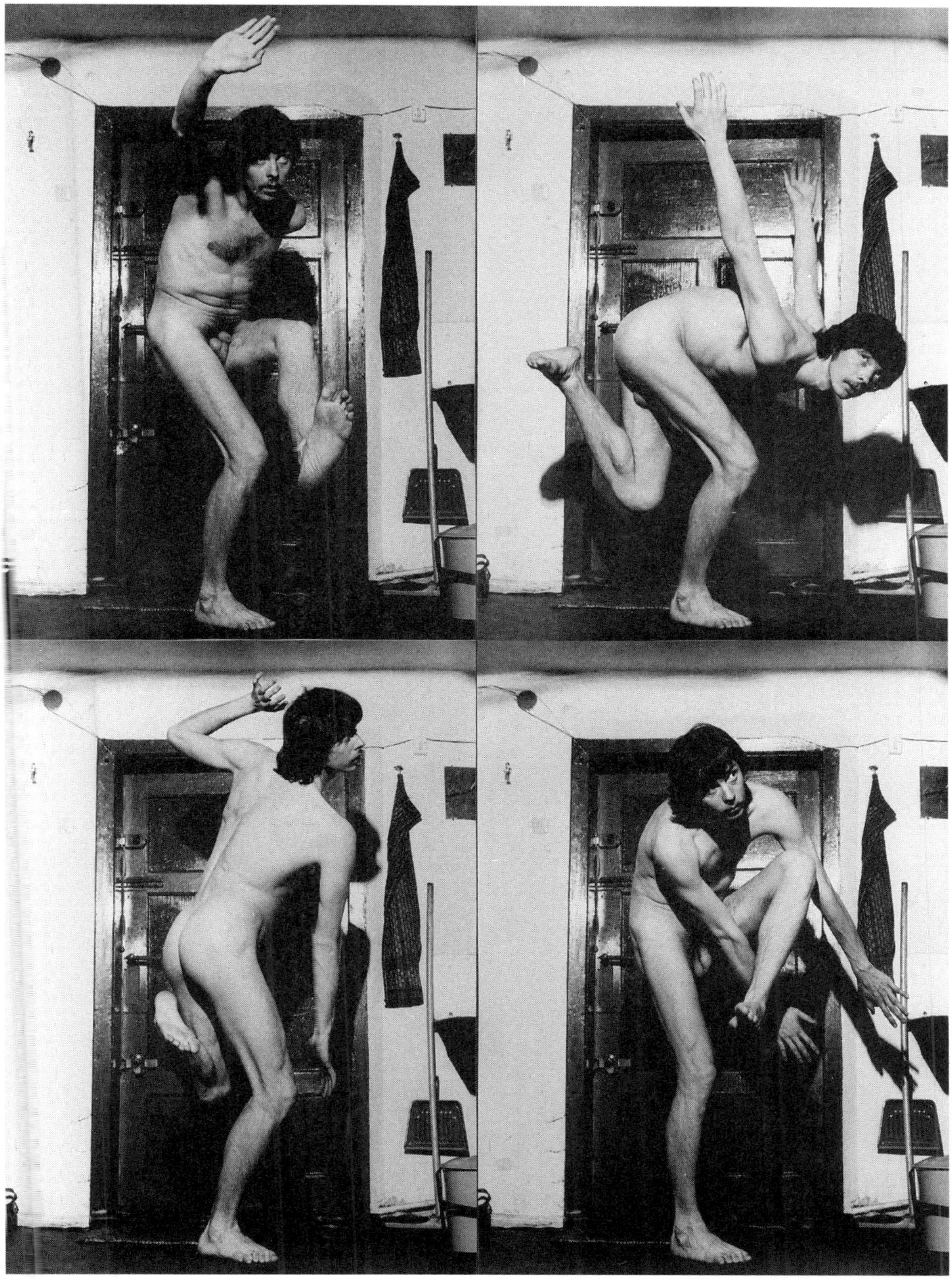

Wojciech Bruszewski, *Język baletowy*, 1973, fot. cz.-b.
Wojciech Bruszewski, *Ballet Language*, 1973, B&W photograph

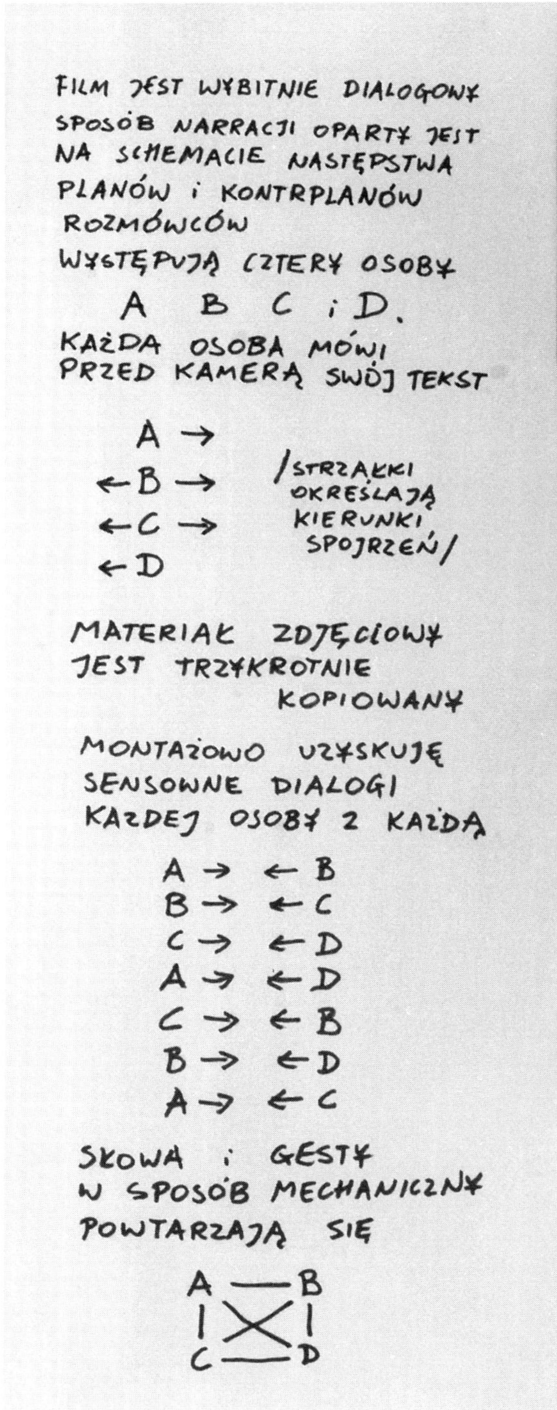
FILM JEST WYBITNIE DIALOGOWY
SPOSÓB NARRACJI OPARTY JEST
NA SCHEMACIE NASTĘPSTWA
PLANÓW i KONTRPLANÓW
ROZMÓWCÓW
WYSTĘPUJĄ CZTERY OSOBY
A B C i D.
KAŻDA OSOBA MÓWI
PRZED KAMERĄ SWÓJ TEKST

A →
← B →
← C →
← D

/STRZAŁKI OKREŚLAJĄ KIERUNKI SPOJRZEŃ/

MATERIAŁ ZDJĘCIOWY
JEST TRZYKROTNIE
KOPIOWANY

MONTAŻOWO UZYSKUJĘ
SENSOWNE DIALOGI
KAŻDEJ OSOBY Z KAŻDĄ

A → ← B
B → ← C
C → ← D
A → ← D
C → ← B
B → ← D
A → ← C

SŁOWA i GESTY
W SPOSÓB MECHANICZNY
POWTARZAJĄ SIĘ

A — B
C — D

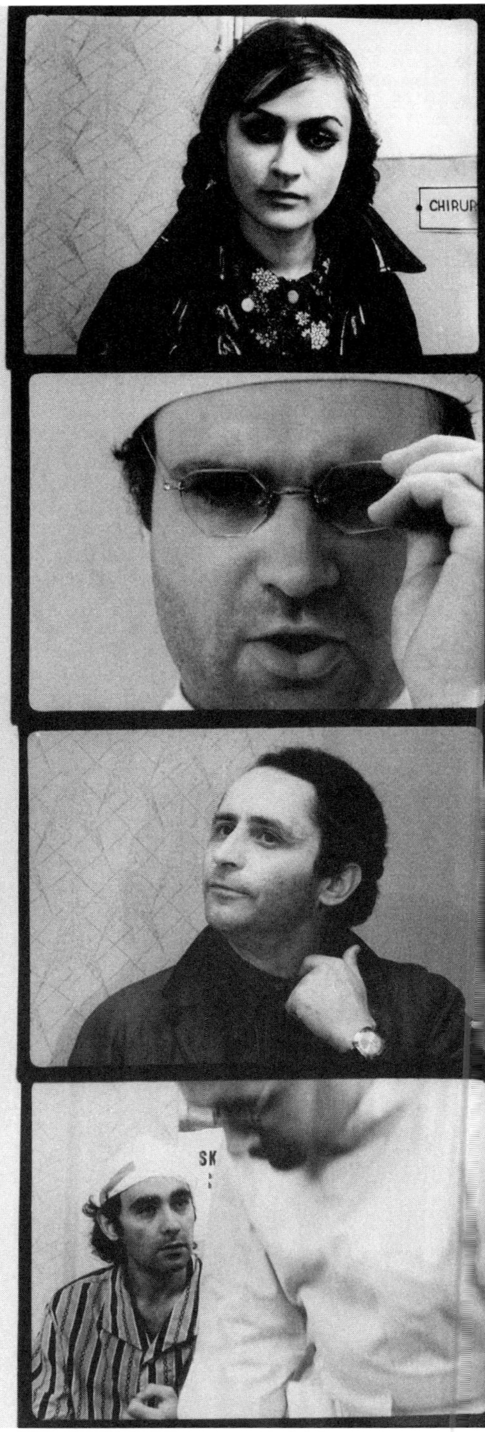

Wojciech Bruszewski, *Bezdech*, 1972, 35 mm, 10'01"
Wojciech Bruszewski, *Apnoea*, 1972, 35 mm, 10'01"

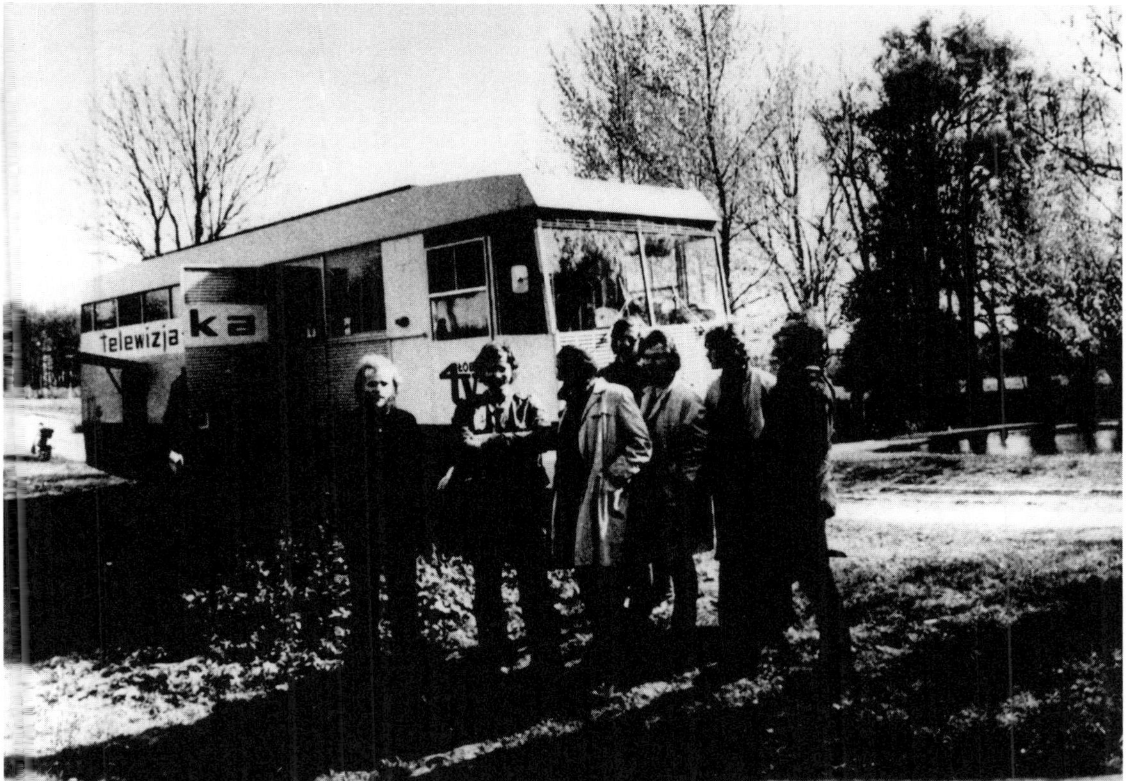

Kwiek Bruszewski Bernacki Lenczewski Łomnicki Wawrzyniak Bobrowski

" JEZYK OBRAZOWY "
widowisko telewizyjne
projekt - Piotr Bernacki
scenariusz - Piotr Bernacki
Wojciech Bruszewski
reżyseria - Wojciech Bruszewski
realizacja TV - Paweł Kwiek
kamery- Ryszard Lenczewski
Jacek Łomnicki
Krzysztof Bobrowski
Krzysztof Wawrzyniak

PROPONUJE SIE WYMIENNOSC ABSTRAKCYJNEGO ZNAKU JAKIM JEST LITERA NA KONKRETNY PRZEDMIOT

w części pierwszej uczy się widzów nowych znaków
w części drugiej nowym kodem przekazuje się tekst
kod stanowią rzeczy znajdujące się w plenerze otwartym

Zanotowano w dniu 9,V,1973 , za pomocą wozu transmisyjnego Telewizji Łódzkiej,czterech kamer, na magnetowidzie "Philips" /taśma półcalowa/. Czas: 25 min.

PICTURES LANGUAGE

Wojciech Bruszewski, *Język obrazkowy*, 1973, wideo (taśma niezachowana)
Wojciech Bruszewski, *Picture Language*, 1973, video (tape unpreserved)

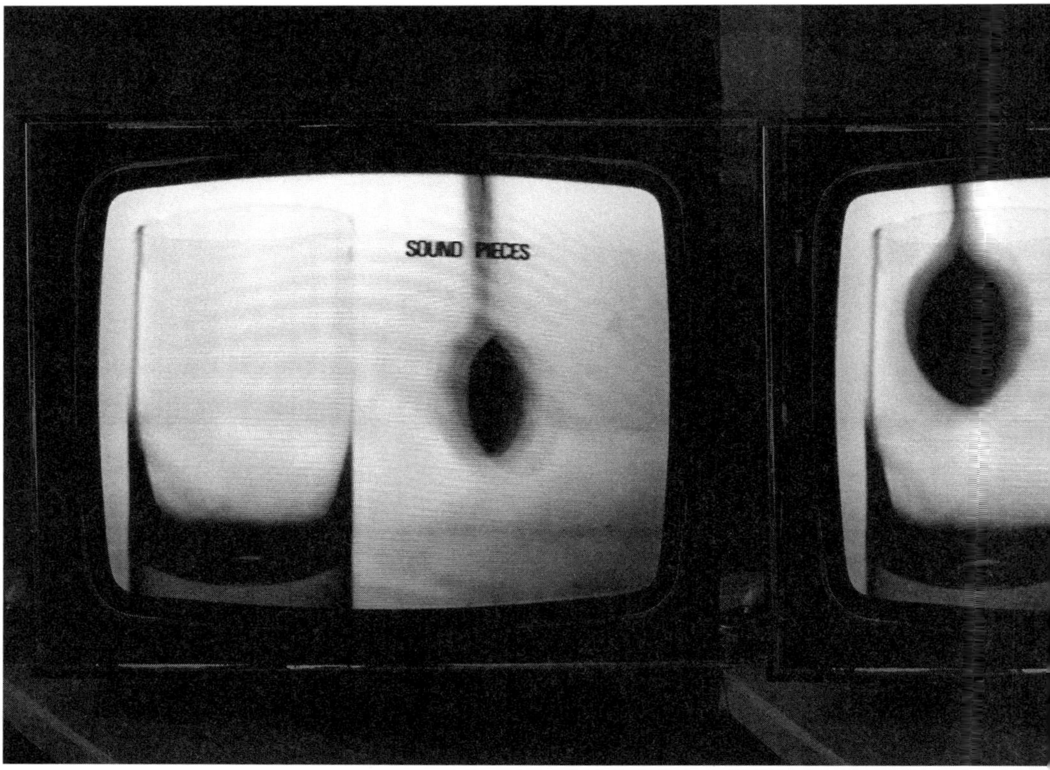

Wojciech Bruszewski, *Łyżeczka*, 1974, wideo, 0'55''
Wojciech Bruszewski, *Tea Spoon*, 1974, video, 0'55''

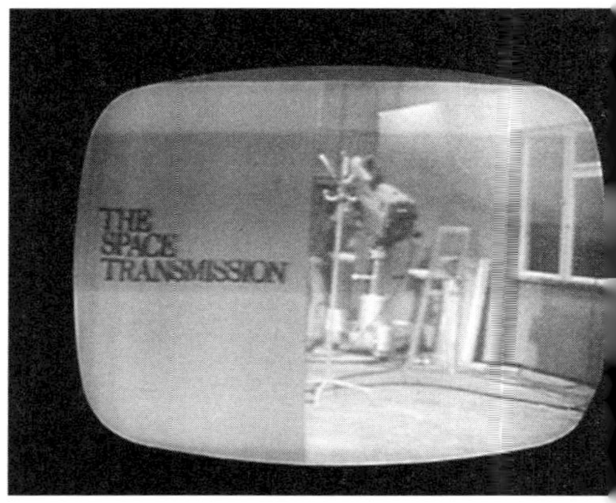

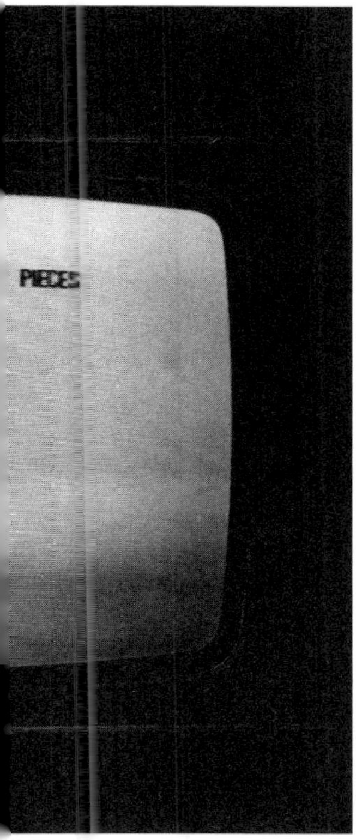

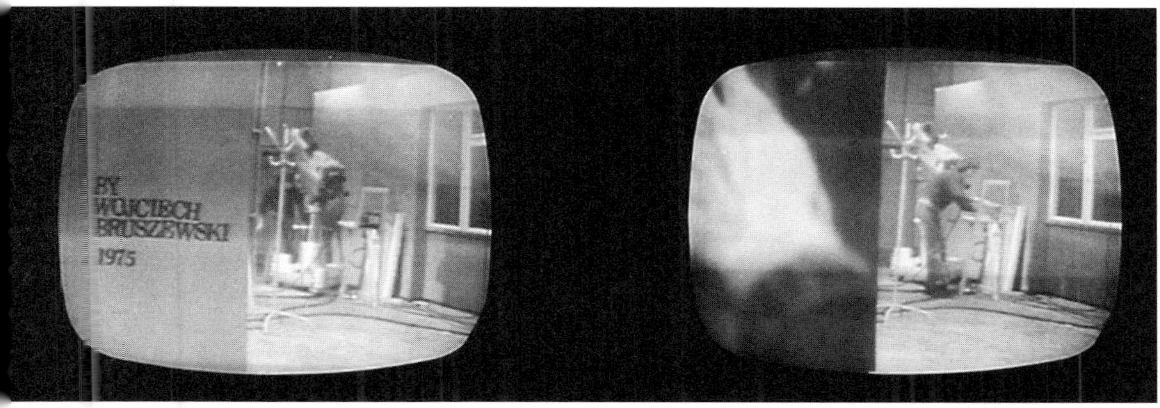

Wojciech Bruszewski, *Transmisja przestrzenna*, 1974, wideo, 1'08''
Wojciech Bruszewski, *A Spatial Transmission*, 1974, video, 1'08''

Wojciech Bruszewski, *Outside*, 1975, instalacja wideo
Wojciech Bruszewski, *Outside*, 1975, video installation

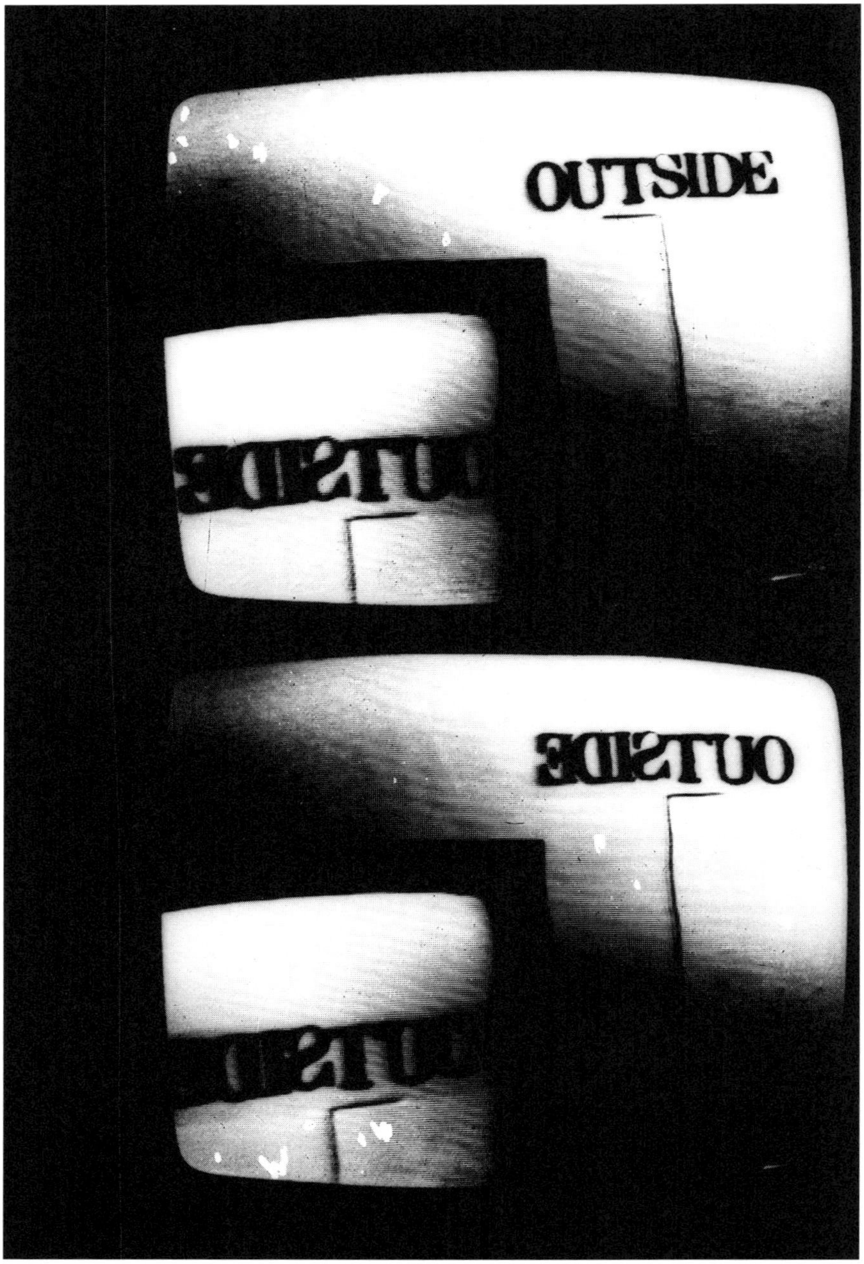

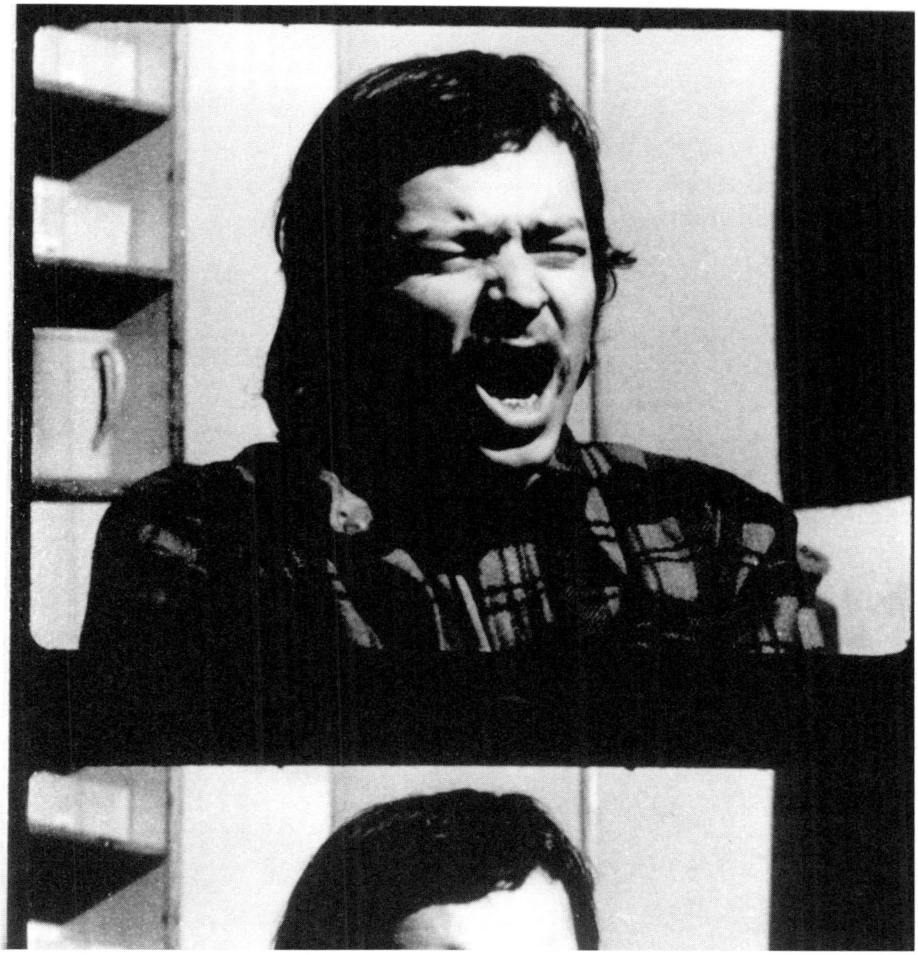

Wojciech Bruszewski, *YYAA*, 1973, 35 mm, 2’59”
Wojciech Bruszewski, *YYAA*, 1973, 35 mm, 2’59”

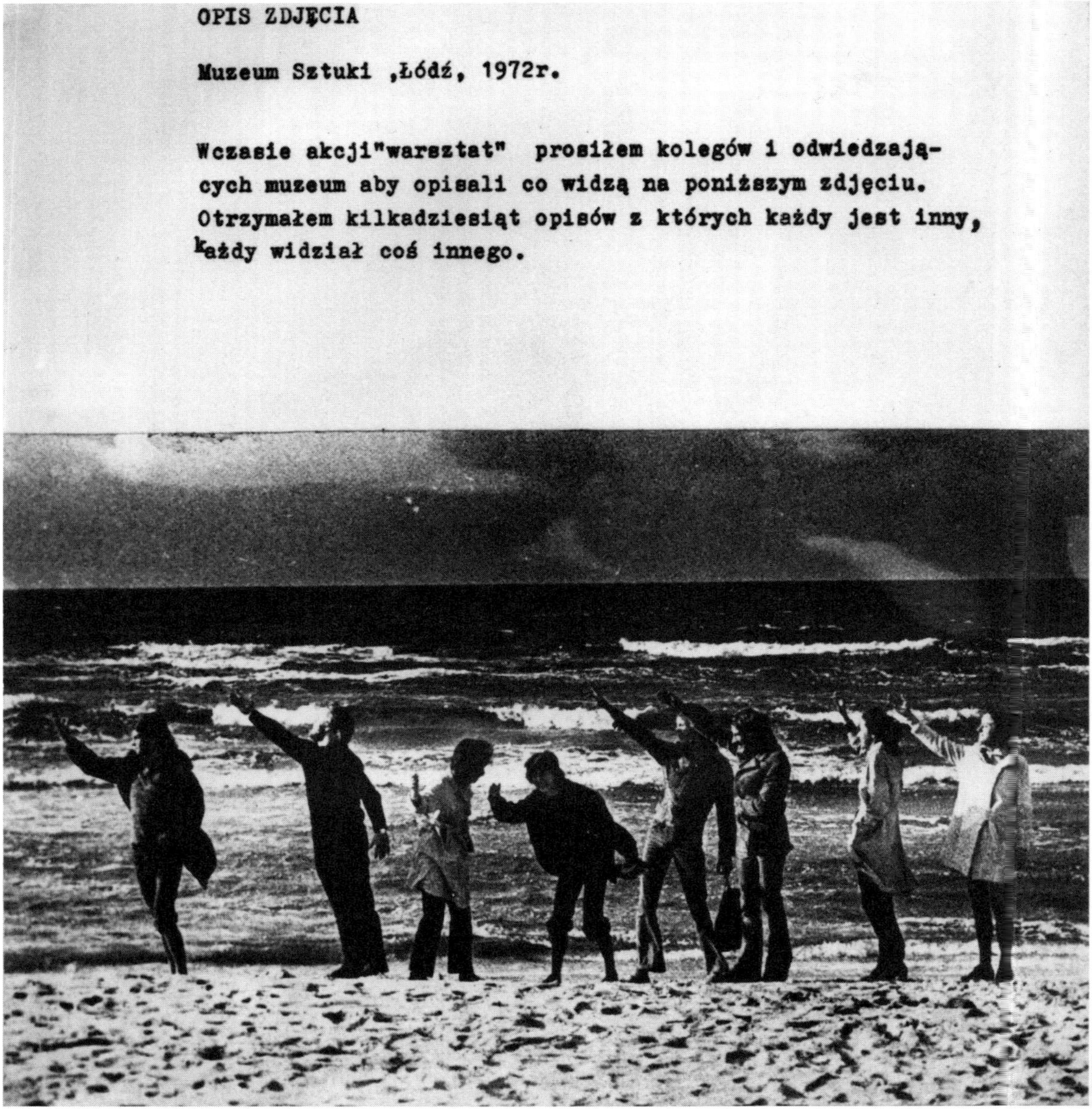

Paweł Kwiek, *Opis zdjęcia*, 1972, fot. cz.-b.
Paweł Kwiek, *Description of a Photo*, 1972, B&W photograph

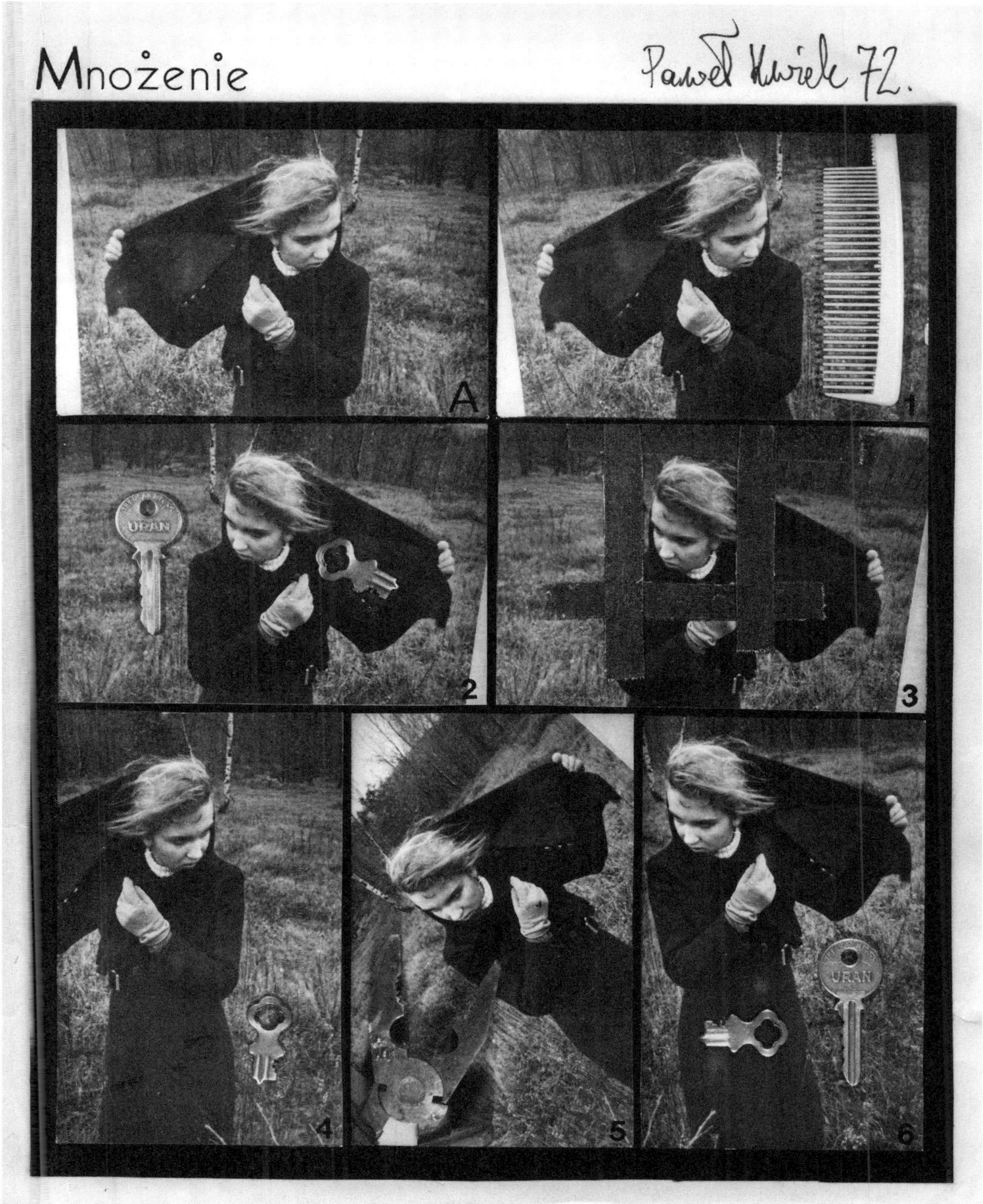

Paweł Kwiek, *Mnożenie*, 1972, fot. cz.-b.
Paweł Kwiek, *Multiplication*, 1972, B&W photograph

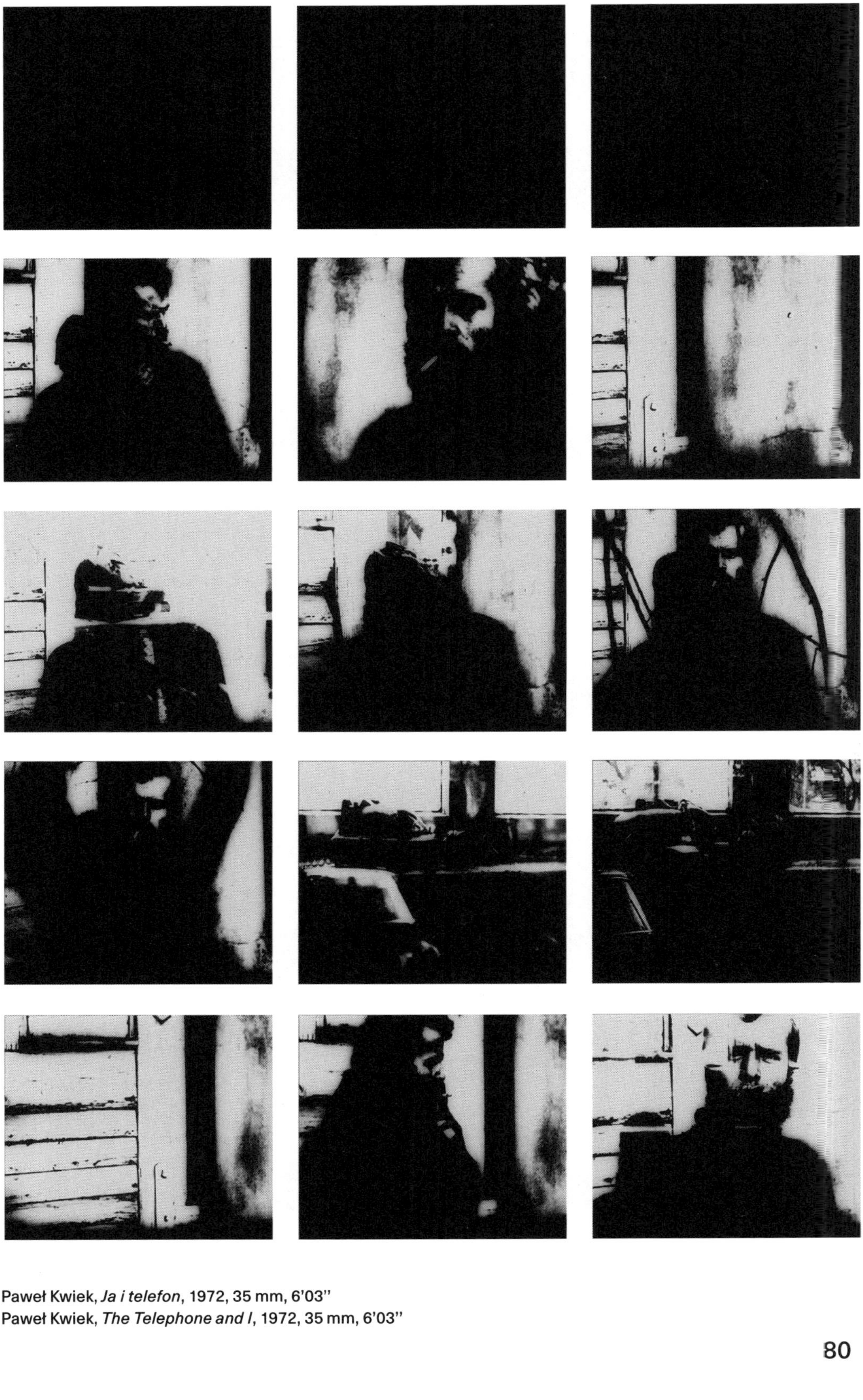

Paweł Kwiek, *Ja i telefon*, 1972, 35 mm, 6’03’’
Paweł Kwiek, *The Telephone and I*, 1972, 35 mm, 6’03’’

Paweł Kwiek, *Numerki*, 1973, 35 mm, 7'52''
Paweł Kwiek, *Numbers*, 1973, 35 mm, 7'52''

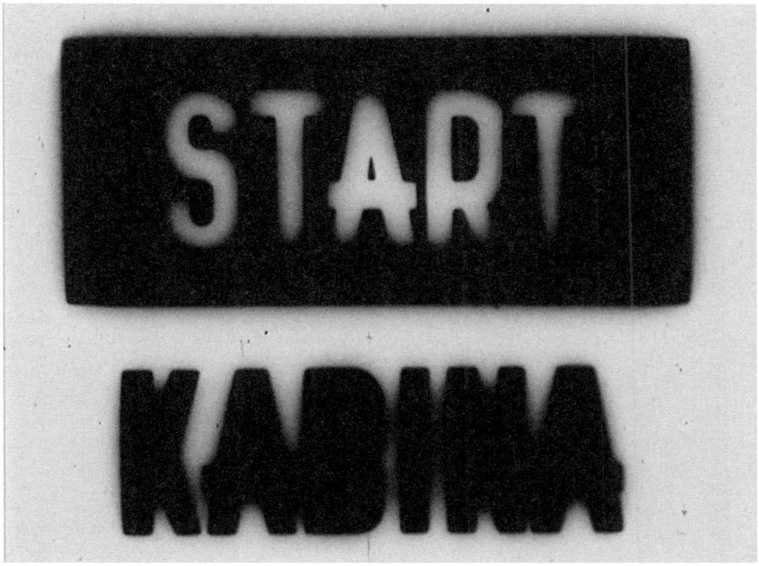

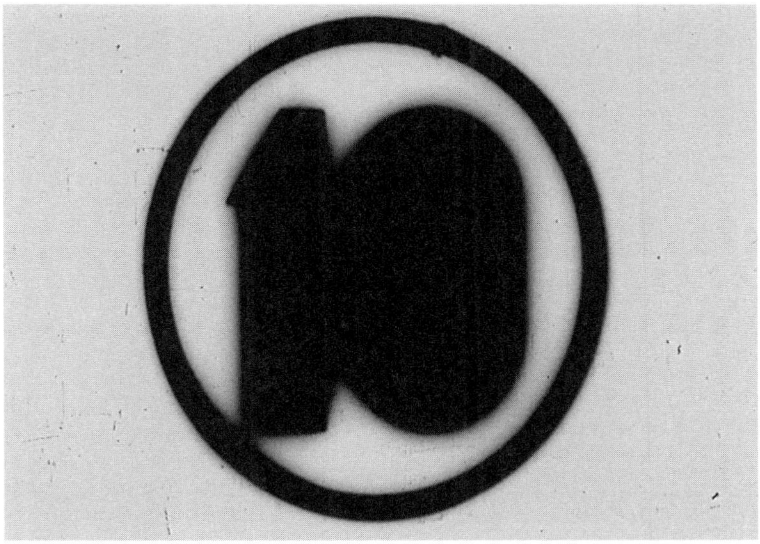

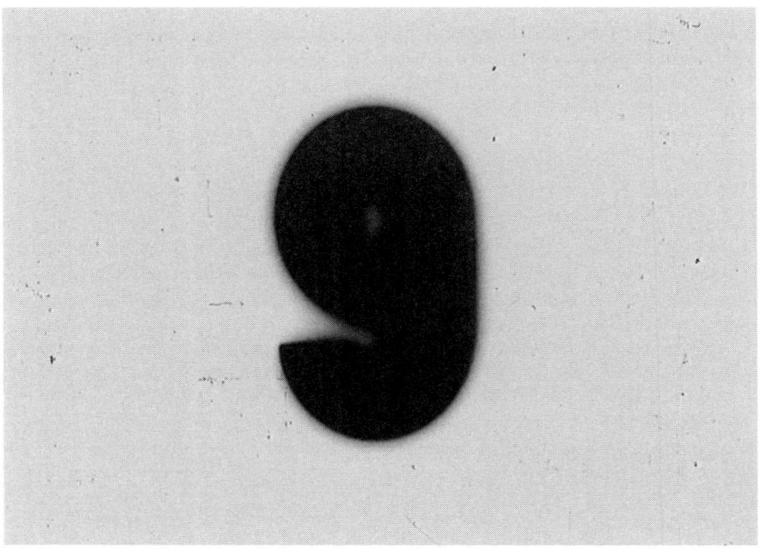

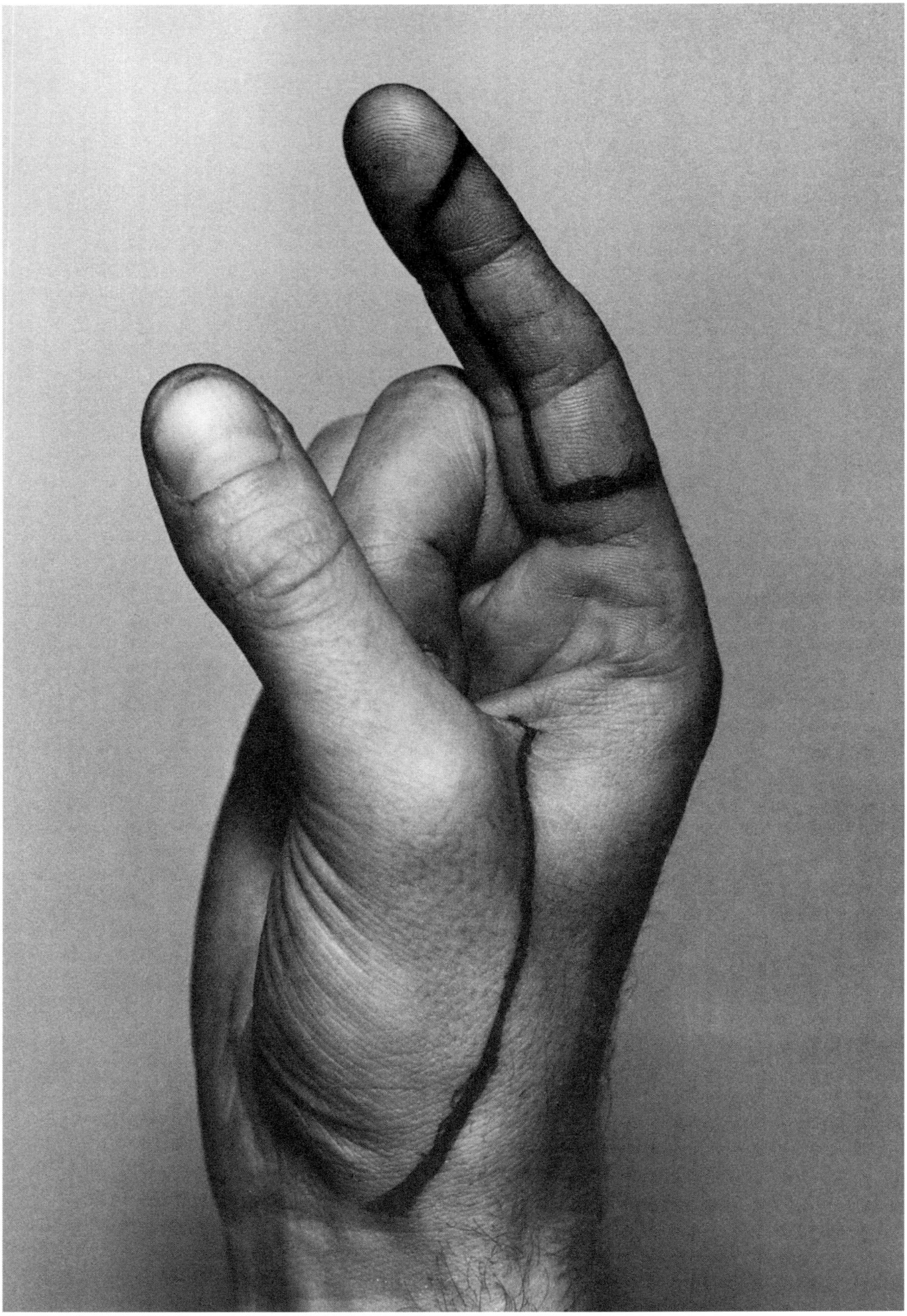

Paweł Kwiek, *Linia 1 i Linia 2*, 1975, fot. cz-b.
Paweł Kwiek, *Line 1 and Line 2*, 1975, B&W photograph

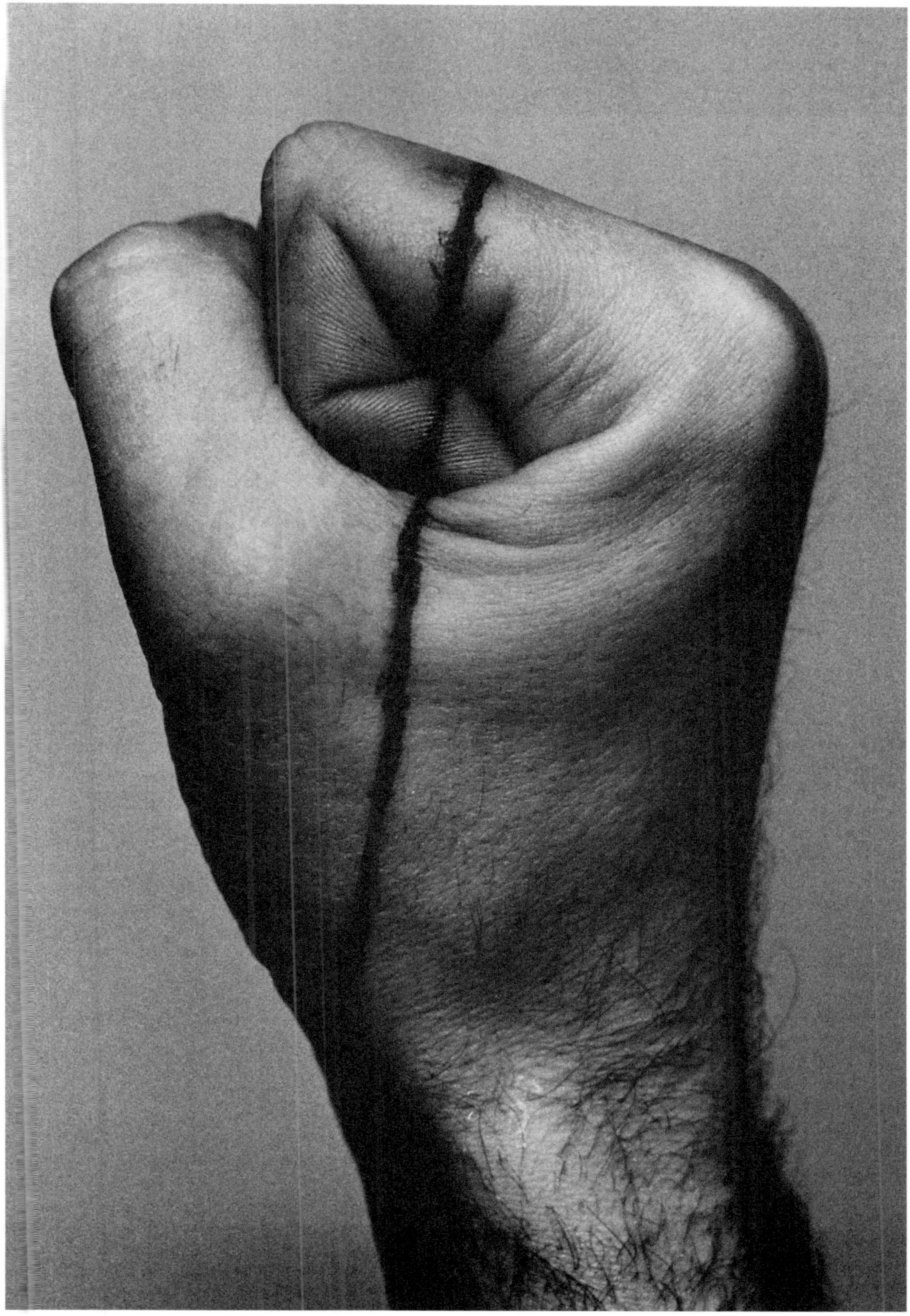

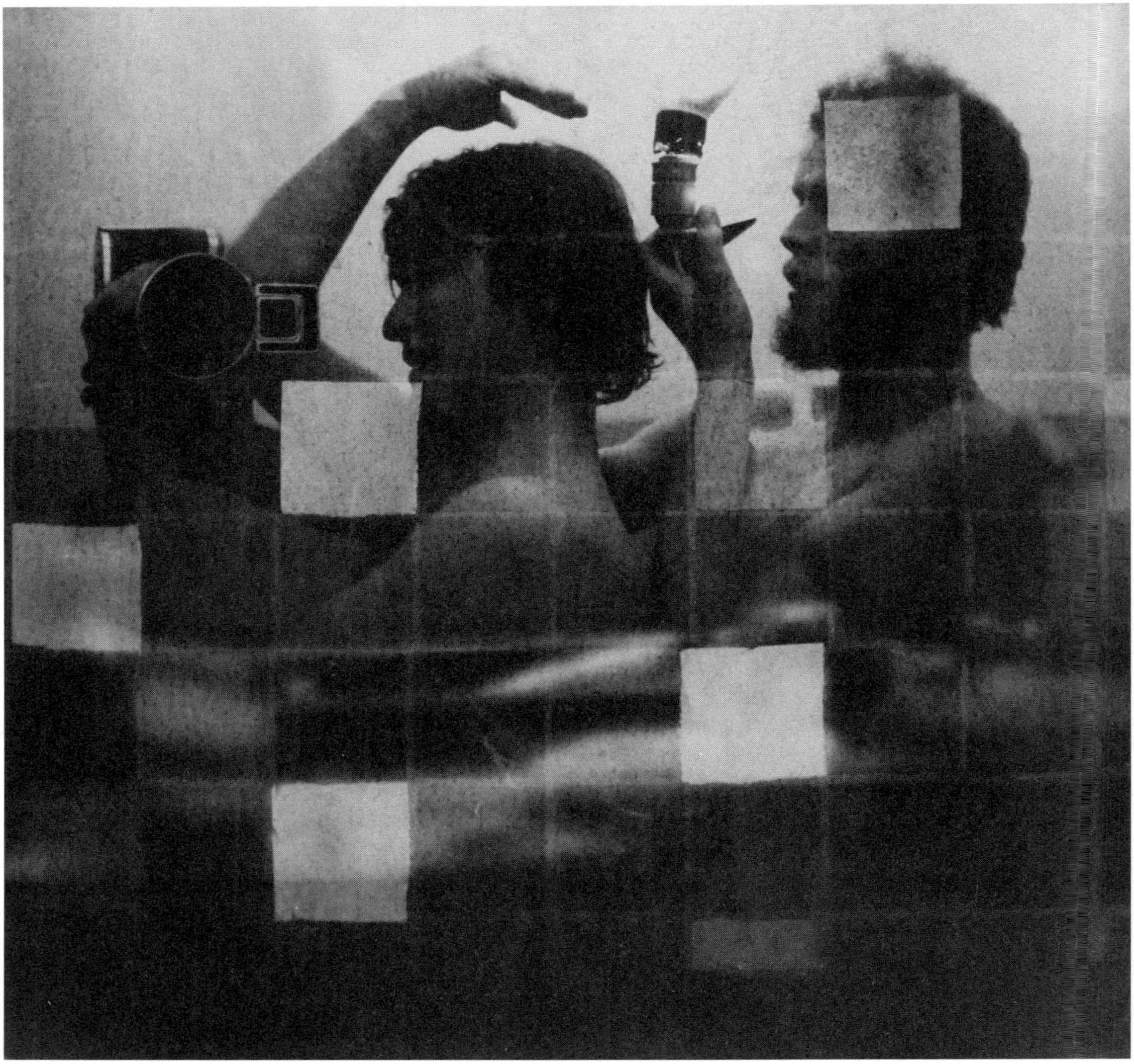

Paweł Kwiek, Jacek Łomnicki, *Łomokwiek*, 1973, fot. cz.-b.
Paweł Kwiek, Jacek Łomnicki, *Łomokwiek*, 1973, B&W photograph

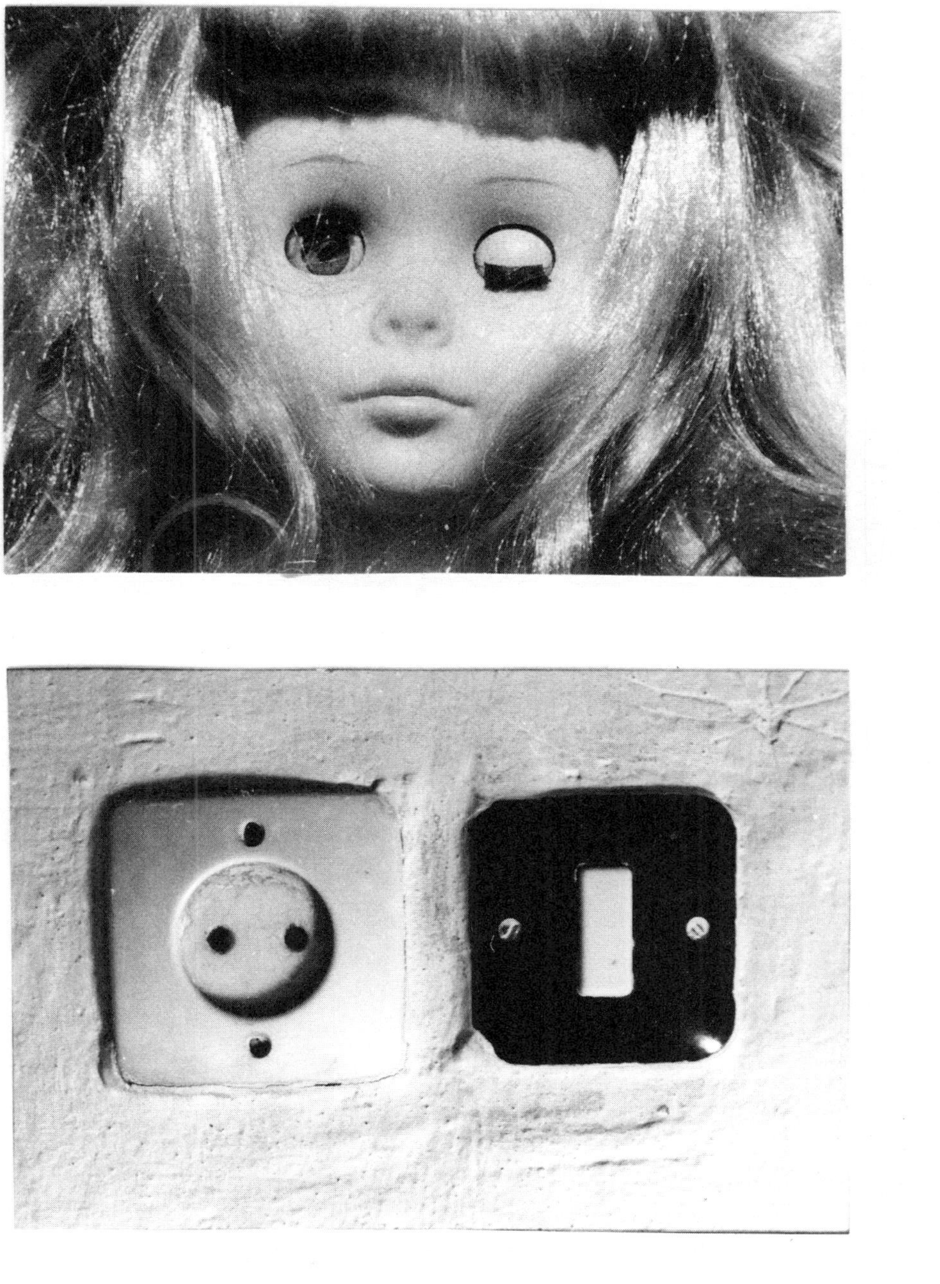

Paweł Kwiek, *Zrobić niemożliwe światło*, 1974, fot. cz.-b.
Paweł Kwiek, *Doing the Impossible Light*, 1974, B&W photograph

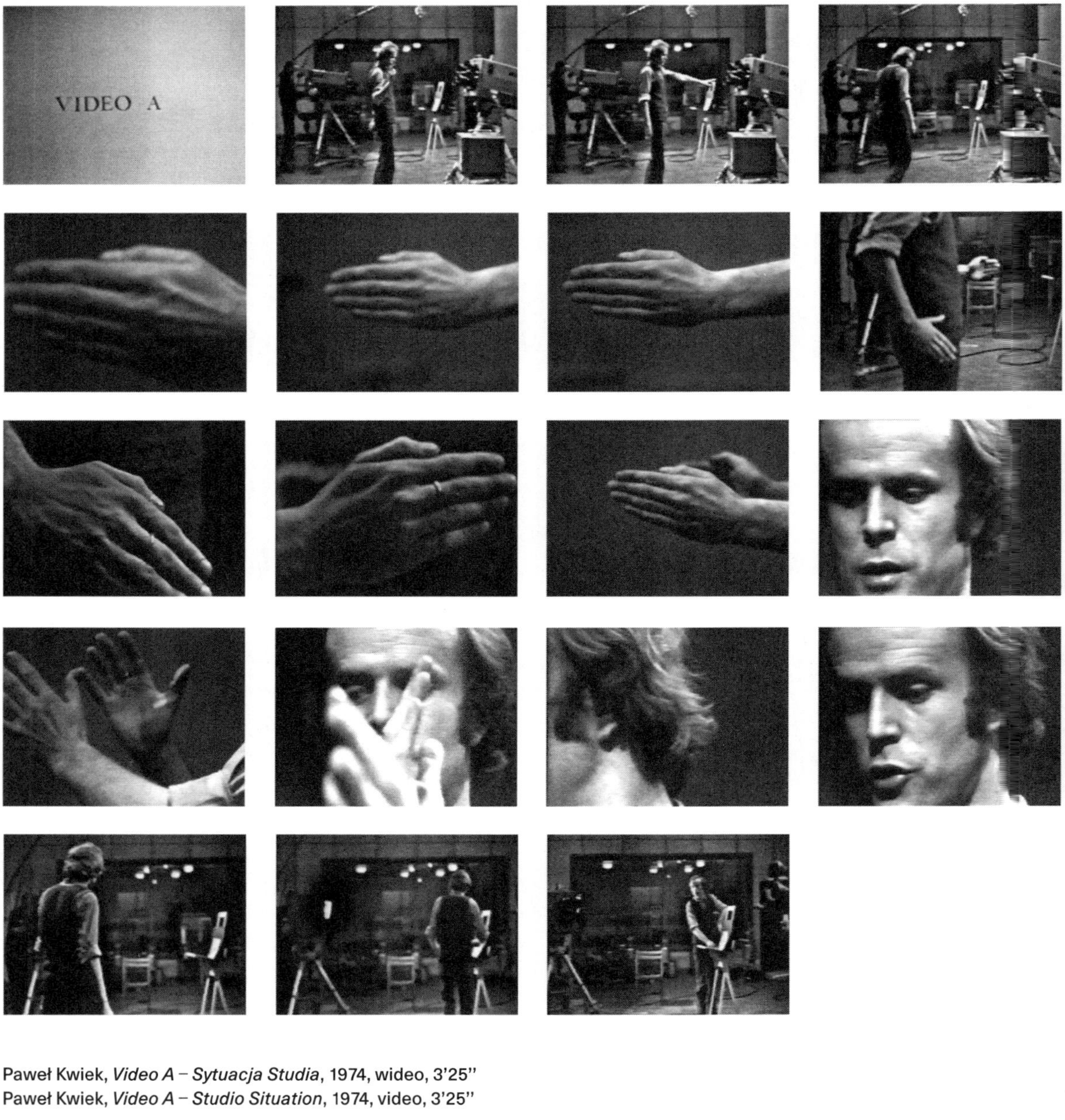

Paweł Kwiek, *Video A – Sytuacja Studia*, 1974, wideo, 3'25"
Paweł Kwiek, *Video A – Studio Situation*, 1974, video, 3'25"

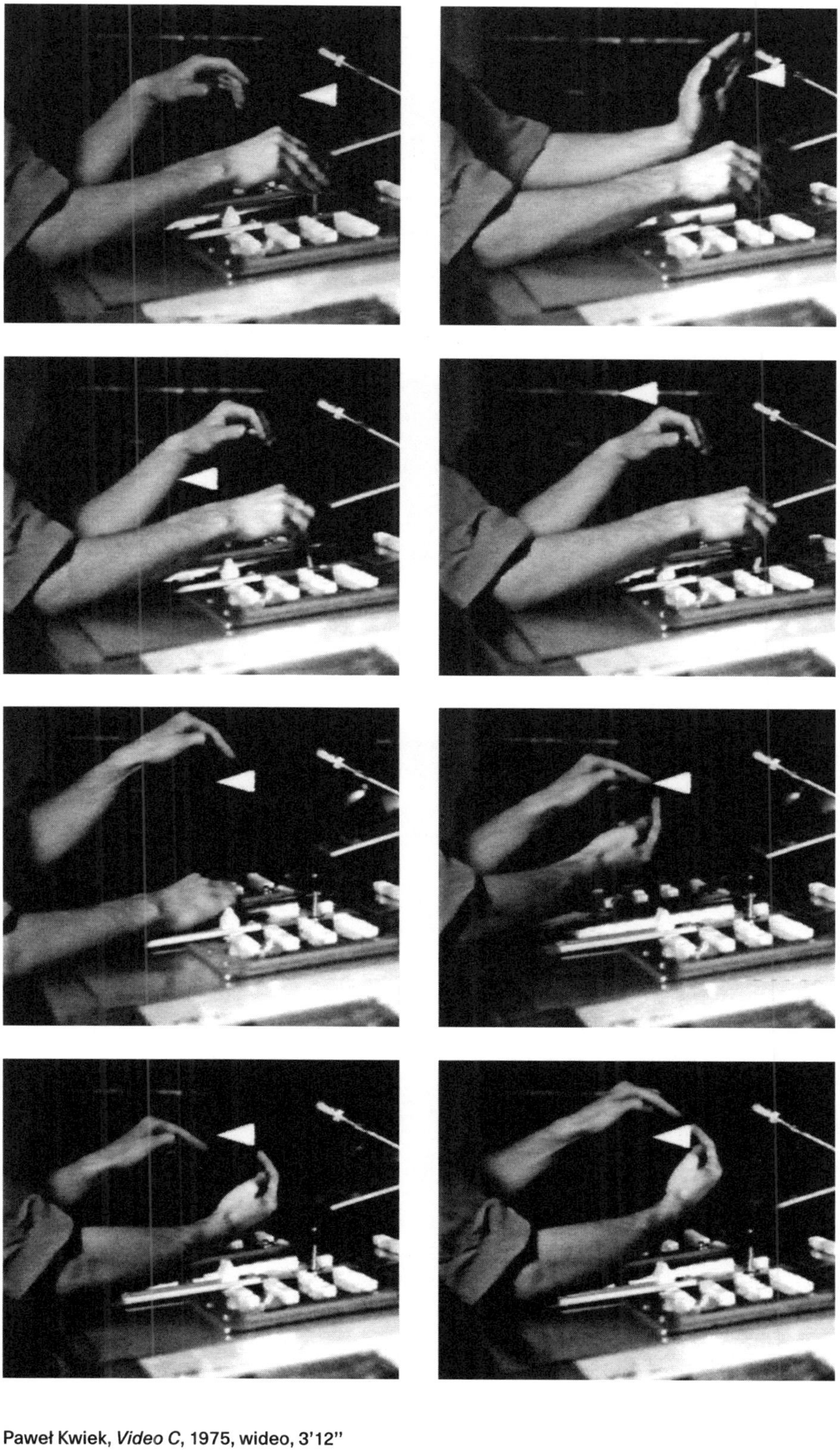

Paweł Kwiek, *Video C*, 1975, wideo, 3'12''
Paweł Kwiek, *Video C*, 1975, video, 3'12''

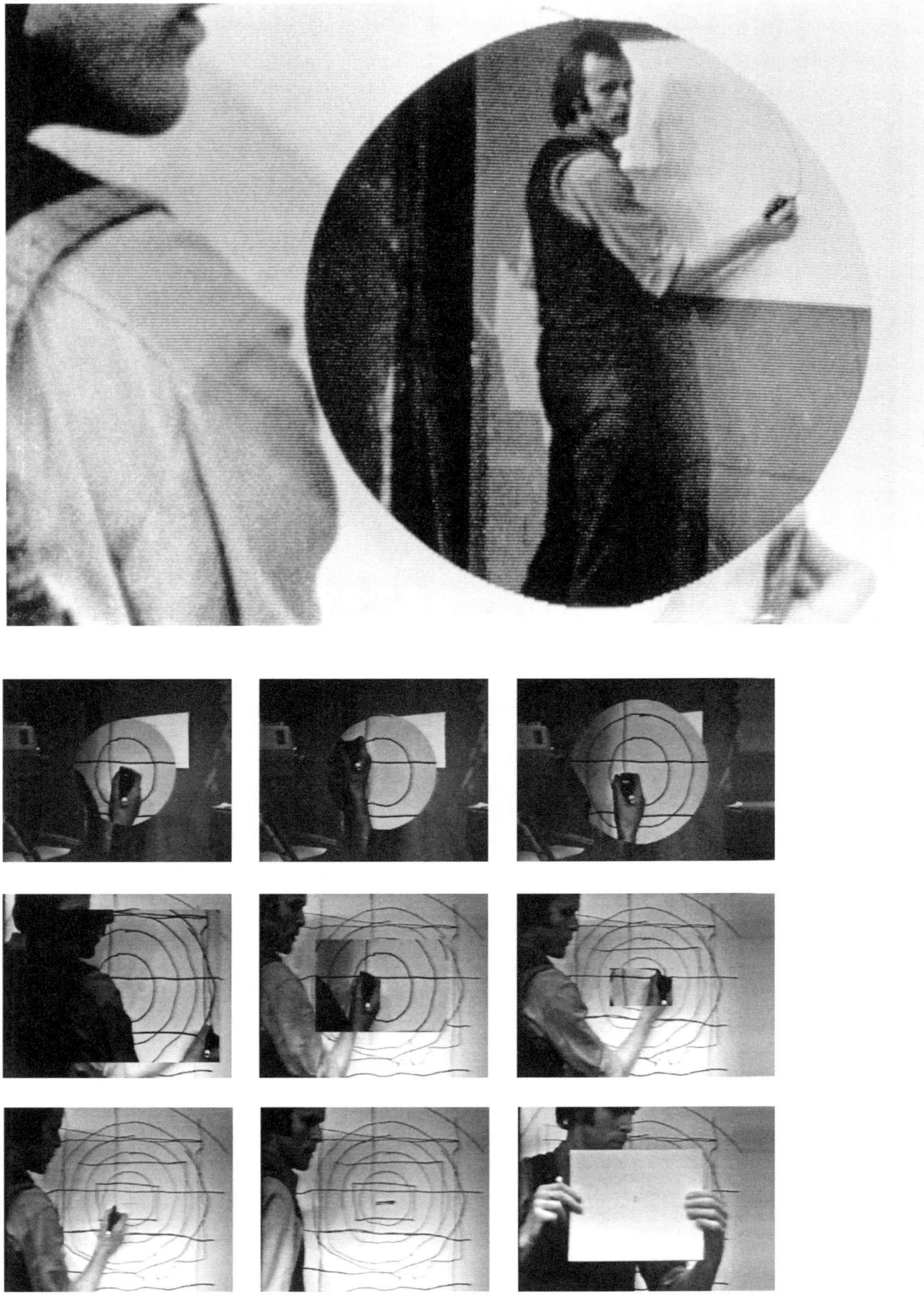

Paweł Kwiek, *Video P*, 1975, wideo, 10'59"
Paweł Kwiek, *Video P*, 1975, video, 10'59"

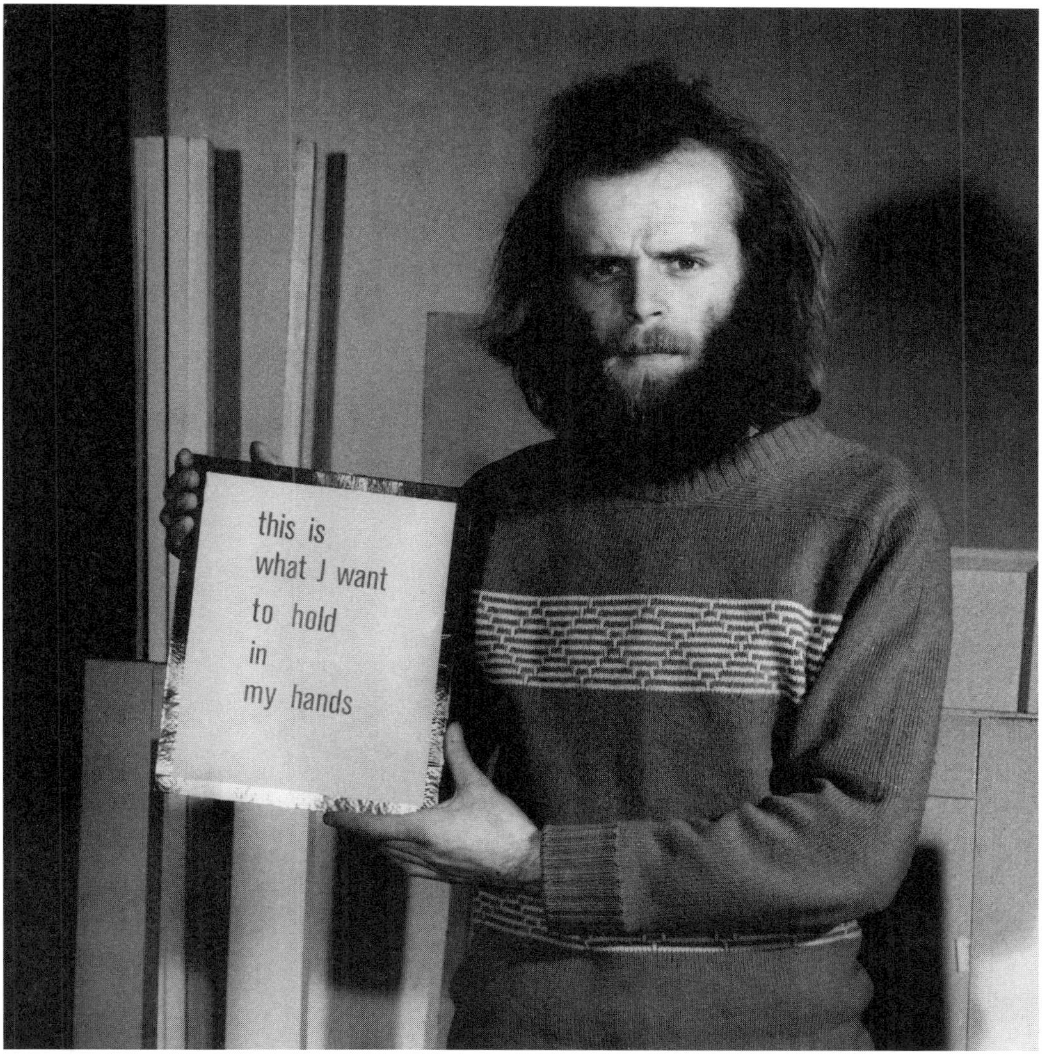

Paweł Kwiek, *To, co chcę trzymać w dłoniach*, 1975, fot. cz.-b.
Paweł Kwiek, *What I Want to Hold in My Hands*, 1975, B&W photograph

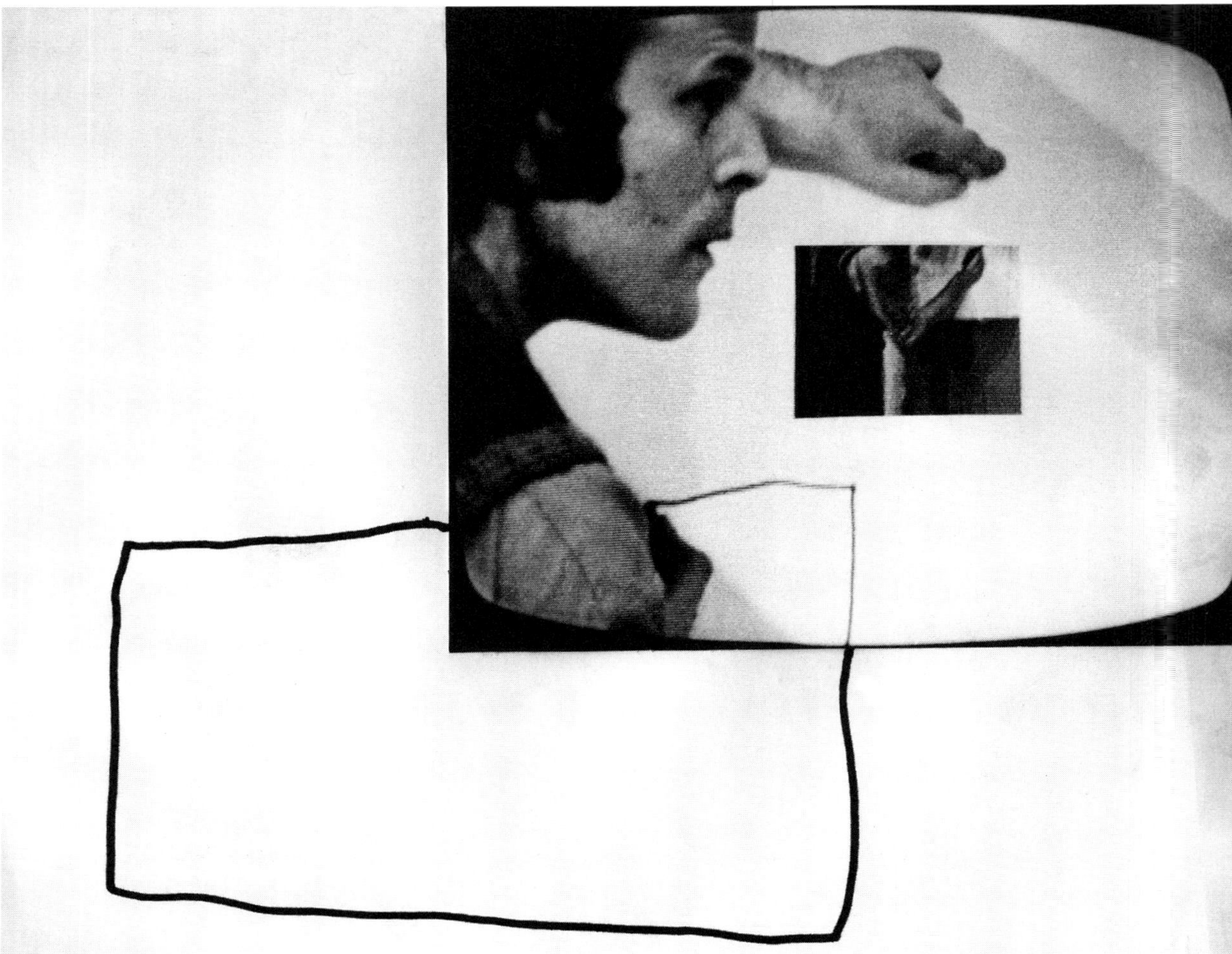

Paweł Kwiek, *Rysunki wideo-fotograficzne*, 1975, fot. cz.-b., flamaster, papier
Paweł Kwiek, *Videophotographic Drawings*, 1975, B&W photograph, marker, paper

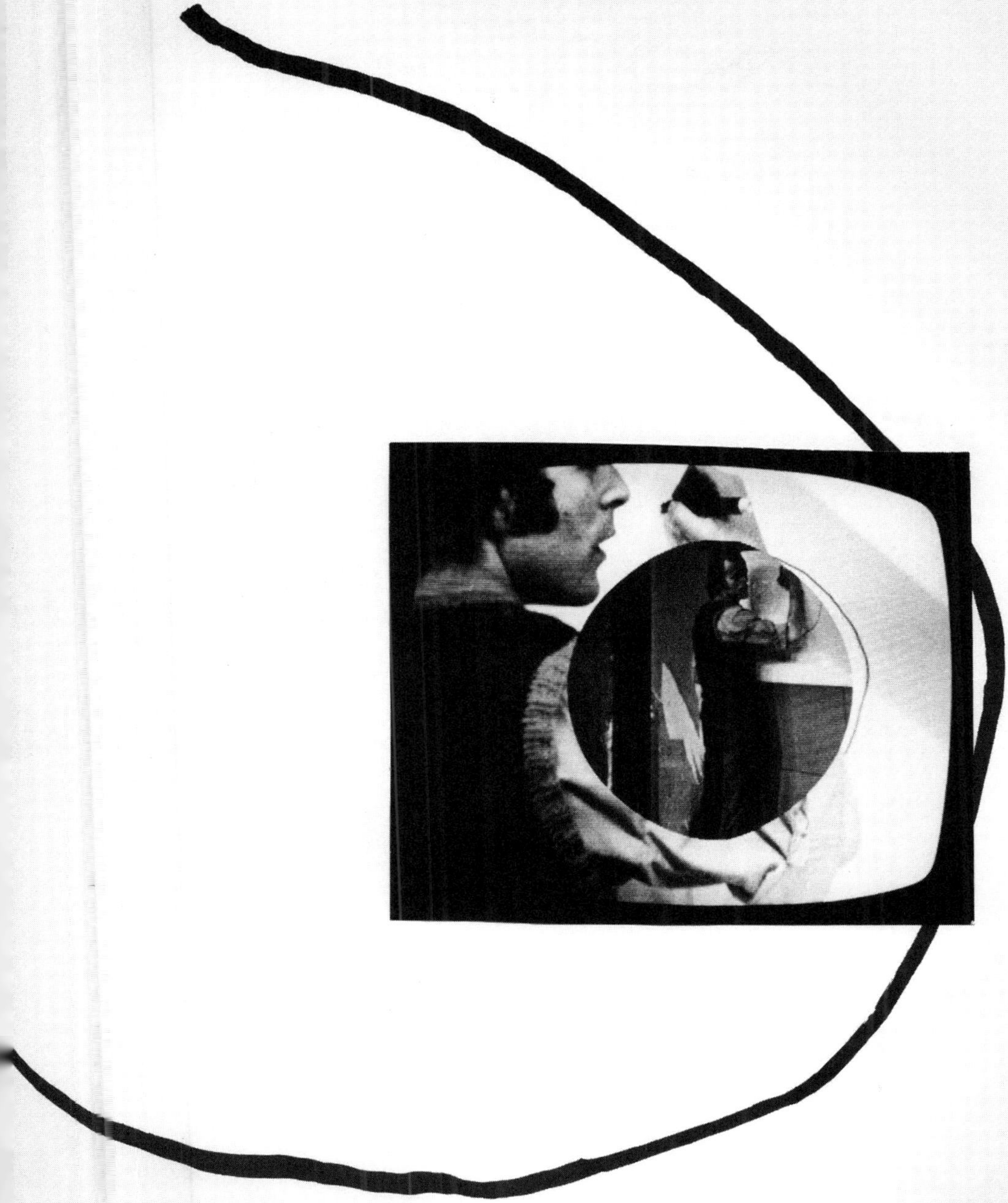

Paweł Kwiek, *System*, 1975, fot. cz.-b.
Paweł Kwiek, *System*, 1975, B&W photograph

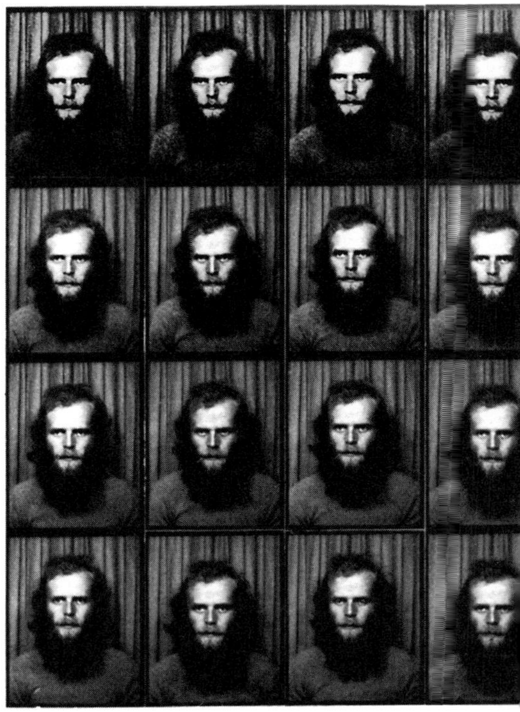

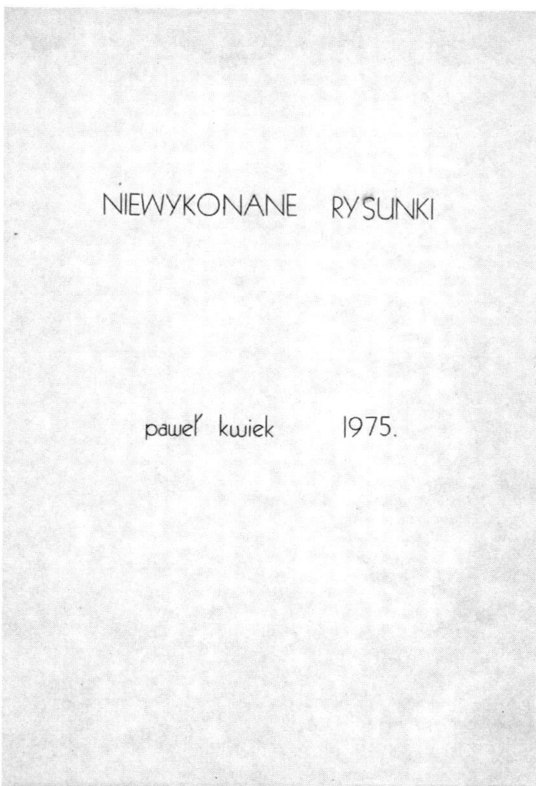

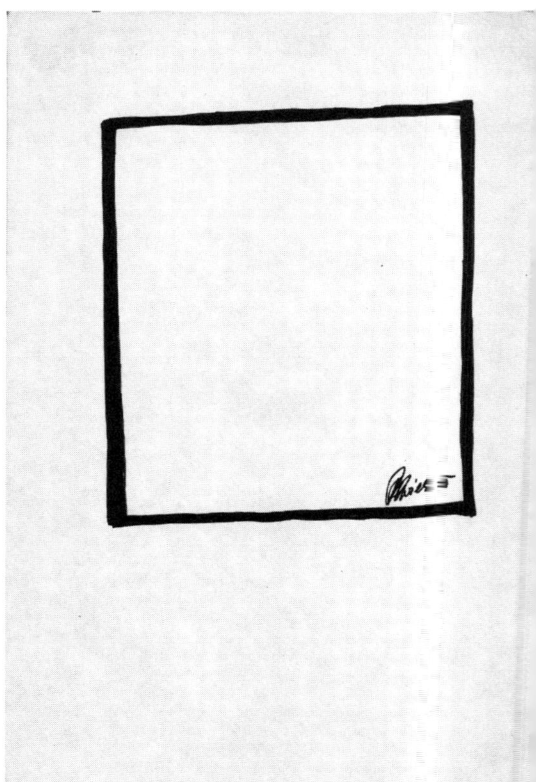

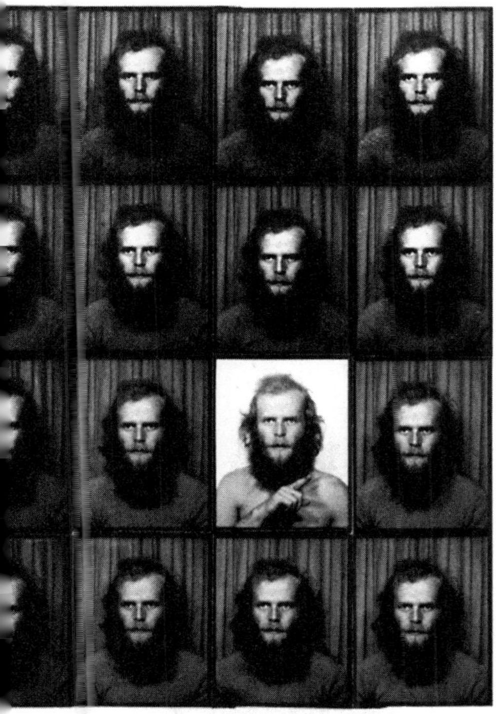

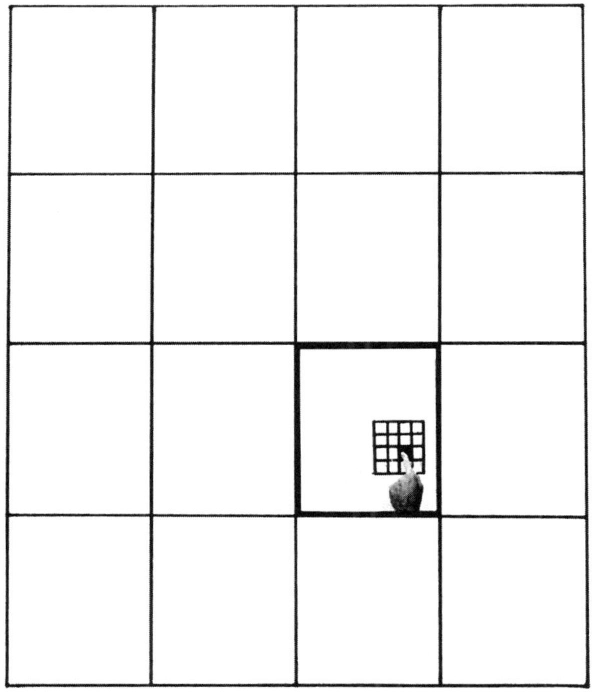

Paweł Kwiek, *Niewykonane rysunki,* 1975, flamaster, papier
Paweł Kwiek, *Never-made Drawings*, 1975, marker, paper

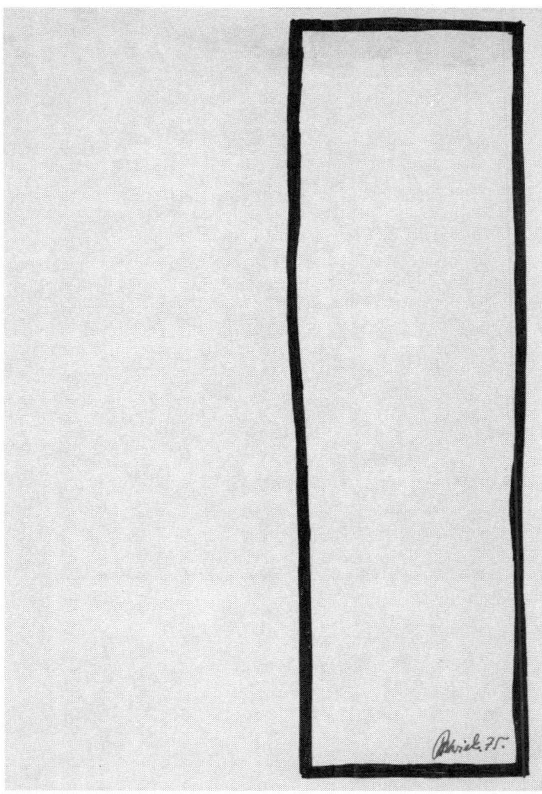

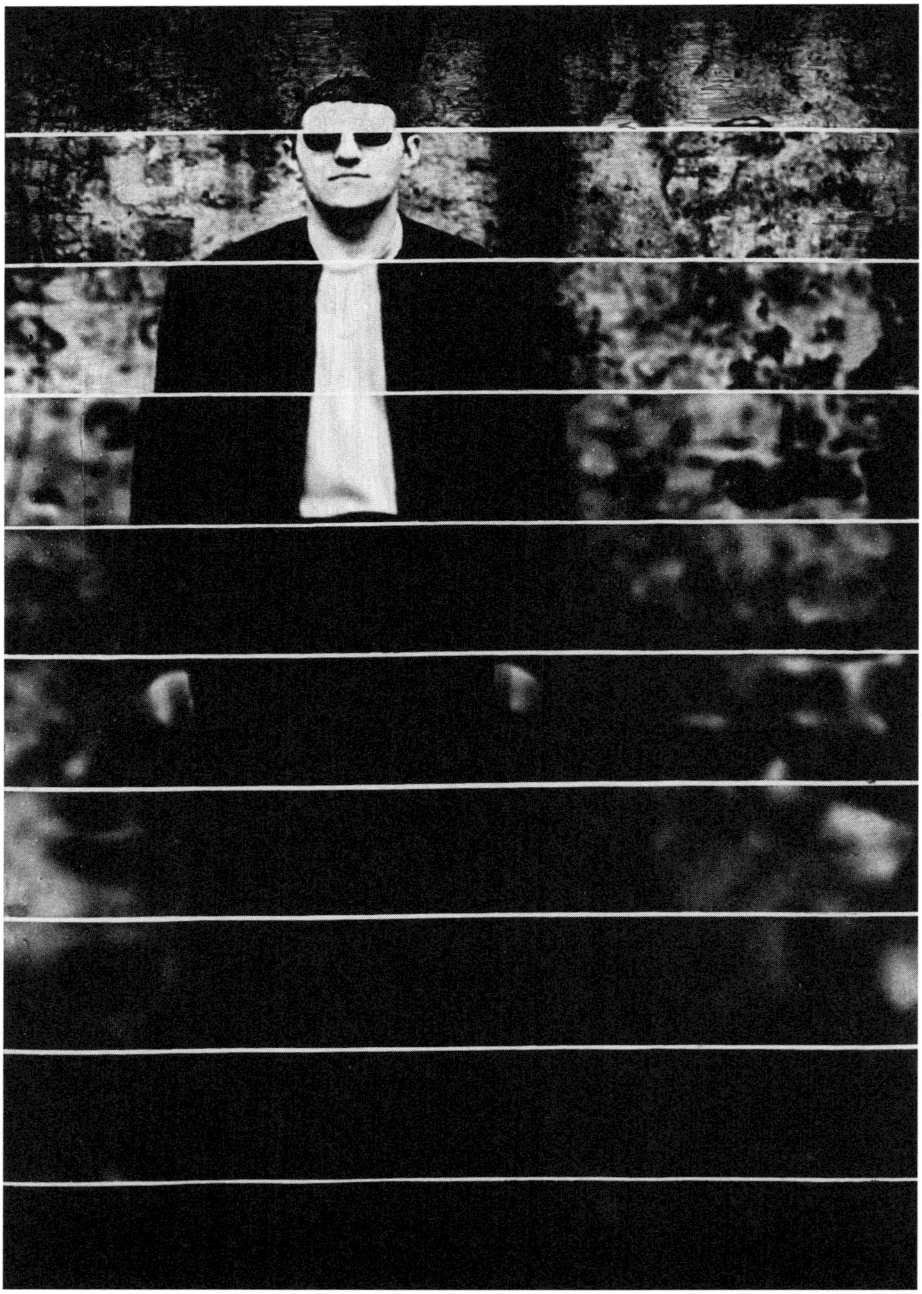

Józef Robakowski, *Dziesięć pól ostrości*, 1969, fot. cz.-b.
Józef Robakowski, *Ten Fields of Sharpness*, 1969, B&W photograph

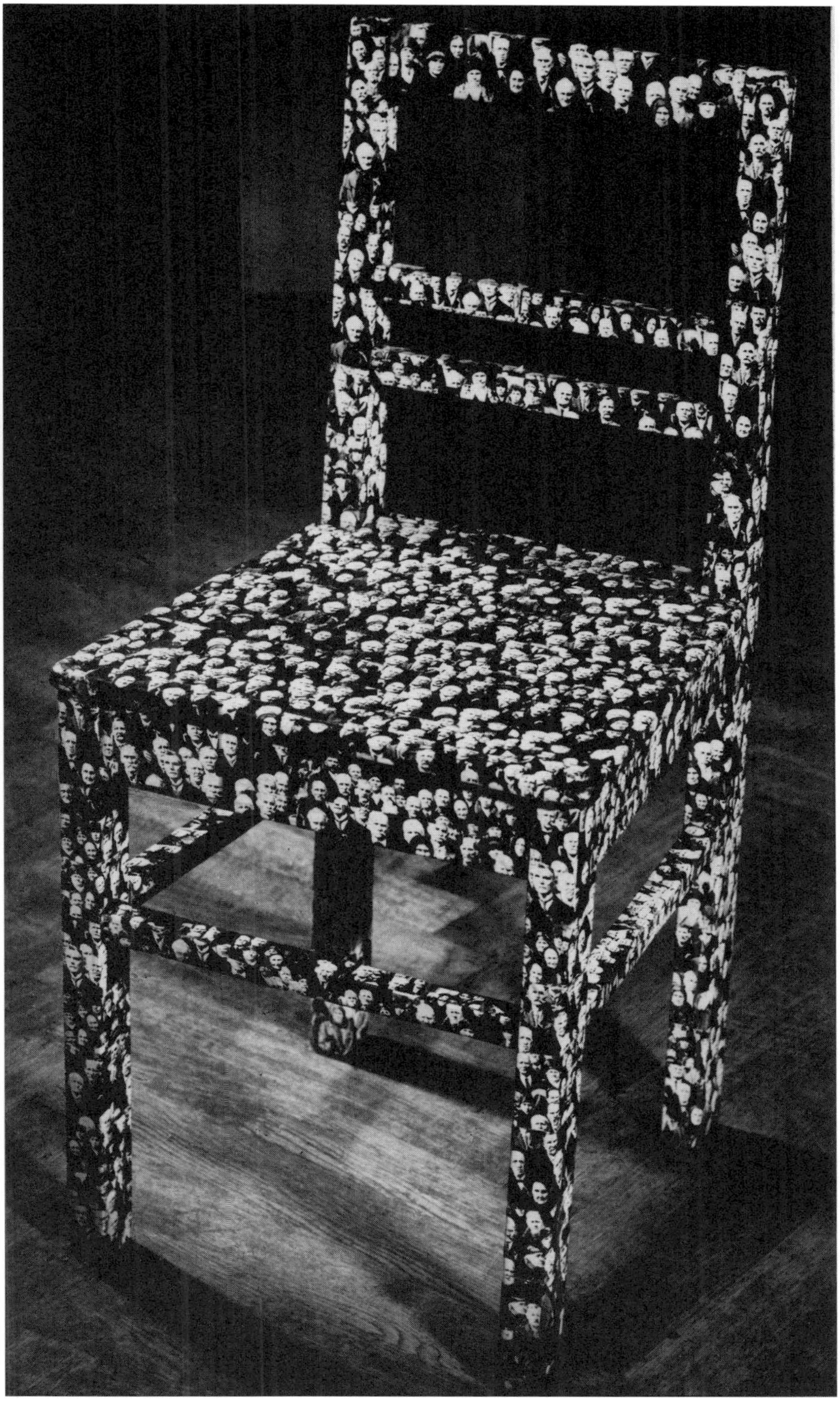

Józef Robakowski, *Krzesło*, 1970, fot. cz.-b., krzesło
Józef Robakowski, *The Chair*, 1970, B&W photograph, chair

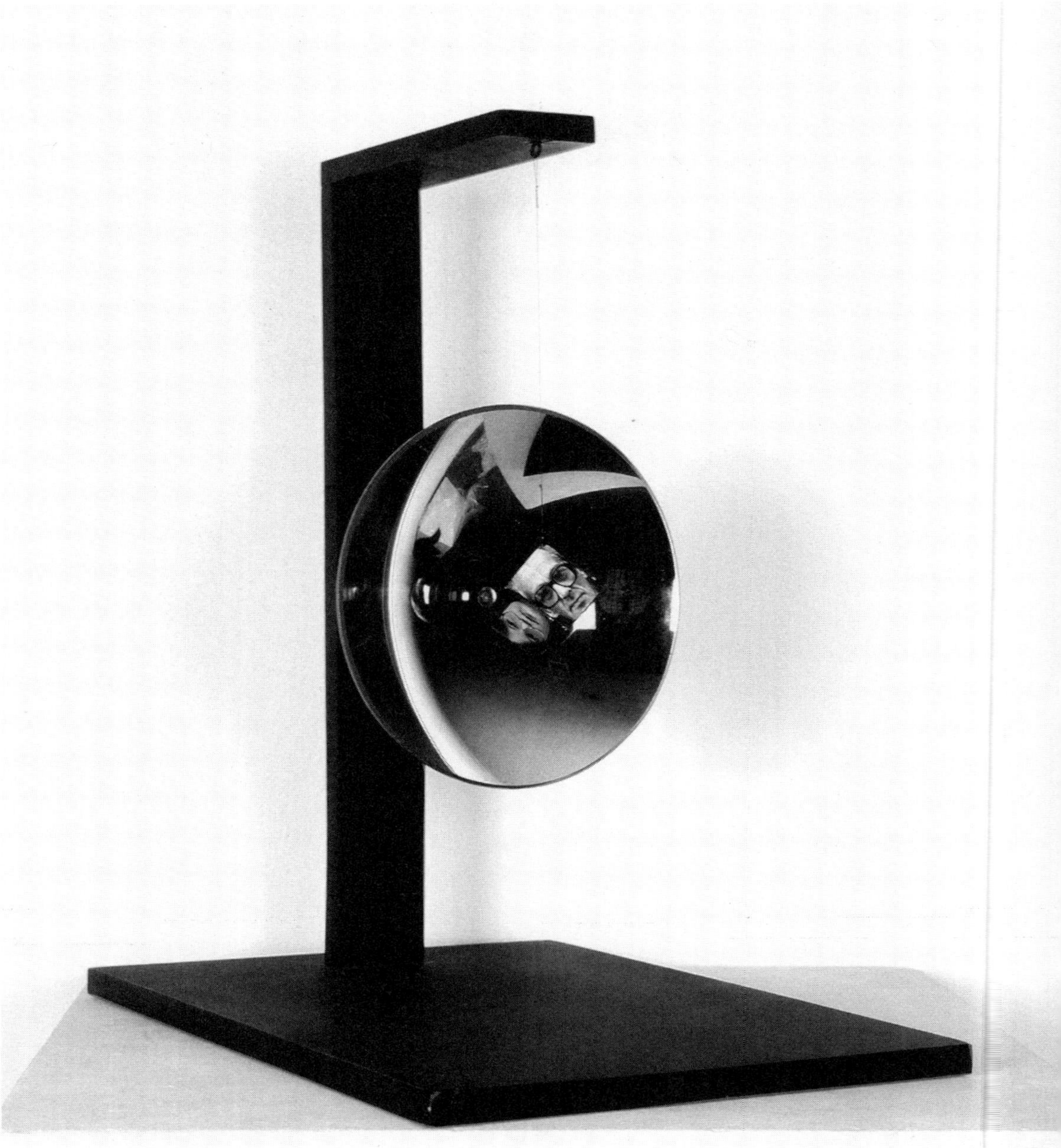

Józef Robakowski, *Kalejdoskop*, 1971, fot. cz.-b., lustro
Józef Robakowski, *Kaleidoscope*, 1971, B&W photograph, mirror

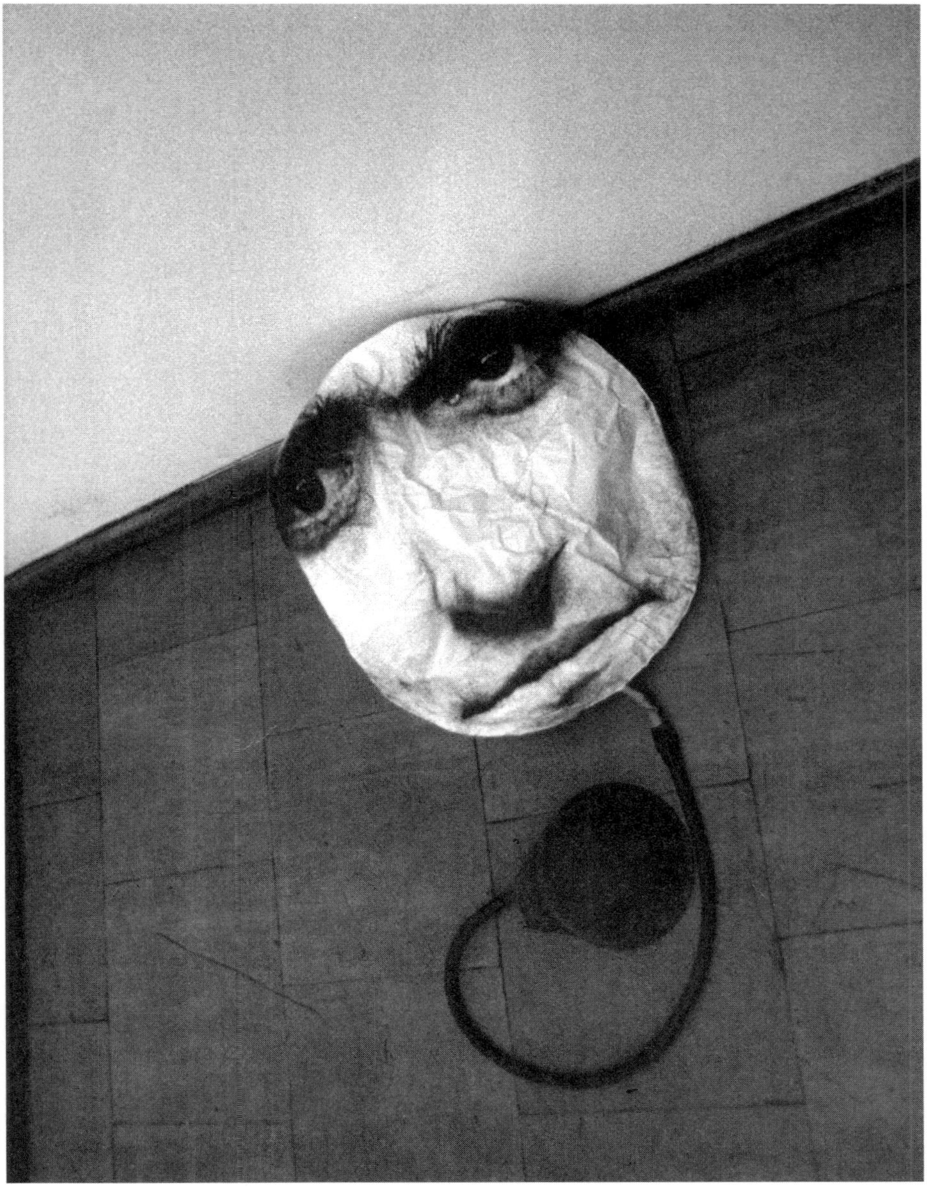

Józef Robakowski, *Dmuchana głowa*, 1971, fot. cz.-b.
Józef Robakowski, *Inflatable head*, 1971, B&W photograph

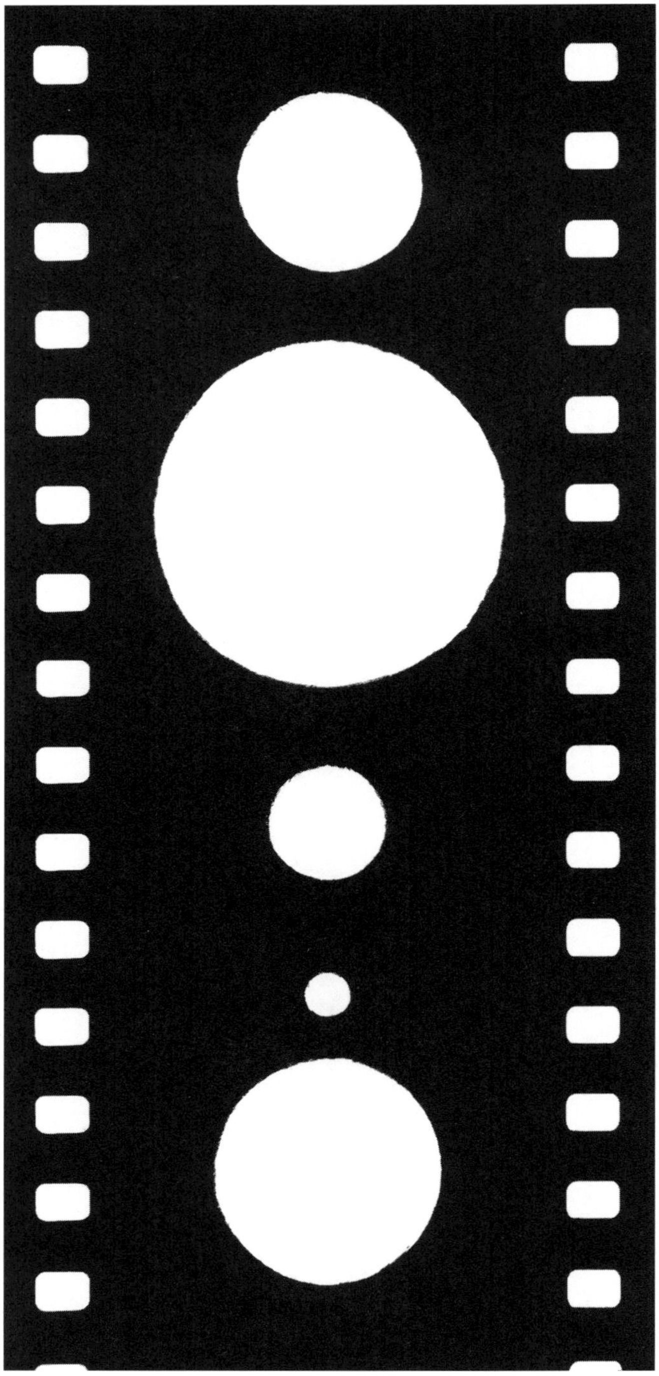

Józef Robakowski, *Test I*, 1971, 35 mm, 5'44''
Józef Robakowski, *Test I*, 1971, 35 mm, 5'44''

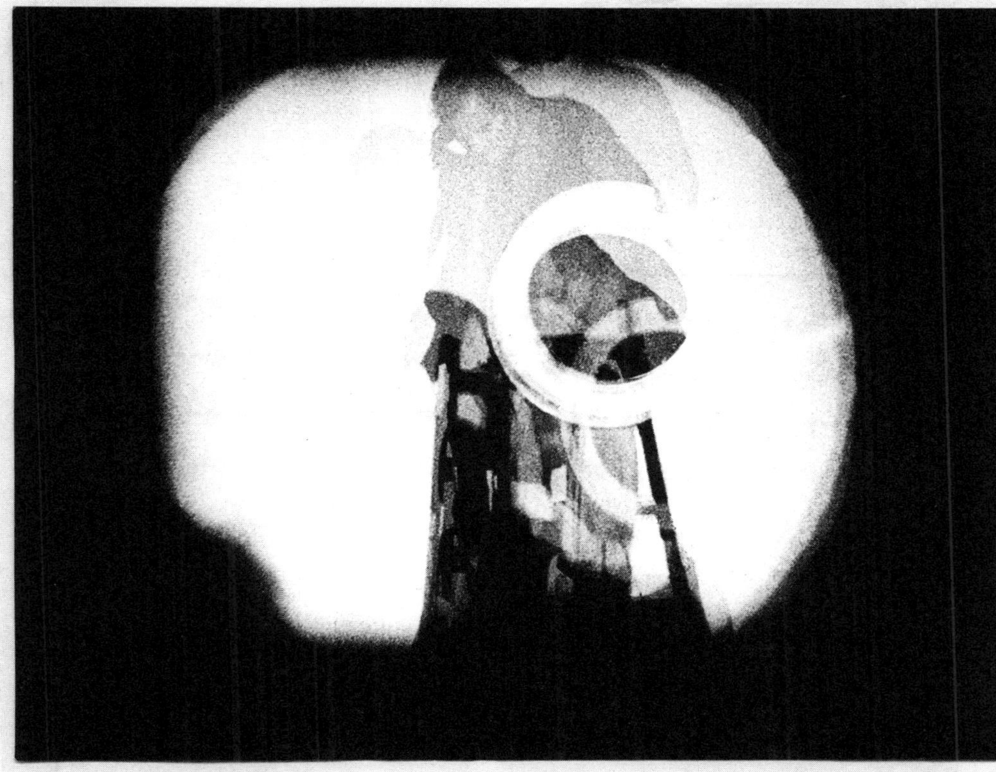

T E S T / film - performance / od 1970 używany w różnych akcjach artystycznych Warsztatu Formy Filmowej.
Zdjęcie dokumentujące akcję TEST w czasie projekcji WFF w Knokke Heist - Belgia,V Festiwal Filmów Eksperymentalnych - 1974 r.

Opis zdarzenia

W czasie projekcji filmu TEST przy pomocy lustra autor kierował strumienie świetlne w strone publiczności,oślepiając widownię silnymi błyskami światła.Ripostą wielu widzów była kontrakcja błysków fleszowych skierowanych w autora prowokacji.

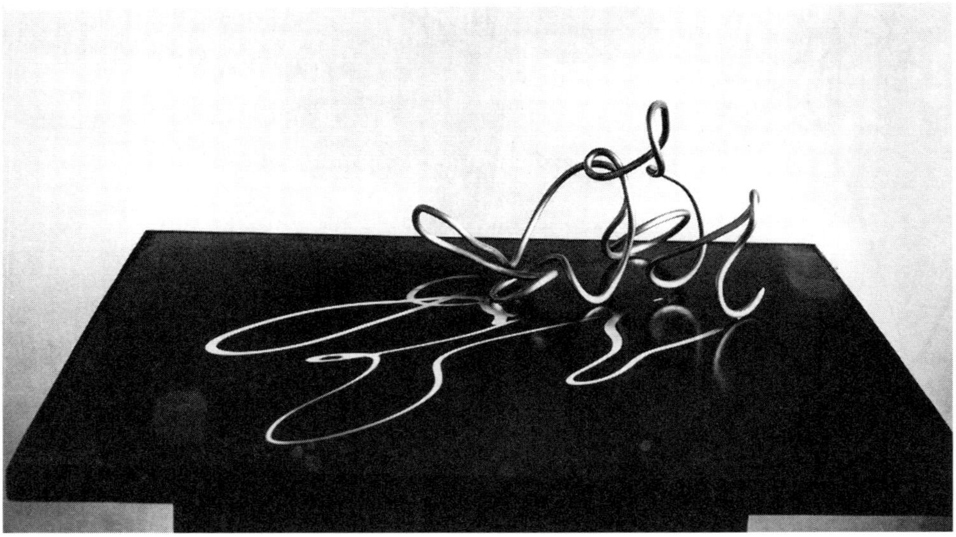

Józef Robakowski, *Studium cienia*, 1971, fot. cz.-b., obiekt
Józef Robakowski, *Study of the Shadow*, 1971, B&W photograph, object

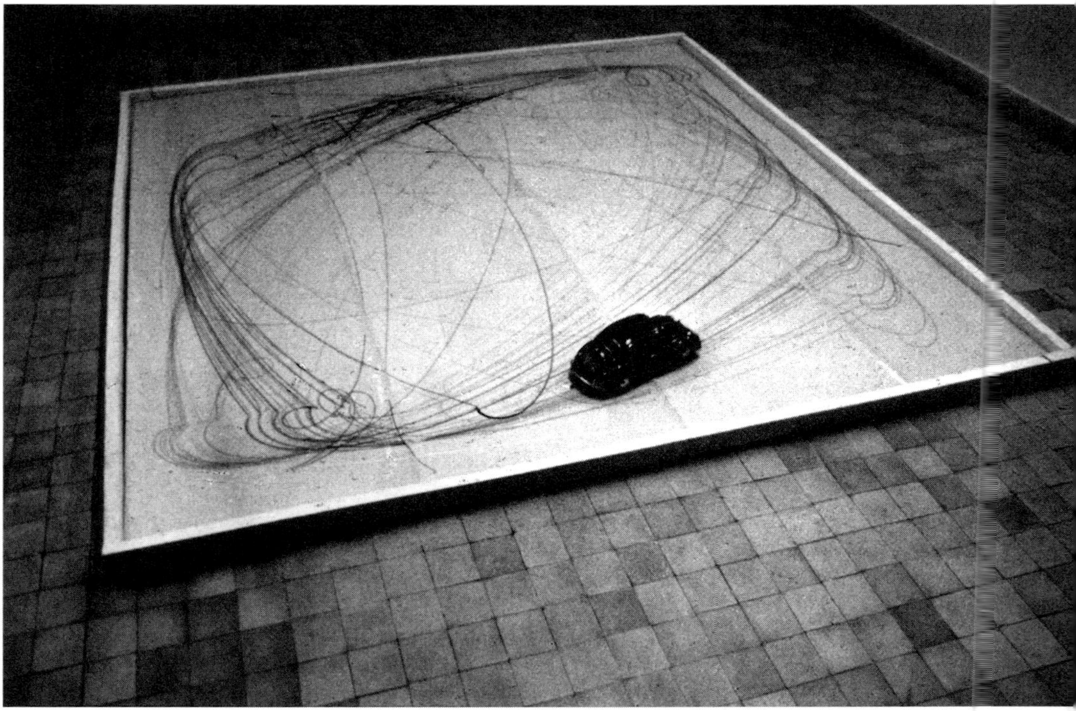

Józef Robakowski, *Samochodzik*, 1972, obiekt interaktywny
Józef Robakowski, *Little Car*, 1972, interactive object

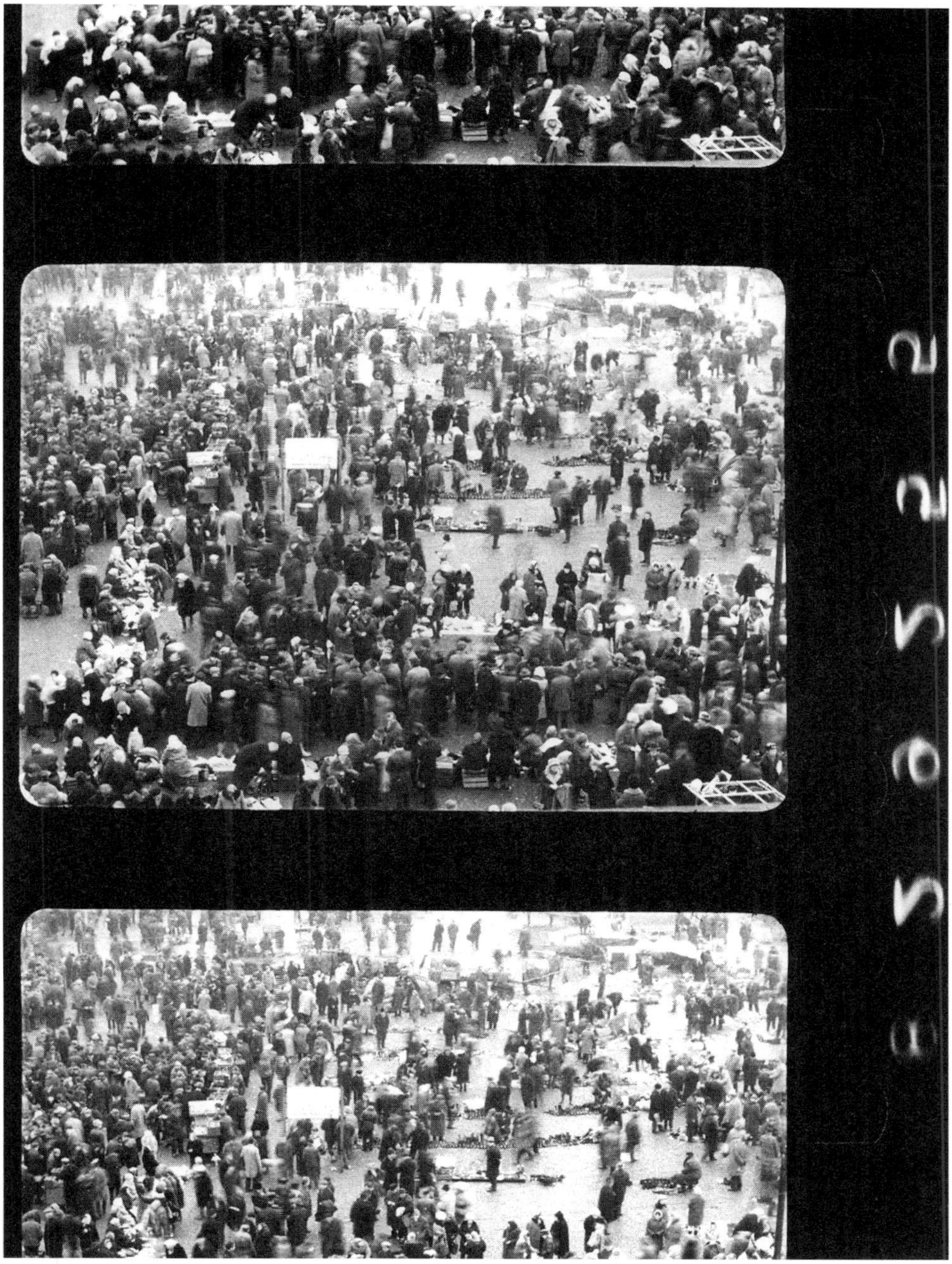

Józef Robakowski, *Rynek*, 1970, 35 mm, 4'20''
Józef Robakowski, *Market*, 197C, 35 mm, 4'20''

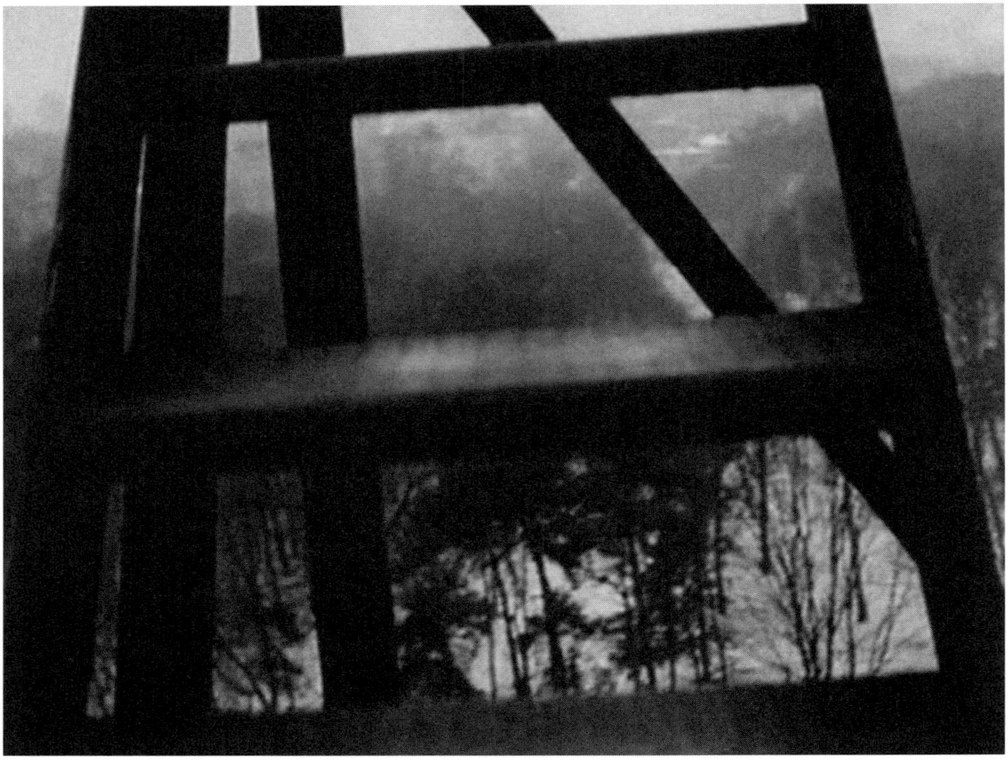

Józef Robakowski, *Idę*, 1973, 35 mm, 2'56"
Józef Robakowski, *I'm Going,* 1973, 35 mm, 2'56"

Józef Robakowski, *Ćwiczenie*, 1972/73, 35 mm, 4'21"
Józef Robakowski, *Exercise*, 1972/73, 35 mm, 4'21"

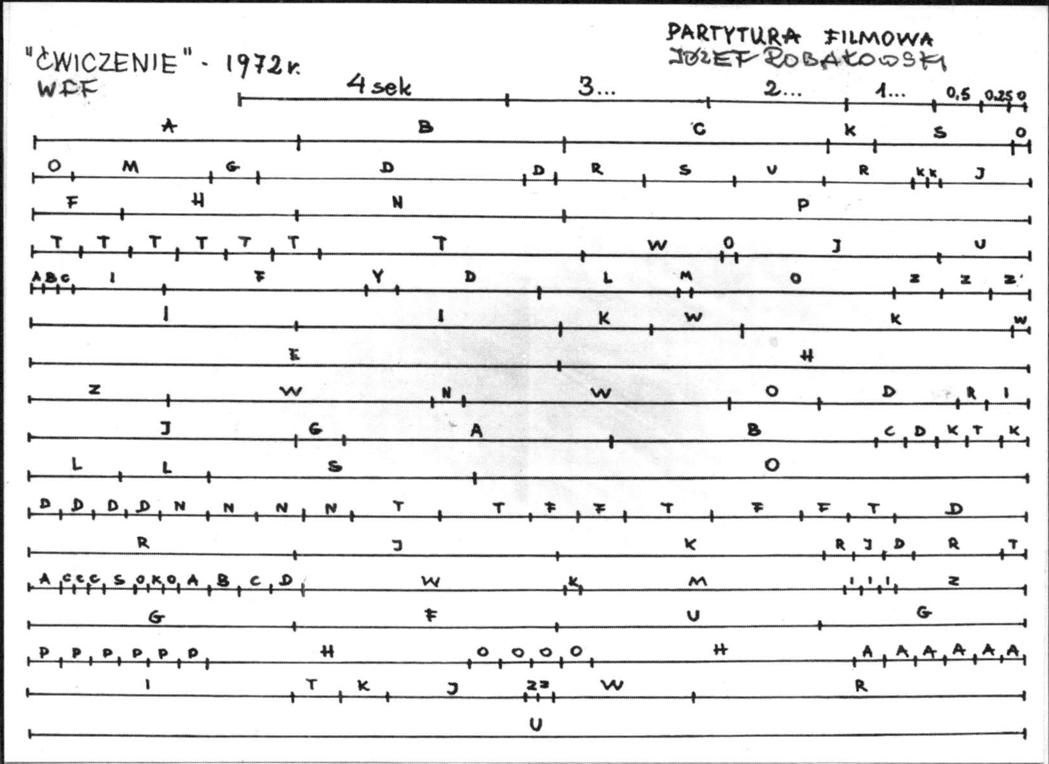

ĆWICZENIE - film 1972/73, real. Józef Robakowski

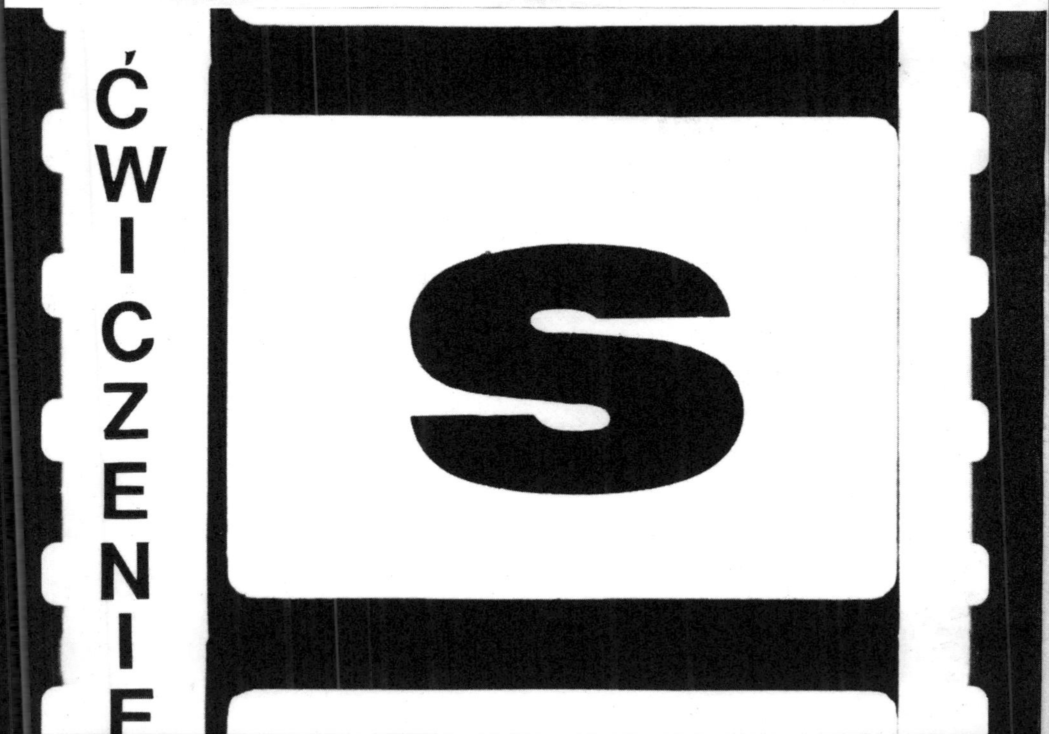

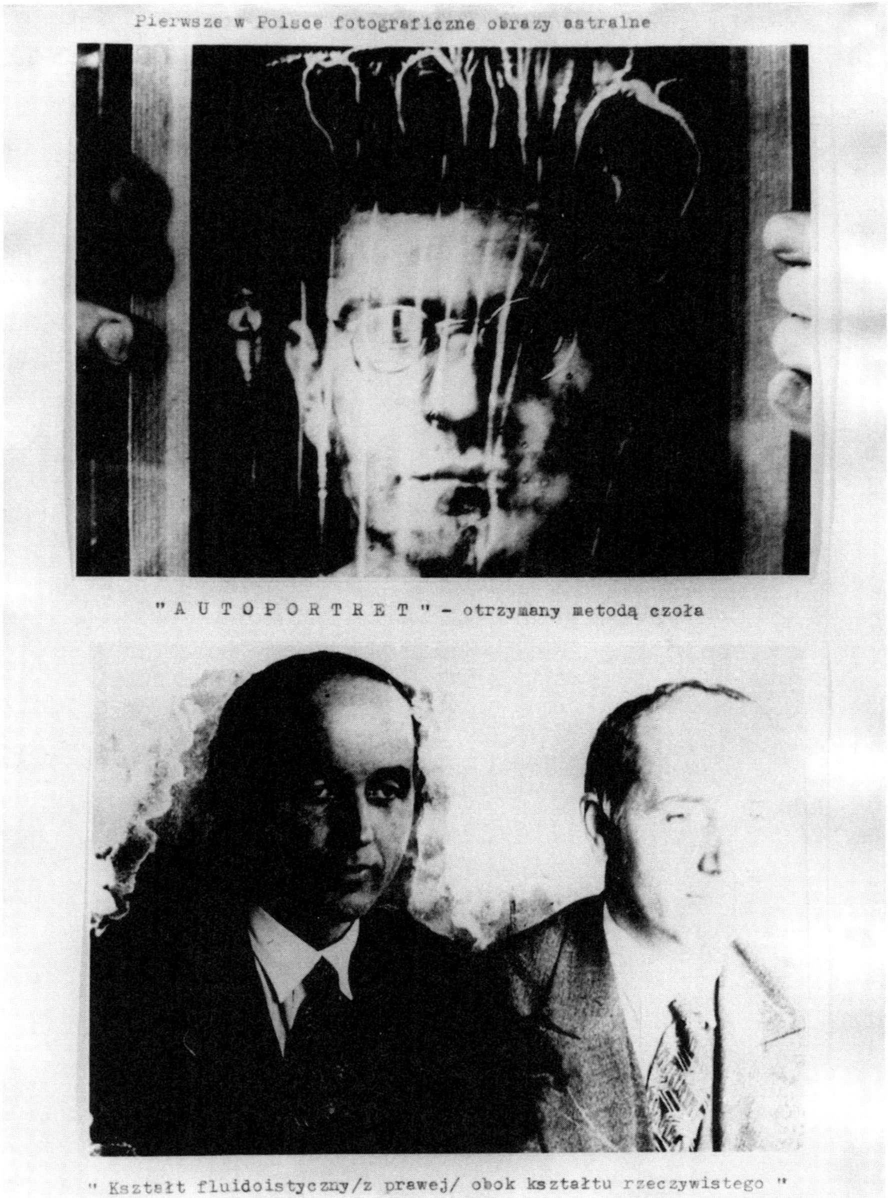

Józef Robakowski, *Fotografia astralna*, od 1972, fot. cz.-b.
Józef Robakowski, *Astral Photopgrahy*, since 1972, B&W photograph

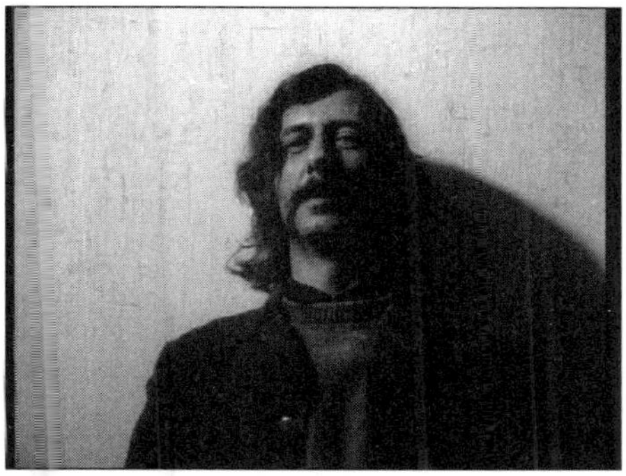

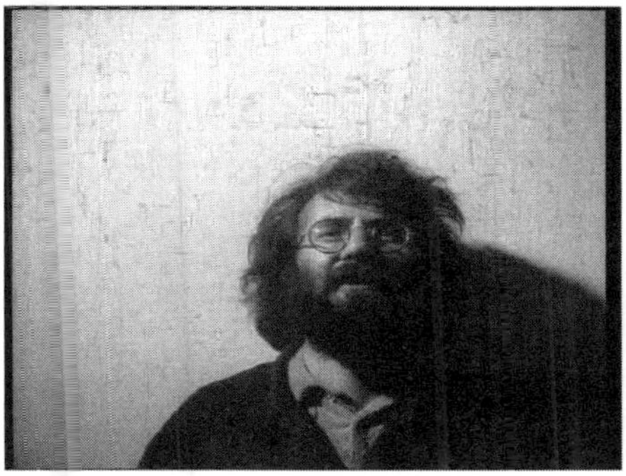

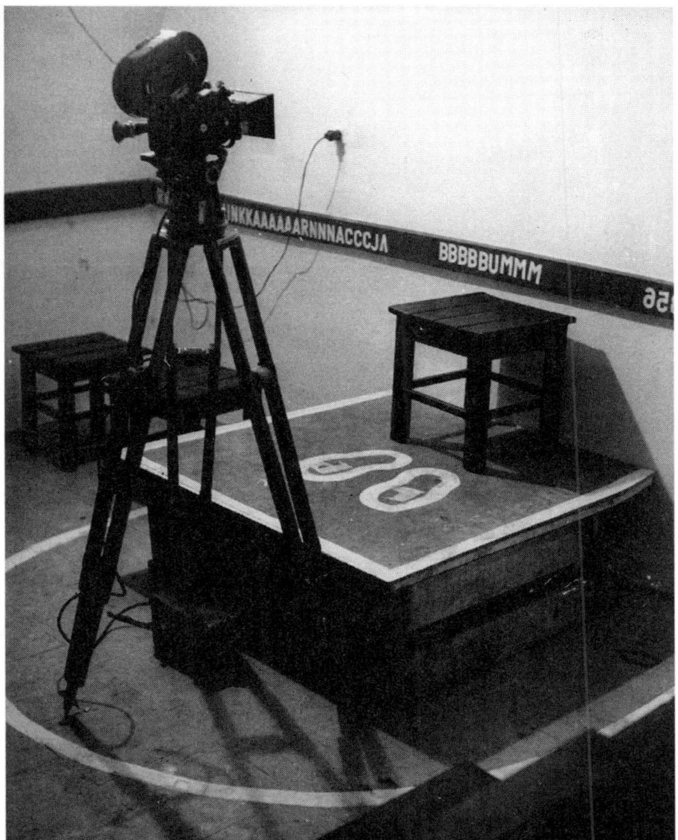

Józef Robakowski (współpraca A. Mikołajczyk), *Zapis*, 1973, 35 mm
Józef Robakowski (cooperation: A. Mikołajczyk), *The Record*, 1973, 35 mm

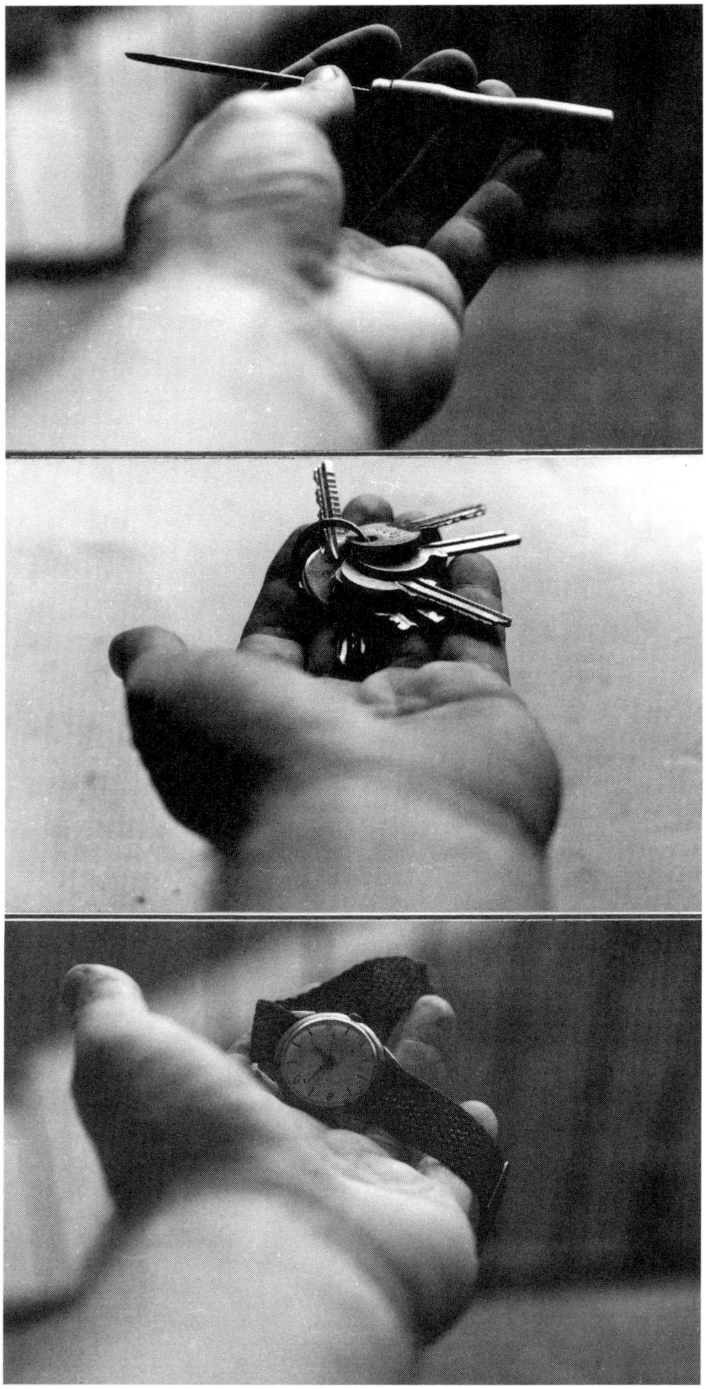

Józef Robakowski, *Fotografia obiektywna*, 1973, fot. cz.-b.
Józef Robakowski, *Objective Photography*, 1973, B&W photograph

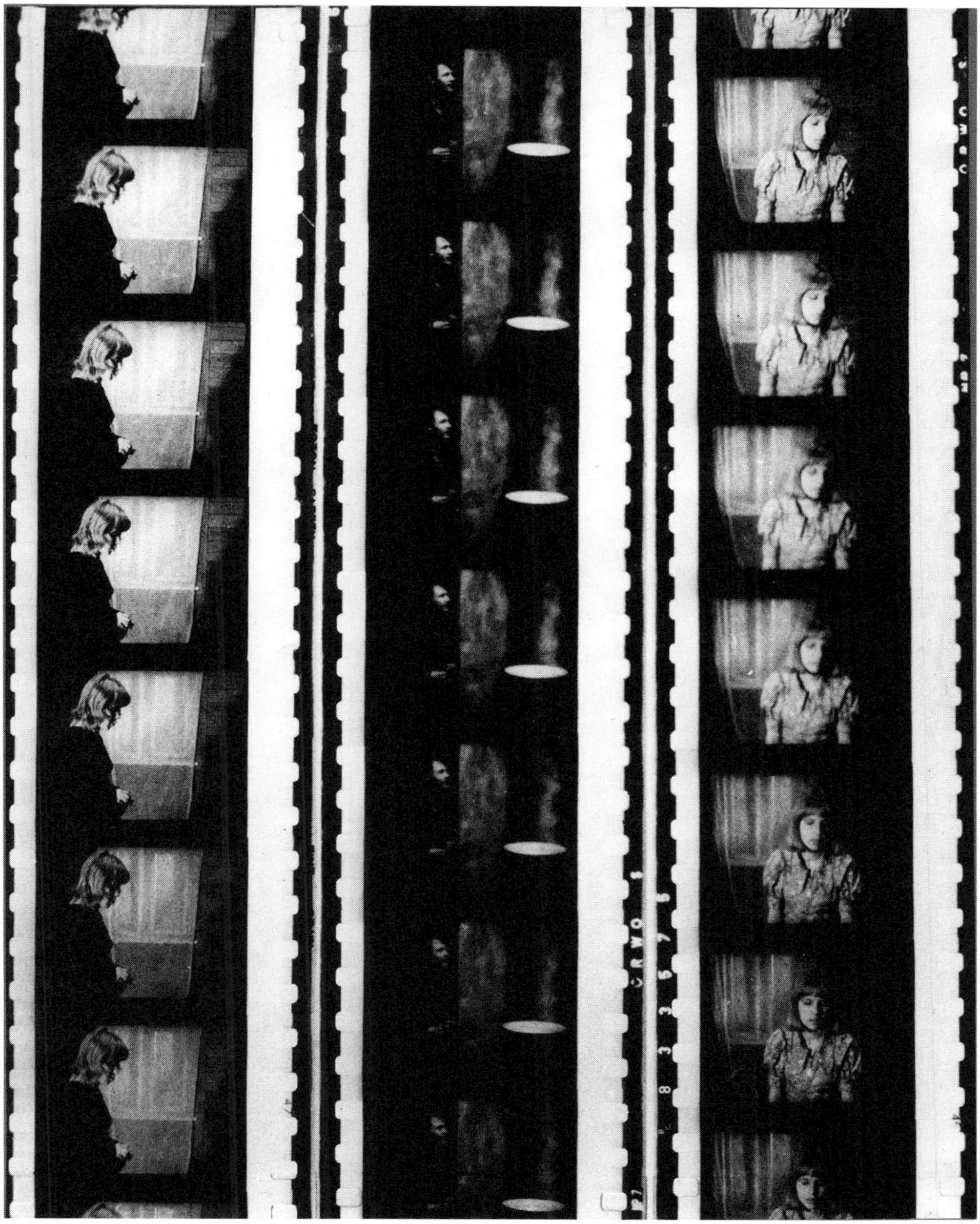

Józef Robakowski, Ryszard Waśko, *Drzwi – okno – krzesło*, 1973, 35 mm, 30’
Józef Robakowski, Ryszard Waśko, *Door-Window-Chair*, 1973, 35 mm, 30’

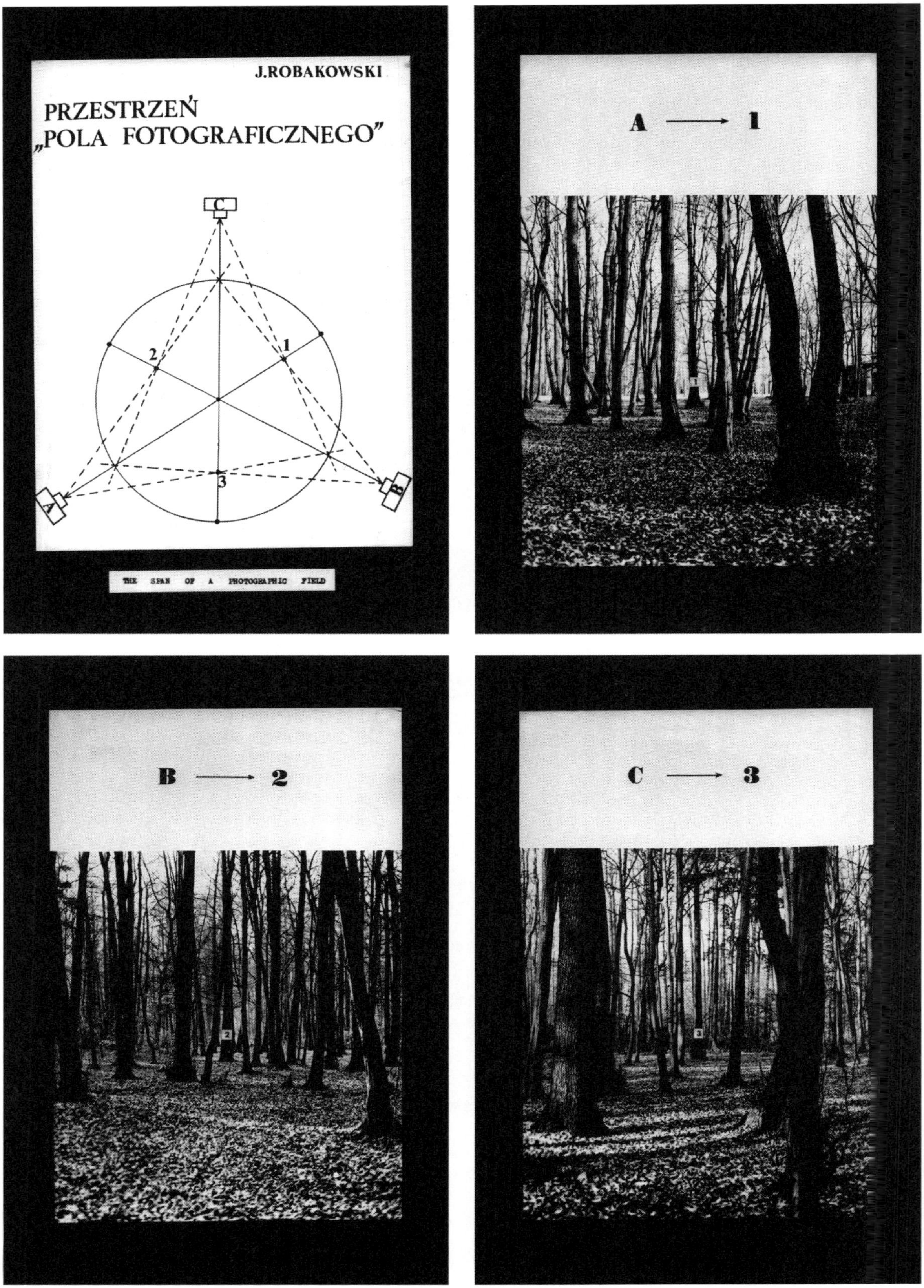

Józef Robakowski, *Przestrzeń pola fotograficznego*, 1975, fot. cz.-b.
Józef Robakowski, *The Space of the Photographic Field*, 1975, B&W photograph

Z cyklu " I N S T R U K C J E " - realizacja: J.Robakowski - 1975

ZAKŁADANIE TAŚMY

/ instrukcja zakładania taśmy do magnetofonu " TONETTE " /

Podczas zakładania taśmy powinien być owinięty jej odcinek długości ok.40cm.Przycisk / wskazany strzałką / służy do zwolnienia hamulców, umożliwiając swobodne obracanie się szpul.Po założeniu taśmy należy upewnić się czy taśma przechodząc wewnątrz obudówki z głowicami jest ułożona prawidłowo na słupkach prowadzących.

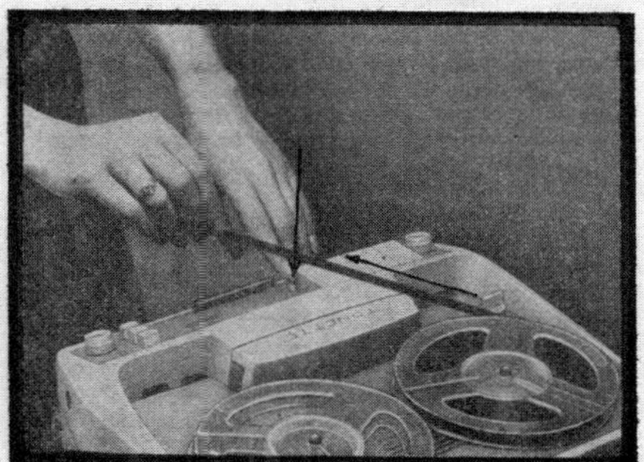

fot.1

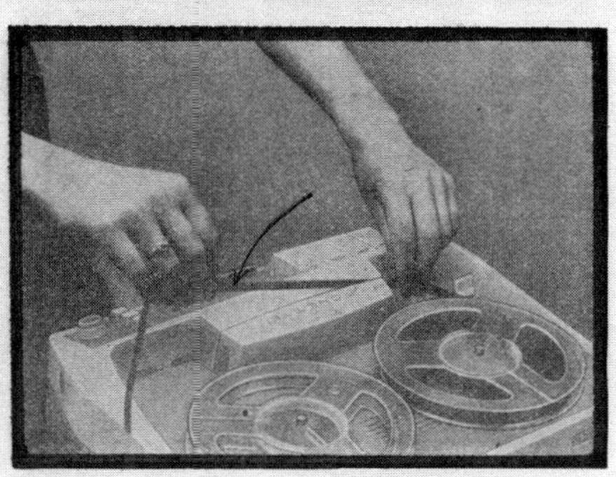

fot.2

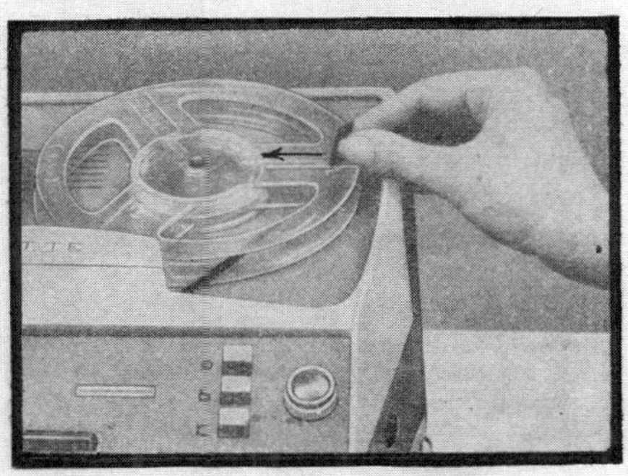

fot.3

Józef Robakowski, *Polecenia*, 1975, wideo, współpraca A. Paruzel
Józef Robakowski, *Instructions*, 1975, video, cooperation with A. Paruzel

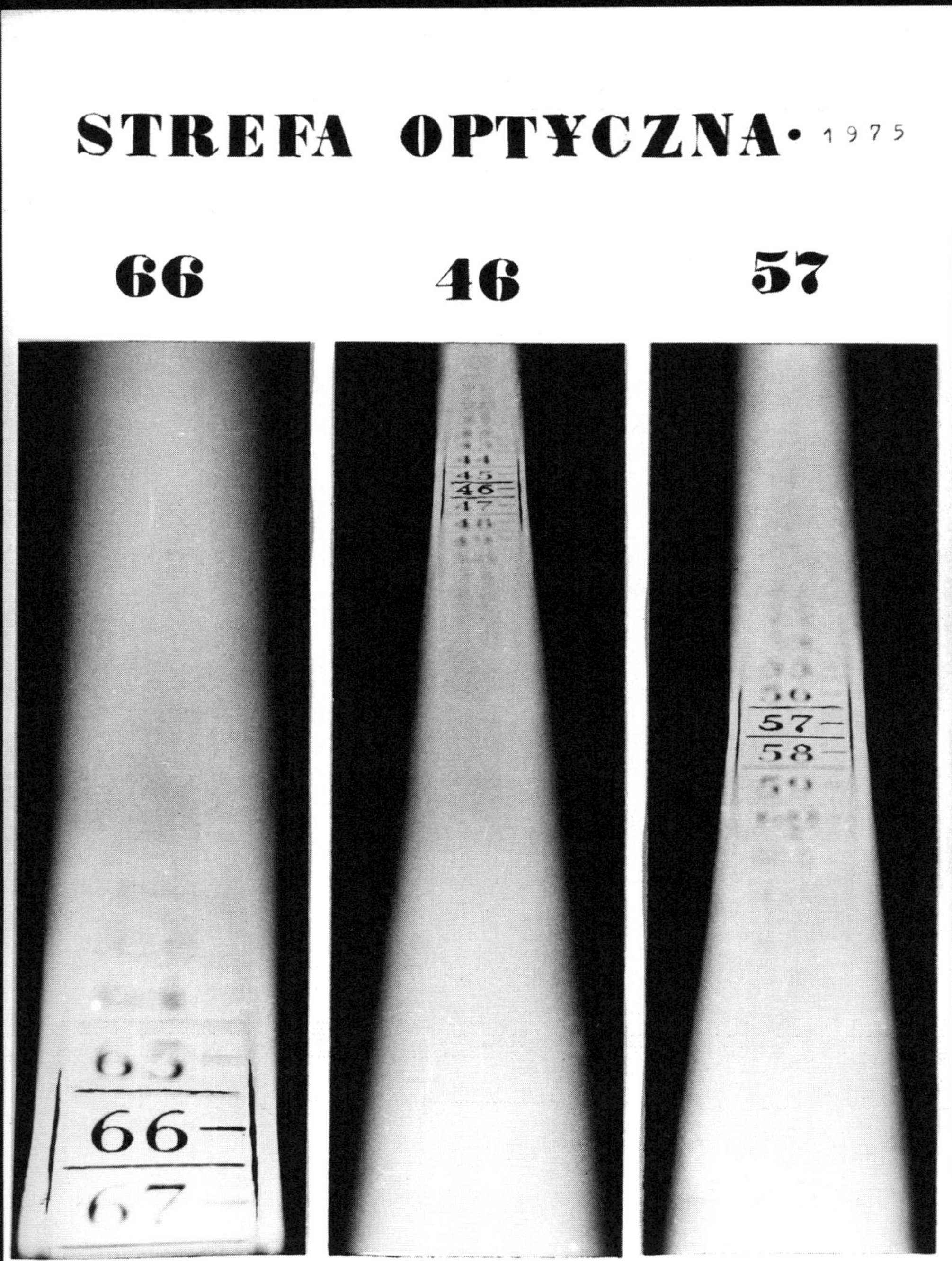

Józef Robakowski, *Sfera optyczna*, 1975, fot. cz.-b.
Józef Robakowski, *The Optical Sphere*, 1975, B&W photograph

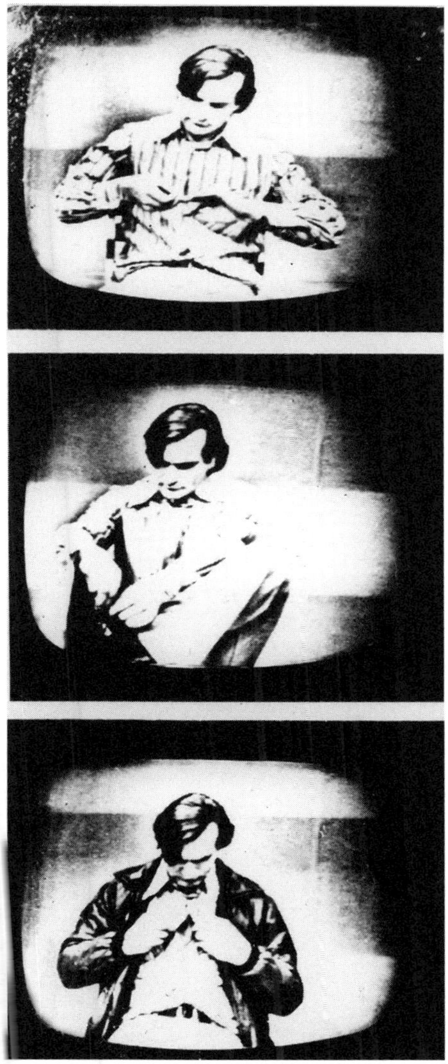

Józef Robakowski, *Czynności*, 1975, wideo, (niezachowane)
Józef Robakowski, *Activities*, 1975, video, (unpreserved)

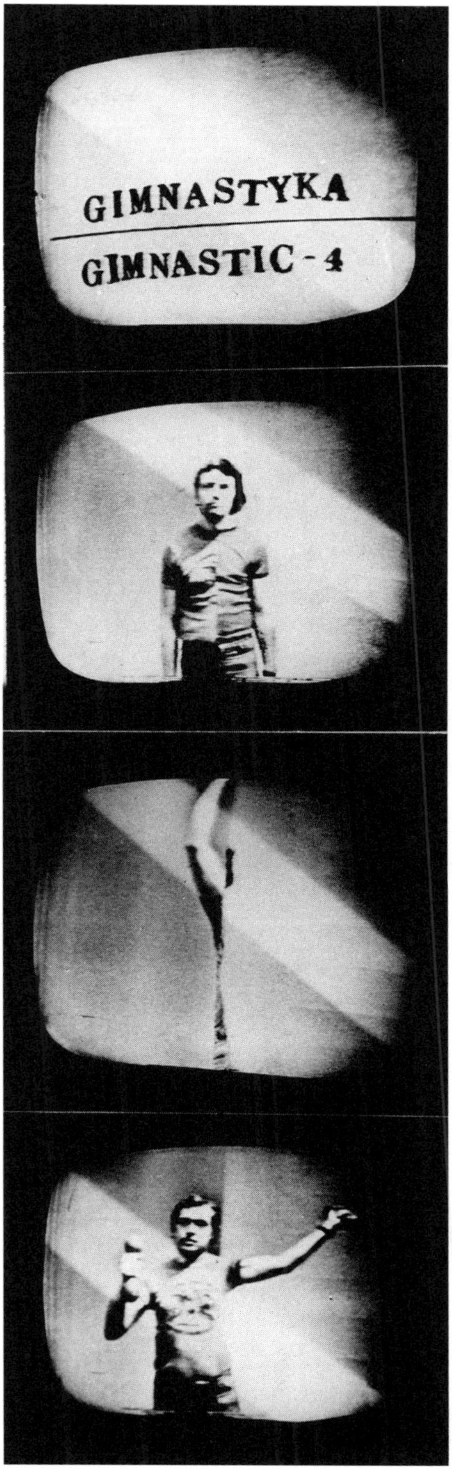

Józef Robakowski, *Gimnastyka*, 1975, wideo, 3', (niezachowane)
Józef Robakowski, *Gymnastics*, 1975, video, 3', (unpreserved)

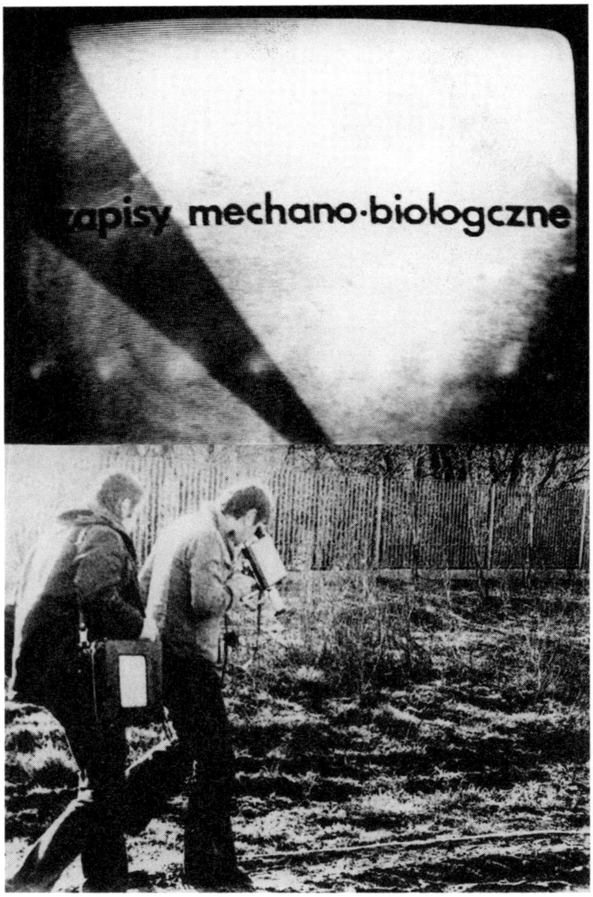

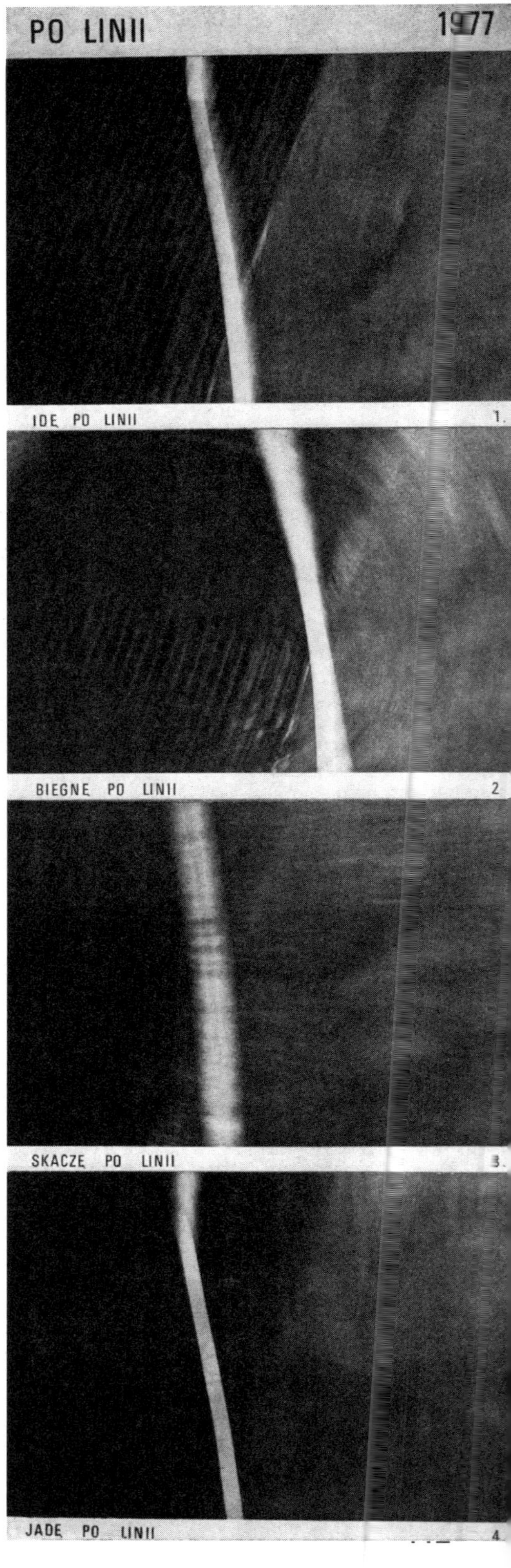

Józef Robakowski, *Po linii (Idę, biegnę, skaczę, jadę...)*, 1977, film-performance, 16 mm
Józef Robakowski, *Follow the Line (I'm Going, I'm Running, I'm Jumping, I'm Driving...)*, 1977, filmic performace, 16 mm

TV·FACE

real. JÓZEF ROBAKOWSKI 1977
/ videoperformance /

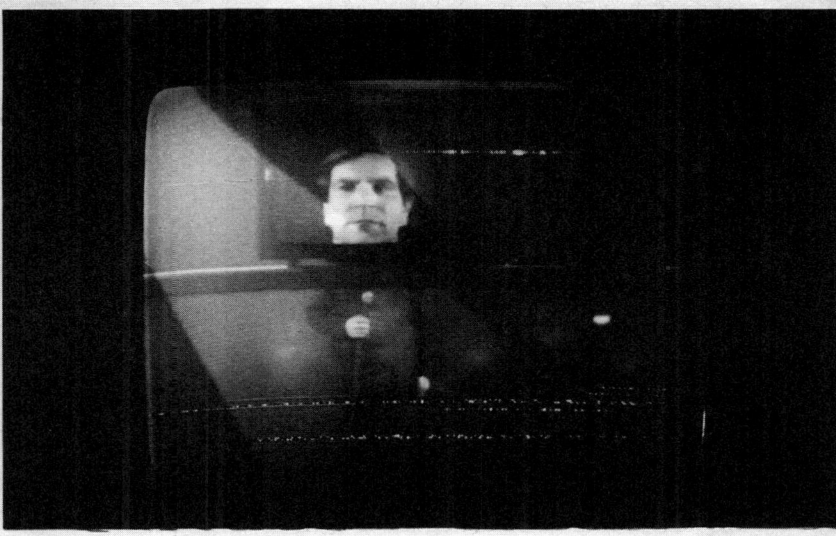

Uwaga !
KAMERA 1 jest sterowana przez operatora na podawane hasła przez autora tej realizacji stojącego przed KAMERA 2. Obraz twarzy widoczny z kamery 2 przeniesiony jest na monitor / M /, by następnie został przekazany przez kamerę 1 do magnetowidu, który go utrwala na kasecie video.

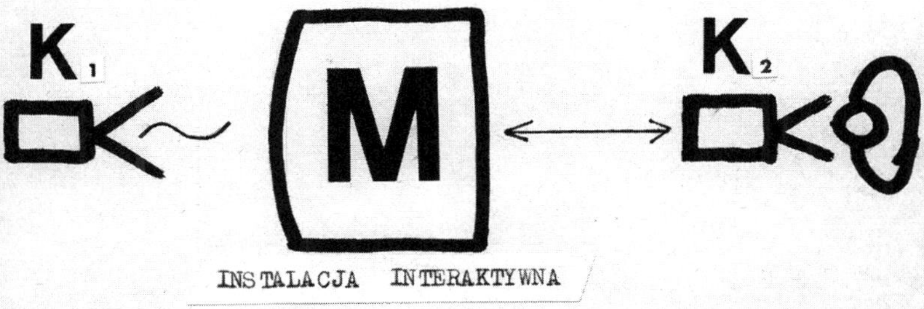

INSTALACJA INTERAKTYWNA

Układ dynamiczny

Układ statyczny

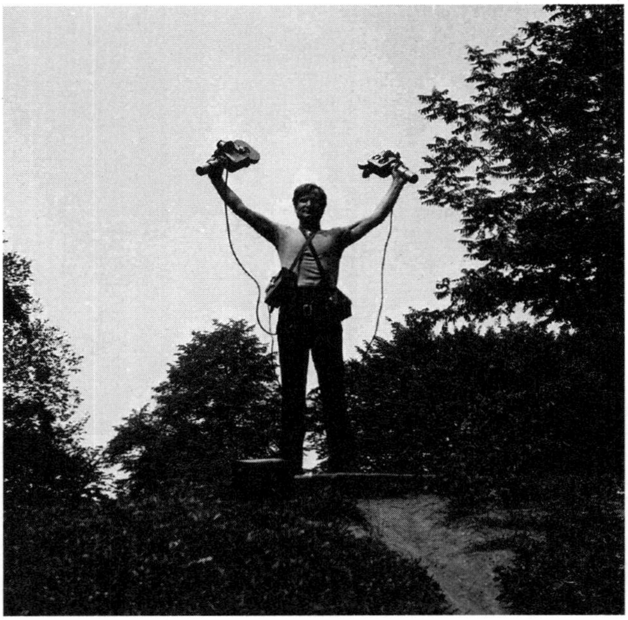

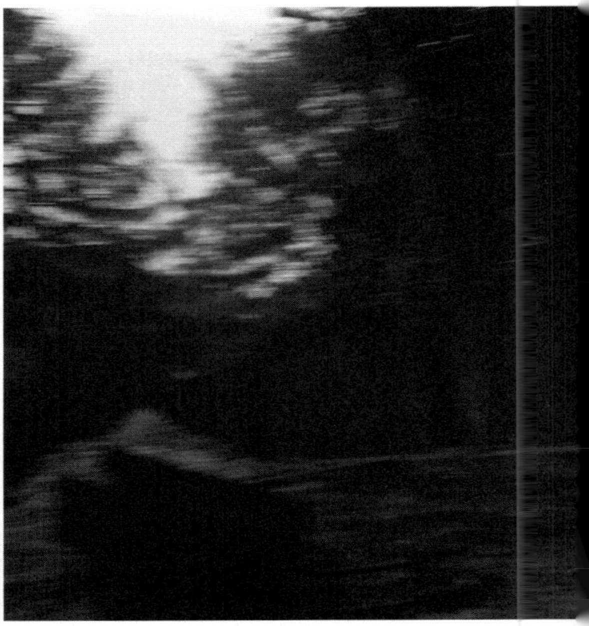

ózef Robakowski *Ćwiczenie na dwie ręce*, 1976, 16 mm, 8'
ózef Robakowski, *Exercise for Both Hands*, 1976, 16 mm, 8'

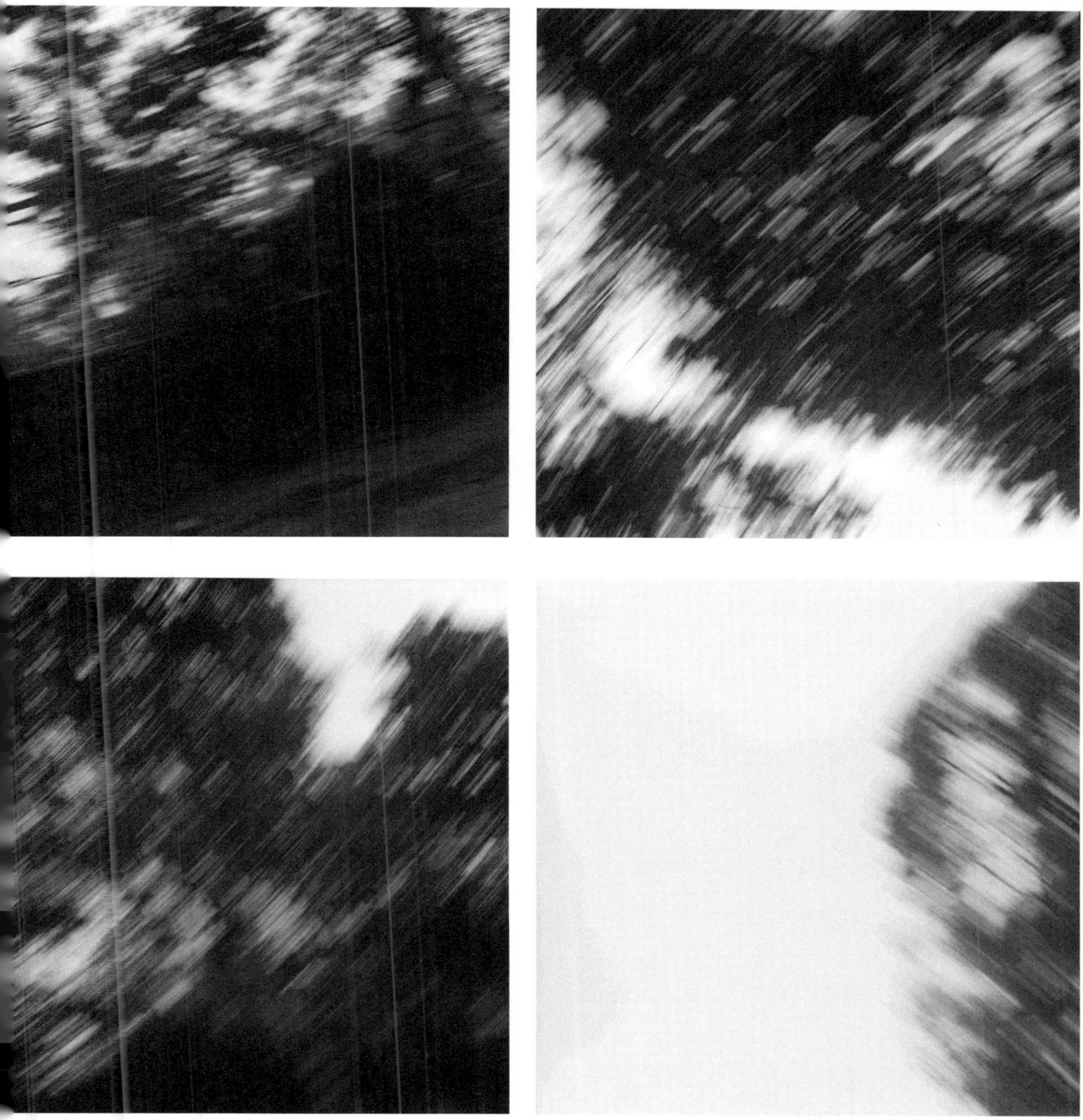

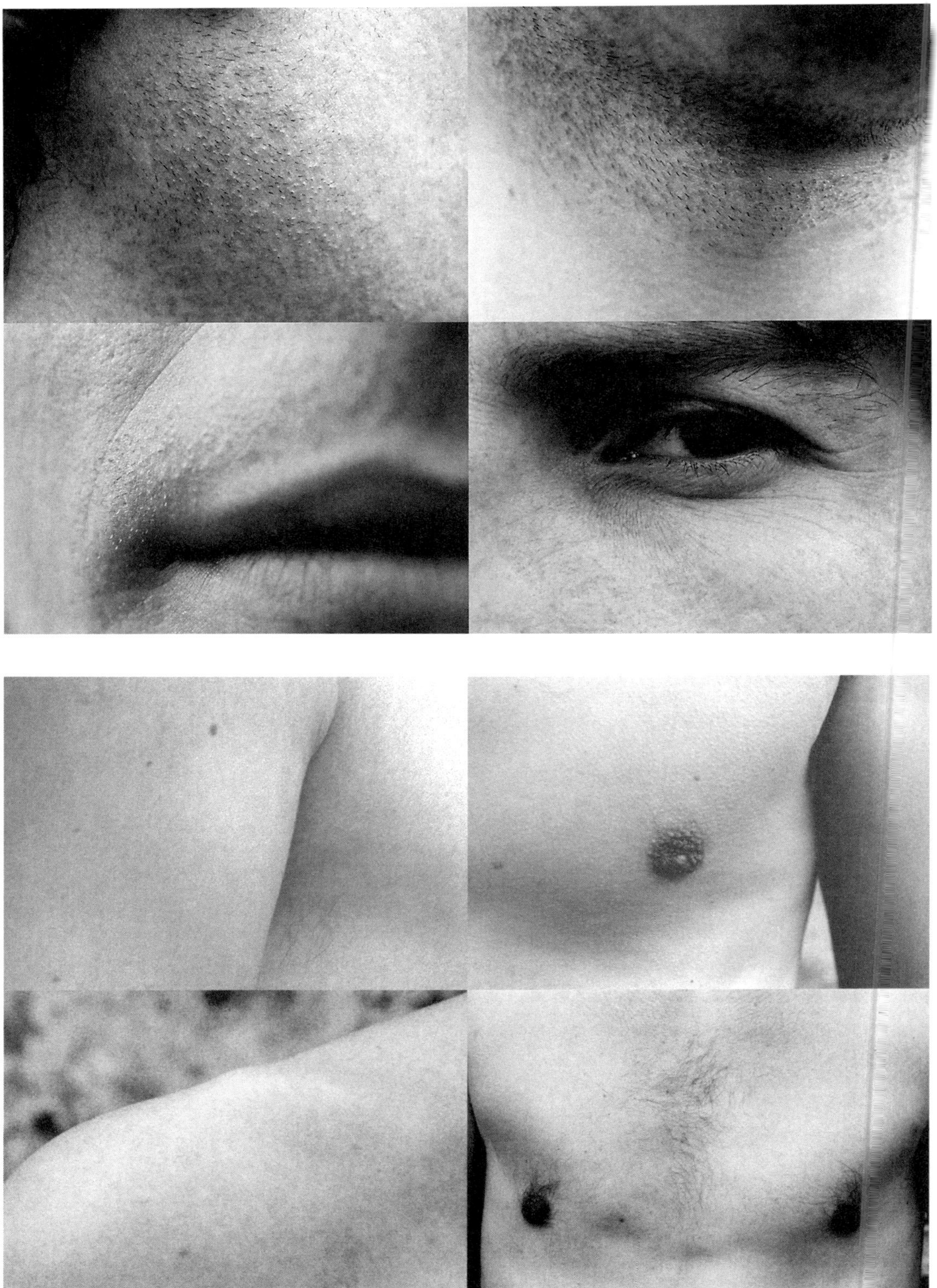

Ryszard Waśko, *Portret pocięty*, 1971, fot. cz.-b.
Ryszard Waśko, *Cut-up Portrait*, 1971, B&W photograph

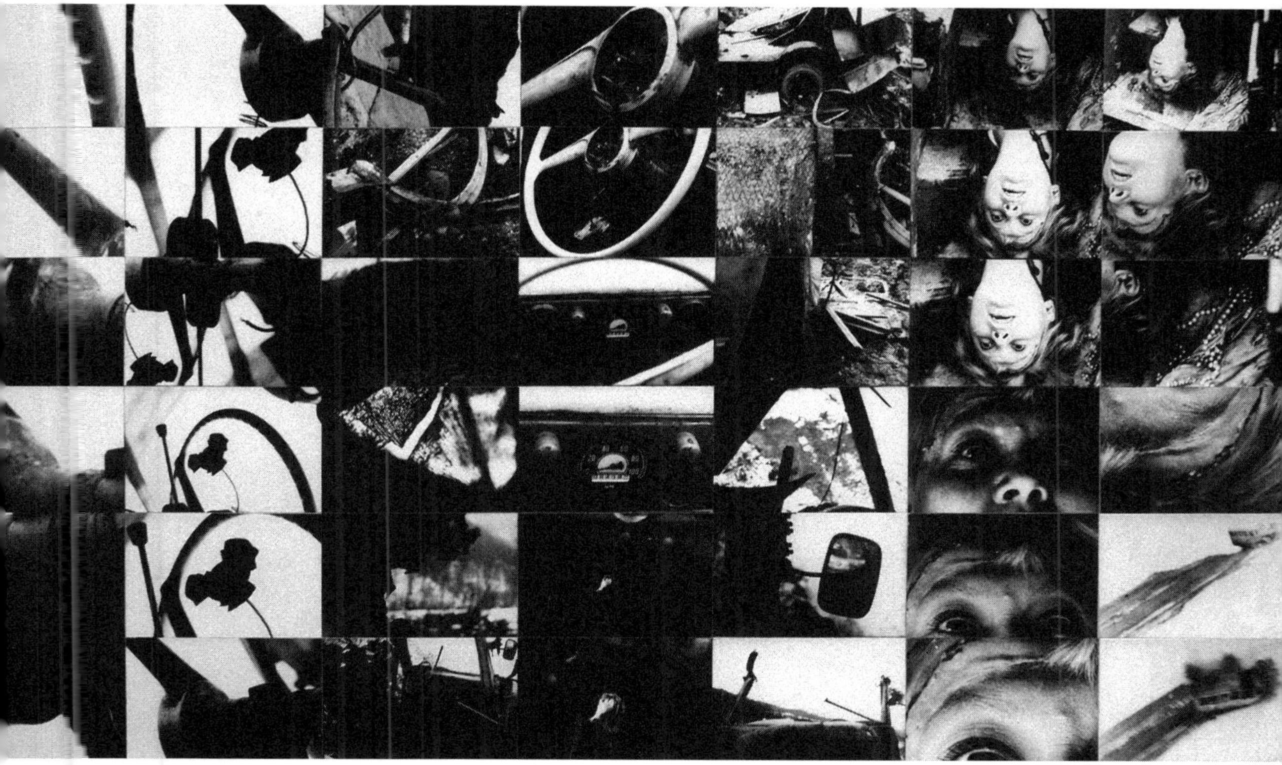

Ryszard Waśko, *Wypadek*, 1971, fot. cz.-b
Ryszard Waśko, *An Accident*, 1971, B&W photograph

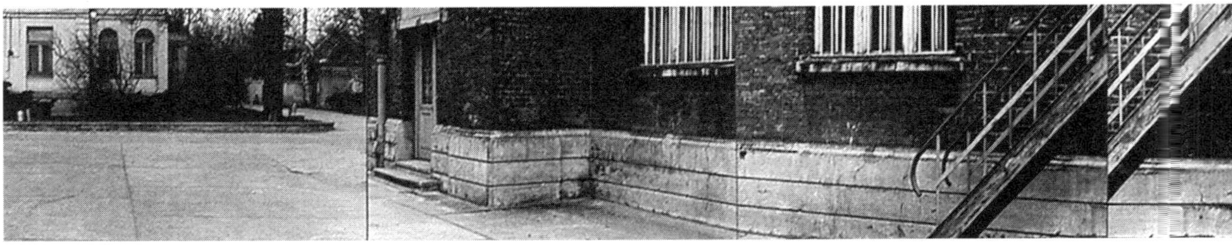

Ryszard Waśko, *Od 0° do 180°*, 1971, fot. cz.-b.
Ryszard Waśko, *From 0° to 180°*, 1971, B&W photograph

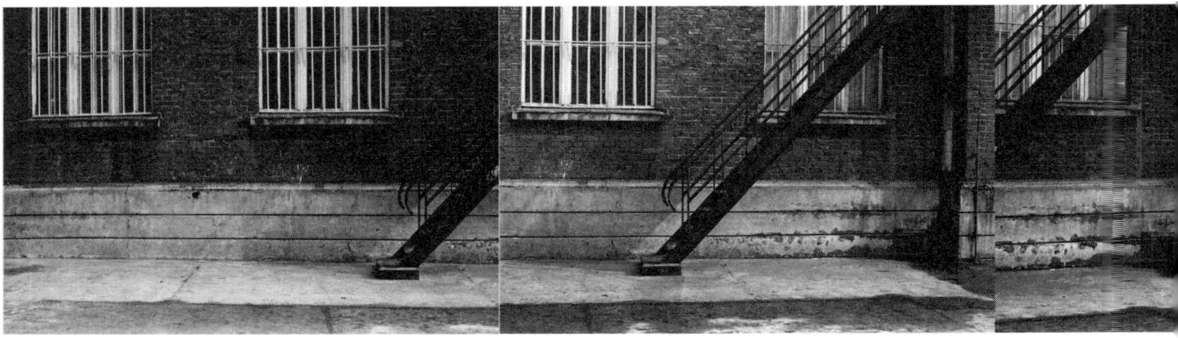

Ryszard Waśko, *Od 0° do 90°*, 1971, fot. cz.-b.
Ryszard Waśko, *From 0° to 90°*, 1971, B&W photograph

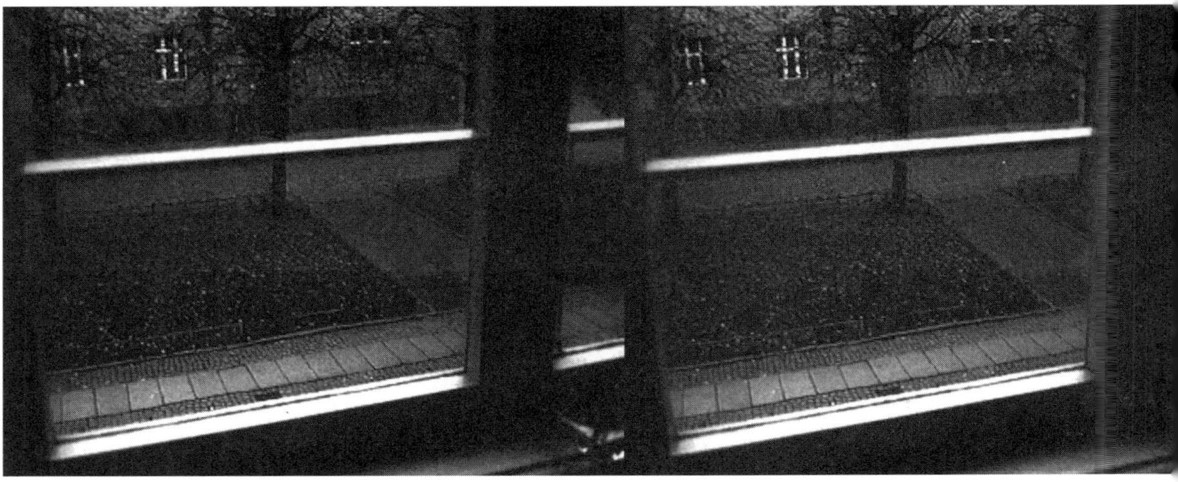

Ryszard Waśko, *Okno*, 1971, 35 mm, 8'26"
Ryszard Waśko, *Window,* 1971, 35 mm, 8'26"

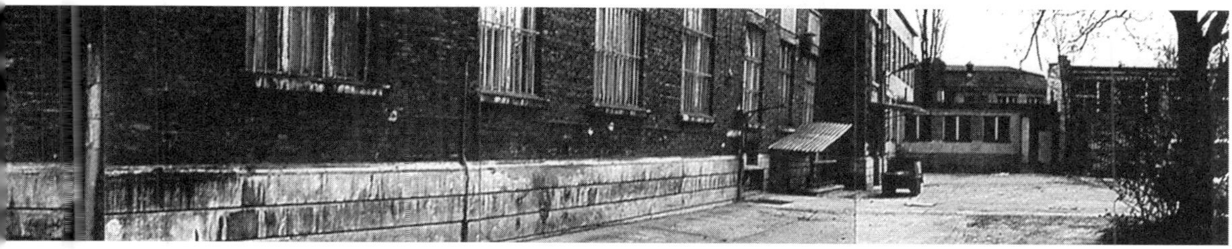

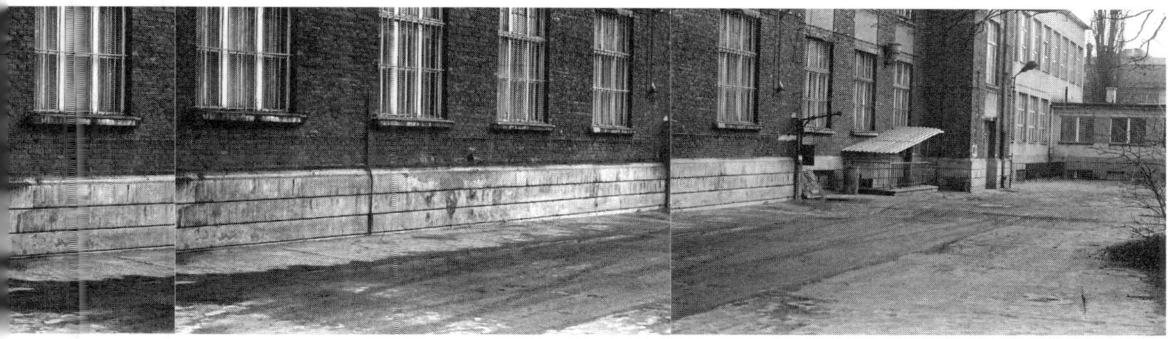

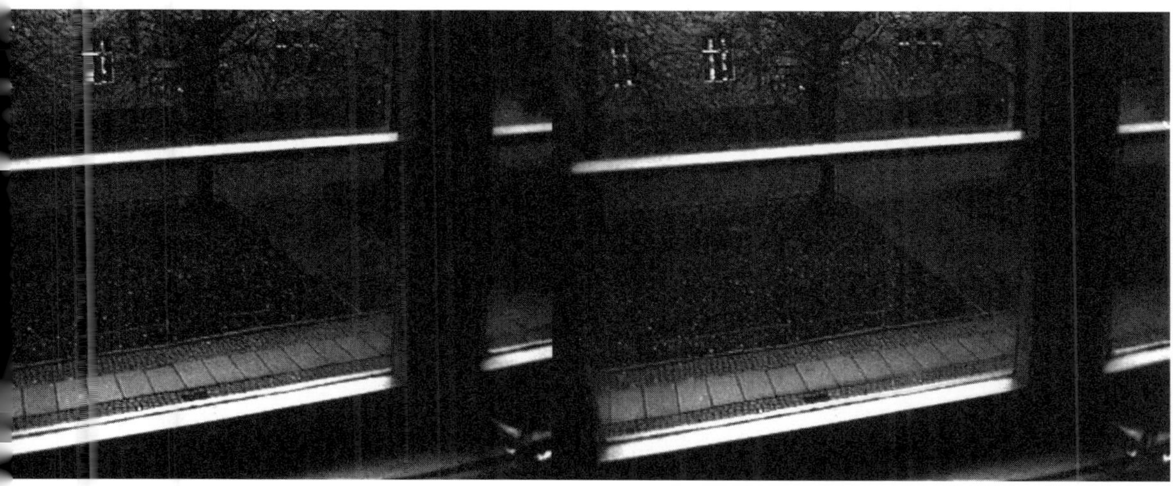

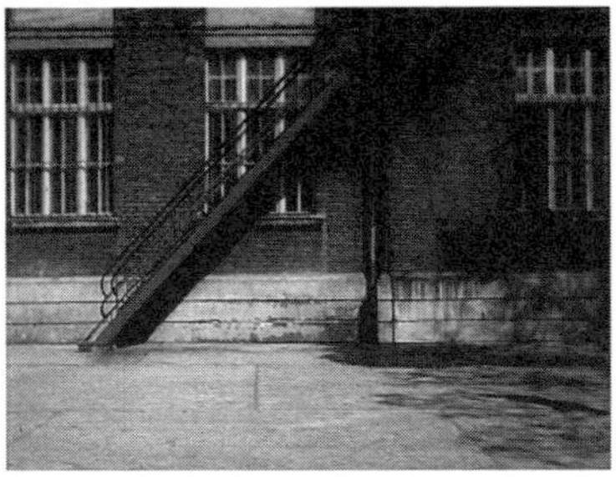
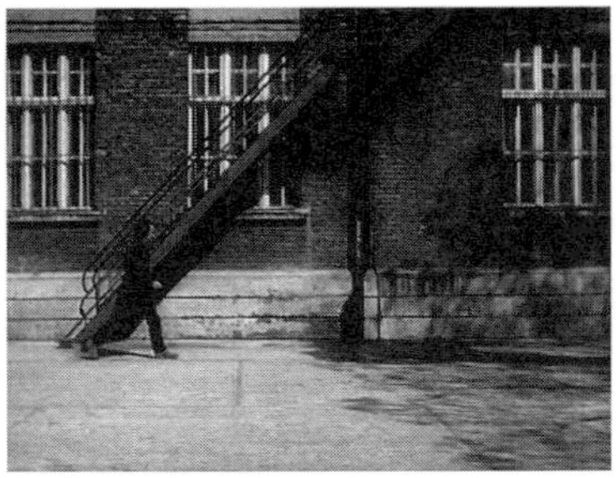
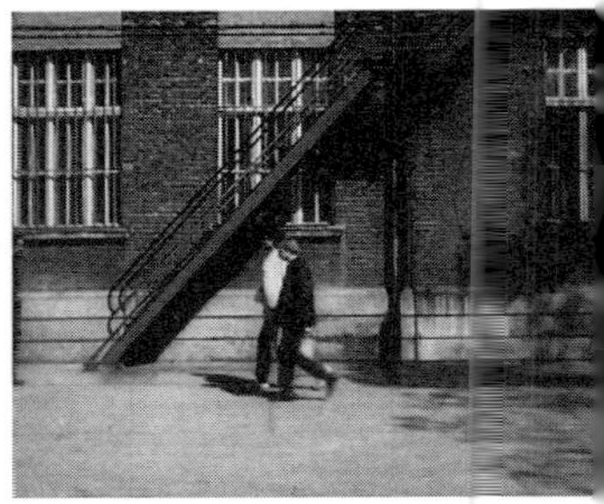
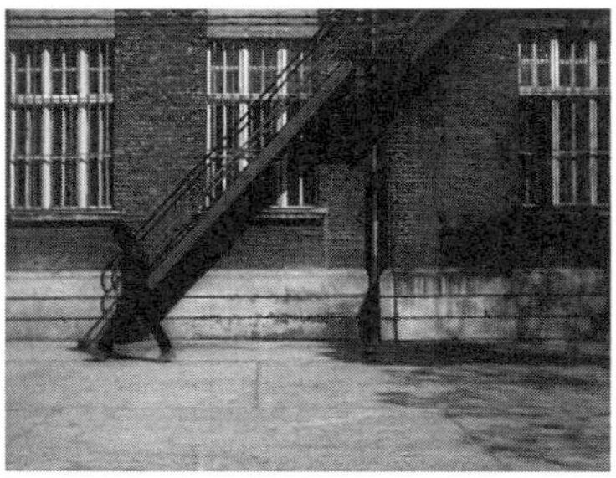
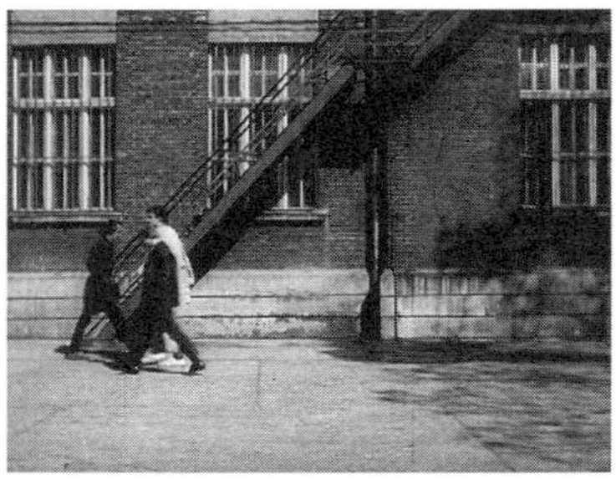
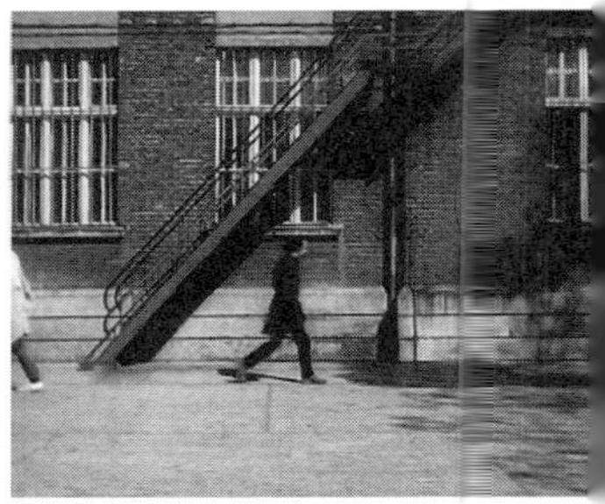
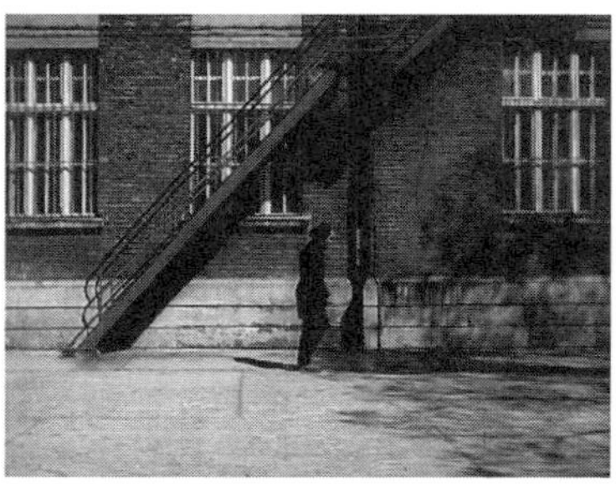
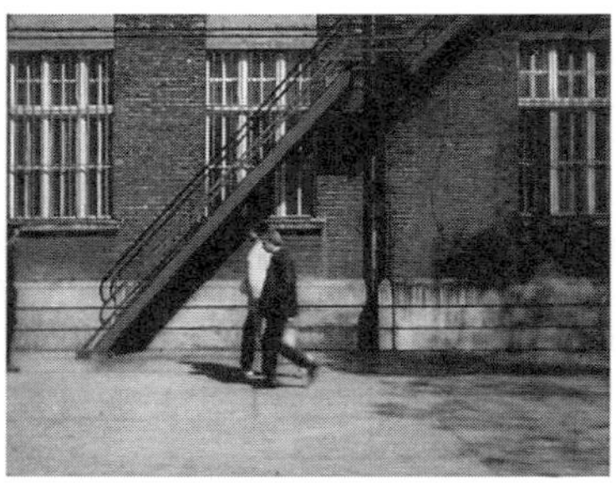
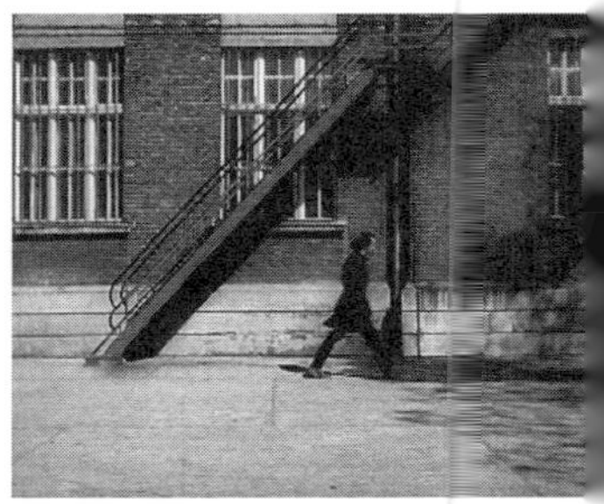

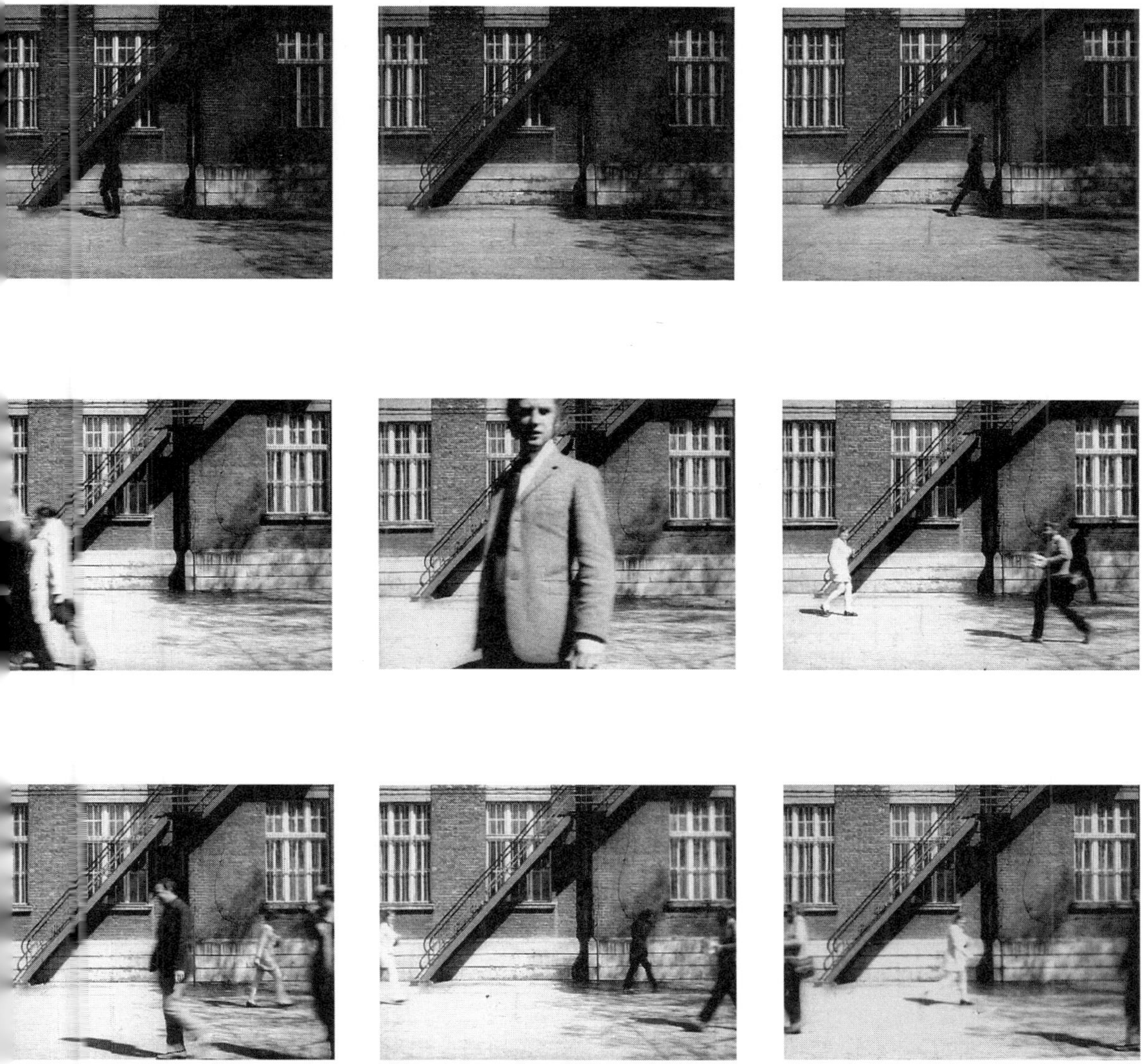

Ryszard Waśko, *Ściana*, 1972, 35 mm, 4'06"
Ryszard Waśko, *The Wall*, 1972, 35 mm, 4'06"

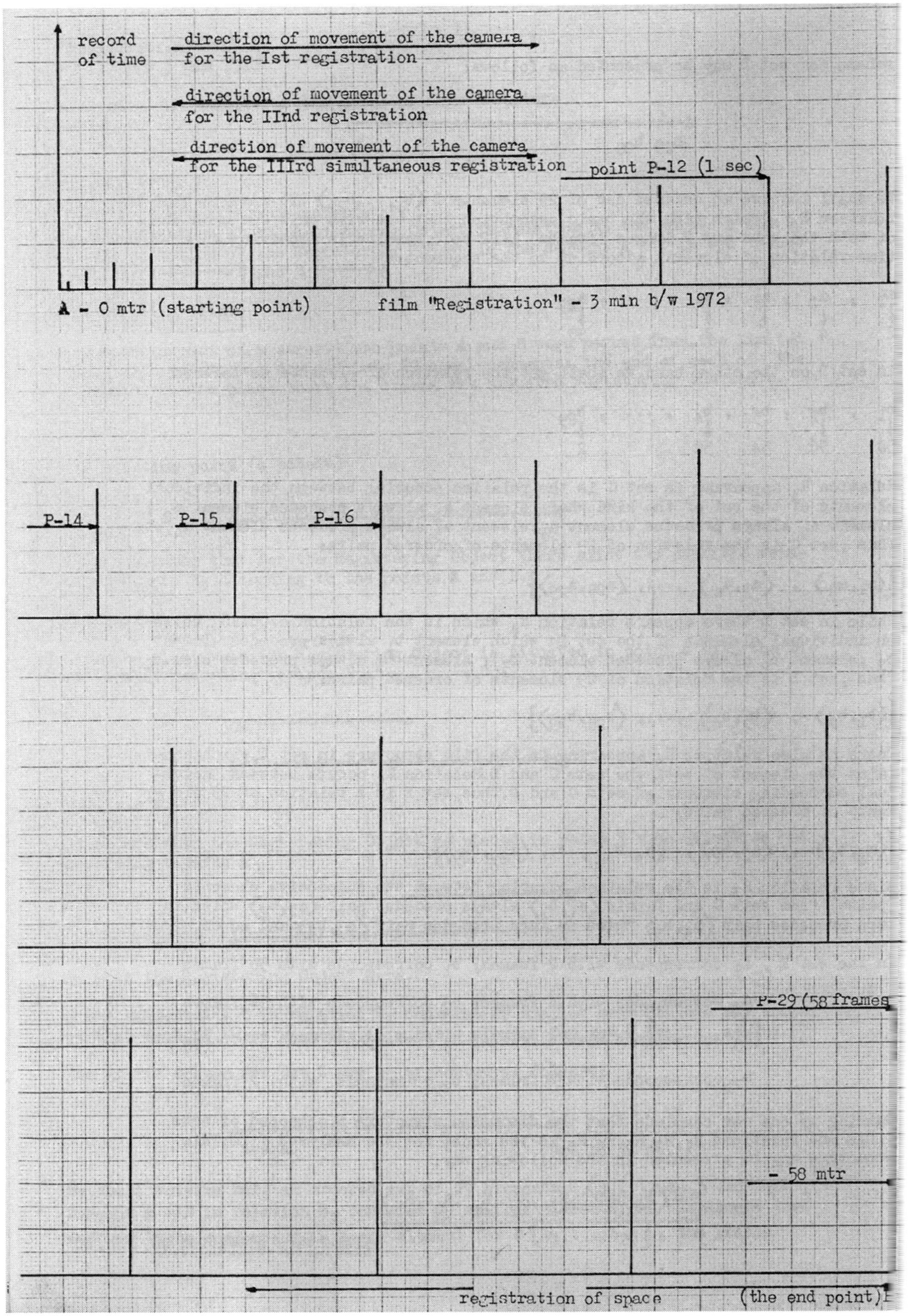

Ryszard Waśko, *Rejestracja*, 1972, 35 mm, 3'
Ryszard Waśko, *Record*, 1972, 35 mm, 3'

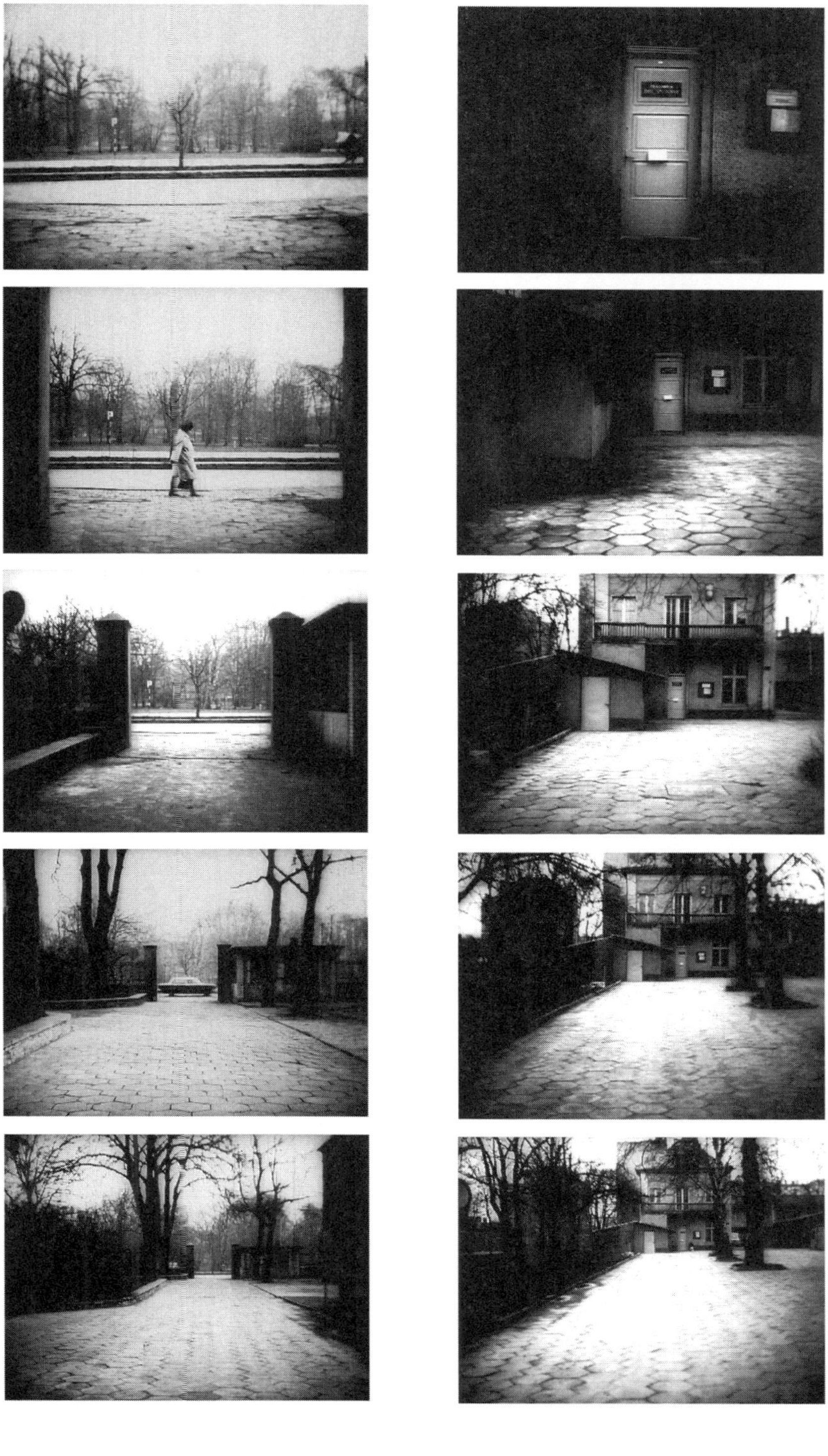

Ryszard Waśko, *Rejestracja*, 1972, 35 mm, 3'
Ryszard Waśko, *Record*, 1972, 35 mm, 3'

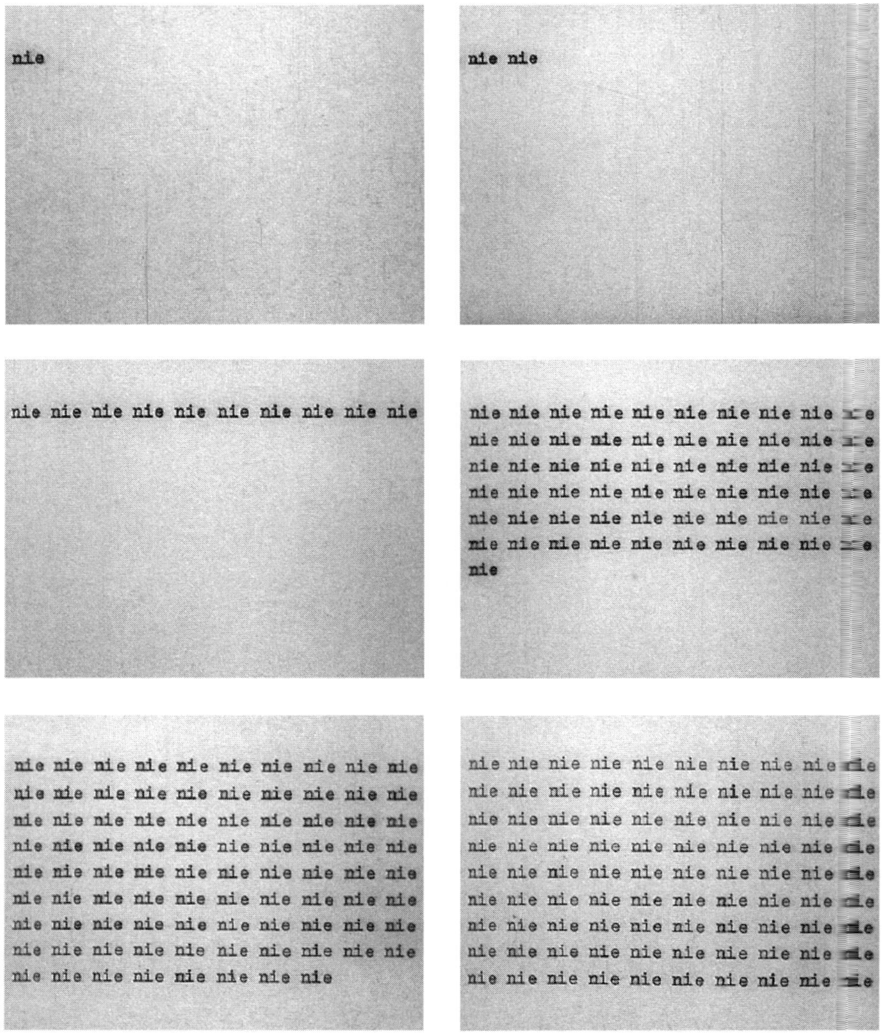

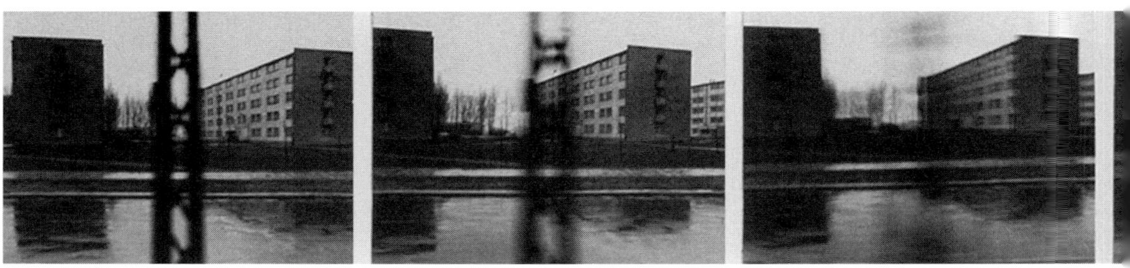

Ryszard Waśko, *Fotografia czterowymiarowa*, 1972, fot. cz.-b.
Ryszard Waśko, *Four-Dimensional Photograph*, 1972, B&W photograph

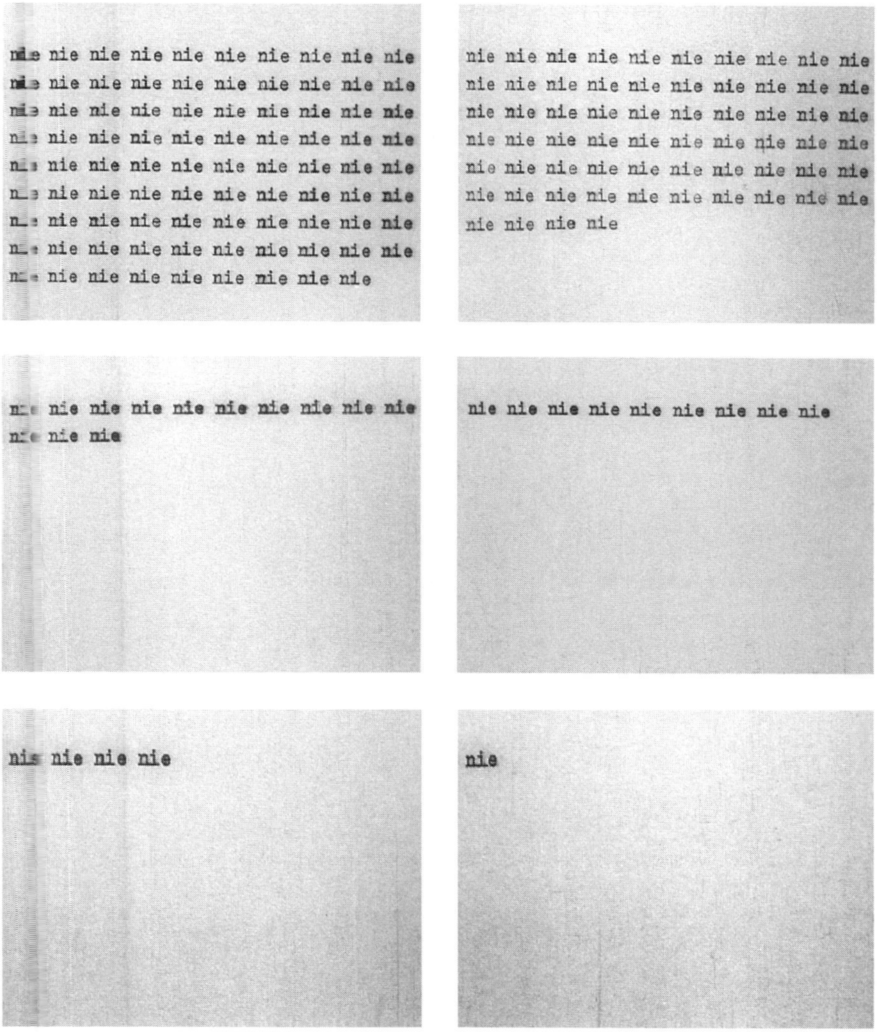

Ryszard Waśko, *Zaprzeczenie*, 1973, 35 mm, 4'05''
Ryszard Waśko, *Negation*, 1973, 35 mm, 4'05''

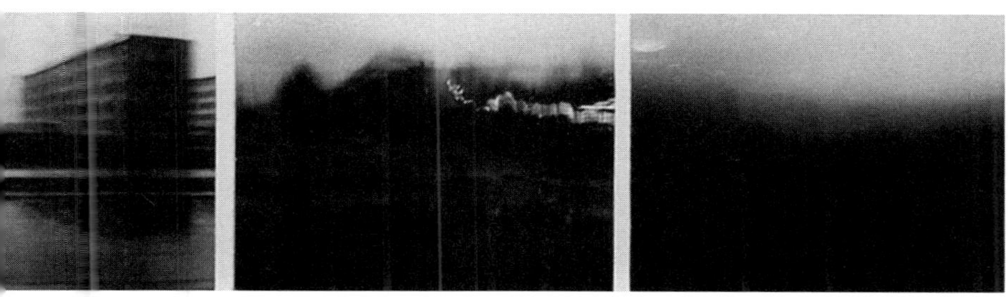

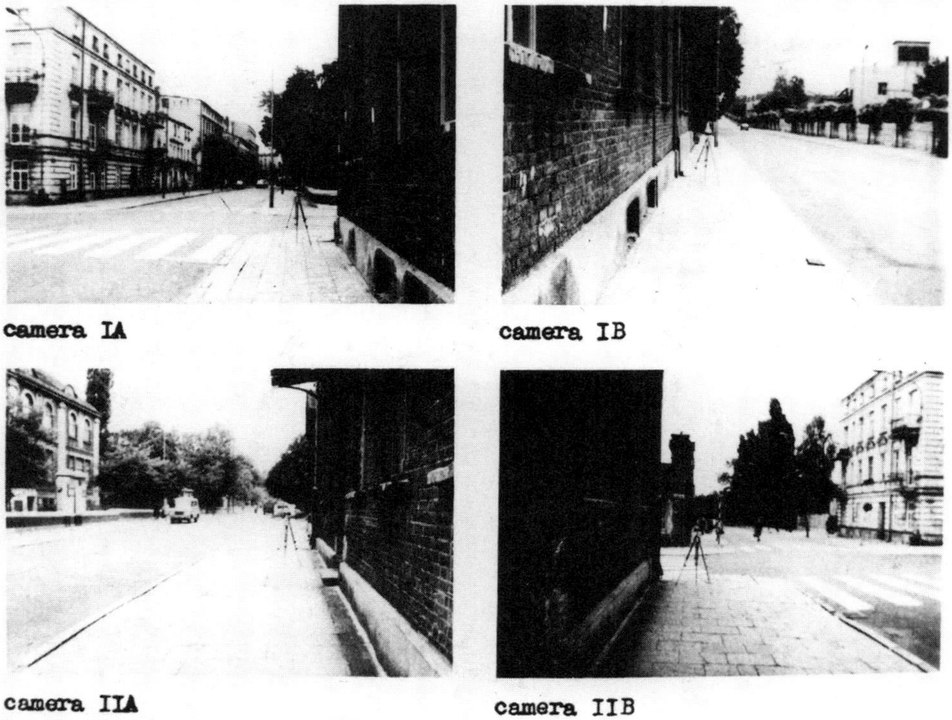

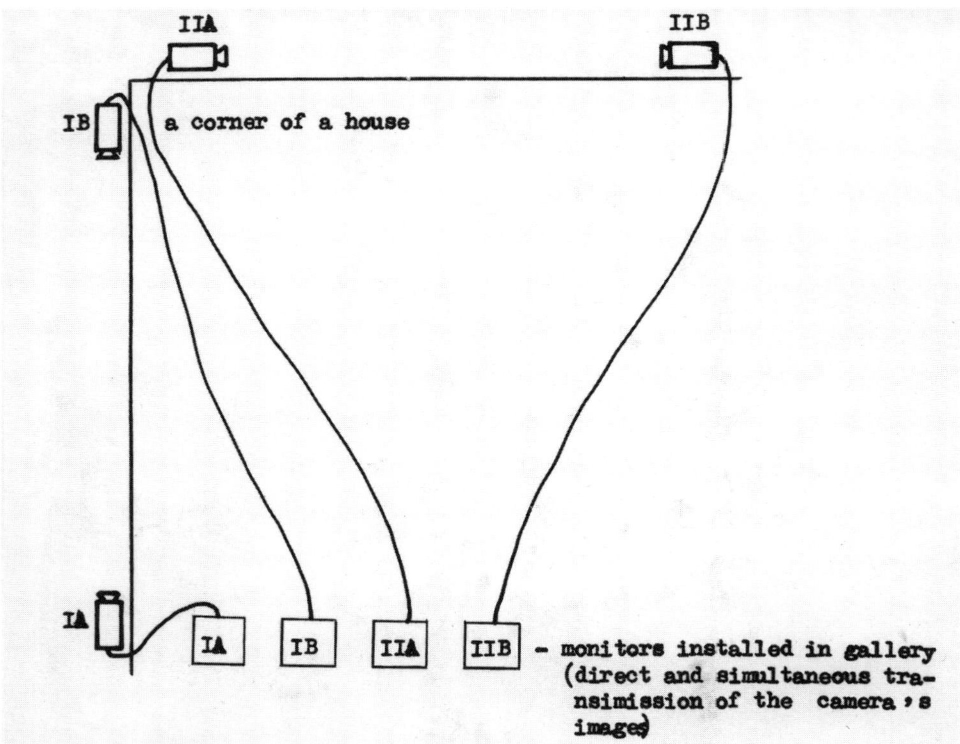

Ryszard Waśko, *Róg domu*, 1975, instalacja wideo
Ryszard Waśko, *A Corner of the House*, 1975, video installation

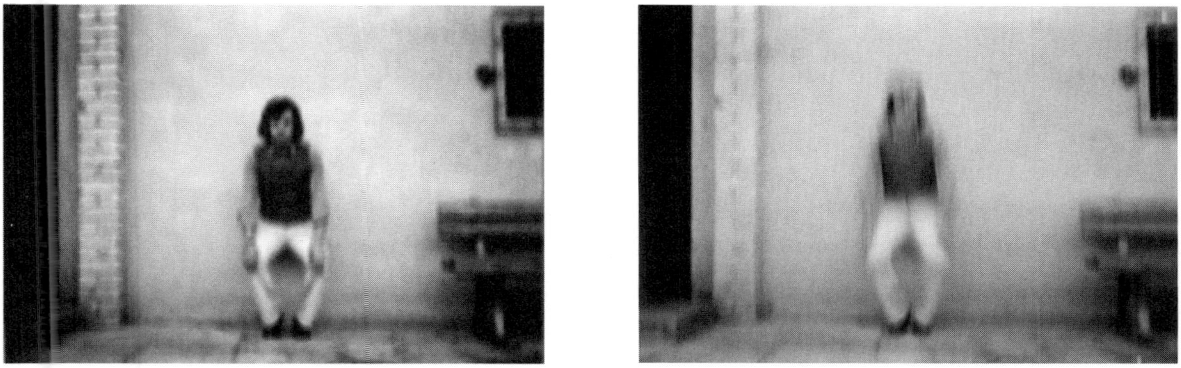

Ryszard Waśko, *Autoportret w ruchu (Wstawanie)*, 1974, fot. cz.-b.
Ryszard Waśko, *Self-portrait in Motion (Getting up)*, 1974, B&W photograph

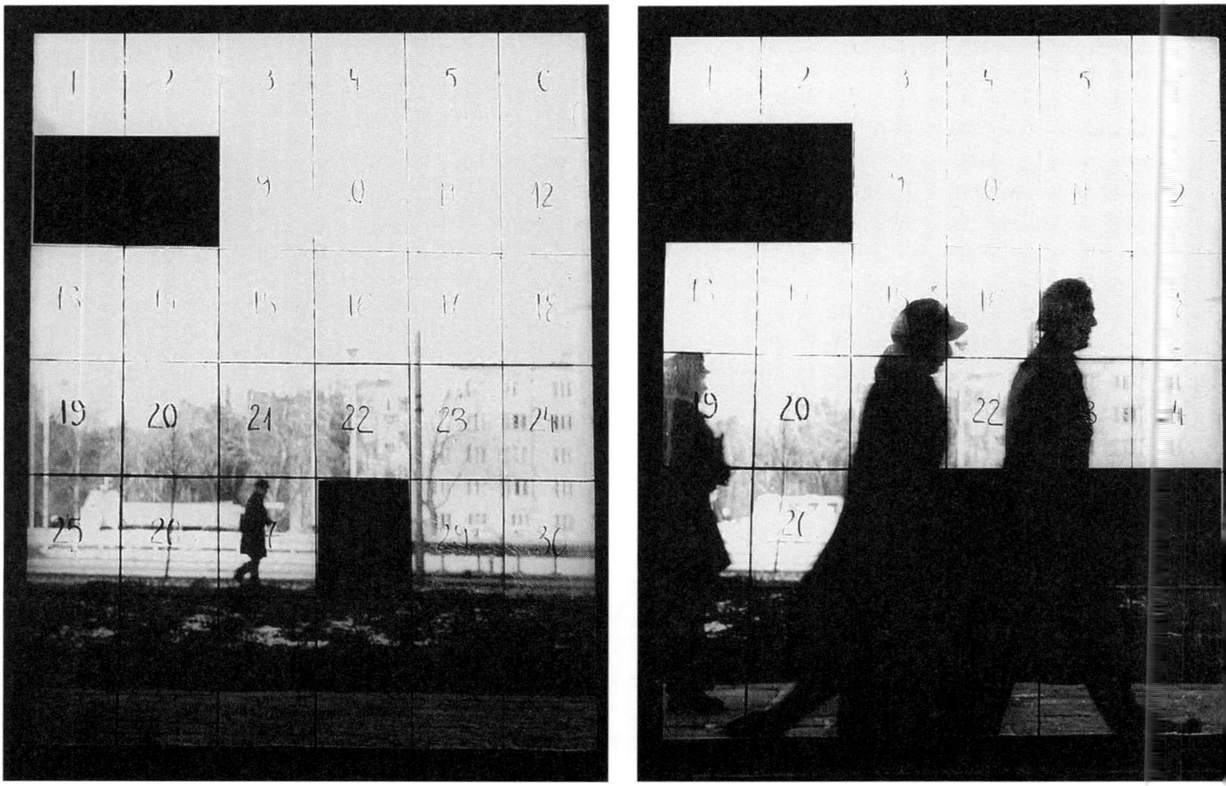

Ryszard Waśko, *Akcja na szybie Galerii Remont*, 1975
Ryszard Waśko, *Action on a Window of the Remont Gallery*, 1975

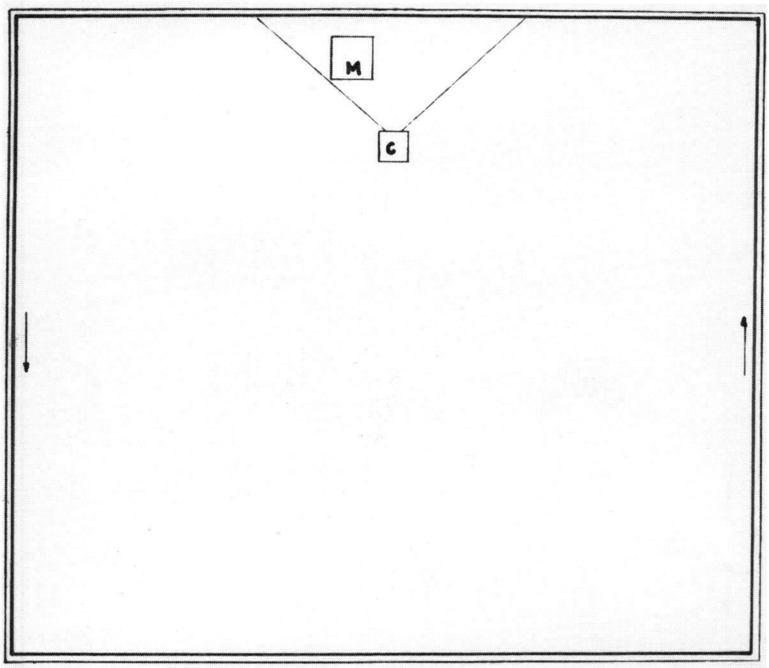

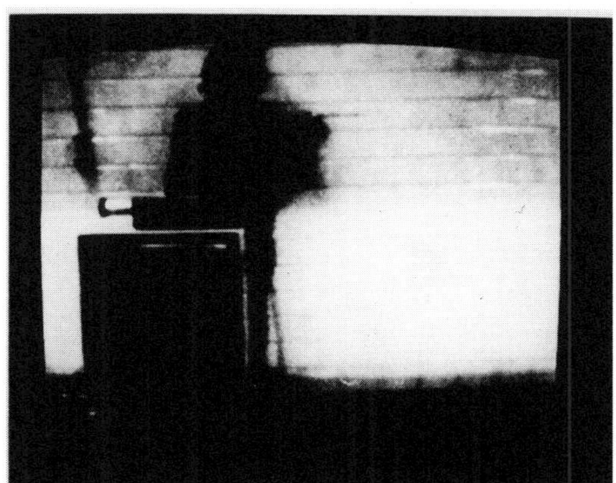

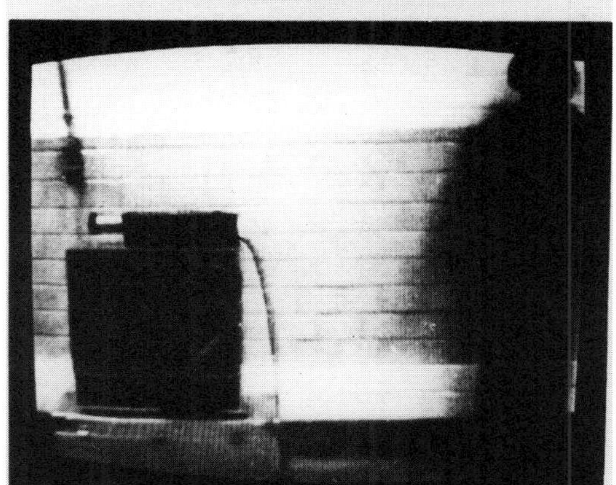

Ryszard Waśko, *Poza przestrzenią*, 1976, wideo-performance
Ryszard Waśko, *Beyond the Space* 1976, video performance

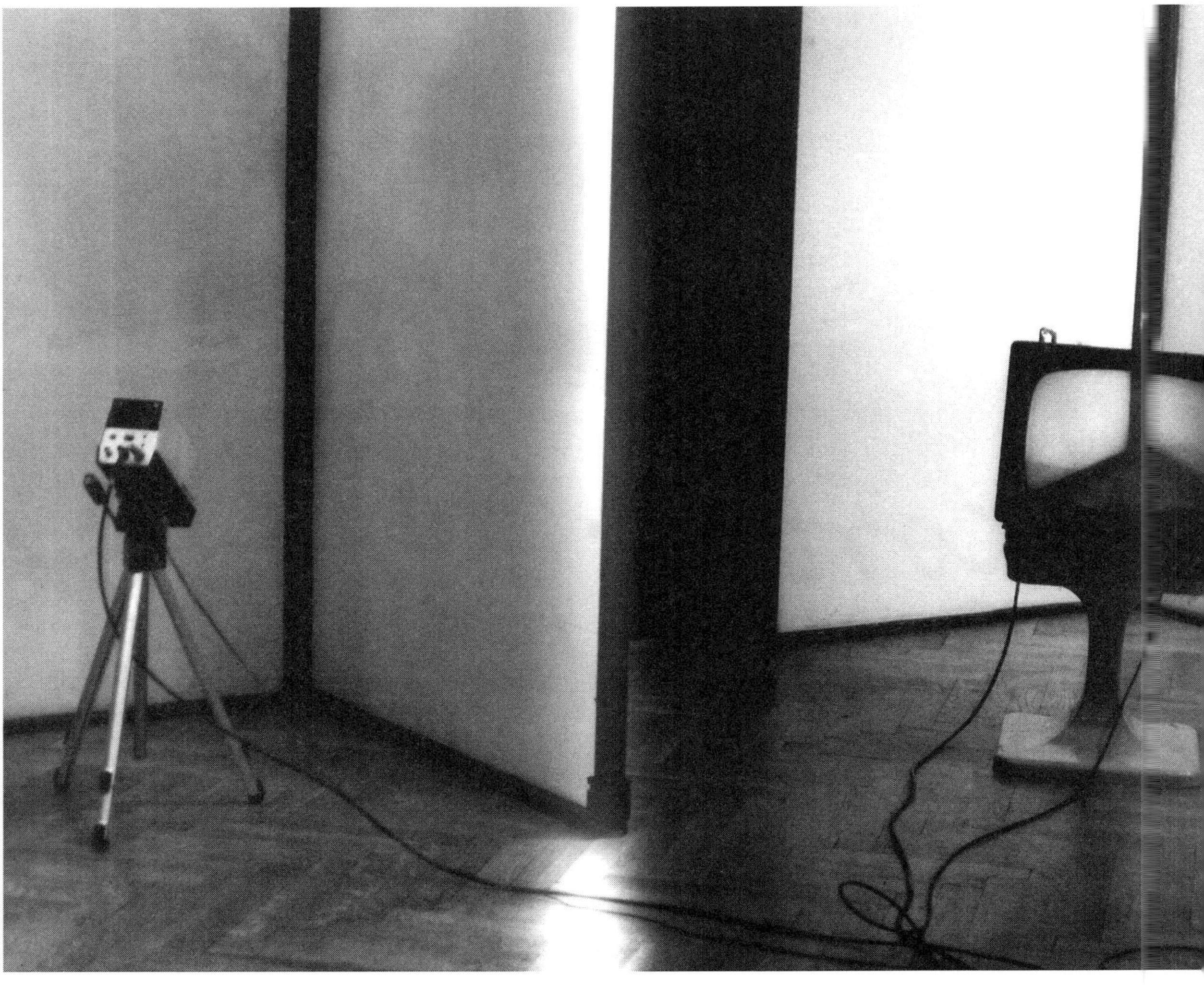

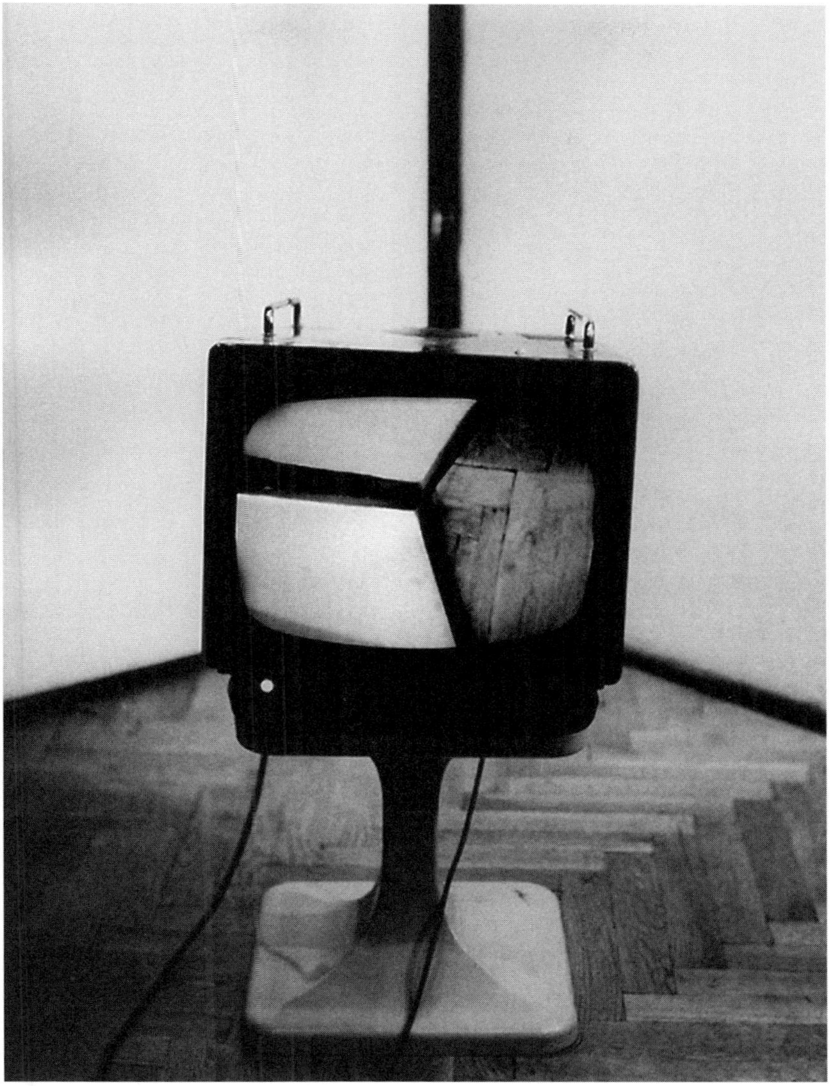

Ryszard Waśko, *Róg*, 1976, instalacja wideo
Ryszard Waśko, *A Corner*, 1976, video installation

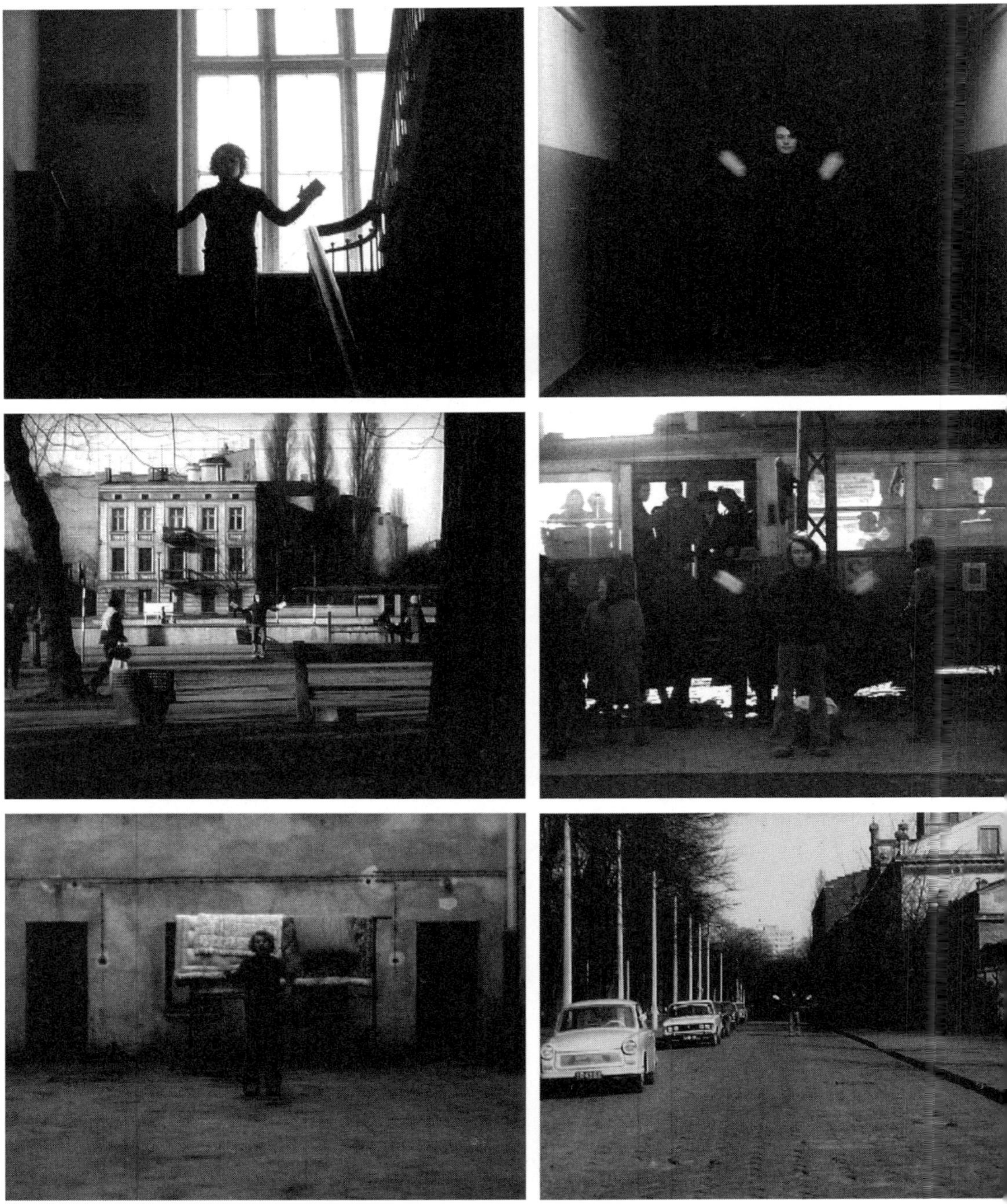

Ryszard Waśko, *30 sytuacji dźwiękowych*, 1975, 35 mm, 9’28”
Ryszard Waśko, *30 Sound Situations*, 1975, 35 mm, 9’28”

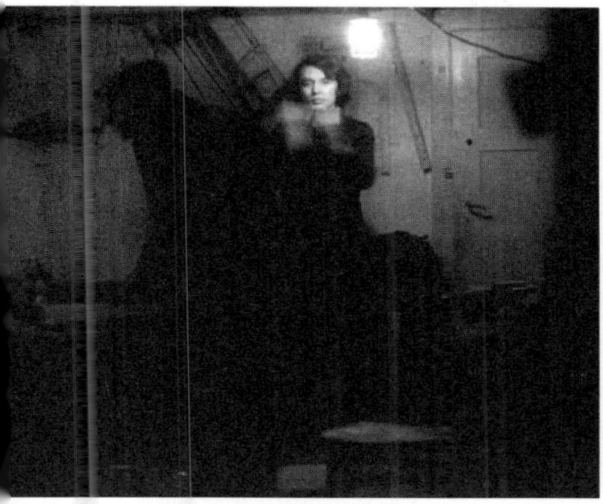
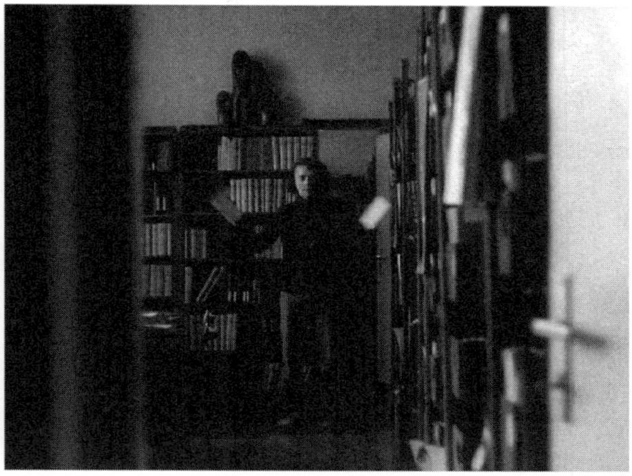
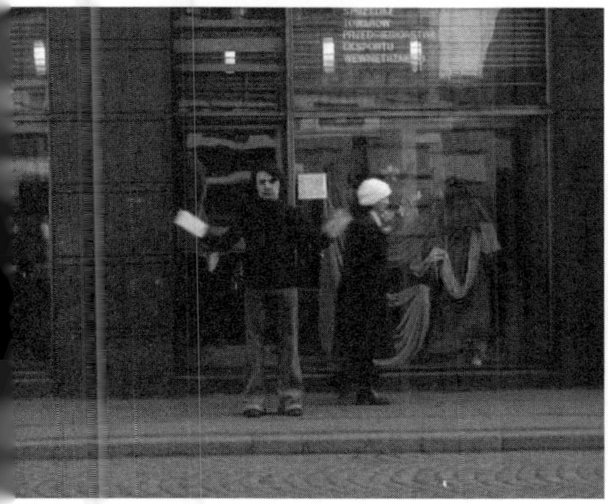
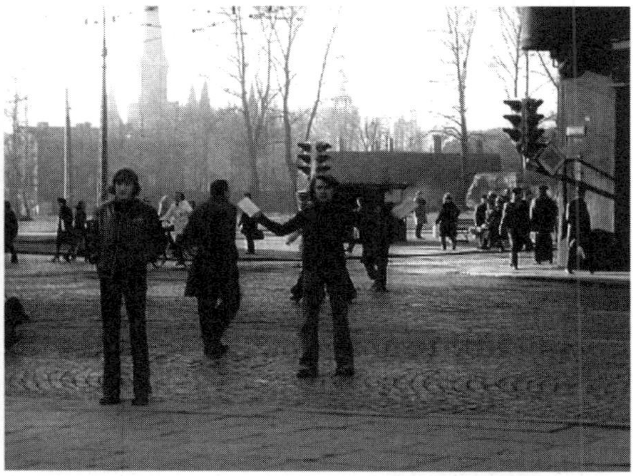
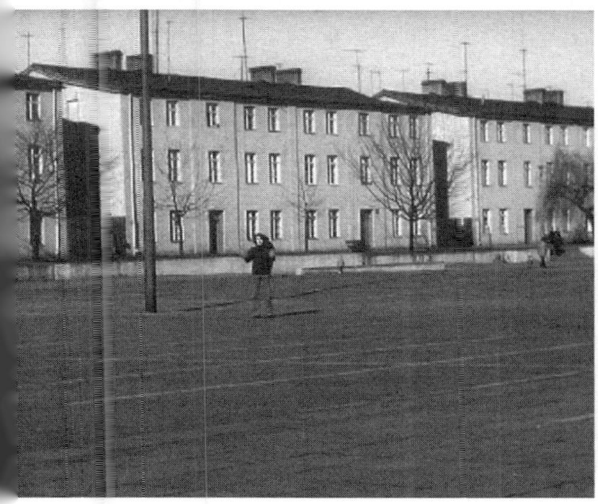
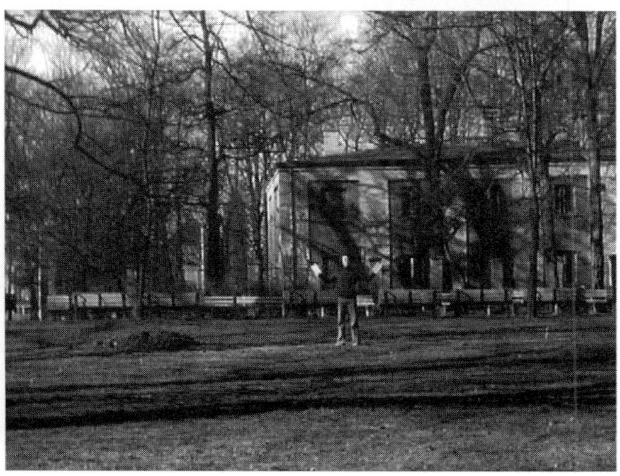

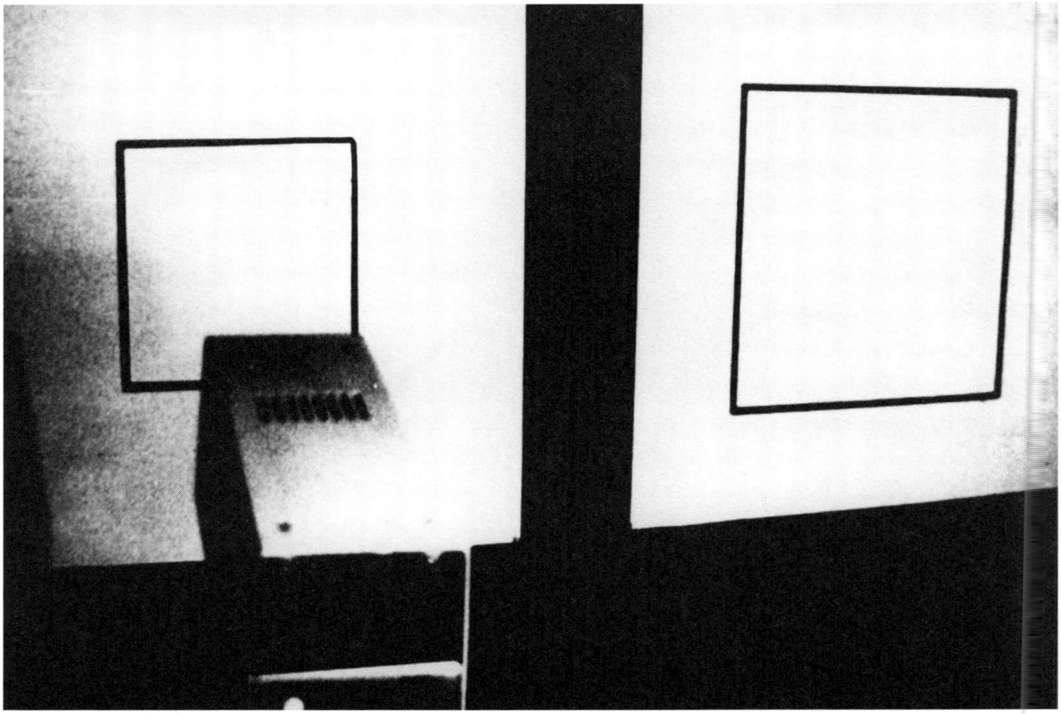

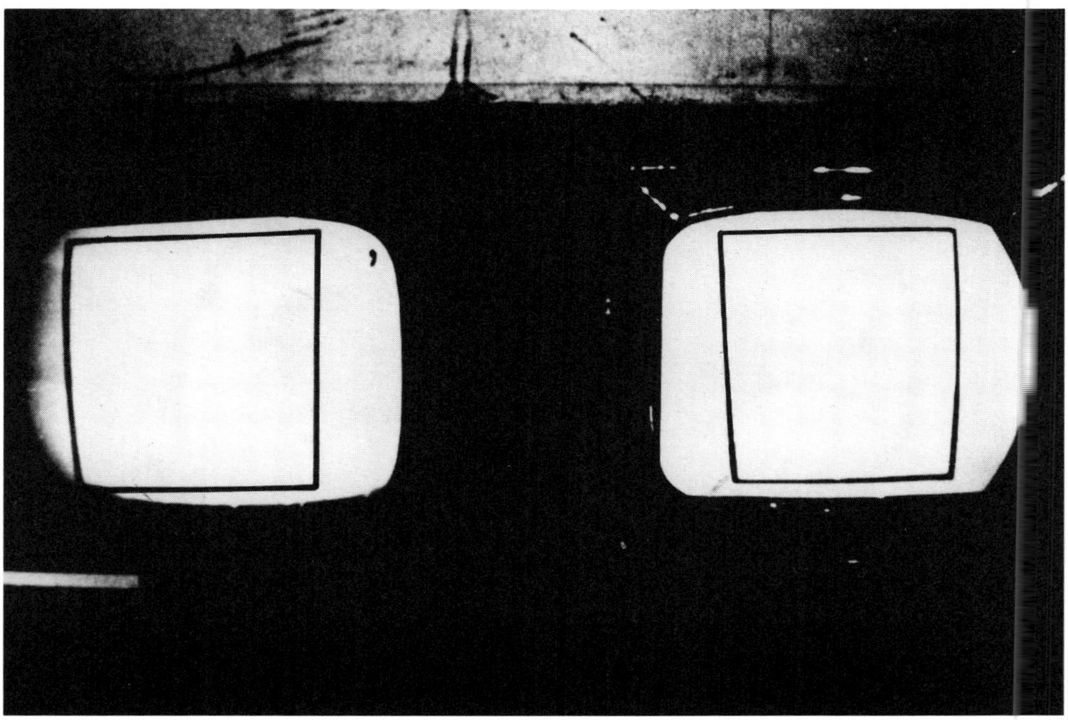

Ryszard Waśko, *Pomiar*, 1976, instalacja wideo
Ryszard Waśko, *Measurement*, 1976, video installation

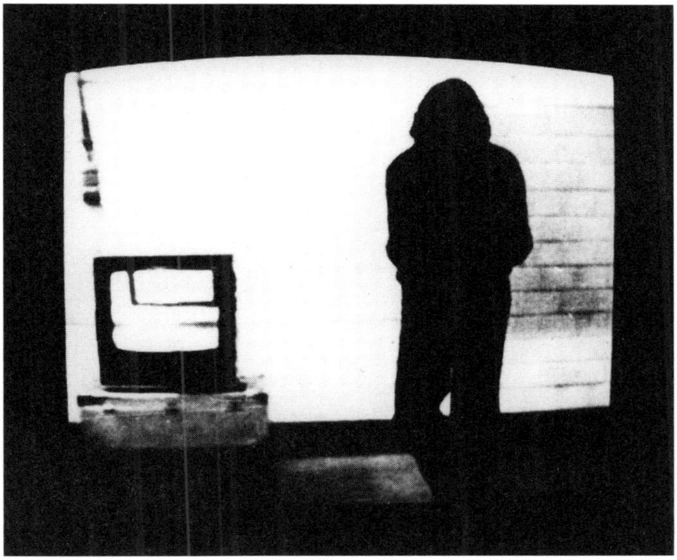

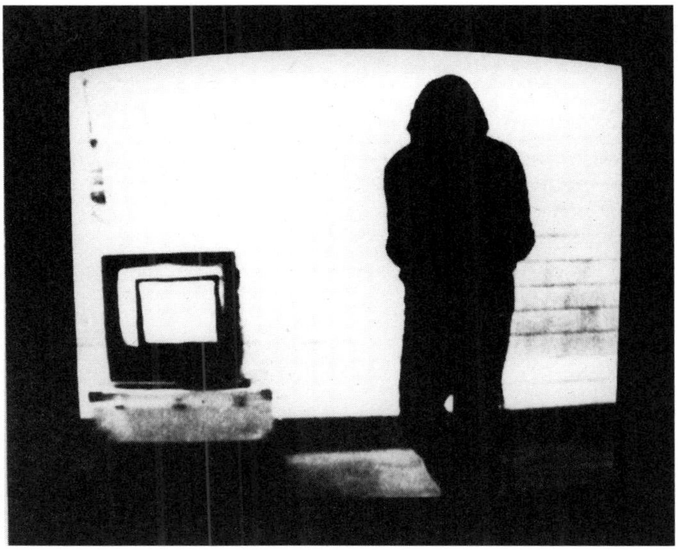

Ryszard Waśko, *Zmęczenie mojej nogi*, 1976, wideo-performance
Ryszard Waśko, *Weariness of My Leg*, 1976, video performance

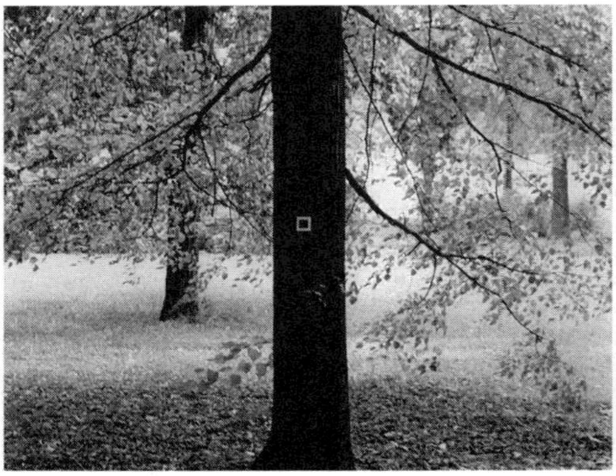

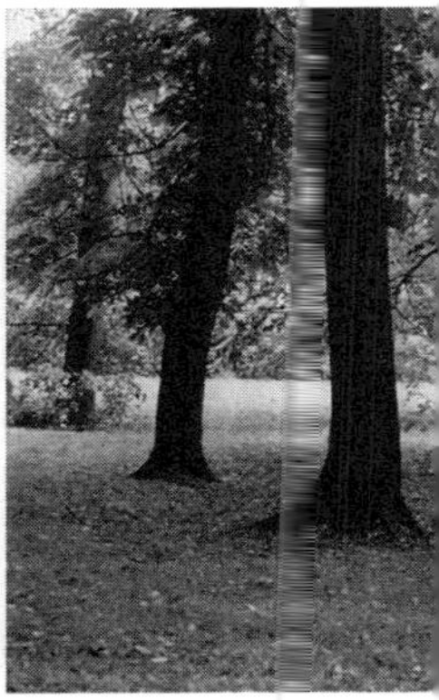

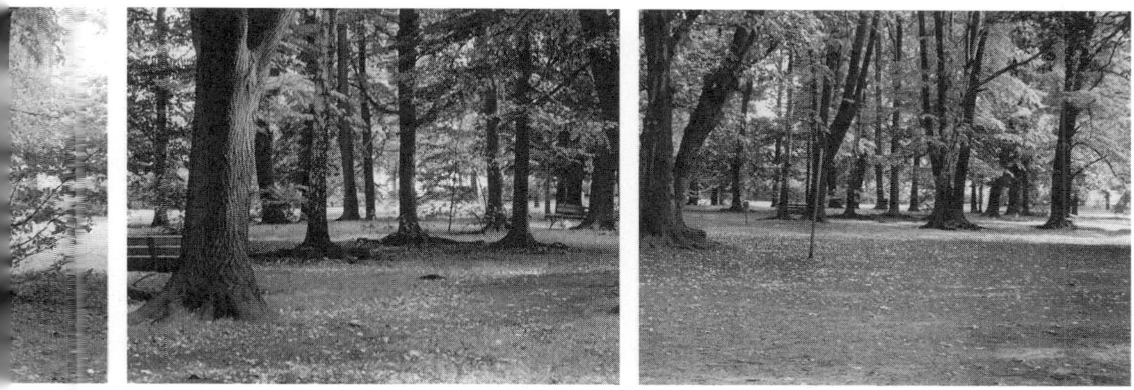

Ryszard Waśko, *Powiększanie-pomniejszanie*, 1976, fot. cz.-b.
Ryszard Waśko, *Zooming-in Zooming-out*, 1976, B&W photograph

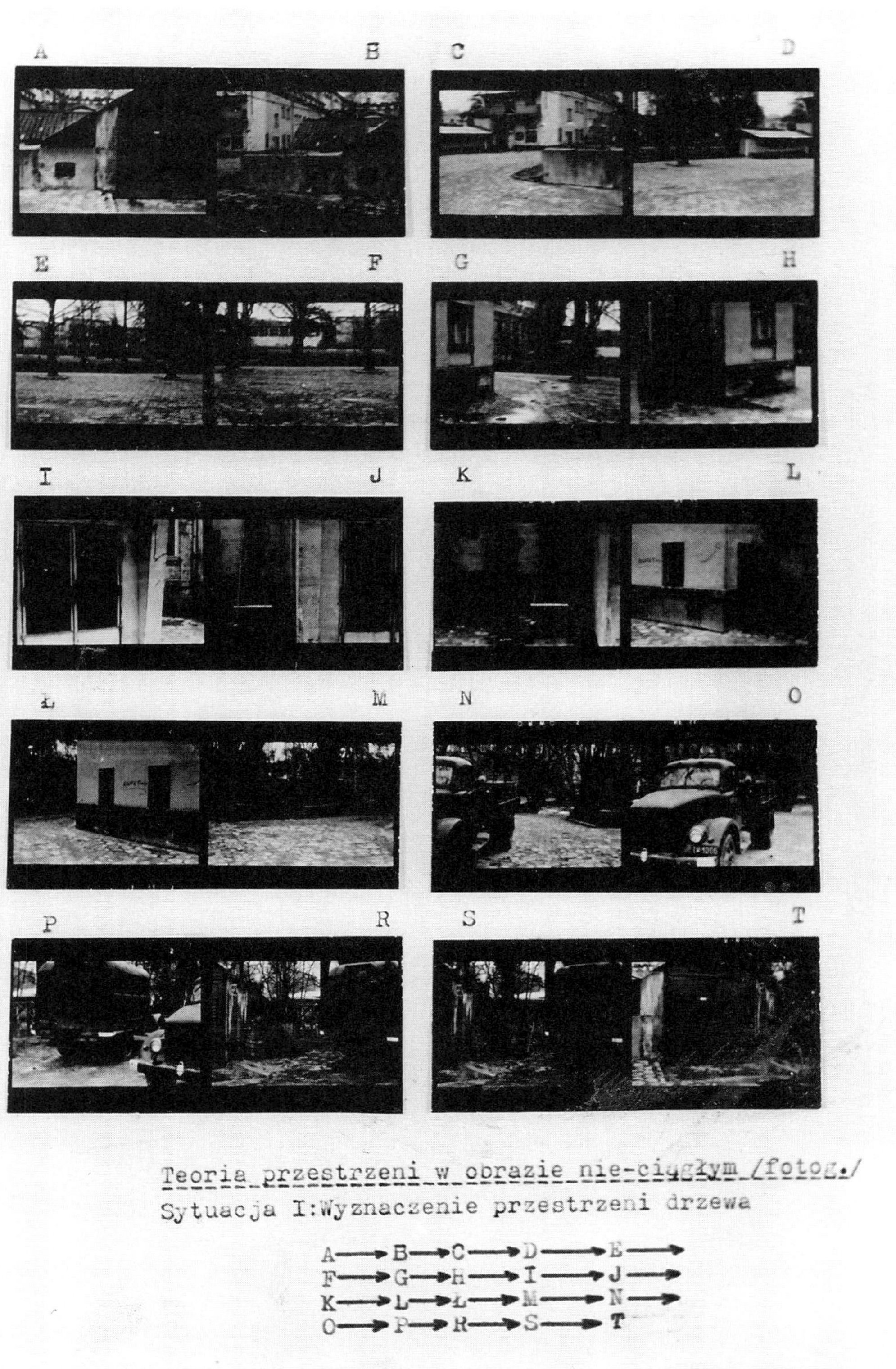

Ryszard Waśko, *Ilustracje do Teorii przestrzeni w obrazie fotograficznym*, 1974, fot. cz.-b., maszynopis
Ryszard Waśko, *Illustrations to the Theory of Space in the Photographic Image*, 1974, B&W photograph, typescript

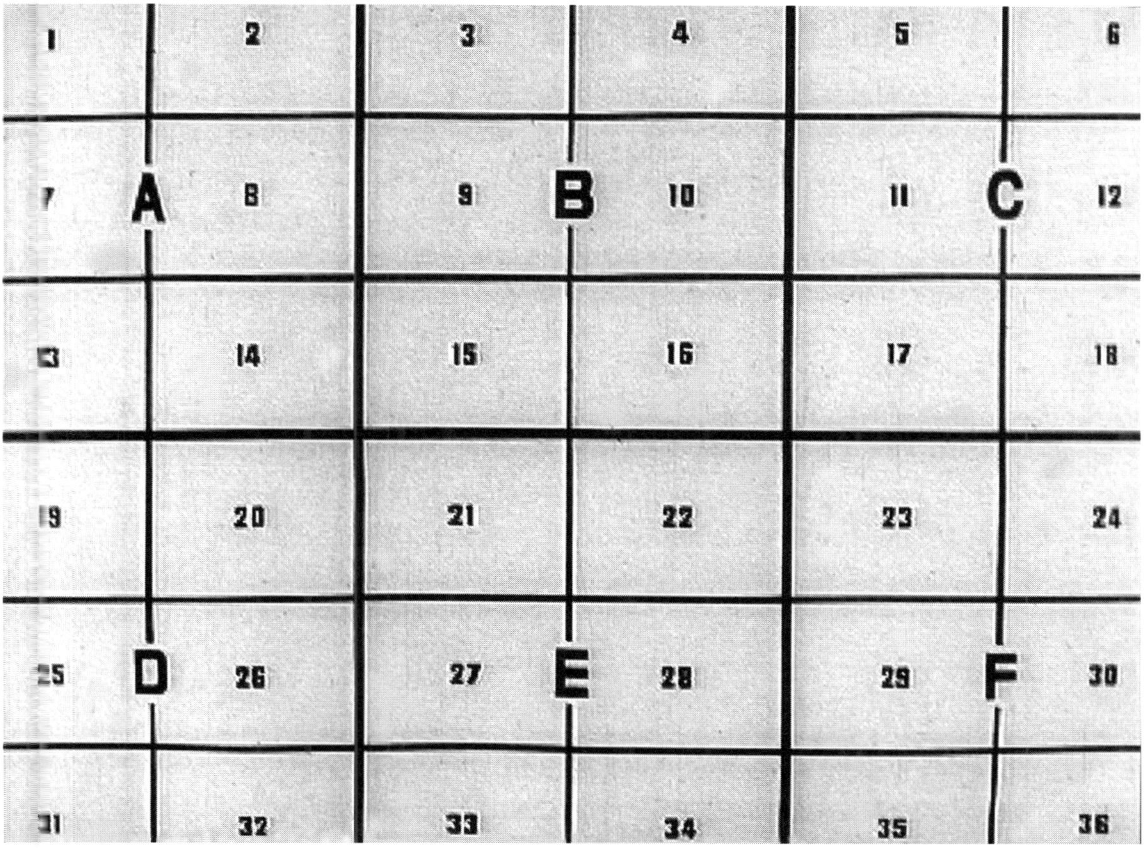

Ryszard Waśko, *A-B-C-D-E-F–1-36*, 1974, 35 mm, 6’24’’
Ryszard Waśko, *A-B-C-D-E-F–1-36*, 1974, 35 mm, 6’24’’

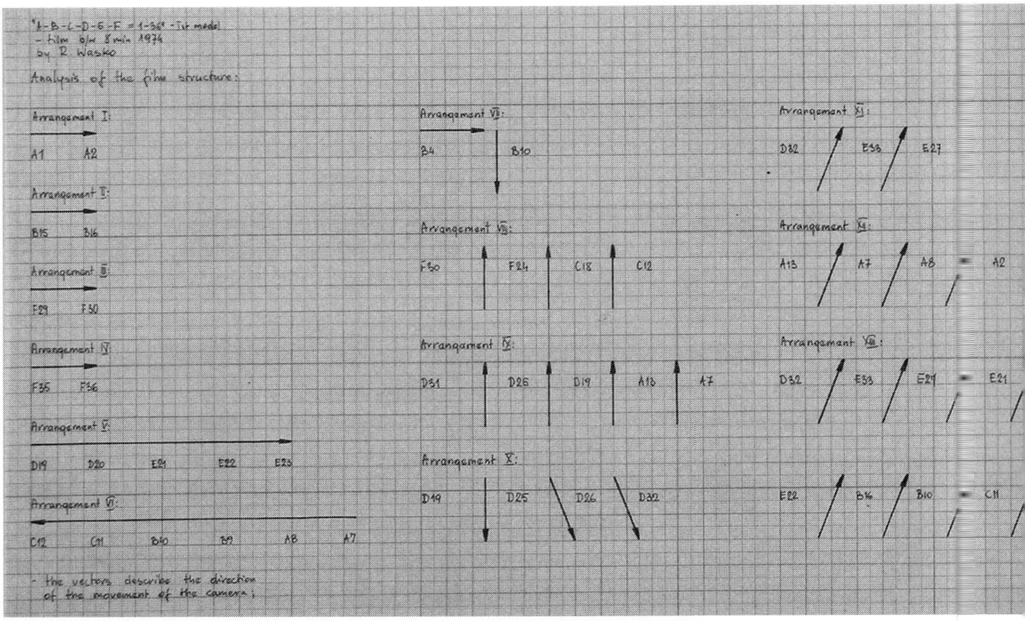

Ryszard Waśko, *Od A do B i z powrotem*, 1974, 35 mm, 7’24’’
Ryszard Waśko, *From A to B and Back*, 1974, 35 mm, 7’24’’

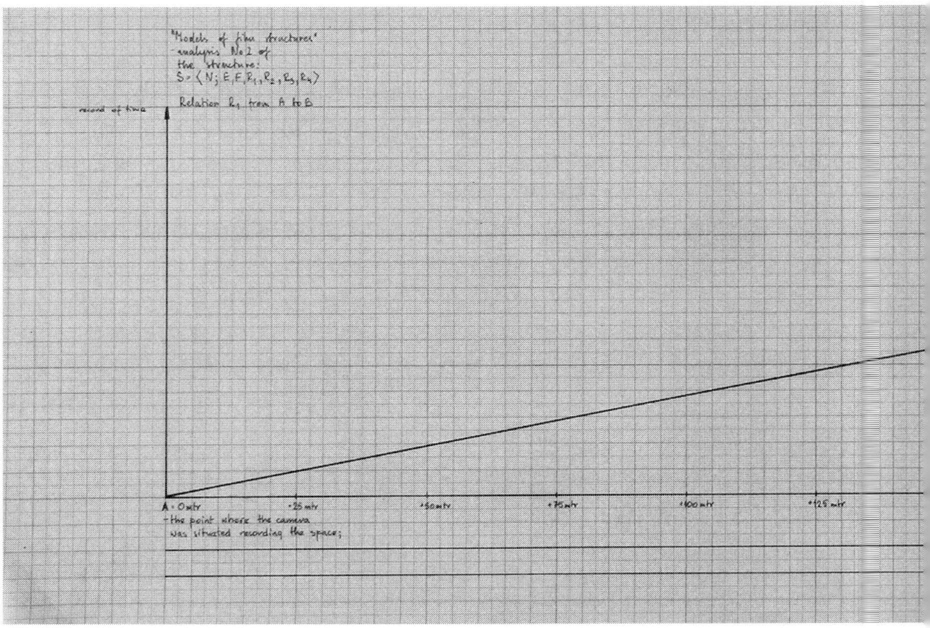

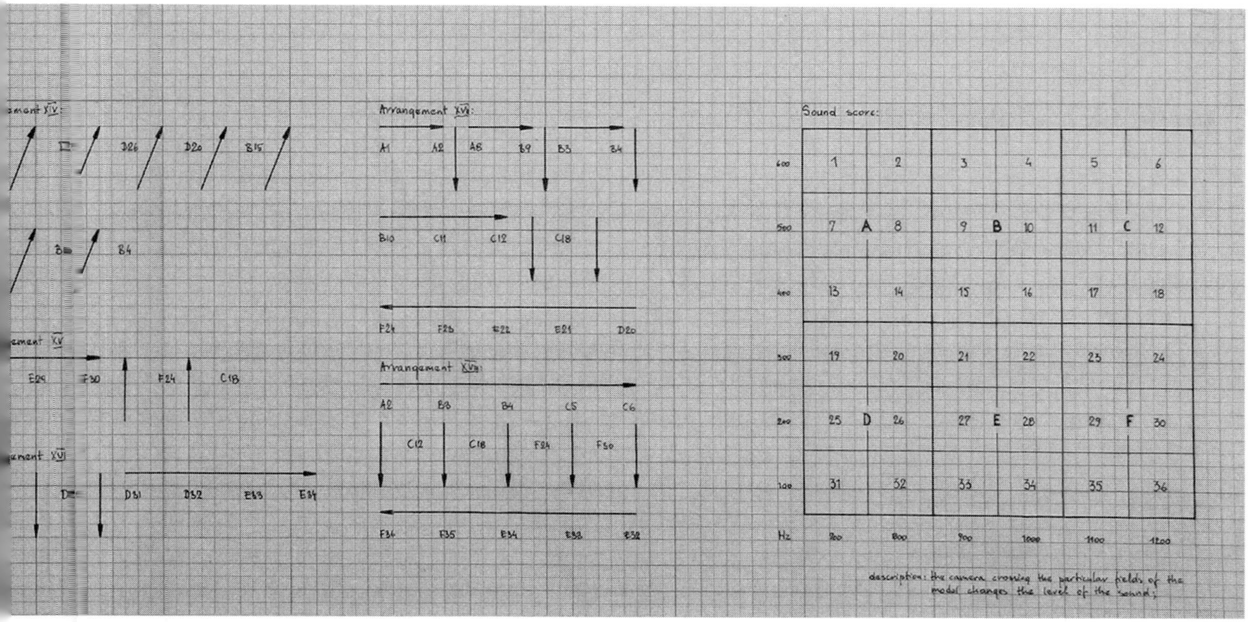

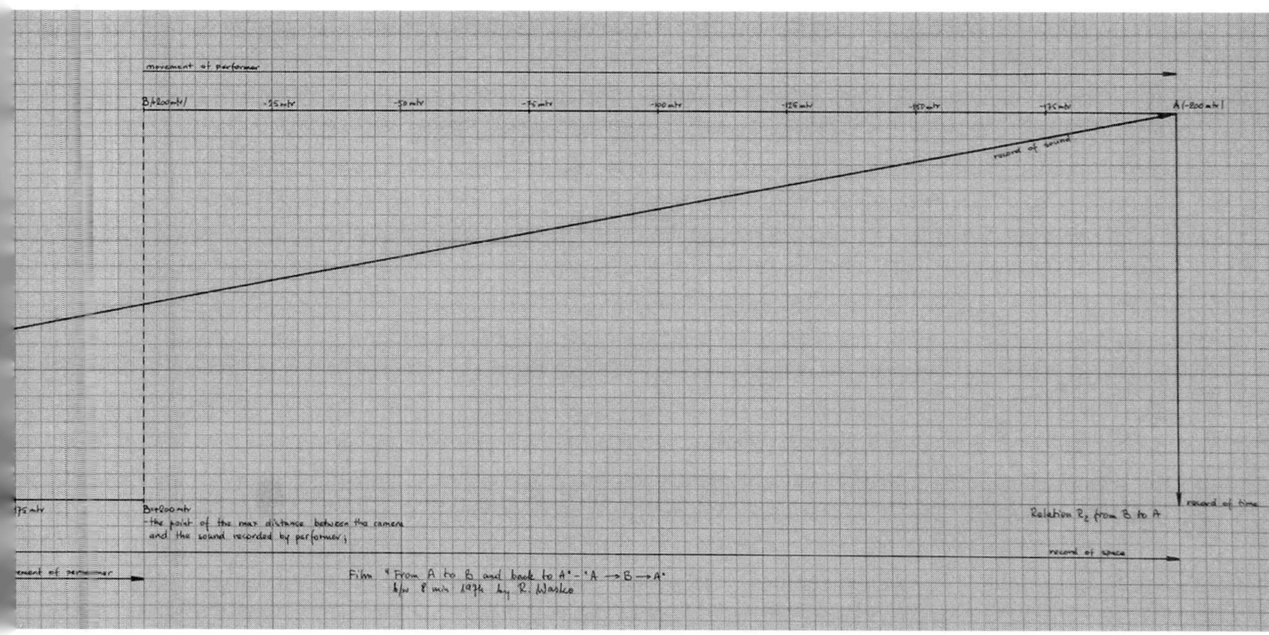

Ryszard Waśko, *Od A do B i z powrotem,* 1974, 35 mm, 7'24''
Ryszard Waśko, *From A to B and Back*, 1974, 35 mm, 7'24''

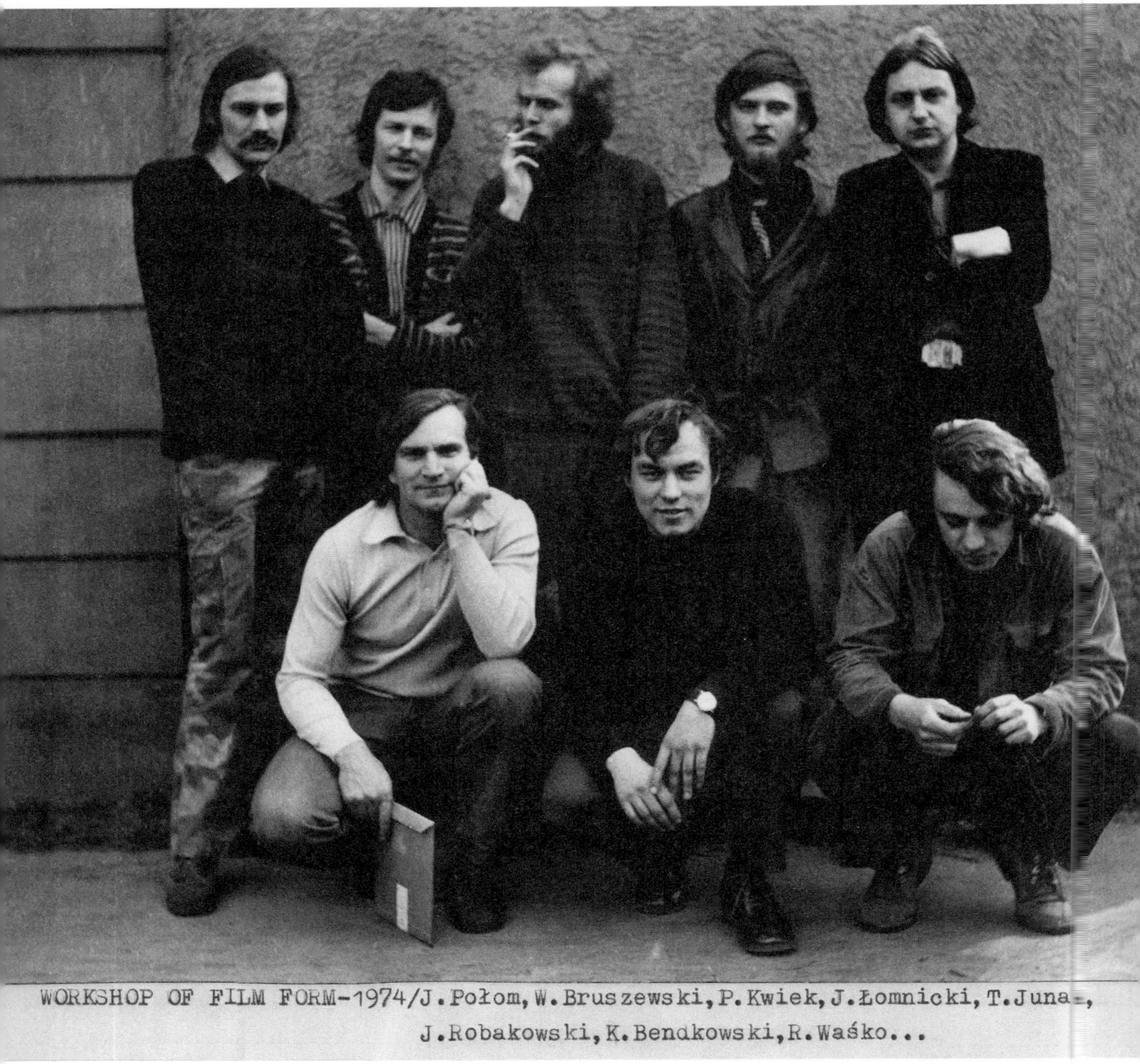

Warsztat Formy Filmowej, Łódź, 1974 (od lewej: J. Połom, W. Bruszewski, P. Kwiek, J. Łomnicki, T. Junak, J. Robakowski, K. Bendkowski, R. Waśko)
Workshop of the Film Form, Łódź, 1974 (from the left: J. Połom, W. Bruszewski, P. Kwiek, J. Łomnicki, T. Junak, J. Robakowski, K. Bendkowski, R. Waśko)

Marika Kuźmicz

Workshop of the Film Form

Introduction

At the beginning of the 1970s several young people at the Film School in Łódź established the Workshop of the Film Form (WFF)[1] – a community founded on a revolt against official cinematography, on an attempt to improve the low level of education at the Film School, but above all on fascination with audiovisual communication, new technologies of image processing, and pre-war avant-garde art. The participants of the group spent time with each other on an almost daily basis, which resulted in an intensive exchange of views. Therefore, despite their extremely varied experiences and interests, they complemented each other. The Workshop grew and operated actively during the following years, during which it went on to become one of the most important millieu to inspire transformations in the art of the 1960s and 1970s in Poland.

We accept the years 1970–77 as the period of the WFF's work, realising at the same time the arbitrariness of these watershed years. This pertains especially to the date of the end of the group's activity, which is two years ahead of their last group presentation.[2] The initial date marks the formalisation of the WFF's activity as an Academic Club at the Film School. It was closed by virtue of the rector's decision in 1975, yet the Workshop continued to operate while the majority of its participants were still students. However, as the WFF members were gaining maturity as artists, ruptures began to emerge within the group and the participants' individual ambitions started to crystallise. In the years 1976–78 Wojciech Bruszewski and Paweł Kwiek resigned from membership in the Workshop. The latter recalls that decision as the very moment when he acquired independence as an artist. The former group members organised film screenings collectively until the end of the 1970s, yet they did not work together.

Those recognised as the 'core' of the Workshop include Józef Robakowski, Wojciech Bruszewski, who shared their prior experience in the group Zero-61, as well as Paweł Kwiek and Ryszard Waśko.[3] It would also be completely justified to include Andrzej Różycki in this circle. Różycki was also a member of Zero-61 and became involved in the Workshop's activity from the

1 The initial name of the group was Workshop of the Film Form 'Content.' It was founded as part of the Academic Club at the Film School in Łodź in October 1970. The founding members were: Wojciech Bruszewski, Ryszard Gajewski, Tadeusz Junak, Andrzej Różycki, Paweł Kwiek, Antoni Mikołajczyk, Józef Robakowski and Zbigniew Rybczyński, supported by Professor Jerzy Kotowski. See: *Żywa Galeria*. Łódzki progresywny ruch artystyczny 1969-1981, ed. J. Robakowski, Łódź: Łódzki Dom Kultury Galeria FF, 2000, p. 32, and R. Waśko, 'Workshop of the Film Form,' MA diss., Film School in Łódź, 1974, http://repozytorium.fundacjaarton.pl/index.php?action=view/collection&colid=24&catid=2&lang=pl#1 [accessed 30-12-2016].

2 The 3rd International Avant-Garde Festival at the National Theatre in London at the turn of June 1979; participants: Wojciech Bruszewski, Tomasz Konart, Józef Robakowski, Janusz Szczerek and Ryszard Waśko. Also held in London at the same time, the exhibition *Film as Film. Formal Experiment in Film 1910–1975* at the Hayward Gallery, featured works by Wojciech Bruszewski, Józef Robakowski and Ryszard Waśko.

3 Ryszard Waśko joined slightly later – in the second term of the academic year 1970/71.

very beginning. What is more, Kazimierz Bendkowski's contribution to the group is recognised as very significant. The artist participated less actively in joint actions and journeys, but created a considerable number of works shown mainly abroad after his departure for Germany in 1982, and very little researched and recognised in Poland.

The enumerated members pursued the Workshop's ethos also in their later practice by choosing to work mainly in the field of art, and not official cinematography. As Józef Robakowski said:

> It's very interesting that some of the colleagues choose such lifestyle, without cinematography: Antoni Mikołajczyk, Kazimierz Bendkowski, Wojciech Bruszewski, Paweł Kwiek, Ryszard Waśko, Andrzej Różycki, Robakowski... It's very interesting that we're professionals, we graduated from the Film School, the most prestigious school in this country, some of us with two diplomas, and we've decided to become such kind of people – artists.[4]

Bearing in mind the particularly important contribution of the above enumerated artists, we have nevertheless decided to examine the Workshop of the Film Form in this book as a certain whole, a community in which an interaction between diverse personalities generated a particular kind of energy. Each of the members co-created in his own way the group's vast oeuvre, which comprises hundreds of works: films, photographs, videos, actions and texts. These works serve as the basis to recognise the Workshop as the most significant formation of structural film in Central and Eastern Europe.[5]

Yet, the history of the Workshop is much more than the works themselves. It embraces extraordinary people and places which they marked with their presence, common inspirations journeys taken together, fascinating moments of what was an authentic team work. It embraces the common experience of historic events, but also everyday life, to which the members of the group were especially open as artists, and to which they opened their audiences.

For the Workshop of the Film Form did not operate in a void – it was established in Poland under the rule of the Polish United Workers' Party (PZPR) under the leadership of the First Secretary Edward Gierek and functioned within an institution of immense importance for the authorities given the propaganda potential of film. In this book, we attempt to examine also this particular thread – the group's functioning in a broader political perspective and the influence of politics on the life and work of its participants.

The presented book is a fruit of not only several years of research, but also meetings and conversations with the members of the Workshop of the Film Form. We conducted interviews at their homes and studios in Łódź, Warsaw and Berlin. That was also where we mostly pursued our research, since relatively few works by the Workshop members entered the holdings of Polish museums and other public art institutions. It was the materials originating from the artists' private archives that helped us to reconstruct a possibly complete picture of the group's activity, even

4 Józef Robakowski, 'The Eighth Cinema,' Józef Robakowski in conversation with Łukasz Ronduda, in *Polish Cine Art, or the Cinematographic Turn in Polish Contemporary Art*, ed. J. Majmurek and Ł. Ronduda, Warsaw: Krytyka Polityczna, 2015, pp. 58–76.

5 Ł. Ronduda, 'The Workshop of the Film Form. Film realizations from the years 1970-1977,' in *The Workshop of the Film Form 1970-1977. Early Film Work from Poland*, ed. G. Joseph-Hunter, Ł. Ronduda, L. Zippay, New York and Warsaw: Electronic Arts Intermix and Centre for Contemporary Art Ujazdowski Castle, 2004, p. 28.

though not a trace – other than oral accounts – has been left after a considerable part of the works.

The text that forms the first part of the book attempts to provide a possibly full account of the group's history. The essays in the second part of the publication aim to provide a new reading of selected works and aspects of the WFF's activity. The third part of the book offers an insight into the artists' biographies and their works (also those unpreserved).

Leaven

The Workshop of the Film Form was founded in Łódź, but its future members had come across each other in different places and circumstances. For instance, Kazimierz Bendkowski, Ryszard Waśko and Lechosław Lenczewski participated in the same amateur documentary film festivals.[6] However, it was the city of Toruń that played the greatest role. After World War II, it became a major academic centre in Poland as well as a landmark on the map of Polish students' culture, and it was there that a numerous group of future members of the WFF met and established collaborations.

In August 1945, the Nicolaus Copernicus University (UMK) was opened in the city. The professors of the university embraced experienced pedagogues from the Stefan Batory University in Vilnius. Alongside the professors, students also appeared in the city. The young generation infused the town with new energy and contributed to creating a particular atmosphere, which Lech Lechowicz described as a result of a combination of the Vilnius tradition and the local Hanseatic culture.[7] After the political 'thaw' in October 1956, the city witnessed the development of cultural life. The Club of the Students' Weekly *Od Nowa*, which was significant on the national scale, inaugurated its activity in 1958. It soon became a dynamic centre of cultural life, frequented by such figures as Ewa Demarczyk, Krzysztof Komeda, Julian Przyboś, Artur Sandauer, Edward Stachura, and Ryszard Bruno Milczewski. In 1960, Toruń hosted the first students' celebrations 'Juwenalia,' which later became a famous event.

It was during that period that the future founders of the Workshop of the Film Form began their studies in Toruń. Józef Robakowski and Andrzej Różycki studied art preservation and knowledge of historic monuments at the faculty of art history. Robakowski considered the studies as a somewhat intermediate stage, a means to achieve his goal, which was to prepare for another attempt at the entry exams to the Film School in Łódź. Andrzej Różycki attempted to enter the faculty of painting at the Academy of Fine Arts in Warsaw,[8] but he was not accepted. Antoni Mikołajczyk studied visual arts training at the Pedagogical Faculty of the UMK since 1962. In 1967, he defended his diploma work in painting under Prof. Bronisław Kierzkowski.

It is noteworthy that Janusz Zagrodzki studied art history in Toruń during the same period. Zagrodzki hailed from Łódź. His goal and dream was to work at the Muzeum Sztuki (Museum of Art) in his home city. He was fascinated by the history of pre-war avant-garde art, particularly the work of the then forgotten Katarzyna Kobro, to whom he devoted his paper at the seminar run by Prof. Gwido Chmarzyński (1906–73). Although the faculty focused mainly on Medieval and Early

6 J. Peltz, 'O filmowcach amatorach bez taryfy ulgowej,' *Fotografia*, 1, 1970, pp. 5–7.

7 L. Lechowicz, 'Grupa Zero-61. Zapomniana tradycja lat sześćdziesiątych,' *Exit*, 2, 1999, p. 19, 54–59.

8 Interview with Andrzej Różycki, September 2016.

Modern art, Zagrodzki strove to use the existing possibilities to expand his knowledge in the field of his interest. He therefore made contact with the future members of the WFF and in the 1970s went on to become one of the first theorists to write about the Workshop's activity[9] as well as a friend of the group who accompanied it during artistic actions and events. Józef Robakowski recalls that he himself and his colleagues tapped into Zagrodzki's knowledge of pre-war art, especially concerning the activity of Katarzyna Kobro, a figure of immense importance for the WFF.[10] When they all settled in Łódź after the studies, Zagrodzki offered the Workshop members access to works in the storage spaces of Muzeum Sztuki. He was also a co-creator of films by the members of the WFF devoted to the representatives of the Polish avant-garde from the period between the two World Wars.[11]

Robakowski and Różycki underline that owing to outstanding professors, who gave proof of complete 'ideological independence,' the university in Toruń offered its students the possibility to 'detach themselves from the official cultural policy.'[12] The lecturers of the Toruń university included eminent artists and scholars, such as Tymon Niesiołowski (1882–1965), painter, graphic artist, representative of the art movement known as the Formists, member of the 'Rytm' group, who became the focus of Robakowski's Master's Thesis;[13] Prof. Stefan Narębski (1892–1966), pedagogue and architect, who worked as the municipal architect of Vilnius prior to World War II; Prof. Jadwiga Puciata – Pawłowska (1902–89), specialist in the history of art of the turn of the 20th century. 'It was them – Robakowski stated – who saved us from the impact of Real Socialism.'[14] What is more, already mentioned Bronisław Kierzkowski hailed from Łódź and studied at the State Higher School of Visual Arts (PWSSP) in that city under Władysław Strzemiński in the years 1946–1947, a fact that undoubtedly establishes him as one of the links between the WFF and the past of the Polish avant-garde, albeit slightly forgotten.

Józef Robakowski described the Toruń period as very creative.[15] The city was home to the dynamic Students' Creative Film Club 'Pętla,' a venue that offered the possibility to create films on 16 mm film stock, as well as the Film Discussion Club, run at a high level by Józef Tęcza.[16] The future members of the WFF profited from the potential offered by those organisations by familiarising themselves with the works of global film avant-garde and creating their first own films.[17]

In parallel to their activity in 'Pętla,' Robakowski, Mikołajczyk ad Różycki also organised their own new groups and associations: OKO (1960), the interdisciplinary Krąg (1965), and above

---

9 See J. Zagrodzki, 'Kino-Laboratorium,' in Żywa Galeria, pp. 112–13, available online: http://repozytorium.fundacjaarton.pl/index.php?action=view/object&objid=3139&colid=75&catid=18 [accessed 30-12-2016].

10 Zagrodzki authored the first monographic book devoted to the sculptress. See J. Zagrodzki, *Katarzyna Kobro i kompozycja przestrzeni*, Warsaw: PWN, 1984.

11 Zagrodzki was a co-writer in such films as *Constructivism in Poland* by Ryszard Waśko. Zagrodzki also co-authored the script of the film *The Spatial Compositions of Katarzyna Kobro* by Józef Robakowski, with music composed by Eugeniusz Rudnik.

12 J. Robakowski, *Art Is Power!*, 2005, http://robakowski.eu/tx13.html [accessed 30-12-2016].

13 See T. Samosionek, *Sztuka video w Polsce*, Łódź: T. Samosionek, 1989, http://robakowski.net/tx23.html [accessed 30-12-2016].

14 J. Robakowski, *Art Is Power!*

15 Interview with Józef Robakowski, October 2015.

16 Interview with Józef Robakowski, November 2015.

17 Józef Robakowski, 'W oczach ekspertów byliśmy amatorami,' interview by A. Mazur, *Fototapeta*, 2002, available online: http://fototapeta.art.pl/2002/jro.php [accessed 30-12-2016].

all Zero-61 (1961). Thus, a powerful film and photography scene emerged in Toruń, which, as Robakowski underlines, was a phenomenon at the time in Poland.

What is more, it was a milieu that enjoyed a considerable margin of freedom. Establishing associations, organising exhibitions, production of films and photographs, as well as formation of approaches to art and life – all of that took place in the spacious sphere of 'students' culture,' which was characterised by a specific autonomy in the totalitarian regime of Poland under Communism and a relative independence from political pressure, especially after March 1968.[18] The students' activities in the field of art and culture undertaken by students did not appeal to mass audiences, and were therefore insignificant from the perspective of the authorities. Yet, as we can see with hindsight, it was the students circles that spawned the most radical stances of the turn of the 1970s. Students' culture provided the Workshop members with a foothold in activities in the art sphere.[19] When asked about the beginnings of his reflection on 'author's cinema,' Robakowski evokes that period:

> It was a kind of our own cinema made on 16 mm, 8 mm film stock. We quite soon realised that we needed to create a completely new configuration – a configuration independent of both photography and film – for all those media activities that emerged at the time.'[20]

The configuration mentioned by Robakowski will provide one of the starting points of the Workshop, and a number of analogies will emerge between the Toruń and Łódź groups. Both groups were founded by young people, close friends studying together. Both groups included many members[21] throughout the entire period of activity (eight and seven years respectively). Both had several most active core members, and – strikingly enough – neither of the groups comprised a single woman artist.[22]

The experience of the members of Zero-61 later contributed significantly to the Workshop's activity, especially in the group's early days. During the Toruń period, they worked through many fundamental problems, such as the status of photography, its dependence/autonomy with regard to reality, as well as the questions related to the materiality of photographic prints. It was then that the WFF member tapped into the potential of photography to make their first attempts to 'deny the traditional techniques and conventions,'[23] which later became their common practice. In May 1966, in the courtyard of the UMK they organised an exhibition, where:

---

18 See L. Burska, *Awangarda i inne złudzenia. O pokoleniu '68 w Polsce*, Gdańsk: Słowo/obraz terytoria, 201, p. 65.

19 According to Józef Robakowski and Andrzej Różycki (Interview in July 2014).

20 'Rozmowa z Józefem Robakowskim,' interview by Adam Mazur, 2001, available online: http://robakowski.eu/tx30.html [accessed 30-12-2016].

21 In 1961, Zero-61 embraced Romuald Chomicz, Czesław Kuchta, Lucjan Oczkowski, Józef Robakowski, Jerzy Wardak and Wiesław Wojczulanis, later joined by Wojciech Bruszewski, Roman Dąbek, Michał Kokot, Antoni Mikołajczyk, Andrzej Różycki and Jan Siennik. The longest and most active members were Kuchta, Robakowski, Wardak, and Różycki, and in the final period of the group's activity also Bruszewski, Kokot and Mikołajczyk. Four of the seven artists later became members of the WFF.

22 Józef Robakowski and Andrzej Różycki explain this situation with a scarce number of female students at the direction of photography department and film direction department of the Film School. This leads to a question about the policy of the Film School regarding women candidates to the studies.

23 L. Olszewski, 'Działalność Warsztatu Formy Filmowej jako przykład strategii sztuki wobec władzy w Polsce lat siedemdziesiątych,' *Artium Quaestiones*, 9 (124), 1998, p. 124 http://repozytorium.amu.edu.pl/handle/10593/10979 [accessed 30-12-2016].

Photographs of fragments of reality were confronted with reality itself. Thus, a photograph of a bulldozer with a heap of sand, photograph of a tree with a real tree, and a photo of a fence was hung on a barrier.[24]

In 1967, a similar idea was implemented at the post-plein exhibition at the 'Od Nowa' club (symptomatically, it coincided with a renovation). Ordinary objects of everyday use were juxtaposed with their large-scale photographic reproductions. It was then that Józef Korbiela appeared among the featured artists, a fictitious character invented by Robakowski. Member of the group used the name 'Korbiela' to sign a variety of peculiar knick-knacks or kitschy works of their own making. The emergence of that character heralds a strategy which Robakowski will pursue also in the 1970s in his actions and activities whose real author became hidden.

In the second half of the 1960s, Robakowski and Bruszewski (who began their studies at the Film School) as well as Mikołajczyk and Zagrodzki (who found his dream job at the Muzeum Sztuki in Łódź after the studies) divided their time and engagement between the two cities. In 1967, the group Zero-61 was joined by Wojciech Bruszewski, who was already a student of the Film School, where he met Robakowski. The Workshop did not yet exist, but the approach of its future founders crystallised and radicalised, a fact that anticipated the decline of Zero-61.

According to the former members of Zero-61, the moment when the group ultimately ceased to exist came with the exhibition 'Smithy' ('Kuźnia'). It was held within a state-wide symposium devoted to the influences of visual arts and other art disciplines on photography (11th–12th May 1969), and therefore the show opening attracted nearly the entire milieu of photography (including avant-garde photography) and independent art of the time. The title of the exhibition bore relation to the site – an old building that used to house a smith's workshop. Far from random, the choice was characteristic of the future work of the WFF. An exhibition located in a space that was publicly available, half-abandoned, seemingly unattractive, and above all – not a gallery or a museum, signalised the artists' willingness to open up themselves and the viewers to reality. Photographs were juxtaposed with objects of everyday use, or even found discarded items. Such a solution, which had also been used by the members of Zero-61, was meant to make viewers realise the material character of the photograph as a three-dimensional entity with its own specific size, which is prone to destruction, highly flammable, which, in turn, was supposed to 'establish new relations between the medium of photography and the viewer.'[25] The artists consistently strove to leave the gallery space, confront their works with reality and investigate the relations between the photographed and photography. Those questions will later become they key problems for the Workshop members.

Some of the Zero-61 artists chose not to participate in the exhibition. Soon after the show, Andrzej Różycki, the last former member of Zero-61, left Toruń for Łódź, where he decided to take up studies at the Film School.[26] Soon afterwards, in September 1969, in a greenhouse on the premises of the Film School in Łodź, Różycki alongside other former members of Zero-61 (Robakowski, Różycki, Mikołajczyk and Bruszewski) and their new colleague Ryszard Gajewski (student of the third year of the faculty of direction of photography) opened an exhibition which they later referred to as a 'garage show.' Once again they presented several dozen of photographs juxtaposed with

24 Ibidem.

25 Ibidem, p. 127.

26 Michał Kokot considered a similar decision, but ultimately resigned from the idea.

objects of everyday use, and once again the exhibition setting was an abandoned and derelict location. This seemingly insignificant gesture is indeed extremely revealing – students of the Film School organise an exhibition of photography, consciously positioning themselves in the field of art, and not cinematography, since they see themselves as artists. Ryszard Gajewski recalls:

> We organised the first photographic exhibition of the Workshop in a greenhouse on the courtyard of the Film School, following the model of the group Zero-61, who exhibited their works in an old smithy. The exhibition, titled 'Greenhouse,' featured works by Józek Robakowski, Wojtek Bruszewski, Ryszard Gajewski, Paweł Kwiek and others. For Józek and Wojtek the exhibition was necessary to close their old chapter of photographic activities in Toruń and begin a new chapter of film activities in Łódź.[27]

Around the same time, Ryszard Waśko, graduate of the secondary technical school of construction in Nysa, and Kazimierz Bendkowski and Tadeusz Junak, graduate of a secondary technical school of motor vehicle engineering from Warsaw, participate in numerous amateur film contests. They are awarded prizes and distinctions, as well as receive mentions in the press.[28] In Olsztyn, high school student Janusz Połom creates his first film on 8 mm film stock. Inspired by his older brother, Połom attends the municipal photographic club 'Giewont.' In Warsaw, another high school student Paweł Kwiek, whose brother, Przemysław, is already a student at the Faculty of Sculpture of the Academy of Fine Arts, receives an 8 mm film camera from his father in recognition of good grades at school and begins his first experiments with photography.

In the same year Bruszewski, Janicki, Gajewski and Robakowski graduated School. In October the same year, they will establish the Workshop of the Film Form.

Community

October 1970 is recognised as the official moment of the establishment of the Workshop of the Film Form. It was the moment when the group, which in fact had informally existed before, became formalised. Ryszard Gajewski, who started his studies at the Film School in 1965, two years later (after a Dean's Leave of absence) joined the year of Józef Robakowski and Wojciech Bruszewski. The School, which had already been in a poor condition as an educational institution, was soon to become a stage of the events of March 1968, which dealt it a heavy blow and assured the then second-year students in their conviction that self-education was the only possible way. Ryszard Gajewski recalls:

> Józef Robakowski, who had already had his Toruń experience, believed that it was necessary to set up another group. He was always interested in the creative work of other people and their way of thinking. When we started to study together he asked me to show him my works. I showed him my film which I made as my student's etude at the end of the first years of studies. It was a still non-creative documentary about how students of the fourth year of the Film School, students from an international exchange, make their end-of-term film. Robakowski liked it a lot, so he asked me if I would want to work with him and Bruszewski. They had plans to create an artistic group. During that period, they

27 Interview with Ryszard Gajewski, January 2016.
28 J. Peltz, op. cit.

divided their time between Toruń and Łódź, but the activity of the group Zero-61 was slowly coming to an end.'[29]

In 1969, after the exhibition 'Smithy' in Toruń, also Andrzej Różycki decided to move to Łódź. He remembers the early days of the WFF as follows:

> I think we were in an ideal situation to create an avant-garde group like the Workshop. For something like that to happen you need intensive co-existence, and that was how we functioned. We spent a lot of time with each other. From the early morning, when we started classes, to the meals we had together, to the evening, when we usually organised social gatherings that lasted until late at night.[30]

The first works were created with very modest, nearly non-existent financial and technological means. Reminiscing about the first screenings of the group's films at the projection hall of the Film School, Ryszard Gajewski mentions Wojciech Bruszewski's attempts to add the 'soundtrack' using a gramophone. Effects were varied, because he did not always manage to 'hit' the right place on the record with the needle. Gajewski recalls:

> Initially, the WFF did not exist as a formal entity. It was simply there. Everybody knew what it was about. When someone made something interesting, he would invite us to a film screening. Józek Robakowski was preparing a sample set of films under the Workshop's label, and when someone's film was included in that set, he could say that he was a member of the Workshop. It was also possible to be removed from the set and to re-appear in it. There were no rules. Józek simply liked to mix those sets. Most films did not have any soundtrack because the School did not provide soundtracks for camera operator's exercises, deeming sheer vision to be sufficient for evaluation. Directors were in a better position because their film etudes were made with a soundtrack. If someone had the money, he would get the soundtrack done 'unofficially.' We resorted to different makeshift ways. In the projection booth we played the sound from a tape recorder, matching it with the image using the rule of thumb. There were more and more films, but we were still stuck in the Stone Age. We couldn't put up with that amateur situation any longer, after all, being in a Film School obliges you to keep a certain level. Someone came up with the idea to piggyback our activity on the Academic Club. Nothing was happening there and the School had funds for its activities. Rector Kotowski was positive about that initiative, but it was still necessary to deal with formalities. As in every state institution, first you needed to make an application, provide a justification, indicate the goals, outline the plan of activity, and so on. If I remember well, it was Józek Robakowski with Wojtek Bruszewski who drew up that beautiful document. It is reprinted in different publications and circulates on different websites as the main manifesto of the Workshop of the Film Form. And yet, the point of the text was to avoid saying anything specific nor promising anything. The level of generality was so high that every film or other kind of activity could be matched to the manifesto. I think it was a very tricky and clever move.[31]

Gajewski reveals the origin of the group's name:

---

29 Interview with Ryszard Gajewski, January 2016.

30 Interview with Andrzej Różycki, July 2016.

31 Interview with Ryszard Gajewski, July 2016.

> Everybody liked the name because different kinds of 'workshops' and 'factories' were in fashion at the time. Our inspiration came from Andy Warhol's 'Factory.' We were interested in juxtaposing our activities with the notion of factory, industry, or the very workshop. And since our activities were related to film, everything became clear, and the name was created.[32]

The 'positive rector' mentioned by Gajewski was Jerzy Kotowski, a maker of animated films (including puppet animations); he 'was not treated very seriously in the filmmakers' circles, who held feature filmmaking in the highest esteem.'[33] Yet, Kotowski was open to explorations related to contemporary art. He realised that the Film School must provide room for experimentation, which was why he agreed to the establishment of the WFF.'[34] It is noteworthy that it was Kotowski who initiated the establishment of the Workshop of Animated Film at the Film School, in which Zbigniew Rybczyński made his first artistic steps.

Therefore, the Workshop was active from 1970 to 1975 within the Academic Club of the Film School, for which they secured financial means for the production and post-production of films. Thus, the group's works acquired a strong professional appeal, which distinguished them amongst other experimental productions of the period (also internationally). The films shot on 35 mm film stock and the production process met the then cinematographic standards. For instance, the members of the group had the funds to employ a production manager as well as provide professional soundtrack and editing for their films.

The short text that was later called *Manifesto I* was drawn up by the entire group.[35] It is synthetic and capacious at the same time, comprising several sentences that carry neither a promise nor a declaration:

> The Workshop was created in 1970 on the initiative of a group of students and graduates of the Łódź Film, TV and Theatre School. Apart from filmmakers, the WORKSHOP includes painters, musicians, cameramen, poets, technicians ... The WORKSHOP creates films and recordings, organises TV transmissions, sound performances, art exhibitions and various events and artistic interventions ... The WORKSHOP also pursues theoretical and critical activity. It researches the potential of audiovisual arts and has the ambition to broaden it. Attention! The WORKSHOP does not engage in any commercial activity and its members work strictly on a non-profit basis. The only condition of taking up work in this SECTION is for filmmakers to subordinate to the above stated programme idea. The programme and organisational work of the Workshop is headed by the Programme Board, which includes seven members.[36]

---

32 Ibidem.

33 Interview with Andrzej Różycki, July 2014.

34 Interview with Ryszard Gajewski, June 2016.

35 The manifesto was not signed with a specific name – neither in the original version nor in any later reprint. The collective authorship was also highlighted by J. Robakowski (correspondence in July 2016).

36 Quoted in R. W. Kluszczyński, *Warsztat Formy Filmowej,* Warsaw: Centrum Sztuki Współczesnej Zamek Ujazdowski, 2000, p. 60. *Manifesto I* (1970) was the first synthetic text to announce the future activities of the group in a way that was not to delimit the field of artists' activity. *Manifesto II* (1975) provided an already more profound presentation of the group's approach and a summary of the five years of its activity. Both texts were published on numerous occasions as leaflets and later reprints. One of the version of the leaflet with *Manifesto I* is available online: http://repozytorium.fundacjaarton.pl/index.php?action-view/object&objid-3178&colid-75&catid-18 [accessed 31-12-2016]. Cf. *Wojciech Bruszewski. Phenomena of Perception*, ed E. Fuchs, J. Zagrodzki, Łódź: Miejska Galeria Sztuki, 2010, pp. 93–4.

Paweł Kwiek remembers that period as a time of very intensive exchange of views and ideas. It was so intensive that sometimes the members of the group would implement ideas of other members. Yet, this does not imply stealing ideas or plagiarism, but an authentic exchange. Paweł Kwiek recalls:

> There were many such situations, they pertained to each of us. I remember that I was sitting in the school cafeteria when one of the colleagues came. I told him about an idea that I had. And he said: 'But you're not going to do it anyway. And it's such a good idea. I'll do it.' And he did it. And it was good, because I wouldn't have done it for sure, I simply had too many ideas.[37]

In order to balance this idealised vision of collective collaboration, let us quote Marek Koterski, who participated in the group's events, trips and shows during the initial years of the WFF's activity:

The formation of the Workshop was always alien to me. I simply didn't like those guys very much. I could sense a lack of acceptance from their side, except for Waśko, with whom we liked each other some more. I was also feeling alienated in content-related terms. In my opinion, the form makes sense as long as it serves the cognition of the ingredients of the film matter. But if it becomes a goal in its own right, it becomes an elitist phenomenon. The Workshop's animators expected their proposals to have a broad audience, who was also expected to have good fun, and for me that is a sign of hubris and lack of understanding. However, indeed, as a forerunner, as an avant-garde that blazes the trail, the Workshop of the Film Form did its job.[38]

An important summary of the community-related aspect of the WFF can be found in a statement by Zbigniew Rybczyński, who said that the existence at the Film School of a group of people who were making films that were 'different' from regular documentary and feature filmmaking emboldened him in his own explorations.

The School

In the period after World War II, tertiary education institutions in Łódź became located in post-industrial spaces or tenement houses. Only artistic schools received better and more presentable seats. Established in 1948, the Film School was seated in a building from 1903 in 61 Targowa St., the former palace of Oskar Kon, owner of the Widzew Manufactory. Kazimierz Kutz recalled: 'When I first came to Łódź, I was so impressed that my legs were trembling, because the School was located in a palace. For a boy from Silesia entering a palace was a shock.'[39]

The graduates of the School from the initial period of its activity – in the 1940s and at the beginning of the 1950s – recall a beautiful garden, which remained under the custody of the same gardener from before the war; given his characteristic appearance, the gardener often featured in students' film etudes created at the School. They also remember quite well preserved pre-war furnishings of the edifice, spacious halls, abundantly decorated walls, colourful flooring, decorative ceilings, mosaics and old-time chandeliers. Unfortunately, the following years brought about

37 Interview with Paweł Kwiek, July 2015.

38 K. Krubski, M. Miller, Z. Turowska, W. Wiśniewski, *Filmówka. Powieść o łódzkiej szkole filmowej*, Warsaw: Prószyński i S-ka, 1998, p. 214.

39 Ibidem, p. 34.

a complete devastation of the villa. Subsequent halls became deprived of original furnishings, which likely adorned later the offices of prominent party members. The school suffered from the lack of halls, therefore toilets were transformed into photographic darkrooms. Also the palace park ultimately fell into disarray. The greenhouse located in the park was adapted for the needs of a small atelier. The long building behind the garden housed a storage space and film editing studios, whereas the main building of the villa housed lecture and projection halls, the rector's and dean's offices, darkrooms and rooms for conducting chemical-photographic experiments. Cafeteria, library, reading room and dormitory were located in a separate edifice.

In the period when the future members of the Workshop began their studies at the School – the second half of the 1960s – the original elegance of the building was already a matter of the past, yet the environment was still emanated a 'high-profile' air. Piotr Szulkin, who studied at the Film School between 1970 and 1975, and created his film *Everything/MPO* (35 mm, 1972), recalled:

> I often had the impression that the old building of the School was struggling with the all-embracing degradation in Łódź and strove to come to life in its own way. Some exotic flora, planted already before the war, would spring up in the garden. It was trampled, covered with coal, but after a while, it would emerge in a different place. When the walls were painted with oil paint, stained glass struck the eye.[40]

Józef Robakowski was the first future WFF member to take the entry exams to the Film School. Studies at the School were his clearly defined goal, therefore the artist made two attempts before being eventually admitted. Robakowski recalls:

> In my opinion, it was impossible to get a place at the School in 1958. It managed to achieve a fantastic level, the best among Polish artistic schools. The teachers, who had a great knowledge of world's art, were at the same time at the cream of the crop of Polish cinematography, and made excellent films. There were no chances for someone as provincial as me from Toruń.[41]

The entry exams were unpredictable. Cinematographer Adam Holender, who took the exams at the same time as Robakowski, recalled:

> The entry exam surprised me, because a twenty-one year old guy comes to a room of experts and expects serious questions, but what they do is to ask him to describe in detail how he enters the loo, takes a pee and flushes the toilet. Terrifying![42]

Robakowski was not accepted, but he managed to visit the Muzeum Sztuki, where he saw 'works by Katarzyna Kobro, Władysław Strzemiński, Karol Hiller.'[43]

> I was accused of bringing someone else's photographic works to the entry exam. They were so good that they didn't want to believe that I could make them myself. A special committee was even set up to solve the matter. I lost my chance. I decided to graduate from different studies, and to prepare well enough to give them no reason to dismiss me. Finally, my third attempt was successful. I had graduated from the Faculty of Fine Arts at the University in Toruń. I had gathered a considerable body of work, presented at exhibitions in Poland

40 Ibidem, p. 203.
41 Ibidem, p. 127
42 Ibidem.
43 Interview with Józef Robakowski, May 2016.

> and abroad. It became impossible to suspect me of bringing someone else's works to the exam. I was accepted with no difficulty as the first or second name on the list.[44]

Józef Robakowski became a student of the Film School in 1966, the same year as his colleague from the group Zero-61, Wojciech Bruszewski. Ryszard Gajewski, an active member of the group in the earliest period of its activity, began his studies one year before (accepted upon his third 'attempt'),[45] followed in 1967 by Marek Koterski, who ultimately devoted his professional life to feature filmmaking,[46] but remained active around the Workshop until 1973.

Students of film direction and direction of photography attended the same classes during the first year of studies. Then, if they managed to emerge successful from the summer exam session, they went on to their chosen faculty. Robakowski and Bruszewski studied direction of photography.[47] In 1969, Paweł Kwiek and Zbigniew Rybczyński were admitted to the direction of photography faculty, whereas Andrzej Różycki – to the film direction faculty. As a high school student, Rybczyński was planning to study film direction at the Film School. He changed his mind under the influence of Professor Ksawery Piwocki, art historian, lecturer at the Academy of Fine Arts in Warsaw, whose son was in Rybczyński's school class:

> Once, I paid a visit to his house and I confessed that I intended to apply to film directing in Łódź. 'Directing is not a profession' – the professor said – 'you should apply to direction of photography, you'll get to know the workshop, you'll be a specialist. [...] I sat my exam in 1969. What mattered at the time was the general level of knowledge of art. Other people were learning that from books, for me it was my whole life, so I got a good grade. I chose the school very consciously. I believed that painting, the static image, had become a matter of the past, and I needed to enliven my passion, set it in motion.[48]

In 1970, Tadeusz Junak, Ryszard Lenczewski and Jacek Łomnicki started their education at the Film School, followed one year later by Janusz Połom and Kazimierz Bendkowski. The latter wanted to become a film director, he recalls, because of his passion for the work of Fellini and Antonioni. While still at high school, Bendkowski belonged to the amateur Film Club in Warsaw and participated as a club member in many amateur film festivals, where he presented films made on 8 mm film stock. One year before his successful attempt at the entry exams to the Film School, he received a special award at the 17th National Amateur Film Contest in Nowa Huta (23rd–26th October 1969) for his film *Glow of Shade*. Ryszard Waśko and Ryszard Lenczewski presented their films at the same festival.[49] In 1973, newcomers to the school included Lechosław Czołnowski, who participated in several actions of the WFF, as well as Janusz Kołodrubiec and Janusz Szczerek, who towards the end of the 1970s established the group Zespół T, which is recognised as somewhat of a continuation of the Workshop's activity.[50]

---

44 K. Krubski et al., op. cit., p. 168.

45 Interview with Ryszard Gajewski, July 2016.

46 Quite revealingly, the members of the group included the information about their 'transfer' to cinematography in their biographical notes. This fact bears testimony to the importance of such decision in the Workshop milieu – it practically marked a rupture with the group. Cf. R. Waśko, op. cit.

47 Since 1970, Bruszewski also studied film directing, graduating five years later.

48 K. Krubski et al., op. cit., pp. 196–97.

49 J. Peltz, op. cit..

50 Ł. Ronduda, *Polish Art of the 70s.*, Warsaw: Centre for Contemporary Art Ujazdowski Castle, 2009, pp. 259–70.

A lot was required from candidates to the Film School, and the students' expectations were even higher. As revealed in the memories of Józef Robakowski, the latter were soon in for a disappointment:

> We hardly had any classes in autumn. The teachers would avoid us or hide from us. Lectures were given only by Lewicki and Karabasz; it was as if the rest of them had evaporated. We realised that we were being tricked. Then, we started the first revolution at the School – we summoned a school parliament, to which we invited the professors and asked them: what do they want to teach us? It turned out that they had little to say. That was a critical moment. There were still outstanding individuals who acted as a driving force. Zanussi, Piwowski, Grzegorz Królikiewicz were on the point of graduating. They managed brilliantly, because that's how outstanding individuals always manage. But we came across nothing but huge chaos in terms of teaching methods.[51]

Similar memories are shared by Tomasz Zygadło, a film and television director, who studied at the Film School since 1970:

> For three months we were hanging around the School, lost and unsupervised. I felt deceived and convinced that I was losing time. Disturbed by such state of affairs, we began to revolt together with our colleagues against the fact that nobody teaches us – students of film directing – how to make films.[52]

Ryszard Gajewski recalls:

> After the successful entry exams, it turned out that the legends about great professors, who are at the same time outstanding 'active' directors, could not be confirmed in reality. It was pure fiction. We were taught virtually nothing that made sense because the professors were largely people who had reached the peak of their creative potential before the war. We were taught the very things that were required from us at those horrible exams. For example, at the first year, we began a course in art history, while our knowledge of it had already been tested. Instead of expanding our knowledge, we were hearing about the basics. We were shown some faded slides in a small dark room. Everybody slept in those classes. It was similar with the subject 'photosensitive materials.' We were taught things that had become completely obsolete at the time, as if they expected us to start making film stock ourselves. Of course, those were theoretical classes, full of chemical formulas, which we gracefully called 'little coffins.' Talented people could not manage to get a credit for that subject and dropped out after the first year. But unfortunately, we weren't taught how to make films.[53]

Zbigniew Rybczyński adds a different perspective to those memories:

> The School gave students complete liberty. If you want to lazy about, just do it; if you want to learn – you've got the possibilities. But my colleagues were mostly playboys and they weren't keen on learning the technique. I was working from one film etude to another, I was greedy to make films. I was the only student to have keys to the School. I wouldn't go on holidays – I would make films.[54]

---

51 K. Krubski et al., op. cit, p. 185.

52 Ibidem.

53 Interview with Ryszard Gajewski in January 2016.

54 K. Krubski et al., op. cit, p. 206.

The Workshop artists changed the atmosphere of the School. A sort of 'foothold' for their activities was the Department of Photography with its staff of older and not very active teachers. The new, creative and bold ideas of the WFF members did not meet with strong resistance.[55] Feridun Erol, a graduate in direction of photography in 1965, and in film direction in 1967, recalled:

> The end of our epoch was imperceptibly approaching [...] the generation of Robakowski came to the School. They brought tape-recorder tapes, loudspeakers, electronics.[56]

In turn, Jacek Korcelli, who graduated from the faculty of direction of photography in 1958, admitted that the group sparked a different way of thinking about cinema: 'The team led by Robakowski may not have dominated the School, but it was a germ of creative anxiety and a point of reference.'[57]

Maeve Connolly remarks that the impact of the group on the cinematographic education model at the Film School has remained unexplored.[58] The School has not tapped into the Workshop's oeuvre to shape its students and itself as an institution. Yet, on a provisional basis, in the School's lengthy and difficult period in the first half of the 1970s, the Workshop became an 'enclave of freedom in a place that lacked breathing air.'[59] The rigid structure of the School not only did not limit the activities of the group, but it even became a breeding ground. The strategy of tapping into niches and loopholes in the system in order to change it became a major part of the WFF's identity, akin to many other progressive artistic groups worldwide.[60]

Łódź

Trembling machines
Howling sirens
And thousands of chimneys
This is our city of Łódź
Anthem of the Workshop acc. to a traditional workers' song

The activity of the Workshop of the Film Form is often described primarily as a self-reflective 'analysis of new media.' This statement is somewhat clichéd and conveys a superficial grasp of the phenomenon, implying that the work of the WFF was isolated from everyday life. Yet, it was the everyday that the Workshop members were particularly open to. One of the manifestations of that approach were the group's frequent 'interventions' in the urban space. The city provided a stage of their activities, whereas their films and photographs have preserved fragments of the urban landscape.

---

55 Ibidem, p. 227
56 Ibidem.
57 Ibidem.
58 See: p. 67.
59 Ibidem, p. 226.
60 For instance, the American group Videofreex, established in the aftermath of the festival in Woodstock. The members were invited by the legendary producer Don West to create the pilot episode of the programme *Subject to Change* on CBS. The programme did not air, but owing to their collaboration with the TV station, Videofreex got hold of television equipment, which they later used in their own activities.

The future members of the WFF were obviously attracted to Łódź by the Film School, but the city itself also became an essential element of their practice. They never intended to create their own isolated studio or gallery space. They did not want to limit and isolate themselves. The urban space was what they wished to explore and conquer.

Importantly, for none of them was Łódź a home town but Józef Robakowski lived there with his mother and younger brother since 1948. Paweł Kwiek, Jacek Łomnicki and Kazimierz Bendkowski came to Łódź from Warsaw, Andrzej Różycki – from his studies in Toruń. Janusz Połom hails from Olsztyn, Ryszard Waśko from Nysa, and Wojciech Bruszewski from Wrocław. Only Zbigniew Rybczyński was born in Łódź, but he later moved with his parents to Warsaw. Therefore, the Workshop members looked at the city from a non-sentimental perspective, without the filters of childhood memories. Instead, they observed it with openness and courage, akin to the way some of them had perceived Toruń, where they were also looking for 'no man's land' – public or semi-public spaces that could be temporarily appropriated. This is also the reason why they spent so much time with each other: they did not have family homes in Łódź, to which they could return after lectures and classes. They stayed together also after the classes, which favoured the consolidation of their community. Indeed, it is obviously easier to annex urban space in a guerilla spirit as a group than individually. Such creative 'appropriation' would have probably occurred in any other city or place where the WFF members had met and started working together. Yet, since it happened in Łódź, let us take a brief look at the city as it was at the time.

World War II destroyed the social tissue of the multicultural workers' city. As a result of the annihilation of the Jewish community, emigration as well as escape and forced resettlement of Germans, the post-war Łódź essentially became a homogeneous, single-nation and single-religion city. Yet, infrastructure and architecture survived. Therefore, among other reasons, after the war the city functioned for around two years as the administrative centre and the capital of Polish culture.[61] It was here, and not in Warsaw, that the Ministry of Culture operated, akin to provisional editorial offices of many magazines, as well as theatres: the Polish Army Theatre was headed by Leon Schiller, whereas the Chamber Theatre – by Erwin Axer. In the years 1948–1949, public institutions and many cultural centres gradually returned to Warsaw, yet many representatives of artistic and cultural milieus stayed in Łódź – a prominent example, among other figures, is Prof. Bolesław Lewicki, with whom the Workshop members had classes in the field of the language and semiotics of film.

That period, known as 'Łódź transit,' stimulated the development of the city which provided an impulse for the city to develop in this direction. By virtue of the decision of the Polish Communist authorities, Łódź was to become a major centre of culture and science, although there was still considerable room for improvement with regard to the level of education, also at the primary level (as late as in 1957, ca. 15 000 inhabitants under 35 were illiterate, and 35% of the city's population did not finish primary school).[62] As for tertiary education, two subsidiary institutions were initially established – of the University of Life Sciences and Warsaw School of Economics. They were followed by subsequent, already independent academic centres: State Higher Pedagogical School (incorporated in 1956 into the University of Łódź), whereas the new artistic education institutions

61 *Ilustrowana Encyklopedia Łodzi. Lata powojenne, czasy PRL*, ed. A. Grzegorzczyk, Łódź: Urząd Miasta Łodzi, 2010, p. 296, http://uml.lodz.pl/get.php?id=2947 [accessed 27-12-2016].

62 Ibidem, p. 302.

included the State Higher School of Visual Arts, State Higher School of Theatre, and State Higher School of Music. The Film School was established in 1948, and two years later it was granted academic rights as the Higher Film School; as of December 1969, it operated as the Leon Schiller National Higher School of Film, Television and Theatre.

The decade of the 1960s marks a period of certain stagnation in the cultural life of the city and another wave of increased pressure from the Communist Party following the political 'thaw' of 1956. In 1968, such situation met with social resistance also in Łódź. In response to the brutal suppression of students' protests in Warsaw, on the 11th of March students in Łódź organised a manifestation, followed by occupations. Many of them were expelled or suspended in the aftermath of the protests. It was similar with the rectors of the University of Łodź and the Film School. The purge that embraced mainly artistic and journalistic circles was accompanied by an anti-Semitic bashing. Some academics were forced to step down from their positions. More or less a thousand people – representatives of intelligentsia and creative milieux – left Łódź as a result of persecutions and emigrated abroad.[63]

The decade of Edward Gierek, the 1970s, came as the period of a seeming opening of the Communist authorities to international collaboration and the needs of the society, as well as a time of a seeming economic success. Vast infrastructural projects financed with loans transformed also the cityscape of Łódź. The city acquired a more metropolitan character – old buildings were demolished and the acquired land served to build urban mass housing. Acting as the showcase of the 'modernity' of Gierek's epoch were, for example, the tower blocks of the City Centre Residential Estate: 14-25-storey buildings crowned with characteristic 'boxes,' which housed artists' studios[64] (in one of such blocks of flats Józef Robakowski created his Exchange Gallery in his apartment in 1978). Besides, modern commercial complexes, monumental hospitals, university buildings were raised in Łódź, such as the Carpet Factory 'Dywilan,' from which Workshop members borrowed CCTV cameras.[65]

The expanding city must have impressed the young people (especially those who came from the provinces), and it certainly became an inspiration. The WFF members did not want to concentrate on self-reflective meditations on the medium of film. They wanted to see what really could be *seen*. If Łódź was their reality and everyday environment, they felt the urge to listen to the rhythm of the city, to see it, to listen to it and to squeeze everything they could out of it. For this reason, broad urban landscape and crowded streets are so frequent to feature in the WFF's films and photographs (particularly in works by Ryszard Waśko). Many of them present an image of the city that is different from the official propaganda – for instance, Bendkowski's film *Area* portrays derelict enclosed backyards and tenement houses whose grim atmosphere is highlighted by the soundtrack. Łódź can also be seen in Robakowski's film *Market* (1971) and *I'm going* (1973) where the artist climbs an old parachute tower, and in video-installations by Mikołajczyk, as well as in photographs by Różycki and Bendkowski. A very interesting project situated in this context was *Television Transmission*, in which the artists used video transmission to 'introduce' live images of the city into an institutional space – Muzeum Sztuki. A noteworthy action in the public space was also Robakowski's and Antczak's *Furniture Sale at Red Market Square*.

63 Ibidem, p. 313.
64 Ibidem, p. 317.
65 Interview with Andrzej Różycki, July 2014.

Another urban thread in the Workshop's oeuvre consists in the impact of the folk culture of Łódź, whose most prominently representative was Wacław Antczak, a charismatic member of the non-professional art world and a full-right member of the WFF. Józef Robakowski met him in the cafeteria of the Film School, where Mister Wacek had become a fixture. He was always seeking contact and conversation with 'the film people,' but they mostly ignored him.[66] Antczak fascinated Robakowski with his personality and a disinterested, radical and engaged approach. He eventually joined the Workshop of the Film Form, accompanied the group in their travels, played the violin and even gave violin lessons to Paweł Kwiek, who had been passionate about music since his childhood. He participated actively in interventions and artistic actions, such as *The Eighth Cinema*[67] or *Permanent Sale of Wares of Dubious Origin* in Red Market Square – an action by Robakowskki in which Antczak played the main role.[68] He carried out his own individual performances. What is more, Antczak appeared as an extra in many feature films, such as Marek Piwowski's *The Cruise*.

The complex relationship between the Workshop and Łódź culminated with the festival *Construction in Process*, organised in 1981 less than one month prior to the imposition of martial law in Poland. The initiative of Ryszard and Maria Waśko materialised in collaboration and with support of the other already former members of the Workshop, for whom it marked the definitive end of the group's activity. Participants included Polish and international artists, who came to Łódź and created their works on site. The public space of Łódź, which was normally subjected to censorship, as well as industrial and postindustrial sites became home to the largest international contemporary art show in Poland after World War II. The motto of the exhibition was a statement by Mieczysław Szczuka, one of the founders of the group Blok: 'Art must not be an empty ornament of the society.' Aleksandra Jach wrote:

> Also the a.r. group was evoked, and thereby the international avant-garde community and the a.r. collection, as well as its educational-social dimension. The folder that accompanied the show featured portraits of Strzemiński and Kobro. The continuation of the legacy of the avant-garde was marked through the figures of the artists themselves, and not merely through a reflection on 'construction.' A similar gesture was the appointment of Henryk Stażewski – one of the members of a.r. – to the honourable committee of the exhibition.[69]

Thus, the tradition of Łódź, a pillar of the Workshop's identity, became manifested through the event that marked the end of the group's activity.

Reclaimed Tradition

Tradition was right here, in Łódź. One just needed to get on the right track

Józef Robakowski in conversation with Tomasz Samosionek

University programmes in museum studies and art history completed in Toruń before the entry exams to the Film School in Łódź by Andrzej Różycki, Józef Robakowski bore the fruit of their

66 Interview with Józef Robakowski, July 2014.

67 Statement by Grzegorz Królikiewicz in the film *A Different City*, dir. Maria Waśko, 1999. Cf. *Żywa Galeria*, p. 39.

68 *Ósme kino*, leaflet, Łódź 1971, archive of the Exchange Gallery, http://repozytorium.fundacjaarton.pl/index.php?action-view/object&objid-3162&colid-75&catid-18 [accessed 30-12-2016].

69 A. Jach, 'Konstrukcja w procesie. Wspólnota, która nadeszła?,' in *Odrzucone dziedzictwo. O sztuce polskiej lat 80.*, Warsaw: Museum of Modern Art, 2014, pp. 136–47.

interest in the oeuvre of artists from the circle of pre-war Constructivism, which influenced their artistic approach. The Workshop members not only to referred to the legacy of the avant-garde, but also confronted it by asking about the same phenomena and problems as those they explored in their own work.

Yet, to make that confrontation possible, they first needed to learn about the past. It was difficult to the extent that at the turn of the 1970s the picture of pre-war Polish art was far from complete. The oeuvre was first destroyed by the war, and later by the Communist authorities.[70] Although the continuity seemed broken, the students of the Film School in Łódź discovered that they did not need to look far. After all, it was Łódź that towards the end of the 1920s became a major landmark not only of Polish but also European avant-garde. It was here that Katarzyna Kobro, Julian Przyboś, Władysław Strzemiński and Henryk Stażewski (joined slightly later by Jan Brzękowski) founded the group a.r. in 1929 and established the International Modern Art Collection. The idea to create the collection originated from Strzemiński's observations from his time in Russia, where the holdings of the modern art collector Shchukin stirred considerable interest when made publicly accessible.[71] Attempts to establish a similar collection in Poland did not yield any results for a long time. It was only on the 15th of February 1931 – after successful talks with the Municipal Council of Łódź – that the collection was made available for viewing. Strzemiński and Kobro worked on complementing the holdings until 1938.[72] Insofar as the Łódź *genius loci* should not be mythologised, the city became home to a collection of artworks that represented the avant-garde currents and tendencies of the end of the 1920s.[73]

The collection formed the core of the holdings of the Muzeum Sztuki in Łódź, an institution that played a major role in the history of the Workshop of the Film Form. It was particularly in the second half of the 1970s – owing to the then director Ryszard Stanisławski – that the museum acted as a link between the first and the second avant-garde. Most importantly, it offered access to its pre-war holdings. Many works were destroyed during the war,[74] but some survived the occupation 'only because the German museum authorities pursued the project of organising a 'degenerated art' exhibition.'[75]

Marian Minich, the Museum director since 1935, attempted to reactivate the institution immediately after the war. Among other contributions, it was made possible by the donations made in 1945 by both Strzemiński and Kobro. Her scarce preserved spatial compositions under-

70 See A. Rottenberg, *Sztuka w Polsce 1945–2005*, Warsaw: STENTOR, 2005, pp. 17–20.

71 A. Turowski, *W kręgu Strzemińskiego. Blok–Praesens–a.r.*, Warsaw: Centralne Biuro Wystaw Artystycznych, 1973, pp. 23–4.

72 Ibidem.

73 Until 1939 the collection comprised at least 112 works, mostly paintings, but also sculptures (Alexander Calder, Katarzyna Kobro) and photomontages (Mieczysław Szczuka). Considering its period, it included an excellent representation of works by abstract artists (Hans Arp and Sophie Taeuber-Arp, Theo van Doesburg, Jean Gorin, Jean Hélion, Vilmos Huszár, Henryk Stażewski and Georges Vantongerloo), Cubists (Fernand Léger and Louis Marcoussis), Futurists (Enrico Prampolini), Dadaists (Kurt Schwitters), Surrealists (Max Ernst, Kurt Seligmann), Formists (Leon Chwistek, Tytus Czyżewski), Constructivists (Aleksander Rafałowski, Andrzej Pronaszko), Unists (Władysław Strzemiński), and the representatives of 'pure form' (Stanisław Ignacy Witkiewicz). See U. Czartoryska, *Kolekcja sztuki XX w. w Muzeum Sztuki w Łodzi*, exhibition catalogue, Warsaw: Zachęta, 1991.

74 'Works by Picasso, Léger, Gleizes, Marcoussis, Ozenfat, Prampolini, Torres-Garcia, Herbin, Seuphor, Gorin, (...) sculptures by Pronaszko from his Expressionist period, and finally *Mobiles* by the American Alexander Calder, disappeared.' M. Minich, 'Szalona Galeria,' in *Marian Minich – pod wiatr*, ed. A. Minich-Scholz, Warsaw: Instytut Wydawniczy Książka i Prasa, 2015, p. 287.

75 Ibidem.

went thorough conservation works under the artist's supervision. The Museum found a new seat in 1948 in the former Poznański palace in Więckowskiego St. It was there that Strzemiński's design of the Neoplastic Room was implemented in 1948, which was destroyed in 1950 and reconstructed in 1960. In turn, in January and February 1973, the same building hosted *Action Workshop*, the culmination of the WFF's history.

Fortunately for the Workshop members, the beginning of the 1970s came as a period of reclaiming and bringing back the tradition of the avant-garde, in which Ryszard Stanisławski became a figure of great merit.[76] Janusz Zagrodzki, affiliated with the Workshop, continued his research into the work of Katarzyna Kobro, who had been almost completely repressed from the collective awareness in the 1950s. In 1973, Zagrodzki was invited by Jerzy Kotowski to deliver lectures in art history at the Film School. Józef Robakowski recalls: 'It turned out that the tradition of analytical thinking on art was present in the work of Władysław Strzemiński and Katarzyna Kobro. Hence the cult of the a.r. group.'[77]
It was therefore a favourable time. In 1973, the Muzeum Sztuki prepared for the Folkwang Museum in Essen and the Kröller-Müller Museum in Otterlo the first international group showcase of Constructivism (Berlewi, Hiller, Kobro, Stażewski, Strzemiński), and the Polish avant-garde began its 'triumphal procession around the most renowned museums worldwide.'[78]

Notwithstanding certain differences in opinions, the analogies between the principles of the a.r. group and the Workshop are essentially clear both in terms of thinking about the artwork and the artistic stance. They can be found, for instance, by analysing Strzemiński's text *B–2*, in which he outlined the rules of 'new art.' In the article, Strzemiński emphasised the role of creativity, opposing it to representational and mimetic procedures. The author claimed that the point of departure for the artwork consists in recognising the 'conditions of its existence – indicating the elements of its structure. The borders of the work of art are its formal borders.'[79]

Those postulates were repeated by the WFF members primarily in relation to the medium of film:

> Here [at the WFF – M.K.], attempts are being made to develop the means of description [of film – M.K.] lying outside the theory of literature, hence the revival of interests in the so-called pure cinema and the efforts to purify film from any possible narrative structures and the methodology of the literary poetics. Again, much attention was given to verify the so-called 'substance of the film structure' based on the characteristics of phono-photographic recording. Any comparative interpretations were rejected, such as juxtaposing film with painting, music, theatre, poetry and literary narrative ... Especially valid is the fact of questioning the links between film and literature, or contradicting the quite common view of the 'literature-bound' nature of the film phenomenon, a concept reasonably backed up by many broadly recognised theorists of film art.[80]

---

76 A. Turowski, *W kręgu Strzemińskiego*, p. 121.
77 T. Samosionek, op. cit.
78 A. Turowski, *W kręgu Strzemińskiego*, p. 121.
79 W. Strzemiński, 'B–2,' *Blok*, 8–9, 1924, quoted in A. Turowski, *Konstruktywizm polski, próba rekonstrukcji nurtu (1921-1934)*, Wrocław: Zakład Narodowy im. Ossolińskich, 1981, pp. 64–5.
80 J. Robakowski, 'Bezjęzykowa koncepcja semiologiczna filmu,' *Zeszyt Warsztatu Formy Filmowej*, 7, 1975, http://robakowski.eu/tx2.html [accessed 30-12-2016].

Both for the Workshop and a.r. found it important to discover the formal borders of the medium and the principles of its structure, as well as to do away with the division into form and content. The latter aspect is prominent in activities and texts by Kobro and Strzemiński[81] and in the Workshop's practice, where it received its fullest manifestation in the WFF's structural films.[82] Both groups also shared a critique of what Strzemiński described as 'provisional-propaganda activities.'[83] An echo of that critique came in the form of the Workshop's resistance to participation in the official cinematographic circulation, which would inevitably lead to an entanglement in the apparatus of propaganda and censorship.

As Ryszard W. Kluszczyński wrote, those examples portray a unification of two discourses – the artistic and the non-artistic – whose co-existence characterised the avant-garde art in the decades between the two World Wars. In structural film, artistic discourse becomes minimised. Its form serves as a pretext for extra-artistic considerations and it does not attract the viewers' attention any more than the content. The opposite is also not the case, because one stems from the other, and even becomes identical. From Kluszczyński's perspective, that strategy of the WFF was supposed to compel the viewer's reflection on the nature of cinema as a medium.[84] From our point of view it is also an interesting example of a building up on the Constructivists' tradition, who entered into polemics with the content-form dualism of the artwork.

It is noteworthy that the WFF members also revealed fascination with Constructivists in their documentary films. In collaboration with Janusz Zagrodzki, the Workshop artists worked in the Studio of Small Film Forms 'Se-ma-for' on the short documentary *The Spatial Compositions of Katarzyna Kobro* (35 mm, 1971) with Tadeusz Junak's voiceover of the fragments of Kobro's and Strzemiński's book *Kompozycja przestrzeni. Obliczenia rytmu czasoprzestrzennego* [Spatial Composition. Calculations of the Temporal-Spatial Rhythm] juxtaposed with her sculptures from the collection of the Muzeum Sztuki. The soundtrack to the film was created by Eugeniusz Rudnik; consultations were provided by Bolesław Utkin, a disciple of Strzemiński and author of the reconstruction of the Neoplastic Room. Robakowski's concept with regard to the film was clear and consisted in possibly the broadest and clearest presentation of works by Katarzyna Kobro, as well as bringing the essence of her theory closer to the viewer. The film comes to an end with the artist's synthetic biographical note. The first monographic book on Kobro was published only a decade later, and therefore the film functioned for a long time as a compendium of knowledge about the artist.[85] Robakowski's memories from the film's pre-release preview reveal a lot about the reception of Kobro's work in the 1970s:

> One of the participants told me: 'Mr Józef, but you've created a mystification here that Kobro was some kind of outstanding artist, and she was just a normal wife of Strzemiński. We need to change it in your commentary because you cannot waste your words like that.'[86]

81 K. Kobro and W. Strzemiński, *Kompozycja przestrzeni. Obliczenia rytmu czasoprzestrzennego*. Łódź: Muzeum Sztuki, 2010.

82 For example, *Text-Door* by Bruszewski (35 mm, 1973), *Test II* by Robakowski (35 mm, 1971), and above all *Configuration I–IV* (35 mm, 1973) and *A-B-C-D-E-F – 1-36* by Waśko (35 mm, 1974).

83 A. Turowski, *W kręgu Strzemińskiego*, p. 22.

84 R. W. Kluszczyński, op. cit., p. 32.

85 J. Zagrodzki, *Katarzyna Kobro i kompozycja przestrzeni*, Warszawa : Państwowe Wydawnictwa Naukowe, 1984.

86 J. Robakowski, 'Kino rozszerzone i kino materiałowe,' interview by G. Borkowski, *Tranzystor–CSWZU*, 4, 2012, pp. 7–8, http://csw.art.pl/upload/file/1207tranzystor_cswzu_4.pdf [accessed 30-12-2016].

In terms of reference points in the history of avant-garde film, once again it turned out that the WFF members did not need to look far – in the archive of the Film School in Łódź they came across the film by Franciszka (1907–1988) and Stefan (1910–1988) Themerson, *The Adventure of a Good Citizen*, a work that provided the starting point for the explorations of the oeuvre of the artists and other representatives of the pre-war film avant-garde.[87]

Since ca 1930, film stirred an increased interest in the Constructivist circles, primarily in the milieu of Praesens (mainly owing to the Themersons and critic Zygmunt Tonecki). Yet, few works did actuallycome into being. Due to the high cost of materials, film was often replaced with photomontage (with all due awareness of the means of expression involved in that medium).[88] Prior to the outbreak of World War II, the Themersons created five films: *Pharmacy* (35 mm, 1930), *Europe* (35 mm, 1931/32) – based on Anatol Stern's poem under the same title, *Moment Musical* (35 mm, 1933) – commissioned by Wanda Golińska's accessories company, *Short Circuit* (35 mm, 1935) – commissioned by the Institute of Social Affairs in Warsaw, and *The Adventure of a Good Citizen* (35 mm, 1937).

The latter film was found by the WFF members in the archive of the Film School, which gave rise to the group's fascination with the Themersons. Thenceforth *The Adventure* was screened by the WFF as often as possible. Robakowski also asked Stefan, who resided in London since 1942, to send the cutting script of the film *Europe*.[89] Robakowski recalls:

> We promoted Stefan Themerson during 'Kinolaboratorium,' and at the Film School we used every opportunity to show *The Adventure of a Good Citizen*, akin to films by Richter, which we came across in the archive and which turned out to be outstanding examples of the pre-war avant-garde traditions in film.[90]

The common denominator between the two generations of film avant-garde artists were not specific works, but an artistic approach that was open to experimentation in a plethora of different disciplines and dimensions of art. Paweł Kwiek recalls:

> I very early realised that I wanted to work in the field of art, and not film. I did want to express myself using that medium, but 'classic' feature or documentary filmmaking was never my goal. At the time I thought that I would become a director of photography after graduating from the School, but above all I was very eager to explore film, its potential, from the technical side. I wanted to understand the medium. When in 1970 I started my studies at the Film School, I discovered that owing to a certain group of people it was a place that favoured art making. An informal master-disciple system was in place at the School. Insofar as it was possible, students chose the people who shaped them. I found myself under the influence of Robakowski, and my first conscious artistic choice was to

---

87 The Workshop members established mail contact with the Themersons. Upon Themerson's invitation, Bruszewski, Robakowski and Waśko participated in 1979 in the exhibition *Film as Film. Formal experimental film 1910–1975* at the Hayward Gallery in London, where they met in person. See I. Schwarz, *Archive für Künstlerpublikationen der 1960er bis 1980er Jahre*, Cologne: Salon Verlag, 2008. Fragment translated by A. Szymanowska available online http://robakowski.eu/tx46.html [accessed 30-12-2016].

88 A. Turowski, *Konstruktywizm polski*, p. 105.

89 B. Cook and Ł. Ronduda, *Films by Franciszka and Stefan Themerson*, Warsaw – London: Centre for Contemporary Art Ujazdowski Castle – LUX, 2007, p. 67.

90 T. Samosionek, *Sztuka video w Polsce*, Łódź: 1989, http://robakowski.eu/tx23.html [accessed 28-12-2016].

join the Workshop of the Film Form. From then on, I started to demonstrate an approach that opposed the history of cinema, the official commercial way of thinking about film.'[91]

Besides their approach to the past of the film avant-garde, a factor that distinguished the WFF members amongst other students was also their perspective on the theory and history of film. They felt the need to consult theoretical text and one of the Workshop's major readings was Karol Irzykowski's (1873–1944) book *X muza* [The Tenth Muse] from 1924.[92] Using the term 'pure cinema,' which was so important for the Workshop members, the author analysed the competences of the medium of film and the potential complexity of the relation between the film image as well as music and words. He assumed that every discipline of art had its borders and potential. Irzykowski wrote: 'All arts have their own distinct properties, which thwart the attempts pursued by aestheticians to embrace them within a uniform system.'[93] In his view, the relation between music and words did not pose a 'threat' to the autonomy of film. Evoking the history of reflection on the borders of painting, poetry and music, Irzykowski claimed that the idea to establish cinema on its 'own' values was worthwhile, but an 'exaggerated penchant for purification,' understood as the willingness to purge film of 'alien elements' may lead to sterilisation:

> To emancipate cinema from theatre, painting, literature, to achieve 'pure cinema'! Well, want it as well, and I continue to talk about it, but it does not mean that cinema should be devoid of life and sterilised. A theorist in his laboratory may ponder upon isolated cinema, yet a visual artist cannot resign from shaping the living entanglement of phenomena that formally seem to belong to different arts. This is the difficulty: to capture the flame. Cinema may therefore – as we have already said – make use of the material of other arts without losing itself.[94]

It was a way adopted several decades later by the Workshop, which on the one hand pursued the goal of purging cinema of narrativity and anecdotes, but on the other hand – broadened the range of its inspirations. This tendency is shown by the fact that at different stages of its activity the group comprised not only the students of the Film School but also, for instance, poets, such as Kader Lagtaa[95] and Wacław Antczak. Another very important matter for the WFF was the question of film's entanglement in broadly understood commercialism. Irzykowski commented on it as follows:

> The development of cinematographic art lends itself to comparison with the development of a plant squashed by stones. These stones are industry and commerce, which impose their own conditions. Cinema, in order to be reborn, must [...] catch a breath of disinterestedness for a brief while.[96]

The reading of *X muza* must have strongly resonated with the beliefs of the Workshop members, who – as if in response to Irzykowski's claim – underscored the problem already in their first manifesto

91 Interview with Paweł Kwiek, July 2015.

92 Interview with Józef Robakowski, July 2014.

93 K. Irzykowski, *Dziesiąta muza. Zagadnienia estetyczne kina*, Warsaw: Wydawnictwa Artystyczne i Filmowe 1960, p. 70.

94 Ibidem, p. 100.

95 R. Waśko, op. cit., p. 9. Lagtaa published his poems in the magazine of the Workshop of the Film Form in 1974, he also collaborated with Andrzej Partum's Office of Poetry and Ewa Partum. Lagtaa was the author of the script for the film *Collage*, based on a poem by André Breton.

96 K. Irzykowski, op. cit., p. 116.

The Workshop does not engage in any commercial activity and its members work strictly on a non-profit basis.[97]

The essence of reflection included in *X muza* consists in the necessity of finding solutions for film that are alternative both to cinematography, which caters for the tastes of the broad audiences, and to the film avant-garde from the years between the two World Wars, whose representatives associated cinema with movement. According to Irzykowski, that situation led to the already mentioned 'isolation of cinema' and its 'sterilisation.' Apart from movement, the author also pointed at the constitutive role of light in cinema – akin to the postulate of using a broad spectrum of means of expression in film, that view proved inspirational for the WFF members. In a chapter of *X Muza* that is very interesting for that matter Irzykowski describes film based on 'photographic reproduction of reality' as equal to animated film. Such perspective will also become reflected in the Workshop's practice, particularly in films by Zbigniew Rybczyński.

Another direct 'link' between the Workshop and the tradition of the pre-war film avant-garde was Professor Bolesław Lewicki (1908–81), who became the rector of the Film School in 1968. A pre-war graduate of the Jan Kazimierz University in Lviv, Lewicki was a disciple of Juliusz Kleiner, among other figures, author of the famous essay *U wrót nowej estetyki*[98] [At the Gates of New Aesthetics], in which the phenomenon of film was noticed probably for the first time in the Polish context as an object of scholarly reflection. Lewicki himself devoted his texts to film already in the 1930s, when he also attended the seminar of Professor Witold Romer at the Lviv University of Technology, devoted to photosensitive materials. In 1932, he was also the initiator (and later the secretary and the head) of the film club 'Avant-garde' in Lviv, based on similar French institutional models to champion 'artistic cinema' and integrate the intellectual milieux. Lewicki also attended the seminar of Roman Ingarden in which cinema became a subject of scholarly reflection.[99] Lewicki arrived in Łódź in 1947, during the period of the city's post-war cultural revival. He took up a position not only at the Film School, but also at the university. Within the Department of Literary Theory, he set up immensely popular film studies. At the Film School, Lewicki headed the Department of Theory and History of Film, where he ran classes in the language and semiotics of film, which the WFF members eagerly attended. Józef Robakowski recalls:

> In his eccentric and lively classes, still in the 1960s, at the Film School we analysed various film editing structures, drawing up virtual scores on paper. It was him who since 1966 gave us historic and current reading, broadly embracing the development of film and photographic thought. Owing to him we became familiar with writings by Irzykowski, Arnheim, Van Lir, Epstein, Helman, Jackiewicz, May, Levi-Strauss, Jakobson, Ingarden, Morin, Schaff, McLuhan, Barthes, Metz... A. Bazin's book *Film i rzeczywistość* [Film and Reality][100], published in Poland (1963) was our essential reading.[101]

---

97 I Manifesto of the WFF, Łódź 1970, quoted in R. W. Kluszczyński, op. cit., p. 60.

98 J. Kleiner, 'U wrót nowej estetyki,' *Tygodnik Ilustrowany*, 4, 1929, p. 62.

99 J. Rek, 'Profesor Bolesław W. Lewicki – między filmem i literaturą,' *Acta Universitatis Lodziensis. Folia Litteraria Polonica*, 9, 2007, p. 334.

100 Collection of A. Bazin's essays published in Poland under the title Film and Reality.

101 J. Robakowski 'Podrzuceni mistrzowie,' no data, http://robakowski.eu/tx19.html [accessed 30-12-2016].

In turn, Ryszard Gajewski remembers Lewicki as follows:

> It was from him that we learnt about Umberto Eco and his 'Open work.' Semantics and semiotics appeared at the School, raising fear among the students. I remember his lecture in which he made impressive scribbles on the board in order to demonstrate that film can be represented by means of formulas. Obviously, the Workshop's first films were not made on the basis of formulas.[102]

A summary of Lewicki's views needs to highlight his view of film as a 'second branch of literature,' which was best exemplified or even incarnated by adaptation. The WFF's declared identification with Lewicki's views may come across as striking, for instance in the light of such a statement by Robakowski:

> In my current work in the Workshop of the Film Form [...] I have the possibility to conduct virtually unlimited tests and experiments that consist in investigating the borders of perception of my films by other people [...] I carry out theoretical and practical tests in order to find and learn certain specific features of film, because I think that [...] this discipline must be 'purged' of the excessive burden of literature.[103]

Yet, it is noteworthy that the WFF's postulated 'purging' of film was not a goal in itself. It was to serve the needs of analysing reality in all its complexity, embracing the relation between the perceiving and the perceived. One of major films that put those postulates to work was Paweł Kwiek's student's etude *1, 2, 3... Cinematographer's Exercises* (35 mm, 1972). The filmmaker freely manipulated stylistically diverse fragments of films and animations in a way that made it impossible to unambiguously read his intentions or the distinct message of the film. 'Purging' therefore consisted in releasing film from the obligation of storytelling, which does not mean that it stood in the way of investigating the relations between film and literature. From such perspective, the work of the WFF and the views of theorists evoked by the group as an inspiration indeed seem close. The WFF members were not vulnerable to the excess of 'laboratory work,' against which Irzykowski warned his readers. Cinema interested them at many levels, also with regard to its social impact and functioning. They deliberately resigned from traditional means of expression in film in order to confront the viewers' habitual expectations seek interaction with them. Such situation often led to tense disputes, even in the circles who shared the WFF's views on art.[104]

The Workshop members functioned freely at the crossroads of various media and therefore they often consciously resigned from the privileges granted by their status as students of the Film School (such as the possibility to use 35 mm film stock or rent a production truck). Therefore, the WFF's body of work also comprised films without camera and films without film stock, as well as films in the form of objects.[105] Such 'soft' use of media, search for intermedia spaces and creating niches for experimentation also brought the Workshop closer to Irzykowski's theories, but above all to the creative practice of the Themersons and such works as *Europe*, based on a poem

---

102 Interview with Ryszard Gajewski, January 2016.

103 J. Robakowski, 'Jeszcze raz o "czysty film",' *Polska*, 10, 1971, http://robakowski.eu/teksty.html [accessed [illegible]-12-2016].

104 For instance, during the 5th Biennial of Spatial Forms in Elbląg in 1973. See: chapter *Elbląg. Cinema in the Service of Rebellion*.

105 For example, Robakowski's *Lightbox* (1971) and Gajewski's *Film Sausage* (1973), *Comb* (1973).

by Anatol Stern under the same title, or the film *Pharmacy*, which the Themersons created in genuinely household conditions with the use of photography.[106]

Summarising the Workshop's search for inspiration in the tradition of the avant-garde, Robakowski stated:

> It was our good tradition. It was needed, it gave us comfort and offered new possibilities of participation in film events, such as Documenta in Kassel, in Cologne, in London. A very important thing was that the tradition was right at hand, and everything certainly would not have been so significant without it. In international discussions we could always say: 'But wait a moment! This is you, but we also have Szpakowski, Hiller, Szczuka, Podsadecki, etc., etc.'[107]

Beyond the Film Form. Video and Television

The Workshop's oeuvre is discussed in detail in the final part of the book. In this section I would like to delineate three lesser known fields of the group's activity: ephemeral video installations, body art and performative actions.

To begin with, it should be noted that the members of the Workshop of the Film Form were the first Polish artists to work with video, and the makers of the vast majority of all Polish works in this medium from the 1970s. Still, this aspect of the group's practice has not yet become a topic of any monographic study. It has also been partly repressed from the scope of research on European and global history of video art.[108] Such a situation results in part from the ephemeral character of those works, known largely from photographic documentation or written descriptions. It is one of the reasons why Polish video works seldom enter museum collections and only few of them exist in artistic circulation. Yet, for some of the WFF members video was particularly significant as a medium, for example Wojciech Bruszewski used it to create some of his most important works.

Video appeared in the circle of the Workshop 'in a natural way,'[109] as Ryszard W. Kluszczyński described it. The properties and the character of the medium fitted ideally in the group's field of interests, so its use was delayed only by technological limitations. Video significantly expanded the potential of transmission and communication – two fields of seminal importance for the WFF. Offering the possibility of simultaneous record and transmission of sound and vision, video created an excellent opportunity to observe the relations between reality and its representation. For this reason, numerous video-installations by the Workshop (created primarily between 1975 and 1977) engaged with the illusory character of the image, and, akin to their films and photographs, they also analysed the tendency of human perception to succumb to that illusion. The seemingly self-reflective character of those works was merely a point of departure for explorations pursued in a wide range of directions. The artists – mainly Kwiek and Robakowski – used it to investigate

106 B. Cook and Ł. Ronduda, op. cit., pp. 44–5.

107 Ibidem.

108 Among international researchers, described only by C. Meigh-Andrews, who presented only part of the WFF's works – mainly by Bruszewski and Kwiek. See C. Meigh-Andrews, *A History of Video Art. The Development of Form and Function*, Oxford: Berg Publishers, 2006, as well as *Analogue. Pioneering Video from the UK, Canada and Poland (1968–88)*, ed. C. Meigh Andrews and C. Elwes, Preston: EDAU, University of Lancashire, 2006.

109 R. W. Kluszczyński, op. cit., pp. 51–5.

the mechanisms of manipulating the viewer in the mass media, and to observe universal laws of physics, to generate various kinds of paradoxes (Bruszewski and Waśko), and to explore human physicality and subjectivity (Bendkowski, Robakowski).

Video works created in the circle of the Workshop need to be analysed in a broader international context, especially because a Polish context was virtually non-existent in 1975. World video art began with the rise in prominence and outreach of television in the mid-20th century. Given its fundamental role in the formation of mass culture, television became an object of artists' interest as well as field and carrier of their experimentation. For them, it became what radio was to Italian Futurists – a tool that allowed them to overcome geographical and cultural distance as well as reach extremely broad audiences.[110] Yet, at the same time, on both sides of the Iron Curtain, television was regarded as a homogenous entity, which was steered top-down and served to spread consumerism (Western Europe, United States) or totalitarian propaganda (countries of the Eastern Bloc). For this reason, artists – fascinated by the medium, but at the same time aware of the need to transform it – began to use TV sets as a material of their activities. The forerunners of video art were artists from the circle of Fluxus, such as Wolf Vostell[111] and Nam June Paik,[112] who confronted the viewers with the fact of television broadcast transmission (Vostell) or tried to elicit an active reaction from them (Paik).

In Poland, the dynamic development of television – which began in 1937 with the first broadcast of an experimental TV station – was interrupted by World War II. Regular broadcasting began only in 1952 (whereas in the USA it began in 1928, in Germany and the USSR – in 1931). The Experimental Television Station of the Institute of Telecommunications in Warsaw began to air a weekly half-hour broadcast. Six years later, the Polish Television launched nationwide broadcasting, and in the 1950s local branches began to operate in seven regional capitals. In 1970, the second channel of Polish Television was inaugurated, which mainly broadcast thematic programmes.

Around the same time – at the beginning of the 1970s – the Workshop members began to use video in their work for the first time. It was indeed still a 'new medium,' because insofar as first works were created in the mid-1960s in the USA and Western Europe (and towards the end of the decade also in Canada, Australia and Japan), the spreading of the medium in Central and Eastern Europe, as well as other regions of the world, was hampered by technological deficiencies due primarily to the inaccessibility of necessary equipment. Therefore, a major breakthrough in the history of video art came when Sony's portable camera Portapak was launched on the market in 1966. It was a handy model which enabled users to single-handedly create transmission as well as record it on tape, which essentially did not require postproduction. For all those reasons, video became recognised as a democratic medium, available for almost everybody, and much more accessible than film. Professional film equipment and 35 mm film stock were often unattainable for visual artists in West Germany, England or the United States. As for the Workshop, the situation was

110 Interestingly, it was the Italian Spatialists that proclaimed in 1952 the first artistic manifesto devoted to television, titled *Manifesto del Movimento Speciale per la Televisione*.

111 Particularly the works *Deutscher Ausblick aus dem Zyklus Schwarzes Zimmer* (1958) and *Television Décollage* (1963).

112 His first work with the use of video is *Exposition of Music – Electronic Television* (1963).

radically different. Video, and not film, was an exclusive medium for the group, or even one beyond its reach. In Poland, akin to the entire Eastern Bloc, portable cameras were not available for sale at all, and therefore every rare opportunity to get hold of such equipment was eagerly used. For instance, with regard to artists from former Yugoslavia – Sanja Iveković, Dalibor Martinis, Goran Trbuljak and Borys Bućan – such key moment came with the participation in the workshop Trigon 73: Audiovisuelle Botschaften in Graz, where each participant was expected to create several video works, while necessary equipment was provided by the organisers.[113]

Around the same time, the Workshop members once again decided to make a creative use of the potential offered by the Film School. Since the curriculum also embraced television production, the School had a truck at its disposal. The members of the WFF used it in 1973 to create the first video works in Poland: *Pictures Language* by Bruszewski, *Television Seance* by Różycki and *Television Transmission*. The latter was a joint idea of the members of the group and it was presented, beside *Television Seance* within *Action Workshop*. Images from three cameras located in different places in Łódź – at an intersection, at a carpenter's workshop, and in a private apartment – were displayed in real time on three monitors at the Muzeum Sztuki. The work was based on transmission itself and highlighted the very principle of transmission. The later 'television' projects by the Workshop were created in the years 1974–1975 and broadcast – owing to a short-lived openness of the authorities – by the second channel of the Polish Television in an afternoon programme on art.[114]

Works by Kwiek, Waśko and Bruszewski form separate chapters in the world history of video art. Each of them used it to face the problems that intrigued them at the time. Therefore, by attempting to find international analogies for those works, we inevitably run the risk of oversimplification. Yet, it is certainly worth evoking the already classic projects by such artists as Steina Vasulka, for instance the installation-object *An Electro/Opto/Mechanical Enviroment* from 1976, in which the artist explored the illusory character of the transmitted image of space, as well as works by David Hall and Steve Patridge, based on the analysis of the video transmission and creation process, and therefore close primarily to Bruszewski's reflection. In turn, the Workshop's works created at the television studio and broadcast by the second channel in May 1974 are situated within a broad international current of artistic activities aired on television. I am referring here to the already canonical works, such as the programmes by Gerry Schum created in 1969–70 for the West Berlin local television station Sender Freies Berlin,[115] as well as *Interruptions* by David Hall for the Scottish TV, and *The Medium Is the Medium*, produced in 1969 by WGBH-TV Boston in collaboration with such artists as Nam June Paik, Aldo Tambellini, Otto Piene and Allan Kaprow.

---

113 B. Borić, I. Panjol, 'Chronology,' in *Video art. In Slovenia 1969–1998*, http://www.videodokument.org/cronology.htm [accessed 30-12-2016].

114 Workshop's presentation was held in the second channel of Polish Television on the 18th of May 1974. Kwiek created the work *Studio Situation – Video A*, and Bruszewski – *Spatial Transmission*. The following films aired: *I'm Going* by Robakowski, *Me and Telephone* by Kwiek, *Ode to Youth* (collective work based on Andrzej Barański's concept) and *Theory of Film Image Space* by Waśko. See *Żywa Galeria*, p. 133.

115 With the participation of Richard Long, Barry Flanagan, Dennis Oppenheim, Marinus Boezem, Robert Smithson, Jan Dibbetsa, Walter De Maria and Michael Heizer, among other artists.

Beyond the Film Form. Body and Portrait

The motifs of the body, portrait and self-portrait are marginalised with respect to the entire post-war avant-garde, and therefore it comes as little surprise that they do not feature prominently in research on the Workshop of the Film Form. Obviously, the reference here is not to aestheticised painterly or photographic female nudes created in bulk in the milieux of the Associations of Polish Artists and Designers (ZPAP), but to conscious and deliberate use of nudity or the body to manifest ideas and views. The only exception are the already canonical works by Ewa Partum and Natalia LL – artists who used the naked female body (their own and someone else's, respectively) in building an artistic strategy. Female nude also sometimes appeared in the work of male avant-garde artists but usually in a very particular role, as it is well demonstrated by the work of Zbigniew Dłubak, who created photographic nudes but at the same time distanced himself by means of language that gravitated towards conceptualism and quasi-science. A deliberate or unconscious repression can be observed here: Polish artists of the period of Gomułka and Gierek justified nudity with their experiments in the field of analytical art. Janusz Haka addressed that position in an ironic and critical way towards the end of the 1970s; he believed that pseudo-analytical concepts served merely as a pre-text to undress a girl in front of the camera.[116]

The female nude persisted despite that repression – as opposed to the male nude, which hardly ever appeared. Or rather never at all if seen through the prism of the consciousness of one's own body. Such a situation does not come as a surprise. As Paweł Leszkowicz wrote, full male nude was considered a taboo in Poland under Communism and images of male genitalia were deemed pornographic. Censorship was particularly active in this sphere; suffice it to mention the untimely closing of the exhibition *Intimate Photography* at the Permafo Gallery[117] or the censor's intervention in Barbara Falender's exhibition, where the artist intended to show sculptures similar to vagina and penis.[118] The only acceptable male nude was the 'Socialist' type which derived its origins from the medieval tradition of deformation, humiliation and shame of the body.[119] Even such performers as Zbigniew Warpechowski and Jerzy Bereś distanced themselves from the body, although it featured prominently in their work. Two exceptions, which only confirmed the general rule, were artists Krzysztof Zarębski, who towards the end of the 1960s posed naked for staged photographs and carried out ephemeral actions in Kraków which involved baring his buttocks as well as Krzysztof Jung, whose performances a decade later at the Repassage Gallery in Warsaw featured the nude artist or invited participants.[120] Also Marek Konieczny could be added to this short list – the artist used nude self-portraits and images of women's breasts, laps and vaginas in order to – as Ronduda wrote – invite the viewer to a sensual experience of the work of art.[121] According to Ronduda, Konieczny suffered a double exclusion – both from the representatives of Modernism, and from the second avant-garde.[122] Also Niemczyk fell prey to social ostracism. In turn, Jung or-

116 Ł. Ronduda, *Polish Art*, p. 337.

117 M. Kuźmicz, 'Ja to ktoś inny,' in *Natalia LL. Doing Gender*, ed. D. Jarecka, A. Rayzacher, Warsaw: Fundacja Lokal Sztuki/lokal_30, 2014, p. 69.

118 Interview with Barbara Falender, November 2009.

119 P. Leszkowicz, *Art Pride. Polska sztuka gejowska*, Warsaw: Abiekt, 2010, p. 18.

120 Cf. *Krzysztof Jung. Przemiana*, ed. J. Zgierski, Warsaw: Academy of Fine Arts, 2016.

121 Ł. Ronduda, *Polish Art*, p. 20.

122 Ibidem, p. 28.

ganised his performances for narrow groups of a dozen people (colleagues and friends). Thus, the presence of the bodily in art led the artist into isolation unless he could 'explain himself' with a pursuit of analytical and Conceptual reflection.

The Workshop members did not undress girls in front of their cameras, nor did they take their own clothes off – it is therefore very easy to overlook the motif of engaged physicality in their work. The austere form of the majority of their projects and the accompanying hermetic terminology[123] contribute to the fact that many texts devoted to the WFF produce the image of artists concentrated on the pursuit of quasi-scientific experimentation, far removed from the everyday. Interpretations do not go beyond the border of the bodily – as if their authors came across an obstacle.

Yet, the real aspirations of the Workshop members were different. The body – however often repressed – was indeed heavily present in their work. Bruszewski, Kwiek, Robakowski, Różycki, Waśko, Bendkowski and Łomnicki very often made use of their own image and engaged physically in the creation of their works. Practically from the beginning of the group's activity, they carried out performative actions in which they appeared in person, and which featured photographic and film cameras, production trucks or the television studio, which seemed to appear in the role of a tool or prop. The bodily engagement was not (or not always) neutral for the tone of a given video installation, film or photograph. In the work of Kwiek, Różycki and Waśko, the body often acquired an existential dimension. For Robakowski, it was a source of physical strength and vitality. It also became manifest in a striking and original way in the work *Ballet Language* (1973) by Bruszewski – a sequence of photographs and drawings of the nude artist who creates a new alphabet with his body. Nudity can be interpreted here as a sign of openness to communication and understanding above the verbal level, but – above all – the work is an extremely rare portrayal of a young vital male body in Polish art. It bears no similarity to other 'laboratory' works by Bruszewski – it looks rather akin to a photographic record of a shamanistic dance.

The motif of the body and portrait evolved in various ways in the work of individual members of the WFF. For instance, Robakowski in the 1960s pursued a deconstruction of his own photographs: he set them on fire, or exposed a number of times so that the image of the face became incomplete or multiplied. On the one hand, it was an example of the exhaustively discussed activity on the medium of photography, yet on the other hand – since Robakowski pursued such an activity on his own portrait – we may venture to adopt a psychological perspective. The aura of anxiety and existential threat that imbues the images yields place in the next decade to an image of a more conscious physicality. Discovering the body, Robakowski combined it with media devices – mainly cameras, which he used akin to limbs. Film equipment was heavy and required considerable physical strength. That struggle with the machine resulted in a record of both competition and collaboration between the human being and the camera. The resulting image is an effect of breaking the resistance of the device, which – seemingly subordinated to the will of the operator-performer – continues to record reality according to its own programme. That problem, highlighted for the first time in the film *I'm Going* (35 mm, 1973), will later become one of the most important motifs in Robakowski's practice, leading to the creation of his cycle of *Biological-Mechanical Records*,

123 Workshop's films were often accompanied by various diagrams and calculations. See: R. Waśko, op. cit.

comprising films, photographs and video works. Such reflection reached its culmination in the video-performance *Exercise for Both Hands* (1976), in which the artist flailed two active cameras. In that work, Robakowski left the position of the camera operator and emerged as a subject, thus complementing the image of his artistic practice.

The opposite pole of this strategy is represented by Ryszard Waśko, who gradually withdrew from the field of vision. His photographs from the series *Self-Portrait in Time* (1972) still featured an artist-subject. Afterwards, the maker not so much disappears, but rather withdraws, limits himself to existence and observation, while preserving a full awareness of his own existence and subjectivity at the same time. In Waśko's works, which essentially provide a record of the relation between time, space and the self, the 'self' is understood literally as a subject that exists in time and space, whose bodiliness can be sensed by the viewer, although it usually remains hidden. We see what we see owing to Waśko's presence in a given place and time. The spatial analysis pursued in such manner serves Waśko as a starting point for existential reflection that bring to mind Buddhist Koans, especially the famous question: 'If a tree falls in a forest and no one is around to hear it, does it make a sound?' The artist seems to ask: 'Do time and space exist when nobody feels them, sees them, perceives them?' In his works (such as *From 0 Degrees to 180 Degrees* and *30 Sound Situations*) Waśko seems to offer a negative answer to that question.

Another artist from the Workshop's circle, Kazimierz Bendkowski, turned self-portrait into the visual axis of his artistic work and used it to explore the relativity of the visual message and photographic manipulation.[124] It can be seen primarily in the cycle *Relative Image*, which the artist developed for many years. It comprises sequences of the same photographic self-portrait, each with a different commentary. With the artist's face as the main motif of the cycle, *Relative Image* went beyond the sphere of meditations on the properties of photography – it became an attempt to determine the relation between oneself and the world. The work can be understood to anticipate or prototype the phenomenon of selfies – photographs usually taken in solitude, in a compulsive way instead of looking in the mirror, which make us look better than in reality. Bendkowski's *Relative Image* is ironic in laying bare the process of ostentatious multiplication of one's own image, which – although it changes depending on the context – essentially remains the same.

In turn, against the Workshop's background the scarce photographic self-portraits by Andrzej Różycki come across as exceptionally personal. Using his own image and playing with meaningful titles of works, Różycki revealed his approach to art and life. One of such works was the multi-part photography *The Project of Launching Photographic Image* (1975), which featured the artist's body multiplied in consecutive photographs akin to film stills. The caption read: 'Akin to the flight of Icarus, this attempt cannot succeed.' It was Różycki's summary of the WFF's pursuit to extract more from photography than it probably ever had.

Another noteworthy work by Różycki, *Seeming Identification* (1973), consisted in a representation – simultaneously by means of photography, film and performance – of the artist performing the same daily activities. It gains more relevance today than at the time of making,

124 See K. Bendkowski, 'Relatywność i obiektywność komunikatów wizualnych,' in R. W. Kluszczyński, op. cit. pp. 62–4.

since it depicts a world in which we need to co-exist alongside our digital avatars. Those multiplied entities have some common points (with us and with each other), but at the same time they compel us to ask which of them is real and if we can ever still talk about reality at all. The tension generated by the work is somewhat neutralised by the triviality of everyday mundane gestures. Such an approach is characteristic of Różycki, who raised fundamental issues in a serious tone in order to counter them with a joke the next moment. The artist combined universality with a personal dimension. Reality turns out to be so complicated that in order to tame it we need not only a deconstruction of machines that dominate our world, but also the ability to look at it from a purely human perspective.

Paweł Kwiek made a permanent and nearly compulsive use of self-portrait in a way that brought to mind an ongoing test of one's capacity of perceiving the world. That approach became the most prominent in video works made by Kwiek in the Polish Television studio in 1974. The artist created a television spectacle in which he himself, as a performer who instructed to the operators, decided about the image of reality seen by the viewers. He used voice commands to generate a transmission of images that portrayed the situation in the studio in a fragmentary way. The most obvious theme of the work is the incompleteness and selectiveness of perception filtered through the media. The theme is the more so resonant that the artist perceived video as a device whose structure was very close to the structure of the human mind. 'It works akin to imagination, to the mind which reviews the perceived, remembered or newly generated images.'[125] Therefore, the work *Video A – Studio Situation* lays bare not only the mechanism of the media, but also the weaknesses of the human mind with its habitual fragmentary and non-holistic vision of reality. Daisetz Teitaro Suzuki, professor of Buddhist philosophy wrote that such a perspective on reality can only yield analytical definitions, which suffice for practical needs, but will never allow us to capture the essence.[126] Suzuki compared such 'objectivism' – drawing on the example of Alfred Tennyson's poem – to an attempt to learn about the flower by tearing it out with its roots. He contrasted it with a different approach, expressed by Bash Matsuo in a haiku that describes an attempt to get to know the flower by embracing it with utter understanding to the point of identification of the exploring and the explored.[127] Strongly echoing such perspective is Kwiek's slightly later work *Video and Breath. Information Channel* (1978), built not on an action, but on a reduction of action to a manifested and conscious presence. The subject of the work sees reality in all its manifestations. He does not evaluate, but remains utterly conscious. He understands, but does not analyse.

In the course of just a few years Kwiek thus radically transformed his understanding of the relation between reality and the perceiving subject. The artist initially used new media as tools to explore the world. Yet, he ultimately confronted it directly – gradually resigning from any props. Towards the end of the 1970s, he finally abandoned para-scientific language and in 1979 created the work *Perception of the Lack of Differences*, which consisted in meditating in front of a smooth white wall. The only trace is a modest photographic documentation.

---

125 P. Kwiek, *Foto-media a struktura czynności myślenia*, leaflet, Galeria Foto-Medium-Art, Wrocław 1978, quoted in Ł. Ronduda, *Polish Art*, p. 285.

126 D. T. Suzuki, 'Lectures on Zen Buddhism,' in D. T. Suzuki, E. Fromm, R. de Martino, *Zen Buddhism and Psychoanalysis*, New York: Grove Press, 1963.

127 Ibidem, pp. 11–14.

It was probably such transformation of consciousness, experienced by the Workshop, that Józef Robakowski described: 'Our goal was never to 'expand visibility by means of technology,' but to change the perception of the world, and therefore the way of thinking. It is a huge difference.'[128]

Beyond the Film Form. Interventions and Actions

Interventions took the form of 'disruptions' to official cultural events, meetings, film reviews screenings, committed by the members of the Workshop of the Film Form on the occasion of their frequent journeys around Poland. Their goal was an attempt to modernise Polish cinematography through criticism, as well as provoke the audience to actively engage with their works or even-co-create them. Some of them were planned beforehand, especially when a film screening was to form part of an intervention, but also in such cases they were not expected by the organisers. Thus, the WFF members 'deflated' the events which – through an excess of awards and titles awarded to mediocre artists and their works – were supposed to create and inflate the seeming successes of Polish cinema. Therefore, the WFF's interventions often bore personal references to specific participants of the disturbed events, especially to cinematographic officials.

That unmasking strategy was described by J. Robakowski in 1973 in his text *Lampoon of Polish Cinematography*:

> Self-contentment about 'fruitful work' is confirmed every year by many festivals and reviews; and they are so many that it is difficult to count. Everywhere sumptuous celebrations, full swing, decorations, best hotels, and many many awards – for mediocrity.[129]

Robakowski reminisced that absurdity was the best strategy to deconstruct a variety of official celebrations.

> Mr Wacek [Antczak – M.K.] was the most skilled at operating in the absurd realm of People's Poland. He was able to generate a situation with which neither the citizens' militia nor the organisers of those festivals couldn't cope.[130]

The first intervention of the Workshop was a carried out during the exhibition *Forward-Looking Photographers* at the Contemporary Gallery in Warsaw. The WFF members prepared leaflets with quotes from reviews and theoretical writings on photography. Statements by Polish scholars, assembled in a more or less logical whole, were supposed to reveal the intellectual state of Polish critics.[131]

The next action was held at the Polish Film Review in Łagów, where three Workshop's films were shown: *Market*, *Inventory* and *Holes* [i.e. *Test I*]. During the projection, the WFF members sat amongst other viewers and provoked them with such questions as: 'Where is the human being?' – ironically reiterating the most frequent accusations with regard to the group's artistic practice. Thus, they managed to unleash a stormy debate.[132]

---

128 J. Robakowski, 'Dziura w historii,' *Studia Artystyczne CDN*, 2, 1980, pp. 76–8.

129 J. Robakowski, 'Paszkwil na polską kinematografię,' *Student*, 3, 1973, quoted in Żywa Galeria, pp. 92–3. http://robakowski.eu/tx16.html [accessed 30-12-2016].

130 Interview with Józef Robakowski, July 2014.

131 See L. Olszewski, 'Gdzie jest człowiek. Interwencje Warsztatu Formy Filmowej,' in *Żywa Galeria*, pp. 306–[illegible]1.

132 Ibidem.

A different kind of intervention was carried out in Zakopane during the Review of Films on Art. During the festival, when the prize was awarded to Andrzej Papuziński for his film on Franciszek Starowieyski *Bull's Glory*, Bruszewski and Koterski went on stage and awarded one of the festival organisers (and at the same time the director of one of presented films) the prize of the Workshop of the Film Form for the worst presented film. It was a gun (popgun) so that he could shoot himself. The director automatically raised the gun to his head and pulled the trigger. Unfortunately, the popgun was loaded.[133] Lechosław Olszewski described that and similar interventions by the Workshop:

> They had the character of provocations. Without a strictly determined form, they were characterised by an uncertainty as to what would follow, and thus they became akin to happenings, whose form was largely derived from Dadaism.[134]

Yet, it is noteworthy that the Workshop's strategy was close primarily to Fluxus. Through happenings, concerts and broadly understood ephemeral actions, the Fluxus artists strove to engage their audiences and eradicate the barrier between life and art. They appeared – akin to the WFF members – amongst 'regular' festival-goers and disturbed the fixed schemes that governed such events as well as engaged the viewers in active participation in a given activity.

Another Workshop's intervention took place in March 1974 at the 'Żak' club in Gdańsk, which was supposed to host a meeting with Andrzej Konic, who experienced difficulties in getting there, however, and was increasingly late. It was then that Józef Robakowski appeared on stage in front of the gathered audience and answered their questions pretending to be the actual director.[135] In December the same year, the WFF members participated in the 5th International Experimental Film Competition in Knokke-Heist, Belgium, where – apart from screening their own films – they carried out a spontaneous intervention during the projection of the film *Cascade* by Dore O, which was a lengthy record of a waterfall. The WFF members took off their clothes and pretended to be swimming against the backdrop of a huge screen. Józef Robakowski remembers his own performance with a mirror at the same event during the screening of the film *Holes* (i.e. *Test I*), as well as a 'forced intervention' during the presentation of a Belgian performer (throwing him into the fountain), bursting ca 100 New Year's Eve balloons, turning off the light at the casino during New Year's Eve celebrations as well as the publication of the 7th WFF magazine in English.[136]

We should also mention interventions carried out in the later period by the group's individual participants, especially the series of *Mysteries*, initiated in Warsaw by Kazimierz Bendkowski as well as *Dustbin* by Paweł Kwiek in Zakopane.[137] *Mysteries* were held in the Rakowiec housing estate in Warsaw since 1971. They took place at night and consisted in 'making use of all kinds of sources of light.'[138] The actions had a spontaneous character. Bendkowski sent out light and sound signals from the windows of his apartment, and the neighbours responded in the same way.[139]

---

133 *Wojciech Bruszewski*, p. 25.
134 L. Olszewski, *Działalność Warsztatu,* p. 129.
135 Ibidem, p. 134.
136 *Żywa Galeria*, pp. 133–34.
137 We should also mention Kwiek's actions carried out alongside Jacek Łomnicki within their ephemeral gallery 'Czyżby', active since May 1972. See R. Waśko, op. cit., p. 10.
138 Ibidem, p. 3.
139 Ibidem, p. 106.

The goal was to create a means of communication between people that would not rely on words.

The action *Dustbin* was also held at night. Paweł Kwiek created ca. 300 photographic prints from the film stills of his film *Face* with Jacek Łomnicki (the son of Tadeusz)[140] and on New Year's eve of 1972 scattered them around Zakopane. It was yet another action that bore reference to the film. One month before Kwiek asked students of one of Warsaw's high schools to 'pull faces to the camera.' It was followed by a screening of the film *Face*, after which the film stills from the work were 'released to the audience' in the form of a long band.[141]

There may have been more interventions which were not documented or preserved in the memory of their witnesses and participants. Yet, it seems that the Workshop's presence in Knokke-Heist marked an end of the period of the group's spontaneous interventions. Such situation is understandable to the extent that at the time the WFF members obtained the possibility to put their postulates into practice within a variety of events, both in Poland and abroad.

Elbląg. Cinema in the Service of Rebellion

Let us begin with Elbląg, which in the 1960s became a major point on the map of Polish art, primarily owing to Gerard Jürgen Blum-Kwiatkowski (1930–2015) as well as the artists he invited to the city. Kwiatkowski settled in Elbląg after World War II. Between 1956 and 1961, he ran the Young Intellectuals' Club 'Czerwona Oberża,' and later established the EL Gallery in 1961, which he operated until his departure for Germany in 1974. During that period, Kwiatkowski organised five editions of the Biennial of Spatial Forms (1965–73). The last Biennial, under the title 'Kino Laboratorium' was created in collaboration with the Workshop of the Film Form.

The idea of the Biennial, which was initially organised in collaboration with the industrial plant 'Zamech' in Elbląg, was to overcome the autonomy of the work of art and to implement the postulate of 'the world as a work of art.' In practice, it consisted in collective work, exploration of the urban space and merging artistic ideas with technological potential. The latter aspect left a particular imprint on the character of the event. In the 1960s it could even seem that it offered a pretext to carry out large scale, technologically complex sculptures, created by artists in collaboration with engineers from 'Zamech.'

Since its first iteration, the event proved highly popular in the artistic avant-garde milieus, yet Kwiatkowski's concept was also met with criticism. For instance, Anka Ptaszkowska accused the organisers of identifying technical means with artistic means and recognising 'spatial forms' as the only righteous effect of artistic activity. In her view, the Biennial thus acquired the characteristics of a totalitarian concept.[142] Although the Biennial did incorporate ephemeral activities (such as those by Stanisław Dróżdż and Ewa Partum), it was only the beginning of the 1970s that witnessed a thorough reconsideration of the event's idea.

The participation of the Workshop members in the final edition in 1973 underlined that change and allowed it to resonate. 'Kino Laboratorium' was devoted to the ties between art and

140 Interview with Paweł Kwiek, March 2010.

141 It took place on the 30th of November 1971 at the Contemporary Gallery in Warsaw within the collective action *Film, Slides, Activities, Theory*, alongside Przemysław Kwiek, Zofia Kulik, Jan S. Wojciechowski and Jacek Łomnicki. See *Kwiekulik*, ed. Ł. Ronduda and G. Schöllhammer, Zürich: JRP Ringier, 2013, p. 90.

142 H. Ptaszkowska, 'Biennale Form Przestrzennych w Elblągu,' *itd*, 45, 1965, quoted in M. Lachowski, *Awangarda wobec instytucji. O sposobach prezentacji sztuki w PRL-u*, Lublin: Towarzystwo Naukowe KUL, 200[illegible], p. 62.

cinema, an issue of fundamental importance for the WFF.[143] It abounded in ephemeral activities and interventions, which provided a more modern, complex and subtle way to explore the relations between art, science and technology. For the Workshop members, the Biennial became a pretext to implement the postulates which they had previously voiced during their impromptu interventions. An invitation leaflet for artists to participate in the event reads:

> Workshop of the Film Form at the Leon Schiller National Higher School of Film, Television and Theatre in Łódź and the Laboratory of Art – EL Gallery in Elbląg announce a call for participants in an international confrontation of new cinema. Our attention will focus exclusively on the problems and methods of a new film language. OUR AIM – PURE CINEMA! Cine-Laboratory resigns from any kind of awards, jurors, classification and evaluation. [...] The space of the EL Gallery will be made available for group artistic activities. Contact with the Polish art avant-garde guaranteed.[144]

The event gathered ca. 120 participants, including artistic groups: Studio Kompozycji Emocjonalnej from Wrocław, Adres Gallery from Łódź, Remont Group from Warsaw, Grupa w Składzie from Warsaw, Wielobranżowa Spółdzielnia Poetycka from Poznań, Balázs Béla Studio from Budapest, as well as individual artists from Spain, Argentina, The Netherlands, Canada, France, Scotland, Hungary.[145] After the ceremonial opening, Eugeniusz Rudnik performed his composition *Us*. The evening saw a screening of films by the Themersons, Léger, Buñuel and Wiene, which were supposed to bring back to memory 'the potential of artistic statement proposed in their era by outstanding representatives of avant-garde cinema.' Late at night, Parajanov's film *The Colour of Pomegranates* was shown, which stirred an abundance of polemics and controversies. The participants celebrated until the early morning at the concert of Grupa w Składzie. The intensive first day also abounded in 'artistic manifestations,' within which the WFF members presented the documentation of *Action Workshop*, carried out in February 1973.

The second day was inaugurated by an afternoon of 'spontaneous-audiovisual spectacle,' carried out by the Workshop members who manipulated colour foil, bands and other objects in front of a projector lamp. The presentation was accompanied by a soundtrack created by Studio Kompozycji Emocjonalnej. If the account is to be believed, the event went beyond its initial frames and was spontaneously joined by the viewers, which resulted in a 'large manifestation that integrated many disciplines.' On the same day, their films were screened by Ryszard Waśko (*Wall*, *Pavement*, *Window*, *Negation*, *Record*, *Flower Pot*) and Paweł Kwiek (*Numbers*), which stirred 'a stormy debate during which the role of such works was discussed.' The filmmakers explained that their works functioned akin to provocations and tests that could broaden the potential of contemporary cinema, even if only by offering the viewers possibility to react during the projection. The same evening saw the screening of Robakowski's *Record*. Interestingly enough, it was interrupted by Andrzej Partum's intervention, who climbed a ladder set by the screen and attached a board reading 'Acupuncture.'

143 J. Robakowski, *Komunikat: Kino Laboratorium,* leaflet, Archive of the Exchange Gallery, 1973, http://repozytorium.fundacjaarton.pl/index.php?action=view/object&objid=3164 [accessed 30-12-2016].

144 *Kino – Laboratorium*, leaflet, Archive of the Exchange Gallery, 1973, http://repozytorium.fundacjaarton.pl/index.php?action=view/object&objid=3163 [accessed 30-12-2016].

145 All information concerning the event from 'Kronika V Biennale Form Przestrzennych – Kino Laboratorium,' in *Notatnik Robotnika Sztuki*, 5, 1973, pp. 4–10. Typescript available online http://repozytorium.fundacjaarton.pl/index.php?action=view/object&objid=3181 [accessed 30-12-2016].

On the third day of the Biennial, Wojciech Bruszewski – in collaboration with Paweł Kwiek and Piotr Bernacki – created the work *Pictures Language*. It was a 'television spectacle' carried out by means of a production truck rented from the Film School and later recorded on video tape and played on a VCR. Akin to the majority of the WFF activities during the Biennial, that action also met with a 'stormy debate' and criticism. The critics pointed out mistakes in sound production and questioned its sense. *Pictures Language* has not been preserved but it went down in history as the first Polish work recorded on video. At the same time, Bruszewski's work was also 'the first attempt made at the Polish Television that went beyond a popular broadcast,' as the organisers of 'Kino Laboratorium' wrote.

On the same day, the members of the WFF announced their *Film Exercises* and offered each participant the possibility to make a one-minute film on 35 mm film stock with the help of Paweł Kwiek as the camera operator. The action lasted until the end of the festival. The makers of those films often had nothing in common with film, neither before nor afterwards – artists such as Włodzimierz Wieczorkiewicz, Milo Kurtis, and Gerard Kwiatkowski himself.[146] Kwiek in collaboration with Karol Cichecki, also took part in the action with his film *The Sprinkler Sprinkled*, which bore a humorous reference to the silent film by the Lumière Brothers, and *My Independence*, which featured a chalk drawing on the floor of the EL Gallery (copy of a restaurant bill paid by the Biennial participants) with the artist's voice-over in which he explains that the film's title is inadequate and should be replaced with *My Senselessness*, because his activity essentially seems to make no sense. Piotr Bernacki created the film *Blade* and Wojciech Bruszewski filled his part of film stock with postulates and mottos that called for a viewers' boycott of official cinematography. In his film Robakowski made use of a mirror, held in his hands as he approached the camera, which revealed the film crew at work.

The evening featured a rich programme of events, including a screening of more films from the Workshop artists: *Confrontation* by Tadeusz Junak, *Take Five* by Zbigniew Rybczyński, as well as *Clapper* and *Inventory* by Wojciech Bruszewski. The projection of Robakowski's *Test II* was disrupted once again by Andrzej Partum's 'intervention group,' who put their motto 'Film doesn't need a screen' into practice by using mirrors to reflect the film image onto the gallery walls. At the same time, Paweł Freisler attached a thread to the screen, which he handed over to Robakowski. The latter himself also replaced the screen for his *Test I* projection with a mirror. The artist used it to reflect the light from the projector to the audience, objects in the gallery and the Gothic vault of the old church building.[147]

The fifth day of the Biennial featured screenings of Junak's *Episode* and Paweł Kwiek's *Face*, followed by films by Javier Aguirre Fernández, which encouraged the viewers to intervene by manipulating the sharpness of the image, turning off the sound and the image, reflecting the projection onto the vault of the church building. The WFF members found themselves on the same wavelength with Fernández and discovered many similarities to the Workshop's strategy in his artistic approach. The Spanish director was also keen to collaborate with musicians and poets; he investigated similar problems related to the medium of film, and, akin to the WFF, he shunned

146 See *Elbląg konceptualny*, ed. J. Denisiuk, Elbląg: Centrum Sztuki Galeria EL, 2010, p. 56.

147 He repeated that action during the festival in Knokke Heist in 1974.

official festivals and contests with prizes. Fernández was therefore nominated an honorary member of the Workshop.

On the last day of the Biennial the film evening belonged entirely to the Workshop – the group showed two hours of its earlier films and Paweł Kwiek created a double screen presentation of film footage spontaneously assembled in real time into an artistic statement by means of effects recorded on the tape and musical effects produced live by Grupa w Składzie. Wojciech Bruszewski screened his then latest film *Apnoea* and Antoni Mikołajczyk 'carried out his artistic manifestation *Fire* on the gallery floor.' The Biennial concluded with an action devised by Gerard Kwiatkowski, which consisted in contemplating the daybreak together.

Workshop's participation in the 5th Biennial of Spatial Forms 'Kino Laboratorium' undoubtedly added a new quality to the event's format. There were no monumental sculptures, replaced by a range of performative activities, and importantly – newly created film and video works. For the Workshop, the festival came as an important opportunity to summarise and expand their work as well as confront it with a lively audience and the oeuvre of international artists. The Biennial resulted in new works: *Pictures Language* by Wojciech Bruszewski, a piece of fundamental art historical importance, and *Kinolaboratorium* by Paweł Kwiek, which exemplified the artist's pursuit of the idea of collective work.

Abroad. Edinburgh, São Paulo, Knokke-Heist, Documenta

The international contacts of the WFF were not limited to incidental encounters, such as the meeting with Javier Aguirre Fernández. The group was gaining recognition abroad, which was bolstered by three key events: the exhibition *Atelier '72* in Edinburgh (1972) – the WFF's first international presentation – and the international experimental film competition in Knokke-Heist (1974), which resulted in an invitation to the sixth edition of the famous exhibition Documenta in Kassel (1977).

A figure who played a key role in those international contacts was Richard Demarco – the owner of the gallery that hosted the show *Atelier '72*. Since the end of the 1960s, Demarco pursued his lively interest in the art of Central and Eastern Europe. He travelled to Romania, Poland, and Yugoslavia for what he called 'educational' trips. He presented the work of artists from those artists respectively in 1971, 1972 and 1973 at the Demarco Gallery in Edinburgh.[148]

It remains unclear whether Demarco visited the Film School on his own initiative or was encouraged by Ryszard Stanisławski, the then director of the Muzeum Sztuki. In any case, he arrived there on a Saturday afternoon, when there was almost no one around. The only staff member was a secretary in the dean's office, who wanted to get rid of the importunate guest by telling him the office was closed. As she could not speak English, she decided to ask the other person who happened to be at the school for help – the young student Ryszard Gajewski, who was working 'overtime' on the soundtrack to his film. Gajewski recalls:

> At the School there was a custom that on Saturday at 3 PM most of the lecturers and students went to Warsaw. I stayed to work on the soundtrack to my film *Pierzgalski*. Suddenly, the secretary calls and asks if I can deal with an intrusive guy who wants to see the School's

148 Demarco hosted the first international presentation by Marina Abramović.

> films. He speaks English, looks like an Italian, but he is Scottish. He won't leave. Could I show him a film? I reluctantly agreed. That stubborn Scotsman was Richard Demarco still relatively unknown in Poland. I showed him *Centrifuge* and *Pierzgalski*. He liked the films and invited me to participate in the exhibition *Atelier'72*, but I didn't believe him. promised to arrange the other films by the Workshop and a meeting with their makers. I don't remember when that meeting happened – then or during Demarco's next visit to Poland. We didn't quite believe that the Ministry of Culture would agree to our participation. We weren't in the officials' good books, and Demarco did not ask for their opinion when he was choosing the artists.[149]

In turn, Demarco remembers his stay in Łódź as follows:

> I went to the great Film School, which created Polański and Wajda, where I witnessed the most exciting film screening I'd ever seen. Józef Robakowski's *Market* [...] is beyond doubt a pure manifestation of the use of the film medium. [...] Another bright young director Wojciech Bruszewski was represented by his two exceptional films *Inventory* and *Clapper*, Ryszard Gajewski and Paweł Kwiek are two other filmmakers who work in the same honest and fresh way, presenting their own point of view. [...] Later the young filmmakers organised an extraordinary party for me in Wojciech Bruszewski's apartment, and it was there that I was entertained by one of those great artists whom I happened to meet – Mister Wacław Antczak. There he was, wearing a tailcoat, white shirt, bow-tie, vest and faded but professionally patched trousers (after all, he's a professional tailor). For two hours he sang songs which he wrote himself, recited his own poems and debated on the role of art and the artist revealing his most profound philosophical reflection. Beyond doubt, his violin was an original Stradivarius, as it was confirmed by words written on them with white paint: 'This is an original Stradivarius.' He sang a soldier's song about Łódź, about the longing for its the smoky factory chimneys, and the bitter-sweet song *Dien Bien Fu* about love and war. I sang a few Scottish songs that I remembered, and he produced even more sounds on his violin that were as important for me as dissonance for John Cage's music. That sixty-year-old gentleman, forever young, full of passion for life, came to embody the extraordinary spirit of Polish artists. [...] I had the impression that if I really understood that man I would also understand Poland.[150]

Robakowski, Gajewski, Bruszewski and Mikołajczyk accepted Demarco's invitation and came to Edinburgh. Although the organisers offered accommodation, the trip was still expensive, and therefore not all members of the group could afford it. The Workshop members took with them a 35 mm film projector, because Demarco was unable to find such equipment in Edinburgh.[151] After arrival, the artists from Poland were given lodging and modest spending money, which was barely enough to survive in Edinburgh. Gajewski writes:

> We were always in good spirits, even when the funds dried up, and they would always dry up. The spending money was enough for bar meals, such as 'two eggs on bacon' or 'fish and chips.' We ate breakfast in our lodging. Every day, the hosts left in the fridge two

149 R. Gajewski, *Warsztat Form Filmowych – początki,* Warsaw 2014 (unpublished manuscript), p. 26.
150 Ibidem, p. 28.
151 Ibidem, p. 41.

> cheese spreads, two jams, bread and instant coffee. Only after a few days we found out that it was for us. Seeing so little food in the fridge we didn't want to eat the host's last cheese spread. When it became clear, we ate every crumb. Free coffee was available all day at the Gallery, as well as roasted bananas with rice for lunch.[152]

The exhibition attracted considerable interest. The workshop members recall that it was seen by Nam June Paik and Charlotte Moorman, among other figures, and even Sean Connery, who belonged to the gallery friends' club and invited the WFF members for an elegant dinner, where they discussed the film *The Hill*, shown at the Film School before, in which Connery played the main role.[153]

The Edinburgh exhibition granted the Workshop other invitations. The same year, the group appeared at the São Paulo Biennial. Initially, the organisers wanted to show only Robakowski's photographic objects,[154] but the artist proposed a group presentation of the Workshop. The proposal was accepted. The members of the group created a collective work *Transmission of the Personality of Wacław Antczak*. Zagrodzki wrote:

> In this multimedia work the artists used photographic, film and sound documentation to transmit the image of the difficult poverty-stricken existence of a folk artist from the margins of the art sphere.[155]

The WFF members wrote in the project description:

> The presentation shall serve to ennoble an artist – a representative of the Łódź urban folk culture, shaped by a specific set of cultural factors:
> beyond official artistic currents
> beyond what we call art
> beyond artistic education
> He is characterised by:
> disinterestedness
> resignation from any possibility to build life stability
> nobility
> belief in his choices
> The presentation shall rely on the following means of transmission:
> written record
> musical notation
> photographic record
> film
> tape recorder[156]

One year later, Bruszewski, Robakowski and Waśko participated in the Fifth International Experimental Film Competition in Knokke-Heist, Belgium, an event which truly opened the Iron Curtain for the Workshop. Their films were shown alongside works by such artists as Birgit

152 Ibidem, p. 101.
153 Ibidem, p. 77.
154 Interview with Józef Robakowski, September 2016.
155 *Wojciech Bruszewski*, p. 68.
156 *Żywa Galeria*, p. 124. Typescript available online: http://repozytorium.fundacjaarton.pl/index.php?action=view/object&objid=3083 [accessed 30-12-2016].

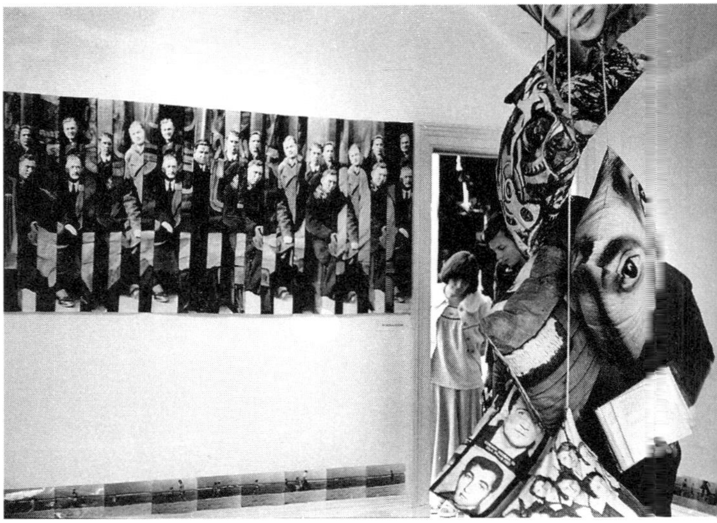

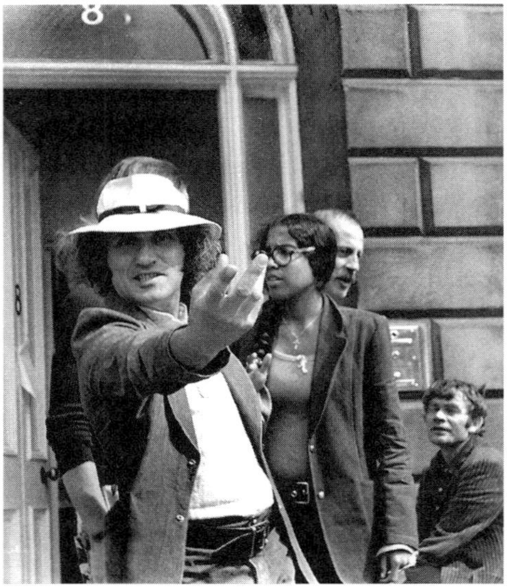

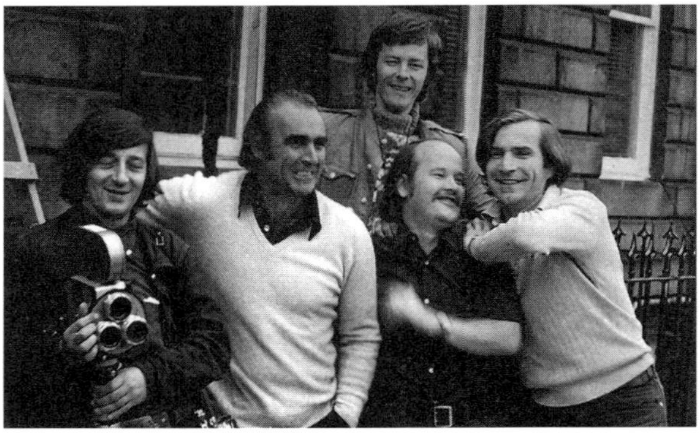

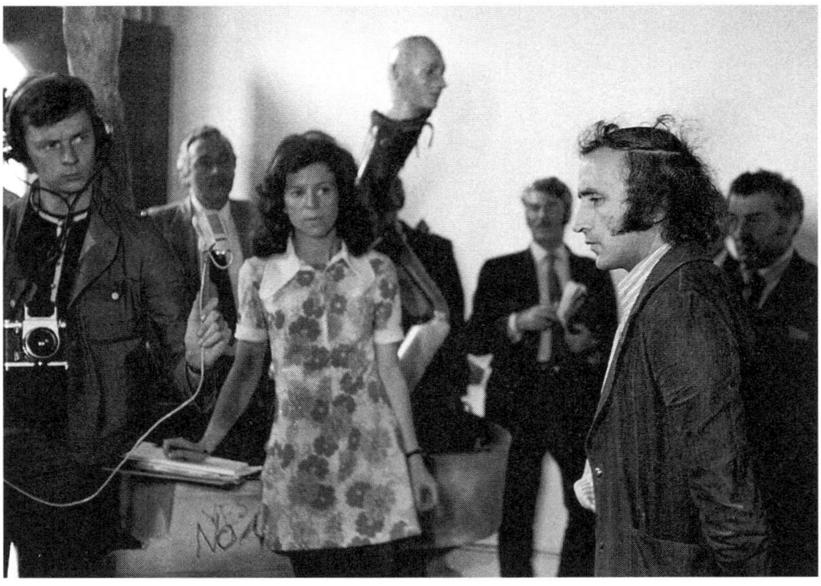

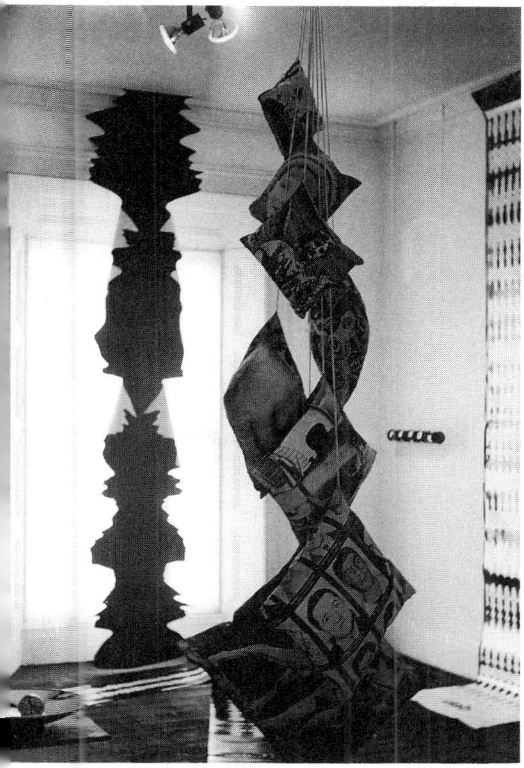

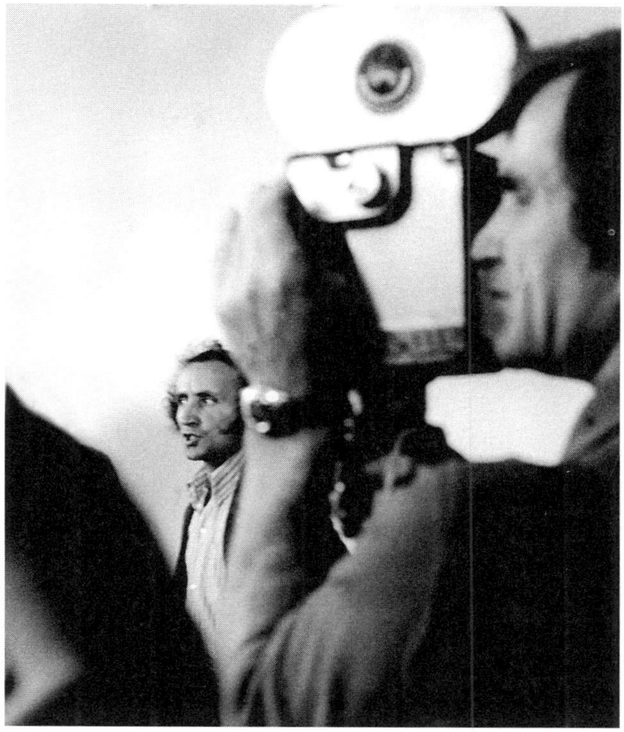

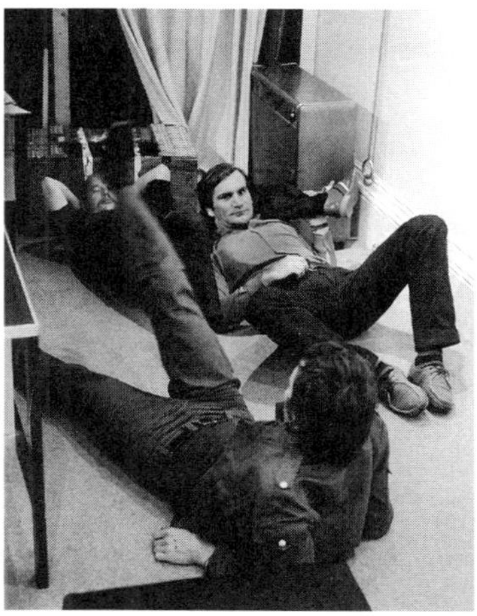

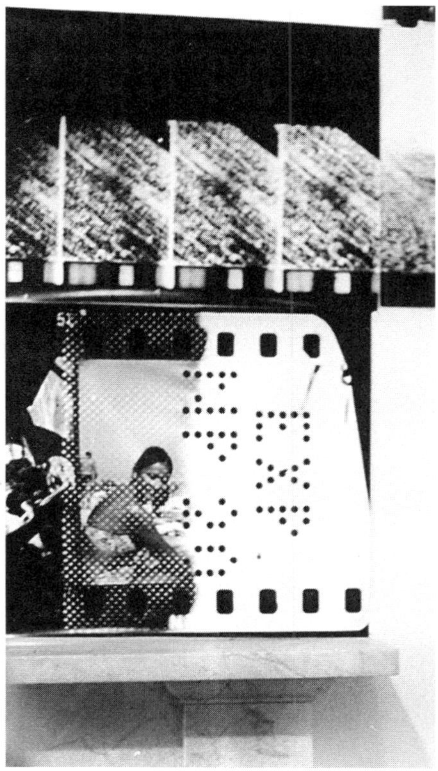

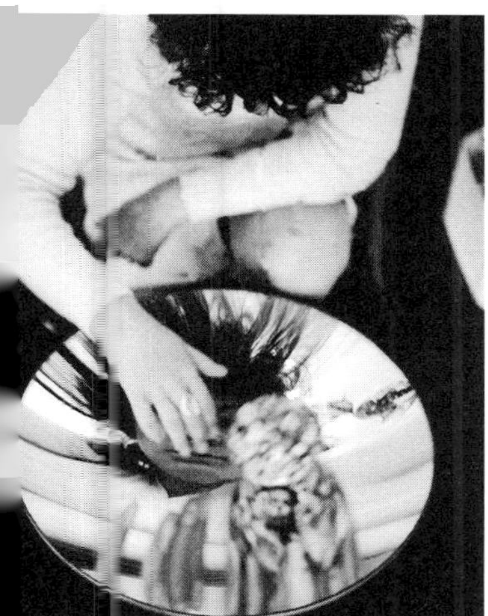

Workshop of the Film Form in Edinburgh, 1972
Warsztat Formy Filmowej w Edynburgu, 1972

and Wilhelm Hein, David Hall, Marilyn Halford, Werner Nekes, Tsuneo Nakai, Anthony McCall, and William Raban. That event led to the group's participation in a range of shows organised in 1975. In January and February alone, WFF's films screened at the Folkwang Museum in Essen, Städtische Kunsthalle in Düsseldorf, X-Screen in Cologne, Abaton Kino in Hamburg, Henie Onstad Kunstsenter in Oslo.

The crowning event marking the interest in the Workshop came with their participation in the exhibition Documenta 6 in Kassel. The show opened between the 24th of June and the 2nd of October 1977, comprising three parts: 1. Painting, sculpture, performance; 2. Photography, film, video; 3. Drawing, book, design. The characteristic edge of that edition was a special focus on the role of new media in contemporary art. New media became the subject of the second volume of the catalogue *Photographs, Film, Video*. The Workshop of the Film Form participated in the film section. Only Wojciech Bruszewski appeared in the video section.

Participation in Documenta consolidated the position of the WFF in the European avant-garde circles. The Workshop members were cut off from those milieux only by the imposition of martial law in Poland. It put an end to any international travels and severely restricted mail correspondence between Polish and international artists. One exception was the ongoing intensive contact between the then former Workshop members (especially Robakowski) with the Hungarian avant-garde.[157]

Culmination. Action Workshop at the Muzeum Sztuki

The WFF members cite *Action Workshop*[158] as the peak moment of their artistic community. It was held at the Muzeum Sztuki in Łódź between the 31st of January and the 25th of February 1973. At the time, the Workshop did not yet witness any competition between its members, there was no hierarchy, ideas were implemented together, and the artists spent a lot of time together offering each other inspiration.[159] Yet, at the same time, it is *Action* Workshop that came as the moment when the artists' individual approaches began to crystallise.

Written sources agree as to the course of the first two days of the action.[160] During the opening on the 31st of January guests were photographed and their images exhibited in the museum hall. The second day featured a screening of films by Bruszewski, Junak, Kwiek, Koterski, Robakowski and Rybczyński. However, the accounts of the further days reveal differences. The order of events in the invitation differs from one provided in Ryszard Waśko's master's thesis. However, the following events certainly took place: *Ocean* – exhibition of photographs by Zbigniew Dłubak; *The Career and Death of Adolf Hitler* – an amateur spectacle directed by Edward Kowalski with the participation of the WFF members; *Musical Facts or a Concert of Dilettantes* – a spontaneous concert on instruments provided by the organisers; *Intersection* and *Doors* by Bruszewski; *Audiovisual Message* by Robakowski; *Electronic Antinomy* by Połom; *Text – Notation – Record*, *Photographic Record* and *Construction* by Mikołajczyk; *Television Seance* and *Seeming Identification* by Różycki; *Kwiekołom*

157 Interview with Józef Robakowski, May 2016.
158 Interviews with Józef Robakowski, Andrzej Różycki, Kazimierz Bendkowski and Ryszard Waśko.
159 Interview with Andrzej Różycki, July 2014.
160 See *Żywa Galeria*, p. 134; R. Waśko, op. cit., pp. 44–74.

and Łomokwiek by Kwiek and Łomnicki;[161] *Sound–Colour–Movement (Mystery in Ultraviolet)* by Bendkowski, and the group action *Artistic Signature*.

The invitation to organise an action at the Muzeum Sztuki came from its then director, Ryszard Stanisławski[162] – somewhat in the aftermath of the exhibition *Atelier '72*. The main premise of the event was that it would remain 'in process.' The halls on the first floor of the Muzeum Sztuki were emptied and became the 'action setting.' Each day featured a different presentation prepared by a specific artist or devised as a group activity. Despite their essentially ephemeral character, some of the actions required quite serious preparations. That was the case, for instance, with the open artistic signature contest. Participants were encouraged in a prior press announcement to submit postcards with their signature proposals. It was one of the many activities intended to engage the audience. Another example was the action *Musical Facts or a Concert of Dilettantes*, within which the WFF members and the museum audience played a concert together on instruments provided by the organisers.

> The Workshop adopted a division into three kinds of events:
> A – borrowed – artists where not the makers of the works, they merely made their presentation possible;
> B – explorations of the problems of language – artists merely activated the means of expression and resigned from creativity;
> C – artistic – the means of expression were entirely subordinated to the artist's idea;[163]

Artistic Signature Contest and *Musical Facts or a Concert of Dilettantes* were classified in Ryszard Waśko's master's thesis as type A. The WFF also included in the same group the spectacle *The Life and Death of Adolf Hitler*, yet another example of Workshop's collaboration with the director Edward Kowalski,[164] as well as Różycki's *Television Seance* – the first Polish work created with the use of television broadcast, which situates it amongst a range of pioneering projects, such as Wolf Vostell's *Television Décollage* and works by Nam June Paik. Against that backdrop, Różycki's gesture is distinguished not so much by openness to interaction with the viewers (which was also characteristic of *Exposition of Music – Electronic Television* by Nam June Paik, where the viewers disturbed television broadcast), but rather by a complete reduction of artistic gesture.

Interestingly enough, group A did not comprise the breakthrough project *Television Transmission*. It was the first work in Poland created with video technology (it was not recorded on tape, let us remind that the first recorded video tape in Poland was *Pictures Language* from the same year, carried out by means of three production trucks belonging to the Film School). It consisted in a mechanical transmission of images from a street, a carpenter's workshop and a private apartment, to the museum hall. The artists made no interventions in the transmission. That radical and austere gesture bore testimony to the group's interest in the everyday not only as a

161 See Paweł Kwiek's own description in R. Waśko, op. cit., p. 57.
162 Interview with Józef Robakowski, September 2016.
163 R. Waśko, op. cit., p. 50.
164 The Workshop members participated in his earlier spectacles and Różycki chose him as the subject of his diploma film *Kowalski*.

source of inspiration, but even as a material of art. *Television Transmission* was classified under type B, akin to Bruszewski's *Intersection*, another transmission, which concentrated on sound. The artist described it:

> Four microphones installed in the corners of the intersection of Więckowskiego St. and Gdańska St. were connected (by means of amplifiers) with four speakers situated in a corresponding way in the corners of the exhibition hall. Throughout the whole day, the sonic space of the intersection existed also at the gallery.[165]

Also Antoni Mikołajczyk created a work that consisted in introducing the outside the Museum interior. The artist described his project:

> Without changing the location of the photo camera, colour diapositive photographs were taken every half hour of the yard with a fragment of a street. As a result, the photographs recorded the changes in the colour of the environment, the ephemerality of the atmosphere of a given moment and the life of the residents on an ongoing basis for 30 hours. The series of diapositives was projected in the exhibition hall without changing their order. The projection was complemented with acoustic effects recorded on tape on the photographed site.[166]

Specific works created during *Action Workshop* can be read nowadays as the beginning of the further individual paths of the majority of the group members. Yet, the project as a whole should be viewed primarily as a contemporary and radical gesture performed by the WFF which consisted in seizing the museum space. That was essentially the nature of the artist's decision to create their works 'on site' and to confront the viewers with the creative process. Also the location of those activities was far from random. The WFF members treated the Muzeum Sztuki – a place with direct ties to the pre-war avant-garde – as a fragment of the city. The works that consisted in transmitting images from the streets of Łódź to the museum echo Katarzyna Kobro's reflection on urban space. The group's gesture opened up the institution to the city and its dwellers, transforming an isolated white cube into a space open to the viewers and their perception of art and the world (an aspect additionally reinforced by activities that engaged the audience).

The Workshop and Politics

> *We began to realise that our creative activity towards reality was possible only in a way that would allow us to avoid being drawn into that reality, being entangled neither in contemplation nor protest, but to act in order to make a landmark as a personality of our time, independently and our own, and yet, for that very reason – to directly influence reality, shape it and describe it critically.*
>
> Józef Robakowski in conversation with Maciej Szybist

At the time of writing, we are witnessing yet another tide of disputes concerning the evaluation of the legacy of the Communist period in Poland. They are pursued in the realm of propaganda, mythicising, repression, oblivion, ignorance, and anything but a real revision of the past.

165 R. Waśko, op. cit., p. 56.
166 Ibidem, p. 64.

few years ago, the situation was still similar in the field of art history. The recent period has seen the release of publications devoted to the phenomena, milieux and particular artists active in that period. Yet, we are still missing a study that would offer a complete diagnosis of the situation of visual artists in Poland under Communism. Still, in order to develop a good understanding of their history, it is impossible to overlook their relations with the political authorities. For this reason, I shall now try to briefly explain what the Workshop members wanted to avoid being drawn into and what they wanted to shape – the political realm of the so-called 'Gierek period' in Poland.

That realm has already been described by Lechosław Olszewski, who in 1998 authored the pioneering essay *Działalność Warsztatu Formy Filmowej jako przykład strategii sztuki wobec władzy w Polsce lat siedemdziesiątych* [The Activity of the Workshop of the Film Form as an Example of a Strategy of Art in Relation to the Authorities in Poland in the 1970s]. The author was the first to embrace the practice of the WFF within a broader political context, providing an insightful examination of the group's functioning at the intersection of visual arts and cinematography. The political decision-makers took a much greater interest in cinema, and therefore the Workshop adopted a unique position towards the authorities. Olszewski highlights this aspect of the group's activity, and his essay could be recognised as an exhaustive discussion of the topic if it had not overlooked one important thread: the activity of the WFF in the structure of the Film School. It was an institution of key importance for the Communist authorities, as well as one that the Workshop wanted to transform.

However, before proceeding to the question of the school, let us briefly outline the historical context. The pressure of censors on artists was the strongest during the period of Socialist Realism. It was followed by a political thaw after 1956, and the Socialist Realist doctrine was relaxed. At the same time, a division emerged between non-official and official art. The official circulation – related to higher education institutions, the Ministry of Culture and Art and creative unions – remained in the hands of the authorities, whereas the opposition circles created their own more or less permanent institutions within various kinds of legal-administrative structures. As Olszewski wrote, in the 1960s those were organisations that postulated rejection of the painterly tradition and its museum context, such as the EL Galery in Elbląg, odNowa Gallery in Poznań, Mona Lisa Gallery in Wrocław, Contemporary Gallery and Foksal in Warsaw. Those centres broke away from the system in a certain way, while they also definitely formed part of it.[167] In the 1970s, author's galleries emerged, such as Permafo, Gallery of Current Art, Remont, which were characterised by less formal or completely informal structures.

The two currents – the official and the non-official – differed from one another. When Socialist Realism was abandoned, the official current became dominated by a 'modernised (post-thaw), but also more contemporary (figurative) Colourist tradition.'[168] Yet, in the 1960s, the avant-garde circles became closed to reality, which can be explained as a reaction to the prior attempts to control their creative work. That tendency was manifested by Conceptual reflection and a self-reflective analysis of the used media. Artists were withdrawing into a field in which the work of art was to remain devoid of references in order to make it impossible to appropriate by ideology.

167 L. Olszewski, op. cit., p. 114.
168 Ibidem, p. 115.

Obviously, a rather naive conviction. It was the fear of the impact of the authorities, the artists' distance to reality and the lack of educated audiences that led to art's diminished influence on reality. In consequence, as Olszewski wrote, 'the ritual of symposia, plein airs, exhibitions, congresses, meetings, presentations supported the creation of a success myth.' Let us underline that it pertains to the 'non-official' current, which did not identify with the system. The avant-garde was therefore enclosed by the authorities. It did not pose threat but functioned as a parallel world.

Art only incidentally interacted with everyday life. Artists sometimes pursued activities in the public space or made scarce attempts to influence state cultural institutions. The instances, rare in the 1960s and 1970s, to deal with explicitly opposition-related themes or erotic motifs met – especially in the latter case – with a strong and quick reaction of the censors. The WFF's resistance to the system manifested itself mainly in the first two ways – through interventions and the organisation of their own events without jurors, verdicts and awards. Akin to their film works, all those activities were carried out entirely within the group's own capacity – in a non-commercial and disinterested manner. Of equal importance were Robakowski's texts, particularly *Lampoon of Polish Cinematography*[169] and a letter from 1975, in which the artist informs the then minister of culture about his 'resignation from further cooperation with Polish Cinematography.'[170] Yet, the most important aspect is the unique way in which the group determined its position in the field of cinematography and how it functioned at the Film School.

The Workshop rejected feature filmmaking controlled by the authorities, which – as Olszewski remarked – marked a significant disruption of the diligently woven network of power and an implementation of the postulate to shape reality through art. The Workshop members were in possession of tools to create mass events and well-funded film productions, but they rejected that potential in favour of disinterested activity, independent programme and ongoing attempts to ridicule the official cultural circulation. In an era of aggressive success propaganda of the Socialist state under Edward Gierek, the WFF members tapped into the structure of the Film School to create films that did not impose a vision of the world. Their works were open to the viewer, who was perceived as a subject able to perceive the world in an individual way. What is more, some of the group's works can be interpreted as attempts to boost viewers' sensitivity to censorship and propaganda strategies, although the former members of the group do not always agree with such understanding of their works.[171]

In this context, we should also mention those works by the WFF which were created by way of handing cameras and film stock over to non-professional artists.

Finally, we should bear in mind that the activity of the WFF aimed to transform the methods of education and model according to which the Film School functioned as an institution that formed part of the system. First such attempts were made already during the winter term of 1966, when the future members of the group – in reaction to the inertia of the professors, lack of materials for work and educational ideas – initiated a students' revolt. Robakowski recalls: 'We summoned a school parliament and invited professors, deans, pro-rectors and the rector Jerzy Toeplitz.'[172] That

169 Józef Robakowski, *Paszkwil na polską kinematografię*, pp. 92–3.
170 Ibidem.
171 Interviews with Paweł Kwiek, July 2015.
172 K. Krubski et al., op. cit., p. 185.

initiative did not bring about any immediate improvement,[173] but the mood at the school changed. In the aftermath of the events of March 1968, students of the Film School joined nationwide protests and supported the demands to democratise education. They were backed by the rector, Jerzy Toeplitz, who lost his office as a result. The later repressions dealt an even heavier blow to the already frail Film School. The oeuvre of the engaged post-war cinematography was discredited by the members of the ruling party. Wajda, Munk and other directors of the Polish Film School, were accused of anti-Polonism and defeatism, and encouraged to seek optimism that could inspire the society to struggle for Socialism.

Given such a situation, the strategy of Robakowski and the entire Workshop appears as the only alternative. It offered the possibility to act and, at the same time, reduced the threat of falling under the influence of the political authorities. Interestingly, after many years the WFF members became associate professors at the Film School: Robakowski, Rybczyński, Lenczewski, Waśko, Junak and Kwiek, while Janusz Połom even became the dean of the Direction of Photography Department in 1981 (chosen with the votes of the students).

Currently, Prof. Józef Robakowski still lectures at the Film School in Łódź (after losing his office during the martial law in Poland), as well as Prof. Ryszard Lenczewski. In 2016, the office of the dean of the Direction of Photography and Television Production Department was conferred to Prof. Zbigniew Wichłacz, who had collaborated with the Workshop on some of the group's film, such as Bruszewski's *Apnoea*.

173 The Workshop members become active in a similar way in 1980, when they establish the Movement for the Renewal of the Film School in the context of the broader political transformations of the period.

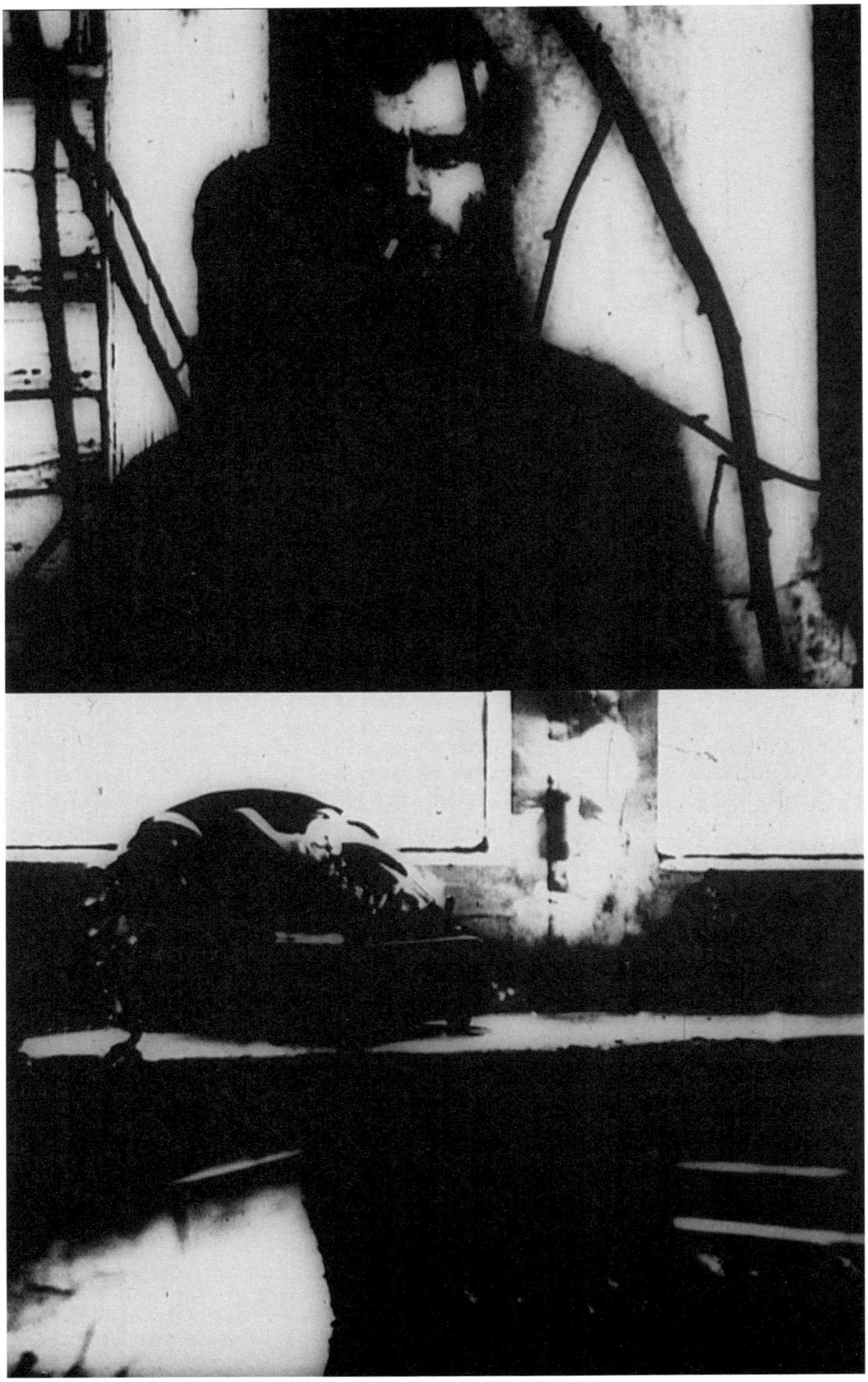

Paweł Kwiek, *Ja i telefon*, 1972, 35 mm, 6’03”
Paweł Kwiek, *The Telephone and I*, 1972, 35 mm, 6’03”

Mike Sperlinger

Tautological Cinema: Some Notes on Self-evidence in the Workshop of the Film Form

Tautology leaves to reality the whole infinite logical space; contradiction fills the whole logical space and leaves no point to reality. Neither of them, therefore, can in any way determine reality.
Ludwig Wittgenstein

Self-evidence has always to be produced.
Alexander García Düttmann

1.

In his final book, *Aesthetic Theory* – published in the same year (1970) that the Workshop of the Film Form was founded – the philosopher Theodor Adorno wrote: 'It is self-evident that nothing concerning art is self-evident anymore, not its inner life, not its relation to the world, not even its right to exist.'[1] Adorno's verdict seems to be open to at least two interpretations, depending on how we relate the two uses of 'self-evident.' The first and most obvious way would be to say that the *only* thing which was self-evident about art, for Adorno, was that nothing could be said to be obvious or self-evident about art any more. This interpretation, however, seems to be haunted by the possibility of a second, more paradoxical one, involving a variant of the famous 'liar's paradox': if *nothing* about art is self-evident any more, might that include precisely this very 'self-evident' assertion itself? And if that is the case – if it *cannot* in fact be self-evident that 'nothing concerning art is self-evident anymore' – what kinds of self-evidence in art might that contradiction allow back in?

Viewed some four decades after they were made, one of the most obvious characteristics of the films produced by the Workshop is their sheer, flagrant obviousness. These are works which often appear to aspire precisely to self-evidence, or even a blunt literalness. Whereas for Adorno the artwork was always associated with 'enigmaticalness' – a resistance to language, programme or paraphrase – many of the films from the artists working in Łódź during this time seem almost philistine in their clarity. Their 'relation to the world' is, by turns, axiomatic, schematic, diagrammatic and didactic. Again and again, they appear to insist on explaining themselves, exposing their own structures, on walking the talk.

If we accept for the moment that the period of the Workshop was a moment when even art's 'right to exist' was no longer self-evident – and not least under the regime in Poland at the time – what to make of these strange works, which seem to defend themselves by insisting they have nothing to hide?

---

1 T. W. Adorno, *Aesthetic Theory*, tr. R. Hullot-Kentor, Minneapolis: University of Minnesota Press, 1998, p. 1.

2.

One common thread to much of the work made at the Workshop of the Film Form was the language of experimentation. This needs be understood, however, as both a more specific and a more freighted use of the term than in the generic term 'experimental film,' for example, as used by both critics and other film co-ops in Western Europe and America at the time.

That latter term – usually employed quite interchangeably with 'avant-garde film' – is commonly the kind of loose, poetic usage of 'experiment' which the philosopher and poet Hans Magnus Enzensberger had in mind when he wrote polemically in 1962 that: '*Experiment* as an aesthetic concept has long since become part of the vocabulary of the consciousness industry [...] this concept is nonsensical and unusable.'[2] For Enzensberger, artists too often borrowed the concept of the experiment illegitimately from science, discarding the rigour of its methodology and using it only to disavow responsibility: 'With the designation *experiment*, the avant-garde excuses its results [...] and unloads all responsibility on the receiver.'[3]

The films of the Workshop seem, on the face of it, to present a very different case. Instead of using 'experimental' as an umbrella term for unlimited licence, Workshop artists often seem to employ it as a form of self-constraint and avowed objectivity. From the very beginning they aggressively framed their own work in the language of specifically scientific enquiry, from Józef Robakowski's early *Test* films to Wojciech Bruszewski's assertion, in the text he wrote for the Workshop's 1975 'manifesto,' that their concern was 'para-scientific activity, cold and calculated artistic theory-practice.'[4] This, in fact, is part of why these works remain so perplexing: they seem to want to *prove* things, in ways that we still do not expect artworks to do. They frequently insist, as Bruszewski put it, on the fact they are 'calculated' rather than spontaneous: they tell us in advance what they are going to do (Ryszard Waśko's *30 Sound Situations*, 1975), or use diagrams to explain their own making (Paweł Kwiek's *Video P*, 1975); they use scientific instruments (like the oscilloscope in Janusz Połom's *ABC*, 1974) and carry out programmatic procedures (like Waśko's taxonomy of camera movements in *Configuration I – VI*, 1973).

3.

Of course, the Workshop produced a variety of films and not all of them fit this template. A film like Kazimierz Bendkowski's *The Area* (1973), for example – a dreamlike and slightly sinister portrait of a semi-derelict backyard and its inhabitants – clearly channels Surrealist and Fluxus energies (and perhaps more specifically those of Franciszka and Stefan Themerson), whilst Marek Koterski's *Ech* (1972) is an uncompromising and visceral political documentary of sorts about alcoholism in the Buñuelian tradition.

One way to frame the varied output of the Workshop more inclusively might be in terms of 'studies,' in the full semantic sense of that word. On the one hand, there are film which are studies

2 H. M. Enzensberger, 'Aporias of the Avant-Garde,' tr. J. Simon, in *The Consciousness Industry*, New York: Continuum, 1974, p. 36.

3 Ibidem.

4 'The manifesto of Workshop of Film Form' (1975), see official website of the Museum of Modern Art, Warsaw, http://artmuseum.pl/en/archiwum/wojciech-bruszewski-2/2408?read=all [accessed 14.10-2016].

in the sense an artistic maquette, or an étude in the musical sense – one might think of a film like Bendkowski's *Centre* (1973), with its dazzling and playful superimpositions of neon, traffic and street-lights, which feels much closer to the poetic explorations of vision to be found in some American artists' films of the period. (It is unsurprising to find these kind of studies being produced in the Workshop, since it was after all part of the Film School in Łódź – David Curtis has also remarked on this 'school exercise' quality to some of the works.[5]) On the other, there are the many works which hew closer to studies in a more scientific idiom, of the kind for example that Waśko developed by moving, in curator Łukasz Ronduda's words, 'his research [...] into the sphere of laboratory operations, building and then testing abstract models.'[6]

The films of the Workshop can thus be located on a kind of spectrum, between the antic and the analytic. Bruszewski's work is a microcosm of this, and his films are often strange admixtures – think of *Audio-Visual Research: Matchbox* (1975) or *Stopwatch* (1976), which present themselves as investigations into visual/acoustic perception with just a hint of deadpan absurdity, as against a film like *YYAA* (1973), in which the structural account of sound and image relations gives way to a more explicit clowning. In the case of other artists, the distinction between these two kinds of study is itself deeply enigmatic.

In Waśko's *The Straight Curve* (1973), we see a series of street scenes over which animated black geometric shapes interpose; this might seem like an archetypal artistic study, a formal investigation of how we read depth into the two-dimensionality of the filmic image – but these images also seem to unwittingly prefigure *TV Solidarity* (1985), the pirate TV interference project mounted by five astronomers from the University of Toruń. In their famous transmissions during September 1985, using a primitive broadcast kit, the astronomers succeeded in superimposing Solidarity slogans ('Solidarity Toruń. Enough of price rises, lies and repression') over images on official Polish state television. In their test transmissions beforehand, they had transmitted small geometrical shapes over the broadcast image – little interventions closely resembling Waśko's floating shapes. In this strange, entirely coincidental echo, there is perhaps a first hint of the potential political subtext to even the seemingly driest 'experiments': the possibility of questioning officially administered and mediated reality.

4.

But what to make of films which so regularly insist on telling you what they will do, implicitly or explicitly, and then doing it? Take Paweł Kwiek's *The Telephone and I* (1972). For three minutes, the screen remains black whilst a voice on the soundtrack describes, in present tense, an improvised film he has made but which we cannot see: 'December 22, 1972, in the morning, I got 90m of TF7 film and now I'm putting it into a camera borrowed for half an hour from a friend making a student film...' He narrates having a fellow student shoot him smoking a cigarette and carrying out a series of simple actions, and then deciding to shoot a superimposition over the whole three minute

5 S. Ball and D. Curtis, 'Poles and Angles: A late-night e-mail conversation about Polish and English Structural Film' in *1,2,3... Avant-Gardes (The Experiment Art and Film)*, ed. Ł. Ronduda and F. Zeyfang, Berlin and New York: Sternberg Press, 2007, p. 60.

6 Ł. Ronduda, *Polish Art of the 70s*, Warsaw: Center for Contemporary Art – Ujazdowski Castle, 2009, pp. 132–33.

sequence, filming a white telephone which happened to be lying nearby. And then... we see the film itself, silent, the actions and superimpositions exactly as described.

Many of the Workshop films have this quality – perhaps less of being experiments than demonstrations or examples: the faithful carrying-out of some baldly-stated premise. Some have a kind of taxonomical approach: Połom's *ABC* – in which, once we have seen the first few letters of the alphabet flash up followed by an oscilloscope registering the sound of that letter being pronounced, we immediately understand the schema and how it will play out. Others carry out even simpler actions, and their titles spell out the results, as in Waśko's *The Journey of Wacław Antczak to the Kiosk in Główna Street* (1973), in which Mr Antczak, standing next to a bicycle, is passed the camera in the first few seconds of the shot and we then get a wobbly tracking shot as he rides to the kiosk with it on his back.

Another variation involves counting. Sometimes the films tell us in advance exactly how many sections they will contain (Waśko's *30 Sound Situations*), or they make counting the central action of the film (Robakowski counting the steps he climbs in *I'm Going*, 1973). Kwiek's *Numbers* (1973) is another good example: a countdown leader, of the kind used for a projectionist to sync the beginning of a film (and which is normally not seen by the audience), is simply looped for almost eight minutes, with a collaged musical soundtrack. Once we have seen the loop a few times, we know exactly how the rest of the film will play out. Kwiek deliberately avoids, for example, an approach such of that of his exact contemporary Guy Sherwin, a member of the London Filmmakers' Coop, who in 1974 made a short 16mm film called *At the Academy*. Also based on 'academy' countdown leader, Sherwin's film starts in identical fashion but quickly develops into a strobing play of superimpositions, using optical printing effects to disrupt the sequence and to make the numbers themselves a kind of formal element. *At the Academy* is transformative, taking this most incidental, throwaway aspect of the filmstrip and turning it into a visual experiment (the title gives the process of discovery additional metaphorical weight). Kwiek's *Numbers*, on the other hand, refuses transformative play and visual interest along with metaphor; instead it is provocatively declines to offer anything more (visually at least) than a literal instantiation of its title.

There is something deeply strange about these works. David Curtis, a sensitive and knowledgeable viewer of the Workshop films, expressed it when he remarked that Polish artists of the period seemed to have 'trapped themselves with over-prescriptive scenarios'[7] – and yet noted, almost in the same breath, how when he first saw these films, 'their wit [...] came as a surprise.'[8] The prescriptiveness – the obviousness, the insistence on the programmatic, the conspicuous abstinence from surprise or narrative development – seems connected, paradoxically, to a subterranean form of wit. It is almost as if art's right to exist was being secretly affirmed, precisely by the abnegation of all of its most cherished unscientific qualities.

5.

There is a famous parable about the Buddha, in which he explains that his teaching is like a finger pointing to the moon: the person who looks only at the finger will never see the moon itself.

7 S. Ball and D. Curtis, op. cit., p. 60

8 Ibidem.

What if we were, to the contrary, to put forward the idea that the films of the Workshop are a case precisely of wanting the viewer to look at the finger?

Film was traditionally thought of as pointing towards an indexical reality, however fictionally framed – hence Jean-Luc Godard's famous remark that every fiction film was a documentary of its actors – and there is, of course, documentary content in most of the Workshop films. Sometimes it is even predominant, as in Koterski's *Ech* or Kwiek's film made with the residents of the eponymous village in *Niechcice* (1973). In many other films, however, what is actually captured on film (even discounting the 'cameraless' productions) seems relatively arbitrary, almost aggressively nondescript – the street scenes in Waśko's *The Journey of Wacław Antczak*, or the view from the tower Robakowski climbs in *I'm Going*, for example. What is being recorded seems to be the *action* of recording, the carrying out of an instruction, as much as what appears in front of the camera lens.

Take another Waśko film, *Wall* (1972): four minutes of footage from a static camera of a wall of the film school in Łódź, cut up and spliced together in random order so that any motion – an occasional figure walking in front of the wall – appears only in flashes of a few frames' duration. The imagery itself could scarcely be more banal, and the lack of conventional documentary curiosity is clearly signalled by taking the camera no further than the bounds of the school itself. At the same time, the soundtrack remains cheerfully and obtrusively continuous: a non-stop chorus of birdsong.

This strange marriage of randomised image track and seemingly innocuous, pseudo-diegetic sound reminds me of a peculiar passage in Immanuel Kant's *Critique of Judgment*, the foundational text for the contemporary understanding of the 'aesthetic'. In the course of reflecting on the experience of beauty in nature, Kant remarks:

> What do poets praise more highly than the nightingale's enchantingly beautiful song in a secluded thicket on a quiet summer evening by the soft light of the moon? And yet we have cases where some jovial innkeeper, unable to find such a songster, played a trick – received with greatest satisfaction [initially] – on the guests staying at his inn to enjoy the country air, by hiding in a bush some roguish youngster who (with a reed or rush in his mouth) knew how to copy that song in a way very similar to nature's. But as soon as one realizes that it was all deception, no one will long endure listening to this song that before he had considered so charming; and that is how it is with the song of any other bird.[9]

For Kant, birdsong is both the supreme expression of natural beauty and yet, at the same time, haunted by the ever-present possibility of its mechanical reproduction (for the purposes, not incidentally, of commerce). But the birdsong in *Wall* would seem to be there precisely to induce such suspicious scepticism: doubly out of place – both because of the urban location, and because its seamlessness means it is clearly not connected to the discontinuous images – it parodies the naturalising effects of sync sound in conventional cinema. If for Kant the discovery of the deception made the sound unendurable because it betrayed nature, Waśko seems to be attempting to emphasise that, in film, we will find only deception and naturalising effects.

These works are not 'pointing' to actuality as much as they are pointing to its construction in film. They are asking us not to look at the world as it appears on film, but to look at film itself (at the finger that points). This is most literally enacted in Kwiek's series of videos made in and

9 I. Kant, *Critique of Judgment*, tr. W. Pluhar, Indianapolis: Hackett Publishing Company, 1987, p. 303.

about the television studio in the mid-1970s, in which we watch his hands as directly or indirectly manipulate the image we see (in the case of *Video A*, 1974, by moving the dials on a video mixer). When it came to celluloid, the fact that the Workshop worked with 35 mm film, rather than 8 mm or 16 mm – something which was a source of some amazement to their contemporaries in London and elsewhere in the west – only emphasised that they were in a critical dialogue with industrial feature film production and reception. It is, in part, the disjunction between their production methods and their subject matter (or lack of it) which gives the Workshop's films their idiosyncratic wit.

6.

A tautology, in logical terms, is both self-evident and – strictly speaking – senseless, in that it is neither true or false. In Wittgenstein's example: 'I know nothing about the weather when I know that it is either raining or not raining.'

'Tautology' was an important critical term in the early 1970s connecting the artists around the Workshop with their contemporaries at the London Filmmakers Coop. It was a strange inheritance, which – in a western context – was the result of a hybridisation of Clement Greenberg's version of modernism with Wittgenstein's theory of language (epitomised by the early work of Joseph Kosuth). In the UK, for example, the film critic Deke Dusinberre used the term repeatedly in relation to what he called 'the formalist dilemma [...] in which radical formal strategies render the processes of representation so arbitrary that they run the risk of lapsing into meaningless tautology.'[10] But if it was a risk, it was one that the Coop filmmakers also courted playfully – Mike Dunford, for example, made a film called *Tautology* (1973), in which the word 'TAUTOLOGY' was superimposed over various shots of buildings.

In Poland, the photographer Zbigniew Dłubak had produced an influential series called *Tautologies* (1971), in which photographs of elements of a gallery space (the parquet floor for example) were placed on or beside those same elements. It directly inspired Bruszewski in his own series of 'anti-tautologies' in the series called *Photography on Canvas* (1979), in which multiple photographs of a white canvas on a stretcher were printed onto canvas and each pulled onto stretchers of their own, with variations caused by the different tensions. In between these two photographic series, were the films of the Workshop and their many variations on the form of tautology: Kwiek's *The Telephone and I*, with its visual recapitulation of its verbal first half; Waśko's *Window* (1972), in which, as Łukasz Ronduda puts it, 'the static, rectangular window frame through which we observe the "images of reality" becomes a tautology for the film frame of this very film,'[11] Waśko's video *A Corner* (1976), in which a monitor with a direct feed from one camera is aligned in front of the second camera so as to reproduce the view of the corner of the room it is physically obscuring; etcetera.

And 'etcetera' is the key term. Perhaps the definitive tautological document from Poland in that period comes from Ewa Partum, a filmmaker never formally involved in the Workshop, although she was in Łódź and in active dialogue with many of its participants. Her *Tautological Cinema* (1973–74) is a series of short films, which each develop a particular conceit; in *10 Metres of Tape*, for example, a series of handmade intertitles mark off, in one-metre increments, the length of film

10 D. Dusinberre, quoted in P. Gidal, *Materialist Film*, London and New York: Routledge, 1989, p. 100.
11 Ł. Ronduda, op. cit., p. 132-33.

that has passed through the projector. Again, we can find parallels in British work of the period – William Raban's *Take Measure* (1973) is effectively a live-performance variant of the same idea. But importantly, Partum's film breaks off after the three metre mark and concludes with an intertitle saying simply 'ETC.' In fact, all of the *Tautological Cinema* sequences end with an 'ETC.' – and one might argue, with only a little overstatement, that almost every film made at the Workshop from this period might have included the same coda. To say 'etcetera' is to say: what should follow is (or would be) a tautology. It is also to mark the point beyond which example or demonstration is no longer necessary, to move from the space of the literal to the conceptual.

Partum wrote, in relation to these films:

> This is not dealing with aesthetics, this is a new kind of philosophical practice in an area where relations between the film image and the movement of the camera exhaust the range of interest in the reality of film. This ensues from the problem of the film as an idea and the capacities of film structure as a medium and this constitutes its only content and is its only meaning. Art that is internally filmic up to the exhaustion of the potential of the cinema as a semantic medium.[12]

Partum's precise formulation offers a clue as to the connection between prescriptiveness and wit in the Workshop films. These are films which seemingly attempt to exhaust film's 'reality' and 'potential... as a semantic medium', by ostentatiously attempting to restrict its operations to what Dusinberre had called 'meaningless tautology.' But the aspiration to exhaustion, in any medium, contains the seeds of parody. Jorge Luis Borges once wrote: 'I would define the baroque as that style that deliberately exhausts (or tries to exhaust) its own possibilities, and that borders on self-caricature.'[13] Here, in these tautological films, we find an art historical and conceptual paradox: a minimalist baroque.

Tautological cinema, as instituted by the artists of the Workshop, appears to give up on claims to reality. And yet, in doing so it holds up a mirror to totalitarianism, which attempts to completely determine (social and political) reality: tautological film reflects tautological ideology. The absurdity of one becomes, cumulatively, an implicit commentary on the absurdity of the other, and self-caricature threatens to flip into political satire. Filmic tautology becomes powerful in its subversive *failure* to become meaningless, or to exhaust its relations to reality. Kwiek reflects in the voiceover for *The Telephone and I*:

> I start wondering what will be on the screen, what this film will be about. I think that actually it will be about nothing. I accept the insignificance of this film, just as those three minutes of my life, and what the camera provoked me to do, were insignificant. I decide to make the film more freaky, more aggressive, so everyone tries to find meaning in it – as I'm doing now.

The supposed insignificance of the film, however, is not necessarily the same as the insignificance of those three minutes. Just as Adorno's aphorism hinges on the relationship between two forms of self-evidence, the political meaning of the Workshop films inhabits the gap between these two insignificances.

---

12 *Ewa Partum 1965–2001*, ed. D. Monkiewicz, Warsaw: Muzeum Narodowe w Warszawie, 2006.

13 J. L. Borges, 'A Universal History of Iniquity, preface to the 1954 edition,' tr. A. Hurley, in *Collected Fictions*. London: Penguin, 1998, p. 4.

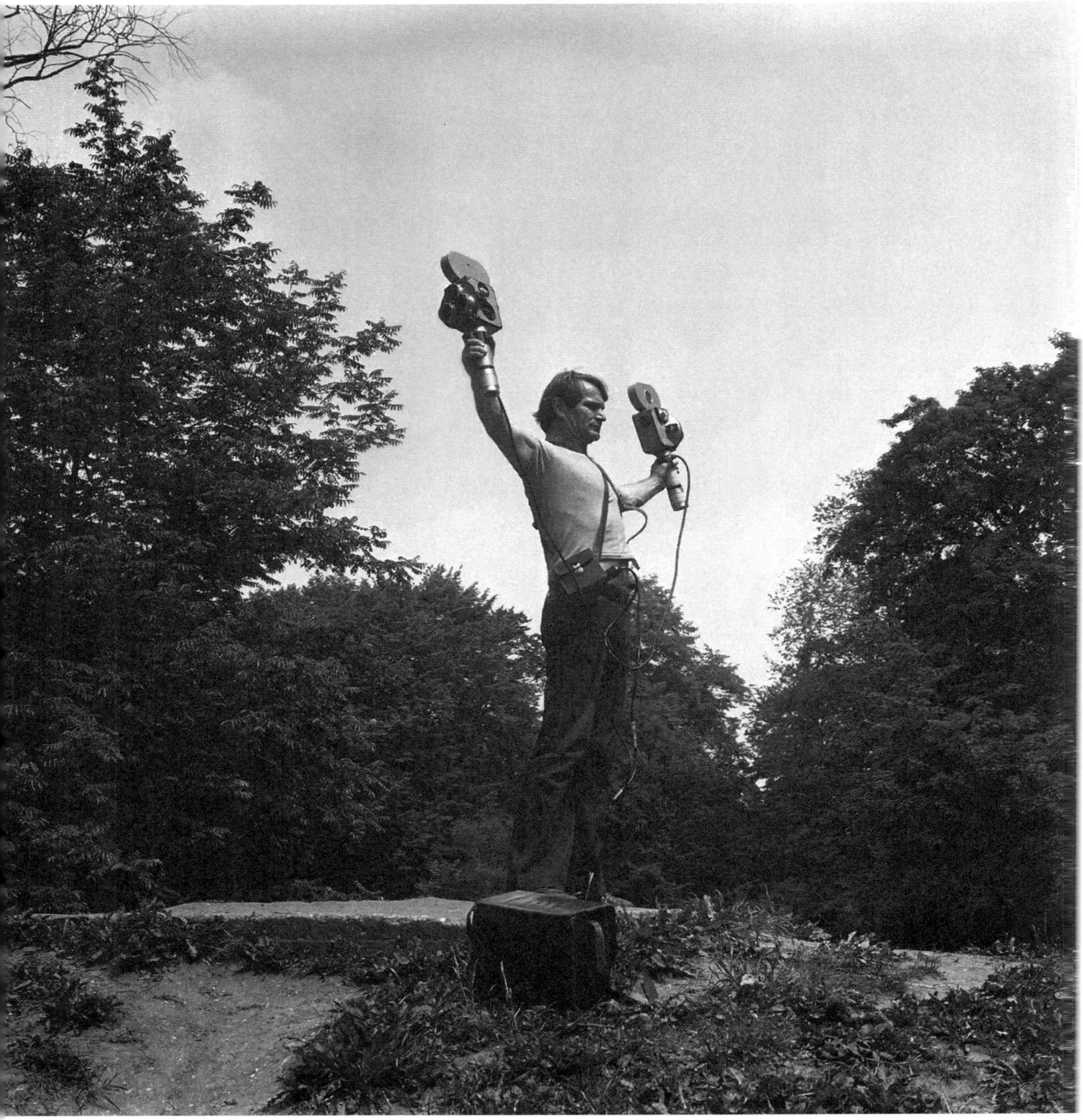

Józef Robakowski, *Ćwiczenie na dwie ręce,* 1976, 2 x 16 mm, 8'
Józef Robakowski, *Exercise for both hands*, 1976, 2 x 16 mm, 8'

Maeve Connolly

'The place of our dreams': Łódź Film School and the Workshop of the Film Form

Introduction

> [...] *at the film school, we developed a concept of an open school, not only a school for cinematography but for all possible disciplines. That concept was elaborated on and articulated in great detail, but martial law ruined all that and we left the film school for a very long time. I returned only in 1995. And today the school is turning into the place of our dreams, a multimedia place.*[1]

In a conversation with Hans Ulrich Obrist published in 2010 – forty years after the formation of the Workshop of the Film Form – Józef Robakowski frames the Workshop as a means to develop and establish an open concept of education. This concept was elaborated within the specific context of Łódź Film School[2], which was (and continues to be) one of the most world's most celebrated national film schools. The Workshop's core members, including Robakowski, were students at the Film School in the late 1960s or early 1970s and, working with its resources, they made numerous short 35 mm films and videos. The Workshop members used every official and unofficial opportunity offered by the Film School to develop international contacts. For example, they would often present their work informally to the various international visitors invited by the School to Łódź, eventually receiving invitations to participate in many prestigious festivals and exhibitions, including Documenta 6 in 1977.

The artistic and cultural significance of the Workshop of the Film Form has been widely recognised by practitioners and scholars of art and experimental film and video. But the impact and legacy of its critique of film education has not yet been fully explored within the context of film and media studies. Workshop members favoured a laboratory-like model of education, emphasising the importance of experiments and tests, exploring a range of media and technologies, extending well beyond the norms of industrial film and television production. Workshop members had extensive knowledge of film theory and of the history of avant-garde art practice directly connected to Poland and to Łódź in particular. The official Film School curriculum, in contrast, tended to prioritise the knowledge gained from practical assignments, closely linked to industry norms and standards, overseen by professors who were well-established in the Polish film industry as directors or cinematographers.

1 'Józef Robakowski in Conversation with Hans Ulrich Obrist,' in *Józef Robakowski: My Own Cinema*, Warsaw: Centre for Contemporary Art Ujazdowski Castle, 2012, p. 29.

2 I have taken the title Łódź Film School from the institution's own official website, but in English language publications of the Workshop of the Film Form, dating from the 1970s, it is usually titled 'Łódź Film, TV and Theatre School.'

Rather than simply rejecting the educational and professional opportunities provided by Łódź Film School, the Workshop members appropriated and repurposed the existing academic structures forming a student society to ensure access to material resources allowing them to make their own films. The Workshop therefore operated differently from student-led protest movements emerging in other educational contexts during the late 1960s. Nonetheless, their struggle for greater creative freedom – achieved in part through their embrace of the role of 'artist'– resonates with aspects of the 'artistic critique'[3] identified by Luc Boltanski and Eve Chiapello in relation to contexts such as the student and worker movements of May 68' in France. According to Boltanski and Chiapello, these movements articulated a demand for increased autonomy, which has since been appropriated and exploited in newer forms of management, which promise workers a high degree of autonomy and creativity, often at the expense of job security and stability.

In this essay, which is informed by interviews with Paweł Kwiek, Janusz Połom, Józef Robakowski and Andrzej Różycki conducted in Łódź and Warsaw,[4] I explore the relationship between the Workshop and the infrastructure and organisation of Łódź Film School in the 1970s. I outline some of the strategies used by Workshop members, collectively or individually, to establish themselves as artists and to develop creative and professional networks extending beyond the Polish film industry. I consider the legacy and ongoing significance of this artistic critique of industry-oriented film education, both in Poland and elsewhere. My discussion is informed by Duncan Petrie and Rod Stoneman's *Educating Film-Makers: Past, Present and Future*. In this study, Petrie and Stoneman examine the history of industry-oriented film education before and after 1989, within many different national contexts, arguing that (in some contexts at least) film schools have begun to emphasise technical and professional specialisation instead of critical and creative development.[5]

I also draw upon research within the fields of cultural industry studies and production studies, including Petr Szczepanik's analysis of the 'state-socialist mode of production' in East-Central Europe, which focuses on the political history of Czech, East German, Hungarian and Polish film production cultures.[6] Szczepanik is careful to differentiate between these cultures, noting that film directors occupied a particularly significant role within the Polish cultural context.[7] Although he does not deal directly with the Polish film school environment, his research indicates that industry professionals in some state-socialist production cultures played a central role in the authorisation of practical film education. In some instances, they rejected state-sanctioned educational models that did not conform to their norms and standards, partly as a way to assert their authority, expertise, and relative autonomy from state controls.[8]

3 E. Chiapello, 'Evolution and Co-optation: The "Artist Critique" of Management and Capitalism', *Third Text*, 18:6, 2004, pp. 585–94. See also L. Boltanski and E. Chiapello, *The New Spirit of Capitalism*, London: Verso Books, 2007.

4 These interviews took place at various locations in Łódź and Warsaw in May 2016 and they were arranged by Marika Kuźmicz of Arton Foundation, who was also the interpreter.

5 D. Petrie and R. Stoneman, 'Introduction', in *Educating Film-Makers: Past, Present and Future*, ed. D. Petrie and R. Stoneman, Bristol: Intellect Ltd, 2014, pp. 3–11.

6 P. Szczepanik, 'The State-Socialist Mode of Production and the Political History of Production Culture', in *Behind the Screen: Inside European Production Cultures,* ed. P. Szczepanik and P. Vonderau, New York: Palgrave Macmillan, 2013, pp. 113–34

7 Ibidem, p. 117. He describes the Polish production units as 'quite unique' within the context of East-Central European industries.

8 Ibidem, p. 129. The example given is of a one-year crash course devised to educate Czech labourers as directors, producers, camera operators and production managers. Industry 'patrons' were assigned to each student but they rejected their roles.

According to Szczepanik, 'historians and filmmakers have noted that in spite of their oppressive aspects, the nationalized film industries of East-Central Europe provided unprecedented levels of material and professional support for those involved in the production of art cinema.'[9] These 'oppressive aspects' were quite varied, including not only state censorship and other mechanisms of direct control but also more complex and subtle 'negotiations of power that [...] involved rewards, punishment, paternalism and corruption.'[10] Significantly, Szczepanik argues that workers in state-socialist film industries may have experienced different levels of exposure to oppression, depending upon their professional role. He differentiates, for example, between the situation of camera operators, editors and production managers, who often 'enjoyed long careers from the 1930s to the 1960s,'[11] and the situation of many directors, screenwriters, dramaturgs, and unit heads.[12] He argues that this latter group of industry workers were more vulnerable to Communist Party ideological and political shifts.

In the years that have passed since the end of the state-socialist system described by Szczepanik, the economic, political and social context for film and television production (and education) has changed radically, in Poland and elsewhere. Film and television workers, including camera operators, editors, production managers, directors, and screenwriters, have had to reconfigure their work practices in order to survive and prosper with a new commercial economy, which is explicitly focused on commercial competitiveness. Szczepanik points out that, even though Polish films have attracted 'sizeable' domestic audiences, the 'media industries of East-Central Europe are still struggling to respond to the dissolution of the state-controlled economy and its organizational structures, and to their marginal geopolitical position, and have been unable to develop internationally competitive strategies.'[13] The widespread use of digital technologies since the early 2000s has also brought about radical changes to film and television production methods and workflows. Consequently, employment instability has become a condition that is now shared by almost all workers in the media industries. This radically-altered environment provides the context for my reconsideration of the relationship between the Workshop of the Film Form and the Film School.

Film Education and the State

In their critical history of practical film and television education, Petrie and Stoneman identify several distinct phases in the development of state-sponsored film education, beginning in 1919 with the establishment of the (highly influential) Vserossiyskiy Gosoudarstvenni Institut Kinematographii/All-Union State Institute of Cinematography (VGIK) in Moscow. They suggest that 'propagandistic aims' were central to the establishment of VGIK and also the next major film school to be founded in Europe – the Centro Sperimentale di Cinematografia, established in Rome by Mussolini's Fascist administration in 1935.[14] But following the end of World War II, a new wave of film schools emerged in many European national contexts, often seeking to 'rejuvenate or create

9 Ibidem, p. 114.

10 Ibidem, p. 114.

11 Ibidem, p. 125.

12 Szczepanik identifies the 'unit' as a mechanism for the organisation of film production within the State-Socialist system. He compares unit heads to producers but notes that they had less control over finance and marketing than Hollywood producers. Ibidem, p. 1[illegible]9.

13 Ibidem, p. 113.

14 D. Petrie and R. Stoneman, op. cit., p. 3.

vibrant national film industries and moving image cultures.'[15] During this immediate post-war period, film schools were founded in Hungary (1945), Czechoslovakia (1946), Poland (1948), Bulgaria (1948), Romania (1950) and East Germany (1954). Numerous Western European countries also established their own schools in the 1940s and 1950s (with Spain, Greece, and Austria followed by the Netherlands and Belgium), a succession of Scandinavian countries, West Germany and, in the 1970s, the UK.

Some of these schools had been preceded by earlier educational initiatives. For example a training workshop for filmmakers had existed in Kraków in 1945, but the decision was made to locate the new Polish national film school in Łódź, in part because the city was already home to a studio, established with equipment captured from the retreating German army. As Petrie points out Łódź Film School benefitted from the expertise of several individuals associated with the Society for the Promotion of Film Art (START), a cine-club founded in the 1930s.[16] Jerzy Toeplitz, one of the cineastes who had established START, was to become a leading figure in Polish film education in the post-war era. Toeplitz was appointed as President of Łódź Film School from 1949 to 1952 and held this role again from 1957 to 1968. During this second period of leadership, the remit of the Film School expanded beyond its initial emphasis on cinematography and directing to include actor training when, in 1958, it merged with the long-established Leon Schiller National Drama School.

Petrie describes the state-socialist model of the film school as a 'cornerstone of state centralization, providing aspiring practitioners with a single approved route'[17] into the industry. Yet he also notes the complex role assigned to film within communist ideology, emphasising that it was often acknowledged as an 'art form' with a role to play in national culture, rather than simply a mass entertainment, a view expounded by Toeplitz among others. By the mid-1950s a new generation of Polish filmmakers, many of them graduates of Łódź Film School, had emerged onto the international stage. Encompassing such celebrated figures as the directors Andrzej Wajda, Andrzej Munk and Janusz Morgerstern and the cinematographers Jerzy Lipman, Jerzy Wójcik, and Mieczysław Jahoda, the new movement (very often termed the 'Polish School') articulated a 'revisionist analysis of the experience of war that resisted the rigid formulations of socialist realism.'[18] While some of these filmmakers migrated, due to pressures faced in the era of Stalinism, others retained a strong association with the Film School and combined their teaching responsibilities with professional commitments as directors and cinematographers.

In 1965, Toeplitz was invited to present a lecture on 'The Creative Impulse in Film-Making' at Edinburgh film festival.[19] According to Petrie, the lecture emphasised the importance of engaging with the history of film art but, more specifically, it outlined a demanding four-year curriculum of production for directors and cinematographers. In accordance with this curriculum, first year students at the Film School worked as a group to devise a documentary, which was shot by a professional director and cinematographer, with each student then required to produce their own edit.

---

15 Ibidem, p. 3.

16 D. Petrie, 'Continental Film Schools: A Brief History of the "National Conservatoire,"' in *Educating Film-Makers*, p. 29.

17 Ibidem, p. 29.

18 Ibidem.

19 D. Petrie, op. cit., p. 30. Petrie lists only the English language title for this paper.

In second year, students made both a silent fiction film short and documentary short with sound, followed in third year by a longer fiction film, a TV show or a 'live' film. Students could then choose from four possible formats for their final year project (fiction, documentary, TV or educational film).

The Łódź Film School model was recognised, even prior to Toeplitz's presentation, as distinctive both because of the emphasis placed on silent, and therefore image-led, assignments and for the sheer volume of material shot by camera students.[20] The school's international standing had also been enhanced by the critical success of student productions such as Polański's film *Two Men and a Wardrobe* (1958), widely screened at festivals. In 1968, however, a pro-nationalist and anti-Semitic campaign led to the expulsion of over 15,000 Polish Jews and Toeplitz was forced out of the Film School. This situation, Petrie notes, allowed 'the return [...] of some of the more conservative "founding members"' of Łódź Film School.[21] The Workshop of the Film Form emerged within this charged context of social, political, and institutional unrest. Robakowski, who began his studies in the school's cinematography department in 1966, after completing an art history degree in Toruń, emphasises that many students protested against government anti-Semitism.[22] But Robakowski also points to some pre-existing difficulties with the curriculum and administration at Łódź. For example, he notes that filmmakers employed as professors in the school were frequently absent, attending international festivals or participating in juries etc. This was a source of frustration for some students, who had succeeded in a highly competitive admission process. They sought a more robust programme of studies, which would not be dominated or disrupted by the demands of the film industry.

Infrastructure and Influences

By 1970, Robakowski would have been coming to the end of his formal studies at Łódź but he had established strong connections within the Film School, contributing as an assistant to the teaching team. So he was highly familiar with the existing institutional structures and systems and played a key role in establishing the Workshop a student association. This meant that members could access material and technological resources such as equipment, film stock and professional broadcasting facilities, and also use the educational context of the school to engage in a range of artistic and pedagogical experiments. The early enthusiasm of some Film School personnel, such as Jerzy Kotowski, had helped to ensure that the new student society was formally accepted by the board of the school. Once this recognition had been achieved, Robakowski describes the activities of the Workshop as a programme of 'self-education' that involved tapping into resources overlooked by many professors. But he also notes that some of the members continued to produce their school assignments, while also working experimentally.[23]

The Workshop seems to have functioned very effectively as a mechanism of self-education, and as a structure for accessing and utilising all available resources. Workshop members knew that the Film School was the main contact point for foreign embassies seeking to promote their

20 This high volume of production was noted in a report on the Film School written by Robert Gessner. R. Gessner, 'Report from Lodz,' *Sight and Sound*, 32:2, 1963, pp. 66–7, quoted in D. Petrie, op. cit., p. 30.

21 D. Petrie, op. cit., p. 31.

22 Interview with Józef Robakowski, May 2016.

23 Interview with Józef Robakowski, May 2016.

national cinemas internationally. Since it had been established as a student society, the Workshop could access preview copies of British, French and US films, screening them for free in the School's own cinema. In addition, as students and associates of the Film School, Workshop members sometimes found opportunities to travel internationally, visiting festivals and schools in Moscow, East Berlin and Budapest and establishing important dialogues with other filmmakers and students, particularly in Hungary.[24]

Robakowski was not the only Workshop member who understood how to utilise the infrastructure and organisation of the Film School to achieve critical and artistic objectives. He was also just one of several Workshop members to be employed by the school and the others included Paweł Kwiek, Janusz Połom, and Ryszard Waśko. Połom, a student in the cinematography department and a member of the Workshop from 1971 onward, maintained a particularly long association with the Film School and he eventually became Dean of the Faculty of Cinematography and Directing in the early 1980s. Połom acknowledges that some of the film professors were absent due to industry commitments during the late 1960s. He emphasises that the workshop initially received significant support from within the Faculty (citing Jerzy Mierzejewski as particularly important).[25] But, Połom notes, when the cinematography students started to make their own short films, independent of the directing students and without conventional scripts, problems arose.[26] By moving away from the established director-led and usually script-based system, the Workshop may have challenged long-standing concepts of authorship, disrupting administrative routines and systems used to govern and regulate production assignments in any Film School.

Workshop Pedagogy and Process

During their primary period of activity, from 1970 to 1977, Workshop members produced a huge variety of films, videos, artworks and performances, both individually and collectively. It is clear that the Workshop's members wanted to develop alternatives to the established norms of cinematography associated with the Polish school.[27] Many works by Robakowski, Kwiek and Różycki, focused attention aspects of the filmmaking process, including camera operation, editing, and direction, which might otherwise be overlooked. It is possible to identify several works that draw attention to the body of the camera operator, the body of the actor, and the body of the film, often by using unconventional techniques or methods, which were sometimes conceived or conducted as pedagogical exercises.

In Robakowski's film *I'm Going* (1973), attention is focuses on the body of the artist in the role of camera operator. This film consists of a single unedited shot filmed by Robakowski as he steadily ascends the steps leading to the top of a metal tower used in parachute training at a pre-World War Two Sports stadium. *I'm Going* can be understood as the document of a performative action, the structure of which is determined by the material bodies of the tower and the

24 Interview with Józef Robakowski, May 2016.

25 Interview with Janusz Połom, May 2016.

26 Połom emphasises that scripts were not used in the making of workshop films, noting that only short descriptions were prepared in advance of films.

27 Różycki notes that, at that time, Łódź Film School was strongly associated with one specific cinematographic style, usually characterised by a slow pace of action, with long takes.

artist. Reflecting upon this work, Robakowski specifically emphasises his intention to remove the camera from the eye and from the role of observer, treating it instead as a part of his body. It is possible to situate *I'm Going* within the context of a much broader investigation of the camera during the early 1970s. There are parallels (for example) with the work of Jonas Mekas, known for his sustained interest in the camera as prosthetic extension. But while Mekas worked primarily with narrow gauge film, and subsequently video, Robakowski was carrying a heavy 35 mm film camera, and the physical effort involved in the climb is vividly registered in the sounds of breathing. Łukasz Ronduda describes him as 'delving into his own materiality' so that the subject 'becomes merely a thing among things, a living fragment of the matter', articulating 'a non-anthropocentric point of perception of the world.'[28]

I'm Going also seems to articulate the experience of the labouring, camera-bearing body that is often absent from cinematography. It is particularly at odds with the vantage point of the disembodied floating perspective enabled by stabilising technologies such as the steadicam, developed in the late 1970s. While *I'm Going* emphasises the bodily presence and agency of the individual filmmaker, Robakowski also realised a number of 'assembled' films, involving the participation of students. In *22x* (1971) he gave each student several metres of unexposed film stock, inviting them to apply their chosen material procedures. Most used chisels and cutters to scratch the emulsion and many of them also manipulated the optical sound strip on the film. Edited by Robakowski into a single sequence, with each strip numbered, this film articulates some of the contradictions integral to the workshop, manifesting a collaborative mode of production, but fusing the roles of director and teacher. *22x* has been described by Robakowski as an attempt to produce an 'objective' cinematic presentation of an artistic community – a community that clearly included students and educators.

It was hugely important for the Workshop to establish a strong artistic community, which was not dependent upon official modes of assessment and validation, but was rather connected to a rich history and legacy of avant-garde practice. Many of the Workshop members were interested in recovering overlooked aspects of Polish avant-garde practice and, for this reason, they made several films about Polish artists, including Katarzyna Kobro, Władysław Strzemiński, Tytus Czyżewski, Leon Chwistek, Witkacy, Wacław Szpakowski, and Henryk Stażewski. The Workshop was also a means to question prevailing definitions of the contemporary 'artistic community'. Robakowski observes that, in the 1970s, it was necessary to be a graduate of the Fine Art academy and a member of the association of artists to be recognised as an artist. In contrast, the Workshop offered a much more open space, reaching out to practitioners who were outside the official systems of art and film education.[29]

The Workshop also engaged in events and actions that extended beyond established contexts and formats such as the cinema screening and the exhibition, often using art galleries and public space as performance spaces. Andrzej Różycki devised several gallery performances, including *Ostensible Identification* (1973) an action involving projection onto his own body. He wanted to use projected photographic images to explore how the film 'protagonist' is defined, questioning whether a protagonist could exist before and after a film. So, for example, he showed slide images of himself engaged in simple activities, such as playing football, and then during the projection he

---

28 Ł. Ronduda, *Polish Art of the 70s*, Warsaw: Center for Contemporary Art - Ujazdowski Castle, 2009, p. 282.

29 For example, Robakowski describes Andrzej Partum, an actor and self-educated practitioner, as 'extremely important' to the art scene. Interview with Józef Robakowski, May 2016.

performed these activities. In another work, entitled *Living Projection (*1975),[30] he investigated the notion that 'film is movement' by suspending a piece of film (just five frames) in front of the projector so that the current of warm air from its motor would cause the film strip to move gently. So this work created an impression of projection, without actually projecting film.

Into the Television Studio

Of all the workshop filmmakers, Paweł Kwiek was the one most influenced by cybernetic theory, approaching the film school as one element of a larger cultural, economic, political and social system.[31] This focus on cybernetics was obviously not specific to the Polish context in the 1970s, and there are many interconnections with (for example) the work of artists such as Hans Haacke and Steven Willats, as well as others working more specifically with film and video, including Les Levine, David Lamelas, Frank Gillette and Ira Schneider. Unlike some of these artists, however, Kwiek (along with other members of the Workshop of the Film Form) had very direct and sustained access to a television studio and could readily experiment with broadcasting technology and organisational systems. In works such as *Video A - A Studio Situation* (1974) Kwiek takes on the role of director and performer, conducting a test involving three camera positions. A subsequent work, *Video C* (1975) introduces a new element in the form of a computer graphic interface. Like Robakowski, Kwiek was interested in the relationship between humans and machines. But while *I'm Going* articulates a continual, and forcefully embodied, movement through space, Kwiek's video deal with a 'studio situation' in which physical motion is both constrained and reduced. This is particularly apparent in *Video C*, which features various details of the human-machine interface, such as the arrows visible on the screen and the levers that form part of the control desk.

Kwiek emphasises that, because the Workshop members 'had professional skills and status' due to their association with Łódź Film School, 'they were not considered as outsiders to the TV studio.'[32] Janusz Połom notes that the Director of Polish national television was 'enthusiastic' about the workshop, ensuring its members had full access to the broadcast facilities, including the mobile broadcast unit.[33] In practice, however, Workshop members had to find ways of operating within existing hierarchies and structures, communicating their requirements to engineers and other studio personnel. Kwiek's performative actions were filmed, under his direction, by colleagues from the camera department at Łódź, but he also required the assistance of a studio engineer who he describes as 'quite cooperative.' Kwiek suggests that his video works have sometimes been (mis)interpreted as a critique of the Polish television institution, and also of 'the system, the communist party and censorship.'[34] It seems that he was more concerned with television (in general) as an institution that involves the control and mediation of communication, through the agency of engineers as well as editors, who determine what is 'seen on TV.'

---

30 Interview with Andrzej Różycki, May 2016.

31 Kwiek was also very interested in psychometric approaches to the study of human intelligence, such as those developed by J. P. Guilford and utilised in the training of soldiers and pilots encompassing 'understanding, systems, relations, changes, classes, independent people, operations, memory, cognition.' Personal interview with Paweł Kwiek, May 2016.

32 Interview with Paweł Kwiek, May 2016.

33 Interview with Janusz Połom, May 2016.

34 Interview with Paweł Kwiek, May 2016.

It is unclear whether Kwiek's studio situation works were ever broadcast, but he recalls that several Workshop members participated in a televised discussion with other filmmakers, devised for an arts programme that was broadcast live on Poland's second TV channel in 1975. There are parallels to be drawn here with other contexts, both in Europe and in the US, since many broadcasters seems to have been interested in radical film and video cultures in the late 1960s and early 1970s. The history of *Black Gate Cologne*, an experimental event devised for German television, broadcast in 1968, is relatively well known. But British broadcasters were also interested in aspects of this experimental culture and, in the late 1960s, London-based artist and activist John Hoppy Hopkins had founded a radical video group called TVX with Cliff Evans, who was then working at the BBC as a trainee cameraman. TVX organised a series of experimental 'happenings' at the New Arts Lab in London, in collaboration with the London Film Makers Co-op, using video equipment donated by John Lennon.[35] In 1969 they were invited, by Tom Corcoran, the director of the BBC2 arts show *Late Night Line Up*, to take advantage of studio downtime by staging a gathering of musicians and friends.[36] The result was *Videospace*, which Hopkins describes as including 'a light show, a studio discussion and some experimentation in the control room with a vision mixer [...] synthesiser or colouriser'.[37] This material was never broadcast but TVX were subsequently commissioned to produce a series of short promotional 'visualisations,' which were aired by the BBC, yet proved to be controversial.[38]

Also worth mentioning in this context is the work of the US-based video group Videofreex, particularly their tape *process video revolution,* which documents a failed attempt to make a public TV show about video collectives in April 1971.[39] The tape was shot in a working television studio and it depicts broadcast personnel struggling to integrate the broadcast system with the portable video technology used by the Videofreex and other collectives. Rather than participating in the discussion with other activist groups, the bearded and casually-dressed 'freex' move around, recording the clean-shaven and smartly-dressed broadcast production personnel at work. One of the broadcast engineers warns that they 'can't shoot in the studio' and when the Videofreex crew persist, they are told, in a vaguely threatening tone 'This is a union shop. You can't do that here.'

At that time, television studios in both the US and Poland would have been staffed by engineers, camera operators, and other workers who were most likely union members, with highly regulated and standardised workflows and roles. John T. Caldwell and Deirdre Boyle have both produced interesting accounts of the tensions between guerrilla TV collectives and broadcasters in the US during the 1970s.[40] These tensions were partly ideological but also linked to labour changes associated with new video technologies. For example, when video was used in television

35 S. Partridge, 'Artists' Television: Interruptions – Interventions,' in *REWIND British Artists' Video in the 1970s & 1980s*, ed. S. Cubitt and S. Partridge, New Barnet: John Libbey Publishing, 2012, p. 75.
36 A. Lockhart, 'A Brief History of Video – Time and Base,' in *REWIND*, pp. 182–83.
37 J. 'Hoppy' Hopkins, cited by S. Partridge, op. cit., p. 76.
38 M. Dickson, 'Vide Verso: Video's Critical Corpus,' in *REWIND*, p. 129. Dickson does not specify whether the 'visualisations' were shown on BBC1 or BBC2, but he notes that TVX were subsequently 'banned from the BBC.'
39 D. Boyle, *Subject to Change: Guerrilla Television Revisited*, New York and Oxford: Oxford University Press, 1997, pp. 17–25.
40 J. T. Caldwell, *Televisuality: Style, Crisis, and Authority in American Television*, New Brunswick, N.J: Rutgers University Press, 1995; D. Boyle, op. cit., pp. 17–25.

news gathering, the smaller handheld cameras meant that the size of the crew could be reduced. Television personnel had to adapt to new production processes and altered workflows, associated with the introduction of each new technology. Writing in the UK context, John Wyver has also highlighted tensions in the relationship between artists and TV workers in the European context, noting that artists often saw themselves as reformers of television and tended to disregard the technical and craft-based knowledges of broadcast engineers, editors, and camera operators.[41] In some instances these conflicts were related to differences in education and it is here that the particularity of the Workshop comes into focus, because the Film School was a recognised pathway into Polish broadcasting and its students had a high level of technical knowledge.

Yet even though they were being trained to work within an industrial context, the Workshop members consciously and consistently sought recognition as artists. This was achieved through their collaborations with other artists, including those associated with the Fine Arts Academy, through their participation in gallery exhibitions, performance and actions, their films about the history of avant-garde, and their development of projects that did not conform to the dominant script-based, director-led model of production in Polish cinema. The position of 'artist' may have been especially appealing to Workshop members seeking to circumvent the dominance of the director as auteur, within the Polish School and within cinematography generally.[42] From this perspective, *I'm Going* is a particularly significant and effective articulation of the camera operator as artist since, like much performance art of the 1970s, it explored and manifested a strong sense of bodily presence and endurance.

Conclusion: Workshop Legacies

By the mid-1970s, Łódź Film School was becoming less hospitable to the Workshop. Robakowski suggests that Stanisław Kuszewski, who was a head of the Film School in Łódź from 1973 until 1980, was frustrated by the attention and interest generated by their activities.[43] Financial support for the society was withdrawn and the members needed to find new sources of funding. But even though their shared activities declined after 1977, following their involvement in Documenta 6, many workshop members remained closely involved in the school. Kwiek taught there in the late 1970s[44] and together with other Workshop members and associates, including Połom, Robakowski and Ryszard Waśko, he contributed to the establishment of new movement for the 'restoration' and reform of the school.[45] The restoration committee organised various strikes and protests, with the aim of opening the school to other media, including photography and, after negotiations with Ministry of Culture, a new system was introduce to ensure a free election of senior faculty.

Połom was subsequently elected as Dean of the Faculty of Cinematography but his appointment in 1981 coincided with the implementation of Martial Law in Poland in an attempt to crush political opposition. This period, which lasted officially until 1983 but continued to affect political, social and cultural life for many subsequent years, was marked by political repression, censorship, travel

41 J. Wyver, 'TV Against TV: Video Art on Television,' in *Film and Video Art*, ed. S. Comer, London: Tate Publishing, 2009, pp. 122–31.

42 C. Greenhalgh, 'Shooting from the Heart – Cinematographers and their Medium,' in *Making Pictures: A Century of European Cinematography*, ed. M. Leitch, New York: Harry N. Abrams, 2003, p. 146.

43 Interview with Józef Robakowski, May 2016.

44 Interview with Paweł Kwiek, May 2016.

45 Interview with Paweł Kwiek, May 2016. This history is documented by Ł. Ronduda, op. cit., p. 273.

restrictions and also economic hardship, all of which led to increased emigration. Although Połom remained in the role of dean for several years (emigrating to Mexico in 1984), it was increasingly difficult to negotiate between the radical aspirations of the students and the demands of a restrictive cultural and political administration. By the end of the 1980s, many of the former Workshop members had left the school or emigrated, but this dissociation was not permanent. In 1995, Robakowski again began teaching at Łódź and he has continued to play a role within the Film School. He has witnessed significant shifts in the institution, to the extent that he now recognises the curriculum 'as the one we wanted to have in the 1970s' since it now encompasses previously excluded media such as animation, electronic art, photography.'[46]

Robakowski's ongoing involvement in the Film School helps to ensure a continued awareness of the Workshop and its critique of film education, at least in Łódź.[47] But the positive developments he describes are in contrast to the broader trends analysed by Petrie and Stoneman in *Educating Film-makers*. While their study is not specifically concerned with developments at Łódź Film School, they identify significant changes in film education after 1989, explicitly shaped by the demands of globalisation and the marketplace. Petrie and Stoneman argue that many film schools have now moved away from the earlier model of cinema as an 'auteur-driven, socially-relevant cultural expression.'[48] In this globalised marketplace, they argue, even the most 'established' school struggles to function as 'a site for innovation and new thinking,' tending instead to 'adopt a more overtly professional role, dictated by the needs of industry, which has served to reproduce commercial forms and arguably discourage genuine originality.'[49]

Interestingly, Petrie and Stoneman are openly in favour of 'innovation,' a buzzword of neoliberal cultural and economic policy, so they do not actually reject the demands of the globalised marketplace. They insist, however, that innovation cannot be fostered by market-driven models of specialisation and they specifically bemoan the emergence of separate spheres of practical and theoretical film education, which has severed practice from critique. It seems difficult, at first, to reconcile Duncan and Petrie's rather grim account of post-1989 developments in industry-oriented film education with the progressive environment described by Robakowski at Łódź and it is certainly possible that the Polish educational context simply differs from the norm. Petrie does acknowledge the existence of 'countervailing tendencies' in film education, citing the critical and commercial success of the Danish model in the late 1990s, a period marked by the emergence of the Dogme 95 movement. He notes that students in all departments in the Danish National Film School are required to study dramaturgy and to work within clearly assigned limits and constraints,[50] engaging in exercises that do not involve reproducing industry formats.

It is clear that new skills and attributes are required to operate in an increasingly unstable labour environment, almost all film and media workers, whether they are above or below the line, must now use a range of new strategies and techniques to negotiate and secure work assignments.

---

46 Interview with Józef Robakowski, May 2016.

47 The curriculum still does not fully address the history of multimedia and histories of art and film tend to remain separate from each other. Personal interview with Andrzej Różycki, Łódź, May 2016.

48 D. Petrie, R. Stoneman, op. cit., pp. 5–6.

49 D. Petrie, R. Stoneman, op. cit., p. 6.

50 D. Petrie, op. cit., pp. 38–9.

So, for example, they must continually extend and maintain their professional networks, engaging with new technologies, radically-altered workflows and hierarchies (particularly in the camera department), insisting upon the employment rates and standards secured by guilds and unions through collective bargaining, while also asserting their adaptability and flexibility.[51] John T. Caldwell has used the term 'worker blowback' to describe some of the strategies used by film and media professionals to assert their professional (and artistic) credentials, while also airing grievances and anxieties, via industry-focused social media. Through these forms of protest and critique, film and media practitioners may frame their own anxieties through reference to concerns about declining standards, appealing to abstract artistic (or craft) values assumed to be under threat.

As students of Łódź Film School in the late 1960 and early 1970s, the Workshop members were being educated to operate within the well-established culture and relatively protected labour structures of state-socialist film production and distribution. Despite the restrictions associated with this system – such as the pressures of censorship – the conditions of employment for technical workers were fairly stable. Yet within the Polish context, production processes and systems were very often organised around the figure of the auteur-director. Through their critique of conventions and norms of filmmaking, the Workshop members imagined, and sought to create, an alternative economy of production and distribution, which offered much greater artistic autonomy for cinematographers, enabled new and unconventional forms of interdisciplinary collaboration and supported experimentation with new media and technologies. In the process, they devised a whole array of strategies that might now prove particularly useful for students seeking to navigate a radically-altered labour environment, characterised by new (and shifting) professional assignments, hierarchies and identities.

Many researchers have highlighted the challenges that are now faced by workers in the film and media industries, particularly those positioned 'below the line,'[52] including precariously employed production researchers, runners, visual effects artists, or self-employed videographers. To date, however, relatively little attention has focused on the industry-oriented film school, as an environment in which professional expectations and entitlements are cultivated and managed.[53] There is much to be gained by analysing the processes through which concepts of 'professionalism' (and related notions of 'labour,' 'craft,' 'art,' and 'innovation') are continuously formed and articulated within film education. National film schools are especially significant, as state-sponsored and professionally-recognised environments that either critique or replicate the behaviour and values of specific production cultures and labour environments. The history of the Workshop of the Film Form, and its complex relationship to Łódź Film School, offers a particularly important resource in thinking about the past, present, and future of film education.

51 J. T. Caldwell, 'Worker Blowback: User-Generated, Worker-Generated, and Producer-Generated Content within Collapsing Production Workflows,' in *Television as Digital Media*, ed. J. Bennett and N. Strange, Durham and London: Duke University Press, 2011, p. 302.

52 V. Mayer, *Below the Line: Producers and Production Studies in the New Television Economy*, Durham and London: Duke University Press, 2011, p. 1.

53 There some exceptions, such as Daniel Ashton's analysis of the expectations and experiences of film and media students and graduates entering the UK industry. D. Ashton, 'Making Media Workers: Contesting Film and Television Industry Career Pathways,' *Television & New Media*, 16:3, 2015, pp. 275–94.

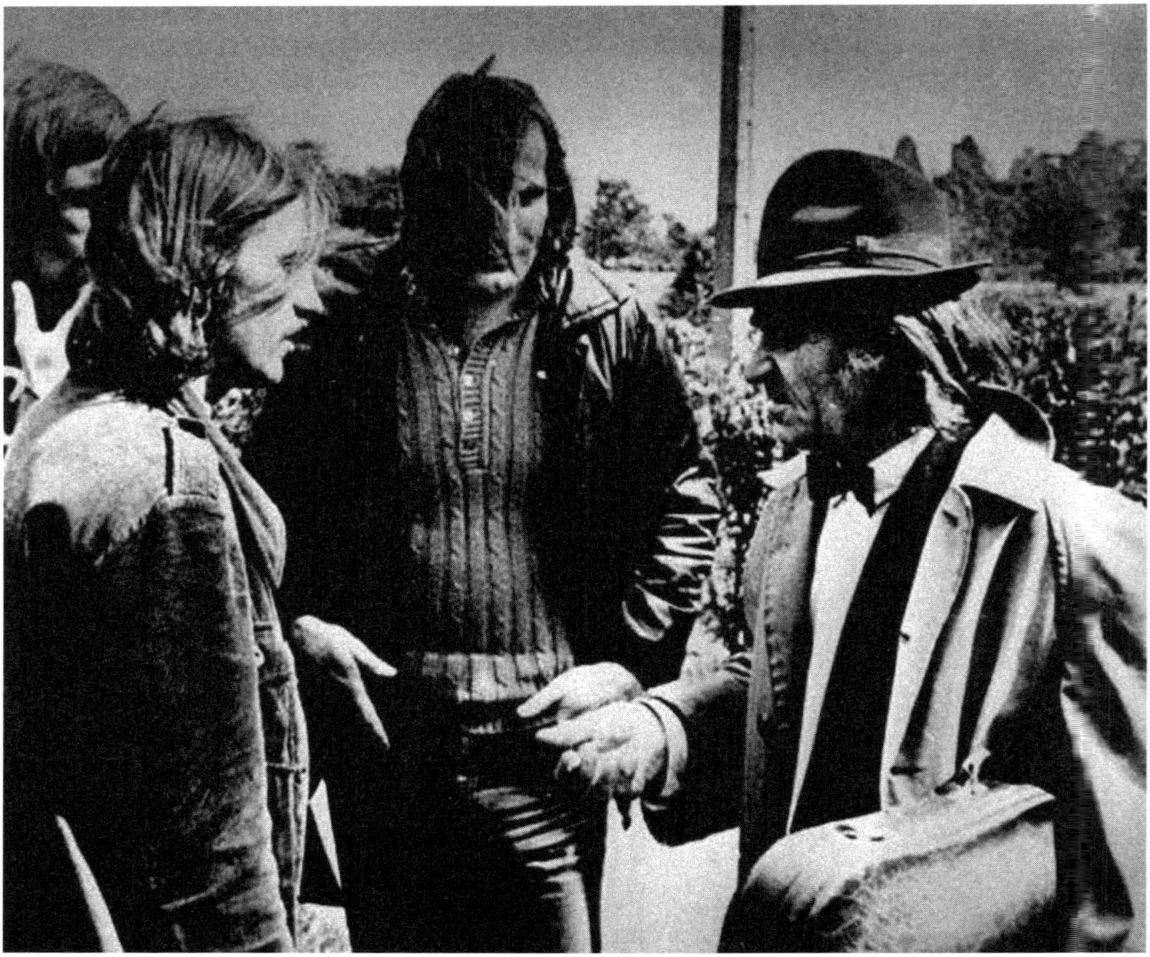

Od lewej: Władysław Wieczorkiewicz, Józef Robakowski, Wacław Antczak
From the left: Władysław Wieczorkiewicz, Józef Robakowski, Wacław Antczak

Łukasz Ronduda

Workshop of the Film Form or the Coalition of Art Workers in a Workers' State

The turn of the 1970s brought an intensified use of the term 'art worker' amongst avant-garde artists on both sides of the Iron Curtain. It is therefore interesting to analyse the differences and similarities between those who employed this term in almost the same period: the New York artists from the Art Workers' Coalition (AWC) operating in the mainstay of the capitalist West, and artists of the Workshop of the Film Form (WFF) on the other side of the Iron Curtain: in Poland under Communism. The members of both groups participated in the Conceptual and Minimalist revolution in art at the turn of the 1970s. Yet, they were immersed in entirely different social, political and economic realms. The AWC were active at the time of 'an emancipatory anomaly within capitalism,'[1] diagnosed by Thomas Piketty, which lasted from the 1950s to the 1970s. That anomaly resulted from Real Socialism – the regime under which the WFF functioned – whose sheer existence compelled capitalism in the Western countries to introduce a higher level of social equality, redistribution, levelling of social inequalities, etc. The AWC used the figure of the art worker in the context of their critique of capitalism with a reference to the general frame set by the above-mentioned anomaly, conditioned by the existence of a universal anti-capitalist emancipatory project, which (at least theoretically) came in the form of Communism. In turn, the WFF made a subversive use of that term in the context of the workers' state, the dictatorship of the proletariat, which was meant to lead to Communism. The WFF artists tapped into such official Marxist terms because for them it was the only form of open critique of reality that was possible in the authoritarian state.

Art Workers' Coalition

Art Workers' Coalition was founded in January 1969 in New York and gathered artists who recognised the necessity to reform the institutions of the contemporary art world, especially in the light of the countercultural and leftist movements that were gaining ground in America during that period. According to Julia Bryan-Wilson, the members of the AWC deliberately referred to themselves as workers in the field of art, and not as artists, since they wanted to remove the focus from Romantic connotations related to the latter term.[2] The term 'art worker' offered a pragmatic possibility to establish a broad trade union of artists engaged in building a community above aesthetic divisions and fighting together more effectively for their rights in relation with the institutions that processed their artistic production. The members of the AWC staged several dozens of protests, manifestations and strikes targeted against institutions (such as New York's MoMA), criticising their instrumental approach to artists and their works, the racism and sexism that was

1 T. Piketty, *Capital in the Twenty-First Century*, tr. A. Goldhammer, Cambridge, Mass: Harvard University Press, 2015.

2 J. Bryan-Wilson, *Art Workers – Radical Practise in the Vietnam War Era*, Berkeley: University of California Press, 2009.

rife in their exhibition policies, and their many-sided entanglement in the Vietnam War. The AWC members even set out to build a broader coalition with workers of other industries (for example they participated in a strike of postal workers), but ultimately to no avail. The term 'art worker' (as opposed to other terms, such as 'cultural producer') seemed very attractive to the AWC members in terms of its political charge (the pursuit of emancipation, equality, the struggle of the exploited classes for their rights), which could be used at the same time in the struggle with the dominant institutions, but also serve to problematize in an interesting way their own artistic practice embedded in the new tendencies of the turn of the 1970s, which were struggling for a broader recognition at the time. For the AWC mostly comprised artists who worked in the field of Conceptualism and Minimalism and stepped against the apolitical, abstract and expressive art of their predecessors, who dominated American institutions of the period. For that reason, those artists (among them Carl Andre, Robert Morris, Dan Graham) were keen to position their highly sophisticated artistic approach and creation – not in the least meant for workers – in the context of such categories as 'art worker,' 'work,' 'production.'

Workshop of the Film Form

Inasmuch as in the context of capitalism the term 'art worker,' which bore distinctively socialist connotations, had an emancipatory dimension, the same term by necessity acquired a different meaning in the anti-capitalist Poland, which was at least theoretically governed by workers, and where the terminology of the Marxist class struggle functioned as the dominant language of describing reality. Generally speaking, the members of the Workshop of the Film Form used the term 'art worker' in three different contexts: to describe their artistic-cognitive approach, to pursue a socio-political critique, and to develop an institutional critique.

The artists of the Workshop of the Film Form described their analytical-minimalist artistic approach with reference to the tradition of Soviet Constructivism and the artist-engineer ethos. Hence the term 'art worker', by means of which they deliberately rejected the term 'artist' in order to counter the Romantic model of artistic practice with a Positivist model. The WFF artists considered their creative practice in materialistic and egalitarian terms as a quasi-scientific cognitive work (tapping into science to investigate the workings of perception, imagination, etc.). It was supposed to be accessible to everyone, and its stake was a critical awareness of the surrounding world. The latter (in the Marxist spirit) was to enhance the 'productive forces' of the human being (art worker) and guide them towards augmenting his or her talents, strengthening his 'psycho-physical posture', thus leading to an increased emancipation, and therefore social equality. Besides such Marxist-oriented understanding of their role as art workers, the members of the WFF appreciated the qualities originating from the realm of industrial work, such as the truth (nature) of the material, the logic of the structure, the rationalism of planning.

The second field in which the term 'art worker' came to be used by the WFF was the sphere of socio-political critique. It is worth noting here that at the beginning of the 1970s artists who originated from intelligentsia used that term in a situation where the position of the working class had changed completely as compared to merely a decade before. Researchers into the class structure of Poland under Communism in the 1970s, such as Henryk Domański[3] and Maciej Gdula

3 H. Domański, *Czy są w Polsce klasy społeczne,* Warszawa: Wydawnictwo Krytyki Politycznej, 2015.

highlight a class conflict that was making itself manifest already at that time in the Communist (and declaratively classless) state, as well as the dichotomist division between the society of exploited workers and the political authorities who exploited them and enjoyed access to privileges, accumulated capital and held power. It was particularly in the 1970s that the party renounced its struggle for equality. According to Maciej Gdula, 'until the end of the 1960s, the political imagination in Poland was dominated by a search for the ways of building a just society. This fact made itself manifest both in the intellectual tendencies in the proximity of the ruling Party and in projects that opposed its authority. The period after 1970 brought about a radical shift away from the ideal of a just society, which was replaced with the idea of an active society. Official language, culture and science changed, and political projects of the opposition were reshaped.'[4] Gdula remarks that in the 1970s the socialist authorities, which were opening up to the West, clearly departed from egalitarianism. 'An idea emerged to build a society that would not be founded on egalitarianism, but to a much larger degree on innovativeness and modernity [...] on a greater engagement of workers. It was supposed to push Socialism onto an entirely new track.'[5]

The above remarks shed a completely new light on the WFF's identification with workers. For the Workshop artists, such identification served as a way to operate with the aporias of the seemingly egalitarian Socialist state, which was essentially becoming more of a class society. In order to manifest their stance as art workers, many artists affiliated with the group chose workers' jackets – donkey jackets – as their everyday attire. Thus, they sought to underline the egalitarian character of their own artistic practice and their willingness to confront the cultural elites.[6] They often praised artists originating from the lumpenproletariat of the city of Łódź, whom they regarded as authentic, such as Wacław Antczak, Irena Iżykowska, Edward Kowalski, Jan Nowacki and many others. Those artists were given significant roles in the WFF's artistic undertakings or were invited to join the group as equal members. That was how Wacław Antczak, tailor by profession and one of the film extras working for the Film School in Łodź, became an active and full right member of the group. For the Workshop artists Antczak was synonymous with a self-made artist, who incarnated all the virtues of a genuine artist: simplicity, authenticity, honesty. They regarded him as a true art worker. Antczak became the focus of the WFF's group project *Transmission from Łódź*, in which they transmitted his personality by way of a variety of media to the São Paulo Art Biennial in 1973.[7] Bearing witness to the fascination with Antczak are predominantly the films: *Reincarnation* from 1974 (created by the entire group and featuring Antczak as he recites his poem), *Execution*

---

4 M. Gdula in conversation with Magdalena Błędowska, 'Jak naród nie obalił komuny,' *Dziennik Opinii Krytyki Politycznej*, 13th June 2014, www.krytykapolityczna.pl/artykuly/rozmowa-dnia/20140604/gdula-4-czerwca-1989-jak-narod-nie-obalil-komuny [accessed: 22nd October 2016].

5 Ibidem.

6 Within their actions members of the Workshop of the Film Form, dressed as workers, would intervene in various intellectual undertakings created with the people in mind. For instance, from the position of 'ordinary workers from the Gdańsk Shipyard,' they publicly mocked the feature film debut of Krzysztof Teodor Toeplitz and Jerzy Gruza *The Woodpecker* (*Dzięcioł*) at the Young Filmmakers' Festival. The reason was that according to Robakowski, the film was 'far removed from any kind of reality, and a typical example of a luxury socialist fad.' Statement from Józef Robakowski's interview with the author.

7 After Antczak's death, the members of the Workshop published a book with his epic literary work, W. Antczak, *Antoś Rozpylacz. Polski Odyseusz. Najsławniejszy wojownik w walce z Niemcami hitlerowskimi*, Łódź: PWSFTviT, 2008.

by Paweł Kwiek (1972, missing), and *As if Better* by Andrzej Różycki (1974). As a full right member of the WFF, Antczak participated in various group excursions: to Zakopane (Festival of Films on Art), Elbląg (Meetings of Young Creative Workshop Kinolaboratorium during the 5th Biennial of Spatial Forms), Warsaw (art event *The Cleaning of Art)*. In 1971, Antczak participated alongside Jan Świdziński in a theoretical session organised at the Film School by the WFF members within the event 'Eighth Cinema,' as well as carried out the action *Furniture Sale* in Czerwony Rynek in Łódź, alongside Józef Robakowski.[8]

In this context it is worth highlighting yet another aspect of the art worker figure as an element of socio-political critique. It consists in the fact that as the members of the WFF, who mostly hailed from intellectual family backgrounds, sought to engage with the working class in the mid-1970s, they preferred to collaborate with the so-called lumpenproletariat than with ordinary factory workers. The group's activity in the context of the Łódź lumpenproletariat, which means people from the margins of the system who constantly need to struggle for survival, can be interpreted as an attempt to create a one-of-a-kind anarchic community of outcasts, outsiders, 'unproductive freeloaders'[9] as Robakowski calls them, who cannot bring any profit to the dominant system and whom the system cannot exploit in any way whatsoever.

Importantly, one of the members of the WFF, Paweł Kwiek, whose political views at the time differed from the rest of the group, engaged in a relatively close collaboration not only with the lumpenproletariat, but also with factory workers. Insofar as the majority of the WFF artists held anti-Communist views (although they were obviously unable to declare it officially), Paweł Kwiek strongly expressed his engagement and support for Socialism, a system that was being built in Poland at the time. He regarded it as an emancipatory and egalitarian project. As an art worker, Kwiek wanted the artist's work, akin to other workers' activities, to contribute to the success of the Socialist state. His understanding of the term 'art worker' differed from the meaning given to it by the other members of the Workshop of the Film Form.

In parallel to his activity in the Workshop of the Film Form, Paweł Kwiek also collaborated with a group of artists gathered around the artistic duo KwieKulik (Zofia Kulik, Przemysław Kwiek),[10] who were also actively engaged in Socialism, and who defined themselves as art workers in a similar fashion to Kwiek. The goal of political art of their making was to enhance communication between people, and in particular between the deprived and the privileged social classes. Founded on Oskar Hansen's theory of Open Form,[11] their projects were underpinned with the postulate of more egalitarian modes of communication, which was supposed to be based on dialogue and improve individual chances of emancipation, self-development and equal treatment. According to those artists, art needed to be treated seriously by the Communist authorities, which betrayed

8 It is worth adding that Różycki also made the film *Kowalski's Theatre* (*Teatr Kowalskiego*) devoted to the theatre group run by Edward Kowalski. In turn, within the action *Workshop* (*Warsztat*) at Muzeum Sztuki in Łódź, carried out upon Ryszard Stanisławski's invitation, the members of the group organised at the museum a costume performance of Edward Kowalski's Pensioners' Theatre (devoted to the fall of Adolf Hitler) as well as events open to all amateur artists—'the dillettanti concert' and an artistic signature contest.

9 Statement from Józef Robakowski's interview with the author.

10 *KwieKulik*, ed. Ł. Ronduda and G. Schollhammer, Zurich and Warsaw: JRP Ringier, 2013.

11 'Oskar Hansen—Opening Modernism', ed. A. Kędziorek and Ł. Ronduda, Warsaw: Museum of Modern Art, 2014.

an ever stronger orientation towards a social class system. One of the most interesting projects created along those lines resulted from a social-artistic action carried out by Paweł Kwiek in a small State Agricultural Farm (PGR) village of Niechcice. The artist made it possible for a group of youth, who mainly comprised children from workers' families in the village, to shoot several one-minute films based on their own scripts. In turn, the artist assumed the role of an obedient camera operator. Kwiek's aim was to 'give the voice to those who have so far been deprived of it.' By offering the young people of Niechcice a chance to make their own films, the artist sought to activate them and develop their critical and creative approach to reality; he wanted to help them realise the conditions that determined the shape of their life experience. In the following years Kwiek returned to Niechcice and went on to establish a long-term processual collaboration with the local workers' community.[12]

The third meaning of the term 'art worker' as used by the WFF artists referred to the context of institutional critique. They employed it mainly to underline their identification as a disregarded group within the official system of art institutions in Poland as part of their pursuit of emancipation. What they understood as the establishment were the official state institutions in charge of culture as well as institutions of the so-called consecrated avant-garde (for instance the Foksal Gallery), which hindered the development (institutionalisation) of new tendencies in avant-garde art – the tendencies which the art workers identified with. Pursuing a critique of art institutions, the WFF proposed a modernisation model that was different from the dominant one. Their critique consisted in posing content-related questions and attacking specific institutions, people, procedures (instead of engaging in abstract philosophical reflection), in laying bear the specific examples of financial, ideological and administrative entanglement of film and artistic practice. The WFF sought to merge institutional and artistic activity, while treating art and cinema in a pragmatic and desacralized way – as opposed to the dominant idealistic-Romantic traditions in art and film. The members of the group attempted to 'deflate' the grandiose events that celebrated the seeming successes of Polish cinema – events which in fact served to create those successes by way of excessive production of prizes and titles awarded to mediocre artists and their works, as well as by deploying insubstantial discourse based on schemes that were meant to grant undeservedly high rank to those films and conceal the nepotism involved in their making.

Conclusion

It was in a similar pragmatic way that the WFF and AWC artists departed from Romantic connotations attached to the terms 'art' and 'artist.' Both groups shared a strong orientation towards institutional critique and defining artists as exploited workers within the labour division of the institutional art world. What the two groups had in common was also the anti-establishment impulse to confront the dominant canon of art.

The AWC gathered artists who focused on the sheer ideas of institutional critique, whereas the WFF grouped artists who mainly shared similar artistic approaches, and it was only from those approaches that their institutional critique followed. Nevertheless, both the AWC and the

12 One of such visits resulted in a very interesting film *Sunday 15 April 1973 – Art Day in Niechcice* (*Niedziela 15.IV.73 – Dniem Sztuki w Niechcicach*).

WFF used the term 'art worker' in direct connection with the Conceptual-Minimalist revolution in art, and with their fascination with qualities that originated from the world of industrial labour. The Workshop members criticised art institutions mainly from an aesthetic, and not political, perspective by laying bear the mystifications and empty gestures of the institutional art world and cinematography. As opposed to the AWC, they did not fight for the rights of women artists, representatives of minorities and their enhanced presence in art institutions. The AWC also attacked official state policies (Vietnam War). In turn, the WFF could not do it openly and therefore focused rather on a critique of the growing class divide in the seemingly classless Socialist state. However, Paweł Kwiek's practice engaged with the contexts of struggle for the emancipation of marginalised and oppressed groups, which was also important for the American art workers. In general, the members of the WFF combined institutional critique with successful coalitions with the working class, which the AWC did not manage to achieve.

A recapitulation of sorts of the history of art workers from the WFF and the AWC came with the exhibition *Construction in Process*, which led to an encounter between the Polish and American art workers (Dan Graham, Carl Andre, among others). That exhibition ushered in a unique collaboration between the neoavant-garde artists gathered around the former members of the WFF and the workers' trade union 'Solidarity,' which became the patron of the show. The motto of the exhibition were the words of Mieczysław Szczuka, who said: 'Art cannot be an empty ornamentation of the society, the artist must co-participate in the organisation of life.'[13] The self-organising artists – 'art workers' – who created a grassroots exhibition of their works found an ally in the self-organising workers' trade union 'Solidarity,' which formed its grassroots structures in the realm of a hostile state – socialist only in its declarations.

13 J. Głowacki, *Konstrukcja w procesie*, in *Muzeum Konstrukcji w Procesie*, ed. M. Szymańska, Łódź: Fundacja Edukacji Wizualnej, 2006).

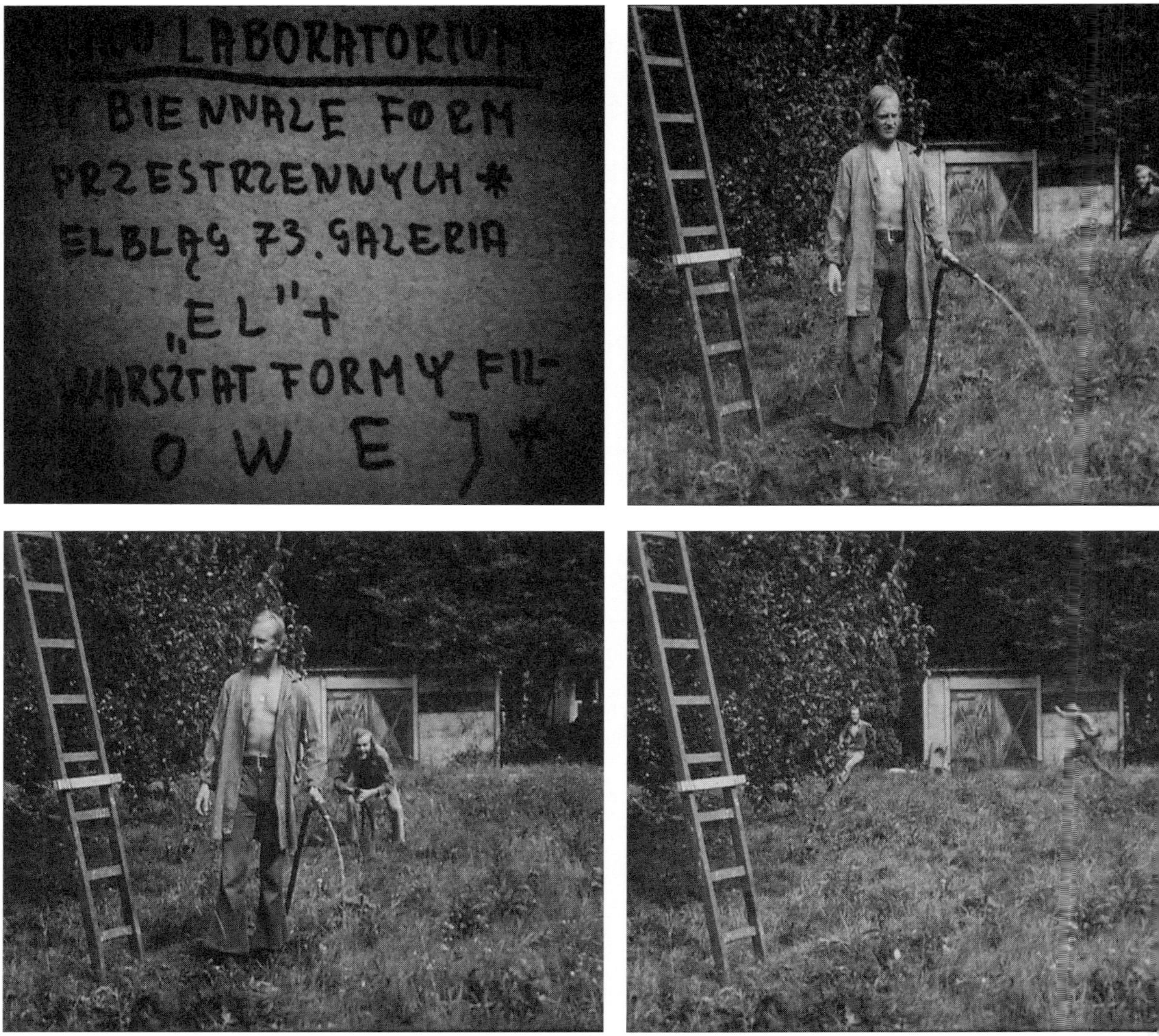

Paweł Kwiek, *Polewacz polany*, (fragment filmu *Kinolaboratorium*), 1973
Paweł Kwiek, *Sprinkler sprinkled*, (part of the film *Cinemalaboratory*), 1973

George Clark

Contact with the Polish Avant-garde Guaranteed: Modes of Exchange in the Workshop of the Film Form

The promised contact with the Polish avant-garde, from which this essay takes its title, was declared in a call for submissions for the Kinolaboratorium[1] in 1973. This five-day event was organised by the Workshop of Film Form and the Laboratory of Art – EL Gallery in Elbląg. The Kinolaboratorium was an early attempt to connect the activities of the Workshop of Film Form to international avant-garde movements of the 1970s. Approaching the works produced under the auspices of the Workshop of Film Form now poses many challenges given the radical shifts in society and politics that have altered how art and film are understood and, crucially, how artists presented and exchanged their work. To explore some of the distinct ways in which these artists and their work operated, this essay will focus on their interventions into networks of exchange and modes of education throughout the 1970s of which the Kinolaboratorium is a crucial instance.

As well as showing works by key members of the Workshop, the Kinolaboratorium presented a selection of pre-war European works from *Ballet mécanique* (Fernand Léger, 1924) and *Un chien andalou* (Luis Buñuel and Salvador Dali, 1929) to *Das Cabinet des Dr. Caligari* (Robert Weine, 1920) and most pertinently Stefan and Franciszka Themerson's *The Adventure of a Good Citizen* (1939), which 'acquired a special significance in the programme as the most outstanding Polish film, a recapitulation of the achievements of the avant-garde.'[2] The selection of contemporary international films was more idiosyncratic as it was dictated in part by connections and access at the time but it did include a range of films by Norman McLaren from Canada, Javier Aguirre from Spain, Sergei Parajanov from USSR and films from the Balázs Béla Studio from Hungary.

The Workshop of Film Form was founded on principles of exchange between practitioners and theorists across media, as stated in early text by founding member Józef Robakowski, 'apart from filmmakers, the Workshop includes painters, musicians, cameramen, poets, technicians.'[3] The desire to develop these modes of exchange can be seen in the adoption of ideas from radical education for how works can be produced, discussed and exchanged. Key works to come out of the Workshop propose new models of exchange, yet paradoxically these are often the least well-travelled or internationally recognised. Films such as *22x* (1971), *Living Gallery* (1974/75) and *Osieki* (197[illegible]), focused on work with film as part of critical pedagogical practice; an analysis of modes of

1 The Kinolaboratorium formed part of the 5th Biennial of Spatial Forms in Elbląg held between the 16th and the 21st of June. The Kinolaboratorium preceded the Biennial and took place between the 15th and the 20th of April 1973

2 Janusz Zagrodzki, 'Cine-laboratory/Kinolaboratium,' typescript, 1973, based on text by Józef Robakowski 'Kronika V Biennale Form Przestrzennych Kinolaboratorium,' 'Notatnik Robotnika Sztuki,' no 5, 1973. http://repozytorium.fundacjaarton.pl/index.php?action=view/object&objid=3523&colid=75&catid=18&lang=eng [accessed 7-12-2016].

3 Quoted in 'The Workshop of the Film Form, 1970–1977. Early Film Work from Poland,' ed. G. Joseph-Hunter, Ł. Ronduda, L. Zippay, New York and Warsaw: Electronic Arts Intermix and Centre for Contemporary Art Ujazdowski Castle 2004, p. 14.

production seeking new methods to make and learn about art, as Józef Robakowski continues '[o]ur activities essentially rest on unlearning everything accrued through education and what we call established culture.'[4]

By the mid-seventies the Workshop had established itself internationally with various film-makers presenting their work in important international showcases, exhibitions and festivals in São Paolo, Knokke-le-Zoute, Edinburgh, Amsterdam, Antwerp, Cologne and Kassel, among other places. Parallel to this, several projects came to fruition that sought to develop new modes of exchange among artists and artist networks. The Workshop's participation in the Biennale of Art, São Paulo in 1973 is an important instance of international exchange that saw the group develop a means to participate in this distant context as well as challenge notions of art and education. The group decided to participate by transmitting the figure of the poet Wacław Antczak (1911–74), a regular workshop collaborator, to São Paolo by way of range of media from photography, video, sound and film, producing the work *Transmission from Łódź* (July–August, 1973). As the accompanying text 'The Transmission of the Personality of Wacław Antczak' states 'the contents of the show will the ennoblement of an artist – representing the Łódź urban folklore, formed by a specific set of cultural factors: outside of the official artistic trends; outside of what we call art; outside of artistic education.'[5] Wacław Antczak's outsider position was important for the Workshop as a means to challenge paradigms of cultural production and cultural value.

One of the key concepts developed in the context of the Workshop was the idea of the collective or assemblage film in which various artists would contribute a statement or 'one minute film' to a collective work. The constraint of a 'one minute film' was a means to challenge notions of privileged expression and authorship and allow the production of works representing multiple positions. The first work realised in this fashion was *22x* (Józef Robakowski, 1971), produced with students of the Łódź Fine Arts College to whom Robakowski gave several lengths of unexposed 35 mm film stock and left them to freely work upon the material. This led many of them to scratch work directly on the emulsion, both of the image field but also the area of the optical soundtrack, creating a direct correlation between mark making and sound. *22x* is significant as one of the first attempts within the Workshop to produce a work as part of an artistic community.

The idea of collective and open enquiry was expanded at the Kinolaboratorium that took place as part of the 5th Biennial of Spatial Forms. The Biennial sought a free and open system of organisation with 120 participants representing all fields of art. As the director of EL Gallery, Gerard Kwiatkowski reflected 'the negation of all artistic conventions and norms had significantly shaped the overall character of events. Spontaneous provocations and artistic reactions released the potential of new notions.'[6] The Biennial featured a diverse range of events and actions including exhibitions and performances featuring new works developed on site as well as works and proposals submitted by post and presentations of artistic documentation. Under the auspices of the Workshop,

4 Ibidem, pp. 20–21.

5 Józef Robakowski, 'The Transmission of the Personality of Wacław Antczak' typescript document, 1973, http://repozytorium.fundacjaarton.pl/index.php?action–view/object&objid–3579&tagid–982&lang–eng [accessed 7-12-2016].

6 Janusz Zagrodzki, 'Cine-laboratory/ Kinolaboratium,' typescript, 1973. Published in the 5th volume of *Notatnik Robotnika Sztuki* with contents related to Kinolaboratium by Józef Robakowski.http://repozytorium.fundacjaarton.pl/index.php?action–view/object&objid–3523&colid–75&catid–18&lang–eng [accessed 7-12-2016].

a collective film was produced with participants called *Kinolaboratorium* (Paweł Kwiek, 1972) with contributions from Javier Aguirre, Piotr Bernacki, Karol Cichecki, Milo Kurtis, Przemysław Kwiek and Zofia Kulik, Stanisław Kowalski, Gerard Kwiatkowski, Antoni Mikołajczyk, Józef Robakowski, and Włodzimierz Wieczorkiewicz. In the context of the screenings of classic avant-garde works some of the contributions mimicked the style of early cinema, from the first work by Paweł Kwiek and Karol Cichecki *The Sprinkler Sprinkled* where to piano accompaniment the artists remake the early Lumière brothers film *The Sprinkler Sprinkled* (1895) in which one artist is tricked into spraying a watering hose into his own face. In Józef Robakowski's film, the artist walks towards the camera holding a mirror reflecting the film crew, reminiscent of the Themersons play with mirrors in *The Adventures of a Good Citizen* as well as Robert Morris early film *Mirror* (1971). What is most striking about the Kinolaboratorium is the way various of the works and artistic strategies can be seen to influence other works, as motifs, actions or characters are repeated in different sections. This dialogue between works is most prominent in the section by Przemysław Kwiek and Zofia Kulik where they re-perform Robakowski's mirror gesture as a mime, repeat shots of typewriter used in earlier film by Stanisław Kowalski and also have an intervention by Wacław Antczak who sprays aerosol into his mouth repeating earlier action by Istwan Sas. Their section also includes self-reflective shots of the artists themselves during production of the work and gather together. The collapsing in of various artistic strategies by Kwiek and Kulik in their contribution is a remarkable feature of *Kinolaboratorium* and the collective film, breaking the idea of the isolated statement and showing how film and art can be made in dialogue with each other.

Following the influential Kinolaboratorium meeting, and the emerging models of collective practice, Józef Robakowski began production on the ambitious 25-minute colour film *Living Gallery* (Józef Robakowski, 1975). Over 20 artists were given 'a chance to make a 1-minute statement'[7] resulting in a rich record of Polish artists active in the art scene of the 1970s with contributions from Henryk Stażewski, Zbigniew Dłubak, Zbigniew Gostomski, Natalia LL, Pawel Freisler and Ryszard Waśko, Zbigniew Warpechowski amongst others with actual works ranging in length from 30 seconds to 3 minutes. Originally conceived as a film about artists associated with the Museum of Art in Łódź (founded by members of the a.r. group, artists Władysław Strzemiński, Katarzyna Kobro, Henryk Stażewski, and the poets Julian Przyboś and Jan Brzękowski), the project grew to reflect on the far ranging contemporary art scene of the mid-1970s seeking to 'uncover at all costs the mentality of currently active artists, to reveal their artistic consciousness.'[8] Utilising the form of a performative or time based gallery, developed through subsequent curatorial projects such as the *Exchange Gallery* established in 1978, *Living Gallery* sought to represent the most vital artistic attitudes and strategies of the period.

Opening with a shot panning down the words of Henryk Stażewski's 1970 painting *L'artiste qui ne lutte pas dans son travail travaille contre l'art*, *Living Gallery* aligns itself with the influential artist and champion of early avant-garde movements to reflect on the nature of art and to situate the contemporary avant-garde in a historical context. Stażewski was a key connection to the first

7 Ibidem.

8 J. Robakowski, 'Aspekty motywujące powstanie filmu Żywa Galeria 1974-75,' in: *Józef Robakowski*, ed. T. Maier and M. Jachuła, Leipzig and New York: MINI/ Goethe-Institut Curatorial Residencies Ludlow 38, Spector Books, 2011, p. 27.

generation of avant-garde artists in Poland through the groups *Blok, Praesens* and *a.r* as well as his important role in establishing context for the exhibition and discussion of modern art.[9] *Living Gallery* is presented and framed by an introductory sequence with voice-over and black and white photographs that document the production of the 'statements.' The individual works or statements operate in different ways from attempts to work directly with conditions of film such as Ryszard Winiarski's film in which black cubes appear seemingly at random until the screen is blacked out in synch with an escalating sine wave or Andrzej Różycki's play with photography, projection and live presence. Other works seek to create a space for performances or actions, most effectively seen in Natalia LL's series of poses in coloured photographic studio and Zbigniew Warpechowski simple yet disturbing action where he releases a bird from a cage that is tied by a ribbon to a fish in a neighbouring tank. Other works take an analytical approach such as the statement by Ryszard Waśko, who continues his examination of sound in film, where he introduces a wall painted with a large numerical grid that will correspond to set sonic tones which change as the camera pans across it or Piotr Bernacki's lecture performance. One of the most renowned works featured within *Żywa Galeria* is by Andrzej Partum and acts as an intervention in the film as it did originally when presented in public. For the project Andrzej Partum hung a large banner across busy street in the Krakowskie Przedmieście Street in Warsaw between the Academy of Fine Arts and the University stating without annotation: *Milczenie awangardowe.*

Living Gallery is one example of the assembly film from this period, the other important work is the film *Osieki* (Paweł Kwiek, 1974), which was created during the International Meetings of Artists, Scientists and Theorists of Art in Osieki in 1974. Kwiek invited 17 participants to create a short one minute film with works ranging from explorations of how painting can be filmed as in *Linia-Stalówka* by Andrzej Ciesielski. in which the camera follows, in extreme close-up, a hand that slowly draws a curved line but we never see the 'final' drawing, to the improvised actions by Wojciech Krzywobłocki and Walenty Gabrysiak, who set up a pole on the beach in order to display large out-door work. A central collective work gives the camera a new mobility through group effort; we see the artists helping push a stalled car, when the car starts the camera is taken with it on a kinetic journey down the country road. Other works functioned as interventions or minimalist provocations: from the unexposed stretch of film by *Cage* by Janusz Zagrodzki, which features only a glimpse of an image at its end, to *Grass* by Wojciech Bruszewski, which was to feature a one minute view but as is announced in a title card 'Wojciech Bruszewski wanted to film the view of grass for 1 minute. I did not make this film as a result of bad organisation.' Revolving around what often seem to be spontaneous actions, the works shift from Józef Robakowski's *Farewells* that functions as a group portrait in which a man attempts to embrace and kiss participants with differing reactions, from affection to resistance, before he finally turns to kiss the camera or Tomas Strauss's *Scenario*, in which the dramatic gesture of a man walking into the sea is rendered as an almost invisible action as we only glimpse in close-up a foot stepping into the waves and then out of the frame leaving only footsteps in the sand that dissolve as the waves break on the shore.

Both works were produced during events that brought a range of artists together, reflecting the pedagogical climate in which the artists functioned and produced work in this period. The

9 Henryk Stażewski was later the subject himself of a film by Workshop member Ryszard Waśko *Documentation 1913–1982. Film about the Artistic Practice and Activity of Henryk Stażewski* (1981).

projects can also be seen to follow the influential models of radical pedagogy developed by Oskar Hansen (1922–2005), related to the concept of Open Form.[10] This way of working and of collective creation can be seen in various collaborative works inspired by Hansen's theories initiated during the 1960s and 1970s. A key precedent that involved Paweł Kwiek is the film *Activities* (KwieKulik, 1972) that was made during a four day collective act with Przemysław Kwiek, Zofia Kulik, Jan S. Wojciechowski, Jacek Łomnicki, Krzysztof Zarębski, Jacek Dobrowolski, and members of the band Grupa w składzie (Milo Kurtis, Jacek Malicki, Andrzej Kasprzyk). During this period other influences, as Robakowski recalls, were 'the pedagogic and artistic work of Zbigniew Dłubak [that] begun to play a very important role among the young artists in Łódź; he was a Warsaw artist who offered very interesting photography courses at the Film School and Art College. Many his students opened up themselves towards new interpretations of understanding and essence of art. For the most part, this new and vigorous movement existed outside of the official art school curricula; and was self-taught.'[11]

The assemblage form of these film projects draws on the model of group presentations such as the biennial or conferences but is also productive to think about in terms of the anthology or magazine as formats to structure, bring together and distribute statements on contemporary practice. The form of the magazine also relates to the desire of these projects to capture contemporary moments, elements of artistic communities as they are coming into being and share them. These projects bare comparison to the television programmes pioneered by German artists Gerry Schum and Ursula Wevers with their influential project *Fernsehgalerie*, which consisted of a short lived gallery and two anthology programmes *Land Art* (1969) and *Identifications* (1970), broadcast on German television. It can be argued that the Workshop produced collective films as an examination of the means of making art rather than seeking to establish alternative institutions through new media such as the *Fernsehgalerie*. As such the project of the Workshop can be understood in contrast to this history as a critical and pedagogical project examining existing structures and their articulation of power rather than seeking to renew the structures through new mediums. As Eric de Bruyn has critically commented with reference to *Fernsehgalerie* 'the "new" television art formed nothing else but the after-image of the "old" gallery art'[12] and as Wevers herself reflected in 1979 'the medium itself proved incapable of discussing the subject in acceptable terms.'[13] In this way the Workshop is markedly distinct from such artistic interventions that helped introduce film and video into the context of contemporary art in Western Europe, such as the exhibition *Prospect 71: Projections*[14] or *Fernsehgalerie*. The Workshop existed within a pedagogical framework and logic with the intention to transform both artists, audiences and society through the analysis of media or, as the early

10 As developed through his work, writings and teaching at the Warsaw Academy of Fine Arts from 1950 onwards and in exhibition projects such as *Oskar Hansen – Searching for a Teaching Method in the Fine Arts*, Warsaw: Muzeum Adama Mickiewicza, 1966.

11 J. Robakowski, 'Live Gallery, Lodz progressive art movement 1969-1992,' Exchange Gallery, 1997, trans. W. Michalak, http://www.robakowski.eu/tx3_ang.html [accessed 7-12-2016].

12 E. de Bruyn, 'Land Art in the Mediascape: On the Politics of Counterpublicity in the Year 1969,' in *Ready to Shoot: Fernsehgalerie Gerry Schum*, Düsseldorf: Kunsthalle Düsseldorf, 2004, p. 146.

13 U. Wevers, 'Gerry Schum: The Television Gallery. The Idea and How it Failed,' in *Museums by Artists*, ed. A A Bronson and P. Gale, Toronto: Art Metropole, 1983, p. 284.

14 The influential exhibition *Prospect 71: Projection* was an early attempt to invite conceptual artists to produce film works for exhibition. Organised by Konrad Fischer, Jürgen Harten, and Hans Strelow the instance of 8 October–17 October 1971, Städtische Kunsthalle, Düsseldorf and included works by predominantly UK and German based artists such as Barry Flanagan, John Hilliard, David Lamelas, John Latham, Bruce McLean, Tony Morgan, and David Tremlett.

manifesto stated, they sought an 'analysis of the means that serve communicative functions.'[15] The ambitions to disband systems around art and education in order to effect change in society at large frame the Workshop closer to projects such as the K3 activities at the Balázs Béla Studio in Budapest or the Artists Placement Group in the UK. The direct address to the audience in the *Living Gallery* and the idea of the one minute statements as a means to peruse 'quasi-scientific activity' is in line with the Workshops aim to analyse 'the essence of cinema' without 'politicising, moralising, anaesthetizing and amusing the spectator.'[16]

One of the most distinct collective projects produced by the Workshop is the 1973 film *Niechcice* (Paweł Kwiek, 13'10"). Produced during the Art Day on Sunday 25 April 1973 in the village of Niechcice, Paweł Kwiek worked with the youth group who lived in the small agricultural village where a State Agricultural Farm (Państwowe Gospodarstwa Rolne) operated. Kwiek supported their activities as camera operator but otherwise gave them freedom to dictate the terms of the film. Parallel to the 'one minute films' this work looks at how the structure of the statements could be played out in communities outside of the direct context of art. Rather than the collectives created through art practice such as the Workshop or temporary groups such as those formed by the International Meetings of Artists, Scientists and Theorists of Art in Osieki or the Biennial of Spatial Forms, Kwiek was here working within the existing community of the state farm, engaging the youth of this collective entity in process of creating their own representations. Seeking to give a 'voice to those who had remained mute' Kwiek's film comes from his interest in the relationship between sociology and art. By supporting a youth group to dictate the terms of the film production in their small community, the project enabled self-reflection through cinema. As Łukasz Ronduda has commented 'the most important thing for the artist was the very social-artistic process that he successfully sparked [...] and only to a lesser extent the final result in the form of a finished film.'[17] This shift from ideas of an authored cinema to a concern with how film and media can operate in the political and sociological context of Poland is an important element of the Workshop and the stated ambition to deconstruct authorship and see how the camera can be used as an active agent to help reflect and reformulate social relationships. The conception of film as manifested in these projects is related to the notion of filmmaking as a social project, the action of the artist lies in the intervention into people's relationship to their image, the camera acts as a prompt for new types of social organisation.

Together these activities can be understood in the context of parallel avant-garde film movements and initiatives in neighbouring countries in Central Europe and beyond during a period marked by growing international dialogue and network formation. The emerging networks in the late 1970s of artist run organisations and initiatives to support film and video practice were founded and formed in relation to the new material and theoretical possibilities that emerged in light of video. Central among these emergent concepts was the notion of feedback, which informed many early formal experiments, performances and installations but also extended out of artists' work to look at new pedagogical models of practice and exhibition. The shift to how technology could develop

15 Józef Robakowski quoted in *The Workshop of the Film Form*, p. 21.

16 Ibidem, p. 19.

17 Ł. Ronduda, 'Warsztat Formy Filmowej. Realizacje filmowe z lat 1970–1977,' *Artpapier.com*, August 2014, http://artpapier.com/pliki/archiwum_sierpien_04/recfilm/warsztaty%20formy.html [accessed 7-12-2016].

new pedagogical systems can be seen in a range of practices that emerged in the 1970s, ranging from the duration studies in schools by Darcy Lange[18] and the political feminist works of Carole Roussopoulos[19] to Paweł Kwiek's live broadcast performance *Video A - A Studio Situation* (1974). At the same time as potential of video to enable new modes of exchange and dialogue artists were also reflecting on this critically such as in the collaborative video made by Gábor Bódy and Marcel Odenbach *Conversation Between East and West* (1978, 3'40"), which reflects ironically on the potential of international communication as the two artists appear as at a conference yet only blow spit bubbles for each other. Many of the Workshop artists explored concepts and processes related to video as part of their interest in ideas of transmission and feedback as seen in early installations and proposals by Wojciech Bruszewski, such as his proposal for *Zapis Video* in 1975,[20] to the live broadcast experiments of Paweł Kwiek. Video was also central to the participatory projects made by members of the Workshop affiliated group Zespół T (Tomasz Kołodrubiec, Tomasz Konart, Janusz Szczerek and Piotr Weychert), such as Andrzej Paruzel's installation *Video Photographic Situation* (1976) or *Experiment with a Specific Group of People and Involving a Video Recording* (1979) created at the State Higher School of Music in Warsaw. As Paruzel commented 'a person entering the video installation stands a chance in the process of discovering its structure to reveal the operation of one's own cognitive structures owing to the potential of manipulation and in the scope of stimuli processed by the system and in itself.'[21]

In this light, we can understand the collaborative projects produced by the Workshop as attempts to utilise technology and art to form new means of reflection, exchange and alternative forms of learning. Central to these is a broader political project, that seeks to understand art within a pedagogical context, as part of a process of feedback distinct from consumption based modes built on fixed notions of the artwork, artist and audience. As Ryszard W. Kluszczyński has observed 'in addition to films, performances and numerous installations, the 1970s also witnessed the appearance of video works that were pre-interactive in nature, that is, works that required audience participation.'[22] The central design of the assemblage works was drawn from ideas feedback related to the material possibilities of the technologies of film and video seeking other forms of collective action and participation.

In the late 1970s, filmmakers from Poland and Hungary sought to establish a new model of exchange built upon distribution possibilities offered by video technology. The potential of video to liberate the spaces and means by which artists could work and exchange with each other are

---

18 Such as his *Study of Three Birmingham Schools* (1976, video, black and white photographs, sound, approx. 6 hours) and *Studies of Teaching in Four Oxfordshire Schools* (UK 1977, video, black and white photographs, sound, approx. 6 hours).

19 Through the group Video Out she founded in 1970 with Paul Roussopoulos she made important documents of political movements such as the video *Le FHAR (Front homosexuel d'action révolutionnaire)* (1971) and in the mid-1970s became increasingly involved with feminist groups facilitating forums and video workshops as well as produced works in collaboration with Delphone Seyrig, most prominatly her video S.C.U.M Manifesto (1976, 26 min).

20 Use image: http://repozytorium.fundacjaarton.pl/index.php?action–view/object&objid–97&colid–11&-catid–3&lang–pl [accessed: 15-10-2016].

21 M. Jankowska, *Wideo, wideo instalacja, wideo performance w Polsce w latach 1973-1994. Historia, artyści, dzieła*, Warsaw: Neriton, 2004, p. 134. See http://artmuseum.pl/en/filmoteka/praca/paruzel-andrzej-video-photographic-situations [accessed 7-12-2016].

22 R. W. Kluszczyński, 'An Outline History Of Polish Video Art,' Culture.pl, 13 April 2005, http://culture.pl/en/article/an-outline-history-of-polish-video-art [accessed 7-12-2016].

centrally important to the formation of media networks at this time from London Video Arts in UK, to Western Front in Canada, FRIGO in Lyon or Video Out in Paris, among others. Following the end of the Workshop in 1977 these networks emerged in Poland against the changing political climate in the late 1970s and early 1980s. As Robakowski reflected 'interrogations, arrests, house searches multiplied while frequent confiscation of priceless parcels that included books, videotapes, and films made any meaningful exchange at best difficult. Finally, the confiscation of passports of many independent artists reduced possibilities of contacts with the world 'outside' to nil.'[23] Robakowski continues that despite these changes 'during a meeting in Budapest we were able to organize an international film co-operative Infermental with great input by a distinguished Hungarian film maker Gábor Bódy. During the martial law in Poland, the Hungarian students were smuggling our video productions through sealed for us borders. Infermental distributed our work world-wide and it became one of the first of its kind video journals anywhere in the world. Thanks to these people our films entered the mainstream of the world art already during the martial law.'

Described as a 'magazine on videocassettes,' the origin of the project was explained in an early call for participants circulated in October 1981 by Gábor Bódy and German artist Astrid Heibach, 'INFERMENTAL is a combination of the words: international, fermentum and experimental. Polish and Hungarian filmmakers found it out during a friendly meeting in autumn 1980.'[24] Despite the importance of this critical instance of exchange and transnational collaboration, the early ambitions of Infermental were fulfilled in a different way to its initial conception. Reflecting the social and political context of the time, Infermental was finally launched in West Berlin with the first of ten issues released in February 1982. Edited by Gábor Bódy and Astrid Heibach and supervised by Gusztáv Hámos, the first issue was supported by the DAAD residency programme rather than through the Hungarian-Polish partnership, as it was originally conceived. Yet, the form of Infermental and its stated aim to build bridges between 'media islands' and desire to create an 'Encyclopaedia of Recorded Imagery,' thus linking avant-gardes groups internationally to extend analysis of film and video, can be traced to the important proposals and projects developed by the Workshop through the anthology and collective films. Most pertinently, *Żywa Galeria* proposed a model for linking and analysing avant-gardes through the one minute statements that was taken up by Infermental on an international scale with later issues produced in France, Hungary, Canada, USA and Japan.

It is interesting to reflect on the early networks formed in the 1920s and 1930s, related to the first wave of Polish avant-garde film, in contrast to the attempts at network formation in the 1970s. Stefan and Franciszka Themerson played important roles in groups such as the STAFT (Association of Film Lovers, 1931–34) and S.A.F, the Polish film makers co-operative, but one of their most important contributions was the formation of the journal *f.a* (standing for *Film Artistique* or *Film Art*) in 1937 drawing on their research in Britain and France. *f.a.* was a pivotal point for the circulation of information between early film avant-gardes. The magazine's rich use of design and photography enabled the circulation of images of artists' works across networks in Europe. The first issue *f.a.1* (February 1937) focused on experimental cinema in Britain with articles on Len Lye, László Moholy-Nagy (then based in London), Basil Wright, and John Grierson; *f.a.2* (March–April

23 J. Robakowski, 'Live Gallery' Live Gallery, 35 mm, 1975, 24'48".
24 Infermental paper archive, ZKM, letter 15 October 1981 from Gábor Bódy and Astrid Heibach.

1937) included substantial material related to French avant-garde film of 1920s and 1930s.[25] The Themersons published the journal in connection with screenings of films they brought to Poland from France and Britain. A third issue of *f.a.* focusing on Polish avant-garde cinema was planned but never published. An extensive range of material was gathered and prepared for this issue and brought by Stefan Themerson with him to London where he would share it with friends and visitors and described the prized documents as his 'bible.'[26]

Through the projects discussed above we can understand that an important part of the Workshop was its focus on ideas of exchange and network formation amongst avant-garde groups with the desire to transcend national borders. The proposition of the 'one minute film' and the development of their collaborative projects can be seen alongside proposals of the time for how the form of the magazine could function in the age of film and video. The shifting notion of the magazine was fundamental to the development of conceptual art that utilised printed matter as well as mail networks to generate new ways for work to exist, networks to be formed and for exchange among artists as discussed extensively by Lucy Lippard in her influential early writing and seen in projects such as diverse as Sol LeWitt's 'Paragraphs on Conceptual Art' published in *Artforum* in summer 1967[27] to Tomislav Gotovac's performance *Showing "Elle" Magazine* in 1962. Publications such as Art & Language's *Art-Language* first published in May 1969 and *ASPEN. The Multimedia Magazine in a Box* established in 1965 prompted a rethinking of the magazine as an exhibition model. In the 1970s these ideas helped to remap the concept of the gallery in the age of video, as the magazine was re-theorised in context of this technology and the new possibilities to circulate actual works between artists. The centrality of video to new modes of exchange marks a fundamental shift at this time, as up to this point works would circulate in limited number of distribution copies predominately on 16mm film (such as the influential *Fluxfilm Anthology* from 1962–70 compiled by George Maciunas) which could only be seen in context of cinemas or independent screenings. To share works prior to this, films were reduced to photographs and textual descriptions to carry them into new contexts. Video brought with it a new carrier for images and sounds providing a model of distribution and documentation previously unavailable. Despite the fact that access to video equipment was scarce and expensive, the new media helped shift conceptually how people understood their work and its potential for exchange. Similar to *f.a.,* the Workshop's ambition to build international networks and its pedagogical models were to remain only partially realised. Yet, the invitation to meet the Polish avant-garde stills stands as the potential of the films and their visions for exchange and artistic production resides in the works completed but also, crucially, in the radical model of the Workshop itself.

---

25 The second issue also included the influential article 'The Urge to Create Visions' by Stefan Themerson, later published in expanded form in 1983 in publication of the same title.

26 As recounted by Jasia Reichardt in dialogue with the author during visit to the Themersons Archive, 2013.

27 S. LeWitt, 'Paragraphs on Conceptual Art,' *Artforum*, 5:10, 1967, pp. 79–83.

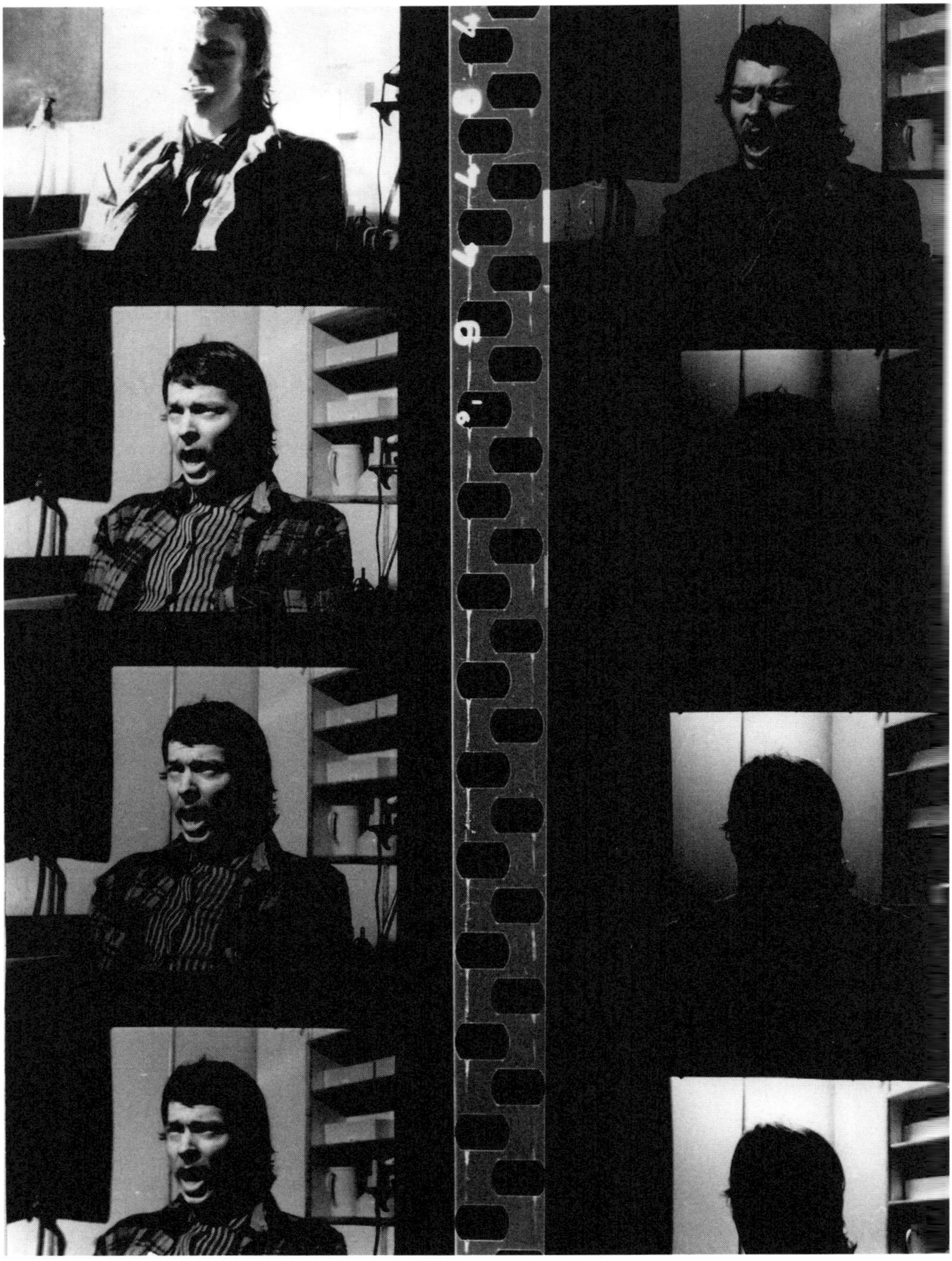

Wojciech Bruszewski, *YYAA*, 1973, 35 mm, 2'59''
Wojciech Bruszewski, *YYAA*, 1973, 35 mm, 2'59''

Jan Verwoert

Gestures Towards a New Life: The Avant-Garde as a Historical Provocation

What to do with the Avant-Garde?

What does an avant-garde want – from art, from people, from society? What is it getting at? How can we find that out? What if we begin by not asking about an avant-garde's motivations, goals, and influences, and instead consider the gestures with which avant-gardists stage themselves? Avant-gardists are never without a gesture, for their appearance on the stage of art history must have the necessary power to unhinge this history (as it previously conceived itself) with a long-lasting effect. The appearance of avant-garde indeed only goes down in history if it successfully performs gestures that make conceivable another course of history. These gestures correspond in their form and status to a coup d'état in art history and its politics. The successful performance of an avant-garde gesture entails a coup, a historical feat. Paradoxically, it lies in the nature of the avant-garde gesture that it is on the one hand *transhistorical*, to the extent that as a singular event it radically interrupts the course of history, exploding its framework and falling out of all previously valid categories of historiography, while at the same time it is deeply *historical*, founding the new history in which it will exist and be conceived from now on – as a revolutionary act of founding a new art. The power of the avant-garde gesture could not even be measured if we didn't somehow feel the impact of the break it causes, and thus did not perceive the break as an event with a still undiminished – that is, transhistorical – effectivity. But adequately describing the significance of this power means nonetheless presenting its long-term impact from an overreaching historical perspective. To grasp the coup of an avant-garde thus entails understanding the force of the gesture at its core in its simultaneously historical and transhistorical dimensions.

Indeed, it seems quite a general characteristics of gestures that the context in which they take on meaning is historical and transhistorical at the same time. On the one hand, historical reality manifests itself so clearly in gestures because they belong to the inventory of means of expression available at a certain point in time. In their function as cultural-historical specific forms of interaction, gestures are signs of their time. On the other hand, the significance of gesture is always also absolutely *contemporary* in the transhistorical sense, for we only understand the gesture if we allow it to have an impact upon us in the moment we perceive it, if it engages us in an exchange in that moment. Gestures demand a direct response. When someone greets, they expect to be greeted back. Someone who makes a scene is courting attention. Whoever cries saddens, and so on. Gestures create presence to the extent that they always commit us to participating in an exchange in that moment. Because it seems to lie in the nature of the gesture that the person who performs it intends to provoke a reaction, it can be said that the gesture is 'provocative' in a literal sense. The practical meaning of the gesture thus lies not least in the provocation that it causes. Provocation is inherent to gestures.

That provocation is the intention of an avant-garde can surely be counted as a commonplace of art history. The slogan *épater le bourgeois* is almost proverbially associated with the context of the avant-garde. The expanded perspective that this understanding of the intrinsically provocative character of the gesture allows in that provocation no longer presents itself as a mere attitude of the avant-garde, but an immanent force of artistic practice. The power of the avant-garde gesture that strives for the historical coup in its performance is its provocative power. But whom does this gesture provoke? Here as well the answer must remain ambivalent: on the one hand, the avant-garde gesture provokes the witness of its performance, that is, both the historical witness as well as those interested in its history, who try to re-experience the power of the provocation in order to attest to it. On the other hand, the avant-garde gesture provokes not just its witnesses, but history itself – here also in a double sense. Avant-gardists *pro-voke*, or indeed *e-voke*, history to the extent that they summon history as the system of references for their artistic practice. It is precisely here that avant-gardists differ from ordinary art producers, for they understand their artistic acts directly as historical acts, as entries in – and rewriting of – the book of history. Through the radical transformation of our habits of perception, they seek to cause an event in art that in its radicalness and explosiveness exceeds art history and constitutes a historically new form of experience – that is, a new form of experiencing history. At the same time, they *pro-voke* history in a still more direct sense, by summoning it, as if calling a ghost to finally show itself: 'Reveal yourself, history, let us see how you will be!' is the true motto of avant-garde provocation. The hope here is that the ghost of history, if it would allow itself to be lured into making an appearance, might take on the shape of a revolution. Through the provocation of their gestures, avant-gardists are interested in nothing less than causing a revolution as an eventful appearance of a new history.

Signs Like Slaps

Let us take a look at three gestures:

The film shows letters in close-up before a bright background. Each shot displays one letter. The shots are sometimes just a few seconds long, sometimes a bit longer. We see the sequence: "a b c k s p f h n p a c o a c o t w o j u a b c i f y d i m o z k w e h z w n w o d r i j g a b c d k t k i n s o a u c d u a n t w f z t f z t d r j y r j d r t a c o z s k..." For the length of each shot, a sound is played on an organ or synthesizer. Each sound has a definite pitch, but neither does the sequence of pitches result in a melody in the conventional sense, nor does the chain of letters from a recognisable term. Nonetheless, the series of letters and sounds does not seem arbitrary, but clear and definite. A film lasts 4'20", is entitled *An Exercise* and was made in 1972/73 by Józef Robakowski.

A film shows a man in close-up. He is sitting in a kitchen, screaming with his eyes closed and his mouth wide open, producing two alternating sounds: a high pitch, that sounds like an E (or a Polish Y), and a deeper sound like an A. He holds this sound for the duration of every shot, so that for each shot only one of the two sounds is made. In each shot, the protagonist is differently lit: sometimes from the front, sometimes from the back, sometimes from the side. The irregular alternation of high and deep pitches thus corresponds to a constant change of the light in the image. In the final shot, the protagonist signals with a wave that the shooting has come to an end. The film lasts three minutes, is entitled *YYAA* and was made in 1973 by Wojciech Bruszewski.

A film alternatively shows a clack screen and a white sheet. When the sheet is seen for the first time, the word 'nie' (no) appears in typing on it. On the second time, the word 'nie' appears twice. This continues, until a number of lines have been filled with the word 'nie.' Then the process is reversed, and with each subsequent shot a word less can be seen, until finally the sheet is again blank. Accompanying each shot, in which the sheet can be seen, a voice sounds that monotonously intones the word 'nie.' Since the black screen and the white sheet with the narrator's voice alternate in rapid sequence, this results in a rhythm of silence and sound and an alternation between black and white that over time produces a nervous flicker. The film lasts four minutes, and is entitled *Negation* and was made in 1973 by Ryszard Waśko. Robakowski, Bruszewski and Waśko were members of The Workshop of the Film Form, an artist group that was founded in 1970 in Łódź and existed until 1977.

Why speak here of gestures? Indeed, the films hardly show what can generally be understood as a gesture. Admittedly, there's a man screaming, but he does not give his screaming any further emphaticness by using other forms of body language; he does not gesticulate, but just sits there restfully. In the two other films, there are no people, but just letters and words to be seen and sound to be heard. All the same, the films have the *impact* of gestures. They have the same intensity. They transfer the power of body language to a language of images, letters, sounds and cuts. The screaming, the illumination of letters, and the appearance and disappearance of the word 'nie,' marked by hard cuts, have the force of a strike. Each cut, each image, each letter and each sound has the sharpness of a slap with the flat palm on a smooth surface. One feels the rhythm of the strikes with each cut. Slap slap slap slap. Nie nie nie nie. A A Y Y. Through a simultaneous reduction of the image's informative content in image and sound to clear, powerful signals and acceleration (if not even brutalisation) of the cuts, the images and cuts are brought closer to one another to the point where the series of cuts is just as present as the series of images and sounds. The series of sounds, pitches, the chain of letters, and the lightning are thus inseparably tied to the rhythm of the series of cuts, fusing them into one. The image, the sound, and light are the cuts, and the cuts are the image, sound, and light. But when we say that the power of a gesture lies in its power to realise a *coup* – 'couper' means in French literally 'making a cut' – and by way of this cut creating a situation that involves the beholder addressed by the gesture, then it becomes all the more clear that the three films are in fact radical gestures.

Using concepts from Gilles Deleuze's cinema theory, Giorgio Agamben in this sense describes the aesthetic of modern film montage as an aesthetic that is marked by '*coupes mobiles*,' images that are themselves in movement, and which Deleuze calls 'movement-images.' He continues, 'It is necessary to extend Deleuze's argument and show how it relates to the status of the image in general in modernity. This implies, however, that the mythical rigidity of the image has been broken, and that here, properly speaking, there are no images but only gestures.'[1] Picking up from this definition, we could speak of the gestures as *coupes mobiles*, moving cuts, that is to say, the films of Robakowski, Waśko, and Bruszewski are avant-garde gestures because they perform this radicalization of visual form. They are resolutely modern

1 G. Agamben, 'Notes on Gesture,' in *Means without End: Notes on Politics*, tr. V. Binetti and C. Cassarino, Minneapolis: University of Minnesota Press, 2000, p. 54.

films, because all the filmic means they mobilise are used in such a way that they don't follow the logic of *coupes mobiles*, but that they also forcefully expose this logic with the entire gestural power of a slap. In other words, the films make us experience what it means when an image as a cut becomes a moving gesture.

But if the power of the gesture, as we established above, cannot be divorced from its provocative impact, this rises the question of whom or what do the film provoke in the gesture inherent to their form? What avant-garde cut do the filmmakers achieve with their 'coupes mobiles'? First of all, we are the addressees of the gesture. The provocation of its avant-garde film language – that is, a language that is condensed into the form of a gesture – is directed at us beholders by subjecting us to sequences of images, sounds, and cuts that cannot be understood in a conventional way, do not correspond to our habits of vision, and thus throw us off balance. Bruszewski yells at us, while Waśko and Robakowski work over our senses with audiovisual information transmitted with the speed, brevity, and density of a technical signal. Their films are like telegrams in Morse code. As recipients, we become tickers that directly process the signals received and spit them out on tape: a b c k s p f h n p a c o a c o t w o j u a b c i f y d i m c z k w e h z w n w o d r i j g a b c d k t k i n s o a u c d u a n t w f z t f z t d r j y r j d r t a c o z s k...A C Y Y... But the medium that processes this information is neither transparent nor functional. It is the body that screams or is yelled at, bombarded with a cannonade of audio-visual signals. As gestures, the films are not just a strike, but a shot or a fusillade. In this way, the military character of the metaphorical concept of avant-garde – the French word originally referred to 'front riders' – is fulfilled.

But wherein lied the impact of this provocation? What reaction do they seek to provoke or tease out? First of all, the provocative effect of all three films lies in bringing the beholders to encounter them with an attitude other than contemplation. Through the high frequency of the moving cuts and processed information (as well as the almost physical proximity created by the audiovisual bombardment), they rob the beholders the time to allow themselves contemplatively – that is slowly and deliberately – to engage with the film. As every engagement is immediately a reaction, the processing of information becomes the production of communication. We are immediately tied and plugged into the feedback loop of signal transmission. To the extent that they rob us of the possibility of contemplation, the films provoke the distanced beholder to become an involved participant. The provocative gestural power of the filmic language changes our attitude in relationship to the object of our perception from an unbinding distance to a binding implication. (Hence Adorno's short and sweet pronouncement on avant-garde provocation: 'Progressive art [...] hardly tolerates a contemplative attitude.'[2])

Apart from this, there isn't really anything to contemplate in these films. Due to the extreme reduction of the filmic language to the simplest means of expression the filmmakers avoid any form of filmic composition that would offer itself to contemplation. It is impossible to immerse oneself, for the films have no depth. They are flat like the palm of a hand ready to strike. They are pure audiovisual information: cut, signal, stimulus. This abolition of depth should be understood as a provocation not just directed at the beholders, but at the filmmakers as well. They refuse them-

2 Theodor W. Adorno, *Ästhetische Theorie*, Frankfurt am Main: Suhrkamp, 1970, p. 495.

selves the depth of expression, and thus the use of all conventional creative techniques that could generate the impression of semantic depth. In that they consciously limit their own possibilities of expression by making the conceptual decision to choose a reduced filmic form, they provoke themselves into taking a different position in relation to their own filmic-artistic ability to act. They thus lure themselves from their reserve, as they do with us as participants in communication. As Łukasz Ronduda sums up, 'In numbing these qualities [the subjective qualities of their works] the artists (or rather 'scientists' in the field of art and aesthetics) sought to 'objectify' their own actions [...] in order to adapt them to the 'intersubjective' sphere of communication.'[3]

The avant-garde sharpening of filmic language to the form of a powerful, flat gesture thus entails a provocation against both the filmmaker and the viewers, which seeks to change their relationship: that they move away from a distanced form of communication that relies on the contemplation of semantically complex artworks. And that they instead allow themselves to engage in a far more direct form of communication that relies entirely on the maximal amplification of the moment of intersubjective communication, because it concentrates on the transmission of the simplest signals, where everything takes place blow after blow. By the way by provoking new forms of intersubjectivity, the avant-garde gesture wants to create new forms of social interaction, and thus connect our social ties in a different way.

Gestures for Another Society

The provocation of the avant-garde gesture of the filmmaker of the Workshop of the Film Form is thus meant to summon a different social situation that at the same time would be a new historical situation, because it would represent an alternative to extant political relations in this historical moment. By developing gestures that are to provoke direct intersubjective communication, the filmmakers formulate their protest against the party dictatorship and the bureaucratic government that determined social life in Poland in the historical moment of their emergence. The transformation of gestures of interpersonal communication is intended to break the authoritarian character of a social order manifests itself most vividly in the most everyday gestures as the ideology maintaining the regime penetrates and determines all areas of social life. In this sense, Ronduda writes: 'In Communist Poland there was no situation outside ideology, just as today there is no situation free from the laws of the market.'[4]

But if the gestures of people in the society in which they live are entirely charged with ideology and alienated by this, then the first step towards liberating gestures must be emptying them of all ideological content. What is at stake in this conscious emptying of significance is in fact the utopian project of inventing gestures that are removed from the grip of ideology because nothing in or about them could be used for any ideological purposes. These motivations explain the provocative flatness of the films discussed. By breaking down filmic language to its simplest, most basic elements, Robakowski, Bruszewski and Waśko strive towards a form of expression that is simultaneously too direct and too open to allow ideology to infiltrate. On the films of Paweł Kwiek, a further member of the Workshop of the Film Form, Ronduda thus states: 'Kwiek's film

---

3 Ł. Ronduda, 'Soc Art – An Attempt in Revitalizing Avant-Garde Strategies in Polish Art of the 1970's,' *Fktogram*, 1, 2005, pp. 121-31.

4 Ibidem, p. 130.

[…] was structurally incapable of promoting the dominant ideology of the time; its basic principle was interpretative openness and deliberate indeterminacy of meaning.'[5]

The avant-garde provocation of the artists of the Workshop of the Film Form therefore effectively lies in the sharpening of the artistic form to a gesture that refuses the historical reality of an ideologically over-formed social life and strives for both a direct and radically open form of intersubjective exchange. In the same historical moment, the artist and theoretician Jan Świdziński formulated in 1974 in his 'theses on contextual art' a program that pointedly expresses these ethics and politics of another form of gesture. Świdziński understands his program of 'contextual art' as a counter-model to Joseph Kosuth's propositions on 'conceptual art.' He emphasizes that an artistic activity freed from the conventional forms of media expression should not primarily be as Kosuth maintained, about defining and ambiguous conceptual positions. Instead it should be about inventing signs and gestures that due to their radical openness only (and always anew) obtain significance in the concrete moment and specific context of an intersubjective social exchange between people. The commitment to the openness of the context-sensitive artistic gesture here means both reflexive recognition of the fact that the significance of artistic activity is dependent on the social context in which it comes to performance, as well as an insistence that such an open and direct context-sensitive artistic gesture might proactively contribute to the opening of existing social relations. Thesis 15 from Świdziński's program reads as follows: 'Contextual Art is a form of acting in reality through the following transformation of meanings: REALITY → INFORMATION → ART → NEW OPEN MEANINGS → REALITY.'[6]

Świdziński's avant-garde program of changing social relations by inventing a language of forms that is simultaneously open and yet intervenes directly in the social reality of interpersonal communication can thus directly be read as an expression of the goals pursued by the artists of the Workshop of the Film Form. In this context, Ronduda's summary of Świdzieński's theses reads like a precise description of the film language developed by Robakowski, Bruszewski and Waśko:

> Instead of obscuring reality, the contextual pure/empty signs were to be stimuli initiating a series of processual, interactive relations, creating an open process of semiosis, blurring the line between the artist and the viewer. […] For contextualism, the ideal of social and cultural communication was radical democracy, i.e, a system completely different from the one in which it was itself born. This aspect reveals the current's [sic] critical attitude towards communist Poland's non-democratic reality. Its anti-authoritarian dimension is contained in the postulate of the impossibility of monopolizing meaning in a single context and the necessity of over-contextual negotiations.[7]

The intersubjective, social, and historical provocation of this avant-garde program thus lies in inventing gestures that in contrast to then extant relations establish openness and directness in communication.

---

5 Ibidem, p. 129.

6 Jan Świdziński, *The 12 Theses of Contextual Art* (1974). (As a gesture of the conscious disturbance of the conventional format of listing theses, the numbering follows no recognisable logic. The numbers of the theses are in random order, and sometimes exceed the number of actual theses.) See *Piktogram*, 3, 2006, p. 31.

7 Ł. Ronduda, 'Flexibility Makes Our Existence Possible: The Contextual Art of Jan Świdziński,' *Piktogram*, 3, 2006, pp. 32–39.

The radicalness of this gesture lies not least in the fact that the political protest appeals directly to the essence of language. The films of Robakowski, Bruszewski, and Waśko want to show language's potential in the state of its liberation from ideology. They want to make clear what language can do when used with the directness and openness inherent in it. It is precisely this performative exhibition of language's basic character that Giorgio Agamben understands as the point of the gesture. The following passages read like a commentary on the films here discussed, in particular Waśko's *Negation*:

> In the same way, if we understand the 'word' as the means of communication, than to show a word does not mean to have at one's disposal a higher level (a metalanguage, itself incommunicable without the first level), starting from which we could make that word an object of communication; it means, rather, to expose the word in its own mediality, in its own being a means, without any transcendence. The gesture is, in this sense, communication of a communicability. It has precisely nothing to say because what it shows is the being-in-language of human beings as pure mediality.[8]

Agamben continues that precisely humanity's 'being in a medium' [*l'essere-in-un-medio*] opens up the 'ethical dimension' of human action.[9]

The provocation and explosiveness of the avant-garde gesture developed by the artists of the Workshop of the Film Form and theorised by Świdziński lies in the act of reclaiming the sphere of communication, communicability, intersubjectivity, and thus the realm of ethics itself from dominant relations, the regime, and ideology. By opening up this sphere as a field of artistic endeavors, the artists turn language, intersubjectivity, and thus ethics into an artistic medium. They reclaim the right to determine their own form of social communication. If with Agamben we understand this realm of communication and being in language as the genuine milieu of intersubjective relations and the ethics of human existence, it becomes clear that reclaiming language means winning back an existential ability to act, and thus reclaiming life from the regime. And that is truly radical. For herein lies the provocation of this avant-garde gesture: by performing a different kind of communication, it seeks to achieve a different and better way of shared living, where direct and open forms of exchange finally liberate social life from the power of ideology.

Translated by Brian Currid

Essay published in: *1,2,3... Avant-Gardes (The Experiment Art and Film)*, ed. Ł. Ronduda and F. Zeyfang, Berlin and New York: Sternberg Press, 2007.

8 G. Agamben, op. cit., p. 55.
9 Ibidem, p. 54.

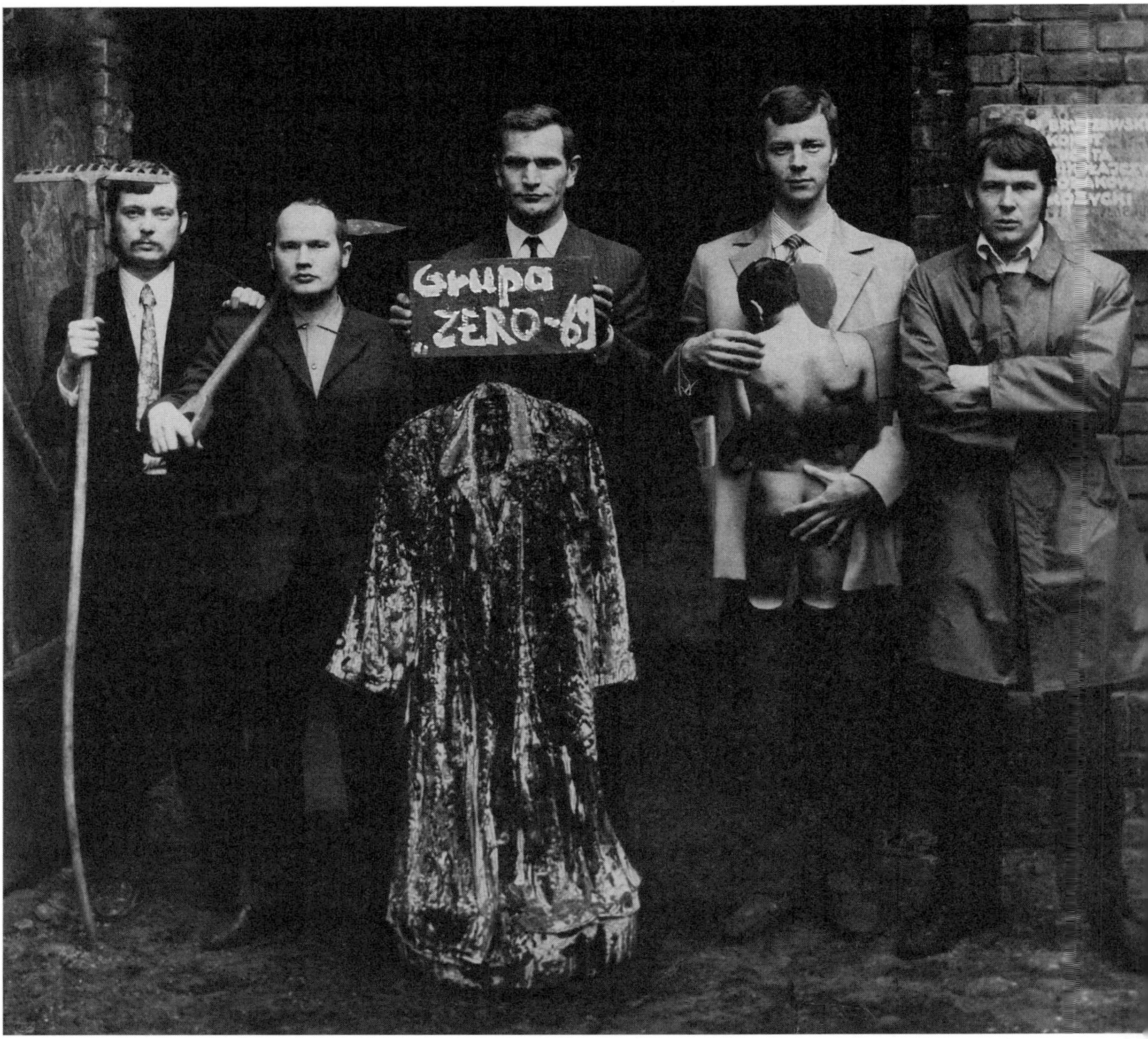

Ostatnia wystawa grupy Zero-61 (Kuźnia), 1969 Toruń, od lewej: A. Różycki, A. Mikołajczyk, J. Robakowski, W. Bruszewski, M. Kokot
Last exhibition of the Zero-61 group (The Smithy), 1969 Torun, from the left: A. Różycki, A. Mikołajczyk, J. Robakowski, W. Bruszewski, M. Kokot

Marika Kuźmicz

Warsztat Formy Filmowej

Wstęp

Na początku lat siedemdziesiątych kilku młodych ludzi założyło w łódzkiej Filmówce Warsztat Formy Filmowej (WFF)[1] – wspólnotę, u podstaw której leżał bunt przeciwko oficjalnej kinematografii, próba zaradzenia niskiemu poziomowi edukacji na uczelni, ale przede wszystkim fascynacja komunikacją audiowizualną, nowymi technikami przetwarzania obrazu i przedwojenną sztuką awangardową. Uczestnicy grupy przebywali ze sobą niemal codziennie, co skutkowało intensywną wymianą poglądów. Dzięki temu – mimo bardzo różnorodnych doświadczeń i zainteresowań – uzupełniali się, a Warsztat rozrastał się i działał intensywnie przez kolejne lata, stając się jednym z najważniejszych środowisk inspirujących przemiany w sztuce lat 60. i 70. w Polsce.

Za okres działalności Warsztatu przyjmujemy lata 1970–1977, zdając sobie sprawę z umowności tych cezur. Dotyczy to zwłaszcza daty końcowej, która przypada na dwa lata przed ostatnim wspólnym wystąpieniem grupy[2]. Data początkowa z kolei wiąże się ze sformalizowaniem działalności Warsztatu pod postacią koła naukowego. Zostało ono zamknięte decyzją rektora w 1975 roku, ale dopóki większość członków grupy była studentami, działała ona dalej. Warsztatowcy dojrzewali jednak jako artyści, w związku z czym wewnątrz grupy zaczęły powstawać pęknięcia i krystalizować się indywidualne ambicje. W latach 1976–1977 z uczestnictwa zrezygnowali Wojciech Bruszewski i Paweł Kwiek, który wspomina tę decyzję właśnie jako moment swojego usamodzielnienia się jako artysty. Dawni uczestnicy grupy do końca lat siedemdziesiątych organizowali wspólne pokazy, ale nie pracowali już razem.

Za trzon wspólnoty uznawani są Józef Robakowski i Wojciech Bruszewski, których łączyło wcześniejsze doświadczenie toruńskiej grupy Zero-61, a także Paweł Kwiek i Ryszard Waśko[3]. Zasadne byłoby dodanie do tego grona Andrzeja Różyckiego, który również był członkiem Zero-61, a w działalność Warsztatu był zaangażowany od samego początku. Istotny był również wkład Kazimierza Bendkowskiego, który wprawdzie mniej aktywnie uczestniczył we wspólnych akcjach

1 Pierwsza nazwa grupy brzmiała: Warsztat Form Filmowych „Treść". Grupa powstała jako część Koła Naukowego w Szkole Filmowej w Łodzi w październiku 1970 roku. Członkami założycielami byli Wojciech Bruszewski, Ryszard Gajewski, Andrzej Różycki, Paweł Kwiek, Antoni Mikołajczyk, Józef Robakowski i Zbigniew Rybczyński, wspierani przez profesora Jerzego Kotowskiego. Zob. *Żywa Galeria. Łódzki progresywny ruch artystyczny 1969–1981,* red. J. Robakowski. Łódź: Łódzki Dom Kultury – Galeria FF, 2000, s. 32 oraz R. Waśko, *Warsztat Formy Filmowej*, praca magisterska, PWSFTviT, Łódź 1974, http://repozytorium.fundacjaarton.pl/index.php?action-view/object&objid-3527&colid-24&catid-2&lang-pl [dostęp 29-12-2016].

2 Chodzi o 3rd International Avant-Garde Festival w National Film Theatre w Londynie, w którym na przełomie maja i czerwca 1979 roku wzięli udział Wojciech Bruszewski, Tomasz Konart, Józef Robakowski, Janusz Szczerek i Ryszard Waśko. Jednocześnie w Londynie odbyła się wystawa *Film as Film. Formal Experiment in Film, 1910–1975* w Hayward Gallery, w której wzięli udział Wojciech Bruszewski, Józef Robakowski i Ryszard Waśko.

3 R. Waśko dołączył nieco później, w drugim semestrze roku akademickiego 1970/71.

i podróżach, ale zrealizował pokaźną liczbę prac – pokazywanych głównie zagranicą od czasu jego wyjazdu do Niemiec w 1982 roku, w Polsce natomiast bardzo mało znanych i nieopracowywanych.

Wymienieni członkowie grupy kontynuowali etos Warsztatu także w swojej późniejszej twórczości, sytuując ją głównie w obszarze sztuki, a nie oficjalnej kinematografii. Jak powiedział Józef Robakowski:

> To jest bardzo ciekawe, że niektórzy z kolegów decydują się na taki styl życia, bez kinematografii. Tak postąpili: Mikołajczyk, Bendkowski, Bruszewski, Kwiek, Waśko, Różycki, Robakowski... To jest niezwykle ciekawe, że jesteśmy profesjonalistami, pokończyliśmy szkołę filmową, czyli najbardziej prestiżową uczelnię w tym kraju, wielu kończyło po dwa fakultety i decydujemy się być ludźmi takimi właśnie – artystami[4].

Mając świadomość szczególnie istotnego wkładu wymienionych powyżej twórców, postanowiliśmy przyjrzeć się w niniejszej książce Warsztatowi jako swoistej całości, wspólnocie, w której interakcja odmiennych osobowości wytworzyła szczególny rodzaj energii. Każdy z uczestników grupy w istotny sposób współtworzył jej ogromny dorobek, na który składają się setki prac – filmy, fotografie, prace wideo, akcje i teksty. To na ich podstawie uznajemy Warsztat za najważniejszą formację filmu strukturalnego w Europie Środkowo-Wschodniej[5].

Ale historia Warsztatu to coś znacznie więcej. To niezwykli ludzie i miejsca naznaczone ich obecnością. To wspólne inspiracje, odbyte razem podróże, fascynujące momenty autentycznej zespołowej pracy. To wspólnie przeżywane historyczne zdarzenia, ale też codzienność, na którą, jako artyści, byli szczególnie otwarci i na którą otwierali odbiorców swojej sztuki.

Warsztat Formy Filmowej nie działał bowiem w próżni – powstał w kraju rządzonym przez Polską Zjednoczoną Partię Robotniczą pod przywództwem Edwarda Gierka i funkcjonował w ramach instytucji, która była dla władzy bardzo istotna ze względu na propagandowy potencjał sztuki filmowej. W książce staramy się przyjrzeć także temu wątkowi – funkcjonowaniu Warsztatu w szerszej perspektywie historycznej i wpływowi, jaki na życie i twórczość jej uczestników miała polityka.

Niniejsza książka powstała w wyniku kilku lat kwerend, a także licznych spotkań i rozmów z członkami grupy. Wywiady przeprowadzaliśmy w ich domach i pracowniach w Łodzi, Warszawie i Berlinie. Tam też najczęściej wykonywaliśmy kwerendy – stosunkowo niewiele prac Warsztatowców znalazło swoje miejsce w polskich muzeach czy innego rodzaju instytucjach publicznych. To właśnie materiały pochodzące z prywatnych archiwów artystów pomogły nam w zrekonstruowaniu możliwie pełnego obrazu działalności grupy, choć trzeba dodać, że po sporej części prac, poza ustnymi relacjami, nie pozostał żaden ślad.

Tekst stanowiący pierwszą część publikacji jest próbą opowiedzenia możliwie pełnej historii grupy. Eseje, stanowiące drugą część publikacji, mają na celu ponowne odczytanie wybranych prac i aspektów działalności Warsztatu. Trzecia część książki pozwala zapoznać się z biografiami artystów oraz ich pracami (także niezachowanymi).

---

4 J. Robakowski, „Ósme kino. Z Józefem Robakowskim rozmawia Łukasz Ronduda", w: *Kino-Sztuka. Zwrot kinematograficzny w polskiej sztuce współczesnej*, red. J. Majmurek, Ł. Ronduda, Warszawa: Krytyka Polityczna, 20[illegible], s. 58–76.

5 Ł. Ronduda, 'The Workshop of the Film Form. Film Realizations from the Years 1970–1977', w: *The Workshop of the Film Form, 1970–1977. Early Film Work from Poland*, red. G. Joseph-Hunter, Ł. Ronduda, L. Zippay, Nowy Jork – Warszawa: Electronic Art Intermix – Centrum Sztuki Współczesnej Zamek Ujazdowski, 2004, s. 28.

Zaczyn

Warsztat Formy Filmowej powstał w Łodzi, ale jego późniejsi uczestnicy odnajdywali się wcześniej w różnych miejscach i okolicznościach. Na przykład Kazimierz Bendkowski, Ryszard Waśko i Ryszard Lenczewski uczestniczyli w tych samych amatorskich festiwalach filmów dokumentalnych[6]. Ważną rolę odegrał Toruń. To w tym mieście, które po wojnie stało się ważnym ośrodkiem akademickiego życia w Polsce i istotnym punktem na polskiej mapie kultury studenckiej, poznała się i rozpoczęła wspólną pracę duża grupa późniejszych Warsztatowców.

W sierpniu 1945 roku w Toruniu został otwarty Uniwersytet Mikołaja Kopernika (UMK), którego kadrę profesorską stworzyli doświadczeni pedagodzy z Uniwersytetu Stefana Batorego w Wilnie. Wraz z nimi w mieście pojawili się studenci. Młode pokolenie wniosło do miasta nową energię, wytworzyła się specyficzna atmosfera, o której Lech Lechowicz pisał, że była wynikiem nakładania się tradycji wileńskiej na hanzeatycką kulturę lokalną[7]. Po odwilży październikowej 1956 roku w mieście zaczęło rozwijać się życie kulturalne. W 1958 roku otworzono ważny w skali kraju Klub Tygodnika Studenckiego Od Nowa, który szybko stał się prężnie działającym centrum życia kulturalnego. Można w nim było spotkać Ewę Demarczyk, Krzysztofa Komedę, Juliana Przybosia, Artura Sandauera, Edwarda Stachurę czy Ryszarda Bruno Milczewskiego. Dwa lata później w Toruniu odbyła się pierwsza edycja słynnych później juwenaliów.

W tym właśnie okresie studia w Toruniu rozpoczęli późniejsi założyciele Warsztatu Formy Filmowej. Józef Robakowski i Andrzej Różycki studiowali konserwatorstwo i zabytkoznawstwo na wydziale sztuk pięknych. Robakowski traktował te studia poniekąd jako etap pośredni – środek do celu, jakim było kolejne podejście do egzaminów do Szkoły Filmowej w Łodzi. Z kolei Andrzej Różycki zdawał wcześniej na wydział malarstwa na warszawskiej Akademii Sztuk Pięknych[8], ale nie został przyjęty. Antoni Mikołajczyk był natomiast od 1962 roku studentem wychowania plastycznego na Wydziale Pedagogicznym UMK, na którym w 1967 roku obronił dyplom z malarstwa w pracowni profesora Bronisława Kierzkowskiego.

Dodajmy, że w tym samym czasie historię sztuki studiował w Toruniu, na tym samym wydziale, Janusz Zagrodzki. Zagrodzki pochodził z Łodzi, a jego celem i marzeniem była praca w tamtejszym Muzeum Sztuki. Fascynowała go historia przedwojennej sztuki awangardowej, szczególnie twórczość zapomnianej wówczas Katarzyny Kobro, której poświęcił referat w ramach seminarium prowadzonego przez profesora Gwidona Chmarzyńskiego (1906–1973). Pomimo tego, że na wydziale zajmowano się przede wszystkim sztuką średniowieczną i nowożytną, Zagrodzki starał się w miarę możliwości pogłębiać swoją wiedzę w interesującej go dziedzinie. Zawarł więc znajomość z późniejszymi uczestnikami WFF, a w latach 70. został jednym z pierwszych teoretyków piszących o działalności Warsztatu[9] i przyjacielem grupy, towarzyszącym jej podczas akcji i wydarzeń artystycznych. Józef Robakowski wspomina, że wraz z kolegami korzystał z wiedzy Zagrodzkiego o sztuce przedwojennej, w szczególności o działalności tak ważnej dla grupy Katarzyny Kobro[10].

6 J. Peltz, *O filmowcach amatorach bez taryfy ulgowej,* „Fotografia", 1, 1970, s. 5–7.

7 L. Lechowicz, *Grupa Zero-61. Zapomniana tradycja lat sześćdziesiątych,* „Exit", 2, 1999, s. 1954–1959.

8 Wywiad z Andrzejem Różyckim, wrzesień 2016.

9 Zob. J. Zagrodzki, *Kino-Laboratorium,* w: *Żywa Galeria*, s. 112–113, http://repozytorium.fundacjaarton.pl/index.php?action=view/object&objid=3139&colid=75&catid=18 [dostęp 28-12-2016].

10 Zagrodzki jest autorem pierwszej monografii rzeźbiarki. Zob. J. Zagrodzki, *Katarzyna Kobro i kompozycja przestrzeni*, Warszawa: PWN, 1984.

Kiedy po studiach wszyscy zamieszkali w Łodzi, to właśnie on umożliwiał im dostęp do dzieł przechowywanych w magazynach Muzeum Sztuki. Był także współautorem filmów członków Warsztatu poświęconych przedstawicielom międzywojennej polskiej awangardy[11].

Robakowski i Różycki podkreślają, że toruński uniwersytet – dzięki wybitnym profesorom, którzy prezentowali „całkowitą ideową niezależność" – pozwalał studentom na „oderwanie się od oficjalnej polityki kulturalnej"[12]. Wśród toruńskich wykładowców znajdowali się wybitni twórcy i badacze tacy jak Tymon Niesiołowski (1882–1965), malarz, grafik formista i członek grupy Rytm któremu Robakowski poświęcił swoją pracę magisterską[13]; Stefan Narębski (1892–1966), pedagog i architekt, który przed II wojną światową pełnił funkcję architekta miejskiego Wilna; Jadwiga Puciata-Pawłowska (1902–1989), specjalistka w zakresie historii sztuki przełomu XIX i XX wieku Jak powiedział Robakowski: „To właśnie oni uchronili nas od wpływów realnego socjalizmu"[14] Ponadto wspomniany już Bronisław Kierzkowski, pochodził z Łodzi i na tamtejszej Państwowej Wyższej Szkole Sztuk Plastycznych w latach 1946–1947 był studentem Władysława Strzemińskiego, co czyni go nieco zapomnianym, ale jednak niewątpliwym łącznikiem Warsztatu z przeszłością polskiej awangardy.

Józef Robakowski określił okres toruński jako bardzo twórczy[15]. W mieście działał prężnie Studencki Twórczy Klub Filmowy „Pętla", który stwarzał możliwość realizacji filmów na taśmie 16 mm, a także Dyskusyjny Klub Filmowy, prowadzony na wysokim poziomie przez Józefa Tęczę[16]. Późniejsi Warsztatowcy efektywnie korzystali z ich oferty, zapoznając się z przeglądem światowej awangardy filmowej i wykonując pierwsze własne filmy[17].

Działając w „Pętli", Robakowski, Mikołajczyk i Różycki organizowali jednocześnie kolejne grupy i stowarzyszenia: OKO (1960), interdyscyplinarny Krąg (1965), a przede wszystkim Zero-61 (1961). Doprowadziło to do powstania w Toruniu silnego środowiska skupionego na filmie i fotografii, co – jak zaznacza Robakowski – było w tamtym czasie fenomenem na skalę krajową.

Co więcej, było to środowisko cieszące się sporym marginesem wolności. Tworzenie stowarzyszeń, organizowanie wystaw, realizacja filmów i fotografii, a także formowanie się postaw artystycznych i życiowych – wszystko to odbywało się w pojemnym obszarze kultury studenckiej, cechującej się, zwłaszcza już po Marcu 1968, swoistą autonomią w totalitarnym systemie PRL i względną niezależnością od nacisków politycznych[18]. Działania w obszarze sztuki i kultury podejmowane przez studentów nie miały przełożenia na masową widownię, w związku z czym władza nie przykładała do nich większego znaczenia. Tymczasem, jak widzimy z perspektywy czasu, to właśnie w kręgu kultury studenckiej kształtowały się najbardziej radykalne postawy przełomu

11 Zagrodzki był między innymi konsultantem filmu *Wielość rzeczywistości Leona Chwistka* i *Konstruktywizm w Polsce* Ryszarda Waśki. Zagrodzki był też współscenarzystą filmu *Kompozycje przestrzenne Katarzyny Kobro* Józefa Robakowskiego, do którego muzykę skomponował Eugeniusz Rudnik (1971).

12 J. Robakowski, *Sztuka to potęga,* 2005, http://robakowski.eu/tx13.html [dostęp 27-12-2016].

13 Zob. T. Samosionek, *Sztuka video w Polsce*, Łódź: T. Samosionek, 1989, http://robakowski.eu/tx23.html [dostęp 28-12-2016].

14 J. Robakowski, *Sztuka to potęga*.

15 Wywiad z Józefem Robakowskim, październik 2015.

16 Wywiad z Józefem Robakowskim, listopad 2015.

17 J. Robakowski, *W oczach ekspertów byliśmy amatorami*, rozmowę przeprowadził A. Mazur, „Fototapeta" 2002, http://fototapeta.art.pl/2002/jro.php [dostęp 28-12-2016].

18 Zob. L. Burska, *Awangarda i inne złudzenia. O pokoleniu '68 w Polsce,* Gdańsk: Słowo/obraz terytoria, 2013, s. 65.

at 60. i 70. Dla Warsztatowców były ona przyczółkiem do działań w sferze sztuki[19]. Robakowski pytany o początek swojego myślenia o „kinie autorskim", przywołuje ten właśnie okres:

> To było takie nasze własne kino tworzone na taśmie 16 mm, 8 mm. W miarę szybko zorientowaliśmy się, że trzeba stworzyć zupełnie nowy układ – układ niezależny zarówno dla fotografii, jak i od filmu – dla wszystkich tych działań medialnych, które się wówczas pojawiły[20].

Układ, o którym mówi Robakowski, stanie się jednym z zaczątków Warsztatu, a między grupami toruńską i łódzką zaistnieje kilka ważnych analogii. Obie grupy stworzyli młodzi ludzie, których łączyły studia i bliskie relacje towarzyskie. Obie były liczne[21], jeśli weźmiemy pod uwagę cały okres działalności (odpowiednio osiem i siedem lat). W obu istniał najbardziej aktywny trzon złożony z kilku osób, w obu też – co zastanawiające – brakowało choćby jednej kobiety[22].

Doświadczenia uczestników Zero-61 stały się później cennym wkładem w działalność Warsztatu, szczególnie we wczesnym okresie jego istnienia. Opracowali oni w okresie toruńskim wiele fundamentalnych problemów, takich jak status fotografii, jej zależność/autonomiczność wobec rzeczywistości czy też kwestie związane z materialnością odbitek. To właśnie wtedy, korzystając z medium fotografii, Warsztatowcy realizowali pierwsze próby „zaprzeczania tradycyjnym technikom i konwencjom"[23], które później stały się ich codzienną praktyką. W maju 1966 roku na dziedzińcu UMK zorganizowali wystawę, na której „Zdjęcia fragmentów rzeczywistości skonfrontowano z nią samą. I tak fotografię spychacza z górą piachu, drzewa z rzeczywistym drzewem, a zdjęcie płotu powieszono na parkanie"[24].

W 1967 roku podobny zabieg zastosowali na wystawie poplenerowej w klubie Od Nowa (co symptomatyczne, odbyła się ona w czasie remontu). Przedmioty codziennego użytku zestawili z ich wielkoformatowymi reprodukcjami fotograficznymi. Wtedy też wśród prezentowanych artystów pojawił się Józef Korbiela, fikcyjna postać wymyślona przez Robakowskiego. Zerowcy podpisywali „Korbielą" różne osobliwe bibeloty lub stworzone przez siebie kiczowate dzieła. Pojawienie się tej postaci zwiastuje strategię, którą Robakowski będzie posługiwał się także w latach 70., przeprowadzając akcje i działania, których rzeczywisty autor pozostawał ukryty.

W drugiej połowie lat 60. Robakowski i Bruszewski (którzy zaczęli studia w Szkole Filmowej), a także Mikołajczyk i Zagrodzki (który po studiach podjął pracę w łódzkim Muzeum Sztuki) dzielili swój czas między dwoma miastami. W 1967 roku do Zero-61 przystąpił Wojciech

19 Wywiad z Józefem Robakowskim i Andrzejem Różyckim, lipiec 2014.

20 *Rozmowa w Józefem Robakowskim*, rozmowę przeprowadził Adam Mazur, 2001, http://robakowski.eu/tx30.html [dostęp 28-12-2016].

21 W 1961 roku do grupy Zero-61 należeli Romuald Chomicz, Czesław Kuchta, Lucjan Oczkowski, Józef Robakowski, Jerzy Wardak i Wiesław Wojczulanis. Później dołączyli Wojciech Bruszewski, Roman Dąbek, Michał Kokot, Antoni Mikołajczyk, Andrzej Różycki i Jan Siennik. Najdłużej i najbardziej aktywnie w grupie działali Kuchta, Robakowski, Wardak i Różycki, natomiast w ostatnim okresie istnienia grupy także Bruszewski, Kokot i Mikołajczyk. Z tych siedmiu artystów czterech weszło potem w skład Warsztatu Formy Filmowej.

22 Józef Robakowski i Andrzej Różycki wskazują przyczynę takiej sytuacji w WFF w znikomej liczbie studentek na Wydziale Operatorskim i Wydziale Reżyserii. Prowadzi to do pytania o ówczesną politykę Szkoły Filmowej wobec kandydatek na studia.

23 L. Olszewski, *Działalność Warsztatu Formy Filmowej jako przykład strategii sztuki wobec władzy w Polsce lat siedemdziesiątych*, „Artium Quaestiones", 9, 1998, s. 124.

24 Ibidem.

Bruszewski – był już wtedy studentem Szkoły Filmowej, na której poznał Robakowskiego. Warsztat jeszcze nie powstał, ale postawa jego późniejszych założycieli krystalizowała się i radykalizowała, zwiastując schyłek Zero-61.

Uczestnicy grupy za moment ostatecznego jej rozpadu uznają wystawę *Kuźnia '69*. Odbyła się w ona ramach ogólnopolskiego sympozjum na temat wpływów plastyki i innych dziedzin sztuki na fotografię (11–12 maja 1969 roku), dzięki czemu w jej otwarciu uczestniczyło niemalże całe ówczesne środowisko związane z fotografią (także awangardową) i sztuką niezależną. Tytuł wystawy był związany z miejscem ekspozycji – starym budynkiem mieszczącym niegdyś warsztat kowalski. Był to wybór nieprzypadkowy i charakterystyczny dla późniejszego dorobku Warsztatu. Ekspozycja usytuowana w przestrzeni ogólnodostępnej, na poły opuszczonej, pozornie nieatrakcyjnej, a przede wszystkim – niebędącej galerią ani muzeum, sygnalizowała chęć otworzenia siebie i swoich odbiorców na to, co realne. Fotografie zostały zestawione z przedmiotami codziennego użytku lub wręcz znalezionymi śmieciami. Zabieg, stosowany już wcześniej przez członków Zero-61, miał na celu uzmysłowienie odbiorcom materialności fotografii jako bytu trójwymiarowego, mającego swoje określone wymiary, możliwego do zniszczenia, łatwopalnego, co z kolei miało prowadzić do ustanowienia „nowych związków między fotograficznym medium a widzem"[25]. Tym samym artyści konsekwentnie starali się wychodzić z przestrzeni galeryjnej, konfrontować swoje prace z rzeczywistością i badać relacje między fotografowanym a fotografią. Te zagadnienia staną się później kluczowymi problemami dla Warsztatowców.

Część członków Zero-61 nie zdecydowała się na udział w wystawie. Niedługo po niej Toruń opuścił na rzecz Łodzi Andrzej Różycki, ostatni z byłych Zerowców, który zdecydował się na studia w Szkole Filmowej[26]. Niewiele później, we wrześniu 1969 roku, w szklarni znajdującej się na terenie łódzkiej Filmówki, zorganizował z innymi byłymi Zerowcami (Robakowskim, Różyckim, Mikołajczykiem i Bruszewskim) oraz ich nowym kolegą Ryszardem Gajewskim (wówczas studentem trzeciego roku wydziału operatorskiego) wystawę nazywaną przez nich potem „garażową". Ponownie zaprezentowali kilkadziesiąt fotografii w zestawieniu z przedmiotami codziennego użytku; ponownie w opuszczonym i zaniedbanym miejscu. Ten pozornie drobny gest jest bardzo znamienny – oto studenci Szkoły Filmowej organizują wystawę fotografii, świadomie sytuując się w obszarze sztuki, a nie kinematografii. Czują się bowiem artystami. Jak wspomina Ryszard Gajewski:

> Pierwszą wystawę fotograficzną Warsztatu zrobiliśmy w szklarni na dziedzińcu Szkoły Filmowej, na wzór grupy Zero-61 wystawiającej w starej kuźni. Nazywała się *Szklarnia*, a swoje fotografie wystawili: Józek Robakowski, Wojtek Bruszewski, Ryszard Gajewski, Paweł Kwiek i inni. Józkowi i Wojtkowi była ta wystawa potrzebna do zamknięcia starego toruńskiego okresu działań fotograficznych i rozpoczęcia nowego łódzkiego okresu filmowego[27].

W tym samym mniej więcej czasie Ryszard Waśko, absolwent technikum budowlanego w Nysie, i Tadeusz Junak, absolwent technikum samochodowego z Warszawy, biorą udział w licznych konkurach filmów amatorskich. Otrzymują nagrody i wyróżnienia. Wspomina o nich

25 Ibidem, s. 127.

26 Analogiczną decyzję rozważał też Michał Kokot, ostatecznie rezygnując z tego pomysłu.

27 Wywiad z Ryszardem Gajewskim, styczeń 2016.

prasa[28]. Z kolei w Olsztynie swój pierwszy film na kamerze 8 mm robi licealista Janusz Połom, który – zainspirowany przez starszego brata – uczęszcza do Miejskiego Klubu Fotograficznego Giewont. W Warszawie kolejny licealista Paweł Kwiek, którego starszy brat Przemysław studiuje już na Wydziale Rzeźby ASP, dostaje od ojca kamerę filmową 8 mm za dobre wyniki w nauce i realizuje pierwsze eksperymenty z fotografią.

We wrześniu 1970 roku wszyscy oni będą już studiować w Szkole Filmowej, którą w tym samym roku skończyli W. Bruszewski, J. Janicki, R. Gajewski i J. Robakowski, a w październiku – założą Warsztat Formy Filmowej.

Wspólnota

Za oficjalny moment powstania Warsztatu Formy Filmowej uważa się październik 1970 roku. Jest to moment sformalizowania działalności grupy, która *de facto* istniała już wcześniej. Ryszard Gajewski, który rozpoczął studia w Szkole Filmowej w 1965 roku, znalazł się dwa lata później (po przerwie na urlop dziekański) na jednym roku z Józefem Robakowskim i Wojciechem Bruszewskim. Wkrótce szkoła, w której działalność dydaktyczna przechodziła wówczas kryzys, miała stać się sceną dla wydarzeń Marca 1968. To osłabiło ją jeszcze bardziej i tylko upewniło ówczesnych studentów w przekonaniu, że współpraca i samokształcenie są dla nich jedyną możliwą drogą. Ryszard Gajewski wspomina:

> Józef Robakowski, który miał już za sobą doświadczenie toruńskie, uważał, że należy powołać kolejną grupę. Był zawsze zainteresowany pracą twórczą i sposobem myślenia innych. Kiedy zaczęliśmy razem studiować, poprosił, żebym pokazał mu swoje prace. Pokazałem film, który zrobiłem jako etiudę na koniec pierwszego roku. Był to niekreacyjny jeszcze dokument o tym, jak studenci czwartego roku Szkoły Filmowej, z wymiany zagranicznej, robią swój film końcoworoczny. Robakowskiemu bardzo się to spodobało, więc zapytał, czy będę chciał pracować razem z nim i Bruszewskim. W planach mieli stworzenie grupy artystycznej. Oni wtedy funkcjonowali między Toruniem a Łodzią, ale działalność grupy Zero-61 powoli się kończyła[29].

W 1969 roku, po wystawie *Kuźnia* w Toruniu, o wyjeździe do Łodzi zdecydował też Andrzej Różycki. Początki WFF wspomina następująco:

> Uważam, że mieliśmy idealną sytuację do tego, żeby stworzyć awangardową grupę, jaką był Warsztat. Do powstania czegoś takiego potrzebne jest intensywne przebywanie ze sobą, a my w taki właśnie sposób funkcjonowaliśmy. Bardzo dużo przebywaliśmy ze sobą. Od wczesnego rana, kiedy zaczynały się zajęcia, przez wspólne posiłki, do wieczora, kiedy organizowaliśmy zwykle spotkania towarzyskie, przeciągające się do późnej nocy[30].

Pierwsze realizacje powstawały przy nader skromnych, praktycznie zerowych środkach finansowych i technicznych. Ryszard Gajewski, wspominając pierwsze pokazy filmów grupy w sali projekcyjnej Szkoły Filmowej, opowiada o Wojciechu Bruszewskim, który starał się je „udźwiękowić" za pomocą magnetofonu. Efekty były różne. Gajewski wspomina:

28 J. Peltz, op. cit.
29 Wywiad z Ryszardem Gajewskim, styczeń 2016.
30 Wywiad z Andrzejem Różyckim, lipiec 2016.

> Początkowo Warsztat formalnie nie istniał. Był i już. Wszyscy wiedzieli o co chodzi. Jak ktoś zrobił coś ciekawego, to zapraszał nas na projekcję. Józek Robakowski przygotowywał pokazowy zestaw filmów i jak ktoś się w nim znalazł, to mógł mówić, że jest członkiem Warsztatu. Można było wylecieć z zestawu i znów się w nim pojawić. Nie było żadnych reguł. Po prostu Józek lubił mieszać w tych zestawach. Większość filmów nie miała ścieżki dźwiękowej, ponieważ szkoła nie udźwiękawiała ćwiczeń operatorskich, wychodząc z założenia, że do oceny wystarczy sam obraz. W lepszej sytuacji byli reżyserzy – ich etiudy były realizowane z dźwiękiem. Jak ktoś miał pieniądze to udźwiękawiał na lewo. Chwytaliśmy się rożnych chałupniczych sposobów. W kabinie projekcyjnej puszczaliśmy dźwięk z magnetofonu, na oko synchronizując go z obrazem. Filmów przybywało, a my ciągle w epoce kamienia łupanego. Nie można było dalej ciągnąć tej amatorki, w końcu Szkoła Filmowa do czegoś zobowiązuje. Ktoś podsunął pomysł, aby założyć Koło Naukowe. Nic tam się nie działo, a szkoła na jego działalność miała pieniądze. Rektor Kotowski był przychylny inicjatywie, niemniej formalności musiały zostać spełnione. Jak w każdej państwowej instytucji – trzeba było złożyć podanie, uzasadnić, wytyczyć cele, naszkicować plan działania i tym podobne. Jeżeli dobrze pamiętam, to Józek Robakowski z Wojtkiem Bruszewskim zredagowali ten piękny dokument. Do tej pory ukazuje się w różnych wydawnictwach i krąży na stronach internetowych jako główny manifest Warsztatu Formy Filmowej. A przecież w tym tekście chodziło o to, aby nie powiedzieć nic konkretnego ani niczego nie obiecać. Stopień ogólności był tak duży, że każdy film lub działanie można było do niego dopasować. Uważam to za bardzo sprytne i mądre posunięcie[31].

Gajewski zdradza też skąd wzięła się nazwa grupy:

> Nazwa spodobała się wszystkim, bo w tamtym czasie były modne różne „workshopy" i „factory". Inspirowaliśmy się Fabryką Andy'ego Warhola. Interesowało nas zestawienie tego co robimy z pojęciem fabryki, przemysłu, warsztatu właśnie. A ponieważ zajmowaliśmy się formą filmu – wszystko było jasne, powstała nazwa[32].

„Przychylnym rektorem", o którym wspomina Gajewski, był prof. Jerzy Kotowski, autor filmów animowanych (w tym lalkowych), „niezbyt poważnie traktowany przez środowisko filmowców, które najwyżej ceniło tworzenie pełnometrażowych filmów fabularnych"[33]. Kotowski był jednak otwarty na poszukiwania związane ze sztuką współczesną. Zdawał sobie sprawę, że w Szkole Filmowej musi być miejsce na eksperyment, dlatego też zgodził się na założenie Warsztatu[34]. Warto dodać, że to właśnie Kotowski był inicjatorem powołania Pracowni Filmu Animowanego. To właśnie w niej pierwsze kroki stawiał Zbigniew Rybczyński.

Warsztatowcy działali więc od 1970 do 1975 roku w ramach Koła Naukowego Szkoły Filmowej, dla którego uzyskali środki finansowe na produkcję i postprodukcję filmów. Nadało to realizacjom grupy silny rys profesjonalizmu, odróżniający je od innych eksperymentalnych produkcji tamtego czasu (także w kontekście międzynarodowym). Filmy były kręcone z wykorzystaniem

31 Wywiad z Ryszardem Gajewskim, lipiec 2016.
32 Ibidem.
33 Wywiad z Andrzej Różyckim, lipiec 2014.
34 Wywiad z Ryszardem Gajewskim, czerwiec 2016.

taśmy 35 mm, a proces ich produkcji był zgodny z ówczesnymi standardami kinematograficznymi. Filmy Warsztatu powstawały przy wsparciu Pracowni Produkcji Filmów Szkolnych.

Krótki tekst założycielski Warsztatu, nazywany później *Manifestem I*, był dziełem całej grupy[35]. Jest syntetyczny i pojemny jednocześnie. Składa się z kilku zdań, które nie są obietnicą ani deklaracją:

> Warsztat powstał w 1970 r. z inicjatywy studentów i absolwentów Łódzkiej Szkoły Filmowej, Telewizyjnej i Teatralnej. Obok realizatorów filmowych w WARSZTACIE pracują plastycy, muzycy, fotografowie, poeci, technicy... WARSZTAT realizuje filmy, zapisy i transmisje telewizyjne, audycje dźwiękowe, wystawy plastyczne, różnego rodzaju zdarzenia i interwencje artystyczne... WARSZTAT uprawia także działalność teoretyczną i krytyczną. Bada i ma ambicje rozszerzyć możliwości sztuk audiowizualnych. Uwaga! WARSZTAT nie uprawia żadnej działalności komercyjnej, a jego realizatorzy pracują całkowicie bezinteresownie. Jedynym warunkiem podjęcia pracy w tej SEKCJI jest podporządkowanie się realizatorów wyżej podanej idei programowej. Pracą programową i organizacyjną Warsztatu kieruje siedmioosobowa Rada Programowa[36].

Paweł Kwiek wspomina tamten okres jako czas bardzo intensywnej wymiany poglądów i pomysłów. Intensywnej do tego stopnia, że członkowie grupy realizowali niekiedy nie swoje pomysły. Nie mówimy jednak o kradzieży czy plagiacie, lecz o autentycznej wymianie. Paweł Kwiek wspomina:

> Takich sytuacji było wiele, dotyczyły każdego z nas. Pamiętam, siedziałem kiedyś w szkolnej stołówce, przyszedł któryś z kolegów. Opowiedziałem mu o jakimś pomyśle, który miałem. A on na to: „Przecież ty tego nie zrobisz i tak. A to taki dobry pomysł. Ja to zrobię". No i zrobił. I dobrze, bo ja bym na pewno tego nie zrobił, miałem za dużo pomysłów po prostu[37].

Aby nieco zrównoważyć ten wyidealizowany obraz kolektywnej współpracy, przytoczę słowa Marka Koterskiego, który w pierwszych latach działalności WFF uczestniczył w wydarzeniach, wyjazdach i pokazach grupy:

> Formacja Warsztatu zawsze była mi obca. Po prostu nie bardzo lubiłem się z tymi facetami. Czułem z ich strony brak akceptacji, poza Waśką, z którym jakoś bardziej przypadliśmy sobie do gustu. Miałem również poczucie obcości merytorycznej. W moim odczuciu forma ma sens dopóki służy poznaniu składników tworzywa filmowego. Ale jeżeli jest celem samym w sobie, staje się zjawiskiem elitarnym. Animatorzy Warsztatu oczekiwali, że ich propozycje winny mieć szerokie audytorium, które w dodatku świetnie się powinno bawić,

---

35 Manifest nie był podpisany konkretnym nazwiskiem – ani w oryginale ani w żadnym późniejszym przedruku. Zbiorowe autorstwo tekstu podkreślał też Józef Robakowski (korespondencja w lipcu 2016 roku).

36 Cyt. za R. W. Kluszczyński, *Warsztat Formy Filmowej,* Warszawa: Centrum Sztuki Współczesnej Zamek Ujazdowski, 2000, s. 60. *Manifest I* (1970) był pierwszym, syntetycznym tekstem mówiącym o przyszłej działalności grupy w sposób mający nie ograniczać twórcom pola działania. *Manifest II* (1975) był już pogłębioną prezentacją stanowiska grupy, podsumowaniem pięcioletniego okresu działalności. Oba teksty były publikowane wielokrotnie w formie ulotek i późniejszych przedruków. Jedna z wersji ulotki z *Manifestem I* jest dostępna online: http://repozytorium.fundacjaarton.pl/index.php?action=view/object&objid=3178&colid=75&catid=18 [dostęp 28-12-2016]. Zob. też *Wojciech Bruszewski. Fenomeny percepcji,* red. E. Fuchs, J. Zagrodzki, Łódź: Miejska Galeria Sztuki, 2010, s. 93–94.

37 Wywiad z Pawłem Kwiekiem, lipiec 2015.

> a to jest moim zdaniem przejaw pychy i niezrozumienie. Owszem, jako forpoczta, jako awangarda, która przeciera szlak, Warsztat Formy Filmowej spełnił zadanie[38].

Ważnym podsumowaniem wspólnotowego aspektu działalności Warsztatu są słowa Zbigniewa Rybczyńskiego, który stwierdził, że istnienie w Szkole Filmowej grupy ludzi robiących filmy „inne" od regularnej dokumentalnej i fabularnej produkcji dawało mu poczucie pewności we własnych poszukiwaniach.

Szkoła

W okresie powojennym szkoły wyższe w Łodzi lokowano w gmachach pofabrycznych albo kamienicach. Lepsze, bardziej reprezentacyjne siedziby otrzymały tylko uczelnie artystyczne. Założona w 1948 roku Szkoła Filmowa została umieszczona w budynku z 1903 roku przy ul. Targowej 61, czyli w dawnym pałacu Oskara Kona, właściciela Manufaktury Widzewskiej. Kazimierz Kutz wspominał:

> Kiedy pierwszy raz przyjechałem do Łodzi, z wrażenia trzęsły mi się nogi, bo Szkoła mieściła się w pałacyku. Dla chłopca ze Śląska wejście do pałacu było wstrząsem[39].

Absolwenci kończący uczelnię w pierwszym okresie jej działalności, czyli w latach 40. i na początku 50., wspominają piękny ogród, o który troszczył się nieprzerwanie ten sam przedwojenny ogrodnik, chętnie obsadzany w etiudach studenckich z uwagi na swój charakterystyczny wygląd. W pamięci utkwiło im także nieźle zachowane przedwojenne wyposażenie gmachu: obszerne sale, bogato zdobione ściany, kolorowe posadzki, ozdobne sufity, mozaiki i żyrandole „z epoki". Niestety następne lata przyniosły szybką dewastację willi. Kolejne pomieszczenia pozbawiano oryginalnego wyposażenia, które zapewne zdobiło później gabinety partyjnych oficjeli. Szkoła cierpiała na brak pomieszczeń, więc łazienki przerabiano na ciemnie. W zaniedbanie popadł też w końcu pałacowy park. Mieszczącą się w nim cieplarnię zaadaptowano na niewielkie atelier. W długim budynku za ogrodem zorganizowano magazyn i montażownie, a w głównym budynku willi – sale wykładowe i projekcyjne, rektorat, dziekanaty, ciemnie i pomieszczenia na doświadczenia chemiczno-fotograficzne. W osobnym gmachu była stołówka, biblioteka, czytelnia i internat.

W okresie, gdy studia rozpoczynali Warsztatowcy, czyli w drugiej połowie lat 60., po pierwotnej elegancji budynku nie było już śladu, choć nadal było to otoczenie „zobowiązujące". Piotr Szulkin, który studiował w Szkole w latach 1970–1975, wspominał:

> Często miałem wrażenie, że stary budynek Szkoły walczy z wszechogarniającą łódzką degradacją i próbuje na swój sposób ożyć. W ogrodzie wybijały się jakieś egzotyczne rośliny posadzone jeszcze przed wojną. Tratowano je, wysypywano na nie węgiel, a one po jakimś czasie wyrastały gdzie indziej. Gdy malowano ściany farbą olejną, kuły w oczy witraże[40].

Józef Robakowski podszedł do egzaminów jako pierwszy spośród późniejszych Warsztatowców. Studia w Szkole Filmowej były jego jasno określonym celem, dlatego zdawał tam aż dwukrotnie (1958, 1966), co wspomina następująco:

---

38 K. Krubski, M. Miller, Z.Turowska, W. Wiśniewski, *Filmówka. Powieść o łódzkiej szkole filmowej*, Warszawa: Prószyński i S-ka, 1998, s. 214.

39 Ibidem, s. 34.

40 Ibidem, s. 203.

> Moim zdaniem w 1958 roku do Szkoły nie można się było dostać. Osiągnięto w niej fantastyczny poziom, najwyższy pośród polskich uczelni artystycznych. Kadra, znakomicie zorientowana sztuce światowej, tworzyła jednocześnie czołówkę polskiej kinematografii, realizując wspaniałe filmy. Nie było szans dla takiego jak ja prowincjusza z Torunia[41].

Egzaminy wstępne były nieprzewidywalne. Zdający równocześnie z Robakowskim operator filmowy Adam Holender wspominał:

> Egzamin wstępny zaskoczył mnie, bo przychodzi dwudziestojednoletni człowiek do pokoju specjalistów i oczekuje poważnych pytań, a tu proszą go o dokładne opisanie wejścia do łazienki, zrobienia siusiu i spuszczenia wody. Przerażające![42]

Robakowski nie zdał, ale udało mu się odwiedzić Muzeum Sztuki, gdzie obejrzał „prace Katarzyny Kobro, Władysława Strzemińskiego, Karola Hillera"[43].

> Posądzono mnie wówczas, że na egzamin wstępny przyniosłem nie swoje prace fotograficzne. Były tak dobre, że nie chciano uwierzyć, abym mógł je sam wykonać. Powołano nawet w tym celu specjalną komisję. Nie miałem już szansy. Postanowiłem skończyć inne studia, a jednocześnie tak się przygotować, żeby nie było już na mnie siły. Ostatecznie sukcesem zakończyło się drugie podejście. Ukończyłem Wydział Sztuk Pięknych na Uniwersytecie w Toruniu. Miałem znaczny dorobek, pokazywany na wystawach w Polsce i zagranicą. Nie sposób było już powtórzyć posądzenia, że przyszedłem na egzamin z nie swoimi pracami. Zdałem bez żadnych kłopotów na pierwszym czy drugim miejscu[44].

Józef Robakowski dostał się na uczelnię w 1966 roku, tym samym co jego kolega z grupy Zero-61, Wojciech Bruszewski. Rok wcześniej studia rozpoczął (zdając za trzecim „podejściem") Ryszard Gajewski, aktywny uczestnik grupy w najwcześniejszym okresie jej działalności[45], a rok później – Marek Koterski, który ostatecznie związał swoje życie zawodowe z filmem fabularnym[46], ale działał w orbicie Warsztatu do 1973 roku.

Na pierwszym roku studenci reżyserii i studiów operatorskich uczyli się razem. Następnie, o ile zaliczyli letnią sesję, trafiali na docelowy wydział. W przypadku Robakowskiego i Bruszewskiego był to wydział operatorski[47]. Również docelowo na „operatorkę" zostali przyjęci w 1969 roku Paweł Kwiek i Zbigniew Rybczyński, na wydział reżyserii natomiast – Andrzej Różycki. Rybczyński w szkole średniej planował zdawać na reżyserię, ale zmienił zamierzenie pod wpływem historyka sztuki i profesora warszawskiej ASP Ksawerego Piwockiego, z którego synem chodził do jednej klasy:

> Kiedyś, kiedy gościłem w jego domu, zwierzyłem się, że zamierzam zdawać do Łodzi na reżyserię. „Reżyseria to nie zawód" – powiedział profesor – „powinieneś zdawać na Wydział Operatorski, poznasz warsztat, będziesz fachowcem". [...] Egzamin składałem w 1969 r.

---

41 Ibidem, s. 127.

42 Ibidem.

43 Wywiad z Józefem Robakowskim, maj 2016.

44 K. Krubski et al., op. cit., s. 168.

45 Na podstawie relacji Ryszarda Gajewskiego (rozmowa w lipcu 2016 roku).

46 Co symptomatyczne, członkowie grupy sami podawali w swoich biogramach informację o „przejściu" do kinematografii. Wskazuje to na rangę tej decyzji w środowisku Warsztatu – w praktyce oznaczała zerwanie z grupą. Por. R. Waśko, op. cit.

47 Bruszewski od 1970 r. studiował także reżyserię, którą ukończył pięć lat później.

Liczył się wówczas ogólny poziom znajomości sztuki. Inni uczyli się tego z książek, dla mnie to było całe moje życie, więc otrzymałem dobrą ocenę. Wybór szkoły był w moim przypadku całkowicie świadomy. Uważałem, że malarstwo, czyli statyczny obraz, przeżyło się i że moją pasję muszę ożywić, poruszyć[48].

W 1970 roku studia rozpoczęli Tadeusz Junak, Ryszard Lenczewski i Jacek Łomnicki. Rok później: Janusz Połom i Kazimierz Bendkowski. Ten ostatni pragnął zostać reżyserem, bo – jak wspomina – fascynowali go Fellini i Antonioni. Jeszcze w szkole średniej należał do amatorskiego klubu filmowego w Warszawie i z jego ramienia brał udział w licznych festiwalach, prezentując nagrania wykonane na taśmie 8 mm. Rok przed zdanymi egzaminami do Filmówki otrzymał za obraz *Blask cienia* nagrodę specjalną na XVII Ogólnopolskim Konkursie Filmów Amatorskich w Nowej Hucie (23–26 października 1969). Na tym samym festiwalu swoje prace prezentowali również Ryszard Waśko i Ryszard Lenczewski[49]. Z kolei w 1973 roku do Szkoły został przyjęty Lechosław Czołnowski, uczestnik kilku akcji Warsztatu, a także Janusz Kołodrubiec i Janusz Szczerek, którzy pod koniec lat siedemdziesiątych utworzyli Zespół T, uważany za swoistą kontynuację Warsztatu[50].

Wymagania wobec kandydatów były wysokie. Oczekiwania studentów względem szkoły – jeszcze wyższe. Jak wynika ze wspomnień Józefa Robakowskiego, szybko spotkało ich rozczarowanie:

> Jesienią nie mieliśmy prawie żadnych zajęć. Pedagodzy albo nas unikali albo się przed nami ukrywali. Prowadzili wykłady jedynie Lewicki i Karabasz, reszta jakby wyparowała. Zorientowaliśmy się, że ktoś nas oszukuje. Zrobiliśmy wtedy pierwszą w Szkole rewolucję – zwołaliśmy sejm, na który zaprosiliśmy profesorów, pytając ich o to, czego zamierzają nas uczyć. Okazało się, że niewiele mają do powiedzenia. To był krytyczny moment. Szkołę jeszcze ciągnęły indywidualności. Kończyli studia Zanussi, Królikiewicz, Piwowski. Radzili sobie świetnie, bo tak jest zawsze z indywidualnościami. W metodach kształcenia zastaliśmy jednak jeden wielki chaos[51].

Podobnie pamięta ten okres Tomasz Zygadło (1947–2011), reżyser filmowy i telewizyjny, który w Szkole Filmowej studiował od 1969 roku:

> Przez trzy miesiące pętaliśmy się po Szkole zagubieni, pozbawieni opieki. Czułem się oszukany i miałem przeświadczenie, że tracę czas. Zaniepokojeni stanem rzeczy, zaczęliśmy wspólnie z kolegami buntować się, że nikt nas – studentów reżyserii – nie uczy robienia filmów[52].

Z kolei Ryszard Gajewski wspomina:

> Po zdanych egzaminach okazało się, że legendy o wielkich profesorach, którzy jednocześnie są wybitnymi czynnymi reżyserami zupełnie się nie potwierdzają. To była fikcja. Niczego sensownego nas nie uczono, dlatego że kadrę w znacznym stopniu stanowili ludzie, którzy byli u szczytu swoich twórczych możliwości przed wojną. Uczono nas

48 K. Krubski et al., op. cit., s. 196–197.

49 J. Peltz, op. cit.

50 Ł. Ronduda, *Sztuka polska lat 70.*, Warszawa: Centrum Sztuki Współczesnej Zamek Ujazdowski, 2009, s. 269–270.

51 K. Krubski et al., op. cit., s. 185.

52 Ibidem , s. 185.

> tego samego, czego wymagano wcześniej na tych strasznych egzaminach. Zaczęliśmy na przykład na pierwszym roku kurs z historii sztuki, którą już zdawaliśmy. Zamiast poszerzać wiedzę, słuchaliśmy jakichś podstawowych rzeczy. W małej ciemnej salce pokazywano nam jakieś wyblakłe slajdy. Wszyscy raczej spali. Podobnie było z zajęciami z materiałów światłoczułych. Uczono nas wielu zupełnie niepotrzebnych rzeczy, jakby spodziewano się po nas, że sami zaczniemy sobie wytwarzać taśmę filmową. To były zajęcia teoretyczne, pełne wzorów chemicznych, które nazywaliśmy wdzięcznie „trumienkami". Zdolni utalentowani ludzie nie byli w stanie zdać tego przedmiotu i odpadali po pierwszym roku. Niestety nie uczono nas robienia filmów[53].

Inną perspektywę do tych wspomnień wnosi Zbigniew Rybczyński:

> Uczelnia pozostawiała studentowi maksymalną swobodę. Chcesz się obijać, proszę bardzo, chcesz się uczyć – masz możliwości. Koledzy byli jednak w większości playboyami i niechętnie uczyli się techniki. Ja pracowałem z etiudy na etiudę, byłem pazerny na robienie filmów. Jako jedyny student miałem klucze do Szkoły. Nie wyjeżdżałem na wakacje – robiłem filmy[54].

Warsztatowcy zmienili atmosferę szkoły. Swoistym przyczółkiem ich działań był Zakład Fotografii, w którym pracowali starsi i mało aktywni członkowie grona pedagogicznego. Nowe, twórcze i odważne pomysły Warsztatowców nie natrafiały na silny opór. Feridun Erol, który ukończył wydział operatorski w 1965, a reżyserski w 1967 roku, wspominał:

> Niezauważenie nadciągał koniec naszej epoki. [...] Do szkoły przyszło teraz pokolenie Robakowskiego. Przynieśli ze sobą taśmy magnetofonowe, kolumny, elektronikę[55].

Z kolei Jacek Korcelli, który ukończył wydział operatorski w 1958 roku, przyznał, że grupa była zaczynem innego myślenia o kinie:

> Zespół prowadzony przez Robakowskiego nie zdominował wprawdzie Szkoły, ale stanowił zarodek twórczego niepokoju i punkt odniesienia[56].

Jak zauważa Maeve Connolly[57], wpływ grupy na model kształcenia w Szkole Filmowej nie został dotąd przebadany. To oznacza, że Szkoła nie wykorzystuje dorobku Warsztatu do kształtowania swoich studentów ani siebie jako instytucji. Doraźnie jednak, w trudnej dla Szkoły pierwszej połowie lat 70., Warsztat pełnił istotną rolę „enklawy wolności w miejscu, w którym brakowało powietrza"[58]. Sztywna struktura Szkoły nie ograniczyła działań grupy, lecz stała się dla nich pożywką. Strategia wykorzystywania nisz i luk w systemie po to, aby go zmieniać, stała się ważnym rysem tożsamości Warsztatu – podobnie jak wielu innych progresywnych grup artystycznych na świecie[59].

---

53 Wywiad z Ryszardem Gajewskim, styczeń 2016.

54 K. Krubski et al., op. cit., s. 206.

55 Ibidem, s. 177-178.

56 Ibidem, s. 227.

57 Zob. s. 299.

58 Ibidem, s. 226.

59 Na przykład amerykańskiej grupy Videofreex, zawiązanej na fali festiwalu w Woodstock. Jej członkowie zostali zaproszeni przez legendarnego producenta Dona Westa do realizacji pilotażowego odcinka programu *Subject to Change* w telewizji CBS. Materiał nie został wyemitowany, ale przy okazji współpracy z telewizją grupa weszła w posiadanie sprzętu telewizyjnego, który wykorzystywała później do własnych działań.

Łódź

Maszyny drżące
Syreny wyjące
I kominów tych tysiące
To jest nasze miasto Łódź

Hymn Warsztatu wg tradycyjnej piosenki robotniczej

Działalność Warsztatu Formy Filmowej często bywa określana mianem autorefleksyjnej „analizy nowych mediów". To stwierdzenie jest swego rodzaju kalką, dotykającą tylko powierzchni zjawiska i sugerujące pewne oderwanie grupy od rzeczywistości. Tymczasem Warsztatowcy byli szczególnie otwarci właśnie na codzienność. Przejawiało się to między innymi w ich częstych „interwencjach", które realizowali w przestrzeni publicznej. To właśnie miasto było sceną ich działań, a na wielu ich filmach i fotografiach zachowały się fragmenty miejskiego krajobrazu.

Do Łodzi przyciągnęła Warsztatowców oczywiście Szkoła Filmowa, ale miasto, samo w sobie, także stało się ważne dla ich twórczości. Ich celem nie było nigdy stworzenie własnej wyodrębnionej pracowni czy galerii. Nie mieli zamiaru ograniczać się i zamykać. Chcieli poznać i podbić przestrzeń miasta.

Co ważne, dla żadnego z nich Łódź nie była miastem rodzinnym. Od 1948 r. mieszkał w niej wraz z matką i młodszym bratem Józef Robakowski. Paweł Kwiek, Jacek Łomnicki i Kazimierz Bendkowski przyjechali z Warszawy, Józef Robakowski i Andrzej Różycki – ze studiów w Toruniu. Janusz Połom pochodzi z Olsztyna, Ryszard Waśko z Nysy, a Wojciech Bruszewski z Wrocławia. W Łodzi urodził się tylko Zbigniew Rybczyński, ale później przeprowadził się wraz z rodzicami do Warszawy. Warsztatowcy patrzyli więc na miasto w sposób pozbawiony sentymentu, nieprzefiltrowany przez wspomnienia z dzieciństwa. Zamiast tego obserwowali je z otwartością i odwagą, tak jak wcześniej kilku z nich przyglądało się Toruniowi, również tam poszukując „miejsc niczyich" – przestrzeni publicznej czy półpublicznej, którą można byłoby na pewien czas zaanektować. Dlatego też tak często przebywali ze sobą: nie mieli w Łodzi swoich rodzinnych domów, do których wracaliby po wykładach i ćwiczeniach. Spędzali razem czas także po zajęciach, co sprzyjało cementowaniu się wspólnoty. A jest przecież oczywiste, że łatwiej jest w grupie, niż pojedynczo anektować przestrzeń miasta w stylu *guerilla*. Taki twórczy „zabór" nastąpiłby prawdopodobnie w każdym innym mieście, w którym spotkaliby się Warsztatowcy. Ponieważ jednak spotkali się w Łodzi, przyjrzyjmy się więc temu, jakim była wówczas miejscem.

Wojna zniszczyła tkankę społeczną tego wielokulturowego, robotniczego miasta. Na skutek zagłady społeczności żydowskiej oraz emigracji i przesiedlenia Niemców, ludność powojennej Łodzi stała się homogeniczna, jednonarodowa i jednowyznaniowa. Ostała się jednak infrastruktura i architektura. Między innymi z tego powodu miasto pełniło po wojnie, przez okres około dwóch lat, rolę nieformalnego centrum administracji i stolicy polskiej kultury Polski[60]. To tu, a nie w Warszawie działało Ministerstwo Kultury. To tu otwarto tymczasowe redakcje wielu czasopism oraz sceny: Teatr Wojska Polskiego objął Leon Schiller, a Teatr Kameralny – Erwin Axer. W okre-

60 *Ilustrowana Encyklopedia Łodzi. Lata powojenne, czasy PRL*, red. A. Grzegorczyk, Łódź: Urząd Miasta Łodzi, 2010, s. 296, http://uml.lodz.pl/get.php?id=2947 [dostęp 27-12-2016].

ie 1948–1949 następowało wprawdzie stopniowe wycofywanie instytucji do Warszawy, ale wiele osób związanych ze sztuką i kulturą pozostało w Łodzi. Ważnym przykładem jest choćby profesor Bolesław Lewicki, który uczył Warsztatowców języka i semiotyki filmu.

Ten okres, zwany „łódzkim tranzytem", dał impuls rozwojowi miasta. Na mocy decyzji władz PRL Łódź miała stać się znaczącym ośrodkiem kultury i nauki, choć na polu oświaty do zrobienia było bardzo dużo, także na poziomie podstawowym (jeszcze w 1957 roku około 15 tysięcy mieszkańców poniżej 35 roku życia była analfabetami, a 35% populacji nie ukończyło szkoły podstawowej)[61]. Jeżeli chodzi o szkolnictwo wyższe, to najpierw utworzono dwie filie: Wyższej Szkoły Gospodarstwa Wiejskiego oraz Szkoły Głównej Handlowej. Następnie powstawały kolejne, samodzielne już ośrodki naukowe, między innymi Państwowa Wyższa Szkoła Pedagogiczna (włączona w 1956 roku do Uniwersytetu Łódzkiego). Jeżeli natomiast chodzi o szkoły artystyczne, to otwarto Państwową Wyższą Szkołę Sztuk Plastycznych, Państwową Wyższą Szkołę Teatralną i Państwową Wyższą Szkołę Muzyczną. Szkoła Filmowa została założona w 1948 roku. Dwa lata później otrzymała uprawnienia akademickie jako Wyższa Szkoła Filmowa, a od grudnia 1969 roku działa jako Państwowa Wyższa Szkoła Filmowa, Telewizyjna i Teatralna im. Leona Schillera.

Lata sześćdziesiąte to czas pewnej stagnacji w życiu kulturalnym miasta i ponownego, po odwilży 1956 roku, zaostrzania kursu partii komunistycznej. W 1968 roku spotkało się to, także w Łodzi, ze społecznym oporem. 11 marca łódzcy studenci na wieść o brutalnym rozpędzeniu protestów w Warszawie zorganizowali wiec, a następnie strajki okupacyjne. Wielu zostało w konsekwencji usuniętych z uczelni lub zawieszonych w prawach studenta. Podobnie postąpiono z rektorami Uniwersytetu Łódzkiego i Szkoły Filmowej. Czystkom, które objęły główne środowiska artystyczne i dziennikarskie, towarzyszyła nagonka antysemicka. Część kadry naukowej zmuszono do rezygnacji z zajmowanych stanowisk. Z Łodzi w wyniku prześladowań wyjechało zagranicę około tysiąca osób – przedstawicieli inteligencji i środowisk twórczych[62].

Dekada Gierka to okres pozornego otwierania się komunistycznej władzy na współpracę zagraniczną i potrzeby społeczeństwa, a także czas pozornego gospodarczego sukcesu. Realizowane na kredyt rozległe inwestycje znalazły swoje odbicie także w pejzażu Łodzi. Miasto nabrało bardziej wielkomiejskiego charakteru – starą zabudowę wyburzano, a pozyskane tereny przekazywano pod wielkomiejskie, wielorodzinne budynki. Wizytówką gierkowskiej „nowoczesności" miały być na przykład bloki Śródmiejskiej Dzielnicy Mieszkaniowej – budowle mające od 14 do 25 kondygnacji, zwieńczone charakterystycznymi „pudłami", w których mieściły się pracownie artystów[63] (w swoim mieszkaniu w jednym z takich bloków Józef Robakowski urządził w 1978 roku Galerię Wymiany). Poza tym w Łodzi wzniesiono nowoczesne obiekty handlowe, szpitale-pomniki, obiekty akademickie i zakłady przemysłowe, między innymi fabrykę dywanów Dywilan, z której Warsztatowcy pożyczali przemysłowe kamery wideo[64].

Rozrastające się miasto musiało robić pewne wrażenie na młodych ludziach (szczególnie tych, którzy przyjechali z prowincji), a z całą pewnością ich inspirowało. Warsztatowcy nie chcieli się koncentrować na autorefleksyjnych dywagacjach o medium filmowym. Chcieli widzieć, to co

61 Ibidem, s. 302.
62 Ibidem, s. 313.
63 Ibidem, s. 317.
64 Wywiad z Andrzejem Różyckim, lipiec 2014.

naprawdę było *widać.* Jeśli rzeczywistością i codziennością była Łódź, to należało wsłuchać się w rytm tego miasta, zobaczyć je, usłyszeć, wycisnąć z niego wszystko, co się da. Dlatego też szerokie miejskie pejzaże i zatłoczone ulice Łodzi tak często pojawiają się w filmach i fotografiach Warsztatu (szczególnie w pracach Ryszarda Waśko). Wiele z nich prezentuje obraz miasta odmienny od oficjalnego – na przykład w filmie *Obszar* Bendkowskiego widzimy zniszczone podwórka-studnie i zaniedbane kamienice, których mroczna atmosfera została podkreślona niepokojącym dźwiękiem. Łódź występuje też w filmach *Rynek* i *Idę* Robakowskiego, który jest zapisem wspinaczki na starą wieżę spadochronową, a także w instalacjach wideo Mikołajczyka oraz fotografiach Różyckiego i Bendkowskiego. W tym kontekście bardzo ciekawa jest praca *Transmisja telewizyjna*, w ramach której Warsztatowcy za pomocą transmisji wideo „wprowadzili" żywe miejskie obrazy do przestrzeni instytucji – Muzeum Sztuki. Warto przywołać też akcję *Permanentna wyprzedaż towarów wątpliwego pochodzenia*, zrealizowaną w przestrzeni miejskiej przez Robakowskiego i Antczaka.

Kolejnym miejskim tropem w dorobku Warsztatu są wpływy łódzkiego folkloru, którego najbardziej znanym przedstawicielem był Wacław Antczak, charyzmatyczny reprezentant nieprofesjonalnego świata sztuki i pełnoprawny uczestnik WFF. Józef Robakowski poznał go w stołówce Szkoły Filmowej, której „Pan Wacek" był stałym bywalcem. Szukał kontaktu i rozmowy z „ludźmi filmu", ale zwykle był przez nich ignorowany[65]. Antczak zafascynował Robakowskiego swoją osobowością oraz bezinteresowną, radykalną i zaangażowaną postawą. Ostatecznie dołączył do Warsztatu Formy Filmowej, towarzyszył w podróżach grupy, grał na skrzypcach i nawet uczył gry na tym instrumencie Pawła Kwieka, który pasjonował się muzyką od wczesnego dzieciństwa. Brał też czynny udział w interwencjach i działaniach artystycznych, między innymi w *Ósmym kinie*[66] czy *Permanentna wyprzedaż towarów wątpliwego pochodzenia* na Rynku Czerwonym – akcji Robakowskiego, w której odegrał główną rolę[67]. Realizował też swoje własne, autorskie performanse. Ponadto statystował w wielu filmach fabularnych, między innymi w *Rejsie* Marka Piwowskiego.

Swoistą kulminacją złożonych związków Warsztatu i Łodzi był festiwal *Konstrukcja w procesie*, zorganizowany w 1981 roku na niecały miesiąc przed wprowadzeniem stanu wojennego. Inicjatywa Ryszarda i Marii Waśko zaistniała przy uczestnictwie i wsparciu byłych już wówczas Warsztatowców, dla których był to moment definitywnego zakończenia działalności grupy. Wzięli w niej udział polscy i zagraniczni artyści, którzy przyjechali do Łodzi i już na miejscu tworzyli swoje prace. W objętej na co dzień cenzurą przestrzeni publicznej, a także na terenach fabrycznych i pofabrycznych, powstała największa w powojennej Polsce wystawa międzynarodowej sztuki współczesnej. Jej mottem była wypowiedź Mieczysława Szczuki – jednego ze współzałożycieli grupy Blok: „Sztuka nie może być pustym ornamentem społeczeństwa". Jak pisała Aleksandra Jach:

> Przywołano także grupę a.r., a przez to międzynarodową wspólnotę awangardową oraz kolekcję a.r. i jej wymiar edukacyjno-społeczny. W folderze towarzyszącym wystawie organizatorzy umieścili portrety Strzemińskiego i Kobro. Kontynuacja dziedzictwa awangardy

---

65 Wywiad z Józefem Robakowskim, lipiec 2014.

66 Wypowiedź Grzegorza Królikiewicza w filmie *Inne kino*, reż. Maria Waśko, 1999. Zob. *Żywa Galeria*, s. 39.

67 *Ósme kino,* druk ulotny, Łódź 1971, archiwum Galerii Wymiany, http://repozytorium.fundacjaarton.pl/index.php?action=view/object&objid=3162&colid=75&catid=18 [dostęp 28-12-2016].

została zawiązana przez postacie samych artystów, a nie tylko refleksję nad „konstrukcją". Podobnym gestem było także włączenie Henryka Stażewskiego – jednego z członków grupy a.r. – do komitetu honorowego[68].

W ten sposób łódzka tradycja, stanowiąca fundament tożsamości Warsztatu, znalazła swój wyraz w wydarzeniu wieńczącym działalność grupy.

Odzyskana tradycja

Tradycja leżała tu, właśnie w Łodzi. Pozostała tylko kwestia wejścia na właściwy trop.

Józef Robakowski w rozmowie z Tomaszem Samosionkiem

Studia z muzealnictwa i historii sztuki, które Andrzej Różycki i Józef Robakowski ukończyli w Toruniu jeszcze przed egzaminami do Szkoły Filmowej, zaowocowały ich zainteresowaniem dla dokonań przedwojennych konstruktywistów. Nie pozostało to bez wpływu na ich postawę artystyczną. Warsztatowcy nie tylko nawiązywali do dorobku awangardy, ale też konfrontowali się z nią – zadawali jej pytania o te same zagadnienia i problemy, które eksplorowali we własnej twórczości.

Zanim jednak mogli się z przeszłością skonfrontować – musieli ją poznać. Było to o tyle niełatwe, że obraz przedwojennej polskiej sztuki był na przełomie lat 60. i 70. niepełny. Jej dorobek został zniszczony najpierw przez wojnę, a następnie przez władze komunistyczne[69]. Chociaż ciągłość wydawała się zerwana, studenci Szkoły Filmowej odkryli, że nie muszą szukać daleko, aby ją przywrócić. W końcu to właśnie Łódź stała się pod koniec lat 20. jednym z najważniejszych punktów na mapie nie tylko polskiej, ale także europejskiej awangardy. To tu w 1929 roku Katarzyna Kobro, Julian Przyboś, Władysław Strzemiński i Henryk Stażewski (nieco później dołączył do nich jeszcze Jan Brzękowski) powołali grupę a.r. i założyli Międzynarodową Kolekcję Sztuki Nowoczesnej. Pomysł stworzenia kolekcji miał swoją genezę w obserwacjach Strzemińskiego z okresu pobytu w Rosji, gdzie duże zainteresowanie wzbudziły udostępnione publicznie zbiory kolekcjonera sztuki nowoczesnej Szczukina[70]. Próby stworzenia podobnej kolekcji w Polsce przez długi czas nie przynosiły rezultatu. Dopiero 15 lutego 1931 roku – w efekcie rozmów z Radą Miejską Łodzi – udostępniono widzom kolekcję, nad której uzupełnianiem do 1938 roku pracowali Strzemiński i Kobro[71]. Łódzkiego *genius loci* nie należy mitologizować, ale to właśnie w tym mieście powstał unikalny zbiór dzieł sztuki stanowiący przegląd awangardowych nurtów i tendencji końca lat 20.[72]

---

68 A. Jach, *Konstrukcja w procesie. Wspólnota, która nadeszła?*, w: *Odrzucone dziedzictwo. O sztuce polskiej lat 80.*, Warszawa: Muzeum Sztuki Nowoczesnej w Warszawie, 2014, s. 136–147.

69 Zob. A. Rottenberg, *Sztuka w Polsce 1945–2005,* Warszawa: STENTOR, 2005, s. 17–20.

70 A. Turowski, *W kręgu Strzemińskiego. Blok–Praesens–a.r.,* Warszawa: Centralne Biuro Wystaw Artystycznych, 1973, s. 23–24.

71 Ibidem.

72 Do 1939 roku kolekcja liczyła co najmniej 112 dzieł, wśród których przeważały obrazy, ale nie zabrakło też rzeźb (Alexandra Caldera i Katarzyny Kobro) czy fotomontaży (Mieczysława Szczuki). Zawierała znakomitą, jak na owe czasy, prezentację prac abstrakcjonistów (Hansa Arpa i Sophie Taeuber-Arp, Theo van Doesburga, Jeana Gorina, Jeana Heliona, Vilmosa Huszára, Henryka Stażewskiego i Georges'a Vantongerloo), kubistów (Fernanda Légera i Louisa Marcoussisa), futurystów (Enrico Prampoliniego), dadaistów (Kurta Schwittersa), surrealistów (Maxa Ernsta, Kurta Seligmanna), formistów (Leona Chwistka, Tytusa Czyżewskiego), konstruktywistów (Aleksandra Rafałowskiego, Andrzeja Pronaszki), unistów (Władysława Strzemińskiego) czy przedstawicieli „czystej formy" (Stanisława Ignacego Witkiewicza). Zob. *Kolekcja sztuki XX w. w Muzeum Sztuki w Łodzi*, red. U. Czartoryska, kat. wyst., Warszawa: Galeria Zachęta, 1991.

Kolekcja stała się trzonem zbiorów łódzkiego Muzeum Sztuki, które odegrało ważną rolę w historii Warsztatu Formy Filmowej. Zwłaszcza w pierwszej połowie lat 70. instytucja ta pełniła – za sprawą ówczesnego dyrektora Ryszarda Stanisławskiego – rolę swoistego łącznika między pierwszą i drugą awangardą. Przede wszystkim dawała dostęp do przedwojennych zbiorów. Wiele prac uległo zniszczeniu w czasie wojny[73], ale część przetrwała okupację – „jedynie dzięki temu, że niemieckie kierownictwo muzeum powzięło projekt urządzenia wystawy „sztuki zdegenerowanej"[74].

Marian Minich, który od 1935 roku sprawował funkcję dyrektora Muzeum, zaraz po wojnie podjął się jego reaktywacji. Udało mu się to między innymi dzięki donacjom, które w 1945 roku poczynili zarówno Strzemiński, jak i Kobro. Jej nieliczne zachowane kompozycje przestrzenne poddano – pod kierunkiem samej artystki – gruntownej konserwacji. Nową siedzibą Muzeum stał się w 1948 roku dawny pałac Poznańskiego przy ul. Więckowskiego. To w nim w 1948 roku zrealizowano projekt Sali Neoplastycznej Strzemińskiego, którą zniszczono w 1950 i zrekonstruowano w 1960 roku. Z kolei w styczniu i lutym 1973 roku w tym samym budynku odbyła się Akcja Warsztatu, stanowiąca punkt kulminacyjny w historii Warsztatu.

Szczęśliwie dla Warsztatowców początek lat 70. był czasem odzyskiwania i przypominania tradycji awangardy, w czym wielki udział miał Ryszard Stanisławski[75]. Swoje badania – poświęcone Katarzynie Kobro, która w latach 50. została niemal całkowicie wyparta ze zbiorowej świadomości – kontynuował również związany z Warsztatem Janusz Zagrodzki. W 1973 roku został on zaproszony przez Jerzego Kotowskiego do poprowadzenia wykładów z historii sztuki w Szkole Filmowej. Józef Robakowski wspomina:

> Okazało się, że tradycja analitycznego myślenia o sztuce miała miejsce w pracy Władysława Strzemińskiego i Katarzyny Kobro. Stąd pojawił się kult dla grupy a.r.[76]

Czasy były więc sprzyjające. W 1973 roku Muzeum Sztuki w Łodzi przygotowało dla Muzeum Folkwang w Essen i Muzeum Kröller-Müller w Otterlo pierwszą zagraniczną zbiorową ekspozycję konstruktywizmu (Berlewi, Hiller, Kobro, Stażewski, Strzemiński), a polska awangarda rozpoczęła „triumfalny pochód po najwybitniejszych muzeach świata"[77].

Analogie założeń a.r. i Warsztatu są – mimo pewnych różnic poglądów – czytelne, zarówno jeśli chodzi o myślenie o dziele sztuki, jak i artystyczną postawę. Można je odnaleźć analizując na przykład tekst *B-2* Strzemińskiego, w którym nakreślał zasady „nowej sztuki". Strzemiński kładł w nim nacisk na rolę twórczej kreacji, przeciwstawiając ją zabiegom odtwórczym, mimetycznym. Twierdził, że punktem wyjścia dla dzieła sztuki powinno być rozpoznanie „warunków jego istnienia – wskazanie elementów jego konstrukcji. Granicami dzieła artystycznego są jego granice formalne"[78].

Te postulaty, przede wszystkim w odniesieniu do medium filmowego, powtórzyli uczestnicy Warsztatu:

---

73 „Zniknęły prace Picassa, Legera, Gleizesa, Marcoussisa, Ozenfata, Prampoliniego, Torres-Garcii, Herbina, Seuphora, Gorina, [...] rzeźby Pronaszki z jego okresu ekspresjonistycznego, a wreszcie *Mobile* Amerykanina Cadlera". M. Minich, *Szalona galeria,* w: *Marian Minich – pod wiatr,* red. A. Minich-Scholz, Warszawa: Instytut Wydawniczy Książka i Prasa, 2015, s. 287.

74 Ibidem.

75 A. Turowski, *W kręgu Strzemińskiego...*, s. 121.

76 T. Samosionek, op. cit.

77 A. Turowski, *W kręgu Strzemińskiego...*, s. 121.

78 Władysław Strzemiński, *B-2*, „Blok", 8–9, 1924, cyt. za A. Turowski, *Konstruktywizm polski. Próba rekonstrukcji nurtu (1921–1934),* Wrocław: Zakład Narodowy im. Ossolińskich, 1981, s. 64–65.

> Usiłuje się tu [w WFF – M.K.] stworzyć narzędzie opisu [filmu – M.K.] leżące poza literaturoznawstwem, stąd ponowne zainteresowanie się tzw. czystym kinem, chęć stworzenia filmu oczyszczonego z wszelkich możliwości struktur narracyjnych oraz metodologii poetyki literackiej. Zaczęto na nowo rozpatrywać tzw. istotę struktury filmowej w oparciu o własności przekazu fonofotograficznego. Porzucono wszelakie interpretacje o charakterze komparatystycznym, czyli zestawianie filmu z malarstwem, muzyką, teatrem, poezją, narracją literacką... Szczególnie istotny jest fakt podważenia związków filmu z literaturą, czyli przeciwstawienie się dość obiegowemu poglądowi o przyliterackiej naturze zjawiska filmowego, koncepcji logicznie umotywowanej przez wielu powszechnie uznanych teoretyków sztuki filmowej[79].

Istotne dla Warsztatu i a.r. było poznanie granic formalnych medium i jego zasad konstrukcyjnych, a także przełamanie podziału na formę i treść. Ten ostatni element wybrzmiewa mocno zarówno w działaniach i tekstach Kobro i Strzemińskiego[80], jak i w twórczości Warsztatowców – najpełniej w ich radykalnych filmach z obszaru kina strukturalnego[81]. Obie grupy łączyła także krytyka działań o – jak pisał Strzemiński – „charakterze doraźno-agitacyjnym"[82]. Echem tej postawy był opór Warsztatu przed udziałem w oficjalnym obiegu kinematograficznym, który nieuchronnie prowadziłby do uwikłania go w machinę propagandy i cenzury.

Te przykłady, jak pisał Ryszard W. Kluszczyński, obrazują unifikację dwóch dyskursów – artystycznego i pozaartystycznego – których współistnienie charakteryzowało sztukę awangardową dwudziestolecia międzywojennego. W filmie strukturalnym dyskurs artystyczny ulega minimalizacji. Jego forma staje się pretekstem do rozważań pozaartystycznych i nie skupia uwagi widzów w większym stopniu niż treść. Nie dzieje się też odwrotnie, ponieważ jedno wynika z drugiego, a wręcz – jest z nim tożsame. W ujęciu Kluszczyńskiego ta właśnie strategia Warsztatu miała skłaniać odbiorcę do refleksji nad naturą kina jako medium[83]. Z naszego punktu widzenia stanowi ona dodatkowo interesujący przykład rozwinięcia strategii konstruktywistów, polemizujących z treściowo-formalnym dualizmem dzieła.

Warto zauważyć, że fascynacja WFF konstruktywistami przejawiała się także w filmach dokumentalnych. Warsztatowcy we współpracy z Januszem Zagrodzkim stworzyli w Studiu Małych Form Filmowych Se-ma-for krótkometrażowy dokument *Kompozycje przestrzenne Katarzyny Kobro* (35 mm, 1971), w którym czytany z offu przez Tadeusz Junaka fragment książki Kobro i Strzemińskiego *Kompozycja przestrzeni. Obliczenia rytmu czasoprzestrzennego* został zestawiony z jej rzeźbami z kolekcji Muzeum Sztuki. Autorem warstwy dźwiękowej filmu jest Eugeniusz Rudnik, a w rolę konsultanta wcielił się Bolesław Utkin, student Strzemińskiego i autor rekonstrukcji Sali Neoplastycznej. Zamysł Robakowskiego odnośnie tej produkcji był klarowny: jak najszersza i jak najbardziej czytelna dla odbiorcy prezentacja prac Katarzyny Kobro, a także esencjonalne przybliżenie istoty jej

79 J. Robakowski, *Bezjęzykowa koncepcja semiologiczna filmu*, „Zeszyt Warsztatu Formy Filmowej, 7", 1975. http://robakowski.eu/tx2.html [dostęp 29-12-2016].

80 K. Kobro, W. Strzemiński, *Kompozycja przestrzeni. Obliczenia rytmu czasoprzestrzennego*, Łódź: Muzeum Sztuki w Łodzi, 2010.

81 Na przykład *Tekst–drzwi* Bruszewskiego (35 mm, 1973), *Test II* Robakowskiego (35 mm, 1971), a przede wszystkim *Układ I–IV* Waśki (35 mm, 1973) i *A-B-C-D-E-F – 1-36* Waśki (35 mm, 1974).

82 A. Turowski, *W kręgu Strzemińskiego...*, s. 22.

83 R. W. Kluszczyński, op. cit., s. 32.

teorii. Pod koniec filmu przytoczono syntetycznie biogram artystki. Pierwsza monografia Kobro ukazała się dopiero ponad dekadę później, więc film przez długi czas pełnił rolę swoistego kompendium wiedzy na jej temat[84]. Wiele o recepcji działalności Kobro w latach 70. mówią wspomnienia Robakowskiego z kolaudacji filmu:

> Jeden z jej uczestników powiedział mi: „Panie Józefie, ale pan jakąś mistyfikację stworzył że ta Kobro to jakaś wybitna artystka, przecież to normalna żona Strzemińskiego. Musimy panu tu zmienić w komentarzu, bo nie wolno tak rzucać słów na wiatr"[85].

Jeżeli chodzi o punkty odniesienia w historii filmu awangardowego, to ponownie okazało się, że Warsztatowcy nie muszą szukać daleko – w szkolnym archiwum w Łodzi znaleźli film Franciszki (1907–1988) i Stefana (1910–1988) Themersonów *Przygoda człowieka poczciwego* (1937), który stał się dla nich punktem wyjścia do poznania dorobku tych i innych twórców polskiej przedwojennej awangardy filmowej[86].

Film budził od około 1930 roku spore zainteresowanie w kręgu konstruktywizmu, szczególnie w środowisku Praesensu (głównie za sprawą Themersonów oraz krytyka Zygmunta Toneckiego). Realizacji nie powstało jednak zbyt wiele. W związku z wysokimi cenami materiałów, film był często zastępowany przez fotomontaż (przy całej świadomości środków wyrazu tego medium)[87]. Themersonowie zrealizowali przed wojną pięć filmów: *Aptekę* (35 mm, 1930), *Europę* (35 mm, 1931/32) – na podstawie poematu Anatola Sterna pod tym samym tytułem, *Drobiazg melodyjny* (35 mm, 1933) – zrealizowany na zamówienie firmy galanteryjnej Wandy Golińskiej, *Zwarcie* (35 mm, 1935) – zamówiony przez Instytut Spraw Społecznych w Warszawie i *Przygodę człowieka poczciwego* (35 mm, 1937).

Ten ostatni film, odnaleziony w archiwum Szkoły Filmowej, wzbudził wśród uczestników Warsztatu fascynację Themersonami. *Przygodę* odtwarzali tak często, jak tylko było to możliwe. Robakowski prosił też przebywającego od 1942 roku w Londynie Franciszka o przesłanie listy montażowej filmu *Europa*[88]. Jak wspomina Robakowski:

> Lansowaliśmy Stefana Themersona podczas Kino Laboratorium, a w Szkole Filmowej przy każdej okazji pokazywaliśmy *Przygodę człowieka poczciwego*, podobnie jak filmy Richtera, które odnajdowaliśmy w archiwum i które okazywały się kapitalnymi przykładami przedwojennych awangardowych tradycji w filmie[89].

Tym, co połączyło dwa pokolenia filmowych awangardzistów, nie były jednak konkretne realizacje, lecz postawa twórcza – nastawiona na eksperyment w wielu różnych dziedzinach i wymiarach sztuki. Jak wspomina Paweł Kwiek:

---

84 J. Zagrodzki, *Katarzyna Kobro...*

85 J. Robakowski, *Kino rozszerzone i kino materiałowe,* rozmowę przeprowadził G. Borkowski, „Tranzystor–CSWZU", 4, 2012, s. 7–8, http://csw.art.pl/upload/file/1207tranzystor_cswzu_4.pdf [dostęp 30-12-2016].

86 Warsztatowcy nawiązali kontakt korespondencyjny z Themersonami. Na zaproszenie Themersona Bruszewski, Robakowski i Waśko wzięli w 1979 roku udział w wystawie *Film as Film. Formal Experimental film 1910–1975* w Hayward Gallery w Londynie, gdzie doszło do bezpośredniego spotkania. Zob. I. Schwarz, *Archive für Künstlerpublikationen der 1960er bis 1980er Jahre*, Kolonia: Salon Verlag 2008. Fragment w tłum. A. Szymanowskiej http://robakowski.eu/tx46.html [dostęp 30-12-2016].

87 A. Turowski, *Konstruktywizm polski...*, s. 105.

88 B. Cook, Ł. Ronduda, *Filmy Franciszki i Stefana Themersonów*, Warszawa – Londyn: Centrum Sztuki Współczesnej Zamek Ujazdowski – LUX, 2007, s. 67.

89 T. Samosionek, op. cit.

Bardzo wcześnie zrozumiałem, że chcę pracować w polu sztuki, a nie filmu. Chciałem co prawda wypowiadać się poprzez to medium, ale tworzenie „klasycznych" fabuł czy dokumentów nigdy nie było moim celem. Myślałem wówczas, że może po skończeniu szkoły będę operatorem, ale przede wszystkim bardzo zależało mi na poznawaniu filmu, jego możliwości, od strony technicznej. Chciałem zrozumieć to medium. Kiedy w 1970 roku dostałem się do Szkoły Filmowej w Łodzi, przekonałem się, że – dzięki pewnej grupie osób – jest to miejsce, które sprzyja tworzeniu sztuki. W szkole panował wówczas nieformalny system mistrz-uczeń. O ile było to możliwe, studenci wybierali osoby, które ich kształtowały. Ja znalazłem się właśnie pod wpływem Robakowskiego, a pierwszym moim świadomym wyborem artystycznym było przystąpienie do grupy Warsztat Formy Filmowej. Od tego momentu zacząłem opozycyjnie odnosić się do historii kina, do oficjalnego, komercyjnego myślenia o filmie[90].

Tym, co wyróżniało Warsztatowców od większości pozostałych studentów Szkoły Filmowej, był nie tylko stosunek do przeszłości filmowej awangardy, ale także do teorii i historii filmu. Odczuwali potrzebę sięgania po teksty teoretyczne, a jedną z najważniejszych dla nich lektur była *Dziesiąta muza* Karola Irzykowskiego (1873–1944) z 1924 roku[91]. Autor, posługując się tak istotnym dla Warsztatowców terminem „czyste kino", analizował kompetencje medium filmowego i potencjalną złożoność relacji obrazu filmowego z muzyką i słowem. Wychodził z założenia, że każda dziedzina sztuki ma swoje granice i możliwości. Pisał: „Wszystkie sztuki mają swoje odrębne właściwości, które psują estetykom próby ujęcia ich w jednolity system"[92]. Relacja z muzyką i słowem nie stanowiła jego zdaniem „zagrożenia" dla autonomii filmu. Przywołując historię refleksji o granicach między malarstwem, poezją i muzyką, Irzykowski stwierdzał, że idea oparcia kina na jego „własnych" walorach jest cenna, ale „przesadny pociąg do puryfikacji", rozumiany jako chęć oczyszczenia filmu z „obcych elementów", prowadzić może do wyjałowienia:

> Wyemancypować kino od teatru, malarstwa, literatury, osiągnąć „czyste kino"! Dobrze, i ja tego pragnę, i o tym wciąż także mówię. Lecz to nie znaczy, żeby kino wypruć z pełni życia i wyjałowić. Teoretyk może w swym laboratorium rozpatrywać kino izolowane, artysta plastyk nie może się zrzec kształtowania żywej plątaniny zjawisk, należących – formalnie – niby do różnych sztuk. Na tym polega trudność: schwytać płomień. Kino może więc – jak się już rzekło – posługiwać się materiałem innych sztuk, nie zatracając się[93].

To była droga, którą kilka dekad później wybrał Warsztat, z jednej strony – próbując oczyścić kino z narratywności i anegdotyczności, a z drugiej – poszerzając obszar swoich inspiracji. Świadczy o tym fakt, że na różnych etapach działalności do grupy należeli nie tylko studenci Szkoły Filmowej, ale także – na przykład – poeci, tacy jak Kader Lagtaa[94] czy Wacław Antczak.

90 Wywiad z Pawłem Kwiekiem, lipiec 2015.

91 Wywiad z Józefem Robakowskim, lipiec 2014.

92 K. Irzykowski, *Dziesiąta muza. Zagadnienia estetyczne kina,* Warszawa: Wydawnictwa Artystyczne i Filmowe, 1960, s. 70.

93 Ibidem, s. 100.

94 Zob. R. Waśko, op. cit., s. 9. Lagtaa publikował swoje wiersze w zeszycie Warsztatu Formy Filmowej w 1974 roku, współpracował z Biurem Poezji Andrzeja Partuma i Ewą Partum, był też autorem scenariusza filmu *Collage*, opartego na poemacie André Bretona.

Dla Warsztatowców bardzo istotna była także kwestia uwikłania filmu w szeroko rozumianą komercję. Irzykowski komentował ją następująco:

> Rozwój sztuki kinowej da się porównać z rozwojem rośliny, przygniecionej kamieniami. Tymi kamieniami są przemysł i handel, której jej narzucają swoje warunki. Kino, aby się odrodzić, musi [...] na chwilę odetchnąć bezinteresownością[95].

Lektura *Dziesiątej muzy* musiała więc silnie rezonować z przekonaniami Warsztatowców, którzy już w pierwszym swoim manifeście – jakby odpowiadając Irzykowskiemu – wyraźnie postawili ten problem:

> WARSZTAT nie uprawia żadnej działalności komercyjnej, a jego realizatorzy pracują całkowicie bezinteresownie[96].

Istotą rozważań zawartych w *Dziesiątej muzie* jest konieczność szukania dla filmu rozwiązań alternatywnych zarówno wobec kinematografii schlebiającej gustom szerokiej publiczności, jak i dla awangardy okresu międzywojennego, której przedstawiciele utożsamiali kino z ruchem. Prowadziło to, zdaniem Irzykowskiego, do wspomnianego „izolowania kina" i jego „wyjaławiania". Oprócz ruchu wskazywał także na konstytutywną dla kina rolę światła – ten pogląd, podobnie jak jego postulat wykorzystywania w filmie różnorodnych środków wyrazu, okazał się inspirujący dla uczestników WFF. Bardzo interesujący pod tym względem jest rozdział *Dziesiątej muzy*, w którym Irzykowski stawia znak równości między filmem opartym na „fotograficznej reprodukcji rzeczywistości", a filmem animowanym. To także znajdzie swoje odbicie w działaniach Warsztatu, w szczególności w filmach Zbigniewa Rybczyńskiego.

Kolejnym bezpośrednim „łącznikiem" z tradycją przedwojennej filmowej awangardy był dla Warsztatowców profesor Bolesław Lewicki (1908–1981), który od 1968 roku pełnił funkcję rektora PWSFTiTv. Lewicki, przedwojenny absolwent Uniwersytetu Jana Kazimierza we Lwowie, był uczniem między innymi Juliusza Kleinera, autora słynnego szkicu *U wrót nowej estetyki*[97], w którym zjawisko filmu zostało – prawdopodobnie po raz pierwszy w Polsce – dostrzeżone jako obiekt refleksji badawczej. Sam Lewicki pisał o filmie już w latach 30., czyli w tym samym czasie, gdy uczył się o materiałach światłoczułych na seminarium profesora Witolda Romera na Politechnice Lwowskiej. W 1932 roku był inicjatorem (a potem sekretarzem i prezesem) opartego na francuskich wzorach klubu filmowego Awangarda, który działał na rzecz promocji „kina artystycznego" i integracji kręgów intelektualnych. Lewicki uczęszczał ponadto na seminarium Romana Ingardena, na którym kino było przedmiotem naukowej refleksji[98]. Lewicki znalazł się w Łodzi w 1947 roku, czyli w okresie powojennego ożywienia miasta. Podjął pracę nie tylko w Szkole Filmowej, ale także na Uniwersytecie Łódzkim, gdzie w ramach Katedry Teorii Literatury powołał bardzo popularne studia z filmoznawstwa. Z kolei w PWSFTiTv Lewicki kierował Katedrą Teorii i Historii Filmu, w ramach której prowadził zajęcia z języka i semiotyki filmu. Warsztatowcy chętnie na nie uczęszczali. Józef Robakowski wspomina:

> Na jego ekscentrycznych, żywych zajęciach, jeszcze w latach sześćdziesiątych, analizowaliśmy w Szkole Filmowej różne struktury montażowe, sporządzając wizualne partytury na

95 K. Irzykowski, op. cit., s. 116.

96 *I Manifest*, Łódź 1970, cyt. za R. W. Kluszczyński, op. cit., s. 60.

97 J. Kleiner, *U wrót nowej estetyki*, „Tygodnik Ilustrowany", 4, 1929, s. 62.

98 J. Rek, *Profesor Bolesław W. Lewicki – między filmem i literaturą*, „Acta Universitatis Lodziensis. Folia Litteraria Polonica", 9, 2007, s. 334.

> papierze. To on od 1966 roku podrzucał nam historyczne i aktualne lektury, uwzględniając w szerokim pojęciu rozwój myśli filmowej i fotograficznej. Dzięki niemu poznaliśmy pisma m. in. Irzykowskiego, Arnheima, Van Lira, Epsteina, Helman, Jackiewicza, Maya, Lévi-Straussa, Jacobsona, Ingardena, Morina, Schaffa, McLuhana, Barthesa, Metza... Wydana w Polsce (1963 rok) książka *Film i rzeczywistość* Bazina, była naszą obowiązkową lekturą[99].

Z kolei Ryszard Gajewski tak wspomina Lewickiego:

> Od niego dowiedzieliśmy się o Umberto Eco i jego *Dziele otwartym*. W Szkole zagościła semantyka i semiotyka budząc postrach wśród studentów. Pamiętam jego wykład, na którym efektownie bazgrząc kredą na tablicy, pokazywał, że film można przedstawić za pomocą wzorów. Oczywiście pierwsze filmy Warsztatu nie powstały na podstawie wzorów[100].

Streszczając poglądy Lewickiego, trzeba zaznaczyć, że uważał on film za „drugą gałąź literatury", czego najlepszym przykładem czy wręcz uosobieniem jest adaptacja. Identyfikacja Warsztatowców z poglądami Lewickiego może więc zastanawiać, jeśli weźmiemy pod uwagę choćby taką deklarację Robakowskiego:

> Pracując obecnie w Warsztacie Formy Filmowej [...] mam możliwość przeprowadzania praktycznie nieograniczonych prób i doświadczeń polegających na badaniu granic percepcji moich filmów przez innych ludzi [...] Próby o charakterze teoretycznym i praktycznym podejmuję w celu znalezienia i poznania pewnych specyficznych cech filmu, uważam bowiem, że [...] musi dojść do „oczyszczenia" tej dyscypliny ze zbędnego balastu literatury[101].

Warto jednak pamiętać, że postulowane przez WFF „oczyszczanie" filmu nie miało być celem samym w sobie. Miało służyć badaniu rzeczywistości w całej jej złożoności, z uwzględnieniem relacji percypującego i percypowanego. Jednym z ważniejszych filmów realizujących te założenia była etiuda studencka Pawła Kwieka pod tytułem *1, 2, 3... ćwiczenia operatorskie* (35 mm, 1972). Autor manipulował w niej różnorodnymi stylistycznie fragmentami filmów i animacji. Robił to w tak swobodny sposób, że odczytanie jego intencji czy też jednoznacznej wymowy filmu stawało się niemożliwe. „Oczyszczanie" wiązało się zatem z uwolnieniem filmu z obowiązku opowiadania historii, co nie oznacza jednak, że zamykało drogę do badania jego relacji z literaturą. W takim ujęciu twórczość Warsztatowców istotnie wydaje się bliska poglądom teoretyków, na których się powoływali. Nie zagrażał im raczej nadmiar „laboratoryjności", przed którą tak przestrzegał Irzykowski. Kino interesowało ich bowiem na wielu poziomach, także na poziomie jego społecznego oddziaływania i funkcjonowania. Rezygnowali z tradycyjnych filmowych środków wyrazu po to, by konfrontować się z oczekiwaniami odbiorców i poszukiwać interakcji z nimi. Często, nawet w gronie osób bliskich ideowo Warsztatowi, kończyło się to ostrymi dyskusjami[102].

Warsztatowcy swobodnie poruszali się na przecięciu różnych mediów, w związku z tym często świadomie rezygnowali z przywilejów, które mieli zapewnione jako studenci Szkoły Filmowej

---

99 J. Robakowski, *Podrzuceni mistrzowie*, b.d., http://robakowski.eu/tx19.html [dostęp 30-12-2016].

100 Wywiad z Ryszardem Gajewskim, styczeń 2016.

101 J. Robakowski, *Jeszcze na koniec o „czysty film"*, „Polska", 10, 1971, http://robakowski.eu/teksty.html [dostęp 30-12-2016].

102 Na przykład podczas V Biennale Form Przestrzennych w Elblągu w 1973 roku. Zob. rozdział *Elbląg. Kino w służbie rebelii*.

(takich jak możliwość użycia taśmy filmowej 35 mm lub wypożyczenia wozu transmisyjnego). W rezultacie powstawały realizacje bezkamerowe i beztaśmowe czy też przybierające formy obiektów[103]. Takie „miękkie" użycie mediów, szukanie przestrzeni intermedialnych i kreowanie eksperymentalnych nisz zbliżało Warsztat do teorii Irzykowskiego, a przede wszystkim do praktyki Themersonów i takich ich realizacji jak *Europa*, do której punktem wyjścia był poemat Anatola Sterna, czy też *Apteka* – film stworzony w autentycznie domowych warunkach przy zastosowaniu fotografii[104].

Robakowski, podsumowując związki Warsztatu z przedwojenną awangardą, powiedział:

> To była nasza dobra tradycja. Ona była potrzebna, dodawała nam otuchy i powodowała następne możliwości udziału w imprezach filmowych takich jak np. Documenta w Kassel w Kolonii, w Londynie. Bardzo ważną rzeczą było to, że ta tradycja była tuż pod nosem bez tej tradycji to wszystko na pewno nie miałoby takiego znaczenia. W dyskusjach zagranicznych zawsze mogliśmy powiedzieć: „Ale chwileczkę! Wy tak, ale my tu jeszcze mamy Szpakowskiego, Hillera, Szczukę, Podsadeckiego itd. itd."[105]

Poza formą filmową. Wideo i telewizja

Dorobek Warsztatu omawiam szczegółowo w ostatniej części niniejszej książki – tu natomiast chciałabym wyodrębnić trzy mniej rozpoznane aspekty działań grupy: efemeryczne instalacje wideo, sztukę ciała oraz akcje performatywne.

Przede wszystkim warto podkreślić, że Warsztatowcy byli pierwszymi artystami w Polsce, którzy pracowali z wideo, a także autorami zdecydowanej większości polskich prac zrealizowanych w tym medium w latach 70. Mimo to ten aspekt twórczości grupy nie doczekał się dotąd monograficznego opracowania. Został też częściowo wyparty z obszaru badań dotyczących europejskiej i światowej historii wideo[106]. Można to częściowo wytłumaczyć efemerycznym charakterem tych prac – znamy je w większości jedynie z dokumentacji fotograficznej lub z opisów. Jest to jedna z przyczyn tego, że wczesne polskie prace wideo rzadko włączane są do muzealnych kolekcji i tylko nieliczne z nich funkcjonują w obiegu sztuki. Tymczasem dla części uczestników Warsztatu wideo było medium szczególnie istotnym – na przykład Wojciech Bruszewski w nim właśnie zrealizował swoje najważniejsze prace.

Wideo pojawiło się w kręgu Warsztatu „naturalnie"[107], jak to określił Ryszard W. Kluszczyński. Właściwości i specyfika tego medium idealnie wpisywały się w obszar zainteresowań grupy, więc jedynie ograniczenia techniczne opóźniały jego wykorzystanie. Wideo istotnie poszerzyło możliwości przekazu i komunikacji – dwóch obszarów kluczowych dla twórców z kręgu WFF. Pozwalało na jednoczesne rejestrowanie i transmitowanie dźwięku i obrazu, co dawało doskonałą sposobność do badania zależności między rzeczywistością i jej odwzorowaniem. Dlatego też liczne instalacje wideo Warsztatu (powstałe przede wszystkim w okresie 1975–1977), podejmowały kwestę

103 Na przykład *Świetlny box* (1971) Robakowskiego, a także *Filmowa kiełbasa* (1973) i *Grzebień* (1973) Gajewskiego.

104 B. Cook, Ł. Ronduda, op. cit., s. 44–45.

105 Ibidem.

106 Spośród zagranicznych badaczy pisał o nich wyłącznie Chris Meigh-Andrews, który przedstawił jednak tylko część realizacji Warsztatu – głównie prace Bruszewskiego i Kwieka. Zob. C. Meigh-Andrews, *A History of Video Art. The Development of Form and Function,* Oksford: Berg Publishers, 2006 oraz *Analogue. Pioneering Video from the UK, Canada and Poland (1968–88)*, red. C. Meigh Andrews, C. Elwes, Preston: EDAU, University of Lancashire, 2006.

107 R. W. Kluszczyński, op. cit., s. 51–55.

iluzoryczności obrazu i, podobnie jak w przypadku filmów i fotografii, analizowały skłonność percepcji do ulegania tej iluzji. Pozornie autorefleksyjny charakter tych prac był dla Warsztatowców tylko punktem wyjścia dla dociekań wybiegających w wielu innych kierunkach. Służyła – głównie Kwiekowi i Robakowskiemu – do badania mechanizmów manipulowania widzem w środkach masowego przekazu, a także do obserwowania uniwersalnych praw fizyki, generowania na tej podstawie różnego rodzaju paradoksów (Bruszewski i Waśko), a także do eksplorowania ludzkiej fizyczności i podmiotowości (Bendkowski i Robakowski).

Prace wideo z kręgu Warsztatu należy analizować w szerszym międzynarodowym kontekście – szczególnie, że w 1975 roku kontekst polski praktycznie nie istniał. Początek sztuki wideo na świecie wiąże się ze wzrostem znaczenia i upowszechnieniem telewizji w połowie XX wieku. Ze względu na swoją fundamentalną rolę w tworzeniu kultury masowej, stała się ona obiektem zainteresowania artystów oraz polem prowadzonych przez nich eksperymentów. Stała się dla nich tym, czym dla włoskich futurystów było radio – narzędziem przekraczania geograficznego i kulturowego dystansu oraz docierania do bardzo szerokiej grupy odbiorców[108]. Jednocześnie jednak telewizja po obydwu stronach Żelaznej Kurtyny postrzegana było jak twór homogeniczny, sterowany odgórnie i szerzący konsumpcjonizm (Europa Zachodnia, Stany Zjednoczone) lub totalitarną propagandę (kraje bloku wschodniego). Dlatego też artyści – z jednej strony powodowani fascynacją, a z drugiej widzący potrzebę zmiany – sięgali po telewizyjne odbiorniki, wykorzystując je jako tworzywo swoich działań. Prekursorami sztuki wideo stali się twórcy z kręgu Fluxusu, m.in.: Wolf Vostell[109] i Nam June Paik[110], którzy konfrontowali widzów z faktem emisji programu telewizyjnego (Vostell) lub też starali się skłonić widzów to aktywnej reakcji (Paik).

W Polsce dynamiczny rozwój telewizji – rozpoczęty w 1937 roku w Warszawie nadaniem pierwszego programu eksperymentalnej stacji telewizyjnej – przerwała II wojna światowa. Regularna emisja rozpoczęła się dopiero w 1952 roku (dla porównania w USA stało się to w 1928, a w Niemczech i ZSRR w 1931 roku). Doświadczalna Stacja Telewizyjna Instytutu Łączności w Warszawie zaczęła wtedy nadawać cotygodniową, półgodzinną audycję. Sześć lat później Telewizja Polska uruchomiła antenę ogólnokrajową, a w połowie lat 50. w siedmiu miastach wojewódzkich zaczęły działać lokalne oddziały. W 1970 roku uruchomiono program drugi TVP, emitujący przede wszystkim programy tematyczne.

Mniej więcej w tym samym czasie – na początku lat 70. – Warsztatowcy po raz pierwszy sięgnęli po wideo. Było ono wtedy faktycznie „nowym medium", bo choć pierwsze realizacje z jego użyciem powstały już w połowie lat 60. w USA i Europie Zachodniej (a pod koniec dekady także w Kanadzie, Australii i Japonii), to w innych rejonach świata kwestie techniczne stanęły na przeszkodzie jego upowszechnieniu. Chodzi przede wszystkim o brak niezbędnego sprzętu. Dlatego tak ważną cezurą w historii sztuki wideo był moment wprowadzenia do sprzedaży przenośnych kamer Sony Portapak w 1966 roku. Był to model poręczny, umożliwiający użytkownikom samodzielną realizację transmisji, a także jej zapis na taśmie niewymagającej zasadniczo postprodukcji. Wszystko to sprawiło, że wideo zaczęło być postrzegane jako medium demokratyczne, dostępne

108 Co ciekawe, to właśnie włoscy spacjaliści ogłosili w 1952 roku pierwszy manifest artystyczny dotyczący telewizji pod tytułem *Manifesto del movimento spaziale per la televisione*.

109 Chodzi w szczególności o prace *Deutscher Ausblick aus dem Zyklus Schwarzes Zimmer* (1958) i *Television Décollage* (1963).

110 Jego pierwsza praca z użyciem wideo to *Exposition of Music – Electronic Television* (1963).

niemal dla każdego i znacznie bardziej przystępne niż film. Profesjonalny sprzęt filmowy i taśma 35 mm były często nieosiągalne dla artystów wizualnych w Niemczech Zachodnich, Anglii czy Stanach Zjednoczonych. W przypadku Warsztatowców sytuacja była odwrotna. To wideo, a nie film, było dla nich medium ekskluzywnym czy wręcz nieosiągalnym. W Polsce, jak i w całym bloku wschodnim, przenośne kamery nie były w ogóle dostępne w sprzedaży, korzystano więc z każdej, nieczęsto się nadarzającej okazji do ich użycia. Na przykład dla artystów z byłej Jugosławii – Sanji Iveković, Dalibora Martinisa, Gorana Trbuljaka i Borisa Bućana – takim kluczowym momentem był udział w warsztacie Trigon '73: Audiovisuelle Botschaften w Grazu, w ramach którego każdy z uczestników miał wykonać kilka prac wideo, a organizatorzy zapewniali niezbędny sprzęt[111].

W tym samym czasie Warsztatowcy po raz kolejny postanowili w twórczy sposób wykorzystać możliwości jakie oferowała im Szkoła Filmowa. Filmówka edukowała także w zakresie realizacji telewizyjnej, dysponowała więc wozem transmisyjnym. Członkowie WFF wykorzystali go w 1973 roku do zrealizowania pierwszych prac wideo w Polsce: *Języka obrazkowego* Bruszewskiego, *Seansu telewizyjnego* Różyckiego i *Transmisji telewizyjnej*. Ta ostatnia była wspólnym pomysłem uczestników grupy i została zaprezentowana obok *Seansu telewizyjnego* w ramach akcji Warsztat. Obraz z trzech kamer umieszczonych w różnych punktach Łodzi – na skrzyżowaniu ulic, w zakładzie stolarskim i w mieszkaniu prywatnym – był wyświetlany w czasie rzeczywistym na trzech odbiornikach znajdujących się w Muzeum Sztuki. Praca opierała się zatem na samym przekazie oraz wyeksponowaniu zasady transmisji. Kolejne „telewizyjne" prace Warsztatu zostały zrealizowane w latach 1974–1975 i wyemitowane – w wyniku chwilowej otwartości władz – przez drugi program TVP w popołudniowym programie o sztuce[112].

Realizacje Kwieka, Waśki i Bruszewskiego są osobnym rozdziałami światowej historii wideo. Każdy z nich wykorzystywał medium wideo do zmierzenia się z nurtującymi ich aktualnie problemami, nie unikniemy więc uproszczeń próbując znaleźć dla nich zagraniczne analogicznie. Z pewnością jednak warto przywołać w tym miejscu klasyczne już dziś prace twórców takich jak Steina Vasulka – na przykład instalację *An Electro/Opto/Mechanical Enviroment* z 1976 roku, w której artystka zgłębiała iluzoryczność transmitowanego obrazu przestrzeni. Warto też wspomnieć realizacje Davida Halla czy Stevena Patridge'a oparte o analizę procesu transmisji i kreacji wideo, a przez to bliskie myśleniu Bruszewskiego. Prace Warsztatu, zrealizowane w studio telewizyjnym i nadane przez TVP2 w maju 1974 r. wpisują się z kolei w szeroki międzynarodowy nurt działań artystycznych emitowanych w telewizji. Mam na myśli kanoniczne już programy Gerry'ego Schuma realizowane w latach 1969–1970 dla zachodnioberlińskiej telewizji regionalnej Sender Freies Berlin[113], a także *TV Interruptions* Davida Halla nadane przez telewizję szkocką czy cykl *The Medium is the Medium* wyprodukowany w 1969 roku przez stację WGBH-TV Boston we współpracy z takimi artystami, jak Nam June Paik, Aldo Tambellini, Otto Piene czy Allan Kaprow.

---

111 B. Borić, I. Panjol, *Chronology*, w: *Video art in Slovenia 1969–1998*, http://www.videodokument.org/cronology.htm [dostęp 30-12-2016].

112 Pokaz odbył się w TVP2 18 maja 1974 roku. Kwiek zrealizował pracę *Video A – Sytuacja studia*, a Bruszewski *Transmisję przestrzenną*. Ponadto wyemitowane zostały filmy: *Idę* Robakowskiego, *Ja i telefon* Kwieka, *Oda do młodości* (praca zbiorowa według pomysłu Andrzeja Barańskiego) oraz *Teoria przestrzeni obrazu filmowego* Waśki. Zob. *Żywa Galeria*, s. 133.

113 Z udziałem między innymi Richarda Longa, Barry'ego Flanagana, Dennisa Oppenheima, Marinusa Boezema, Roberta Smithsona, Jana Dibbetsa, Waltera De Marii i Michaela Heizera.

Poza formą filmową. Ciało i portret

Wątki cielesności, portretu i autoportretu są marginalizowane w odniesieniu do całej powojennej awangardy, nic więc dziwnego, że pomija się je także w badaniach nad działalnością Warsztatu. Nie chodzi tu, rzecz jasna, o estetyzowane kobiece akty malarskie, rzeźbiarskie czy fotograficzne, których obfitość powstawała w kręgach Związku Polskich Artystów Plastyków, ale o świadome i celowe posłużenie się nagością lub fizycznością w celu zamanifestowania idei i poglądów. Wyjątkami od tej reguły są kanoniczne już dziś przykłady Ewy Partum czy Natalii LL – artystek używających nagiego kobiecego ciała (odpowiednio: swojego i cudzego) do budowania strategii artystycznej. Żeński akt pojawiał się również niekiedy w twórczości awangardzistów-mężczyzn, ale zazwyczaj w bardzo szczególnej roli, czego dobrym przykładem może być dorobek Zbigniewa Dłubaka, który tworzył akty fotograficzne, jednocześnie dystansując się od nich za pomocą konceptualizującego, paranaukowego języka. Mamy tu do czynienia z uświadomionym lub nieuświadomionym wyparciem: polscy artyści i artystki czasów Gomułki i Gierka powoływali się na zamiar realizowania eksperymentów na polu sztuki analitycznej, aby uzasadnić nagość. Do tej sytuacji ironicznie i krytycznie odnosił się pod koniec lat 70. Janusz Haka, uważając, że pseudoanalityczne koncepcje są jedynie pretekstem do rozebrania dziewczyny przed obiektywem[114].

Motyw kobiecego aktu, choć wypierany, był jednak obecny – w przeciwieństwie do aktu męskiego, który pojawiał się sporadycznie. A właściwie: wcale, jeśli mówimy świadomej cielesności. Nic w tym dziwnego. Jak pisał Paweł Leszkowicz, pełen akt męski stanowił tabu w czasach PRL, a przedstawianie męskich genitaliów uznawano za pornografię. Cenzura działała na tym polu ze szczególną energią, by wspomnieć choćby przedwczesne zamknięcie wystawy *Fotografia intymna* w Galerii Permafo[115] czy ingerencję cenzora w wystawę Barbary Falender, na której artystka zamierzała pokazać rzeźby przypominające waginę i penisa[116]. Dopuszczalny był jedynie oficjalny, „socjalistyczny" akt męski, który sięgał swoimi korzeniami do średniowiecznej tradycji deformacji, poniżenia i wstydu ciała[117]. Nawet performerzy tacy jak Zbigniew Warpechowski czy Jerzy Bereś dystansowali się od cielesności, mimo że ustawicznie ją eksponowali. Wyjątkami potwierdzającymi regułę byli dwaj artyści: Krzysztof Niemczyk, który pod koniec lat 60. pozował nago do inscenizowanych fotografii oraz przeprowadzał w Krakowie efemeryczne akcje polegające między innymi na obnażaniu pośladków, a także Krzysztof Jung, którego performanse, realizowane o dekadę później w warszawskiej Galerii Repassage, powstawały z udziałem nagiego artysty lub zaproszonych uczestników[118]. Do tej krótkiej listy można dołączyć jeszcze Marka Koniecznego, który używał nagich autoportretów oraz obrazów kobiecych biustów, łon i wagin, po to, by – jak pisał Ronduda – zaprosić widza do zmysłowego doświadczania dzieła sztuki[119]. Według Rondudy Konieczny doznał podwójnego wykluczenia – zarówno ze strony przedstawicieli modernizmu, jak i drugiej awangardy[120]. Społecznego ostracyzmu doświadczył też Niemczyk. Jung z kolei organizował

114 Ł. Ronduda, *Sztuka polska lat 70.*, s. 337.
115 M. Kuźmicz, *Ja to ktoś inny*, w: *Natalia LL. Doing Gender*, red. D. Jarecka, A. Rayzacher, Warszawa: Fundacja Lokal Sztuki / lokal_30, 2014, s. 69.
116 Wywiad z Barbarą Falender, listopad 2009 roku.
117 P. Leszkowicz, *Art Pride. Polska sztuka gejowska,* Warszawa: Wydawnictwo Abiekt, 2010, s. 18.
118 Zob. *Krzysztof Jung. Przemiana*, red. J. Zgierski, Warszawa: Akademia Sztuk Pięknych, 2016.
119 Ł. Ronduda, *Sztuka polska lat 70.*, s. 20.
120 Ibidem, s. 28.

swoje performanse dla wąskich grup kilkunastu widzów (znajomych i przyjaciół). Wykorzystywanie cielesności przynosiło więc izolację artyście, chyba że ten „tłumaczył się” zamiarem podjęcia analitycznej i konceptualnej refleksji.

Warsztatowcy nie rozbierali dziewczyn przed obiektywami, nie rozbierali też samych siebie – bardzo łatwo jest więc przeoczyć wątek zaangażowanej fizyczności w ich twórczości. Surowa forma większości ich realizacji i towarzysząca im hermetyczna terminologia[121] sprawiają, że z wielu tekstów o działalności WFF wyłania się obraz artystów zajmujących się prowadzeniem mniej lub bardziej wyabstrahowanych z codzienności paranaukowych eksperymentów medialnych. Interpretacje zatrzymują się na granicy cielesności – jakby ich autorzy napotykali jakąś przeszkodę.

Tymczasem faktyczne aspiracje Warsztatowców sytuowały się gdzie indziej. Cielesność – choć często wyparta – była jak najbardziej obecna w ich twórczości. Bruszewski, Kwiek, Robakowski, Różycki, Waśko, Bendkowski i Łomnicki bardzo często posługiwali się swoim wizerunkiem i angażowali się fizycznie w realizację swoich prac. Praktycznie od początku istnienia grupy realizowali działania performatywne ze swoim osobistym udziałem, w których – niejako w roli narzędzia lub rekwizytu – pojawiały się aparaty, kamery, wozy transmisyjne czy studio telewizyjne. Cielesne zaangażowanie nie było (lub nie zawsze było) neutralne dla wymowy danej instalacji wideo, filmu czy fotografii. U Kwieka, Różyckiego i Waśki ciało miało często wymiar egzystencjalny. U Robakowskiego było źródłem fizycznej siły i witalności. Z kolei u Bruszewskiego objawiło się w zdumiewający i oryginalny sposób w pracy *Język baletowy* (1973) – sekwencji zdjęć i rysunków przedstawiających nagiego artystę, który za pomocą swojego ciała tworzy nowy alfabet. Nagość może być tu interpretowana jako otwartość na komunikację i porozumienie ponad przekazem werbalnym, ale – ponad wszystkim – jest to nader rzadki w polskiej sztuce przypadek pokazania witalnego, młodego, męskiego ciała. Nie przypomina innych „laboratoryjnych” prac Bruszewskiego – wygląda raczej jak fotograficzny zapis szamańskiego tańca.

Motyw ciała i autoportretu ewoluował na różne sposoby w twórczości poszczególnych członków Warsztatu. Na przykład Robakowski w latach 60. dekonstruował fotografie ze swoją podobizną: nadpalał je lub naświetlał wielokrotnie w taki sposób, że obraz twarzy stawał się niepełny lub zwielokrotniony. Z jednej strony mamy tu do czynienia z wielokrotnie już opisywanym działaniem na medium fotograficznym, z drugiej jednak – ponieważ te działania Robakowski prowadził na własnym portrecie – możemy się pokusić o przyjęcie psychologicznej perspektywy. Obecna w nich aura niepokoju i egzystencjalnego zagrożenia ustępuje w kolejnej dekadzie bardziej świadomej fizyczności. Odkrywając ciało, Robakowski łączy je z narzędziami medialnymi – głównie kamerami, których używa tak, jakby były jego kończynami. Sprzęt filmowy był ciężki i wymagał użycia siły fizycznej. To próbowanie się z maszyną dawało efekt w postaci zapisu zarówno walki, jak i współpracy człowieka z kamerą. Powstały w ten sposób obraz jest rezultatem przełamania oporu urządzenia, które – pozornie podporządkowując się woli operatora-performera – nie przestaje rejestrować rzeczywistości według swojego własnego programu. Ten problem, zaznaczony po raz pierwszy w filmie *Idę* (35 mm, 1973), stanie się z czasem jednym z najważniejszych wątków w twórczości Robakowskiego. W rezultacie powstał cykl *Zapisy biologiczno-mechaniczne*, na który składały się filmy, fotografie i prace wideo. Swoistym apogeum tego myślenia był wideoperformans *Ćwiczenie*

121 Filmom Warsztatu towarzyszyły często różnego rodzaju wykresy i obliczenia. Zob. R. Waśko, op. cit.

na dwie ręce (1976), w którym artysta wymachiwał dwoma pracującymi kamerami. Robakowski wyszedł w tej realizacji z roli operatora i objawił się jako podmiot, dopełniając tym samym obraz swojej praktyki artystycznej.

Na przeciwległym biegunie tej strategii sytuuje się Ryszard Waśko, który stopniowo wycofywał samego siebie z pola widzenia. Jego fotografie z serii *Autoportret w czasie* (1972) dopuszczały jeszcze istnienie twórcy-podmiotu. Później autor nie tyle znika, ile wycofuje się, ogranicza się do istnienia i patrzenia, zachowując przy tym jednak pełną świadomość własnej egzystencji i podmiotowości. W pracach Waśki, będących w istocie zapisem relacji czas–przestrzeń–ja, owo „ja" rozumiane jest dosłownie, jako podmiot istniejący w czasie i przestrzeni, którego cielesność, pozostając zazwyczaj niewidoczna dla widza, jest jednak wyczuwalna. To, co widzimy, widzimy dzięki obecności Waśki w danym miejscu i czasie. Realizowana w ten sposób analiza przestrzeni jest dla Waśki punktem wyjścia do egzystencjalnych rozważań, przywodzących na myśl buddyjskie koany, zwłaszcza słynne pytanie: „Czy wówczas, gdy nikt nie słyszy trzasku upadającego w lesie drzewa, drzewo upada?". Zdaje się pytać: „Czy czas i przestrzeń istnieją, gdy nikt ich nie odczuwa, nie widzi, nie odbiera?". Odpowiedź Waśki zawiera się w zawiera się pracach, takich jak *Od 0 stopni do 180 stopni* czy *Powiększenie czy 30 sytuacji dźwiękowych* i wydaje się negatywna.

Kolejny artysta z kręgu Warsztatu, Kazimierz Bendkowski, uczynił autoportret wizualną osią swojej twórczości, używając go do badania relatywności przekazu wizualnego i fotograficznej manipulacji[122]. Dotyczy to w szczególności rozwijanego latami cyklu *Obraz relatywny*. Składały się na niego sekwencje tych samych fotograficznych autoportretów, opatrzonych za każdym razem innym komentarzem. Wybór twarzy twórcy jako głównego motywu cyklu sprawił, że *Obraz relatywny* przekroczył ramy dywagacji nad właściwościami fotografii – stał się próbą ustalenia relacji między samym sobą a światem. Praca może być też postrzegana jako antycypacja czy też swoista „makieta" fenomenu *selfies* – zdjęć robionych zazwyczaj w samotności, w sposób kompulsywny, zastępujących spojrzenie w podręczne lusterko i prezentujących nas korzystniej niż wyglądamy w rzeczywistości. *Obraz relatywny* Bendkowskiego ironicznie obnaża ten proces ostentacyjnego multiplikowania własnego wizerunku, który – choć pozornie zmienia się w zależności od kontekstu – w gruncie rzeczy pozostaje taki sam.

Nieliczne fotograficzne autoportrety Andrzeja Różyckiego były z kolei wyjątkowo – jak na Warsztat – osobiste. Wykorzystując swój wizerunek i grając znaczącymi tytułami prac, Różycki opowiadał o swojej postawie artystycznej i życiowej. Jedną z tego typu realizacji była wieloelementowa fotografia *Projekt uruchomienia obrazu fotograficznego* (1975), która przedstawiała ciało artysty, zmultiplikowane na kolejnych fotografiach w sposób przywodzący na myśl filmowe stopklatki. Podpis głosił: „Podobnie jak lot Ikara, tak i ta próba nie może skończyć się powodzeniem". Różycki podsumował w ten sposób usiłowania Warsztatowców, zmierzające do wydobycia z fotografii czegoś, czego prawdopodobnie nigdy nie miała ona do zaoferowania.

Warto tu przywołać jeszcze jedną pracę Różyckiego, *Identyfikację pozorną* (1973), która polegała na przedstawieniu – równocześnie za pomocą fotografii, filmu i performansu – artysty wykonującego te same codzienne czynności; czytającego, drącego gazetę. Ta realizacja jest

122 Zob. K. Bendkowski, *Relatywność i obiektywność komunikatów wizualnych*, w: R. W. Kluszczyński, op. cit., s. 62–64.

dziś bardziej aktualna niż w momencie powstania, opowiada bowiem o świecie, w którym musimy współegzystować obok naszych cyfrowych awatarów. Te zwielokrotnione byty mają punkty wspólne (z nami i między sobą), ale jednocześnie zmuszają nas do zapytania o to, który z nich jest realny i czy w ogóle możemy jeszcze mówić o realności. Napięcie, które generuje ta praca jest poniekąd niwelowane przez banalność codziennych, błahych gestów. To charakterystyczny zabieg dla Różyckiego. Fundamentalne kwestie podnosił poważnym tonem, aby potem zbić je swoistym żartem. Uniwersalność mieszał z wymiarem osobistym. Rzeczywistość okazuje się bowiem na tyle skomplikowana, że do jej oswojenia potrzebna jest nie tylko dekonstrukcja maszyn dominujących nasz świat, ale także umiejętność spojrzenia na nią z czysto ludzkiej perspektywy.

Paweł Kwiek używał autoportretu permanentnie i niemal kompulsywnie, w sposób przypominający ciągłe testowanie własnych możliwości percepcji świata. Najpełniejszą manifestacją tej postawy były prace wideo, które Paweł Kwiek zrealizował w studiu TVP w 1974 roku. Powstało wówczas widowisko telewizyjne, w którym Kwiek, jako performer wydający polecenia operatorom, decydował o tym, jaki obraz rzeczywistości zobaczą widzowie. Za pomocą komend głosowych stworzył transmisję, składającą się z obrazów przedstawiających sytuację w studiu we fragmentaryczny sposób. Najbardziej oczywistym tematem tej pracy jest niepełność i wybiórczość percepcji zapośredniczonej przez media. Motyw ten wybrzmiewa tym mocniej, że artysta postrzegał wideo jako narzędzie bardzo bliskie struktury ludzkiego umysłu: „Działa podobnie jak nasza wyobraźnia, jak umysł, który przegląda percypowane, zapamiętane lub właśnie wytwarzane obrazy"[123]. A zatem praca *Wideo A. Sytuacja studia* demaskuje nie tylko mechanizm mediów, lecz także słabości ludzkiego umysłu, nawykowo przyzwyczajonego do postrzegania rzeczywistości fragmentarycznie, nigdy holistycznie. Daisetz Teitaro Suzuki, profesor filozofii buddyjskiej, pisał, że takie spojrzenie na rzeczywistość może nam zaoferować jedynie analityczne definicje, co wystarczy nam dla celów praktycznych, ale nie pozwoli uchwycić istoty rzeczy[124]. Suzuki porównał taki „obiektywizm" – na przykładzie poematu Alfreda Tennysona – do próby poznania kwiatu poprzez wyrwanie go z korzeniami. Przeciwstawił go odmiennej postawie, uchwyconej przez Bash Matsuo w haiku będącym zapisem próby poznania kwiatu poprzez całkowite objęcie go zrozumieniem, aż do utożsamienia się poznającego i poznawanego[125]. Z taką postawą silnie rezonuje nieco późniejsza praca Kwieka *Wideo i oddech. Kanał informacji* (1978), zbudowana nie na działaniu, lecz na jego redukcji do zamanifestowanej i uświadomionej obecności. Podmiot tej pracy widzi rzeczywistość we wszystkich jej przejawach. Nie ocenia, ale jest w pełni świadomy. Pojmuje, ale nie analizuje.

Tym samym Kwiek, na przestrzeni kilku zaledwie lat, dokonał zasadniczej zmiany w swoim sposobie rozumienia relacji między rzeczywistością a odbierającym ją podmiotem. Początkowo używał nowych mediów jako narzędzi poznania świata. Ostatecznie jednak skonfrontował się z nim bezpośrednio – stopniowo rezygnując z jakichkolwiek rekwizytów. Pod koniec lat 70. porzucił ostatecznie paranaukowy język i w 1979 roku zrealizował pracę *Percepcja braku zróżnicowań*, polegającą na medytowaniu przed białą gładką ścianą. Jedynym jej śladem jest skromna dokumentacja fotograficzna.

123 P. Kwiek, *Foto-media a struktura czynności myślenia*, druk ulotny, Galeria Foto-Medium-Art, Wrocław 1978, za: Ł. Ronduda, *Sztuka polska lat 70*, s. 285.

124 D. T. Suzuki, *Wykłady o buddyzmie zen*, w: E. Fromm, D. T. Suzuki, R. de Martino, *Buddyzm zen i psychoanaliza*, Poznań: Rebis, 2011, s. 46–48.

125 Ibidem, s. 11–14.

Prawdopodobnie o takiej właśnie zmianie świadomości, która miała stać się udziałem Warsztatu, pisał Józef Robakowski:

> Nigdy nie chodziło nam o „rozszerzenie widzialności przy pomocy urządzeń technicznych", ale o zmianę percypowania świata, a więc sposobu myślenia. Jest to zdecydowana różnica[126].

Poza formą filmową. Interwencje i akcje

Interwencje były zakłóceniami oficjalnych wydarzeń kulturalnych, spotkań, przeglądów filmowych i pokazów, które Warsztatowcy przeprowadzali przy okazji swoich częstych podróży po Polsce. Ich celem była próba modernizacji polskiej kinematografii poprzez jej krytykę oraz prowokowanie publiczności do czynnego odbioru prac czy wręcz ich współtworzenia. Niektóre z nich były z góry zaplanowane, szczególnie gdy elementem interwencji miał być pokaz filmów, ale także wówczas działy się one niespodziewanie z punktu widzenia organizatorów. W ten sposób Warsztatowcy spuszczali powietrze z imprez, które miały – przez nadprodukcję nagród i tytułów przyznawanych miernym twórcom i dziełom – kreować i nadmuchiwać pozorne sukcesy polskiego kina. W związku z tym interwencje WFF często odnosiły się personalnie do konkretnych uczestników zakłócanych imprez, w szczególności do urzędników oficjalnej kinematografii.
Taką demaskatorską strategię opisywał w 1973 roku w *Paszkwilu na polską kinematografię* Józef Robakowski:

> Samozadowolenie z „owocnej pracy" potwierdzane jest corocznie wieloma festiwalami i przeglądami; a jest ich taka ilość, że trudno zliczyć. Wszędzie wystawne fety, pełna gala, dekoracje, najlepsze hotele, no i wiele, wiele nagród – za byle co[127].

Robakowski wspominał, że najbardziej skutecznym narzędziem dekonstruowania różnego rodzaju oficjalnych fet był absurd:

> Pan Wacek [Antczak – M.K.] potrafił najlepiej poruszać się w rzeczywistości PRL-owskiego absurdu. To on potrafił wygenerować taką sytuację, z którą nie umiała sobie poradzić ani milicja, ani organizatorzy tychże festiwali[128].

Pierwsza interwencja odbyła się na wystawie *Fotografowie poszukujący* w Galerii Współczesnej w Warszawie. Warsztatowcy przygotowali ulotki składające się z cytatów z recenzji i rozpraw teoretycznych dotyczących fotografii. Wypowiedzi polskich badaczy i krytyków, złożone w mniej więcej logiczną całość, miały pokazywać stan intelektualny polskiej krytyki[129].

Następna akcja miała miejsce na Przeglądzie Polskich Filmów w Łagowie, gdzie pokazywano trzy filmy Warsztatu: *Rynek*, *Inwentaryzację* i *Dziury* (czyli *Test I*). W czasie projekcji członkowie WFF usiedli pomiędzy widzami, prowokując ich pytaniami typu: „Gdzie jest człowiek?" – ironicznie powtarzając w ten sposób najczęstsze zarzuty stawiane twórczości grupy. Udało im się w ten sposób rozpętać burzliwą dyskusję[130].

---

126 J. Robakowski, *Dziura w historii*, „Studia Artystyczne CDN", 2, 1980, s. 76–78.

127 J. Robakowski, *Paszkwil na polską kinematografię*, „Student", 3, 1973, cyt. za *Żywa Galeria*, s. 92–93, http://robakowski.eu/tx16.html [dostęp 30-12-2016].

128 Wywiad z Józefem Robakowskim, lipiec 2014.

129 Zob. L. Olszewski, *Gdzie jest człowiek. Interwencje Warsztatu Formy Filmowej*, w: *Żywa Galeria*, s. 306–311.

130 Ibidem.

Odmienny charakter miała interwencja wykonana podczas Przeglądu Filmów o Sztuce w Zakopanem. Gdy w ramach tego wydarzenia przyznawano nagrodę Andrzejowi Papuzińskiemu za dokument o Franciszku Starowieyskim *Bykowi chwała*, Bruszewski i Koterski wyszli na scenę i wręczyli jednemu z organizatorów festiwalu (a zarazem reżyserowi jednego z prezentowanych na nim filmów) nagrodę Warsztatu Formy Filmowej za najgorszy film. Był nią pistolet (korkowiec) – aby laureat mógł się zastrzelić. Reżyser automatycznie podniósł go do głowy i nacisnął spust. Niestety, korkowiec był nabity[131].

Lechosław Olszewski pisał o tej i podobnych interwencjach Warsztatu:

> Miały charakter prowokacji. Nie mając ściśle określonej formy, charakteryzowały się niepewnością tego, co nastąpi, i w tym upodabniały się do happeningów, których forma wiele zawdzięczała dadaizmowi[132].

Warto jednak zauważyć, że strategia Warsztatu była bliska przede wszystkim Fluxusowi. Poprzez happeningi, koncerty i szeroko rozumiane efemeryczne akcje, Fluxusowcy usiłowali zaangażować publiczność oraz znieść bariery między życiem a sztuką. Pojawiali się – podobnie jak członkowie WFF – wśród „regularnej" publiczności festiwalowej, naruszając utarte schematy funkcjonowania tego typu wydarzeń, a także angażując widzów w czynne uczestnictwo w danym działaniu.

Kolejna interwencja Warsztatu miała miejsce w marcu 1974 roku w gdańskim klubie Żak. Miało się w nim odbyć spotkanie z Andrzejem Koniczem, który miał jednak problem z dojazdem. Jego nieobecność przedłużała się. Wtedy przed zgromadzoną publicznością pojawił się Józef Robakowski i, wcielając się w rolę reżysera, zaczął odpowiadać na pytania padające z sali[133]. W grudniu tego samego roku Warsztatowcy wzięli udział w V International Experimental Film Competition w Knokke-Heist w Belgii, gdzie – poza prezentacją swoich filmów – przeprowadzili spontaniczną interwencję w trakcie pokazu filmu Dore O *Kaskada*, będącego długą rejestracją wodospadu. Warsztatowcy rozebrali się i zaczęli symulować pływanie na tle wielkiego ekranu. Józef Robakowski wspomina z tej samej imprezy własny performans z lustrem, wykonany podczas projekcji filmu *Dziury* (czyli *Test I*), a także „interwencję siłową w czasie wystąpienia belgijskiego performera (wrzucenie go do fontanny), rozbicie ok. 100 balonów sylwestrowych, wyłączenie światła w kasynie podczas nocy sylwestrowej oraz wydanie VII Zeszytu WFF w wersji angielskiej"[134].

Należy tu wspomnieć jeszcze o interwencjach realizowanych w późniejszym okresie przez poszczególnych uczestników akcji *Śmietnik*, w szczególności *Misteriach*, które w Warszawie zainicjował Kazimierz Bendkowski oraz *Śmietniku* zrealizowanym przez Pawła Kwieka w Zakopanem[135].

Misteria odbywały się od 1971 roku na osiedlu Rakowiec w Warszawie. Działy się w nocy i polegały na „użyciu wszelkiego rodzaju źródeł światła"[136]. Miały charakter spontaniczny. Bendkowski wysyłał sygnały świetlne i dźwiękowe z okien swojego mieszkania, a sąsiedzi odpowiadali tym samym[137]. Celem akcji było wytworzenie innego niż słowa środka porozumienia między ludźmi.

---

131 *Wojciech Bruszewski*, s. 25.

132 L. Olszewski, *Działalność Warsztatu*, s. 129.

133 Ibidem, s.134.

134 *Żywa Galeria*, s. 133–134.

135 Warto też wspomnieć o akcjach Kwieka, które realizował wspólnie z Jackiem Łomnickim w ramach działającej od maja 1972 r. dwuosobowej efemerycznej galerii *Czyżby*. Zob. R. Waśko, op. cit., s. 10.

136 Ibidem, s. 3.

137 Ibidem, s. 106.

Akcja *Śmietnik* również odbyła się w nocy. Paweł Kwiek wykonał około 300 odbitek fotograficznych ze stopklatek ze swojego filmu *Twarz* z udziałem Jacka Łomnickiego (syna Tadeusza)[138] w Sylwestra 1971/1972 rozrzucił je w Zakopanem. Była to kolejna akcja nawiązująca do tego filmu. Miesiąc wcześniej Kwiek poprosił uczniów jednego z warszawskich liceów o „robienie min do kamery". Następnie odbył się pokaz *Twarzy*, po którym fotograficzne odbitki kadrów z filmu zostały „puszczone w publikę" w formie długiej wstęgi[139].

Interwencji mogło być więcej. Mogły nie zostać udokumentowane ani nie przechować się w pamięci świadków i uczestników. Wydaje się jednak, że pobyt w Knokke-Heist w 1974 roku zakończył okres spontanicznych wystąpień w wykonaniu grupy. Jest to o tyle zrozumiałe, że Warsztatowcy zyskali w tym okresie możliwość wprowadzania w życie swoich postulatów – także w ramach prestiżowych zagranicznych wydarzeń.

Elbląg. Kino w służbie rebelii

Zacznijmy od Elbląga, który w latach 60. stał się ważnym miejscem na mapie polskiej sztuki – przede wszystkim za sprawą Gerarda Jürgena Bluma-Kwiatkowskiego (1930–2015) oraz zapraszanych przez niego artystów. Kwiatkowski zamieszkał w Elblągu po II wojnie światowej. W latach 1956–1961 prowadził Klub Młodej Inteligencji Czerwona Oberża, a następnie, w 1961 roku, otworzył Galerię EL, którą prowadził aż do swojego wyjazdu do Niemiec w 1974 roku. W tym czasie zorganizował pięć edycji Biennale Form Przestrzennych (1965–1973). Ostatnią z nich, pod nazwą Kino Laboratorium, zrealizował we współpracy z Warsztatem Formy Filmowej.

Ideą Biennale, organizowanego pierwotnie we współpracy z elbląskimi zakładami Zamechu, było przekraczanie autonomii dzieła sztuki i realizacja postulatu „świata jako dzieła sztuki". W praktyce oznaczało to pracę kolektywną, eksplorację przestrzeni miasta oraz sprzężenie artystycznych idei z możliwościami technologicznymi. Ten ostatni wątek szczególnie mocno ukształtował charakter wydarzenia. W latach 60. mogło się wręcz wydawać, że jest ono pretekstem do realizacji pokaźnych, technologicznie skomplikowanych rzeźb, produkowanych przez artystów we współpracy z inżynierami Zamechu.

Wydarzenie było od początku bardzo popularne w środowiskach awangardowych, ale koncepcja Kwiatkowskiego spotykała się także z krytyką. Anka Ptaszkowska sformułowała na przykład zarzut, że organizatorzy utożsamiają środki techniczne z artystycznymi i uznają „formy przestrzenne" za jedynie słuszny rezultat twórczego działania. Prowadziło to jej zdaniem do nadania Biennale cech koncepcji totalitarnej[140]. W ramach Biennale miały też wprawdzie miejsce działania efemeryczne (na przykład Stanisława Dróżdża czy Ewy Partum), ale dopiero początek lat 70. przyniósł gruntowne przewartościowanie idei tego wydarzenia.

Udział Warsztatowców w jego ostatniej edycji w 1973 roku podkreślił tę zmianę i pozwolił jej wybrzmieć. Kino Laboratorium zostało poświęcone związkom sztuki i kina, a więc kwestii

---

138 Wywiad z Pawłem Kwiekiem, marzec 2010.

139 Miało to miejsce 30 listopada 1971 roku w Galerii Współczesnej w Warszawie w ramach zbiorowej akcji *Film, Przeźrocza, Działania, Teoria* zrealizowanej wspólnie z Przemysławem Kwiekiem, Zofią Kulik, Janem S. Wojciechowskim i Jackiem Łomnickim. Zob. Ł. Ronduda, G. Schöllhammer, *Kwiekulik,* Zurych: JRP Ringier, 2013, s. 90.

140 H. Ptaszkowska, *Biennale Form Przestrzennych w Elblągu,* „itd", 45, 1965, cyt. za M. Lachowski, *Awangarda wobec instytucji. O sposobach prezentacji sztuki w PRL-u,* Lublin: Towarzystwo Naukowe KUL, 2006, s. 62.

fundamentalnej dla Warsztatowców[141]. Obfitowało w działania efemeryczne i interwencje, które w bardziej nowoczesny, skomplikowany i subtelny sposób eksplorowały relacje między sztuką, nauką i techniką. Dla Warsztatowców stało się pretekstem do wprowadzenia w życie postulatów głoszonych wcześniej w formie incydentalnych interwencji. W ulotce zapraszającej artystów do udziału w imprezie, czytamy:

> Warsztat Formy Filmowej przy Państwowej Wyższej Szkole Filmowej, Telewizyjnej i Teatralnej w Łodzi oraz Laboratorium Sztuki – Galeria El w Elblągu wzywają do udziału w międzynarodowej konfrontacji nowego kina. Rozważane będą wyłącznie problemy oraz metody nowego języka filmowego. NASZYM CELEM – KINO CZYSTE! Kino-Laboratorium rezygnuje z wszelkiego rodzaju nagród, jurorów, klasyfikacji i ocen. [...] Na wspólne działanie oddajemy Wam teren Galerii–El. Zapewniamy kontakt z polską awangardą artystyczną[142].

W wydarzeniu wzięło udział stu dwudziestu uczestników, w tym grupy artystyczne: Studio Kompozycji Emocjonalnej z Wrocławia, Galeria Adres z Łodzi, Grupa Remont z Warszawy, Grupa w Składzie z Warszawy, Wielobranżowa Spółdzielnia Poetycka z Poznania, Studio Béla Balázs z Budapesztu, a także artyści indywidualni z Hiszpanii, Argentyny, Holandii, Kanady, Francji, Szkocji czy Węgier[143]. Po uroczystym otwarciu Eugeniusz Rudnik wykonał swoją kompozycję *My*, a wieczorem odbyły się projekcje filmów Themersonów, Légera, Buñuela i Wienego, które miały przypomnieć „jakie możliwości wypowiedzi artystycznej proponowali w swoich czasie wybitni przedstawiciele kina awangardowego". W późnych godzinach nocnych pokazano film Paradżanowa *Owoc granatu*, który wzbudził wiele polemik i kontrowersji. Uczestnicy bawili się potem do rana na koncercie Grupy w Składzie. Intensywny pierwszy dzień obfitował także w liczne „manifestacje artystyczne", w ramach których Warsztatowcy zaprezentowali dokumentację przeprowadzonej w lutym 1973 roku akcji Warsztat.

Drugi dzień rozpoczął popołudniowy „spektakl spontaniczno-audiowizualny", realizowany przez Warsztatowców poprzez manipulowanie kolorowymi foliami, taśmami i innymi przedmiotami przed lampą projektora kinowego. Pokazowi towarzyszyła oprawa dźwiękowa Studia Kompozycji Emocjonalnej. Wydarzenie to, jeśli wierzyć relacji, wymknęło się z założonych ram. Spontanicznie włączyli się w nie widzowie, co poskutkowało „dużą manifestacją integrującą wiele dyscyplin". Tego dnia swoje filmy pokazał Ryszard Waśko (*Ściana*, *Chodnik*, *Okno*, *Zaprzeczenie*, *Rejestracja*, *Doniczka*), oraz Paweł Kwiek (*Numerki*), co wywołało „burzliwą dyskusję, w której zastanawiano się nad rolą takich propozycji". Autorzy wyjaśniali, że są to prowokacje i testy, które mają rozszerzać możliwości współczesnego kina – choćby przez fakt umożliwienia widzom wyrażania swoich reakcji w trakcie projekcji. Wieczorem odbył się jeszcze pokaz *Zapisu* Robakowskiego. Co ciekawe, został on przerwany interwencją Andrzeja Partuma, który wspiął się na przystawioną do ekranu drabinę i umieścił na nim tabliczkę z napisem „Akupunktura".

Trzeciego dnia Biennale Wojciech Bruszewski wykonał – we współpracy z Pawłem Kwiekiem i Piotrem Bernackim – pracę *Język obrazkowy*. Było to „widowisko telewizyjne" zrealizowane przy

---

141 J. Robakowski, *Komunikat: Kino Laboratorium,* druk ulotny, Archiwum Galerii Wymiany, 1973, http://repozytorium.fundacjaarton.pl/index.php?action=view/object&objid=3164 [dostęp 30-12-2016].

142 *Kino – Laboratorium*, druk ulotny, Archiwum Galerii Wymiany, 1973, http://repozytorium.fundacjaarton.pl/index.php?action=view/object&objid=3163 [dostęp: 30-12-2016].

143 Wszystkie informacje na temat wydarzenia pochodzą z: *Kronika V Biennale Form Przestrzennych – Kino Laboratorium*, „Notatnik Robotnika Sztuki", 5, 1973, s. 4–10. http://repozytorium.fundacjaarton.pl/index.php?action=view/object&objid=3181 [dostęp 30-12-2016].

użyciu wozu transmisyjnego wypożyczonego ze Szkoły Filmowej, a następnie zapisane na taśmie video i odtworzone na magnetowidzie. Praca spotkała się, jak większość działań WFF podczas Biennale, z „burzliwą dyskusją" i krytyką. Zarzucano jej błędy w realizacji dźwięku i podważano jej sens. *Język obrazkowy* nie zachował się, ale przeszedł do historii jako pierwsza polska praca zarejestrowana na taśmie wideo. Jednocześnie praca Bruszewskiego była, jak pisali organizatorzy, „pierwszą próbą w Telewizji Polskiej, wychodzącą poza program popularny".

Tego samego dnia członkowie Warsztatu ogłosili Ćwiczenia filmowe, w ramach których każdy uczestnik Biennale mógł zrealizować – z operatorską pomocą Pawła Kwieka – jednominutowy film na taśmie 35 mm. Akcja trwała do końca festiwalu. Twórcy tych prac często nie mieli nic wspólnego z filmem, ani wcześniej ani później. Tak było chociażby w przypadku Włodzimierza Wieczorkiewicza, Milo Kurtisa czy samego Gerarda Kwiatkowskiego[144]. W akcji wziął udział także sam Kwiek, który zrealizował *Polewacza polany*[145], nawiązującego w zabawny sposób do filmu niemego braci Lumière, a także *Moją niezależność*, przedstawiającą rysunek, który Kwiek wykonał kredą na podłodze Galerii EL (było to odwzorowanie rachunku, który uczestnicy Biennale zapłacili w restauracji). Kwiek mówi w filmie z offu, że tytuł *Moja niezależność* jest nieadekwatny i powinien brzmieć *Moja bezsensowność* – ponieważ całe działanie wydaje się pozbawione sensu. Inni członkowie grupy również wzięli udział w akcji. Piotr Bernacki zrealizował film *Źdźbło*, a Wojciech Bruszewski wypełnił swoją część taśmy filmowej postulatami i hasłami przekonującymi widzów do bojkotu oficjalnej kinematografii. Z kolei Robakowski zbliżył się z lustrem w dłoniach do rejestrującej go kamery, kierując w ten sposób spojrzenie widza na ekipę filmową przy pracy.

Wieczorem – jako jeden z elementów bogatego programu – zaprezentowano kolejne filmy Warsztatu: *Konfrontację* Tadeusza Junaka, *Take five* Zbigniewa Rybczyńskiego oraz *Klaskacza* i *Inwentaryzację* Wojciecha Bruszewskiego. Pokaz *Próby II* Robakowskiego został ponownie zakłócony przez „grupę interwencyjną" Partuma, która – działając pod hasłem „Film nie potrzebuje ekranu" – przeniosła obraz filmowy na ściany galerii za pomocą lustra. Jednocześnie Paweł Fleisler przymocował do ekranu nić, którą wręczył Robakowskiemu. Sam Robakowski też użył lustra, zastępując nim ekran podczas projekcji *Testu I*. Za jego pomocą kierował światło z projektora w stronę publiczności, na przedmioty znajdujące się w galerii i na gotyckie sklepienia[146].

Piątego dnia festiwalu widzowie zobaczyli *Epizod* Junaka oraz *Twarz* Kwieka. Zaraz po nich wyświetlono eksperymentalne filmy Javiera Aguirre Fernándeza, które stały się pretekstem dla interwencji ze strony widzów, którzy manipulowali ostrością obrazu, wyłączali dźwięk i obraz i sterowali projekcję na sklepienie kościoła. Warsztatowcy znaleźli z Fernándezem wspólny język i odkryli w jego postawie twórczej wiele podobieństw do własnej strategii. Hiszpański reżyser również chętnie podejmował współpracę z muzykami i poetami, badał podobne problemy dotyczące medium filmu oraz, podobnie jak WFF, nie uczestniczył w oficjalnych festiwalach ani premiowanych konkursach. Został w związku z tym mianowany honorowym członkiem grupy.

Ostatniego dnia wieczór filmowy należał już całkowicie do Warsztatu – grupa zaproponowała dwugodzinną prezentację swoich wcześniejszych filmów, a Paweł Kwiek pokazał na dwóch ekranach materiał filmowy komponowany na bieżąco i spontanicznie w wypowiedź artystyczną,

144 Zob. *Elbląg konceptualny*, red. J. Denisiuk, Elbląg: Centrum Sztuki Galeria EL, 2010, s. 56.
145 We współpracy z Karolem Cicheckim.
146 Działanie to powtórzył podczas festiwalu w Knokke Heist w 1974 roku.

posługując się efektami nagranymi na taśmie oraz efektami muzycznymi powodowanymi na miejscu przez Grupę w Składzie. Oprócz tego Wojciech Bruszewski pokazał swój najnowszy wówczas film *Bezdech*, a Antoni Mikołajczyk „zrealizował na posadzce galerii demonstrację artystyczną *Ogień*". Biennale zakończyło się akcją według pomysłu Gerarda Kwiatkowskiego, która polegała na wspólnym kontemplowaniu nadchodzącego świtu.

Udział Warsztatu w V Biennale Form Przestrzennych – Kino Laboratorium bezsprzecznie wniósł nową jakość do formuły wydarzenia. Nie powstały monumentalne rzeźby, przeprowadzono natomiast szereg działań performatywnych i, co szczególnie ważne, zrealizowano prace filmowe i wideo. Dla Warsztatu festiwal był z kolei istotnym pretekstem do podsumowania i poszerzenia swojej działalności, a także do skonfrontowania się z żywiołowo reagującą publicznością i dorobkiem artystów zagranicznych. Rezultatem tego doświadczenia były kolejne prace: fundamentalna z perspektywy historii sztuki realizacja wideo *Język obrazkowy* Wojciecha Bruszewskiego, a także film *Kinolaboratorium* Pawła Kwieka, stanowiący egzemplifikację rozwijanej przez niego idei pracy kolektywnej.

Za granicą. Edynburg, São Paulo, Knokke-Heist, Documenta

Kontakty międzynarodowe Warsztatu nie ograniczały się do incydentalnych spotkań takich jak to z Javierem Aguirre Fernándezem. Grupa budowała coraz większą rozpoznawalność na Zachodzie, w czym kluczową rolę odegrały trzy wydarzenia: wystawa Atelier '72 w Edynburgu (1972), która była pierwszym zagranicznym wystąpieniem WFF, a także konkurs filmów eksperymentalnych w Knokke-Heist (1974), który z kolei przyniósł grupie zaproszenie na szóstą edycję słynnej wystawy Documenta w Kassel (1977).

Osobą, która odegrała w tych międzynarodowych kontaktach kluczową rolę był Richard Demarco, właściciel galerii, w której odbyła się wystawa Atelier '72. Demarco od końca lat 60. intensywnie interesował się sztuką Europy Środkowej i Wschodniej. Odbywał podróże, które nazywał „edukacyjnymi": do Rumunii, Polski i Jugosławii. Prace artystów z tych krajów zaprezentowano odpowiednio w 1971, 1972 i 1973 roku – w Demarco Gallery w Edynburgu[147].

Nie jest pewne, czy Demarco wybrał się do Szkoły Filmowej z własnej inicjatywy, czy też został do tego zachęcony przez Ryszarda Stanisławskiego, ówczesnego dyrektora Muzeum Sztuki. Niemniej zjawił się na uczelni w sobotę popołudniu, kiedy prawie nikogo w niej nie było. W pracy była tylko sekretarka z dziekanatu, która chciała jak najszybciej pozbyć się natrętnego gościa, mówiąc mu, że biuro jest nieczynne. Gajewski wspomina to następująco:

> W Szkole Filmowej był taki zwyczaj, że w sobotę o godzinie piętnastej większość wykładowców i studentów wyjeżdżała do Warszawy. Ja zostałem, aby popracować nad ścieżką dźwiękową do mojego filmu *Pierzgalski*. Nagle zadzwoniła sekretarka z pytaniem czy mógłbym się zająć jakimś natarczywym facetem, który chciałby zobaczyć szkolne filmy. Mówi po angielsku, wygląda na Włocha, ale jest Szkotem. Nie daje się spławić. Pyta czy mógłbym pokazać mu jakiś film. Zgodziłem się niechętnie. Tym upartym Szkotem był mało jeszcze znany w Polsce Richard Demarco. Pokazałem mu *Wirówkę* i *Pierzgalskiego*. Filmy mu się spodobały. Zaprosił mnie do udziału w wystawie Atelier '72, ale mu nie

147 Pokaz u Demarco był pierwszym zagranicznym wystąpieniem Mariny Abramović.

uwierzyłem. Obiecałem jednak załatwić pozostałe filmy Warsztatu oraz spotkanie z ich autorami. Nie pamiętam, kiedy do niego doszło – wtedy czy w trakcie następnej jego wizyty w Polsce. Nie wierzyliśmy za bardzo, że Ministerstwo Kultury zgodzi się na nasz udział. Urzędnicy mieli o nas nienajlepszą opinię, a Demarco nie zapytał ich o zdanie przy wyborze artystów[148].

Z kolei Demarco tak wspomina pobyt w Łodzi:

> Pojechałem do wielkiej Szkoły Filmowej, która stworzyła Polańskiego i Wajdę, gdzie nastąpił najbardziej ekscytujący pokaz filmowy jaki kiedykolwiek widziałem. *Rynek* Józefa Robakowskiego [...] jest bezwzględnie czystą manifestacją wykorzystania medium filmowego. [...] Inny jasno myślący młody reżyser Wojciech Bruszewski był reprezentowany przez dwa niezwykłe filmy *Inwentaryzacja* i *Klaskacz*. Ryszard Gajewski i Paweł Kwiek to dwaj inni filmowcy, którzy pracują w ten sam szczery i świeży sposób, przedstawiając swój punkt widzenia. [...] Później młodzi filmowcy wyprawili dla mnie wyjątkowe przyjęcie w małym mieszkaniu Wojciecha Bruszewskiego i właśnie tam bawił mnie jeden z tych wielkich artystów, jakich zdarzyło mi się poznać – pan Wacek Antczak. Oto on, we fraku, białej koszuli, muszce, kamizelce i wyblakłych, ale fachowo połatanych spodniach (w końcu jest zawodowym krawcem). Przez dwie godziny śpiewał piosenki, które napisał, recytował własne wiersze i z najgłębszym filozoficznym namysłem dyskutował o roli sztuki i artysty. Jego skrzypce były z całą pewnością oryginalnym Stradivariusem, co potwierdzały namalowane na nich białą farbą słowa: „To jest oryginalny Stradivarius". Zaśpiewał żołnierską piosenkę o Łodzi, o tęsknocie za jej dymiącymi fabrycznymi kominami, i słodkogorzką pieśń *Dien Bien Phu* o miłości i wojnie. Odśpiewałem kilka szkockich piosenek, które pamiętałem, a on wydobył ze swoich skrzypiec jeszcze więcej dźwięków, które były dla mnie tak znaczące, jak dysonans dla muzyki Johna Cage'a. Ten sześćdziesięcioletni gentleman, wiecznie młody, pełen pasji życia, uosabiał wyjątkowego ducha polskich artystów. [...] Miałem wrażenie, że jeśli naprawdę zrozumiem tego człowieka, zrozumiem też Polskę[149].

Na zaproszenie Demarco do Edynburga pojechał Robakowski, Gajewski, Bruszewski i Mikołajczyk. Wyjazd, nawet przy zapewnieniu przez organizatorów noclegów, był kosztowny, dlatego nie wszyscy uczestnicy grupy mogli sobie na niego pozwolić. Warsztatowcy zabrali ze sobą projektor do filmów 35 mm, bo Demarco nie mógł znaleźć takiego sprzętu w Edynburgu[150]. Na miejscu artyści z Polski zostali zakwaterowani w domach klubu przyjaciół galerii i otrzymali skromne kieszonkowe, które ledwo starczało na przeżycie w Edynburgu. Gajewski pisze:

> Dobry humor nie opuszczał nas ani na moment. Nawet jak brakowało pieniędzy, a brakowało ich zawsze. Kieszonkowe starczało na dania barowe na przykład „dwa jajka na bekonie" czy „rybę z frytkami". Śniadanie jedliśmy na kwaterze. Gospodarze codziennie zostawiali nam w lodówce dwa serki topione, dwa dżemiki, pieczywo i kawę rozpuszczalną. O tym, że to było dla nas, dowiedzieliśmy się dopiero po kilku dniach pobytu. Widząc w lodówce takie małe ilości jedzenia, kulturalnie nie chcieliśmy wyjadać gospodarzom

148 R. Gajewski, *Warsztat Form Filmowych – początki*, Warszawa 2014 (tekst niepublikowany), s. 26.
149 Ibidem, s. 28.
150 Ibidem, s. 41.

ostatnich serków. Jak się sprawa wyjaśniła – zjadaliśmy wszystkie okruszki. W galerii przez cały dzień była darmowa kawa i zapiekane banany z ryżem na lunch[151].

Wystawa cieszyła się dużym zainteresowaniem. Członkowie WFF wspominają, że obejrzeli ją między innymi Nam June Paik, Charlotte Moorman, a nawet Sean Connery, który należał do klubu przyjaciół galerii i zaprosił Warsztatowców na elegancką kolację. Tematem rozmowy był prezentowany swego czasu w łódzkiej szkole film *Wzgórze*, w którym Connery zagrał główną rolę[152].

W rezultacie wystawy w Edynburgu Warsztat otrzymał kolejne zaproszenia. W tym samym roku grupa pojawiła się na Biennale w São Paulo. Pierwotnie organizatorzy planowali wystawić wyłącznie obiekty fotograficzne Robakowskiego[153], ten jednak zaproponował zbiorowy udział Warsztatu. Propozycja została przyjęta. Członkowie grupy zaproponowali kolektywną realizację *Przekaz osobowości Wacława Antczaka*. Jak pisał Zagrodzki:

> W multimedialnej realizacji artyści, poprzez dokumentację fotograficzną, filmową i dźwiękową, starali się przekazać obraz umiejscowionej na marginesie sfery sztuki, zdeterminowanej biedą, trudnej egzystencji ludowego artysty[154].

W opisie akcji Warsztatowcy informowali:

> Treścią pokazu będzie nobilitacja artysty – przedstawiciela łódzkiego folkloru miejskiego, ukształtowanego przez specyficzny zespół czynników kulturowych:
> poza oficjalnymi prądami artystycznymi
> poza tym, co nazywamy sztuką
> poza wykształceniem artystycznym
> Charakteryzuje go:
> bezinteresowność
> rezygnacja z możliwości stabilizacji życiowej
> szlachetność
> przekonanie o słuszności swego wyboru
> Do realizacji pokazu zostaną zastosowane następujące środki przekazu:
> zapis słowny
> zapis nutowy
> zapis fotograficzny
> filmowy
> magnetofonowy[155]

Rok później Bruszewski, Robakowski i Waśko wzięli udział w V International Experimental Film Competition w Knokke-Heist w Belgii – wydarzeniu, które na dobre uchyliło Warsztatowi bramę Żelaznej Kurtyny. Ich filmy zostały pokazane obok prac takich artystów jak Birgit i Wilhelm Hein, David Hall, Marilyn Halford, Werner Nekes, Tsuneo Nakai, Anthony McCall czy William Raban. Następstwem tego wydarzenia był udział grupy w szeregu pokazów organizowanych w 1975

151 Ibidem, s. 101.
152 Ibidem, s. 77.
153 Wywiad z Józefem Robakowskim, wrzesień 2016.
154 *Wojciech Bruszewski*, s. 68.
155 *Żywa Galeria*, s. 124. Opis dostępny http://repozytorium.fundacjaarton.pl/index.php?action=view/object&objid=3083 [dostęp 30-12-2016].

roku. W samym tylko styczniu i lutym filmy WFF wyświetlono w Folkwang Museum w Essen, Städtische Kunsthalle w Düsseldorfie, X-Screen w Kolonii, Abaton Kino w Hamburgu, Henie Onstad Kunstsenter w Oslo.

Ukoronowaniem zainteresowania twórczością Warsztatowców był ich udział w Dokumenta 6 w Kassel. Wystawa była otwarta od 24 czerwca do 2 października 1977 i składała się z trzech części: 1. Malarstwo, rzeźba, performans; 2. Fotografia, film, wideo; 3. Rysunek, książka, projektowanie. Specyfiką tej edycji wystawy było szczególne podkreślenie roli nowych mediów w sztuce współczesnej. Poświęcono im drugi tom katalogu: *Fotografie, Film, Video.* Prace Warsztatu zostały zakwalifikowane do sekcji filmowej. Tylko Wojciech Bruszewski uczestniczył w sekcji wideo.

Udział w Documenta umocnił pozycję WFF w kręgach europejskiej awangardy. Dopiero stan wojenny wytrącił uczestników grupy z tej wspólnej orbity. Na kilka lat położył kres jakimkolwiek możliwościom podróżowania, znacznie ograniczył też korespondencję polskich artystów z zagranicą.

Kulminacja. Akcja Warsztat w Muzeum Sztuki

Uczestnicy Warsztatu pytani o to, który moment był apogeum ich artystycznej wspólnoty, wskazują akcję Warsztat[156], która odbyła się w Muzeum Sztuki w Łodzi w dniach 31 stycznia – 25 lutego 1973 roku. W tym czasie w grupie nie pojawiły się jeszcze elementy rywalizacji nie obowiązywała hierarchia, pomysły realizowane były wspólnie, a jej członkowie spędzali ze sobą dużo czasu, wzajemnie się inspirując[157]. Jednocześnie to właśnie akcja Warsztat jest tym momentem, w którym zaczęły krystalizować się indywidualne postawy twórców.

Źródła są zgodne co do przebiegu pierwszych dwóch dni akcji[158]. Podczas wernisażu 31 stycznia wykonano fotografie gości, które następnie wyeksponowano w salach muzealnych. Drugiego dnia odbył się natomiast pokaz filmów Bruszewskiego, Junaka, Kwieka, Koterskiego, Robakowskiego i Rybczyńskiego. W opisie kolejnych dni pojawiają się już rozbieżności. Inną kolejność znajdziemy w zaproszeniu na wydarzenie, inną w pracy magisterskiej Ryszarda Waśko. Wiemy jednak z pewnością, że odbyły się następujące działania: *Ocean* – wystawa fotografii Zbigniewa Dłubaka; *Kariera i śmierć Adolfa Hitlera* – spektakl amatorski w reżyserii Edwarda Kowalskiego z udziałem członków Warsztatu; *Fakty muzyczne, czyli koncert dyletantów* – spontaniczny występ z wykorzystaniem instrumentów dostarczonych przez organizatorów; *Skrzyżowanie* i *Drzwi* Bruszewskiego; *Komunikat audiowizualny* Robakowskiego; *Elektroniczna antynomia* Połoma; *Tekst–zapis–rejestracja, Zapis fotograficzny* oraz *Konstrukcja* Mikołajczyka; *Seans telewizyjny* i *Identyfikacja pozorna* Różyckiego, *Kwiekołom* i Łomokwiek Kwieka i Łomnickiego[159], *Dźwięk–barwa–ruch (misterium w świetle ultrafiolet)* Bendkowskiego oraz akcja zbiorowa *Podpis artystyczny.*

Do realizacji akcji w Muzeum Sztuki zaprosił Warsztatowców jego ówczesny dyrektor, Ryszard Stanisławski[160] – poniekąd w rezultacie ich udziału w Atelier '72. Głównym założeniem wydarzenia było to, że odbędzie się „w procesie". Sale na pierwszym piętrze zostały opróżnione i stały się „miejscem akcji". Każdego dnia odbywał się inny pokaz, przygotowany przez konkretnego

156 Na podstawie relacji Józefa Robakowskiego, Andrzeja Różyckiego, Kazimierza Bendkowskiego i Ryszarda Waśki.
157 Wywiad z Andrzejem Różyckim, lipiec 2014.
158 Zob. *Żywa Galeria*, s. 134 oraz R. Waśko, op.cit., s. 44–74.
159 Zob. autorski opis Pawła Kwieka w: R. Waśko, op. cit., s. 57.
160 Wywiad z Józefem Robakowskim, wrzesień 2016.

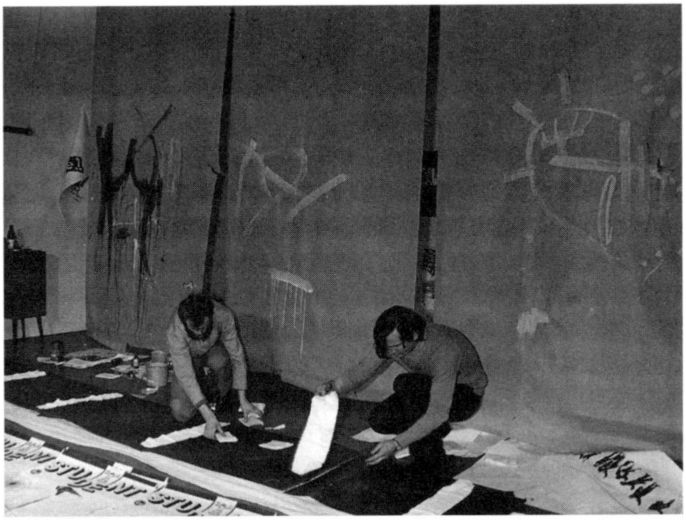

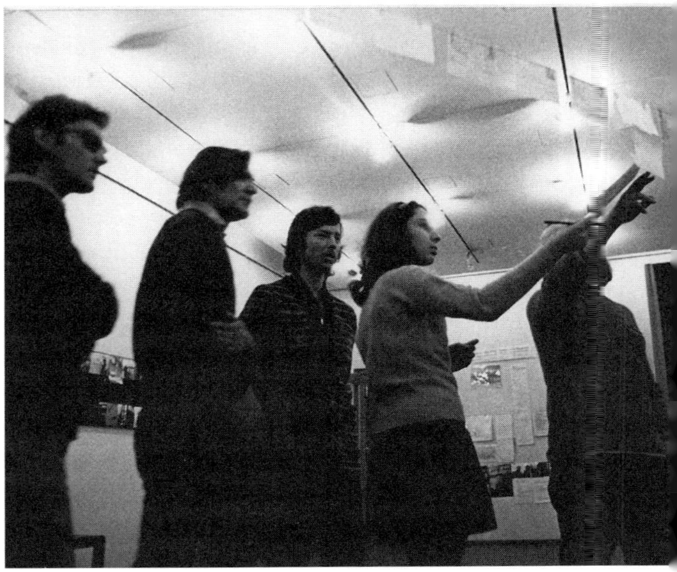

Akcja Warsztat w Muzeum Sztuki, 1973
Action Workshop, Museum of Art, Łódź, 1973

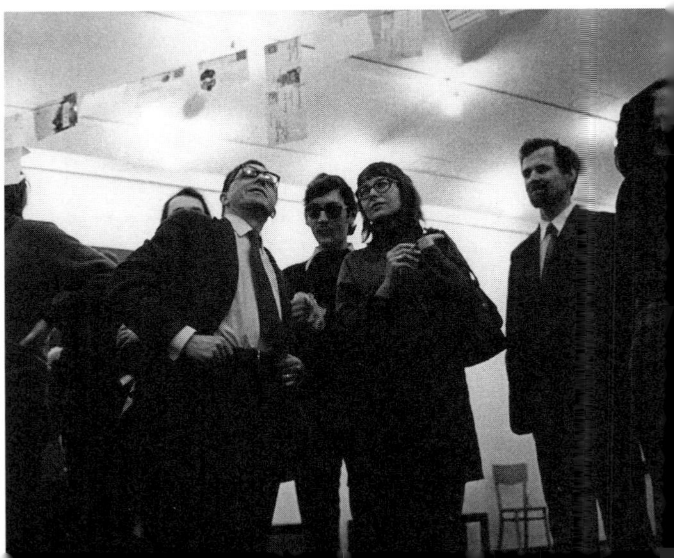

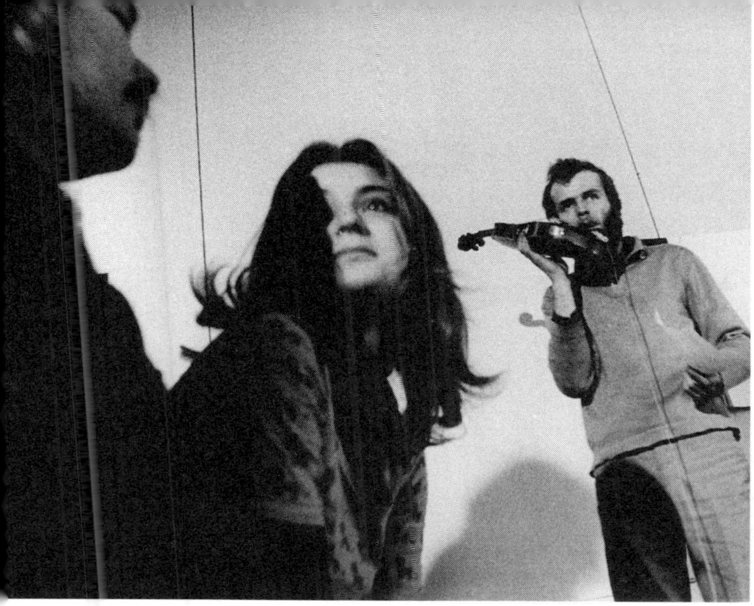

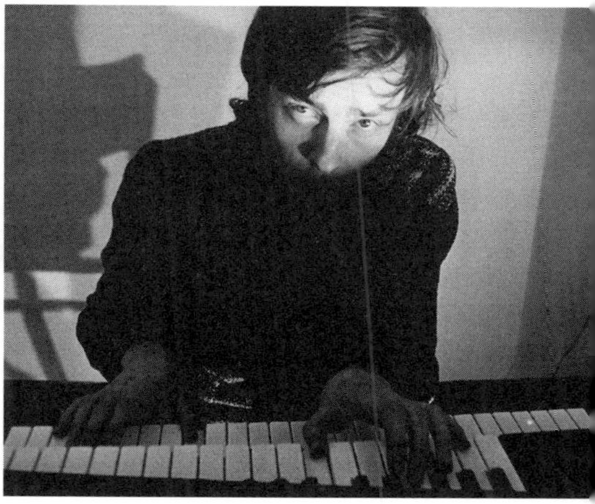

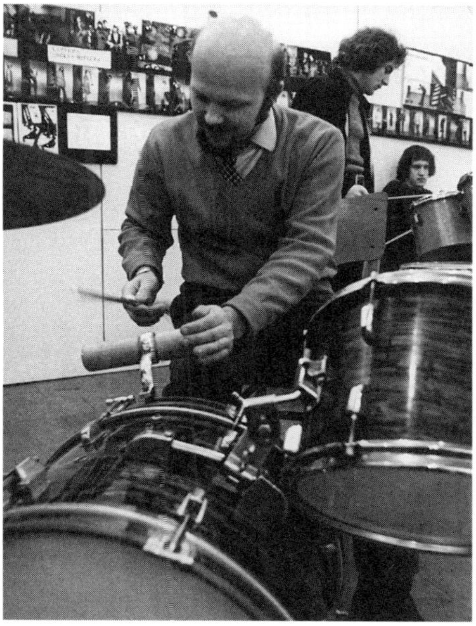

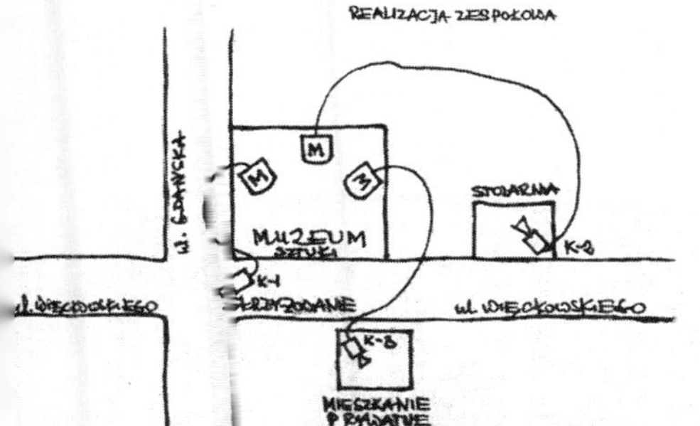
REALIZACJA ZESPOŁOWA
MUZEUM
SZTUKI
STOLARNIA
K-1
K-2
K-3
W. WIĘCKOWSKIEGO
MIESZKANIE
PRYWATNE
TRANSMISJA TELEWIZYJNA /INSTALACJA/
/MUZEUM SZTUKI - AKCJA "WARSZTAT" 11.2.'78 r./

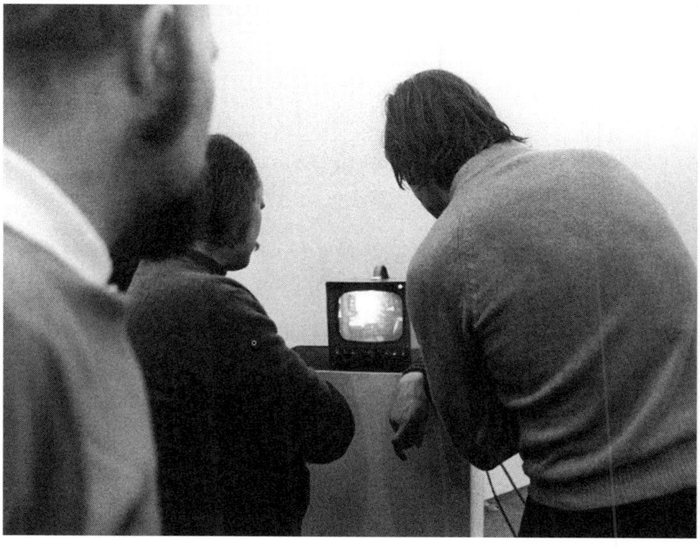

autora lub pomyślany jako działanie zbiorowe. Część z nich, pomimo zasadniczo efemerycznego charakteru, wymagała dość poważnych przygotowań. Tak było na przykład z otwartym konkursem na podpis artystyczny. Uczestnicy mieli nadsyłać swoje propozycje na kartkach pocztowych, co odpowiednio wcześniej ogłoszono w prasie. Było to jedno z wielu działań, mających na celu angażowanie publiczności. Inny przykład to akcja *Fakty muzyczne, czyli koncert dyletantów*, podczas której Warsztatowcy i muzealna publiczność odegrali wspólny koncert na instrumentach dostarczonych przez organizatorów.

Warsztatowcy przyjęli, że na akcję Warsztat złożą się trzy rodzaje pokazów: zapożyczone – realizatorzy nie byli autorami, umożliwili jedynie ich zaistnienie; penetrujące problemy języka – autor uruchamiał jedynie środek przekazu, rezygnując z kreacyjności; artystyczne – środki przekazu były całkowicie podporządkowane idei autora.[161]

Konkurs na podpis artystyczny i *Fakty muzyczne, czyli koncert dyletantów* zostały w pracy magisterskiej Ryszarda Waśko opisane jako działanie typu A. Do tej grupy Warsztatowcy zaliczyli również spektakl *Kariera i śmierć Adolfa Hitlera*, który był kolejnym przykładem ich współpracy z reżyserem Edwardem Kowalskim[162], a także *Seans telewizyjny* Różyckiego, który był pierwszą polską pracą zrealizowaną z wykorzystaniem emitowanego przez telewizję programu, wpisującą się tym samym w szereg prekursorskich realizacji, takich jak *Television Décollage* Wolfa Vostella czy realizacje Nam June Paika. Na ich tle gest Różyckiego wyróżnia nie tyle otwartość na interakcję z odbiorcami (co charakteryzowało też na przykład pracę *Exposition of Music – Electronic Television* Nam June Paika, w której widzowie zakłócali program telewizyjny), co całkowitą redukcją gestu artystycznego.

Co ciekawe do grupy A nie została zaliczona przełomowa *Transmisja telewizyjna*. Była to pierwsza w Polsce praca wykonana w technice wideo (realizacja nie była rejestrowana na taśmie; przypomnijmy, że pierwszą zarejestrowaną taśmą w Polsce był *Język obrazkowy* z tego samego roku zrealizowana za pomocą trzech wozów transmisyjnych należących do Szkoły Filmowej). Polegała na mechanicznym przekazie obrazów z ulicy, warsztatu stolarskiego i prywatnego mieszkania do sali muzealnej. Artyści nie poczynili żadnej ingerencji w transmisję. Ten radykalny i oszczędny gest świadczył o tym, że uczestnicy grupy są zainteresowani codziennością nie tylko jako źródłem inspiracji, lecz wręcz jako tworzywem sztuki. *Transmisja telewizyjna* została oznaczona symbolem B. Podobnie jak *Skrzyżowanie* Bruszewskiego, które również było transmisją, tym razem dźwiękową. Tak opisuje ją sam twórca:

> Cztery mikrofony zainstalowane na rogach skrzyżowania Więckowskiego i Gdańskiej połączono (poprzez wzmacniacze) z czterema kolumnami głośnikowymi odpowiednio ustawionymi w rogach sali wystawowej. Przez cały dzień przestrzeń dźwiękowa skrzyżowania ulic istniała również w galerii[163].

Również Antoni Mikołajczyk zrealizował pracę, która polegała na wprowadzeniu tego, co na zewnątrz do wnętrza muzeum. Artysta opisał projekt następująco:

> Nie zmieniając położenia aparatu fotograficznego, dokonywano co pół godziny zdjęcia wi-

161 R. Waśko, op. cit., s. 50.

162 Warsztatowcy brali udział we wcześniejszych jego przedstawieniach, a Różycki zrealizował o nim swój film dyplomowy *Kowalski*.

163 R. Waśko, op. cit., s. 56.

doku podwórka z fragmentem ulicy na barwnym diapozytywie. W efekcie rejestrowano na zdjęciach zmiany barwy otoczenia, ulotność nastroju chwili i życia mieszkańców nieprzerwanie przez 30 godzin. W sali wystawowej wyświetlono, nie zmieniając kolejności, serię otrzymanych diapozytywów. Projekcję tę uzupełniono efektami akustycznymi nagranymi na taśmie magnetofonowej, pochodzącymi z miejsca fotografowanego[164].

Poszczególne prace zrealizowane w ramach akcji Warsztat mogą być dziś odczytywane jako początek indywidualnej drogi twórczej większości uczestników grupy. Całość tego działania powinna być jednak rozpatrywana przede wszystkim jako współczesny i radykalny gest Warsztatu, polegający na zawładnięciu przestrzenią muzealną. Tym w istocie była decyzja artystów o realizowaniu prac „na miejscu" oraz konfrontowaniu widzów z procesem ich powstawania. Nieprzypadkowa była też przestrzeń tych działań. Warsztatowcy potraktowali Muzeum Sztuki – miejsce związane wprost z łódzką przedwojenną awangardą – jako fragment miasta. Realizacje polegające na transmisji do muzeum obrazu z łódzkich ulic są echem rozważań Katarzyny Kobro o przestrzeni miejskiej. Gest ten otwierał instytucję na Łódź i jego mieszkańców, zamieniając wyizolowanyo *white cube* w przestrzeń otwartą na widza oraz jego postrzeganie sztuki i świata (co dodatkowo podkreśliły działania angażujące publiczność).

Warsztat i polityka

Zaczęliśmy sobie wtedy zdawać sprawę, że działalność twórcza wobec rzeczywistości jest możliwa tylko w ten sposób, żeby nie dać się w tę rzeczywistość wciągnąć, nie dać się wplątać ani w kontemplację ani protest, natomiast działać tak, żeby zaistnieć jako osobowość swojego czasu, niezależnie i samoistnie, a jednak właśnie dlatego – bezpośrednio oddziaływać na rzeczywistość, kształtować ją i krytycznie opisywać.

Józef Robakowski w rozmowie z Maciejem Szybistem

W momencie, w którym pracujemy nad niniejszą publikacją, mamy do czynienia z kolejną falą sporu o ocenę spuścizny PRL. Odbywa się on na gruncie zbudowanym z propagandy, mitologizacji, wyparcia, niepamięci, niewiedzy, nie zaś na faktycznej rewizji przeszłości. Podobnie sytuacja wyglądała jeszcze kilka lat temu w obszarze historii sztuki. W ostatnim okresie wydawane są kolejne publikacje dotyczące ówczesnych zjawisk, środowisk czy poszczególnych twórców, nadal jednak brakuje opracowania, które stanowiłoby pełną diagnozę sytuacji artystów wizualnych w PRL. Tymczasem, aby dobrze zrozumieć ich historię, nie możemy abstrahować od ich relacji wobec władzy. Dlatego postaram się teraz pokrótce opowiedzieć o tym, w co członkowie Warsztatu nie chcieli dać się wciągnąć i co chcieli kształtować – czyli o politycznych uwarunkowaniach tak zwanego „okresu gierkowskiego" w Polsce.

Przed nami zrobił to Lechosław Olszewski, który w 1998 roku napisał prekursorski esej *Działalność Warsztatu Formy Filmowej jako przykład strategii sztuki wobec władzy w Polsce lat siedemdziesiątych.* Autor jako pierwszy ujął twórczość WFF w szersze polityczne ramy, wnikliwie przyglądając się funkcjonowaniu grupy na przecięciu sztuk wizualnych i kinematografii. Decydenci interesowali się kinem w daleko większym stopniu, dlatego też Warsztat – pozycjonując się w ten sposób –

164 Ibidem, s. 64.

ustawił się na wyjątkowej pozycji względem władzy. Olszewski uwypukla ten aspekt działalności grupy, a jego esej mógłby być uznany za wyczerpujące omówienie zagadnienia, gdyby nie pomijał jednego ważnego wątku – tego, że WFF działał w strukturach Szkoły Filmowej. Z punktu widzenia władzy komunistycznej była to instytucja kluczowa, Warsztatowcy natomiast – próbowali ją zmienić.

Zanim jednak przejdziemy do tematu szkoły, zarysujmy pokrótce kontekst historyczny. Presja wywierana na artystów przez cenzurę była najsilniejsza w okresie realizmu socjalistycznego. Po 1956 roku nastąpiła odwilż, a socrealistyczna doktryna uległa złagodzeniu. Jednocześnie zarysował się podział sztuki na sztukę nieoficjalną i oficjalną. Oficjalny obieg – związany z wyższym uczelniami, Ministerstwem Kultury i Sztuki oraz związkami twórczymi – pozostawał w rękach władzy, a kręgi wobec niej opozycyjne tworzyły własne mniej lub bardziej trwałe instytucje w ramach różnego rodzaju struktur prawno-administracyjnych. W latach 60. były to organizacje związane z, jak pisał Olszewski, odrzuceniem tradycji obrazu i jego muzealnego kontekstu, takie jak Galeria EL w Elblągu, Galeria odNowa w Poznaniu, Galeria Pod Moną Lizą we Wrocławiu, Galeria Współczesna i Galeria Foksal w Warszawie. Ośrodki te wyłamywały się w pewnym sensie z systemu, pozostając jednocześnie jego częścią[165]. W latach 70. pojawiły się natomiast galerie autorskie, takie jak Permafo, Galeria Sztuki Aktualnej czy Remont, które charakteryzowały się mniej formalnymi (lub całkiem nieformalnymi) strukturami.

Obydwa nurty – oficjalny i nieoficjalny – różniły się między sobą. Kiedy porzucono socrealizm, nurt oficjalny zdominowała „unowocześniona (post-odwilżowa), ale też uwspółcześniona (figuratywna) tradycja kolorystyczna"[166]. Z kolei kręgi awangardowe zamknęły się w latach 60. na rzeczywistość, co można tłumaczyć reakcją na wcześniejsze próby kontrolowania ich twórczości. Przejawiło się to refleksją konceptualną i autotematyczną analizą wykorzystywanych mediów. Artyści wycofywali się w obszar, w którym dzieło sztuki miało być pozbawione odniesień, tak by uniknąć zawłaszczenia przez ideologię. Było to oczywiście dość naiwne przekonanie. To właśnie lęk przed wpływem ze strony władzy, oddalenie się od rzeczywistości i brak wyedukowanych odbiorców spowodowały, że sztuka straciła wpływ na rzeczywistość. W efekcie, jak pisał Olszewski, „rytuał sympozjów, plenerów, wystaw, zlotów, spotkań, prezentacji [...] wspierał tworzenie mitologii sukcesu". A działo się to, przypomnijmy, w obiegu „nieoficjalnym", nieutożsamiającym się z systemem. Awangarda została więc przez władzę „otorbiona". Nie stanowiła zagrożenia, lecz świat równoległy.

Sztuka tylko incydentalnie wchodziła w interakcję z codziennością. Artyści realizowali czasem działania w przestrzeni publicznej lub podejmowali nieliczne próby oddziaływania na państwowe instytucje kultury. Rzadkie próby poruszania w latach 60. i 70. tematów wprost opozycyjnych lub erotycznych kończyły się – szczególnie w tym drugim przypadku – zdecydowaną i szybką reakcją cenzury. Opór Warsztatowców wobec systemu objawiał się głównie na dwa pierwsze sposoby – poprzez wykonywanie „interwencji" i organizowanie własnych imprez pozbawionych jurorów, werdyktów i nagród. Wszystkie te działania, podobnie jak realizacje filmowe, realizowali od początku do końca własnym sumptem – niekomercyjnie i bezinteresownie. Równie ważne były teksty Robakowskiego, w szczególności *Paszkwil na kinematografię*[167] i list z 1975 roku, w którym artysta informuje ówczesnego ministra kultury o „rezygnacji z dalszej współpracy z Polską

165 L. Olszewski, op. cit., s. 114.

166 Ibidem, s. 115.

167 Józef Robakowski, *Paszkwil...*, s. 92–93.

kinematografią”[168]. Najważniejszy jest jednak wyjątkowy sposób, w jaki grupa określiła swoje miejsce w obszarze kinematografii i w jaki funkcjonowała w obrębie Szkoły Filmowej.

Warsztat odrzucał kontrolowaną w znacznym stopniu przez władzę twórczość fabularną. Warsztatowcy posiadali narzędzia do realizowania masowych wydarzeń i wysokobudżetowych produkcji filmowych, ale porzucili tę możliwość na rzecz bezinteresownego działania, niezależnego programu i ustawicznych prób skompromitowania oficjalnego obiegu kultury. W dobie nachalnie lansowanego socjalistycznego sukcesu epoki Gierka, członkowie Warsztatu wykorzystywali struktury Filmówki do tego, aby tworzyć filmy nienarzucające widzowi wizji świata. Były to dzieła otwarte na odbiorcę. Widz był w nich traktowany jako podmiot obdarzony indywidualną zdolnością percypowania świata. Ponadto niektóre prace grupy mogą być interpretowane jako próby uwrażliwienia publiczności na strategie cenzorskie i propagandowe, choć byli uczestnicy grupy nie zawsze zgadzają się z takim odczytaniem ich prac[169].

Warto wspomnieć w tym kontekście o realizacjach Warsztatu, które powstawały dzięki przekazaniu kamer i taśm filmowych nieprofesjonalnym twórcom.

Nie należy wreszcie zapominać o tym, że działalność Warsztatu była obliczona na zmianę metod kształcenia i modelu funkcjonowania Szkoły Filmowej – instytucji, stanowiącej istotną część systemu władzy. Do pierwszych takich prób doszło już w semestrze zimowym 1966 roku, kiedy to przyszli członkowie grupy – w reakcji na inercję kadry, niedobory materiałów oraz brak pomysłu na kształcenie – zainicjowali bunt studentów. Jak wspomina Robakowski: „Zwołaliśmy sejm, na który zaprosiliśmy profesorów, dziekanów, prorektorów i Toeplitza”[170]. Inicjatywa ta nie przyniosła natychmiastowej poprawy[171], ale nastroje w Szkole zmieniły się. Na fali Marca 1968 studenci Filmówki dołączyli do ogólnopolskich protestów i poparli żądania dotyczące demokratyzacji szkolnictwa. Wstawił się za nimi rektor Jerzy Toeplitz, który w rezultacie został usunięty ze stanowiska. Późniejsze represje osłabiły i tak już wątłą kondycję Filmówki. Dorobek zaangażowanej, powojennej kinematografii był dyskredytowany przez partię. Wajdzie, Munkowi i innym reżyserom Polskiej Szkoły Filmowej wytykano antypolskość i defetyzm, zalecając poszukiwanie optymizmu, który miałby natchnąć społeczeństwo do walki o socjalizm.

W tej sytuacji strategia Robakowskiego i całego Warsztatu wydaje się być jedyną alternatywą. Dawała grupie możliwość działania, jednocześnie oddalając groźbę dostania się w strefę wpływów władzy. Co ciekawe, członkowie Warsztatu zostali po latach asystentami w Szkole Filmowej. Udało się to Robakowskiemu, Rybczyńskiemu, Lenczewskiemu, Waśce, Junakowi i Kwiekowi, a Janusz Połom w 1981 roku został nawet dziekanem Wydziału Operatorskiego (wybranym głosami studentów Filmówki). Obecnie w Szkole Filmowej w Łodzi nadal uczy prof. Józef Robakowski (zwolniony z uczelni w okresie stanu wojennego), a także prof. Ryszard Lenczewski. W 2016 roku dziekanem Wydziału Operatorskiego i Realizacji Telewizyjnej został prof. Zbigniew Wichłacz, który współpracował z Warsztatem przy realizacji niektórych filmów, między innymi *Bezdechu* Bruszewskiego.

168 Ibidem.

169 Na podstawie rozmów z Pawłem Kwiekiem, lipiec 2015.

170 K. Krubski et al., op. cit., s. 185.

171 Członkowie Warsztatu uaktywnią się w podobny sposób w 1980 roku, tworząc – w kontekście szerszych politycznych zmian tamtego czasu – Ruch Odnowy Uczelni.

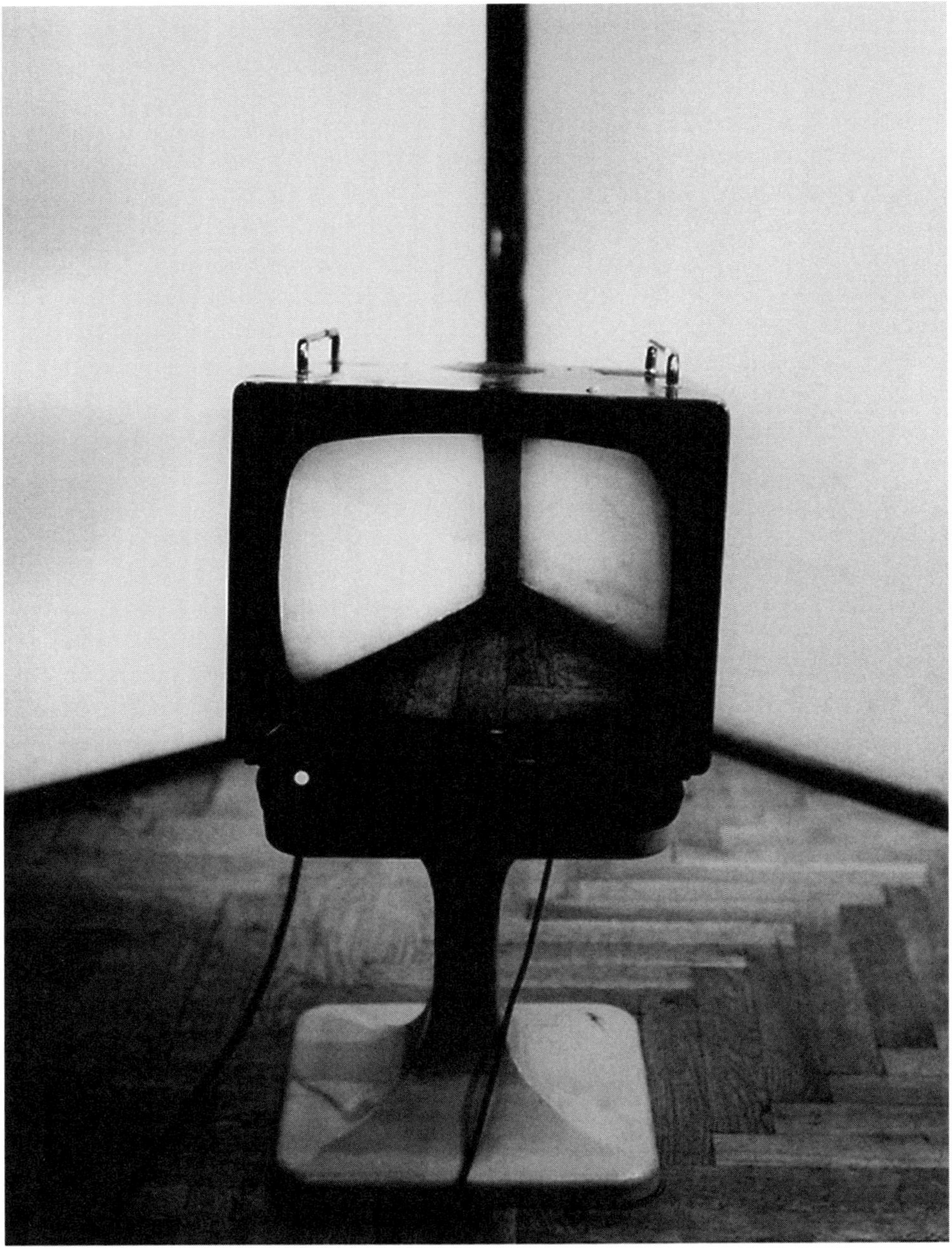

Ryszard Waśko, *Róg*, 1976, instalacja wideo
Ryszard Waśko, *A Corner*, 1976, video installation

Mike Sperlinger

Tautologiczne kino: kilka uwag na temat oczywistości w działach twórców Warsztatu Formy Filmowej

Tautologia zostawia rzeczywistości całą — nieskończoną — przestrzeń logiczną; sprzeczność wypełnia całą przestrzeń logiczną, nie zostawiając rzeczywistości ani punktu. Stąd żadna z nich nie może nijak rzeczywistości określać.
Ludwig Wittgenstein, *Traktat logiczno-filozoficzny* (przeł. Bogusław Wolniewicz)

Oczywistość zawsze musi być wytworzona.
Alexander García Düttmann

1.

W swym ostatnim dziele, *Teorii estetycznej* – wydanej w tym samym roku (1970), gdy utworzono Warsztat Formy Filmowej – Theodor Adorno pisał: „Stało się oczywiste, że wszystko, co dotyczy sztuki, przestało być oczywiste, zarówno w obrębie jej samej, jak i w jej stosunku do całości, nawet jej racja istnienia" [1]. Zdanie Adorno wydaje się być otwarte na co najmniej dwie interpretacje, które zależą od tego, jak pojmujemy dwa znaczenia słowa „oczywistość". Pierwsza i najbardziej jednoznaczna interpretacja to taka, według której j e d y n ą oczywistą rzeczą na temat sztuki jest dla Adorno to, że już nic nie można o niej powiedzieć jednoznacznego i oczywistego. Jednak pod tą interpretacją wydaje się skrywać możliwość drugiej, bardziej paradoksalnej, będącej wariantem słynnego „paradoksu kłamcy": jeśli nic na temat sztuki nie jest już oczywiste, to czy objęte tym prawem jest także owo „oczywiste" stwierdzenie? A jeśli tak – jeśli w rzeczy samej nie może być oczywiste to, że „wszystko, co dotyczy sztuki, przestało być oczywiste" – jakie rodzaje oczywistości w sztuce mogłaby ta sprzeczność wyrazić dla odbiorców?

Z perspektywy czterech dekad, które minęły od ich powstania, jedną z najbardziej rzucających się w oczy cech filmów stworzonych przez artystów związanych z Warsztatem jest ich totalna, rażąca oczywistość. To są dzieła, które wydają się dopominać oczywistości, a nawet tępej dosłowności. Podczas gdy dla Adorno dzieło sztuki zawsze łączyło się z „enigmatycznością" – oporem stawianym językowi, programowi czy parafrazie – wiele filmów artystów tworzących w tym czasie w Łodzi wydaje się niemal bezmyślnymi w swojej klarowności. Ich „stosunek do świata" jest kolejno aksjomatyczny, schematyczny, diagramatyczny i dydaktyczny. Wydają się wciąż uparcie tłumaczyć same siebie, wyjawiając swoją strukturę, realizując swój zamysł.

Jeśli na chwilę zgodzimy się, że lata funkcjonowania Warsztatu był czasem, gdy nawet „prawo do istnienia" nie było już dla sztuki oczywiste – a z pewnością nie w peerelowskim reżimie

---

1 T. W. Adorno, *Teoria estetyczna*, przeł. K. Krzemieniowa, Warszawa: PWN, 1994. s. 1.

tamtego okresu – jak mamy odczytać te zadziwiające dzieła, które wydają się bronić swych racji, uparcie ukazując, iż nie mają nic do ukrycia?

2.

Znakiem rozpoznawczym wielu dzieł stworzonych w Warsztacie Formy Filmowej jest wykorzystywanie języka eksperymentu. Należy jednak dodać, że chodzi tu o bardziej konkretne i głębsze znaczenia tego terminu niż w generycznym „kinie eksperymentalnym", którego to określenia używali w tym samym czasie filmowcy w Europie Zachodnie i Stanach Zjednoczonych.

To ostatnie wyrażenie – zwykle stosowane zamiennie z „kinem awangardowym" – jest w języku potocznym rodzajem luźnej, poetyckiej impresji na temat „eksperymentu", którą miał na myśli filozof i poeta Hans Magnus Enzensberger, kiedy pisał w 1962 roku, że „eksperyment jako koncept estetyczny długo był częścią słownika przemysłu świadomości (...) ten koncept jest nonsensowny i bezużyteczny"[2]. Według Enzensbergera artyści zbyt często bezprawnie nadużywali pojęcia „eksperyment" , ignorując rygor metodologii i używając go wyłącznie po to, żeby zrzucić z siebie odpowiedzialność: „Nazwa e k s p e r y m e n t pozwala awangardzie usprawiedliwiać rezultaty swoich poczynań [...] i obarczać całą odpowiedzialnością odbiorcę"[3].

Filmy artystów związanych z Warsztatem wydają się – przynajmniej na pierwszy rzut oka – należeć do innej kategorii dzieł. Zamiast używać terminu „eksperyment" jako parasola ochronnego o nieograniczonym zastosowaniu, twórcy Warsztatu często wydają się go stosować jako rodzaj techniki ograniczającej i deklarację obiektywności. Od samego początku bardzo agresywnie posługiwali się oni w swoich dziełach językiem konkretnych naukowych badań, co widać we wczesnych filmach Józefa Robakowskiego z cyklu *Test*, a także „Manifeście Warsztatu" z 1975 roku, który mówił, iż obszarem zainteresowań twórców grupy jest „działalność paranaukowa, zimna i wykalkulowana artystyczna teoria i praktyka"[4]. Właśnie to sprawia, że ich dzieła są tak trudne do analizy: u d o w a d n i a j ą istnienie problemów w sposób, który wciąż wydaje się zaskakujący dla dzieła sztuki. Często kładą nacisk na fakt, że są raczej „wykalkulowane" niż spontaniczne: mówią nam z góry, co mają zamiar przedstawić, jak *30 sytuacji dźwiękowych* (1975) Ryszarda Waśki; lub używają diagramów, żeby wytłumaczyć swoje powstanie, jak *Video P* (1975) Pawła Kwieka; używają naukowych instrumentów, jak oscyloskop w *Alfabecie* (1974) Janusza Połoma; realizują zaprogramowane procedury, jak taksonomia ruchów kamery w *Układ I-VI* (1973) wspomnianego już Waśki.

3.

Oczywiście w Warsztacie powstawały różnorodne filmy i nie wszystkie pasują do powyższego wzoru. Na przykład obraz Kazimierza Bendkowskiego *Obszar* (1973) – wykonany w poetyce snu nieco złowieszczy portret mieszkańców walącej się kamienicy – ucieleśnia tę samą energię, co surrealizm czy Fluxus (a może konkretniej, co twórczość Franciszki i Stefana Themersonów),

---

2 H. M. Enzensberger, 'Aporias of the Avant-Garde', przeł. J. Simon, w: *The Consciousness Industry*, Nowy Jork: Continuum, 1974, s. 36.

3 Ibidem.

4 „Manifest Warsztatu Formy Filmowej autorstwa Bruszewskiego", Muzeum Sztuki Nowoczesnej w Warszawie, http:// artmuseum.pl/pl/archiwum/wojciech-bruszewski-2/2408?read=all [dostęp 14-10-2016].

zaś wyreżyserowany przez Marka Koterskiego film *Ech* (1972) to bezkompromisowy i emocjonalny dokument o alkoholizmie utrzymany w buñuelowskiej poetyce.

Żeby łatwiej opisać zróżnicowane produkcje Warsztatu, można by użyć terminu „studia", w pełnym, semantycznym sensie tego słowa. Z jednej strony mamy filmy, które są studiami w sensie modelu w sztukach wizualnych albo etiudy w sensie muzycznym – przychodzi tu na myśl film Bendkowskiego *Centrum* (1973), z oślepiającym i wesołym nakładaniem się neonów, lamp ulicznych i świateł samochodów, które wydaje się dużo bliższe poetyckim eksploracjom patrzenia, typowym dla niektórych artystów amerykańskich tego okresu. (Nie może zaskakiwać, że tego rodzaju studia powstały w Warsztacie, ponieważ był on mimo wszystko częścią Państwowej Wyższej Szkoły Filmowej – David Curtis również zauważył charakter „szkolnego ćwiczenia" w niektórych dziełach twórców tej placówki[5].) Z drugiej strony wiele dzieł ma charakter studiów w bardziej naukowym sensie; studiów, które rozwinął na przykład Waśko – według kuratora Łukasza Rondudy – przesuwając „swoje poszukiwania w sferę laboratoryjnych operacji, budowania a następnie testowania modeli abstrakcyjnych[6]".

Filmy autorstwa uczestników Warsztatu można zatem umieścić w kompozycyjnym spektrum, gdzieś pomiędzy błazenadą a naukową analizą. Powyższa obserwacja dobrze charakteryzuje dzieło Bruszewskiego, a jego obrazy są często dziwną mieszanką stylów. Na przykład *Audiowizualne poszukiwanie: zapałki* (1975) czy *Stoper* (1976), które okazują się dociekaniami na temat wizualnej/dźwiękowej percepcji, doprawionej odrobiną śmiertelnie poważnego absurdu, są przeciwieństwem takich dzieł jak *YYAA* (1973), gdzie strukturalny opis relacji między dźwiękiem a obrazem przechodzi w bardziej bezpośrednią clownadę. W przypadku innych artystów rozgraniczenie pomiędzy powyższymi dwoma rodzajami studiów jest samo w sobie wysoce enigmatyczne.

W filmie Waśki *Prosto-krzywa* (1973) widzimy serię scen ulicznych, na które nakładają się animowane, czarne kształty geometryczne; może się to wydawać archetypicznym studium artystycznym, formalnym dociekaniem na temat tego, jak odczytujemy głębię w dwuwymiarowości filmowego obrazu – ale kształty te także nieświadomie zapowiadają *Telewizję Solidarność* (1985), czyli akcję sabotażową polegającą na zakłócaniu programu Telewizji Polskiej, rozpoczętą przez naukowców z Uniwersytetu im. Mikołaja Kopernika w Toruniu. W słynnych transmisjach we wrześniu 1985 roku naukowcy zdołali nałożyć na obraz rządowego Dziennika Telewizyjnego slogany solidarności, używając prymitywnego sprzętu nadawczego („Dość podwyżek cen, kłamstw i represji. Solidarność Toruń"). Wcześniej w testowych transmisjach nakładali na obraz telewizyjny proste figury geometryczne – te zabiegi bardzo przypominały pływające kształty Waśki. Właśnie owo artystyczne echo – dziwne i zupełnie przypadkowe – jest chyba pierwszym śladem politycznego potencjału pozornie najbardziej beznamiętnych „eksperymentów": wskazuje na możliwość zakwestionowania oficjalnie sterowanej i przekazywanej rzeczywistości.

---

5 S. Ball., D. Curtis, 'Poles and Angles: A Late-Night E-mail Conversation about Polish and English Structural Film', w: *1,2,3... Avant-Gardes (The Experiment Art and Film)*, red. Ł. Ronduda, F. Zeyfang, Berlin – Nowy Jork: Sternberg Press 2007, s. 60.

6 Ł. Ronduda, *Sztuka polska lat 70.*, Warszawa: Centrum Sztuki Współczesnej Zamek Ujazdowski, 2009, s. 291.

4.

Ale jak oceniać filmy, które natarczywie mówią odbiorcy, co mają zamiar przedstawić – aluzyjnie czy bezpośrednio – a następnie ten zamiar wykonują? Weźmy film *Ja i telefon* (1972) Pawła Kwieka. Przez trzy minuty ekran pozostaje czarny, podczas gdy głos na ścieżce dźwiękowej opisuje w czasie teraźniejszym improwizowany film, który wykonał autor, ale którego nie możemy zobaczyć: „22 grudnia 1972 roku rano dostałem 90m filmu TF7 i teraz wkładam go do kamery pożyczonej na pół godziny od przyjaciela, który robi film na pracę zaliczeniową..." Głos opowiada, jak poprosił kolegę ze studiów, żeby go sfilmował, gdy pali papierosa i wykonuje serię prostych czynności. W drugiej części filmu widzimy niemą projekcję obrazu, o którego „produkcji" opowiadał Kwiek w części pierwszej, a na postaci narratora pojawia się przebitka białego, masywnego aparatu telefonicznego z odłożoną na bok słuchawką, który przypadkowo znalazł się w zasięgu kamery artysty, a także przebitki gałęzi drzewa, czy też może choinki.

Wiele filmów twórców związanych z Warsztatem posiada tę właściwość – może nie tyle są eksperymentami, co przykładami czy egzemplifikacjami: wiernie realizują bezpośrednio wyrażone artystyczne przesłanki. Niektóre stosują taksonomiczne podejście: *Alfabet* (1974) Janusza Połoma pokazuje pierwsze litery alfabetu a później oscyloskop rejestrujący dźwięk litery, która jest wymawiana, i widz natychmiast rozumie schemat i sposób, w jaki zostanie odegrany. Niektóre rejestrują jeszcze prostsze działania, których rezultaty opisane są w ich tytułach, jak na przykład *Podróż Wacława Antczaka do kiosku na ulicy Głównej* (1973) autorstwa Waśki, gdzie w pierwszych kilku sekundach ujęcia kamera mija pana Antczaka, stojącego obok roweru, a później chwiejące się ujęcie z kamery na jego plecach ukazuje przybliżający się kiosk.

Inna wariacja wykorzystuje odliczanie. Niektóre filmy mówią nam z góry, ile dokładnie sekcji będą zawierały, co ma miejsce w filmie *30 sytuacji dźwiękowych* Waśki, inne robią z odliczania główną z przedstawianych czynności, jak w obrazie *Idę* (1973) Robakowskiego, gdzie narrator liczy stopnie, które pokonuje. *Numerki* (1973) Kwieka to kolejny dobry przykład: odliczanie na rozbiegówce taśmy filmowej, które pomaga operatorowi w synchronizacji (i jest normalnie niewidoczne dla publiczności), zostaje zapętlone i puszczane przez 7 minut i 52 sekundy z kolażowym podkładem muzycznym. Kiedy obejrzymy pętlę kilka razy, dokładnie wiemy, jak będzie wyglądała reszta filmu. Kwiek celowo unika podejścia swojego rówieśnika, Guya Sherwina – członka grupy London Filmmakers' Coop – który w 1974 roku stworzył na taśmie 16mm krótki film pod tytułem *At the Academy* [*W Akademii*]. Film Sherwina jest także oparty na odliczaniu z rozbiegówki i rozpoczyna się identycznie, ale szybko zamienia się w grę migoczących nakładek, wykorzystującą optyczne nadruki do zakłócenia kolejności wyświetlania liczb, i prezentuje same liczby jako element formalny. *W Akademii* to dzieło same siebie modyfikujące – dzieło, które wykorzystuje przypadkową jednorazowość taśmy filmowej i zamienia ją w wizualny eksperyment (tytuł nadaje procesowi odkrywania dodatkową, metaforyczną wagę). *Numerki* Kwieka, wprost przeciwnie, odrzucają grę modyfikacji i wizualnej atrakcyjności, które wynikają z metafory; w zamian prowokacyjnie oferują widzowi jedynie dosłowne (przynajmniej w warstwie obrazu) odtworzenie swojego tytułu.

Jest coś osobliwie dziwnego we wszystkich tych dziełach. David Curtis, wrażliwy i pełen fachowej wiedzy ekspert w tematyce Warsztatu, dotknął sedna tego problemu, gdy zauważył, iż polscy artyści z tamtego okresu „wpadli w pułapkę nadmiernych nakazów", choć mimo to – dodał niemal jednym tchem – gdy zobaczył ich filmy pierwszy raz, „ich inwencja był niespodzianką"[7]. Preskryptywność – czyli oczywistość, nacisk na programowość, wyraźne unikanie niespodzianki czy narracyjnego rozwoju – paradoksalnie wydaje się łączyć z formą inwencji popularną w kręgach organizacji podziemnych. To niemal tak, jakby prawo sztuki do istnienia zostało potajemnie potwierdzone właśnie poprzez porzucenie najbardziej pielęgnowanych w niej, nienaukowych zalet.

5.

Jest słynna przypowieść o Buddzie, w której mędrzec ten tłumaczy, że jego nauki są jak palec pokazujący księżyc: osoba, która patrzy tylko na palec, nigdy nie zobaczy samego księżyca. A gdybyśmy przyjęli, że artyści Warsztatu chcą – odwrotnie niż Budda – żeby widz patrzył właśnie na palec?

Tradycyjnie uważano, że film pokazuje indeksyjną rzeczywistość, choć w fikcyjnych ramach – stąd słynna uwaga Jean-Luca Godarda, mówiąca że każdy film fabularny jest dokumentem na temat występujących w nim aktorów – i oczywiście dokumentalna treść jest obecna w większości filmów artystów Warsztatu. Niekiedy nawet ma ona dominujące znaczenie, jak w *Ech* Koterskiego czy w *Niechcicach* (1973) Kwieka, który to obraz opowiada o mieszkańcach tytułowej, pegeerowskiej wioski. Jednak w wielu innych filmach to, co jest faktycznie przedstawione w filmie (nawet gdy odrzucimy „bezkamerowe" produkcje), wydaje się dość przypadkowe, niemal agresywnie nieokreślone – na przykład obrazy ulicy, które pokazuje Waśko w *Podróży Wacława Antczaka do kiosku na ulicy Głównej*, czy widok z wieży, na którą Robakowski się wspina w *Idę*. Tym, co jest filmowane, wydaje się sama czynność filmowania, wypełnianie instrukcji, a nie tylko świat, który znajduje się przed obiektywem.

Weźmy inny film Waśki zatytułowany *Ściana* (1972): czterominutowy materiał ze statycznej kamery skierowanej na ścianę łódzkiej filmówki, pocięty na kawałki i pomieszany w przypadkowej kolejności, tak że jakikolwiek ruch – przechodząca niekiedy na tle ściany postać – pojawia się tylko na mgnienie kilku klatek. Symbolika nie może już być bardziej banalna, a brak typowej dla filmu dokumentalnego ciekawości wynika z faktu, że kamera nigdy nie przekracza granic uczelni. Jednocześnie ścieżka dźwiękowa pozostaje radośnie i natrętnie ciągła: to niekończący się chór ptasich treli.

To dziwne połączenie obrazów poddanych działaniu przypadkowości i pozornie bezbronnej i pseudonarracyjnej ścieżki dźwiękowej kojarzy się z pewnych szczególnym fragmentem *Krytyki władzy sądzenia* Immanuela Kanta – tekstu fundamentalnego dla współczesnego rozumienia „estetyki". Rozmyślając nad doświadczeniem piękna w naturze, Kant zauważa:

> Cóż bardziej wielbią poeci aniżeli czarująco piękne trele słowika w ustronnych zaroślach w cichy letni wieczór przy łagodnym świetle księżyca? Ale znane są przykłady, że z braku takiego śpiewaka jakiś krotochwilny gospodarz swych gości, którzy przybyli do niego po to, ażeby rozkoszować się wiejskim powietrzem, wyprowadza – ku ich najwyższemu zadowoleniu – w pole, gdzie schował w krzaku swawolnego chłopaka, który potrafi (za pomocą trzciny czy rurki) naśladować owe trele w sposób zupełnie podobny do występujących w naturze. Lecz wystarczy stwierdzić, że jest to oszustwo, i nikt nie będzie w stanie

7 S. Ball, D. Curtis, op. cit., s. 60.

dłużej przysłuchiwać się śpiewowi, który przedtem uważał za tak powabny. Analogicznie ma się rzecz z każdym innym śpiewającym ptakiem[8].

Dla Kanta ptasi trel jest najwyższym wyrazem naturalnego piękna, mimo iż filozofa prześladuje możliwość mechanicznego powielenia jego estetycznej wartości (dla celów – nieprzypadkowo – komercyjnych). Ale ptasi trel w *Ścianie* wydaje się być wykorzystany w filmie dokładnie po to, żeby prowokować podejrzliwy sceptycyzm: podwójnie nie na miejscu – lokalizacja znajduje się w mieście, a jego dźwięk rozbrzmiewa bez przerwy, będąc przez to oderwanym od nieciągłych obrazów – parodiuje naturalistyczny efekt zsynchronizowanego dźwięku w konwencjonalnym kinie. Jeśli według Kanta odkrycie oszustwa sprawiało, że trel ptaka stawał się nieznośny, ponieważ zdradzał naturę, Waśko wydaje się podkreślać, że w filmie znajdziemy tylko oszustwo i naturalistyczne efekty.

Dzieła twórców związanych z Warsztatem nie tyle „wskazują" na jakąś realność, co wskazują na jej konstruowanie w filmie. Nakazują nam, żebyśmy nie patrzyli na świat, który wyłania się w filmie, ale żebyśmy patrzyli na sam film (palec, który pokazuje). Ta koncepcja w najbardziej dosłownym ujęciu pojawia się w połowie lat 70. w cyklu realizacji video Kwieka, które traktowały o studiu telewizyjnym: widzimy na nich ręce artysty, jak bezpośrednio lub pośrednio manipulują obrazem, który oglądamy (w przypadku *Video A* z 1974 roku poruszają suwakami na mikserze video). Jeśli chodzi o rodzaj używanej taśmy filmowej, fakt że artyści związani z Warsztatem pracowali na filmie 35 mm, a nie na formatach 8 mm czy 16 mm – co dziwiło ich rówieśników z Londynu i innych miejsc na Zachodzie – tylko podkreślał, iż byli zaangażowani w krytyczny dialog z przemysłem filmowym i kwestiami recepcji filmu. W dużej części właśnie ta niespójność pomiędzy technikami produkcji filmowej a jej tematyką (lub jej brakiem) stanowi o idiosynkratycznej inwencji obrazów twórców Warsztatu.

6.

Tautologia, w logicznym sensie, jest zarówno oczywista, jak i – ściśle mówiąc – bezsensowna, ponieważ nie jest prawdziwa ani fałszywa. Wittgenstein podaje przykład: „Nie wiem nic o pogodzie, gdy wiem tylko, że pada lub nie pada".[9]

„Tautologia" była ważnym terminem krytycznym we wczesnych lata 70. XX wieku, łącząc artystów skupionych wokół Warsztatu z ich rówieśnikami z grupy London Filmmakers' Coop. Było to dziwne pokrewieństwo, które – w zachodnim kontekście – wynikało z połączenia wersji modernizmu propagowanej przez Clementa Greenberga z wittgensteinowską teorią języka, co uosabiała wczesna twórczość amerykańskiego konceptualisty Josepha Kossutha. Na przykład w Wielkiej Brytanii krytyk filmowy Deke Dusinberre wielokrotnie używał tego terminu w odniesieniu do tego, co nazywał „formalistycznym dylematem [...] w którym radykalne strategie formalne sprawiają, że proces przedstawienia staje się tak arbitralny, iż ociera się o bezsensowną tautologię"[10]. Lecz jeśli używanie tautologii było ryzykiem, artyści z grupy London Filmmakers' Coop podejmowali je świadomie: na przykład, w filmie *Tautologia* (1973) Mike'a Dunforda słowo „TAUTOLOGIA" było nakładane na różne ujęcia budynków.

8 I. Kant. *Krytyka władzy sądzenia*, przeł. M. Żelazny, Toruń: Wydawnictwo Naukowe UMK, 2014. s. 180

9 L. Wittgenstein, *Traktat logiczno-filozoficzny*, przeł. B. Wolniewicz, Warszawa: PWN, 2011, s. 38.

10 D. Dusinberre, cytat za: P. Gidal, *Materialist Film*, Londyn – Nowy Jork: Routledge, 1989, s. 100; Ł. Ronduda, op. cit., s. 289.

W Polsce fotograf Zbigniew Dłubak stworzył inspirujący cykl prac pod tytułem *Tautologie* (1971), w którym fotografie elementów przestrzeni galerii (na przykład parkietu podłogi), były umieszczone na tych elementach lub obok nich. To bezpośrednio zainspirowało Bruszewskiego do stworzenia swojego własnego pojęcia „antytautologii" w cyklu prac zatytułowanym *Fotografia na płótnie* (1979), w którym powtarzające się fotografie białego płótna na blejtramie były nadrukowane na płótno i naciągnięte na swój własny blejtram, gdzie różne naprężenie płótna tworzyło odmienne wersje prac. Oprócz tych dwóch wystaw fotografii „Warsztatowcy" stworzyli wiele dzieł filmowych , które dotyczyły tautologii: *Ja i telefon* Kwieka, w drugiej części wizualnie powtarzający swój początek; *Okno* (1972) Waśki, gdzie – jak to ujmuje Łukasz Ronduda – „statyczna, prostokątna rama okna, przez którą obserwujemy »obrazy rzeczywistości« staje się tautologią klatki filmowej w tymże filmie"[11]; czy wideo Waśki *Róg* (1976), gdzie monitor z bezpośrednim obrazem jednej kamery jest ustawiony przed drugą kamerą, tak żeby odtwarzać widok kąta pokoju, który fizycznie zasłania. Et cetera, et cetera.

„Et cetera" jest tu kluczowym terminem. Może najlepszy tautologiczny dokument z Polski tamtego okresu stworzyła Ewa Partum – artystka, która nigdy nie była formalnie związana z warsztatem, choć mieszkała w Łodzi i brała aktywny udział w dialogu między uczestnikami całego przedsięwzięcia. Jej *Tautologiczne kino* (1973–1974) to seria krótkich filmów, z których każdy rozwija konkretny koncept: na przykład w *10 metrach taśmy* seria ręcznie wykonanych podtytułów oznacza w metrowych odstępach długość taśmy filmowej, która przeszła przez projektor. Także tutaj możemy znaleźć paralele z pracami brytyjskich artystów tego okresu – film Williama Rabana *Take Measure* [*Zmierz*] (1973) jest w gruncie rzeczy performensową wariacją tego samego pomysłu. Ale – co istotne – film Partum urywa się po napisie oznaczającym trzeci metr i kończy się po prostu słowem „ETC". Tak naprawdę wszystkie odcinki cyklu *Tautologicznego kina* kończą się słowem „ETC." i można by stwierdzić bez większej przesady, że niemal każdy obraz twórców Warsztatu mógłby zawierać tę samą kodę. Powiedzieć „et cetera" oznacza: to, co nastąpi teraz, jest (albo mogłoby być) tautologią. Oznacza to także dotarcie do punktu, poza którym przykład czy dowód nie są już potrzebne, bo przemieściliśmy się z przestrzeni dosłowności do przestrzeni konceptualnej.

Partum pisała o tych filmach:

> Nie jest to zajmowanie się estetyką, jest to nowego rodzaju praktyka filozoficzna w obszarze, w którym relacje między obszarem filmowym, a pracą kamery wyczerpują zakres zainteresowań rzeczywistością filmu. Wynika to z problemu filmu jako idei i możliwości struktury filmu jako medium i to stanowi jedyną treść i jest jedynym znaczeniem. [Jest to] sztuka wewnętrznie filmowa aż do wyczerpania możliwości kina jako medium semantycznego[12].

Precyzyjna formuła Partum stanowi klucz do zrozumienia związku pomiędzy preskryptywnością oraz inwencją w filmach twórców Warsztatu. Obrazy te próbują wyczerpać filmową „rzeczywistość" i „potencjał [...] jako semantyczne medium", chcąc ograniczyć ich operacje do tego, co Dusinberre nazwał „bezsensowną tautologią". Ale poetyka wyczerpania, w jakimkolwiek medium, zawiera ziarno parodii. Jorge Luis Borges pisał kiedyś: „Zdefiniowałbym barok jak styl, który

11 Ibidem, s. 291.

12 *Ewa Partum 1965-2001*, red. D. Monkiewicz, Warszawa: Muzeum Narodowe w Warszawie, 2006.

celowo wyczerpuje (lub próbuje wyczerpać) swoje własne możliwości i który graniczy z autoka-rykaturą[13]." W tautologicznych filmach autorów Warsztatu odnajdujemy historyczny i koncepu-alny paradoks sztuki: minimalistyczny barok.

Tautologiczne kino, zapoczątkowane przez artystów Warsztatu, wydaje się rezygnować z aspiracji do opisu rzeczywistości. Jednak – czyniąc to – skierowuje zwierciadło sztuki w oblicze totalitaryzmu, który chce całkowicie podporządkować sobie (społeczną i polityczną) rzeczywistość: tautologiczny film odzwierciedla tautologiczną ideologię. Absurdalność jednej z tych sfer staje się – poprzez kumulację znaczeń – niewypowiedzianym komentarzem na temat absurdalności drugiej, co grozi obróceniem się autokarykatury w polityczną satyrę. Filmowa tautologia staje się najistotniejsza w momencie, gdy wywrotowo nie udaje jej się porzucić sensu lub wyczerpać relacji z rzeczywistością. Kwiek rozmyśla w ścieżce dźwiękowej obrazu *Ja i telefon*:

> Zaczynam się zastanawiać, co będzie na ekranie, o czym będzie ten film? Myślę, że tak naprawdę będzie o niczym. Akceptuję nieistotność tego filmu, jak i to, że te trzy minuty mojego życia, i to, do czego sprowokowała mnie kamera, są nieistotne. Mam zamiar zrobić dziwniejszy film, bardziej agresywny, tak żeby każdy próbował znaleźć w nim znaczenie – tak jak ja próbuję teraz.

Jednak rzekoma nieistotność filmu jest niekoniecznie tym samym, co nieistotność trzech minut z życia artysty. Podobnie jak aforyzm Adorno, który istnieje w relacji pomiędzy dwoma formami oczywistości, polityczne znaczenie filmów Warsztatowców istnieje w przestrzeni pomiędzy tymi dwoma nieistotnościami.

przeł. Paweł Marcinkiewicz

13 J. L. Borges, *A Universal History of Iniquity. Preface to the 1954 edition*, przeł. A. Hurley, w: *Collected Fictions*, Londyn: Penguin, 1998, s. 4.

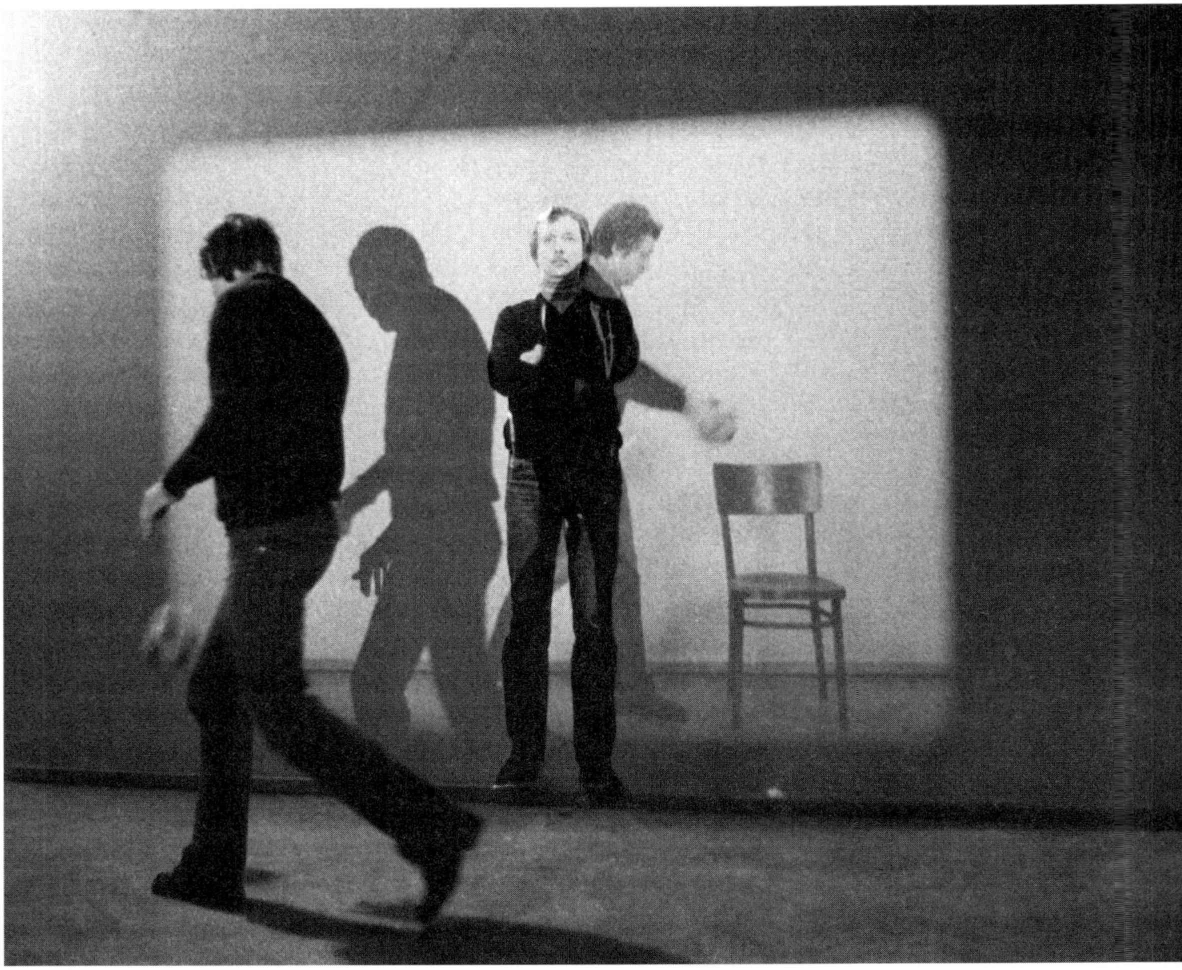

Andrzej Różycki, *Identyfikacja pozorna (Żywa Galeria)*, 1974
Andrzej Różycki, *Seeming Identification (Living Gallery)*, 1974

Maeve Connolly

„To jest miejsce naszych snów". Działalność Warsztatu Formy Filmowej w Szkole Filmowej w Łodzi

Wstęp

> [...] *w Szkole Filmowej rozwijaliśmy koncepcję „szkoły otwartej", nie tylko szkoły dla operatorów, ale szkoły uczącej wszystkich możliwych dziedzin. Ta koncepcja została przez nas opracowana bardzo szczegółowo. Niestety wszystkie plany, dotyczące Szkoły, które mieliśmy zniszczyło wprowadzenie stanu wojennego – musieliśmy wówczas z niej odejść. Wróciłem do pracy dopiero w 1995 roku. Ale dziś Szkoła zmienia się w miejsce, staje się bardziej multimedialna, staje się takim miejscem, jakim marzyliśmy, że będzie.*[1]

Józef Robakowski, w cytowanej powyżej rozmowie z Hansem Ulrichem Obristem, która odbyła się w 2010 roku, a więc czterdzieści lat po utworzeniu Warsztatu Formy Filmowej, stwierdził, że grupa miała posłużyć stworzeniu modelu otwartej edukacji. Model ten powstał w specyficznym kontekście Łódzkiej Szkoły Filmowej[2], która była (i wciąż jest) jedną z najbardziej cenionych na świecie państwowych szkół filmowych. Założyciele grupy, w tym Józef Robakowski, byli jej studentami pod koniec lat sześćdziesiątych i na początku lat siedemdziesiątych XX wieku. Wówczas, w ramach działalności Warsztatu Formy Filmowej i w oparciu o możliwości, jakie dawała im struktura Szkoły zrealizowali liczne krótkometrażowe filmy na taśmie 35 mm oraz prace wideo. Jako studenci, a później pracownicy Szkoły, wiele podróżowali i prezentowali swoje prace na festiwalach i wystawach w Polsce i zagranicą, otrzymywali liczne zaproszenia do udziału w różnych wydarzeniach, między innymi na Documenta 6 w 1977 roku.

Artystyczne i kulturowe znaczenie Warsztatu Formy Filmowej zostało rozpoznane przez praktyków i badaczy sztuki, filmu eksperymentalnego i wideo. Ale nadal, w kontekście badań nad filmem i mediami, nie został zbadany wpływ krytycznego podejścia grupy do klasycznej edukacji filmowej i jego skutki.

Warsztatowcy preferowali laboratoryjny model edukacji, kładąc nacisk na znaczenie eksperymentów i badań, odkrywając różne media i technologie, wykraczając znacznie poza zasady obowiązujące w przemyśle filmowym i w produkcji telewizyjnej.

Uczestnicy Warsztatu zdobyli gruntowną wiedzę z zakresu teorii filmu i historii polskiej, a szczególnie łódzkiej przedwojennej awangardy artystycznej. Z drugiej jednak strony w oficjalnym program nauczania w Szkole Filmowej kładziono nacisk na zdobywanie wiedzy poprzez wykonywanie zadań praktycznych, które były powiązane ściśle ze standardami obowiązującymi w przemyśle

---

1 *Józef Robakowski w rozmowie z Hansem Ulrichem Obristem*, w: *Józef Robakowski: Moje własne kino*, Warszawa: Centrum Sztuki Współczesnej Zamek Ujazdowski, 2012, s. 29.

2 Nazwa „Łódzka Szkoła Filmowa" pochodzi z oficjalnej strony internetowej, jednak w anglojęzycznych publikacjach Warsztatu Formy Filmowej z lat siedemdziesiątych jest ona nazywana Państwową Wyższą Szkołą Filmową, Telewizyjną i Teatralną.

filmowym. Wykonywanie tych zadań przez studentów było nadzorowane przez profesorów, którzy mieli wysokie pozycje w polskim przemyśle kinematograficznym, jako uznani reżyserzy, scenarzyści czy operatorzy.

Członkowie Warsztatu Formy Filmowej, zamiast odrzucić i zanegować te metody, wykorzystali do swoich potrzeb niektóre aspekty struktury Szkoły, tworząc stowarzyszenie studenckie, po to, aby zyskać dostęp do materiałów i w rezultacie móc pracować nad własnymi filmami. Strategia Warsztatu była zatem zasadniczo inna niż ta, która cechowała większość ruchów studenckich, formujących się w różnych ośrodkach akademickich na całym świecie pod koniec lat sześćdziesiątych, ale ich walka o poszerzenie granic twórczej wolności, do której drogą miało być między innymi przyjęcie roli „artystów" (zamiast filmowców, wpisuje się w koncepcję *artistic criticism* [artystycznego krytycyzmu] sformułowaną przez Luca Boltanskiego i Eve Chiapello w odniesieniu do studenckich i robotniczych protestów w maju 1968 roku we Francji. Ta forma sprzeciwu, według Boltanskiego i Chiapello, w odróżnieniu od postawy *social criticism* [społecznego krytycyzmu][3], przejawiała się postulowaniem większej autonomii dla jednostki, co zresztą stosuje się w nowych formach zarządzania, w których pracownicy mają obiecywaną samodzielność i możliwość rozwijania kreatywności często kosztem bezpieczeństwa i stabilności zatrudnienia.

W niniejszym tekście, który powstał w oparciu o wywiady z Pawłem Kwiekem, Januszem Połomem, Józefem Robakowskim i Andrzejem Różyckim[4], przeprowadzonymi w Warszawie i Łodzi, badam związki pomiędzy działalnością Warsztatu Formy Filmowej a infrastrukturą i strukturą organizacyjną Szkoły Filmowej w Łodzi w latach siedemdziesiątych. Na potrzeby eseju zarysowuję strategie wybranych uczestników Warsztatu, jak również strategię całej grupy, która były przez nich stworzona po to, aby zbudować statut artystów, a także po to, aby rozwinąć kontakty twórcze i zawodowe, sięgające poza obszar polskiego przemysłu filmowego. Rozważam spuściznę i dzisiejsze znaczenie krytyki edukacji filmowej opartej o zasady przemysłu filmowego podjętej w przeszłości przez artystów w Polsce i zagranicą. Moje rozważania opartam także na publikacji autorstwa Duncana Petrie i Roda Stonemana *Educating Film-Makers: Past, Present and Future*. Jej autorzy omawiają historię edukacji filmowej zorientowanej na kształcenie kadr dla przemysłu filmowego przed i po 1989 rokiem w wielu krajach, zauważając, że szkoły filmowe rezygnowały z rozwijania intelektualnych i artystycznych umiejętności i zainteresowań. W zamian kładziono w nich nacisk na doskonalenie umiejętności technicznych, czysto zawodowych[5].

W mojej pracy korzystałam ponadto z badań dotyczących branży kultury i przemysłu filmowego, w tym z analizy Petra Szczepanika, poświęconej „socjalistycznemu modelowi produkcji" i ukazującej polityczną historię produkcji filmowej w Czechach, Niemieckiej Republice Demokratycznej, na Węgrzech i w Polsce[6]. Szczepanik wnikliwie analizuje różnice, które istniały pomiędzy tymi krajami, zwracając uwagę, że w Polsce szczególną rolę w kształtowaniu się kultury filmowej odegrali

3 E. Chiapello, *Evolution and Co-optation: The 'Artist Critique' of Management and Capitalism*, „Third Text" 18:6, 2004, s. 585–594. Patrz także L. Boltanski, E. Chiapello, *The New Spirit of Capitalism*, Londyn: Verso Books, 2005.

4 Wywiady zostały przeprowadzone przez autorkę w różnych miejscach w Łodzi i Warszawie w maju 2016 roku. Zostały zorganizowane przez Marikę Kuźmicz, która była naszą tłumaczką.

5 D. Petrie, *Continental Film Schools: A Brief History of the 'National Conservatoire'*, w: *Educating Film-Makers: Past, Present and Future*, red. D. Petrie, R. Stoneman, Bristol: Intellect Ltd, 2014, s. 15–48.

6 P. Szczepanik, *The State-Socialist Mode of Production and the Political History of Production Culture*, w: *Behind the Screen: Inside European Production Cultures*, ed. P. Szczepanik, P. Vonderau, Nowy Jork: Palgrave Macmillan, 2013, s. 113–134.

reżyserzy[7]. Pomimo że Szczepanik nie odnosi się bezpośrednio do środowiska Szkoły Filmowej w Łodzi, jego badania wykazują, że to profesjonalni filmowcy odegrali kluczową rolę w kształtowaniu się edukacji kinematograficznej. Znane są przypadki, gdy oponowali oni przeciwko wprowadzaniu alternatywnych modeli edukacji, takich, które byłyby w jakiś sposób niezgodne z ich przekonaniami i standardami zawodowymi. W pewnym sensie był to ich sposób na budowanie własnego autorytetu oraz na uzyskanie częściowej autonomii od kontroli władzy[8].

Szczepanik pisze: „twórcy filmowi dostrzegli, że pomimo swoich opresyjnych aspektów racjonalizacja przemysłu filmowego w Europe Środkowo-Wschodniej przyniosła bezprecedensowy poziom wsparcia materialnego i zawodowego dla osób zaangażowanych w produkcję filmową"[9]. Wspomniana opresja przybierała różne formy. Była to cenzura państwowa i wiążące się z nią mechanizmy kontroli, ale też bardziej wyrafinowane formy nacisku „nagradzanie,karanie, paternalizm i korumpowanie[10]. Zauważa, że pracownicy kinematografii w państwie socjalistycznym byli narażeni w różnym stopniu na opresję w zależności od swojej specjalizacji. Rozróżnia na przykład sytuację operatorów montażystów, kierowników produkcji, którzy często „cieszyli się długimi karierami od lat trzydziestych do lat sześćdziesiątych"[11], od sytuacji wielu reżyserów, scenarzystów, dramaturgów (w nomenklaturze hollywoodzkiej określanymi mianem *above-the-line*). Twierdzi on, że druga z wymienionych grup pracowników przemysłu filmowego była bardziej podatna na zmiany ideologiczne i polityczne wprowadzane przez partię komunistyczną, chociaż nadal nie w tak dużym stopniu, jak kierownicy zespołów filmowych.

Na przestrzeni czasu, który minął od zmiany systemu socjalistycznego opisywanego przez Szczepanika, kontekst polityczny i społeczny produkcji filmowej, telewizyjnej, a także edukacji kinematograficznej, zmienił się radykalnie w Polsce i w innych krajach regionu. W rezultacie twórcy filmowi i telewizyjni: operatorzy, montażyści, producenci, reżyserzy i scenarzyści musieli zmienić swój sposób pracy, aby przetrwać i funkcjonować w nowym systemie społecznym, który wymusza komercyjną konkurencyjność. Szczepanik zauważa, że nawet pomimo tego, że polskie filmy przyciągają do kin liczną krajową widownię, „przemysł kinematograficzny w tym regionie i w całej Europie Środkowo-Wschodniej nadal nie potrafi wypracować strategii, która uczyniłaby go konkurencyjnym i zmaga się nadal z konsekwencjami likwidacji gospodarki państwowej i struktur państwa socjalistycznego, jak również z sytuacją pewnej geopolitycznej marginalizacji."[12] Ponadto szerokie zastosowanie technologii cyfrowej w kinematografii od około 2000 roku przyniosło kolejne radykalne zmiany w dotychczasowych zasadach produkcji filmowej i telewizyjnej. W rezultacie, tym co łączy obecnie wszystkie grupy zawodowe w przemyśle filmowym, to brak stabilnej sytuacji zatrudnienia. Ta zmiana w sytuacji środowiska filmowego jest dla mnie kontekstem do zrewidowania relacji pomiędzy Warsztatem Formy Filmowej a Szkołą Filmową w Łodzi.

7 P. Szczepanik, op. cit., s. 117. Autor opisuje polskie jednostki produkcyjne jako „dość wyjątkowe" w kontekście przemysłu filmowego w Europie Środkowo-Wschodniej.

8 P. Szczepanik, op. cit., s. 129. Przykładem może być roczny intensywny kurs w Czechosłowacji, którego celem uczenie zawodu reżysera, producenta, operatora i menedżera produkcji. Każdemu uczestnikowi kursu przypisywano w założeniu „opiekuna" – wykonującego dany zawód przedstawiciela branży filmowej - ale filmowcy odmawiali wykonywania tych obowiązków.

9 P. Szczepanik, op. cit., s. 114.

10 Ibidem, s. 114.

11 Ibidem, s. 125.

12 Ibidem, s. 113.

Edukacja filmowa a państwo

W swojej krytycznej historii edukacji filmowej i telewizyjnej, Patrie i Stoneman wskazują kilka określonych faz budowania edukacji filmowej dotowanej przez państwo, zaczynając od roku 1919, kiedy w Moskwie powstał Wszechrosyjski Państwowy Uniwersytet Kinematografii im. S.A. Gierasimowa. Badacze sugerują, że głównym celem założenia szkoły była propaganda. Podobnie było w przypadku Eksperymentalnego Centrum Kinematografii, założonego w Rzymie w 1935 roku przez faszystowską administrację Mussoliniego[13]. Po II wojnie światowej wiele szkół filmowych, zakładanych w Europie powstawało w związku z polityką władz, polegającą na „budowaniu lub odmładzaniu prężnie działającego przemysłu filmowego i kultury ruchomego obrazu”[14]. W okresie powojennym szkoły filmowe założono na Węgrzech (1945), w Czechosłowacji (1946), w Polsce (1948), Bułgarii (1948), Rumunii (1950), Niemieckiej Republice Demokratycznej (1954). Ponadto, w latach czterdziestych i pięćdziesiątych, liczne szkoły filmowe powstawały także w Europie Zachodniej (w Holandii, Belgii, Austrii, a także Hiszpanii i Grecji), w Skandynawii, Republice Federalnej Niemiec, w latach siedemdziesiątych również w Wielkiej Brytanii.

Powstanie niektórych ze szkół było poprzedzone podjętymi wcześniej inicjatywami edukacyjnymi. Przykładowo, w Polsce rodzaj warsztatu szkoleniowego dla filmowców działał w Krakowie już w 1945 r. Ostatecznie podjęto decyzję o tym, że Szkoła Filmowa powstanie w Łodzi, ponieważ to w tym mieście istniało wówczas studio filmowe wyposażone w sprzęt przejęty przez Polaków od wycofującej się niemieckiej armii.

Petrie wskazuje, że w skład kadry pedagogicznej Szkoły Filmowej w Łodzi weszło kilka wybitnych indywidualności tworzących już wcześniej, w latach trzydziestych, Stowarzyszenie Miłośników Filmu Artystycznego START[15]. Na przykład Jerzy Toeplitz (1909–1995), historyk kina, jeden z założycieli START-u, z czasem stał się jedną z najważniejszych postaci powojennej polskiej edukacji kinematograficznej. Najpierw w latach 1949–1952 i ponownie, w okresie 1957–1968 Toeplitz pełnił funkcję rektora Szkoły Filmowej. Podczas swojej drugiej kadencji, rozszerzył propozycję edukacyjną dla studentów, m.in. tworząc wydział aktorski, który powstał w 1958 roku w wyniku połączenia Szkoły Filmowej i Państwowej Wyższej Szkoły Teatralnej im. Leona Schillera.

Petrie określił model socjalistycznej szkoły filmowej, jako „kamień węgielny państwowej centralizacji, zapewniający aspirującym do zawodu osobowościom jedyną obowiązującą ścieżkę”[16], po której można było wejść do przemysłu filmowego. Jednocześnie zauważa on złożone zadania stawiane filmowi przez ideologię komunistyczną. Petrie podkreśla, że dla Toeplitza i innych, film jako „dziedzina sztuki” miał raczej uczestniczyć w kształtowaniu kultury narodowej, niż dostarczaniu rozrywki dla mas.

Już w połowie lat pięćdziesiątych nowe pokolenie filmowców, z których wielu było absolwentami Szkoły Filmowej w Łodzi, zaczęło funkcjonować na arenie międzynarodowej, by wymienić choćby słynnych reżyserów: Andrzeja Wajdę, Andrzeja Munka, Janusza Morgensterna, a także operatorów, m.in. Jerzego Lipmana, Jerzego Wójcika, Mieczysława Jahodę. Ten nowy ruch (określany jako Polska Szkoła Filmowa), przejawiał „silne zainteresowanie rewizją niedawnych doświadczeń

13 D. Petrie, R. Stoneman, *Introduction*, w: *Educating Film-Makers...*, s. 3.

14 Ibidem.

15 D. Petrie, op. cit., s. 29.

16 Ibidem.

wojennych Polaków, co stanowiło sprzeczność w stosunku do obowiązujących założeń socrealizmu"[17]. W związku z naciskami władzy w okresie stalinizmu w Polsce, niektórzy filmowcy emigrowali, ale wielu pozostało w kraju i zdecydowali się, mimo wszystko, pracować w zawodzie. Wielu z nich funkcjonowało w bliskiej relacji ze Szkołą Filmową – łączyli oni praktykę reżyserską czy operatorską z działalnością pedagogiczną.

W 1965 roku Toepliz otrzymał zaproszenie do wygłoszenia w Edynburgu, podczas odbywającego się tam festiwalu filmowego wykładu pod tytułem „The Creative Impuls in Film-Making"[18]. Podkreślił w nim konieczność zgłębiania przez twórców filmowych historii filmu i czerpania z niej, a także nakreślił szczegółowo czteroletni program kształcenia operatorów i reżyserów filmowych. W myśl tej koncepcji studenci pierwszego roku Szkoły Filmowej mieli pracować w grupach nad filmem dokumentalnym, pod opieką zawodowego reżysera. Zdjęcia do tych produkcji wykonywać mieli doświadczeni już operatorzy. Następnie każdy student z grupy samodzielnie pracował nad montażem powstałego materiału. Na drugim roku studenci wykonywali film niemy, krótkometrażowy film fabularny i krótkometrażowy dokument dźwiękowy, a na trzecim roku dłuższy film fabularny, program telewizyjny lub film „na żywo". Studenci następnie wybierali sposób wykonania pracy dyplomowej, decydując się na realizację filmu fabularnego, dokumentu, filmu edukacyjnego bądź programu telewizyjnego.

Jeszcze przed wykładem Toeplitza model realizowany w łódzkiej Szkole Filmowej i uznawany był za wyjątkowy, zarówno ze względu na nacisk kładziony na nieme ćwiczenia filmowe, które koncentrowały się przez to przede wszystkim na obrazie, jak i na samej ilość materiału realizowanego przez przyszłych operatorów[19]. Mocną międzynarodową pozycję szkoły wzmacniał także pozytywny odbiór prac jej studentów przez krytyków, jak choćby filmu Romana Polańskiego *Dwaj ludzie z szafą* (1958), prezentowanego na wielu festiwalach filmowych. Pomimo tego Toepliz został wyrzucony ze Szkoły Filmowej na fali antysemickiej nagonki zainicjowanej przez komunistyczne władze PRL w 1968 roku, która zmusiła do emigracji blisko 15 000 obywateli polskich pochodzenia żydowskiego. Petrie zauważa, że wydarzenia polityczne Marca 1968 spowodowały powrót do Szkoły Filmowej części jej niegdysiejszych konserwatywnych założycieli, którzy zastąpili wyrzuconych profesorów[20].

W tej właśnie napiętej sytuacji politycznego, społecznego i instytucjonego niepokoju powstał Warsztat Formy Filmowej. Robakowski, który zaczął studia na wydziale operatorskim Szkoły Filmowej w 1966 roku po wcześniejszym uzyskaniu dyplomu z historii sztuki na uniwersytecie w Toruniu, podkreśla, że wielu studentów protestowało przeciwko antysemickiej polityce rządu. Jednocześnie wskazuje on na niedostatki wcześniejszej propozycji edukacyjnej i trudności administracyjne panujące w Szkole Filmowej[21]. Wielu z profesorów, jak wspomina Robakowski, było często nieobecnych podczas zajęć, ponieważ korzystali skwapliwie z możliwości uczestniczenia w licznych polskich i zagranicznych festiwalach filmowych, zasiadali w różnego rodzaju jury. Przynosiło to doraźne profity i swoisty środowiskowy prestiż, ale głęboko rozczarowywało ich studentów, którzy, aby dostać się do obleganej przez kandydatów Szkoły, musieli zdać wyjątkowo wymagające egzminy

17 Ibidem.

18 Ibidem, s. 30.

19 Dużą liczbę produkcji odnotował raport Roberta Gessnera o Szkole Filmowej, opublikowany w *Sight and Sound* 32:2, 1963; za: D. Petrie, op. cit., s. 30.

20 D. Petrie, op. cit., s. 31.

21 Wywiad z Józefem Robakowskim, Łódź, maj 2016.

wstępne. W związku z tym oczekiwali oni solidnej edukacji, która nie będzie zdominowana czy zakłócana innymi obowiązkami profesorów związanych z przemysłem filmowym.

Infrastruktura i jej wpływ

W 1970 roku Józef Robakowski skończył studia w Szkole Filmowej, ale nadal był z nią związany jako asystent. Doskonale znał strukturę i system funkcjonowania Filmówki i to on odegrał kluczową rolę podczas zakładania Warsztatu Formy Filmowej, który formalnie zaistniał jako studenckie koło naukowe. W praktyce oznaczało to, że uczestnicy grupy mieli niezbędny do pracy twórczej dostęp do materiałów filmowych, do taśmy filmowej, kamer, wozów transmisyjnych, a także, że mogli używać kontekstu szkoły po to, by angażować się w różnego rodzaju artystyczne i pedagogiczne eksperymenty. Powstaniu grupy towarzyszył entuzjazm niektórych członków szkolnej kadry, przede wszystkim Jerzego Kotowskiego, co ułatwiło formalną rejestrację WFF i pozwoliło zdobyć akceptację szkoły dla jego powstania. Kiedy już cel, jakim było założenie grupy, został osiągnięty, Warsztat wypracował program nazywany przez Robakowskiego „samokształceniem", a który polegał między innymi na zgłębianiu wielu cennych źródeł, przeoczonych i zaniedbanych przez profesorów w Szkole Filmowej. Robakowski wspomina także, że praca eksperymentalna była dla większości uczestników grupy równoległymi zajęciami, obok wykonywania przez Warsztatowców ich szkolnych obowiązków i zadań[22].

Warsztat funkcjonował jako grupa samokształceniowa bardzo efektywnie, wykorzystując do swoich celów wszystkich dostępnych źródeł i zasobów. Członkowie grupy mieli na przykład dostęp do pokazowych, premierowych w Polsce, kopii filmów brytyjskich, francuskich, niemieckich i amerykańskich, które były wyświetlane w szkolnym kinie, ponieważ to Szkoła Filmowa była instytucją, której te kopie powierzały różne ambasady, promujące w Polsce sztukę i kulturę swoich krajów.. Ponadto, jako studenci Szkoły, uczestnicy WFF dostawali niekiedy możliwość odbycia zagranicznego wyjazdu, przy okazji festiwali albo pod pretekstem odwiedzenia szkoły filmowej w Moskwie, Berlinie Wschodnim czy Budapeszcie, co pozwoliło im z czasem zbudować relacje z innymi studentami kinematografii, szczególnie na Węgrzech[23].

Robakowski nie był jedynym uczestnikiem Warsztatu, który rozumiał w jaki sposób można wykorzystać infrastrukturę Szkoły Filmowej do swoich artystycznych i krytycznych celów. Nie był także jedynym Warsztatowcem, który po skończeniu studiów rozpoczął pracę w Szkole Filmowej. Asystentami zostali także m. in. Ryszard Waśko i Paweł Kwiek. Janusz Połom, który przyłączył się do WFF w 1971 roku i był studentem wydziału operatorskiego, na początku lat osiemdziesiątych objął funkcję Dziekana Wydziału Operatorskiego i Realizacji Telewizyjnej. Połom wspomina, że niektórzy pedagodzy uczących na wydziale operatorskim (szczególnie, jego zdaniem, cenne było zaangażowanie po stronie Warsztatu Jerzego Mierzejewskiego)[24], udzielili wsparcia Warsztatowi, ale też przyznaje, że wówczas, gdy uczestnicy grupy zaczęli tworzyć własne, niezależne od programu szkolnego krótkometrażowe filmy, powstające często bez scenariuszy, pojawiły się ze strony kadry pedagogicznej pewne problemy[25]. Odchodząc od przyjętych i utrwalonych przez lata schematów

22 Wywiad z Józefem Robakowskim, maj 2016.

23 Wywiad z Józefem Robakowskim, maj 2016.

24 Wywiad z Januszem Połomem, maj 2016.

25 Połom kładzie nacisk na to, że w filmach kręconych w ramach Warsztatu nie korzystano ze scenariuszy, opracowywano jedynie krótkie opisy poprzedzające właściwą realizację.

robienia filmów, Warsztat rzucił jednocześnie wyzwanie wieloletniej rutynie administracyjnej, zasadom i systemowi stworzonemu w celu regulacji procesu produkcji filmów panującym w łódzkiej Szkole, ale też w zasadzie, w każdej innej szkole filmowej.

Dydaktyka Warsztatu – twórczość jako proces

W głównym okresie działalności grupy, w latach 1970–1977, uczestnicy Warsztatu zrealizowali bardzo wiele filmów, prac wideo, performansów, zarówno indywidualnie, jak i wspólnie. Nie jest moim celem podsumowywanie wszystkich aspektów ich działalności i dorobku, ale jest jasne, że Warsztatowcy chcieli wypracować alternatywne wobec zastanych w szkole metod pracy[26]. Wiele prac Józefa Robakowskiego, Pawła Kwieka i Andrzeja Różyckiego i innych uczestników grupy powstało jako wynik refleksji nad procesem realizacji filmu, włączając w to analizę pracy operatora, reżysera, montażysty, których wkład w ten proces łatwo mógłby zostać przeoczony.

W innym filmie Robakowskiego *Idę* (1973) nie występują aktorzy. Zamiast tego film koncentruje się na zagadnieniu jaką rolę w procesie powstania filmu odgrywa fizyczność, ciało operatora. Film składa się z jednego ujęcia, którego autorem jest sam Robakowski, trzymający kamerę i wchodzący po schodach przedwojennej łódzkiej wieży spadochronowej. *Idę* może być rozpatrywane jako dokumentacja performans, ponieważ struktura tego filmu jest całkowicie determinowana przez czynność wspinaczki artysty po schodach, a więc opiera się o materialność spadochronowej wieży i ludzkiego ciała. Mówiąc o tej pracy, Robakowski podkreśla, że zrealizował w niej zamiar oderwania kamery od oka operatora, uwalniając się tym samym od roli operatora, a w zamian traktując ją jak przedłużenie własnego ciała. *Idę* można rozpatrywać w szerokim kontekście licznych prób podejmowanych przez artystów z użyciem kamery we wczesnych latach siedemdziesiątych. Próby te miały na celu poszerzenie możliwości jej użycia, zmianę utartych sposobów posługiwania się nią. Można w tym miejscu przywołać prace Jonasa Mekasa, który rozpatrywał rolę kamery jako protezy, jako „uzupełnienie" ciała operatora. O ile jednak Mekas posługiwał się najpierw kamerą małoobrazkową a potem lekką kamerą wideo, to Robakowski użył ciężkiej kamery do filmu 35 mm, w związku z tym na filmie utrwalony został jego autentyczny fizyczny wysiłek i zmęczenie, nasilające się w miarę wspinaczki w górę, słyszymy jego oddech, który staje się coraz głośniejszy.

Łukasz Ronduda opisał działanie Robakowskiego, jak „zagłębianie się we własną materialność", w taki sposób, że podmiot staje się „rzeczą między rzeczami" i „żywymi fragmentami materii"[27], posiadający nieantropocentryczny punkt widzenia świata. Film *Idę* zawiera też doświadczenie pracującego, dźwigającego kamerę ciała, które zwykle jest dla nas niedostępne, znajduje się poza ekranem. Ten sposób filmowania w ujęciu klasycznej kinematografii był niezgodny z płynnym sposobem prowadzenia kamery, które stało się możliwe dzięki rozwijanym technikom stabilizacji kamery, takim jak technologia *steadicam* rozwinięta w drugiej połowie lat siedemdziesiątych XX w. Podczas gdy zarówno tytuł jak i forma filmu *Idę* podkreślają cielesność i obecność operatora, zależnego od kamery i wpływającego na nią jednocześnie, Robakowski realizował także filmy realizowane zespołowo, w tym z udziałem studentów, czego przykładem jest praca *22x* (1971). Każdy student otrzymał od

26 Andrzej Różycki zwraca uwagę na fakt, że w tamtym czasie Szkoła Filmowa była pod silnym wpływem pewnego stylu w kinematografii, charakteryzującego się powolną akcją i długimi ujęciami w celu zbudowania konkretnego nastroju w danym filmie.

27 Ł. Ronduda, *Sztuka polska lat 70.*, Warszawa: Centrum Sztuki Współczesnej - Zamek Ujazdowski, 2009, s. 281.

niego kilka metrów nienaświetlonej taśmy filmowej i był poproszony o dowolną obróbkę tego materiału. Większość studentów podrapała emulsję przy użyciu różnych narzędzi, wielu z nich także manipulowało paskiem dźwiękowym widocznym na taśmie. Poszczególne fragmenty taśmy zostały następnie zmontowane przez Robakowskiego w jedną sekwencję. Sam Robakowski opisywał ten film jako próbę stworzenia filmu, który będzie „obiektywnym" obrazem wspólnoty twórczej, która co oczywiste składała się z nauczycieli i studentów.

Pytanie o to, czym jest w istocie taka wspólnota, było dla uczestników Warsztatu bardzo istotne i wiązało się z definiowaniem własnej roli, jako artysty w określonym kontekście. To dlatego Warsztatowcy byli zainteresowani rewizją i upowszechnianiem dokonań polskiej przedwojennej awangardy, czego przejawem są liczne filmy poświęcone jej twórcom, m.in. Katarzynie Kobro, Tytusowi Czyżewskiemu, Leonowi Chwistkowi, Witkacemu i Henrykowi Stażewskiemu autorstwa członków WFF. Warsztat stał się narzędziem do redefinicji pojęcia artystycznej wspólnoty. W tym czasie, aby być postrzeganym jako artysta, należało mieć dyplom szkoły artystycznej i należeć do Związku Plastyków Polskich. W opozycji do tej sytuacji Warsztat oferował sytuację daleko bardziej otwartą, przyjmując w swoje szeregi osoby wywodzące się z różnych środowisk, także spoza Szkoły Filmowej[28].

WFF angażował się uczestnictwo w różnego rodzaju działania, które zmieniały i poszerzały ustalone formy prezentacji sztuki, takie jak wystawa albo pokaz filmu w sali kinowej, często przy tych okazjach wykorzystując przestrzenie galerii (oraz przestrzeń publiczną) do realizacji działań performatywnych. Przykładem może być działanie Andrzeja Różyckiego *Identyfikacja pozorna* (1973), która została zbudowana w oparciu o projekcję slajdów wyświetlanych na ciele Różyckiego – performera. Pomiędzy projekcją a jej autorem dochodziło do interakcji; obydwie postaci, wyświetlana i realna, uzupełniały się. Różycki chciał użyć projekcji slajdów na których widoczna była jego postać podczas wykonywania różnych czynności, po to by zdać pytanie o los bohatera filmu: czy mógł on istnieć także przed i po rozpoczęciu filmowej projekcji?

W innej realizacji *Żywa projekcja* (1975)[29], Różycki analizuje problem ruchu w filmie, odnosząc się do koncepcji formułowanych przez przedstawicieli pierwszej filmowej awangardy, mówiącej o tym, że „film to ruch". Różycki umieścił fragment taśmy filmowej przed włączonym projektorem. Ruch ciepłego powietrza wydobywającego się z projektora powodował ruch taśmy filmowej, a tym samym ruch widoczny na ekranie, pomimo tego, że projekcja w zasadzie nie miała miejsca.

W studiu telewizyjnym

Ze wszystkich uczestników WFF to właśnie na Pawła Kwieka największy wpływ wywarła cybernetyczna teoria charakteru, skłaniająca go do traktowania Szkoły Filmowej jako element większego systemu kulturowego, ekonomicznego, politycznego i społecznego[30]. Zainteresowanie cybernetyką w tamtym okresie było oczywiście dość powszechne, także poza Polską, by przywołać w tym miejscu przykłady artystów takich jak Hans Haake, Steven Willats, czy twórców zajmują-

28 Józef Robakowski podaje przykład Andrzeja Partuma, jako samouka, który był osoba kluczową w ówczesnym środowisku artystycznym. Wywiad z Józefem Robakowskim, maj 2016.

29 Wywiad z Andrzejem Różyckim, maj 2016.

30 Kwiek interesował się także podejściami psychometrycznymi do badania lidzkiej inteligencji, takimi jak metody opracowane przez J. P. Guilforda wykorzystywane w szkoleniach żołnierzy i pilotów, obejmujące „rozumienie, systemy, relacje, zmiany, klasy, niezależnych ludzi, działania, pamięć, pojmowanie." Wywiad z Pawłem Kwiekiem, maj 2016.

cych się, podobnie jak Kwiek, przede wszystkim filmem i wideo: Les Levine, David Lamelas, Frank Gillete czy Ira Schneider. Jednak w przeciwieństwie do większości z nich, Kwiek, jako student Szkoły Filmowej, miewał bezpośredni dostęp do studia telewizyjnego, w którym mógł eksperymentować ze zjawiskiem transmisji i organizacją pracy w studio. Widzimy to na przykładzie pracy *Video A – Sytuacja Studia* (1974), w której Kwiek wziął na siebie równocześnie rolę performera występującego przed kamerą i reżysera, wydającego polecenia operatorom kamer. W kolejnej zrealizowanej w podobny sposób pracy *Video C* (1975), Kwiek wprowadza nowe elementy, w formie efektów specjalnych – czarnego trójkąta, który widzowie widzieli na ekranie – był to rezultat użycia miksera trickowego. Podobnie jak Robakowski, Kwiek interesował się relacjami zawiązującymi się między ludźmi a maszynami, fizyczności ludzkiej i techniki. Jednak o ile *Idę* okazywało wysiłek, forsowny ruch w człowieka w przestrzeni, o tyle ruch fizyczny Kwieka w jego pracach wideo w studio podlega różnym zależnościom w większym systemie. Widać to wyraźnie w *Video C*, w którym widzimy różne punkty styku człowiek-maszyna, takie jak strzałki widoczne na ekranie i czy dźwignie na panelu miksera trikowego.

Paweł Kwiek podkreśla, że on sam i inni uczestnicy WFF, mieli status i umiejętności profesjonalnych filmowców, w związku z tym przez zespół pracujący w studio telewizyjnym nie byli traktowani jak osoby „z zewnątrz"[31]. Z kolei Janusz Połom wspomina, że Warsztat był traktowany wręcz entuzjastycznie przez dyrektora TVP, w związku z czym, członkowie grupy mieli dostęp do sprzętu telewizyjnego[32]. Niemniej jednak, w praktyce musieli wypracować własny sposób na funkcjonowanie w istniejących instytucjonalnych strukturach i w hierarchii, na przykład zespołu w studiu telewizyjnym, znaleźć język komunikacji podczas współpracy z inżynierami dźwięku, obrazu i z pozostałymi pracownikami telewizji. I tak na przykład działania Kwieka w studiu były filmowane przez jego kolegów z wydziału operatorskiego, ale podczas realizacji prac wideo konieczna była także współpraca z inżynierem studia, którą z perspektywy czasu Kwiek opisuje jako „całkiem zadowalającą". Należy dodać, że podkreśla on fakt, że jego prace zrealizowane w telewizji są często nadinterpretowane, jako realizacje zabarwione politycznie, odnoszące się do kwestii cenzury panującej wówczas w Polsce, co nie było wówczas jego intencją[33]. Był skoncentrowany raczej na analizie instytucji telewizji w sensie ogólnym, na tym, że ma ona wpływ na nasz sposób postrzegania świata, ponieważ pośredniczy w tym procesie, a wszystko to z kolei odbywa się przy zaangażowaniu wydawców programu, inżynierów obrazu i dźwięku, a więc osób, które determinują to, co widzimy na ekranie odbiornika telewizyjnego i na to chciał w swoich realizacjach uczulić odbiorcę.

Kilku uczestników Warsztatu (Kwiek, Bruszewski, Robakowski, Waśko) wzięło udział w transmisji programu wyemitowanym w drugim programie TVP. Był to program o sztuce, transmitowany na żywo w 1975 roku. Ta sytuacja ma swój szeroki kontekst, ponieważ zarówno w Europie Zachodniej, jak i w Stanach Zjednoczonych wielu artystów zajmujących się pod koniec lat sześćdziesiątych i na początku lat siedemdziesiątych kinem eksperymentalnym, realizowało swoje prace w studiach telewizyjnych. Znamy słynny przykład *Black Gate Cologne*, eksperymentalnego telewizyjnego widowiska przygotowanego przez Otto Piene i Aldo Tamelliniego dla niemieckiej telewizji WDR w 1968 roku. Także brytyjskie stacje telewizyjne przejawiały zainteresowanie tego typu eksperymentami.

31 Wywiad z Pawłem Kwiekiem, maj 2016.
32 Wywiad z Jerzym Połomem, maj 2016.
33 Wywiad z Pawłem Kwiekiem, maj 2016.

Pod koniec lat sześćdziesiątych John Hopkins Hoppy, utworzył radykalną grupę TVX, zajmującą się sztuką wideo, razem z Cliffem Evansem, który w tym okresie pracował jako operator dla BBC.

TVX zorganizowało serię eksperymentalnych „happeningów" w New Arts Lab w Londynie, we współpracy z London Film Makers co-op, używając do tego sprzętu wideo sponsorowanego przez Johna Lennona[34]. W 1969 roku zostali zaproszeni przez Toma Corcorana, dyrektora artystycznego BBC 2 do programu *Late Night Line Up*, który oddał im do dyspozycji studio telewizyjne, w którym urządzili spotkanie muzyków i przyjaciół grupy[35]. W rezultacie powstało *Videospace,* którą Hoppkins opisał jako eksperyment z użyciem światła, miksera trickowego, syntetyzatora, zawierający elementy dyskusji w studio[36]. Ten materiał nie został nigdy wyemitowany, ale stał się początkiem zrealizowanych przez TVX prac, zwanych „wizualizacjami", które zostały wyemitowane przez BBC, choć budziły sporo kontrowersji[37].

W tym kontekście warto także wspomnieć o amerykańskiej grupie artystycznej Videofreex, a szczególnie o ich taśmie wideo *process video revolution*, która jest dokumentacją nieudanej próby realizacji programu telewizyjnego przez kilka kolektywów artystów pracujących z wideo w kwietniu 1971 roku[38]. Nagranie pokazuje zmagania ekipy technicznej usiłującej zintegrować i zsynchronizować ze sobą różne przenośne kamery i rekordery używane przez Videofreex i inne grupy uczestniczące w eksperymencie. Widać, na nim, jak brodaci, ubrani w codzienne stroje członkowie Videofreex swobodnie poruszają się po studio nagrywając miotających się po nim gładko ogolonych i elegancko ubranych pracowników telewizji. W pewnym momencie któryś z nich mówi do trzymającego kamerę, że nie wolno mu nagrywać. Gdy zostaje zignorowany, wypowiada zakamuflowaną nieczytelną groźbę: „Nie wolno wam tu filmować, to studio należy do związków zawodowych."

W tym okresie, zarówno w Polsce jak i w USA w studiach telewizyjnych zatrudniano osoby na jasno określonych warunkach, podział obowiązków był klarowny. John T. Caldwell i Deirdre Boyle w interesujący sposób zarysowują napięcia, które pojawiły w się w latach siedemdziesiątych pomiędzy kolektywami *guerilla,* które pracowały z medium telewizyjnym, a nadawcami telewizyjnymi[39]. Były to po części napięcia ideologiczne, ale nie tylko – wiązały się także ze poważnymi zmianami w sposobie pracy stacji telewizyjnych, co z kolei wiązało się z udoskonalaniem techniki wideo. Zaczęto na przykład używać przy pracy w telewizji mniejszych kamer wideo, w związku z czym mogła zostać zmniejszona ilość pracowników stacji telewizyjnych. Pracownicy telewizji musieli przystosować się do tych zmian i zapoznawać się z nowymi technologiami. Pisząc o tej sytuacji John Wyver zwrócił także uwagę na zaistnienie na tym tle napięć między artystami a pracownikami telewizji, również w Europie, co miało wynikać przede wszystkim z tego, że artyści postrzegali samych siebie jak reformatorów telewizji i często ignorowali wiedzę techniczną, którą dysponowali zatrudnieni w tych

34 S. Partridge, *'Artists' Television: Interruptions – Interventions*, w: *REWIND British Artists' Video in the 1970s & 1980s*, red. S. Cubitt, S. Partridge, New Barnet: John Libbey Publishing, 2012, s. 75.

35 A. Lockhart, *A Brief History of Video – Time and Base*, w: *REWIND...*, s. 182–183.

36 John 'Hoppy' Hopkins, cytowany w S. Partridge, op. cit., s. 76.

37 M. Dickson, *Vide Verso: Video's Critical Corpus*, w: *REWIND...*, s. 129. Dickson nie precyzuje czy „wizualizacje" zostały pokazane przez BBC1 albo BBC2, ale zauważa, że TVX zostało później „zakazane przez BBC".

38 D. Boyle, *Subject to Change: Guerrilla Television Revisited*, Nowy Jork – Oksford: Oxford University Press, 1997, s. 17–25.

39 J. T. Caldwell, *Televisuality: Style, Crisis, and Authority in American Television*, New Brunswick, N.J. Rutgers University Press, 1995; D. Boyle, op. cit., s. 17–25.

stacjach inżynierowie dźwięku i obrazu, kamerzyści, wydawcy, montażyści[40]. W wielu przypadkach było to spowodowane różnicami w edukacji, którą otrzymywali przedstawiciele jednej i drugiej grupy. Na tym tle wyraźnie widzimy wyjątkowość WFF: Szkoła Filmowa była bowiem główną i oczywistą drogą, umożliwiającą pracę w telewizji, a uczestnicy grupy prezentowali wysoki poziom umiejętności technicznych. Jednak pomimo faktu, że Warsztatowcy, jako studenci Szkoły Filmowej byli w niej przygotowywani do pracy w przemyśle kinematograficznym i filmowym, świadomie poszukiwali dla siebie miejsca w polu sztuki i postrzegali siebie jako artystów. Nawiązywali współpracę z innymi artystami, także z twórcami z kręgu Akademii Sztuk Pięknych, uczestniczyli w wystawach, performansach i różnego rodzaju działaniach artystycznych, tworzyli filmy o artystach i filmy eksperymentalne, które powstawały w oparciu o zasady odmienne od tych, które rządziły oficjalną kinematografią w PRL. Status „artysty" mógł być szczególnie atrakcyjny dla członków Warsztatu, którzy starali się podważyć dominującą pozycję reżysera jako autora zarówno w polskiej szkole filmowej, jak i w kinematografii w ogóle . Z tej perspektywy film Idę zdaje się w istotny sposób i niezwykle skutecznie artykułować pozycję operatora kamery jako artysty, ponieważ podobnie jak większość działań sztuki performance w latach siedemdziesiątych XX wieku praca ta eksploruje i ukazuje silne poczucie fizycznej obecności i wytrzymałości.

Konkluzja: dziedzictwo Warsztatu

W połowie lat siedemdziesiątych przychylność władz Szkoły Filmowej w Łodzi dla działalności Warsztatu zmniejszyła się. Robakowski sugeruje wprost, że ówczesnemu rektorowi Szkoły, Stanisławowi Kuszewskiemu, nie podobało się zainteresowanie jakie budziły działania WFF[41]. Wycofano wsparcie finansowe dla grupy, która musiała szukać innych źródłach finansowania. Po 1977 roku, po udziale grupy w Documenta 6, działalność Warsztatu zaczęła zamierać, ale wielu z jej członków pozostało w ścisłych związkach ze Szkołą. W Szkole uczył Paweł Kwiek, a także Janusz Połom, Józef Robakowski i Ryszard Waśko[42]. Mieli oni swój istotny udział w stworzeniu Ruchu Odnowy Uczelni[43], organizacji inicjującej strajki i protesty, które miały na celu rozluźnienie struktur Szkoły, stworzenie możliwości mianowania starszej kadry pedagogicznej w trybie wyborów (co udało się, po negocjacjach z Ministerstwem Kultury i Sztuki), a także otwarcie Filmówki na nowe media, w tym na fotografię[44].

Janusz Połom został wybrany dziekanem Wydziału Operatorskiego, ale jego wybór zbiegł się w czasie z wprowadzeniem w Polsce stanu wojennego w grudniu 1981 roku. Stan wojenny trwał do lipca 1983, ale jego wprowadzenie było nadal odczuwalne. Życie polityczne, społeczne i kulturalne było naznaczone represjami, cenzurą i trudnościami ekonomicznymi, zmuszając wiele osób do emigracji. Pomimo tego, że Janusz Połom pełnił swoją funkcję przez kilka lat (w 1984 roku wyemigrował do Meksyku), wspomina, że szukanie kompromisów pomiędzy aspiracjami studentów a restrykcyjną polityką władz było w tym okresie szczególnie trudne. W latach osiemdziesiątych

40 J. Wyver, *TV Against TV: Video Art on Television*, w: *Film and Video Art*, ed. S. Comer, Londyn: Tate Publishing, 2009, s. 122–131.

41 Wywiad z Józefem Robakowskim, maj 2016.

42 Wywiad z Pawłem Kwiekiem, maj 2016.

43 Wywiad z Pawłem Kwiekiem, maj 2016. Zob. Ł. Ronduda, op. cit., s. 273.

44 Wywiad z Józefem Robakowskim, maj 2016.

niewielu dawnych uczestników WFF pozostało w Szkole Filmowej, część z nich została zwolniona z pracy, część wyemigrowała. Józef Robakowski powrócił na uczelnię w 1995 roku i odegrał ponownie istotną rolę w strukturach Szkoły. Był inicjatorem i świadkiem wielu zmian w wprowadzonych w programie Szkoły i dziś ocenia jej program nauczania, uwzględniający przedmioty takie jak fotografia, animacja, animacja komputerowa, jako taki, jakiego on i jego koledzy z Warsztatu domagali się w latach siedemdziesiątych.

Zaangażowanie Robakowskiego na przestrzeni dekad w działalność Szkoły pomaga zapewnić ciągłość świadomości o działalności Warsztatu wśród studentów kinematografii, a przynajmniej wśród studentów łódzkiej Filmówki[45]. Ale ten pozytywny wątek jest raczej odosobniony, wobec szerszego kontekstu, który był opisywany przez Petrie i Stonemana w *Educating Film-Makers*. Jakkolwiek ich rozważania nie dotyczą bezpośrednio Szkoły w Łodzi, to opisują oni ogólnie zmiany, jakie zaszły w edukacji kinematograficznej po 1989 roku pod wpływem postępującej globalizacji i pojawienia się gospodarki wolnorynkowej w Europie Środkowej i Wschodniej. Badacze dowodzą, że wiele szkół filmowych odeszło od wcześniejszych modeli kina rozumianego jako „kino autorskie, pełniące ważną funkcję społeczną, kształtujące obraz kultury"[46]. W nowej sytuacji powstania wolnego rynku, wobec globalizacji, każda, nawet najbardziej szacowna placówka edukacyjna musi obecnie zafunkcjonować jako „miejsce, wykazujące tendencję do „przyjmowania jawnie zawodowej roli podyktowanej potrzebami branży, co prowadzi do reprodukowania komercyjnych formatów i szkodzi zapewne autentycznej oryginalności"[47].

Co ciekawe, Petrie i Stoneman popierają otwarcie „innowacyjność", słowo-wytrych neoliberalnej kulturowej i ekonomicznej polityki, tym samym nie sprzeciwiając się dyktatowi wolnego rynku i globalizacji. Jednocześnie podkreślają, że innowacyjność nie może być osiągana kosztem oddzielenia się praktyki od teorii w procesie nauczania kinematografii, co ich zdaniem ma miejsce, ponieważ rynek wymusza na nas zdobywanie coraz węższych zawodowych specjalizacji. Początkowo trudno jest odnieść dość przygnębiającą wizję branży filmowej po 1989 roku przedstawioną przez Duncana i Petrie, do obrazu progresywnego środowiska, jakie pojawiło się na gruncie Szkoły Filmowej w Łodzi, które opisuje Robakowski i nie jest wykluczone, że charakter polskiego kształcenia po prostu różni się od przyjętej w innych miejscach normy. Petrie przywołuje zresztą także przykłady modeli edukacyjnych, których celem jest równoważenie tych tendencji, jak na przykład zainicjowany w Danii pod koniec lat dziewięćdziesiątych ruch Dogme 95. Badacz zauważa, że wszyscy studenci w Duńskiej Szkole Filmowej są zobowiązani do odbywania zajęć z dramaturgii i muszą pracować z jednej strony według jasno określonych zasad i reguł[48], ale z drugiej wolno im nie odtwarzać schematów narzucanych przez przemysł filmowy.

Jest oczywiste, że sytuacja zatrudnienia w środowisku filmowym wymaga zdobywania nowych umiejętności, a wszyscy pracownicy filmu i mediów muszą obecnie stosować nowe strategie i techniki w negocjowaniu i zapewnianiu pracy. Dlatego muszą stale poszerzać i utrzymywać sieć swoich zawodowych kontaktów, uczyć się nowych technologii, walczyć o stawki i standardy zapewniane przez związki poprzez umowy zbiorowe, przy jednoczesnym zwiększaniu zdolności

45 Program Szkoły nadal nie omawia wspólnej historii multimediów, historii sztuki i filmu, sprawiając, że te dziedziny są omawiane jako oderwane od siebie. Wywiad Andrzejem Różyckim, maj 2016.

46 D. Petrie, P. Stoneman, op. cit., s. 5–6.

47 Ibidem, s. 6.

48 D. Petrie, op. cit. s. 38–39.

adaptacyjnych i elastyczności[49]. John T. Caldwell użył terminu *worker blowback* („silny opór pracowników"), opisując niektóre ze strategii stosowanych przez pracowników filmu i mediów w celu ochrony pozycji zawodowej (i artystycznej), przy jednoczesnym wyrażaniu niezadowolenia z sytuacji zawodowej w mediach społecznościowych. Dzięki takim formom protestu pracownicy filmu i mediów mogą dać upust swojej frustracji, odnosząc ją do swoich obaw dotyczących obniżających się standardów.

Jako studenci Łódzkiej Szkoły Filmowej pod koniec lat sześćdziesiątych i na początku siedemdziesiątych, uczestnicy Warsztatu byli przygotowani do funkcjonowania w określonej i stosunkowo stabilnej strukturze socjalistycznej produkcji i dystrybucji filmowej. W ówczesnej Polsce produkcja filmowa była często zorganizowana wokół osoby reżysera. Uczestnicy Warsztatu marzyli o stworzeniu alternatywnych metod produkcji i dystrybucji filmowej, oferujących znacznie większą autonomię twórczą operatorom, umożliwiających nowe i niekonwencjonalne formy interdyscyplinarnej współpracy, wspieranych eksperymentami z nowymi mediami i technologiami. W tym procesie wypracowali oni cały szereg strategii, które mogą obecnie okazać się bardzo przydatne dla studentów kinematografii, poszukujących sposobów na funkcjonowanie w radykalnie odmiennym środowisku charakteryzującym się nowymi (i zmiennymi) wyzwaniami.

Wielu badaczy podkreśla wyzwania, przed jakimi stoją obecnie pracownicy kinematografii, szczególnie ci nieposiadając stałego zatrudnienia, jak researcherzy produkcji, asystenci, inżynierowie efektów specjalnych czy samozatrudnieni operatorzy[50] Jak dotąd nie poświęcano wiele uwagi szkołom filmowym jako miejscom, w których rozwija się zawodowe umiejętności i aspiracje.[51] W moim przekonaniu, cennym byłoby przeanalizowanie procesów formowania się i artykułowania „profesjonalizmu" (i powiązane z nimi pojęcia „pracy", „rzemiosła", „sztuki" i „innowacyjności") w edukacji filmowej. Państwowe szkoły filmowe mają w tym procesie szczególne znaczenie, ponieważ są finansowanymi przez państwo uznanymi środowiskowo placówkami, których propozycja edukacyjna może być krytyczna lub bierna wobec oficjalnej kinematografii i zasad przemysłu filmowego. Historia Warsztatu Formy Filmowej i jego złożonych relacji ze Szkołą Filmową w Łodzi stanowi szczególnie ważny materiał dla rozważań o przeszłości, teraźniejszości i przyszłości edukacji filmowej.

---

49 J. T. Caldwell, *Worker Blowback: User-Generated, Worker-Generated, and Producer-Generated Content within Collapsing Production Workflows*, w: *Television as Digital Media*, red. J. Bennett, N. Strange, Durham – Londyn: Duke University Press, 2011, s. 302.

50 V. Mayer, *Below the Line: Producers and Production Studies in the New Television Economy*, Durham – Londyn: Duke University Press, 2011, s. 1.

51 Jednym z wyjątków jest praca Daniel Ashtona analizująca oczekiwania i doświadczenia studentów i absolwentów studiów filmowych rozpoczynających pracę w brytyjskim przemyśle. D. Ashton, *Making Media Workers: Contesting Film and Television Industry Career Pathways*, "Television & New Media", 16:3, 2015, s. 275–294.

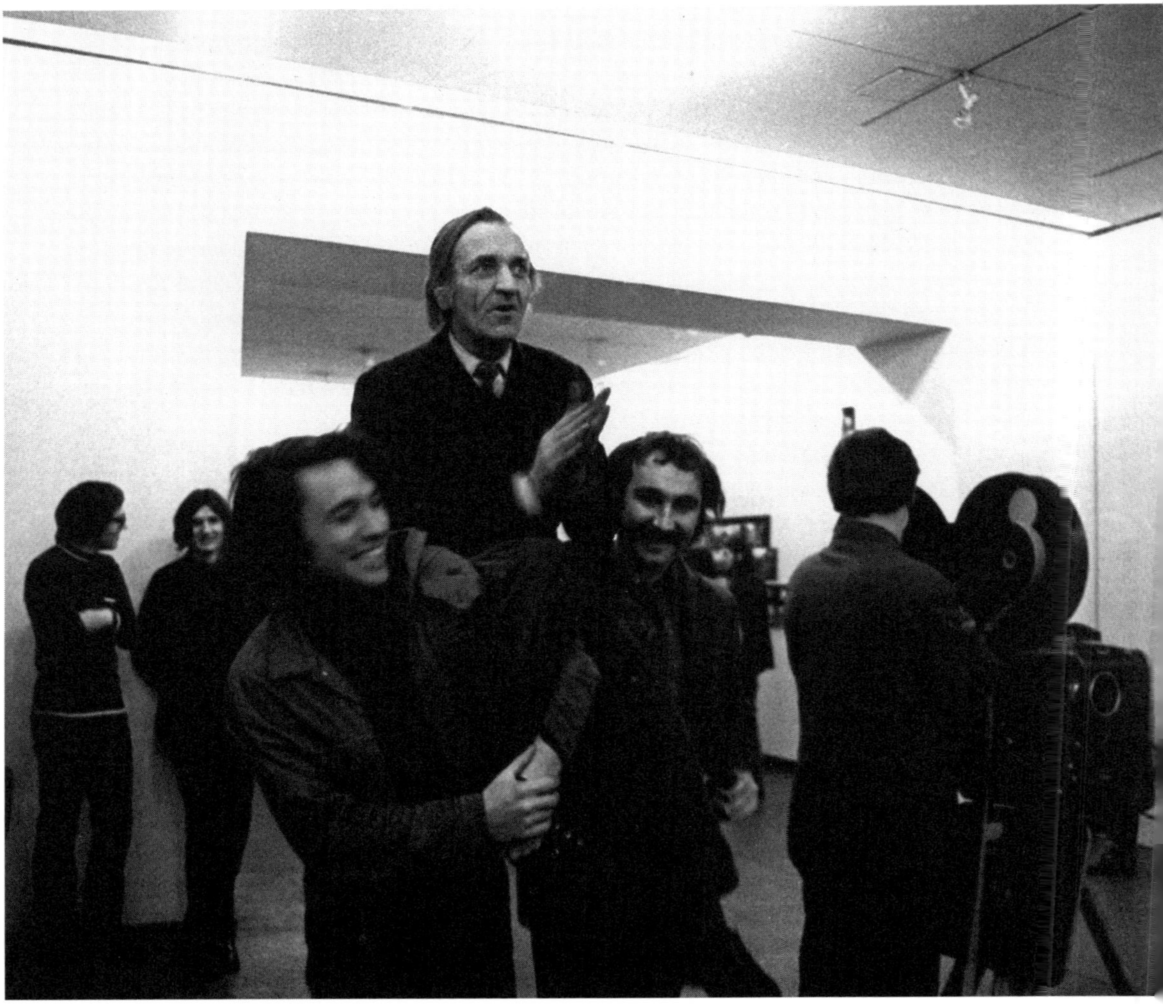

Akcja Warsztat, Muzeum Sztuki, Łódź, 1973 (od lewej: R. Waśko, W. Antczak, J. Cyrus)
Action 'Workshop,' Museum of Art, Łódź, 1973 (from the left: R. Waśko, W. Antczak, J. Cyrus)

Łukasz Ronduda

Warsztat Formy Filmowej czyli koalicja robotników sztuki w robotniczym państwie

Na przełomie lat 60. i 70. możemy zaobserwować wśród artystów awangardowych po obu stronach żelaznej kurtyny zintensyfikowane użycie terminu „robotnik sztuki". Interesująca wydaje się analiza różnic i podobieństw pomiędzy tym jak używali tego terminu, w tym samym niemal czasie nowojorscy artyści Art Workers Coalition w stolicy kapitalistycznego zachodu oraz jak używali go artyści Warsztatu Formy Filmowej po drugiej stronie żelaznej kurtyny, w komunistycznej Polsce. Członkowie obu formacji uczestniczyli w konceptualnej i minimalistycznej rewolucji w sztuce przełomu lat 60. i 70., niemniej jednak zanurzeni byli w zupełnie innych rzeczywistościach społeczno-polityczno-gospodarczych. AWC działali w czasie, diagnozowanej przez Thomasa Piketty'ego „emancypacyjnej anomalii w obrębie kapitalizmu"[1] trwającej od lat 50. do 70. XX wieku. Spowodowana była ona realnym socjalizmem – w ramach którego z kolei działał WFF – którego samo istnienie wymuszało na kapitalizmie w krajach zachodnich wprowadzenie większej równości społecznej, redystrybucji, niwelowania nierówności ekonomicznych etc. AWC używali figury robotnika sztuki w kontekście krytyki kapitalizmu, odnosząc się do generalnej ramy jaką była wymieniona anomalia warunkowana przez istnienie uniwersalnego, antykapitalistycznego projektu emancypacyjnego, którym (przynajmniej w sensie teoretycznym) był komunizm. Z kolei WFF używał tego terminu subwersywnie w kontekście robotniczego państwa dyktatury proletariatu na drodze do komunizmu. Artyści WFF sięgali po takie oficjalne marksistowskie terminy traktując je jako jedyne możliwe w autorytarnym państwie formy otwartej krytyki rzeczywistości.

Art Workers Coalition

Koalicja Robotników Sztuki powstała w styczniu 1969 roku w Nowym Jorku i grupowała artystów uznających konieczność reformy instytucji świata sztuki współczesnej szczególnie w świetle rozwijających się wtedy w Ameryce emancypacyjnych i lewicowych ruchów kontrkulturowych. Wg Julii Bryan-Wilson[2], Członkowie AWC nazywali siebie celowo pracownikami pola sztuki a nie artystami, chcąc odwrócić uwagę od romantycznych konotacji związanych z tym drugim pojęciem. Słowo „pracownik sztuki" dawało pragmatyczną szansę na powołanie szerokiego związku zawodowego artystów, którzy stworzą wspólnotę ponad estetycznymi podziałami i razem będą walczyć bardziej skutecznie o swoje prawa w relacjach z instytucjami zajmującymi się wytwarzaną przez nich sztuką. Członkowie AWC przeprowadzili kilkadziesiąt akcji protestacyjnych, manifestacji i strajków wymierzonych w instytucje (takie jak m.in. MoMA) krytykując instrumentalne traktowanie artystów i ich dzieł, ponadto kwitnący w ich polityce wystawienniczej rasizm i seksizm,

1 T. Piketty, *Kapitał w XXI wieku*, Warszawa: Wydawnictwo Krytyki Politycznej, 2015.

2 J. Bryan-Wilson, *Art Workers - Radical Practice in the Vietnam War Era*, Berkeley: University of California Press, 2009, s. 5.

oraz wielowymiarowe uwikłanie w wojnę w Wietnamie. Członkowie AWC przymierzali się nawet do budowy szerszej koalicji z pracownikami innych branż (brali m.in. udział w strajku poczty) ale ostatecznie nic z tego nie wyszło. Termin „robotnik sztuki" (w przeciwieństwie do innych terminów np. producent kultury) wydawał się członkom AWC bardzo atrakcyjny ze względu na zawarty w nim ładunek polityczny (dążenia do emancypacji, równości, walki wykorzystywanych klas o swoje prawa), który zarazem mógł być wykorzystany do walki z dominującymi instytucjami ale również służyć do ciekawego sproblematyzowania własnej twórczości artystycznej związanej z nowymi trendami w sztuce przełomu lat 60. i 70. walczącymi wówczas o szersze rozpoznanie. AWC składała się bowiem głównie z artystów związanych z konceptualizmem i minimalizmem występujących przeciwko apolitycznej, abstrakcyjnej i ekspresyjnej sztuce poprzedników dominujących ówcześnie w amerykańskich instytucjach. W związku z tym artyści ci (m.in. Carl Andre, Robert Morris, Dan Graham) swoją bardzo wyrafinowaną postawę i kreację artystyczną – nie przeznaczoną bynajmniej dla robotników – chętnie interpretowali w kontekście kategorii takich jak „robotnik sztuki", „praca", „produkcja".

Warsztat Formy Filmowej

O ile w kontekście systemu kapitalistycznego użycie terminu robotnik sztuki, z ewidentnie socjalistycznymi konotacjami, miało emancypacyjny wymiar, tak użycie tego terminu w antykapitalistycznej Polsce rządzonej przynajmniej teoretycznie przez robotników, w której terminologia marksistowskiej walki klas była dominującym językiem opisu rzeczywistości, musiało mieć nieco inne znaczenie. Generalnie członkowie Warsztatu Formy Filmowej używali terminu robotnik sztuki w trzech różnych kontekstach: opisu postawy artystyczno-poznawczej, krytyki społeczno-politycznej oraz krytyki instytucjonalnej.

Artyści Warsztatu Formy Filmowej opisywali swoją analityczno-minimalistyczną postawę artystyczną nawiązując do tradycji radzieckiej sztuki konstruktywistycznej i etosu artysty inżyniera. To stąd wzięli termin „robotnik sztuki", świadomie odrzucając termin artysta w ramach przeciwstawienia się romantycznemu modelowi twórczości artystycznej – modelu pozytywistycznego. Warsztatowcy swą twórczość traktowali w sposób materialistyczny i egalitarny jako paranaukową pracę poznawczą (poprzez naukę jak działa nasza percepcja, wyobraźnia itp.). Dostęp do niej miał mieć każdy, a stawką jej była krytyczna świadomość otaczającego świata. Ta ostatnia (w marksistowskim duchu) powinna wzmacniać „siły wytwórcze" człowieka (robotnika sztuki), kierować je dla pomnożenia jego zdolności, wzmocnienia jego „konstrukcji psychofizycznej", w rezultacie prowadząc do jego większej emancypacji i co za tym idzie równości społecznej. Poza takim marksistowskim rozumieniem swojej roli jako robotników sztuki Warsztatowcy cenili jakości pochodzące ze świata pracy przemysłowej takie jak prawda (natura) materiału, logika konstrukcji, racjonalizm planowania.

Drugim polem wykorzystania terminu „robotnik sztuki" przez WFF była sfera krytyki społeczno-politycznej. Warto tutaj zaznaczyć, iż użycie tego terminu na początku lat 70. przez artystów wywodzących się ze środowisk inteligenckich dokonywało się w sytuacji zupełnie innego położenia klasy robotniczej niż jeszcze dekadę wcześniej. Badacze struktury klasowej PRL-u lat 70. tacy jak

Henryk Domański[3] i Maciej Gdula podkreślają, że wyraźnie zaznaczał się już wtedy konflikt klasowy istniejący w obrębie komunistycznego (deklaratywnie bezklasowego) państwa na dychotomiczny podział na eksploatowane społeczeństwo robotnicze i eksploatująca je władzę partyjną, mającą dostęp do przywilejów, akumulującą kapitał i rządzącą. Szczególnie w latach 70. Partia zrezygnowała z walki o równość. Według Macieja Gduli „do końca lat 60. wyobraźnia polityczna w Polsce zdominowana była przez poszukiwanie dróg budowy sprawiedliwego społeczeństwa. Znajdowało to wyraz zarówno w prądach intelektualnych zbliżonych do Partii jak i projektach opozycyjnych wobec jej władzy. Po roku 1970 nastąpił radykalny odwrót od ideału sprawiedliwego społeczeństwa, który zastąpiła idea społeczeństwa aktywnego. Zmienił się oficjalny język, kultura, nauka, przekształceniu uległy opozycyjne projekty polityczne"[4]. Według Gduli otwierająca się w latach 70. na Zachód socjalistyczna władza wyraźnie odchodziła od egalitaryzmu: „Powstał pomysł, żeby budować społeczeństwo, które zamiast na egalitaryzmie, będzie się w o wiele większym stopniu opierało na innowacyjności, nowoczesności [...] na większym zaangażowaniu pracowników. To miało pchnąć socjalizm na zupełnie inne tory"[5].

Wszystko to stawia w zupełnie innym świetle identyfikację Warsztatowców z Robotnikami. Była ona dla nich sposobem na operowanie aporiami pozornie egalitarnego państwa socjalistycznego, które w istocie było coraz bardziej klasowe. Manifestując swą postawę jako robotników sztuki wielu artystów z grupy chodziło codziennie w tzw. robotniczych kufajkach, watówkach. Podkreślali w ten sposób egalitarność własnej praktyki artystycznej jak i chęć walki z kulturowymi elitami[6]. Często sławili autentycznych ich zdaniem artystów pochodzących z lumpenproletariatu łódzkiego, Wacława Antczaka, Irenę Iżykowską, Edwarda Kowalskiego, Jana Nowackiego i wielu innych, powierzając im znaczącą rolę w swoich przedsięwzięciach artystycznych czy też zapraszając na równych prawach do członkostwa w WFF. W ten sposób aktywnym i równoprawnym członkiem grupy stał się krawiec z zawodu Wacław Antczak, przedstawiciel statystów skupionych przy szkole filmowej. Był on dla Warsztatowców synonimem artysty naturszczyka, który ucieleśniał za swego życia wszystkie cnoty prawdziwego artysty: prostotę, autentyczność, szczerość. Był dla nich prawdziwym robotnikiem sztuki. To właśnie jemu poświęcili Warsztatowcy wspólną pracę *Przekaz z Łodzi* wysyłając jego osobowość w wielu mediach na Biennale Sztuki do São Paulo w 1973 roku[7]. Świadectwem fascynacji Antczakiem są w szczególności filmy: *Reinkarnacja* z 1974 roku (zrealizowany przez całą grupę i przedstawiający Antczaka recytującego swój wiersz), *Egzekucja* Pawła Kwieka (1972, zaginiony) oraz *Jakby lepiej* Andrzeja Różyckiego (1974). Antczak jako rów-

3 H. Domański, *Czy są w Polsce klasy społeczne*, Warszawa: Wydawnictwo Krytyki Politycznej, 2015.

4 Maciej Gdula w rozmowie z Magdaleną Błędowską, *4 czerwca 1989. Jak naród nie obalił komuny*, „Dziennik Opinii Krytyki Politycznej", 13.06.2014, http://www.krytykapolityczna.pl/artykuly/rozmowa-dnia/20140604/gdula-4-czerwca-1989-jak-narod-nie-obalil-komuny [dostęp 8-12-2016].

5 Ibidem.

6 W ramach swojej akcyjnej działalności, członkowie Warsztatu Formy Filmowej przebrani za robotników interweniowali w różnego rodzaju inteligenckie przedsięwzięcia skierowane dla ludu. Na przykład jako „zwykli robotnicy ze stoczni gdańskiej" obśmiewali publicznie na Festiwalu Młodych Filmowców debiut fabularny Krzysztofa Teodora Toeplitza i Jerzego Gruzy pt. *Dzięcioł*. Był to bowiem wg Robakowskiego „oderwany od jakichkolwiek realiów, typowy przykład luksusowej fanaberii socjalistycznej" Wypowiedź Józefa Robakowskiego w rozmowie z autorem.

7 Antczakowi po śmierci byli członkowie Warsztatu wydali książę z jego życiowym eposem literackim, Wacław Antczak, *Antoś Rozpylacz. Polski Odyseusz. Najsławniejszy wojownik w walce z Niemcami hitlerowskimi*, Łódź: PWSFTviT, 2008.

noprawny członek Warsztatu uczestniczył w różnych wyjazdach grupy: do Zakopanego (Festiwal Filmów o Sztuce), Elbląga (Zbliżenia Młodego Warsztatu Twórczego, Kinolaboratorium podczas V Biennale Form Przestrzennych), Warszawy (*Czyszczenie sztuki*). W roku 1971 Antczak wziął udział obok Świdzińskiego w sesji teoretycznej organizowanej w szkole filmowej przez członków WFF w ramach imprezy *Ósme kino*, a także wspólnie z Robakowskim przeprowadził akcję *Wyprzedaż mebli* na Czerwonym Rynku w Łodzi[8].

Warto tutaj zwrócić uwagę na kolejny element figury robotnika sztuki jako elementu krytyki społeczno-politycznej. Otóż, pochodzący raczej z inteligenckich rodzin członkowie WFF w połowie lat 70. wcielając się w klasę robotniczą preferowali współpracę z tzw. lumpenproletariatem niż zwyczajnymi robotnikami przemysłowymi. Działalność grupy w kontekście lumpenproletariatu łódzkiego, czyli ludzi, którzy znajdują się na marginesie systemu i muszą wciąż walczyć o przeżycie, można interpretować jako próbę stworzenia jedynej w swoim rodzaju anarchicznej wspólnoty wyrzutków, outsiderów, jak to określa Robakowski – „bezproduktywnych trutni"[9], z których dominujący system nie ma żadnego pożytku i nie może go w żaden sposób zinstrumentalizować.

Warto dodać, iż jeden z głównych członków grupy – Paweł Kwiek, reprezentujący wówczas odrębne poglądy polityczne niż reszta grupy, oprócz lumpenproletariatu wchodził dość silnie we współpracę z robotnikami przemysłowymi. O ile większość artystów WFF określała swoje poglądy jako antykomunistyczne (nie mogąc oczywiście robić tego oficjalnie), tak Paweł Kwiek wyraźnie deklarował swoje zaangażowanie i poparcie dla rozwijającego się wtedy w Polsce socjalizmu. Traktował go jako projekt emancypacyjny i równościowy. Paweł Kwiek jako robotnik sztuki pragnął, aby artysta w swojej pracy podobnie jak inni robotnicy budował sukces socjalistycznego państwa. Jego rozumienie interesującego nas terminu było różne od tego, które nadawała mu reszta grupy Warsztat Formy Filmowej.

Paweł Kwiek symultanicznie do działalności w Warsztacie Formy Filmowej współpracował z grupą artystów skupionych wokół KwieKulik (Zofia Kulik, Przemysław Kwiek)[10], również aktywnie zaangażowanych w socjalizm, którzy w podobny co on sposób definiowali się jako robotnicy sztuki. Celem sztuki politycznej tworzonej przez nich było udoskonalenie komunikacji pomiędzy ludźmi, w szczególności zaś pomiędzy niższymi a uprzywilejowanymi klasami społecznymi. Ich realizacje, poparte teorią Formy Otwartej Oskara Hansena[11], postulowały wprowadzenie bardziej egalitarnych sposobów komunikacji, opierających się na dialogu, zwiększającej szanse jednostki ludzkiej na emancypację, samorozwój i równe traktowanie. Według nich sztuka ta powinna być poważnie potraktowana przez coraz bardziej klasowo zdeterminowane władze komunistyczne. Jedna z najciekawszych realizacji w tym duchu powstała w wyniku akcji społeczno-artystycznej przeprowadzonej przez Kwieka w małej PGR-owskiej osadzie Niechcice. Artysta umożliwił grupie młodzieży, głównie dzieci z robotniczych rodzin z tej miejscowości, nakręcenie kilku krótkich, jed-

---

8 Warto dodać, że Różycki nakręcił jeszcze film *Teatr Kowalskiego* poświęcony tytułowej amatorskiej grupie teatralnej. Z kolei w ramach akcji *Warsztat* w łódzkim Muzeum Sztuki, przeprowadzonej na zaproszenie Ryszarda Stanisławskiego, członkowie grupy zorganizowali w jej przestrzeniach wystawienniczych kostiumowe wystąpienie Teatru Emerytów Edwarda Kowalskiego (tematem sztuki był upadek Hitlera) oraz imprezy otwarte dla każdego artysty-amatora – „koncert dyletantów" i konkurs na podpis artystyczny.

9 Józef Robakowski, wypowiedź w rozmowie z autorem.

10 *KwieKulik*, red. Ł. Ronduda, G. Schollhammer, Warszawa: Muzeum Sztuki Nowoczesnej w Warszawie, 2012.

11 *Oskar Hansen — Opening Modernism*, red. A. Kędziorek, Ł. Ronduda, Warszawa: Museum of Modern Art, 2014, s. 52.

rominutowych, filmów według jej własnego scenariusza. Natomiast sam przyjął rolę posłusznego operatora kamery filmowej. Kwiekowi chodziło o – „przekazanie głosu tym, którzy go do tej pory nie mieli". Umożliwiając młodym ludziom z Niechcic realizację własnych filmów, artysta pragnął ich zaktywizować, rozbudzić w nich postawę krytyczną i kreatywną wobec rzeczywistości, pragnął im pomóc w uświadomieniu sobie uwarunkowań determinujących kształt ich doświadczenia życiowego. Kwiek powracał w następnych latach do Niechcic, nawiązując długotrwałą, procesualną współpracę z miejscową robotniczą wspólnotą[12].

Trzecim znaczeniem terminu robotnik sztuki artyści Warsztatu operowali w kontekście krytyki instytucjonalnej, głównie aby podkreślić, że identyfikują się jako grupa lekceważona w obrębie istniejącego oficjalnie systemu instytucji sztuki w Polsce, walcząc o emancypację. Establishment stanowiły dla nich oficjalne instytucje państwa odpowiedzialne za kulturę oraz instytucje tzw. konsekrowanej awangardy (np. Galeria Foksal), blokujące rozwój (instytucjonalizację) nowych tendencji sztuki awangardowej, z którymi artyści – robotnicy sztuki się utożsamiali. Przeprowadzając krytykę instytucji sztuki WFF proponował odmienny od dominującego model ich modernizacji. Krytyka ta polegała na stawianiu merytorycznych pytań i atakach na określone instytucje, osoby, procedury (a nie na snuciu abstrakcyjnych filozoficznych rozważań), na ujawnianiu konkretnych uwikłań finansowych, ideologicznych, administracyjnych twórczości filmowej i artystycznej. WFF starał się łączyć działalność instytucjonalną i artystyczną, oraz traktował sztukę i kino w sposób pragmatyczny i zdesakralizowany – w odróżnieniu od dominujących idealistyczno-romantycznych tradycji artystycznych i filmowych. Członkowie grupy starali się „spuszczać powietrze" z nadmiernie rozbuchanych imprez celebrujących pozorne sukcesy polskiego kina, mających *de facto* te sukcesy kreować poprzez nadprodukcję nagród i tytułów przyznawanych miernym twórcom i ich dziełom, operowanie miałkim dyskursem opartym na schematach, nadającym tym filmom niewspółmiernie wysoką rangę, kryjącym nepotyzm.

Zakończenie

Artyści WFF i AWC w podobnie pragmatyczny sposób odchodzili od romantycznych konotacji związanych z terminem sztuka i artysta. Obie grupy łączył silny rys krytyki instytucjonalnej i definiowanie artystów jako eksploatowanych robotników w podziale pracy w instytucjonalnym świecie sztuki. Wspólny dla obu grup był również antyestablishmentowy impuls występowania przeciwko dominującemu kanonowi sztuki.

AWC gromadziło artystów skupionych wokół samych idei krytyki instytucjonalnej, podczas gdy WFF gromadziło artystów głównie ze względu na wspólne artystyczne przekonania, z nich dopiero wynikały akcje krytyki instytucjonalnej. Niemniej jednak AWC i WFF używali terminu „robotnik sztuki" w ścisłym powiązaniu z konceptualno-minimalistyczną rewolucją w sztuce, z fascynacją jakościami pochodzącymi ze świata pracy przemysłowej. Warsztatowcy krytykowali instytucje sztuki głównie z perspektywy estetycznej a nie politycznej, obnażając mistyfikacje, puste gesty instytucjonalnego świata sztuki i kinematografii. W przeciwieństwie do AWC nie walczyli jednak o prawa kobiet artystek, przedstawicieli mniejszości i ich większą obecność w instytucjach sztuki. AWC atakowali oficjalną politykę państwa (wojna w Wietnamie), z kolei WFF nie mogli tego robić

12 Podczas jednej z takich wizyt powstał bardzo ciekawy film *Niedziela 15.IV.73 – Dniem Sztuki w Niechcicach.*

otwarcie i skupiali się raczej na krytyce rosnących podziałów klasowych w pozornie bezklasowym państwie socjalistycznym. Przy tym działalność Pawła Kwieka podejmuje ważne dla amerykańskich robotników sztuki konteksty walki o emancypację grup marginalizowanych i represjonowanych. Generalnie członkowie WFF łączyli krytykę instytucjonalną z wchodzeniem w udane koalicje z klasą robotniczą, co z kolei nie udało się AWC.

Swoistym podsumowaniem historii robotników sztuki z WFF i AWC była wystawa *Konstrukcja w Procesie* w ramach, której doszło do spotkania przedstawicieli amerykańskich robotników sztuki (m.in. Dan Graham, Carl Andre) i polskich. W przypadku tej wystawy doszło do unikalnej współpracy artystów neoawangardowych skupionych wokół byłych członków WFF z „Solidarnością", robotniczym związkiem zawodowym, która przejęła patronat nad organizacją wystawy. Przyświecającym jej mottem stały się słowa Mieczysława Szczuki: „Sztuka nie może być pustym ornamentem społeczeństwa, artysta musi współuczestniczyć w organizacji życia"[13]. Samoorganizacja artystów – robotników sztuki – tworzących oddolnie wystawę swych dzieł znalazła sojusznika w samoorganizacji zawiązku zawodowego robotników „Solidarność" tworzącego oddolnie swoje niezależne struktury w ramach wrogiego mu, tylko deklaratywnie socjalistycznego, państwa.

13 Por. J. Głowacki, *Konstrukcja w procesie*, w: *Muzeum Konstrukcji w Procesie*, Łódź: Fundacja Edukacji Wizualnej, 2006.

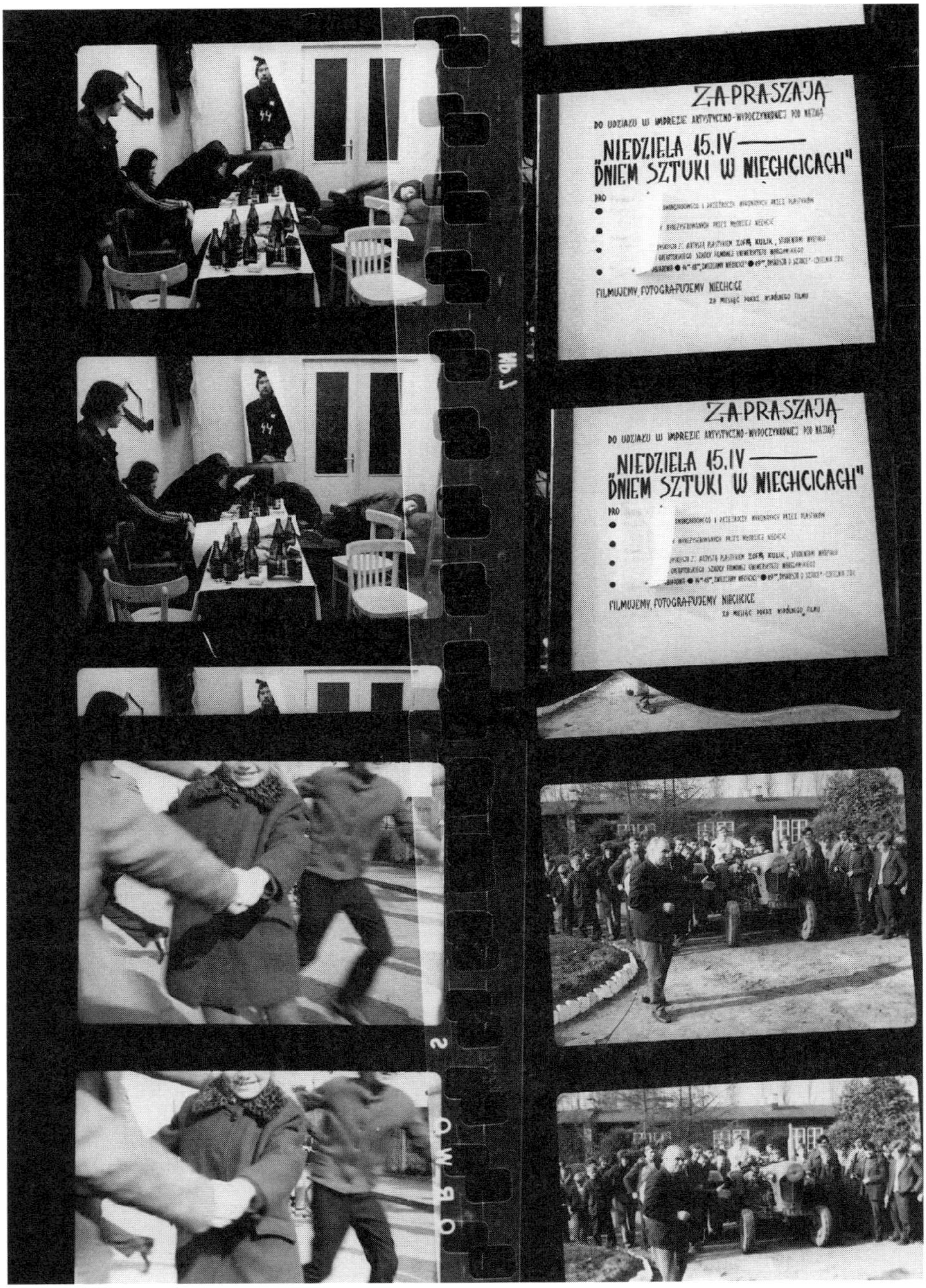

Paweł Kwiek, *Niechcice*, 1973, 35 mm, 5'01''
Paweł Kwiek, *Niechcice*, 1973, 35 mm, 5'01''

George Clark

Zapewniamy kontakt z polską awangardą artystyczną: tryby wymiany w Warsztacie Formy Filmowej

Obiecany kontakt z polską awangardą, do którego nawiązuje tytuł eseju, został zadeklarowany w zaproszeniu do nadsyłania zgłoszeń do Kinolaboratorium w 1973 roku[1]. To pięciodniowe wydarzenie zostało zorganizowane wspólnie przez Warsztat Formy Filmowej (WFF) oraz Laboratorium Sztuki – Galerię EL w Elblągu. Kinolaboratorium stanowiło wcześnie podjętą próbę włączenia działalności Warsztatu Formy Filmowej w międzynarodowy ruch awangardowy lat 70. XX w. Badanie prac powstałych w ramach WFF stawia obecnie wiele wzywań wynikających z ważnych przekształceń społecznych i politycznych, które zmieniły pojmowanie sztuki i filmu oraz, co istotne, metody prezentacji prac i ich wymiany. Niniejszy tekst stanowi próbę przyjrzenia się poszczególnym sposobom funkcjonowania tych artystów i ich prac koncentrując się na podejmowanych przez nich interwencjach w sieci wymiany i mechanizmy kształcenia w latach 70. XX wieku, których kluczowym przykładem jest Kinolaboratorium.

Obok prac głównych członków Warsztatu Formy Filmowej, w ramach Kinolaboratorium zaprezentowano także wybór filmów przedwojennych, począwszy od *Baletu mechanicznego* (Fernand Léger, 1924) i *Psa andaluzyjskiego* (Luis Buñuel i Salvador Dali, 1929) po *Gabinet Doktora Caligari* (Robert Weine, 1920) oraz, co dla nas najistotniejsze, *Przygodę człowieka poczciwego* Stefana i Franciszki Themersonów (1939), która „w tym zestawie miała znaczenie szczególne jako najwybitniejszy film polski, podsumowanie dorobku awangardy"[2]. Wybór współczesnych filmów zza granicy był bardziej arbitralny, jako że podyktowały go istniejące w tamtym czasie powiązania. Obejmował on prace Normana McLarena z Kanady, Javiera Aguirre z Hiszpanii, Siergeja Paradżanowa z ZSRR oraz filmy z kręgu Balázs Béla Studio z Węgier.

Warsztat Formy Filmowej opierał się na wymianie prowadzonej pomiędzy praktykami i teoretykami na polu różnorodnych mediów, zgodnie z treścią manifestu grupy: „Obok realizatorów filmowych w WARSZTACIE pracuje grupa plastyków, muzyków, fotografików, poetów i techników"[3]. O dążeniu do rozwijania tego rodzaju trybów wymiany artystycznej świadczy otwarcie się na idee radykalnej edukacji w zakresie tworzenia i omawiania prac oraz wymieniania się nimi. Kluczowe osiągnięcia twórców Warsztatu były propozycjami nowych modeli wymiany, choć paradoksalnie to właśnie te prace należą do najrzadziej prezentowanych i najmniej znanych za granicą. W realizacjach takich, jak *22x* (1971), *Żywa Galeria* (1974/75) i *Osieki* (1974) akcent padał na pracę nad filmem w ramach krytycznej praktyki

---

1 Kinolaboratorium odbyło się w ramach V Biennale Form Przestrzennych w Elblągu w dniach 15-20 czerwca 1973 roku.

2 J. Zagrodzki, „Kinolaboratorium", maszynopis, 1973, tekst opracowany w oparciu o artykuł J. Robakowskiego Kronika V Biennale Form Przestrzennych Kinolaboratorium „Notatnik Robotnika Sztuki", 1973 nr 5. 5http://repozytorium.fundacjaarton.pl/index.php?action-view/object&objid-3139&colid-75&catid-18&lang-pl [dostęp 7-12-2016].

3 *Warsztat Formy Filmowej*, w: *Żywa Galeria. Łódzki progresywny ruch artystyczny 1969–1981*, red. J. Robakowski, Łódź: Łódzki Dom Kultury – Galeria FF, 2000, s. 35.

pedagogicznej, analizę trybów produkcji artystycznej w poszukiwaniu nowych metod tworzenia i uczenia się o sztuce, zgodnie ze stwierdzeniem zawartym w manifeście grupy: „Działalność nasza jest więc w istocie oduczaniem się tego wszystkiego, co dało nam wykształcenie i to, co nazywamy kulturą zastaną"[4]. W połowie lat 70. XX w. Warsztat cieszył się już międzynarodową renomą, a poszczególni twórcy prezentowali swoje prace na ważnych pokazach, wystawach i festiwalach za granicą, m.in. w São Paulo, Knokke-Heist, Edynburgu, Amsterdamie, Antwerpii, Kolonii i Kassel. Równolegle zrealizowanych zostało kilka projektów, które miały na celu wytworzenie nowych trybów wymiany pomiędzy artystami oraz w ramach sieci artystycznych. Uczestnictwo Warsztatu w Biennale Sztuki w São Paulo w 1973 roku stanowiło istotny przykład wymiany na skalę międzynarodową, dzięki któremu grupa mogła rozwijać środki służące partycypacji w tym jakże odległym kontekście, jak również podważaniu istniejących koncepcji sztuki i edukacji. Wkładem członków WFF w Biennale była transmisja postaci poety Wacława Antczaka (1911–1974), regularnie współpracującego z Warsztatem, za pośrednictwem rozmaitych mediów, takich jak fotografia, wideo, dźwięk i film, w ramach pracy *Przekaz z Łodzi* (lipiec–sierpień 1973). Jak głosił towarzyszący jej tekst *Przekaz osobowości Wacława Antczaka*, „treścią pokazu będzie nobilitacja artysty-przedstawiciela łódzkiego folkloru miejskiego, ukształtowanego przez specyficzny zespół czynników kulturowych: poza oficjalnymi prądami artystycznymi; poza tym co nazywamy sztuką; poza wykształceniem artystycznym"[5]. Pozycja Wacława Antczaka jako *outsidera* była istotna dla członków Warsztatu i służyła im do podważania paradygmatów produkcji i wartości kulturowej.

Jedną z kluczowych koncepcji rozwijanych w obrębie Warsztatu była idea filmu tworzonego kolektywnie, czy też filmu „składkowego", w ramach którego poszczególni artyści przygotowywali jednominutowe fragmenty wspólnej pracy. Ograniczenie czasu trwania pojedynczej „składki" do jednej minuty było drogą do podważenia uprzywilejowanej ekspresji i autorstwa oraz stworzenia prac reprezentatywnych dla wielu punktów widzenia. Pierwszym filmem zrealizowanym w ten sposób był film Józefa Robakowskiego *22x*, stworzony wraz ze studentami Państwowej Wyższej Szkoły Sztuk Plastycznych w Łodzi, którym Robakowski powierzył odcinki nienaświetlonej taśmy 35 mm i dał wolną rękę w pracy z tym materiałem. Wielu z nich rysowało bezpośrednio na emulsji, zarówno w polu obrazu, jak i dźwięku optycznego, wiążąc w ten sposób bezpośrednio nanoszone rysy z dźwiękiem w filmie. Film *22x* jest istotny także jako jedna z pierwszych prób w kręgu Warsztatu, której celem było stworzenie pracy przez wspólnotę artystyczną.

Idea wspólnotowych, otwartych dociekań artystycznych była rozwijana w ramach wydarzenia Kinolaboratorium, stanowiącego część V Biennale Form Przestrzennych w Elblągu. Biennale, w którym uczestniczyło 120 twórców reprezentujących różne dziedziny sztuki, cechować miała nieskrępowana i otwarta formuła organizacyjna. Według dyrektora Galerii EL, Gerarda Kwiatkowskiego, „negacja wszystkich konwencji i norm artystycznych miała znamienny wpływ na całokształt wydarzeń. Spontaniczne prowokacje i reakcje artystyczne wyzwoliły możliwości dla nowych pojęć"[6].

4 Cyt. za *The Workshop of the Film Form, 1970–1977. Early Film Work from Poland*, red. G. Joseph-Hunter, Ł. Ronduda, L. Zippay, Nowy Jork – Warszawa: Electronic Art Intermix – Centrum Sztuki Współczesnej Zamek Ujazdowski, 2004, s. 21–22.

5 „Przekaz osobowości Wacława Antczaka", maszynopis, 1973. http://repozytorium.fundacjaarton.pl/index.php?action-view/object&objid-3083&tagid-982&lang-pl [dostęp 7-12-2016].

6 J. Zagrodzki, op. cit.

Biennale obejmowało szereg różnorodnych wydarzeń i działań, takich jak wystawy i performanse – prezentowano prace realizowane na miejscu, bądź też projekty nadesłane pocztą, jak również dokumentację artystyczną. Pod auspicjami Warsztatu wraz z uczestnikami imprezy stworzono film zatytułowany Pawła Kwieka *Kinolaboratorium*, w którego powstaniu udział wzięli Javier Aguirre, Piotr Bernacki, Karol Cichecki, Milo Kurtis, Przemysław Kwiek i Zofia Kulik, Stanisław Kowalski, Gerard Kwiatkowski, Antoni Mikołajczyk, Józef Robakowski oraz Włodzimierz Wieczorkiewicz. Odnosząc się do wyświetlanych na Biennale awangardowych klasyków, niektórzy uczestnicy podszywali się pod styl znany z wczesnych dziejów kina. Pierwszą taką pracą był *Polewacz polany* Pawła Kwieka i Karola Cicheckiego, gdzie przy akompaniamencie fortepianu artyści dokonali remake'u wczesnego filmu braci Lumière *Polewacz polany* (1895), w którym mężczyzna zostaje podstępem skłoniony do tryśnięcia sobie w twarz wodą ze szlaucha. Film Józefa Robakowskiego przedstawiał artystę zmierzającego w stronę kamery z lustrem, w którym odbijali się członkowie ekipy filmowej, co przywodzi na myśl grę luster w *Żywocie człowieka poczciwego* Themersonów, jak również wczesny film Roberta Morrisa *Lustro* (1971). Tym, co najbardziej rzuca się w oczy w przypadku Kinolaboratorium jest sposób, w jaki rozmaite prace i strategie artystyczne wpływały na inne prace, a motywy, działania i postacie powtarzały się w różnych sekwencjach. Tego rodzaju dialog pomiędzy pracami najłatwiej zauważyć w sekwencji Przemysława Kwieka i Zofii Kulik, w której twórcy powtórzyli gest Robakowskiego z lustrem jako mimowie oraz ujęcia maszyny do pisania obecne wcześniej w filmie Stanisława Kowalskiego, a także zawarli interwencję Wacława Antczaka, który pryska sobie aerozolem do ust, powtarzając w ten sposób wcześniejsze działanie Istvána Sasa. Ich sekwencja zawiera także ujęcia samych artystów przygotowujących pracę. Połączenie przez Kwieka i Kulik różnych strategii artystycznych jest niezwykłą cechą Kinolaboratorium. Wspólnie stworzony film przełamuje ideę odrębnej wypowiedzi artystycznej i pokazuje sposób, w jaki film i sztuka powstawać mogą na drodze dialogu.

Na bazie brzemiennego w skutki wydarzenia Kinolaboratorium i wyłaniających się modeli kolektywnej twórczości artystycznej Józef Robakowski przystąpił do realizacji ambitnego projektu 25-minutowego filmu barwnego *Żywa Galeria*. Ponad dwudziestu twórców otrzymało „możliwość jednominutowej wypowiedzi"[7], dzięki czemu powstał bogaty zapis twórczości artystów czynnych w latach 70. XX w., m.in. Henryka Stażewskiego, Zbigniewa Dłubaka, Zbigniewa Gostomskiego, Natalii LL, Pawła Freislera, Ryszarda Waśki i Zbigniewa Warpechowskiego. Poszczególne fragmenty trwały od 30 sekund do trzech minut. Film pierwotnie miał prezentować artystów związanych z Muzeum Sztuki w Łodzi (założonym przez członków grupy a.r., artystów Władysława Strzemińskiego, Katarzynę Kobro, Henryka Stażewskiego oraz poetów Juliana Przybosia i Jana Brzękowskiego), lecz ostatecznie objął swoim zasięgiem szeroką scenę sztuki współczesnej połowy lat 70. XX wieku, aby "odkryć za wszelką cenę mentalność aktualnie działających artystów, ujawnić ich świadomość artystyczną"[8]. Bazując na formacie galerii performatywnej, czy też galerii rozgrywającej się w czasie (rozwijanym w ramach kolejnych projektów kuratorskich, takich jak powstała w 1978 roku Galeria Wymiany), *Żywa galeria* miała reprezentować najważniejsze postawy i strategie artystyczne tamtego okresu.

Za sprawą otwierającego ujęcia, w którym kamera prześlizguje się po słowach widocznych na obrazie Henryka Stażewskiego z 1970 roku: *L'artiste qui ne lutte pas dans son travail travaille contre*

7 Ibidem.

8 J. Robakowski, „Aspekty motywujące powstanie filmu *Żywa Galeria*" *1974-75*, w: *Józef Robakowski*, red. T. Mayer, M. Jachuła, Lipsk–Nowy Jork: MINI/ Goethe-Institut Curatorial Residencies Ludlow 38, Spector Books, 2011, s. 27.

l'art. („Artysta, który nie walczy w swojej pracy, pracuje przeciwko sztuce"), *Żywa galeria* stała się filmem natchnionym duchem tego wpływowego artysty awangardowego i propagatora wczesnych ruchów awangardowych, podejmując refleksję nad naturą sztuki i sytuując współczesną awangardę w kontekście historycznym. Stażewski był bardzo istotnym łącznikiem z pierwszym pokoleniem artystów awangardowych w Polsce, skupionych w grupach Blok, Praesens i a.r., a także odegrał ważną rolę w tworzeniu kontekstu dla prezentacji i dyskusji o sztuce współczesnej.[9] *Żywa galeria* zostaje ujęta w ramę otwierającej sekwencji z głosem z offu i czarno-białymi fotografiami dokumentującymi powstawanie "wypowiedzi artystycznych". Poszczególne prace i wypowiedzi operują na rozmaite sposoby, począwszy od prób działania odnoszącego się bezpośrednio do uwarunkowań filmu, jak np. film Ryszarda Winiarskiego, gdzie czarne sześciany pojawiają się na ekranie w pozornie przypadkowej kolejności, by następnie wyczernić cały ekran w synchronizacji z narastającą falą dźwiękową, bądź też gry Andrzeja Różyckiego z fotografią, projekcją i żywą obecnością. Inne prace tworzą przestrzeń dla prezentacji performansów lub akcji – najlepsze przykłady to fragment w którym Natalia LL przybiera różne pozy w barwnym studiu fotograficznym oraz akcja Zbigniewa Warpechowskiego, gdzie artysta wypuszcza z klatki ptaka przypiętego wstążką do ryby znajdującej się w stojącym obok akwarium. Jeszcze inne prace dają wyraz analitycznej postawie twórców: Ryszard Waśko kontynuuje badania nad dźwiękiem w filmie ukazując ścianę pokrytą dużych rozmiarów siatką numeryczną, która odpowiada wysokościom dźwięków zmieniających się w miarę najazdu kamery. Taka postawa obecna jest też w wykładzie performatywnym Piotra Bernackiego. Jedną z najbardziej znanych prac ukazanych w *Żywej galerii* jest działanie Andrzeja Partuma, które przybiera tu postać interwencji w film, podobnie jak pierwotnie stanowiło interwencję w przestrzeń publiczną. Andrzej Partum wywiesił nad Krakowskim Przedmieściem w Warszawie, pomiędzy Akademią Sztuk Pięknych i Uniwersytetem Warszawskim, dużych rozmiarów transparent, na którym widniał tylko i wyłącznie napis „Milczenie awangardowe".

Żywa galeria stanowi przykład filmu „składkowego" z tamtego okresu. Kolejną ważną pracą jest film *Osieki* Pawła Kwieka (1974), który powstał w czasie Międzynarodowych Spotkań Artystów, Naukowców i Teoretyków Sztuki w Osiekach w 1974 roku. Kwiek zaprosił 17 uczestników do stworzenia krótkich, jednominutowych filmów. Obejmowały one rozmaite prace, począwszy od tych, których twórcy badali sposoby filmowania malarstwa, jak *Linia-stalówka* Andrzeja Ciesielskiego, gdzie kamera w dużym zbliżeniu podąża za ręką z wolna kreślącą falistą linię, ale „finalny" rysunek nigdy nie zostaje ukazany, po improwizowane akcje Wojciecha Krzywobłockiego i Walentego Gabrysiaka, ustawiających na plaży słup w celu prezentacji wielkoformatowej pracy w plenerze. W głównej, zrealizowanej wspólnie części filmu kamera zostaje wprawiona w ruch wysiłkiem całej grupy. Artyści pchają samochód aż do momentu, w którym pojazd rusza i zabiera ze sobą kamerę w kinetyczną podróż polną drogą. Inne prace przybierały charakter interwencji lub minimalistycznych prowokacji, począwszy od nienaświetlonego odcinka taśmy w *Cage* Janusza Zagrodzkiego, gdzie oglądamy jedynie przebłysk obrazu na końcu, skończywszy na filmie *Trawa* Wojciecha Bruszewskiego, który przez minutę ukazywać miał pewien widok, lecz jak głosi plansza tytułowa: "Wojciech Bruszewski chciał sfilmować widok trawy przez 1 minutę.

9 Henrykowi Stażewskiemu poświęcony został film zrealizowany później przez członka WFF Ryszarda Waśko *Dokumentacja 1913–1981. Film o twórczości i działalności artystycznej Henryka Stażewskiego* z 1981 roku.

Nie zrobiłem tego filmu w wyniku złej organizacji pracy." Wśród prac, które często jawią się jako zapisy spontanicznych akcji odnajdziemy *Pożegnania* Józefa Robakowskiego, czyli grupowy portret, w którym mężczyzna usiłuje objąć i pocałować poszczególnych uczestników, spotykając się z różnymi reakcjami, od czułości po opór, by w końcu pocałować kamerę, bądź też *Scenariusz* Tomasa Straussa, gdzie dramatyczny gest wejścia do morza ukazany zostaje w niemal niewidoczny sposób poprzez zbliżenie stóp, które wkraczają w fale i wychodzą poza kadr, pozostawiając jedynie ślady na piasku rozmywane roztrzaskującymi się o brzeg falami.

Obie prace powstały podczas wydarzeń gromadzących szereg różnych artystów podejmujących refleksję nad panującym w tamtym okresie klimatem pedagogicznym, w którym twórcy funkcjonowali i tworzyli swoje prace. Projekty te uznać można także za kontynuację wpływowych modeli radykalnej pedagogiki rozwijanych przez Oskara Hansena (1922–2005), związanych z jego teorią Formy Otwartej[10]. Tego rodzaju sposób pracy i wspólnej twórczości dostrzec można w rozmaitych kolektywnych działaniach zainspirowanych teoriami Hansena z lat 60. i 70. XX wieku. Najwcześniejszym z nich stał się film *Działania* (KwieKulik, 1972), w który zaangażowany był także Paweł Kwiek. Powstał on w czasie czterodniowej akcji grupowej, w której uczestniczyli Przemysław Kwiek, Zofia Kulik, Jan S. Wojciechowski, Jacek Łomnicki, Krzysztof Zarębski, Jacek Dobrowolski oraz członkowie zespołu Grupa w Składzie (Milo Kurtis, Jacek Malicki, Andrzej Kasprzyk). Jak wspomina Robakowski, innym źródłem inspiracji w tamtym okresie była „praca pedagogiczna i artystyczna Zbigniewa Dłubaka – artysty warszawskiego, który zaczął prowadzić interesujące zajęcia z fotografii w Szkole Filmowej (PWSFTviT) i Plastycznej (PWSSP). W wyniku tego studenci otwierają się na inną jeszcze perspektywę rozumienia istoty sztuki. Na ogół ten nowy, witalny ruch rozwija się poza oficjalnymi programami uczelni artystycznych, mając charakter samokształceniowy"[11].

Realizowany przez te projekty filmowe model „składkowy" zaczerpnięty został z formatu prezentacji grupowych, takich jak biennale czy konferencja, choć warto przyjrzeć mu się także w kontekście antologii czy magazynu jako formatów służących strukturyzowaniu, gromadzeniu i dystrybucji współczesnych praktyk artystycznych. Format magazynu koresponduje także z celem przyświecającym tym projektom, jakim było uchwycenie współczesności i wspólnot artystycznych w momencie ich powstawania, jak również szerzenie informacji na ich temat. Projekty te porównać można do programów telewizyjnych zapoczątkowanych przez niemieckich artystów Gerry'ego Schuma i Ursulę Wevers, a zwłaszcza wpływowej *Galerii telewizyjnej* (*Fernsehgalerie*), na którą składała się krótkotrwale istniejąca galeria oraz dwa programy antologiczne *Land Art* (1969) i *Identifications* (1970) wyemitowane przez niemiecką telewizję. Można postawić tezę, że członkowie Warsztatu realizowali filmy wspólnie po to, by prowadzić badania nad środkami tworzenia sztuki, nie zaś po to, by za pomocą nowych mediów kreować alternatywne instytucje, jak działo się to w przypadku *Fernsehgalerie*. Działania Warsztatu można wobec tego pojmować jako przeciwstawne wobec wspomnianych inicjatyw – jako projekty krytyczne i pedagogiczne, które miały na celu badanie istniejących struktur i sposobów ich artykulacji, nie zaś odnawianie tych struktur przy pomocy nowych mediów. Krytyczny komentarz Erica de Bruyna dotyczący *Fernsehgalerie* brzmiał następująco „»nowa sztuka

10 Rozwijanej w jego pracy, tekstach i działalności dydaktycznej na Akademii Sztuk Pięknych w Warszawie od 1950 roku oraz w ramach projektów wystawienniczych, takich jak *Oskar Hansen – Poszukiwanie metody kształcenia w plastyce*, Warszawa: Muzeum Adama Mickiewicza, 1966.

11 J. Robakowski, *Żywa galeria, Łódź 1995–1997*, http://www.robakowski.eu/tx11.html [dostęp 7-12-2016].

telewizyjna« nie wytwarzała niczego oprócz powidoku »dawnej galerii sztuki«"[12]. Sama Wevers zreflektowałasię w 1979 roku, stwierdzając: „samo medium okazało się niezdolne do omówienia tematu w możliwy do przyjęcia sposób"[13]. Dlatego też działania Warsztatu wyraźnie odróżniają się od interwencji artystycznych, które wspomogły włączenie filmu i wideo w kontekst sztuki współczesnej w Europie Zachodniej, jak choćby wystawa *Prospect 71: Projections*[14], czy właśnie *Fernsehgalerie*. Warsztat funkcjonował w ramie i logice pedagogicznej z zamiarem reformowania artystów, publiczności i społeczeństwa poprzez analizę mediów, bądź też, jak głosił wczesny manifest grupy, poprzez "analizę funkcjonowania środków kontaktowania się [...]"[15]. Ambicja rozmontowywania systemów rządzących sztuką i edukacją w imię szeroko zakrojonej transformacji społecznej zbliża Warsztat do takich inicjatyw, jak działania K3 prowadzone w Balázs Béla Studio w Budapeszcie, bądź też Artist Placement Group w Wielkiej Brytanii. Bezpośredni zwrot ku widzowi w *Żywej galerii* oraz idea jednominutowych wypowiedzi filmowych jako sposobu dogłębnego odczytania „działalności quasi-naukowej" idą w parze z celem Warsztatu, jakim było analizowanie „istoty kina" bez „politykowania, moralizowania, estetyzowania, i bawienia widza"[16].

Jednym z najbardziej wyrazistych kolektywnych dzieł powstałych w obrębie Warsztatu jest film *Niechcice* Pawła Kwieka (1973), stworzony w czasie akcji *Niedziela 15 IV 1973 – Dzień sztuki w Niechcicach*. Paweł Kwiek współpracował z grupą młodzieży z tej PGR-owskiej wsi przy tworzeniu przez nią jej własnego filmu. Artysta wspierał działania młodzieży jako operator kamery, pozostawiając jej swobodę w kwestii pozostałych aspektów filmu. Podobnie jak "jednominutówki", praca ta ukazuje sposób, w jaki tego rodzaju strukturę wypowiedzi artystycznej usytuować można w społecznościach spoza świata sztuki. W odróżnieniu od grup artystycznych, takich jak Warsztat, bądź też tymczasowych społeczności zawiązywanych w czasie Międzynarodowych Spotkań Artystów, Naukowców i Teoretyków Sztuki w Osiekach, czy też Biennale Form Przestrzennych, Kwiek pracował tu z już istniejącą społecznością PGR-owskiej wsi, angażując młodzież w proces tworzenia pracy, która odzwierciedli ją samą. Starając się „dać głos tym, którzy go do tej pory nie mieli", Kwiek oparł film na swoim zainteresowaniu punktem styku socjologii i sztuki. Wspierając grupę młodzieży w samodzielnym kształtowaniu uwarunkowań twórczości filmowej w obrębie jej małej społeczności, projekt ten sprawił, że kino stało się środkiem autorefleksji. Łukasz Ronduda pisał: „Najważniejszy dla artysty był sam proces społeczno-artystyczny, który udało mu się wywołać [...], a mniej jego finalny element, jakim był skończony film"[17]. Ten zwrot

---

12 E. de Bruyn, *Land Art in the Mediascape: On the Politics of Counterpublicity in the Year 1969*, w: *Ready to Shoot: Fernsehgalerie Gerry Schum*, Düsseldorf: Kunsthalle Düsseldorf, 2004, s. 146.

13 U. Wevers, *Gerry Schum: The Television Gallery. The Idea and How it Failed*, w: *Museums by Artists*, red. A. A. Bronson, P. Gale, Toronto: Art Metropole, 1983, s. 284.

14 Wpływowa wystawa „Prospect 71: Projection" stanowiła wcześnie podjętą próbę zaproszenia artystów konceptualnych do stworzenia prac filmowych na wystawę. Została zorganizowana przez Konrada Fischera, Jürgena Hartena i Hansa Strelowa w dniach 8 – 17 października 1971 w Städtische Kunsthalle w Düsseldorfie. Prezentowano głównie prace artystów zamieszkałych w Wielkiej Brytanii i w Niemczech, m.in. Barry'ego Flanagana, Johna Hilliarda, Davida Lamelasa, Johna Lathama, Bruce'a McLeana, Tony'ego Morgana i Davida Tremletta.

15 *Warsztat Formy Filmowej 7*, Łódź 1975. Cyt. za *Wojciech Bruszewski. Fenomeny percepcji*, red. E. Fuchs, J. Zagrodzki, Łódź: Miejska Galeria Sztuki, 2010, s. 94.

16 Ibidem.

17 Ł. Ronduda, *Warsztat Formy Filmowej. Realizacje filmowe z lat 1970–1977*, Artpapier.com, sierpień 2004, http://artpapier.com/pliki/archiwum_sierpien_04/recfilm/warsztaty%20formy.html [dostęp 7-12-2016].

od idei kina autorskiego w stronę zainteresowania funkcjonowaniem filmu i mediów w polskim kontekście politycznym i społecznym stanowi istotny element działalności Warsztatu. Jest też świadectwem dążenia jego członków do dekonstrukcji autorstwa oraz zweryfikowania możliwości kamery jako czynnika umożliwiającego refleksję i przemianę relacji społecznych. Realizacje te ukazują pojmowanie praktyki filmowej jako projektu społecznego, gdzie działanie artysty polega na interwencji w relacje między ludźmi oraz ich obraz; kamera służy tu wyzwalaniu nowych typów organizacji społecznej.

Wszystkie te działania ująć można w kontekście rozwijających się równolegle ruchów i inicjatyw filmowych w sąsiednich krajach Europy Środkowej i poza nią w okresie naznaczonym postępującym umiędzynarodowieniem dialogu i formowaniem się sieci. Powstające w późnych latach 70. XX w. sieci organizacji i inicjatyw prowadzonych przez artystów w imię wspierania twórczości filmowej i wideo rozwijały się na bazie nowego materialnego i teoretycznego potencjału wynikającego z pojawienia się technologii wideo. Jedną z kluczowych nowych koncepcji był *feedback* – informacja zwrotna. Przyświecała ona wielu wczesnym eksperymentom formalnym, działaniom *performance* i instalacjom, lecz także modelom praktyk pedagogicznych i wystawienniczych spoza obszaru twórczości samych artystów. Zwrot w stronę sposobów, w jakie technologia umożliwiała rozwój nowych systemów kształcenia zaobserwować można w szeregu działań z lat 70. XX wieku, począwszy od *duration studies* prowadzonych w szkołach przez Darcy'ego Lange[18] oraz polityczno-feministycznych prac Carole Roussopoulos[19] po transmitowany na żywo *performance* Pawła Kwieka *Video A –Sytuacja Studia* z 1974 roku. Artyści podejmowali także krytyczną refleksję nad możliwościami, jakie oferowało wideo w zakresie umożliwiania nowych form wymiany i dialogu. Przykładem jest film wideo zrealizowany wspólnie przez Gábora Bódy i Marcela Odenbacha *Dialog między Wschodem a Zachodem* (1978), który w ironiczny sposób odnosi się do potencjału komunikacji międzynarodowej. Artyści występują wspólnie na konferencji, lecz ograniczają się do puszczania baniek ze śliny. Wielu artystów Warsztatu eksplorowało koncepcje i procesy związane z technologią wideo zgłębiając swoje zainteresowania transmisją i przekazem zwrotnym. Tego rodzaju eksploracje zaobserwować można we wczesnych instalacjach i projektach Wojciecha Bruszewskiego, takich jak propozycja *Zapisu video* z 1975 roku[20], w eksperymentach Pawła Kwieka z transmisją na żywo, jak również partycypacyjnych projektach realizowanych przez członków działającego przy Warsztacie Zespołu T (Tomasz Kołodrubiec, Tomasz Konart, Janusz Szczerek i Piotr Weychert), takich jak instalacja Andrzeja Paruzela *Sytuacje video-fotograficzne* (1976), czy też *Doświadczenie z określoną grupą osób z wykorzystaniem zapisu video* (1979), stworzone w Wyższej Szkole Muzycznej w Warszawie. Jak stwierdził Paruzel: „Osoba wchodząca w video instalację ma szansę w procesie poznawania jej struktury, równocześnie

18 Na przykład jego prace *Study of Three Birmingham Schools* [1976, wideo, fotografie czarno-białe, dźwięk, ok. 6 godzin] oraz *Studies of Teaching in Four Oxfordshire Schools* [1977, wideo, fotografie czarno-białe, dźwięk, ok. 6 godzin].

19 Wraz z grupą Video Out, założoną w 1970 roku z Paulem Roussopoulosem, artystka stworzyła ważne dokumenty poświęcone ruchom politycznym, takie jak *Le FHAR* [*Front homosexuel d'action révolutionnaire*] [1971], a w połowie lat 70. XX w. coraz bardziej angażowała się w działalność grup feministycznych wspomagając organizację forów i warsztatów wideo, jak również realizując prace wspólnie z Delphone Seyrig, zwłaszcza wideo „S.C.U.M Manifesto" [1976, 26 min].

20 Dokument dostępny na stronie internetowej Fundacji Arton: http://repozytorium.fundacjaarton.pl/index.php?action=view/object&objid=97&colid=11&catid=3&lang=pl [dostęp 15-10-2016].

ujawnić funkcjonowanie własnych struktur poznawczych, dzięki możliwościom manipulacji i w obrębie oddziaływań przetwarzanych przez ten system i w nim samym”[21].

W tym świetle, na kolektywne projekty Warsztatu spojrzeć można jako na próby wykorzystania technologii i sztuki w celu wygenerowania nowych środków refleksji i wymiany oraz alternatywnych form uczenia się. U ich podstaw leży szerszy projekt polityczny, którego celem jest ujęcie sztuki w kontekście pedagogicznym, jako części procesu przekazywania informacji zwrotnej, który różni się od konsumpcyjnego trybu opartego na utrwalonych pojęciach dzieła sztuki, artysty i widza. Jak zauważył Ryszard W. Kluszczyński, „Obok taśm, performances i licznych instalacji należy jeszcze odnotować pojawienie się w latach siedemdziesiątych prac wideo o pre-interaktywnym charakterze wymagających uczestniczącej postawy odbiorców”[22]. Bazowy model prac „składkowych” czerpie z idei *feedbacku* powiązanej z materialnym potencjałem, jakie oferowały technologie filmu i wideo, a celem stało się znalezienie nowych form kolektywnego działania i partycypacji.

W późnych latach 70. XX wieku twórcy filmowi z Polski i Węgier dążyli do stworzenia nowego modelu wymiany w oparciu o możliwości dystrybucji, jakie dawała technologia wideo. Potencjał wideo w wyzwalaniu przestrzeni i środków, dzięki którym artyści mogli tworzyć i prowadzić między sobą wymianę nabiera istotnej wagi w kontekście formowania się w tamtym okresie sieci medialnych, takich jak m.in. London Video Arts w Wielkiej Brytanii, Western Front w Kanadzie, FRIGO w Lyonie, czy też Video Out w Paryżu. Po zakończeniu działalności Warsztatu w 1977 roku, tego rodzaju sieci wyłoniły się w Polsce na przekór klimatowi politycznemu, który uległ zmianie pod koniec dekady lat 70. i we wczesnych latach 80. Jak wspomina Robakowski: „Mnożyły się jednak uciążliwe przesłuchania i aresztowania, rewizje, nagminne konfiskaty bezcennych przesyłek (książki, kasety video, filmy). Wreszcie zablokowano niektórym paszporty i możliwości kontaktowania się z wolnym światem”. Jak mówi dalej artysta, mimo tych przemian „w czasie grupowego pobytu w Budapeszcie udało nam się utworzyć międzynarodową kooperację video-filmową INFERMENTAL – według projektu wybitnego filmowca węgierskiego Gábora Bódy. W czasie zablokowania granic można było przez studentów węgierskich przemycać prace video-filmowe. INFERMENTAL rozpowszechniał je na cały świat jako pierwszy na kuli ziemskiej Międzynarodowy Magazyn Video. Dzięki tej współpracy nasze filmy weszły jeszcze w stanie wojennym do obiegu sztuki światowej”[23].

Podstawy projektu opisywanego jako „magazyn na kasetach wideo” opisane zostały we wczesnym zaproszeniu do nadsyłania zgłoszeń rozpowszechnianym w październiku 1981 roku przez Gábora Bódy'ego i niemiecką artystkę Astrid Heibach: „INFERMENTAL to połączenie słów: international, fermentum i experimental. Polscy i węgierscy filmowcy utworzyli tę inicjatywę podczas spotkania towarzyskiego jesienią 1980”[24]. Mimo istotnej wagi tego kluczowego przykładu wymiany i współpracy międzynarodowej, początkowe ambicje projektu INFERMENTAL urzeczywistniły się w sposób inny, niż pierwotnie zakładano. Za sprawą społecznego i politycznego kontekstu tamtego okresu inicjatywę uruchomiono ostatecznie w Berlinie Zachodnim, a pierwsze dziesięć wydań „ma-

21 M. Jankowska, *Wideo, wideo instalacja, wideo performance w Polsce w latach 1973-1994. Historia, artyści, dzieła*, Neriton, Warszawa 2004, s. 134. Film dostępny pod adresem: http://artmuseum.pl/en/filmoteka/praca/paruzel-andrzej-video-photographic-situations [dostęp 7-12-2016].

22 R. W. Kluszczyński, *Zarys historii sztuki wideo w Polsce*, Culture.pl, 13 kwietnia 2005, http://culture.pl/pl/artykul/zarys-historii-sztuki-wideo-w-polsce [dostęp 7-12-2016].

23 J. Robakowski, *Żywa galeria*, 35 m, 1975, 24'48''.

24 Archiwum Infermental, ZKM, list 15 października 1981 od Gábora Bódy i Astrid Heibach.

gazynu" ukazało się w lutym 1982 roku. Pierwsze wydanie, przygotowane pod redakcją Gábora Bódy i Astrid Heibach oraz pod okiem Gusztáva Hámosa, uzyskało wsparcie programy rezydencyjnego DAAD, a nie partnerstwa polsko-węgierskiego, jak początkowo zakładano. Jednak format działalności INFERMENTAL i deklarowany cel polegający na budowaniu mostów pomiędzy „medialnymi wyspami" oraz pragnienie stworzenia „Encyklopedii Rejestrowanych Obrazów", co służyć miało powiązaniu grup awangardowych w różnych krajach w celu rozszerzenia zasięgu analizy filmu i wideo, wywieść można z propozycji i projektów Warsztatu związanych z antologiami i filmami powstającymi kolektywnie. Zwłaszcza *Żywa galeria* stworzyła model łączenia i przyglądania się awangardom za pośrednictwem jednominutowych wypowiedzi artystycznych, który podjęty został następnie przez INFERMENTAL na skalę międzynarodową – kolejne wydania powstawały we Francji, na Węgrzech, w Kanadzie, USA i Japonii.

Warto spojrzeć także na wczesne sieci powstające w latach 20. i 30. XX wieku w obrębie pierwszej fali polskiej awangardy, jak również to, co różni je od prób formowania sieci w latach 70. Stefan i Franciszka Themerson odegrali znaczącą rolę w takich grupach, jak START (Stowarzyszenie Miłośników Filmu Artystycznego, 1931–1934) oraz S.A.F (Spółdzielnia Autorów Filmowych), lecz jednym z ich najważniejszych dokonań było powołanie pisma *f.a* („film artystyczny") w 1937 roku na bazie badań prowadzonych przez nich w Wielkiej Brytanii i we Francji. Pismo *f.a.* odegrało kluczową rolę w obiegu informacji wśród wczesnych awangard filmowych. Dzięki szerokiemu zastosowaniu projektowania graficznego i fotografii, pismo umożliwiło rozpowszechnianie wizerunków prac artystów w obrębie istniejących w Europie sieci. Pierwsze wydanie *f.a.1* (luty 1937) koncentrowało się na eksperymentalnym kinie brytyjskim i zawierało artykuły poświęcone Lenowi Lye, László Moholy-Nagy (mieszkającemu wówczas w Londynie), Basilowi Wrightowi oraz Johnowi Griersonowi, natomiast w *f.a.2* (marzec-kwiecień 1937) znalazły się obszerne materiały dotyczące francuskiej awangardy filmowej lat 20. i 30.[25] Publikacje wydań magazynu przez Themersonów zbiegły się w czasie z organizowanymi przez nich w Polsce pokazami filmów przywiezionych z podróży do Francji i Wielkiej Brytanii. Planowano także trzecie wydanie *f.a.*, poświęcone polskiemu kinu awangardowemu, lecz nigdy się ono nie ukazało. Na potrzeby tego wydawnictwa zgromadzono i przygotowano szeroki zasób materiałów, które Stefan Themerson zabrał ze sobą do Londynu, gdzie dzielił się nimi z przyjaciółmi i gośćmi, określając cenne dokumenty mianem swojej „biblii"[26].

Omówione powyżej projekty pozwalają nam dostrzec, że istotnym aspektem działalności Warsztatu była koncentracja na ideach wymiany i formowania sieci w obrębie grup awangardowych w celu przekraczania granic poszczególnych krajów. Propozycję „jednominutówek" oraz realizację projektów współpracy postrzegać można jako analogiczne do wysuwanych w tamtym okresie postulatów dotyczących funkcjonowania formatu magazynu w erze filmu i wideo. Zmiana w pojmowaniu tego formatu miała niebagatelne znaczenie dla rozwoju sztuki konceptualnej, w której druki i przesyłki pocztowe wykorzystywane były do kreowania nowych sposobów istnienia twórczości, formowania sieci i wymiany między artystami, co zostało szczegółowo omówione przez Lucy Lippard w jej wpływowych wczesnych tekstach, i co zaobserwować można w tak różnych projektach jak

25 Drugie wydanie zawierało także głośny artykuł Stefana Themersona pt. „O potrzebie tworzenia widzeń", którego rozszerzona wersja została opublikowana w 1983 roku w wydawnictwie pod tym samym tytułem.
26 Wg Jasi Reichardt w rozmowie z autorem w czasie wizyty w Archiwum Themersonów, 2013.

tekst Sola LeWitta „Paragraphs on Conceptual Art"[27], opublikowany w *Artforum* latem 1967 roku, czy performans Tomislava Gotovaca *Showing "Elle" Magazine* z 1962 roku. Takie wydawnictwa, jak *Art-Language* grupy Art & Language z maja 1969 roku, czy też powstałe w 1965 roku *ASPEN. The Multimedia Magazine in a Box* otworzyły drogę do przemyślenia formatu magazynu jako modelu wystawienniczego. W latach 70. idee te wspomogły proces rewidowania koncepcji galerii sztuki w erze wideo, jako że magazyn poddany został na nowo refleksji teoretycznej w kontekście tej właśnie technologii oraz nowych możliwości cyrkulacji prac wśród artystów. Kluczowe znaczenie wideo dla nowych trybów wymiany wiąże się z fundamentalnym przesunięciem, jakie dokonało się w tamtym czasie – prace filmowe nie musiały być już rozpowszechniane jak do tej pory w ograniczonej liczbie kopii dystrybucyjnych głównie na taśmach 16 mm (jak wpływowa antologia *Fluxfilm anthology* z 1962–1970 zebrana przez George'a Maciunasa), które wyświetlano wyłącznie w kinach lub na niezależnych pokazach. Aby móc dzielić się nimi i wprowadzać w nowe konteksty, filmy należało wcześniej redukować do postaci stopklatek lub opisów tekstowych. Technologia wideo dostarczyła nowego nośnika obrazów i dźwięków, tworząc model dystrybucji i dokumentacji, który nie był wcześniej dostępny. Mimo że dostęp do sprzętu wideo był ograniczony i kosztowny, nowe media zmieniły sposób pojmowania przez artystów własnej twórczości i jej potencjału wymiany. Podobnie jak w przypadku pisma *f.a.*, ambicją Warsztatu była budowa międzynarodowych sieci, a proponowany model pedagogiczny został zrealizowany tylko częściowo. Jednak zaproszenie do kontaktu z polską awangardą pozostaje aktualne, jako że potencjał filmów oraz wizji ich wymiany i produkcji artystycznej tkwi nie tylko w zrealizowanych pracach, lecz przede wszystkim w samym radykalnym modelu działalności Warsztatu.

27 S. LeWitt, *Paragraphs on Conceptual Art*, „Artforum", 5:10, 1967, s. 79–83.

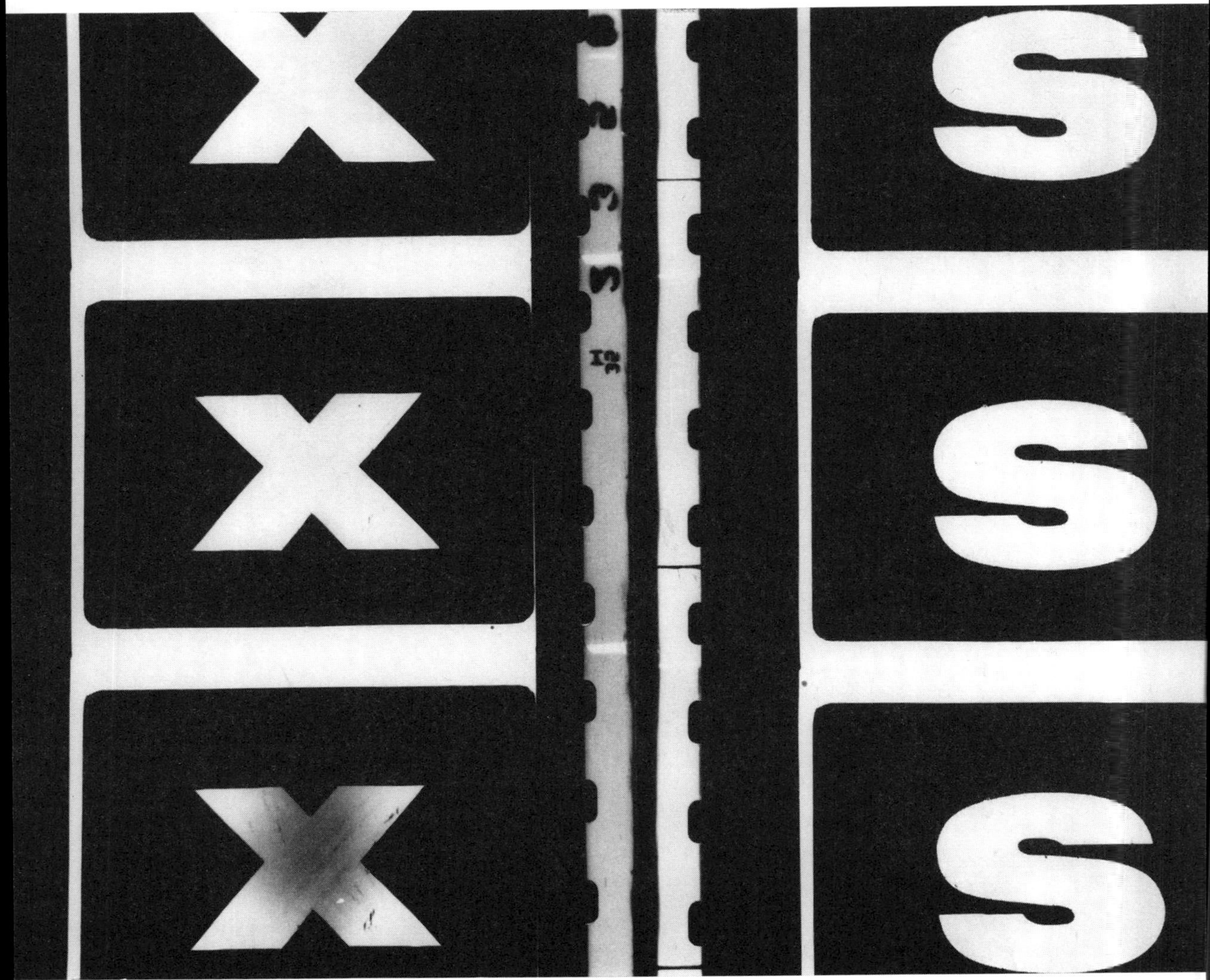

Józef Robakowski, *Ćwiczenie*, 1972/73, 35 mm, 4'21"
Józef Robakowski, *Exercise*, 1972/73, 35 mm, 4'21"

Jan Verwoert

Gesty na Rzecz Nowego Życia: Awangarda jako historyczna prowokacja

Co zrobić z awangardą?

Czego chce awangarda? Od sztuki, od ludzi, od społeczeństwa? O co jej chodzi? W jaki sposób możemy się tego dowiedzieć? Co by było gdybyśmy raz zapytali nie o przyczyny jej ruchu, cele i wpływy, a zamiast tego wzięli pod uwagę gesty, za pomocą których awangardziści prezentują się na scenie artystycznej? Awangardziści nigdy nie są zażenowani gestami, ponieważ ich wystąpienie na scenie historii sztuki musi mieć konieczną siłę, aby tę historię (tak, jak prezentowała się ona uprzednio) na stałe zmienić. Wystąpienie awangardy staje się częścią historii jedynie wtedy, gdy wprowadza w czyn gesty, od momentu zaistnienia których możliwy wydaje się inny bieg historii. Owe gesty odpowiadają w swojej formie i statusie *coup d'état* w historii sztuki i jej polityce. Udane wykonanie awangardowego gestu oznacza wprowadzenie do historii przewrotu. Paradoksalnie, awangardowy gest jest z natury *ponadhistoryczny*, w tym znaczeniu, że jako pojedyncze wydarzenie radykalnie przerywa bieg historii, wykracza poza jej ramy i wypada ze wszystkich do tego momentu liczących się kategorii historiografii. Ale jest też jednocześnie głęboko *historyczny*, jako że sam ustanawia nową historię, w której od tej pory istnieje i jest pojmowany jako rewolucyjny akt wprowadzania nowej sztuki. Siły awangardowego gestu nie można by nawet zmierzyć, gdybyśmy sami w jakiś sposób nie odczuwali działania przełomu, który wprowadził, nie postrzegając go jedynie jako zamkniętą część historii, lecz doświadczając jako wydarzenia o wcale nie mniejszym, współczesnym (czyli ponadhistorycznym) oddziaływaniu. Opisanie znaczenia tej siły oznacza jednak wyjaśnienie również długofalowego oddziaływania z historycznej perspektywy. Pojąć awangardowy przewrót oznaczałoby tym samym zrozumieć siłę kryjącego się u jego podstaw gestu, w jej jednocześnie historycznym i ponadhistorycznym wymiarze. W rzeczy samej, wydaje się charakterystyczne dla gestów, że kontekst, w którym zyskują swoje znaczenie, jest w równej mierze historyczny i ponadhistoryczny. Z jednej strony w gestach ujawnia się historyczna rzeczywistość, ponieważ w określonym momencie historii uwidaczniają dostępny zasób środków wyrazu danej kultury. Pełniąc funkcję kulturowo-historycznych specyficznych form interakcji, gesty są znakami swojego czasu. Z innej jednak strony znaczenie gestu jest zawsze absolutnie *współczesne* w sensie ponadhistorycznym, ponieważ rozumiemy go jedynie wtedy, gdy oddziałuje również na nas w momencie, w którym go postrzegamy, to znaczy, jeśli uda mu się nas momentalnie włączyć w wymianę. Gesty wymagają bezpośredniej odpowiedzi. Kto pozdrawia, oczekuje, że też zostanie pozdrowiony. Kto wstępuje na scenę stara się o uwagę. Kto płacze, wywołuje smutek i tak dalej. Gesty tworzą współczesność o tyle, że zawsze zobowiązują nas do udziału w wymianie w danym momencie. Ponieważ wydaje się, że w naturze gestu leży to, że ten, kto go wykonuje, czyni tak, by *wywołać reakcję*, można powiedzieć, że charakter gestu jest w dosłownym znaczeniu *prowokacyjny*. W związku z tym praktyczne znaczenie gestu kryje się w szczególności w prowokacji, którą wywołuje. W gestach tkwi ich własna prowokacyjność.

To, że prowokacja jest motorem awangardy, należy już niejako do pewników historii sztuki. Hasło *épater le bourgeois* niemalże dosłownie łączy się z pojęciem awangardy. Szersza perspektywa, wynikająca jednakże ze zrozumienia wewnętrznie prowokacyjnego charakteru gestu, polega na tym, że prowokacyjność nie prezentuje się już jako jedynie postawa awangardy, ale jako immanentna siła praktyki artystycznej. Siła awangardowego gestu, która poprzez jego realizację dąży do historycznego przewrotu, jest jego prowokacyjną siłą. *Kogo* jednakże przywołuje ów gest? Również w tym wypadku odpowiedź jest niejednoznaczna: z jednej strony awangardowy gest prowokuje świadków jego wykonania, i to zarówno świadków z danego historycznego czasu, jak i nas, zainteresowanych historią, którzy w tym momencie próbują uzmysłowić sobie siłę tej prowokacyjności, aby także samemu móc o niej zaświadczyć. Z drugiej strony awangardowy gest prowokuje nie tylko swoich świadków, ale w zasadzie także samą historię, również w podwójnym znaczeniu. Awangardziści prowokują bądź bardziej ewokują historię o tyle, że wywołują ją jako system odniesienia dla swojej artystycznej praktyki. Tym właśnie różnią się od innych twórców, że pojmują swoje artystyczne działania zawsze bezpośrednio jako działania historyczne, jako wkład w historię – i pisanie jej od nowa. Poprzez zmianę naszych percepcyjnych przyzwyczajeń chcą wprowadzić do sztuki wydarzenie, które swoim zasięgiem i siłą wybuchu wykroczy poza historię sztuki i ustanowi historycznie nową formę doświadczenia – co oznacza jednocześnie nową formę doświadczania historii. Jednocześnie jednak prowokują oni historię w jeszcze bardziej bezpośrednim znaczeniu, poprzez wywołanie, tak jak przywołuje się ducha, aby w końcu się ukazał: „Ukaż się historio i pozwól nam zobaczyć, jaka będziesz!", to jest właściwe motto awangardowej prowokacji. Nadzieją jest, że duch historii, jeśliby się pozwolił przywołać, mógłby przyjąć kształt rewolucji. Poprzez prowokacyjność swoich gestów awangardziści liczą na nie mniej, niż na wywołanie rewolucji jako pełnego wydarzeń objawienia nowej historii.

Znaki jak wymierzane policzki

Przyjrzyjmy się trzem gestom:

Film pokazuje w zbliżeniu litery na jasnoniebieskim tle. Na każde ujęcie przypada jedna litera. Ujęcia trwają czasem zaledwie kilka sekund, czasem nieco dłużej. Widzimy sekwencję: a b c k s p f h n p a c o a c o t w o j u a b c i f y d i m o z k w e h z w n w o d r i j g a b c d k t k i n s o a u z d u a n t w f z t f z t d r j y r j d r t a c o z s k... W czasie trwania jednego ujęcia rozbrzmiewa ton organów bądź syntezatora. Każdy ton ma określoną wysokość dźwięku. Ani kolejność dźwięków nie oddaje żadnej (w konwencjonalnym znaczeniu rozpoznawalnej) melodii, ani ciąg liter żadnego pojęcia. Mimo to kolejność liter i dźwięków nie wydaje się przypadkowa, ale jasna i określona. Film trwa cztery minuty i dwadzieścia sekund, jest zatytułowany *Ćwiczenie* i został zrealizowany przez Józefa Robakowskiego w 1972/73.

Film ukazuje zbliżenie mężczyzny. Siedzi w kuchni, krzyczy z zamkniętymi oczami i szeroko otwartymi ustami, tworząc przy tym zmiennie dwie głoski, wysoki dźwięk, który brzmi jak Y, i głęboki, który brzmi jak A. Utrzymuje ten dźwięk przez czas trwania każdego ujęcia, tak że w każdym z nich brzmi tylko jedna z dwóch głosek. W każdym ujęciu bohater jest w różny sposób oświetlony, raz z przodu, raz od tyłu, raz z boku. Nieregularnej zmianie wysokich i niskich dźwięków odpowiada tym samym ciągła zmiana oświetlenia obrazu. W ostatnim ujęciu bohater machając, sygnalizuje, że ujęcie jest skończone. Film trwa trzy minuty, jest zatytułowany YYAA i został zrealizowany przez Wojciecha Bruszewskiego.

Film pokazuje na zmianę czarny obraz i białą kartkę. Kiedy widać po raz pierwszy kartkę, jest na niej jedynie napisane na maszynie pojedyncze słowo „nie". Za drugim razem są to dwa słowa „nie". Zabieg ten powtarza się, aż kolejne linijki wypełniają się słowem „nie". Wtedy proces się odwraca, widać za każdym razem o jeden wyraz mniej, aż ostatecznie kartka staje się na nowo pusta. Każdemu ujęciu kartki towarzyszy głos, który monotonnie wypowiada wyraz „nie". Ponieważ czarny obraz i biała kartka oraz głos mówiący zamieniają się w szybkich sekwencjach, powstaje rytm ciszy i dźwięku, jak również zmiany czerni i bieli, które przez dłuższy czas tworzą nerwowe migotanie. Film trwa cztery minuty, jest zatytułowany *Zaprzeczenie* i został zrealizowany w 1973 roku przez Ryszarda Waśko. Robakowski, Bruszewski i Waśko byli członkami grupy artystycznej Warsztat Formy Filmowej, która została założona w 1970 roku w Łodzi i działała do roku 1977.

Dlaczego mowa w tym wypadku o gestach? Właściwie filmy nie pokazują prawie niczego, co można by rozumieć pod pojęciem gestu. Zgoda, jest człowiek, który krzyczy, ale nie wzmacnia tego krzyku innymi formami języka ciała; nie gestykuluje, jedynie spokojnie siedzi. W dwóch pozostałych filmach nie występują w ogóle ludzie, a widać jedynie litery i wyrazy oraz słychać dźwięki. Mimo to filmy te działają jak gesty. Mają tę samą intensywność. Przenoszą siłę języka ciała na język obrazów, liter, dźwięków i cięć. Zaznaczony ostrymi cięciami krzyk, rozbłysk liter oraz pojawianie się i znikanie słowa „nie" ma siłę uderzenia w policzek. Każde cięcie, każdy obraz, każda litera i każdy dźwięk mają wyrazistość uderzenia płaską dłonią w gładką powierzchnię. Z każdym cieciem czuje się rytm uderzeń. Pac pac pac. Nie Nie Nie Nie. AA YY. Poprzez jednoczesne zredukowanie treści informacyjnej obrazu i dźwięku do czytelnych, silnych sygnałów i przyspieszenia (o ile nie wręcz brutalizacji) cięć, obraz i cięcie zbliżają się do siebie aż do momentu, w którym kolejność cięć jest tak samo obecna jak sekwencje obrazów i dźwięków. Następstwo dźwięków, wysokość dźwięku, ciąg liter i wyciemnienie są tak bezpośrednio związane z rytmem kolejności ujęć, że stają się jednym. Obraz, dźwięk i światło są cięciem, a cięcie jest obrazem, dźwiękiem i światłem. Kiedy jednak mówimy, że siła gestu tkwi w jego sile pozwalającej dokonać przewrotu (*coup*) – w języku francuskim *couper* znaczy dosłownie „ciąć" – i poprzez to cięcie stworzyć sytuację, która angażuje widza, do którego adresowane są owe gesty, staje się jasne, że w wypadku tych trzech filmów chodzi o radykalne gesty.

Giorgio Agamben, używając pojęć zaczerpniętych z teorii kina Gillesa Deleuze'a, opisuje stworzoną poprzez radykalne techniki montażu filmowego współczesną estetykę obrazów jako estetykę, którą określają: *coups mobiles,* ruchome cięcia: obrazy, które same są w ruchu, nazwane przez Deleuze'a „obrazami-ruchu" (*l'image-mouvement*). Rozwijając analizę Deleuze'a, można pokazać, że dotyczy ona statusu obrazu w nowoczesności w ogóle. Oznacza to jednak, że mityczna dyscyplina obrazu została tutaj przełamana i należałoby mówić w tym miejscu nie o obrazach, ale właśnie o gestach[11]. Można w uzupełnieniu do tej definicji gestu jako *coup mobile*, ruchomego cięcia, dodać, że filmy Robakowskiego, Waśki i Bruszewskiego są awangardowymi gestami, ponieważ właśnie radykalizują formę obrazu. Są to filmy, które są absolutnie nowoczesne, ponieważ

11 G. Agamben, *Noten zur Geste*, w: *Mittel ohne Zweck. ...Noten zur Politik*, przeł. S. Schulz, Zurych – Berlin: Diaphanes-Verlag, 2006, s. 52.

wszystkie występujące w nich środki filmowe zostały celowo tak wykorzystane, że nie tylko podążają za logiką *coup mobile*, lecz wręcz ową logikę eksponują w przerysowanej formie, z całą siłą gestu uderzenia w policzek. Inaczej mówiąc, filmy te pozwalają nam doświadczyć, co znaczy, gdy obraz jako cięcie staje się ruchomym gestem.

Jeśli więc siła gestu, jak uznaliśmy powyżej, nie da się oddzielić od swojego prowokacyjnego oddziaływania, pojawia się pytanie: kogo – bądź co – prowokują filmy poprzez gesty kryjące się w ich formie? Jaki awangardowy przewrót realizują filmowcy poprzez swoje *coupes mobiles*? Adresatami tych gestów jesteśmy przede wszystkim my i oni sami. Prowokacja ich awangardowego (czyli celowego i skondensowanego gestu) języka filmowego skierowana jest o tyle przeciw nam, widzom, o ile sekwencje obrazów, dźwięków i cięć, które nie są zrozumiałe w konwencjonalny sposób, nie odpowiadają naszym percepcyjnym przyzwyczajeniom i w pierwszym momencie wytrącają nas z równowagi. Bruszewski na nas krzyczy, Waśko i Robakowski pracują nad naszymi zmysłami za pomocą audiowizualnych informacji, które przekazywane są nam z szybkością, zwięzłością i gęstością technicznego przekazu sygnału. Ich filmy są jak przekazy telegraficzne kodem Morse'a. Jako odbiorcy stajemy się odbiornikiem, który bezpośrednio przetwarza nadchodzące sygnały i wypluwa na taśmę: a b c k s p f h n p a c o a c o t w o j u a b c i f y d i m o z k w e h z w n w [illegible] d r i j g a b c d k t k i n s o a u c d u a n t w f z t f z t d r j y r j d r t a c o z s k...AAYY... Medium, które te informacje przetwarza, nie jest jednak ani przejrzyste, ani funkcjonalne. Jest to ciało, które krzyczy bądź na które się krzyczy i które jest bombardowane sygnałami audiowizualnymi. Jako gesty filmy te są nie tylko uderzeniem, lecz także wystrzałem bądź salwą. W ten sposób wojskowy charakter metaforycznego pojęcia „awangarda" (dosłownie: straż przednia) zostaje spełniony.

Na czym polega jednakże działanie owej prowokacji? Jaką reakcję chce ona wywołać albo sprowokować?

Przede wszystkim prowokacyjne działanie tych filmów tkwi w skonfrontowaniu widzów z postawą inną niż kontemplacja. Poprzez zwiększoną częstotliwość ruchomych cięć i przetwarzanych informacji (jak również dzięki wytworzonej poprzez audiowizualny ostrzał niemal fizycznej bliskości) odbierają widzom czas na kontemplacyjne, to znaczy powolne i celowe, zaangażowanie się w filmy. Ponieważ każdy odbiór powoduje natychmiast reakcję, przetwarzanie informacji staje się wytwarzaniem komunikacji. Jesteśmy natychmiast włączeni w pętlę reakcji na przekaz sygnału. Poprzez odebranie możliwości kontemplacji i przemienieniu zdystansowanego widza w zaangażowanego uczestnika procesu komunikacji, filmy te prowokują nas, celowo wytrącając zachowywanej rezerwy. Prowokacyjna siła języka filmowego wyostrzonego do formy gestu zmienia naszą postawę wobec przedmiotu naszej percepcji, z niezobowiązująco zdystansowanej do zobowiązująco zaangażowanej. Odnośnie prowokacyjności awangardy Adorno stwierdza krótko i zwięźle, że „zaawansowana sztuka [...] prawie nie jest już w stanie znieść postawy kontemplacyjnej[2]."

Abstrahując od tego, w filmach tych faktycznie niewiele jest do kontemplowania. Poprzez ekstremalną redukcję języka filmowego do najprostszych środków wyrazu filmowcy unikają kompozycji formy filmowej, która nadawałaby się do kontemplacji. Niemożliwe jest pogrążenie się w obserwacji, ponieważ filmy nie mają żadnej głębi. Są płaskie niczym wnętrze dłoni wyciągnięte do uderzenia w policzek. Są czystą informacją audiowizualną, co oznacza cięcie, sygnał i stymu-

2 T. W. Adorno, *Ästetische Theorie,* Frankfurt: Suhrkamp 1970, s. 495.

lację. Owo zaniechanie głębi należy rozumieć jako prowokację, która nie kieruje się jedynie przeciw nam, widzom, ale także przeciw samym filmowcom. Oni sami zabraniają sobie głębi wyrazu, a tym samym wykorzystania konwencjonalnych środków wyrazu, które mogłyby stworzyć wrażenie semantycznej głębi. Filmowcy poprzez konceptualną decyzję o wyborze zredukowanej formy filmowej świadomie ograniczają swoje własne możliwości, sami prowokując się do przyjęcia innej postawy względem własnej filmowo-artystycznej zdolności działania. W ten sam sposób sami wytrącają się z dystansu, podobnie jak czynią to z nami jako uczestnikami procesu komunikacji. Zasady własnego języka filmowego doprowadzają ich do przyjęcia nowej postawy czy pozycji wobec produkcji artystycznej. Sami prowokują się do tego, aby z autorów stać się przekazującymi sygnał uczestnikami komunikacji. Łukasz Ronduda podsumowuje ów rozwój w następujący sposób: „Artyści (czy już teraz bardziej »naukowcy« zajmujący się estetyką i sztuką) poprzez znieczulenie tych własności pragnęli »zobiektywizować« własne postępowanie (...), aby bardziej dostosować je do »intersubiektywnej« sfery komunikacji.[3]"

Awangardowe wyostrzenie języka filmowego do formy pełnego siły płaskiego gestu oznacza więc prowokację wymierzoną przeciw filmowcom i publiczności, która powinna spowodować zmianę ich relacji: odejście od zdystansowanej formy komunikacji, polegającej na kontemplacji semantycznie złożonego dzieła sztuki. Zamiast tego dopuszczają o wiele bardziej bezpośrednią formę komunikacji, która jest totalnie nastawiona na maksymalne wzmocnienie momentu międzypodmiotowego spotkania, ponieważ koncentruje się na przekazywaniu najprostszych sygnałów, w której wszystko dzieje się bezpośrednio jedno po drugim. Poprzez prowokowanie nowych form międzypodmiotowości awangardowy gest chce wpływać na nowe formy stosunków społecznych i tym samym w inny sposób zawiązywać więzi społeczne.

Gesty dla innego społeczeństwa

Prowokacja awangardowych gestów filmowców z Warsztatu Formy Filmowej zmierza więc tym samym do wywołania innej społecznej sytuacji, która jednocześnie byłaby nową sytuacją historyczną, mogącą przedstawić alternatywę wobec istniejących w określonym historycznym momencie stosunków politycznych. Poprzez stworzenie gestów, które miały prowokować bezpośrednią międzypodmiotową komunikację, filmowcy formułują swój protest przeciw dyktaturze partii i biurokratycznemu państwu, które w historycznym momencie ich aktywności określały życie społeczne w Polsce.

Zmiana gestów należących do komunikacji interpersonalnej miała przełamać autorytarny porządek istniejących stosunków. Decydujące przy tym było to, że autorytarny charakter porządku społecznego wywierał najbardziej radykalne piętno właśnie poprzez fakt, że określał nawet najbardziej codzienne ludzkie gesty, ponieważ ideologia reżimu przenikała wszystkie sfery życia społecznego. Ronduda pisze o tej sytuacji: „W socjalistycznej Polsce nie było miejsca poza ideologią, podobnie jest i dziś, gdy nie ma miejsca wolnego od »praw rynku«"[34]. Kiedy jednak gesty ludzi w społeczeństwie, w którym żyją, są przeładowane ideologią i przez to wyobcowane, pierwszy krok ku ich uwolnieniu stanowić musi ich całkowite oczyszczenie z wszelkich ideologicznych treści. W tym akcie świadomego opróżnienia z sensu chodzi jednak jednocześnie o utopijny projekt wynalezienia gestów, które wymykałyby się ideologii, ponieważ w żaden sposób nie nadawałyby

3 Ibidem, s. 119.

się do ideologicznego wykorzystania. Te motywy wyjaśniają prowokacyjną płaskość dyskutowanych filmów. Poprzez sprowadzenie języka filmowego do najprostszych podstawowych elementów Robakowski, Bruszewski i Waśko pracują nad stworzeniem formy wyrazu, która jednocześnie jest zbyt bezpośrednia i zbyt otwarta, aby ideologia mogła się w niej osadzić. Ronduda w kontekście filmów Pawła Kwieka, kolejnego członka Warsztatu stwierdza: „[Film Kwieka] był strukturalnie niezdolny do lansowania panującej wówczas, jedynej słusznej ideologii. Jego naczelną zasadą była bowiem otwartość interpretacyjna, celowe niedeterminowanie znaczenia”[45].

Właściwą dla awangardy prowokacją artystów Warsztatu byłoby więc wyostrzenie formy artystycznej do gestu, który – w sprzeciwie wobec historycznej rzeczywistości ideologicznie przeformowanego życia społecznego – dąży do jednocześnie bezpośredniej i radykalnie otwartej międzypodmiotowej wymiany. Artysta i teoretyk Jan Świdziński sformułował w roku 1974, czyli w tym samym historycznym momencie, w swoich *Tezach sztuki kontekstualnej* program, który dokładnie artykułuje ową etykę i politykę innej formy gestu. Świdziński rozumie swój program „sztuki kontekstualnej” jako kontrprojekt wobec wyłożonych przez Josepha Kosutha tez „sztuki konceptualnej”. W przeciwieństwie do Kosutha podkreśla, że w artystycznym działaniu uwolnionym od konwencjonalnych medialnych form wyrazu nie powinno chodzić w pierwszej linii o jasne, jednoznaczne konceptualne zasady, a o wiele bardziej o wynalezienie znaków i gestów, które wskutek swojej radykalnej otwartości zyskają znaczenie dopiero (i zawsze od nowa) w konkretnym momencie i za każdym razem w specyficznym kontekście międzypodmiotowej społecznej wymiany między ludźmi.

Deklaracja otwartości artystycznego gestu wrażliwego na kontekst oznacza przy tym zarówno rozpoznanie faktu, że znaczenie artystycznego działania jest zależne od społecznego kontekstu, w którym powstało, jak również nacisk na to, że tego rodzaju otwarte i bezpośrednie, wrażliwe na kontekst gesty artystyczne mogą się aktywnie przyczynić do otwarcia istniejących społecznych relacji. Teza numer 15 z programu Świdzińskiego brzmi: „Sztuka kontekstualna jest działaniem w rzeczywistości poprzez następujące transformacje znaczeń: RZECZYWISTOŚĆ → INFORMACJA → NOWE OTWARTE ZNACZENIA → RZECZYWISTOŚĆ”[56].

Awangardowy program Świdzińskiego, dotyczący zmiany stosunków społecznych poprzez wynalezienie języka formalnego, jednocześnie otwartego i bezpośrednio sięgającego w głąb społecznej rzeczywistości komunikacji interpersonalnej, tym samym może być rozumiany również jako bezpośredni wyraz dążeń artystów Warsztatu. Na tym tle można odczytać podsumowanie tez Świdzińskiego, dokonane przez Rondudę, także jako precyzyjny opis języka filmowego stworzonego przez Robakowskiego, Bruszewskiego i Waśkę:

> Kontekstualne znaki czyste/puste miały być bodźcami nie przesłaniającymi rzeczywistości, inicjującymi szereg procesualnych, interaktywnych relacji, kreującymi otwarty proces semiozy, rozmywającymi granice pomiędzy twórcą a odbiorcą. [...] Kontekstualizm za swój ideał komunikacji społecznej i kulturowej przyjmował radykalną demokrację, czyli rzeczywistość skrajnie różną od tej, w której powstał. W tym aspekcie ujawnia się (sic) krytyczność tego kierunku wobec niedemokratycznej rzeczywistości PRL-u. Jego

4 Ibidem, s. 117.

5 J. Świdziński, *Sztuka kontekstualna (1) wersja druga,* „Piktogram”, 3, 2006, s. 31. Jako gest świadomego zakłócenia konwencjonalnego formatu wyliczania tez ich numeracja nie kieruje się żadną rozpoznawalną logiką. Numery są pomieszane i przekraczają liczbę rzeczywiście przedstawianych tez.

antyautorytarny wymiar zawiera się w postulatach niemożności monopolizacji znaczenia w jednym kontekście i konieczności negocjacji ponadtekstowych[67].

Międzypodmiotowa, społeczna i historyczna prowokacja owego awangardowego programu tkwi zatem w wynalezieniu gestów, które – w opozycji wobec istniejących relacji – w silny sposób ustanawiają jednocześnie otwartą i bezpośrednią komunikację. Radykalność takiego gestu nie polega jedynie na tym, że zawarty w nim polityczny protest powołuje się bezpośrednio na istotę języka. Filmy Robakowskiego, Bruszewskiego i Waśki pokazują potencjał języka w stanie jego uwolnienia od ideologii. Chcą wykazać, co może język, kiedy używa się go z otwartością i bezpośredniością, które w nim tkwią. Właśnie to wyeksponowanie i pokazanie podstawowego charakteru językowości Giorgio Agamben rozumie z kolei jako puentę gestu. Następujący fragment odczytać można jako komentarz do omawianych filmów, zwłaszcza *Zaprzeczenia* Waśki:

> W tym samym stopniu przekazanie słowa nie oznacza, że dysponuje ono jakimś wyższym poziomem (metajęzykiem, który na niższym poziomie sam jest nieprzekazywalny), na którym stać się może przedmiotem przekazu, lecz oznacza wyeksponowanie słowa bez jakiejkolwiek transcendencji w jego własnej przekazywalności, w jego własnym byciu środkiem (jeśli pod słowem środek rozumie się przekaz). W tym znaczeniu gest jest przekazem przekazywalności. Nie ma właściwie niczego do powiedzenia, ponieważ to, co pokazuje, jest byciem-w-języku człowieka jako czystą przekazywalnością[78].

Agamben mówi dalej, że właśnie owo „bycie-w-medium [*l'essere-in-un-medio*] człowieka" otwiera „etyczny wymiar" ludzkiego działania.[89]

Jeśli podążyć za tą myślą, okazuje się, że prowokacyjność i krusząca siła idei awangardowego gestu stworzonego przez Świdzińskiego i artystów Warsztatu Formy Filmowej tkwi właśnie w tym, aby sferę komunikacji, przekazywalności, międzypodmiotowości – a tym samym sam obszar etyki – odzyskać z dominujących relacji reżimu i ideologii. Dzięki temu, że artyści otworzyli ową sferę jako pole działania sztuki, domagali się języka, międzypodmiotowości i tym samym etyki jako mediów artystycznych. Wysunęli żądanie prawa do samostanowienia formy ich społecznej komunikacji. Jeśli rozumieć za Agambenem ów obszar komunikacji, *bycie-w-języku* człowieka, jako właściwe środowisko międzyludzkie i tym samym w ogóle jako sferę etyki, wtedy staje się jasne, że ich artystyczne działanie skierowane było na odzyskanie języka, ponowne zdobycie egzystencjalnej zdolności działania i tym samym niejako odzyskania życia od reżimu. I to jest rzeczywiście radykalne. Wówczas bowiem, prowokacyjność tego awangardowego gestu tkwi w woli wprowadzenia, poprzez odmienny rodzaj komunikacji, nowego i lepszego sposobu wspólnego życia, w którym bezpośrednie i otwarte formy wymiany ostatecznie uwalniają życie społeczne od władzy ideologii.

Tłum. Kaja Pawełek

Tekst publikowany w: *1,2,3... Awangarda. Film/sztuka pomiędzy eksperymentem a archiwum*, red. Ł. Ronduda, F. Zeyfang, Warszawa: Centrum Sztuki Współczesnej Zamek Ujazdowski, 2007.

6 Ł. Ronduda, *Elastyczność pozwala nam istnieć. Sztuka kontekstualna Jana Świdzińskiego,* „Piktogram", 3, 2006, s. 28–29.

7 G. Agamben, op. cit., s. 55.

8 Ibidem, s. 54.

Biographies

Wacław Antczak

(1911–1974)

Wacław Antczak was a tailor by profession:

> After finishing primary school I became a tailor's apprentice. I simultaneousy attended a vocational school. Having received a master diploma as a tailor, I entered the workers' university in 1937, and in 1939, on the 1st of September, the war broke out.[1]

After the outbreak of the war, Antczak travelled to Warsaw in order to "join other patriots in the defence [of the capital city] against Hitler's invasion."[2] He fought in a workers' battalion, and returned to Łódź after its capitulation, where he stayed in hiding for fear of denunciation. Arrested during a street round-up, he was sent to the camp in Radogoszcz, from which he managed to flee. Around the same time, Antczak began to write his first poems. After the war, he left for Gdynia, where he attempted to run a tailor's workshop. He returned to Łódź, where he stayed until the end of his life, living off a pension and writing poetry, as well as appearing as an extra in films.[3]

Antczak declared:

> I write poems. I want to use them to give to the young generation, which did not see and experience the things that my and the older generation did, not only people of Polish nationality, but also the nationality which did not experience Hitler's yoke, regardless of their political views, but is wholeheartedly dedicated to mankind, to preserving peace worldwide.[4]

Antczak – a charismatic representative of the non-professional art world – fascinated the Workshop members with his personality and eventually went on to become a full-right member of the group. He actively participated in interventions and artistic actions, such as *The Eighth Cinema* in 1971 (whose name he invented).[5] He played the main role in in Robakowski's activity *Furniture Sale* in Red Market Square;[6] in 1972, he accompanied the WFF members in their intervention in Zakopane during the 5th Festival of Films on Art; he took part in the spectacle *The Career and Death of Adolf Hitler* in Toruń; in the action *Cleaning of Art* in Warsaw,[7] as well as in the activity *Artistic Exercises, Oskar Hansen's Visual Games* on Morel Hill in Elbląg.[8] He carried out his own performances, such as the one during the festival Young Cinema in Gdańsk in

---

1 W. Antczak, *Antoś Rozpylacz. Polski Odyseusz. Najsławniejszy wojownik w walce z Niemcami hitlerowskimi*, Łódź: PWSFTviT, 2008, p. 247.

2 Ibidem.

3 Ibidem.

4 Ibidem p. 247.

5 Statement by Grzegorz Królikiewicz in the film *A Different Cinema* (*Inne Kino*), dir. Maria Waśko, 1999. See J. Robakowski, *Żywa Galeria,* p. 39.

6 *The Eighth Cinema*, leaflet, Łódź 1971, archive of the Exchange Gallery, Arton Foundation, http://repozytorium.fundacjaarton.pl/index.php?action=view/object&objid=3162&colid=75&catid=18 [accessed 30-12-2016].

7 *Żywa Galeria. Łódzki progresywny ruch artystyczny 1969-1981*, ed. J. Robakowski, Łódź: Łódzki Dom Kultury Galeria FF, 2000, p. 67.

8 *Elbląg konceptualny*, ed. J. Denisiuk, Elbląg: Centrum Sztuki Galeria EL, 2010, p. 49.

February 1973.[9] The same year, Antczak participated in *Action Workshop*, one of the most important events in the Workshop's history,[10] as well as in the event "Kinolaboratorium" within the 5th Biennial of Spatial Forms in Elbląg, organised by the Workshop.[11] The members of the group paid homage to Wacław Antczak in their project for the 12th São Paulo Biennial – *Transmission of the Personality of Wacław Antczak from Łódź*.[12]

Wacław Antczak died in Łódź in 1974. After his death, on several occasions the Workshop members undertook efforts with a view to commemorating him. In 1984, the exhibition *Hommage à Wacław Antczak* was held at the STK Gallery in Łódź.[13]

In 2008, the Film School in Łódź published the book *Antoś Rozpylacz. Polski Odyseusz. Najsławniejszy wojownik w walce z Niemcami hitlerowskimi. Epopeja partyzantów z czasów powstania w Warszawie*, a literary piece by Antczak with a preface by E. Janicka. The typescript of the text was preserved by Józef Robakowski in the archive of his Exchange Gallery.

9 J. Robakowski, *Żywa Galeria*, p. 88.

10 It seems that in this case Antczak's participation was rather passive, Józef Robakowski does not mention him as a participant (see J. Robakowski, *Żywa Galeria*, p. 88), but Antczak can be seen in the photographic documentation of the activity created by Z. Sowiński, available on the website of the Arton Foundation, http://repozytorium.fundacjaarton.pl/index.php?action-view/object&objid-3074&colid-75&catid-18&lang-pl [accessed 31-12-2016].

11 *Kronika V Biennale Form Przestrzennych Kinolaboratorium,* op. cit.

12 J. Robakowski, *Żywa Galeria*, p. 91.

13 Brochure accompanying the exhibition from the archive of the Exchange Gallery available on the website of the Arton Foundation http://repozytorium.fundacjaarton.pl/index.php?action-view/object&objid-3078&colid-75&catid-18&lang-pl [accessed 30-12-2016]; script of *Hommage à Wacław Antczak*, manuscript, from the archive of the Exchange Gallery available on the website of the Arton Foundation, http://repozytorium.fundacjaarton.pl/index.php?action-view/object&objid-3080&colid-75&catid-18&lang-pl [accessed 30-12-2016].

Andrzej Barański

(1941)

Andrzej Barański studied at the Film School between 1969 and 1973. His *Winding Paths* (1971) were included into the set of Workshop's films. The film oscillates between experimental and feature filmmaking, in which two protagonists roam the streets of Łódź – their paths do not cross and the characters do not interact. The film, which presents Łódź as a rather provincial place immersed in the slow rhythm of everyday life, provides one of examples of the Workshop members' interest in the cityscape of Łódź.

Barański also authored the concept of the film *Ode to Youth* (1974). The group members created it together, encouraging random passers-by to recite a single word from Adam Mickiewicz's eponymous piece and composing their statements into a single whole by editing very short cuts. *Ode* is one of a range of collective works by the Workshop which mark an attempt to go beyond the narrow circle of professional artists and to create a record of collective consciousness.

FILMOGRAPHY:

Winding Paths (35 mm, 6'11, 1970, B&W)

Kazimierz Bendkowski

(1948)

While still at high school, Bendkowski belonged to the amateur Film Club in Warsaw, and as a member of the club he participated in numerous amateur film festivals, where he presented films made on 8 mm film stock. One year before successfully passing entry exams to the Film School, he received a special award at the 17th National Amateur Film Contest (Nowa Huta, 23rd–26th October 1969) for his film *The Glow of Shade*.

Akin to nearly all other Workshop members, Bendkowski declared his interest in the problem of the relativity of media transmission. In 1975, the artist wrote in his essay:

> Humans encounter information that originates from mass media, which primarily make use of visual communication — [...] for instance, someone who watches a fragment of the Gobi Desert on television will find it difficult to differentiate it from the Sahara. My work serves to determine the border between objectivity and relativity of visual messages.[14]

Bendkowski also pursued his explorations in fields that were not particularly characteristic of the Workshop's activity, such as mysticism. He believed that art bears connection to a kind of mystery – not only is it supposed to activate the viewers' senses, but also to expand their potential of spiritual cognition. These two spheres became intertwined in his works, characterised both by an analytical use of the media and openness to metaphysics. This can be seen, for instance, in a series of photographs *Gold*, created within the cycle *Relative Image* (which Bendkowski began in 1970, and on which he carries on working, according to his own declaration).

The artist refers to the works that form *Relative Image* as "performances for camera." The use of self-portrait was therefore not an indifferent gesture the project does no consist merely in an analysis of the properties of the photographic medium and its potential to convey the truth, but rather with an epic (several thousand prints) attempt at self-identification. In *Gold*, Bendkowski created a kind of comic book with himself as the protagonist who struggles with a golden element within a secondary painted layer of the works. In some photographs, he becomes crushed by a golden triangle or drenched with golden liquid. In a simple manner – introducing an unexpected and mysterious element to photography – the artist activated the viewer's imagination.

Characteristic of the artist, the elements of surprise, mystery and engagement can also be found in *Mysteries*, which Bendkowski organised in Warsaw in the Rakowiec housing estate since 1971,[15] as well as in *Action Workshop* in 1973, where he carried out the activity *Sound–Movement–Colour*. A darkened tent became a stage of an ephemeral audio-visual spectacle. The artist used audio tape painted with fluorescent paint to create a moving projection akin to a starry sky, which was accompanied by experimental music recorded on tape. The second part of the installation consisted of an isolated space in which two people were closed. They could be seen by the viewers through small holes covered with different 'converters', such as colour foil or mesh.[16] The third fragment of the work was a mirror in which the viewers – illuminated with fluorescent light – could see themselves transformed.

Within his activity in the Workshop, Kazimierz Bendkowski produced six films: *A Wheel* (1973), *An Area* (1973), *A Point* (1973), *Centre* (1973), unpreserved *Laughter* (1973) and *Soley* (1976). As Łukasz Ronduda wrote, the first three are interpretations of the eponymous spatial forms, while at the same time they testify to the artist's declared fascination with grand film productions.[17] These are analytical

14 K. Bendkowski, *Relatywność i obiektywność komunikatów wizualnych*, in R. W. Kluszczyński, *Warsztat Formy Filmowej*, Warsaw: Centrum Sztuki Współczesnej Zamek Ujazdowski, 2000, pp. 62–4.

15 See note on p.44.

16 Interview with Kazimierz Bendkowski, September 2016.

17 Ł. Ronduda, *Polish Art of the 70s*, Warsaw: Centre for Contemporary Art Ujazdowski Castle, 2009, p. 295.

films, yet they do not mark a protest against cinematography, but propose enriching it with additional means. As opposed to the majority of the Workshop members, Bendkowski considered it possible to subordinate formal experiments to the narrative layer. For instance, in the film *Area* he tapped into such experiments to build a surrealist image of the city (a destroyed tenement house and the yard with the residents of the house). The mood of anxiety is based on frequent changes in the sharpness of the image, but also on the dynamics of shots, static at the beginning of the film and very expressive at the end. Thus, Bendkowski demonstrates a broad range of skills in direction of photography and film editing, the artist attempts to use them to balance poetic and structural discourse.[18] We can also observe it in the film *Centre* (1976), one of the most visually refined works created in the Workshop circle, in which the view of a city illuminated with neon signs transforms into an increasingly abstract play of lights.

At the turn of 1976, Bendkowski took a scholarship at the Internationaal Cultureel Centrum (ICC) in Antwerp. At that time, the artist created several works using video technology, which was highly inaccessible in Poland. In the film *An Image of Speaking* (1976), he juxtaposed the image of a speaking person with a visual representation of their voice on the bottom of the screen (it was a continuation of the missing film *Laughter* from 1972, in which the artist carried out a similar procedure). In turn, the work *I Like It...* (1976) offered an interesting perspective of an Eastern European guest on a Western metropolis – the portrayed girl pointed at the elements of the cityscape which she found attractive, saying: 'I like it.'

Kazimierz Bendkowski finished his studies at the Film School with a certificate of completion, after which he began working at the Academy of Fine Arts in Warsaw. In 1982 he emigrated to the German Federal Republic. From 1984 to 2010, he worked at the Faculty of Visual Communication of Kunsthochschule in Kassel.

FILMOGRAPHY AND VIDEO WORKS:
A Wheel (35 mm, 1973, 4', B&W)
An Area (35 mm, 1973, 4'47", B&W)
A Point (35 mm, 2'50", 1973 B&W)
Centre [*Roundabout*] (35 mm, 5'20", 1973, colour)
View from a Window (35 mm, 1974, B&W., unpreserved)
Solei (35 mm, 1975/76, B&W, unpreserved)
Replica 35 mm, 8'30", 1975, colour)
Laughter (35 mm, 1974/75, B&W, unpreserved)
I Like It (video, 1976)
Mine (video, 1976)
An Image of Drinking (video, 1976)
An Image of Speaking (video, 1976)

PHOTOGRAPHY:
Relative Image (series of B&W photographs; the cycle includes smaller series of photographs, such as *Gold*, created by Bendkowski from the 1970s until the present day)

OTHER WORKS:
Ultraviolet Mystery (environment at the Muzem Sztuki [Museum of Art] in Łódź, during *Action Workshop*, 1973)
Various Variants of Record of Light, work made during the exhibition *Mechanical Record of Image*, Remont Gallery, Warsaw, 1975

18 Ł. Ronduda, *Workshop.*

Wojciech Bruszewski

(1947–2009)

Wojciech Bruszewski studied at the Direction of Photography Department of the Film School in Łódź between 1966 and 1970, and later continued his education at the Film Direction Department (until 1974).

A co-founder of the Workshop of the Film Form, Bruszewski previously belonged to the group Zero-61 since 1967. At that time, among other projects, the artist created an important work in the form of a series of photograms (1967–1969) under the common title *xxx*. By their principle, they were supposed to be devoid of any connotations and avoid eliciting any memories or associations from the viewer. Already in that work Bruszewski questioned the mimetic properties of photography, drew attention to the materiality of the medium and manifested his conviction that the most complete form of creative work consists in the experience of transmission.[19]

In his entire later practice Bruszewski consistently developed that premise, examining the media, investigating their relation with reality (the artist would probably say 'with nature' – with what can be seen and heard), as well as deconstructing our convictions concerning media. That led him to abandoning the tested ways of using them.[20] Such an approach was represented essentially by all the Workshop members, but in Bruszewski's case it acquired a particular undertone. Media served him as a tool of struggle with the division into art and nature as well as the resulting mimesis. The artist used them not to imitate but to investigate reality – also in areas that were difficult to access and required creating experiments and paradoxical situations. Bruszewski's early photograms were such a perception trap. They were supposed to function as an 'imprint' of the real, and not its record. Bruszewski used them to verify the possibility to create such a photograph that would become intertwined with reality not only at the visual, but also at the haptic, sensual and material level. The artist tested how much of the world could be contained by the medium. He wrote:

> Photography, as well as all its related techniques, lives a double life. It is a thing, paper, celluloid film, silver particles, pigment molecules, gelatine, projection, etc. [...], and at the same time it is: a representation, a relation about something, an image of something; something which it itself is not.[21]

During the early period of the Workshop's practice, Bruszewski went out into space beyond the sphere of the photographic print. His approach is exemplified by the works *Continuation – Hand* (1971) and *Continuation – Ear* (1971), which became autonomous structures composed of fragments of photographs. Bruszewski used them to deconstruct the popular conviction that photography is able to represent merely a fragment of the world – in his installation the frame became not a fragment, but an autonomous infinity.

The last such polemical work by Bruszewski was *Photographs of Sounds* (1971) – visual records of soundtracks on photosensitive paper. Yet, a gesture that ultimately recapitulated that period of his practice was *Ballet Language* (1973) – a sequence of photographs and drawings that portrayed the nude artist using his body to create a new alphabet. That work, which was essentially a performance documentation, bears testimony to the artist's growing interest in the problems of language. At the same

19 *Wojciech Bruszewski*, pp. 11–12.

20 Ibidem, p. 13.

21 Wojciech Bruszewski, *Ciąg dalszy*, „Fotografia", 9, 1969, quoted in *Wojciech Bruszewski. Phenomena of Perception*, ed. E. Fuchs, J. Zagrodzki, Łódź: Miejska Galeria Sztuki, 2010, p. 13.

time, the presented sequence brings to mind a shamanistic dance, as if Bruszewski was trying to distance himself from attempts to codify any system of signs whatsoever.

From 1973 to the end of the 1980s, Bruszewski explored a different medium: video, which – owing to its intimacy, flexibility and openness to interventions – provided him with the most complete means to lay bare the paradoxes of reality and implement a strategy which the artist referred to as 'setting traps':

> What I do is nothing short of setting traps for WHAT EXISTS. I am trying to set the traps in a place of contact between the 'spiritual' and 'material,' between what 'we know and think,' and what 'is'. [22]

Bruszewski authored the first Polish work recorded on video tape, *Pictures Language* (1973). The 'television spectacle' was created in Elbląg according to a script prepared alongside Piotr Bernacki, with production assistance of Paweł Kwiek, by means of a production truck and four cameras borrowed from the Film School. The artists proposed to transform the alphabet into a visual code. For instance, the letter 'e' corresponded to an image of a ploughed field. They used the new code to convey a text – information about the transport of luggage by the Polish airline LOT. The language imposed the manner of representing reality. The work can be interpreted as an activity in the field of semantic archaeology with the goal of tracing the initial stages of the formation of a sign system.[23]

Pictures Language anticipated Bruszewski's further explorations in the field of communication methods – other than speech or film. In another work, *Spatial Transmission* (1974), the artist rode a bicycle around a Polish Television studio in the field of vision of three cameras, while observing himself on monitors. Acting as both a participant and an observer of transmission, he disturbed the linear structure of the medium.

Bruszewski also created video installations. Such works functioned akin to 'mental and visual paradoxes,'[24] often based on a specific configuration of cameras, mirrors or screens. That was the case in the work *Tap* (1976), in which viewers could see water running upwards. In turn, in the installation *From x to x* (1976) an appropriate configuration of the camera and monitor in connection with a drawing combined the image on the monitor with a drawing (of the line and the sign 'x') visible on the gallery wall into a single whole. Bruszewski implemented a similar procedure in the work *Speaker* (1976), which he described as follows:

> A real fan blows onto a 'false' flag; an image of a line connects to the actual line itself; a piece of paper and its reflection in the mirror are combined into a single rectangular shape; I often ask myself why I accept these obvious absurdities with so much kindness. 'Since this is the human condition,' the spirit of René Magritte replies. 'Nonsense exists only in the sphere of language,' the master continues, 'if something does not fit, one should appeal to the Office of Logic. And we, after all, you and me, we do pictures.' Only recently, I have noticed that one of my works (*Loud-Speaker* from the cycle: *The Video Touch*) is a direct replica of the painting presented above. [Magritte's *Human Condition*].

---

22 Wojciech Bruszewski, *Co robię?*, 1976, http://repozytorium.fundacjaarton.pl/indexzphp?action–view/object&objid–63 [accessed 2-01-2016], quoted in *Wojciech Bruszewski*, p. 112.

23 See M. Kuźmicz, "Magister ludi," in *Across Realities*, Warsaw: Arton Foundation, 2014, p. 67.

24 *Wojciech Bruszewski*, p. 114.

> What happens on the TV screen and what takes place outside it is a unity in terms of time, space and action.[25]

In 1977, Bruszewski became an owner of a video camera, which gave him the possibility to record the above works on tape and present them at Documenta 6 in Kassel under the common title *The Video Touch*. It is the ten works that form this cycle that provide the fullest representation of his primordial and vigilant way of seeing the world. Reality according to Bruszewski was a universe of signs, signs that can be read if we reject the egocentric belief in the objective and obligatory character of our own perspective. Therefore, Bruszewski created audiovisual loops that transported the viewer from one reality to another, without answering the question: Which of them, if any of them at all, is not so much the *real one* but the one that can serve as the basis to verify the other ones? The artist wrote that he intended to set traps for reality. Indeed, his creativity was self-restrained, oriented not toward the generation of new phenomena, but to a careful observation of the fundamental matters of the world that pass every day in front of our very eyes. Bruszewski set his traps in the best of places – where situations occurred which inhabited the borderland of reality and which seemed to contradict the laws of nature; where it was possible to 'catch' the world in a paradox, to capture and confine it in a video installation, as if in a trap.

FILMOGRAPHY AND VIDEO WORKS:

Inventory (35 mm, 5', 1970, B&W)
A Clapper (35 mm, 5'53", 1971, B&W)
Apnoea (35 mm, 10'01", 1972, B&W)
YYAA (35 mm, 2'59", 1973, B&W)
Door–Text (35 mm, 1'50", 1973, B&W)
System of a New Alphabet (35 mm, 5', 1973)
Pictures Language (video, 1973, B&W, unpreserved, collaboration: P. Bernacki, P. Kwiek)
Spatial Transmission, (video, 1'08", 1974, B&W)
Zapłon mózgu (35 mm, 4'5", 1974, cz.-b.)
Brain Ignition (35 mm, 4'5", 1974, B&W)
Chairs (35 mm, 15', 1975, B&W)
Music Score for Individual and Collective Performance (35 mm, 3'12", 1975, B&W)
Voting (part of the film *Living Gallery,* 35 mm, 4'5", 1975, colour)
Audiovisual Experiment – Matchbox (two versions: 35 mm and video, 2', 1975, B&W)
Audiovisual Experiment – Spoon (two versions: 35 mm, video, 2', 1976, B&W)
Between March and June (video, 10', 1977)

PHOTOGRAPHY:

Text (photographic object, 1970)
Continuation – Ear (photo-installation, B&W photograph, 1971)
Continuation – Hand (photo-installation, B&W photograph, 1971)
Photographs of Sounds (B&W photograph, 1970)
Sixteen Lighting Situations (an installation, unpreserved, B& W photograph, 1975)

OBJECTS:

New Words (1972)

VIDEO INSTALLATIONS:

Installation for the Labirynt Gallery (1976)
Input – Output 1 (1976)
Speaker (1976)
Tap (1976)
Outside (1976–1977)
Time Structure – Stopwatch (1977)
My Five Fingers (1977)

25 Ibidem, p. 116.

Positive Memory, Negative Memory (1977)
Object in Motion – Observer in Motion (1977)

PERFORMANCE, AUDIOVISUAL ACTIVITIES:
Intersection (1973)
Wojciech Bruszewski Is Dancing (photographic documentation of Bruszewski's performance, part of work *Ballet Language,* B&W photograph, pencil, paper, 1973)
Trans-translocation (1974)
When I say (1974)
Spatial Transmission at the Dziekanka Gallery (1977)
I count (video-performance, 1977)
The Structure of Time – Points (video-performance, recorded on 16 mm tape, 10', 1977)

Wojciech Chyła

(1950)

Graduate of a musical high school in a piano class, Chyła studied later at the Faculty of Musical Direction at the Higher State School of Music. His biographic note created for the needs of Ryszard Waśko's diploma work read:

> Established a range of musical contacts with a view to investigating the potential of intervention of phonographic structures into musical codes. [...] Those experiences resulted in an open composition technique leading to a synthesis of sound.[26]

Within his activity in the Workshop, Chyła created the soundtrack to Ryszard Waśko's films, such as *Wall II* (1974) and *Configuration I-VI* (1974).

Lechosław Czołnowski

(1946)

Studied at the Film School between 1973 and 1977. Collaborator in the production of some of the works by the WFF, primarily films by Waśko: *Window*, *Padlock*, *Pavement*, and *Backyard*. In the later period Czołnowski worked primarily as a director of photography in documentary and feature films, such as *Constructivism in Poland* (1979) by Ryszard and Maria Waśko, among other productions.

Jan Freda

(1948)

Sound engineer, co-producer of many feature and documentary films. Freda contributed with the soundtrack to some films by the WFF, such as Ryszard Waśko's *A-B-C-D-E-F-1-35* from 1976.

Ryszard Gajewski

(1944)

Ryszard Gajewski began his studies at the Film School in 1965 – the earliest among all the Workshop members. The choice of the school was a result from his interest in the history of photography, and later in the history of avant-garde film, which he explored in the dynamically operating Gorzów Photographic Society.[27]

Gajewski was an active member of the Workshop until 1973. His collaboration with the group began already before its official establishment, when he participated in the exhibition *Greenhouse* in September 1969. Yet, Gajewski had created his first experimental film etude *Her and Him* before – in 1967. Unfortunately, it has not been preserved, akin to his next film *Professionals* from 1969, which was an experimental documentary devoted to the stay of inter

---

26 R. Waśko, 'Warsztat Formy Filmowej', MA diss., Film School in Łódź, 1974, http://repozytorium.fundacjaarton.pl [accessed 30-12-2016].

27 Interviews with Ryszard Gajewski, January and July 2016.

national exchange students at the Film School. Also missing is his vivid impressionistic documentary about the hippie environment in Poland, titled *Hippie* (1970). All we know are film stills and the filmmaker's memories:

> The School offered even less film stock for exercises in colour than for exercises in black and white. Fortunately, Orwo Color launched a new type of film stock, and I was the first one to test it. Everyone was afraid of the Orwo film stock, because the effects were often a nightmare. At the Educational Film Studio (WFO) laboratory, together with its head, we decided to treat the film stock in a different way than recommended by the German manufacturer. I can't remember all the details, but we increased the sensitivity, we changed the time of development and after a few attempts we achieved similar colours to the Kodak film stock. I made a 'hippie' film that sought to render an altered state of consciousness after drug consumption. It was only my imagined vision, because I never tried drugs and I couldn't check if my visions were true.[28]

Later, probably between 1970 and 1972, Gajewski worked on the film *Centrifuge*, which was included in the first set of the Workshop's films and shown at Atelier '72 in Edinburgh. Gajewski made use of a centrifugal movement of the camera to the music of Led Zeppelin's 'Whole Lotta Love' – the featured takes were supposed to correspond to the lyrics of the song. Gajewski's last film within the Workshop was *Pierzgalski* (1971) – an experimental documentary about the lecturer at the Film School in Łódź, painter and photographer Ireneusz Pierzgalski.

After 1973, Gajewski devoted himself entirely to work in the field of professional cinematography, where he attempted to implement some of the solutions developed within the Workshop, especially different innovative and unconventional procedures in direction of photography. Unfortunately, given a variety of compromises which the directors of those films had to accept, Gajewski's ideas were usually significantly reduced.[29]

FILMOGRAPHY:
Centrifuge (35 mm, 2'50", 1970/72, colour)
Pierzgalski (35 mm, 8'20", 1971, colour)

PHOTOGRAPHIC OBJECTS:
Comb (used film stock, 1973, the work was presented during *Action Workshop*, 1973)
Film Sausage (film stock, 1973, the work was presented during *Action Workshop*, 1973)

Tadeusz Junak

(1945–2009)

Studied at the Film School since 1970. Co-founder of the Workshop. Junak created two films within the group. *Confrontation* (1972) comprises aesthetic close-ups of a jukebox that plays a record by Ewa Demarczyk. Thus, Junak attempted to show the eponymous confrontation of two machines: one that plays music, and another that records the image. In turn, in *Episode* (1973), Junak reversed a 15-minutes fragment of the Hollywood film *Sweet Bird of Youth* in such a way that the last take of the original film became

28 R. Gajewski, *Warsztat Form Filmowych – początki*, unpublished manuscript, Warsaw 2014.

29 That was the case in the film *Scorpio, Virgo and Sagittarius*, directed by Andrzej Kondratiuk in 1972 roku, in which Ryszard Gajewski and Ryszard Waśko worked as camera operators.

the first. The work was a direct, but also ironic and perverse, expression of the Workshop's attitude towards the main cinematographic current.

FILMOGRAPHY:
Confrontation (35 mm, 4'29", 1972, B&W)
Episode (35 mm, 15'27", color)

Marek Koterski

(1942)

Marek Koterski studied at the Film School since 1967. He distances himself from his affiliation with the Workshop,[30] but he was an active member of the group in the early days of its activity. Koterski also participated in some of its actions and interventions, and his film *Ah* (1972) was often show within the Workshop's screenings. *Ah* was somewhat of a by-product of Koterski's work for a public institution which commissioned a film about alcoholism. He edited the unused takes into a new film, which was later transposed from 16 mm to 35 mm film stock and presented in such form as a Workshop film.

FILMOGRAPHY:
Ah (35 mm, 10'47", 1972, B&W)

Paweł Kwiek

(1951)

In 1969, Paweł Kwiek was admitted to the Direction of Photography Department of the Film School. The beginning of his studies coincided with the establishment of the Workshop of the Film Form, in which he participated. Thus, Kwiek inaugurated his extremely intensive decade of the 1970s.

Included in Waśko's MA dissertation, Kwiek's biographic note enumerates not only student film etudes, but also performance and quasi-theatrical activities, which were often pursued with another member of the group, Jacek Łomnicki, as well as with the 'Warsaw group,' comprising Jan Stanisław Wojciechowski as well as the KwieKulik duo (Zofia Kulik and Przemysław Kwiek). Thus, Paweł Kwiek became a 'link' between the Film School and the Academy of Fine Arts in Warsaw. Among other works, that collaboration resulted in the film *Open Form* (1972), which, as Kwiek wrote, became 'the first large-scale collaboration between the students of the above-mentioned schools, which consisted in carrying out a range of exercises with the use of film camera.'[31]

Kwiek's simultaneous participation in several artistic initiatives bears testimony to his need to unite and work collectively. In the creative process, the artist attached particular importance to communication: with colleagues from the group, but also with the viewers, who often became co-creators of works. Kwiek consistently developed the idea of democratic approach to art, including film – and it is important to remember that in the 1970s film was an elitist medium (from the perspective of production) and entangled in relations with the political authorities. Kwiek wrote:

> Documentary strives to deliver the truth on man. Until now however no one could avoid the deformation of that truth resulting from the influence of the producer on the work. [...] I claim that the truth of a man can be a product of a face to face contact, regardless of what s/he would like to say [...] In film the situation is present when all the decisions of the maker are taken by the person, or the group, which is the subject of the film. That means that s/he will make the film on herself/himself, or in other

30 K. Krubski, M. Miller, Z. Turowska, W. Wiśniewski, *Filmówka. Powieść o łódzkiej szkole filmowej*, Warsaw: Prószyski i S-ka, 1998, p. 214.

31 R. Waśko, op. cit., p. 41.

> words s/he would be allowed to make a free realization on any subject.[32]

Kwiek put that concept into practice on several occasions – for the first time during the 5th Biennial of Spatial Forms in Elbląg (1973). The event resulted in several dozen one-minute recordings created by different makers, which Kwiek composed within a single film *One Laboratory*. In turn, within the action 'Art Day on Sunday 15th April, 1973 in Niechcice,' the local community with the youth from the State Agricultural Farm (PGR) in the village of Niechcice created the film *Niechcice* (1973). It comprised the scenes of hooligan fight, jostling an elderly man by a group of youngsters walking on the pavement, pre-empting a suicide attempt of a young girl. Kwiek also briefly described the unrealised ideas: a scene of saving a drowning man from in ice-hole, a little boy waiting for a phone call, a lesbian love scene, a scene of pick-pocketing, licking the wall (with someone's name written on it), and showing an injured tongue to the camera.[33] It was not the final effect that enjoyed prominence here, but the sheer social-artistic process. The artist's goal was to "give voice to those who had remained mute."[34]

Among the WFF members, Paweł Kwiek most often explored the borderlands of film, creating what R. Kluszczyński described as 'a vision of open cinema, which was unspecified, negated norm and conventions, and opened up to the unknown.'[35] The artist created films without camera and films without film stock, such as *Commentary* (1972), a kind of performance in which Kwiek narrated the plot of a non-existent film to the gathered audience (Kwiek carried out the performance on many occasions, such as Atelier '72 in Edinburgh[36]), and *Mirror* (1971), where he used a mirror to reflect light from the projector in the direction of the audience. Those works aimed to deconstruct the norms of perceiving the medium of film, as well as to elicit the viewers' reactions and observe them. *Commentary* had yet another function: The banal love story told by Kwiek was supposed to trigger mental clichés in the minds of the viewers and make them realise the extent to which they were immersed in such clichés.

In the mid-1970s, Kwiek embarked on intensive investigations into theories that could describe human intelligence and human cognitive engagement with the world along the lines that differed from the Marxist school. The artist found such an alternative in the cybernetic theory of character, which provided an important context for his experiments with the use of video technology. From that theory Kwiek adopted the association of new audiovisual technologies with the cognitive structures of the human mind. He wrote:

> We thus have a tool that works much like our imagination, like our mind, which processes perceived, remembered, or currently produced images. The discovery of successive parallels, relations, analogies, and oppositions between the functions of means of mechanical recording, playback, and transmission happens to be on the one hand the process of learning about those means and, on the other, learning about the analogous structures of our minds. The reality of the television studio was like a piece of the human brain that has such characteristics as: perception, cognitive structure, some ability to

32 P. Kwiek, *Objective Documentary about a Man*, in *The Struggle for Form: Perspectives on Polish Avant-Garde Film 1916—1989*, ed. K. Kuc and M. O'Pray, New York: Columbia University Press, 2014, p. 126.
33 Ibidem.
34 Interview with Paweł Kwiek, July 2014.
35 R. W. Kluszczyński, op. cit., p. 33.
36 See R. Waśko, op. cit., p. 129.

operate on objects, on what it perceives, and some ability to operate on the objects of thought, that is, filming itself. And when one adds to this the structure of live intellect that enters this system, the model of reality created by television, the opportunity for the penetration of reality becomes doubled: a human being resides in the reality which is a model, and simultaneously this model becomes the reality inhabited by that human being. [...]Models [...] give one the opportunity to observe what is over the horizon of everyday life, what is at the limits of cognition.[37]

That theory provided a basis for Kwiek's further experiments related to the impact of the media on the human body and psyche. In May 1974, during a live broadcast from the studio of the Polish Television, the artist carried out the performance *Video A – A Studio Situation*, which consisted in providing camera operators and producers with guidelines as to framing, choice of the current camera and changing the takes. In this simple way, Kwiek demonstrated to thousands of viewers that any attempt at reporting a given event is necessarily selective, fragmentary and distorted.

In 1977, Paweł Kwiek chose to leave the Workshop of the Film Form, while continuing his investigations into human cognitive capacities. In that process, the artist gradually rejected the tool of new media, which he had used in the WFF period, and turned instead to transcendental experiences.

FILMOGRAPHY AND VIDEO WORKS:

Forma Otwarta (activity outside the Workshop of the Film Form, in collaboration with Przemysław Kwiek, Zofia Kulik, Jan S. Wojciechowski – 7-day action of exercises for camera, which resulted in the film *Open Form*, screened within the sets of the Workshop's films, 35 mm, 15-17', depending on the version, 1971, colour)
Face (35 mm, 6', 1971, B&W, collaboration: J. Łomnicki)
Feature Film (35 mm, 4', 1971, B&W, unpreserved)
Mirror (film without film stock, film performance, first presented in December 1970 at the Współczesna Gallery in Warsaw)
Face II (16 mm, 1', 1971, B&W, collaboration: J. Łomnicki)
Camera Exercise (35 mm, 7', 1972, B&W, film based on the idea of Paweł Kwiek, with the participation of J. Robakowski, A. Mikołajczyk, P. Kwiek, D. Roberts, W. Bruszewski, T. Junak, A. Bogusławski
A Commentary (film without film stock, 1972, collaboration: W. Bruszewski)
Chinese (35 mm, 7', 1972, colour)
Colour (35 mm, 5', 1972, unpreserved)
1, 2, 3... Cinematographer's Exercise 35 mm, 8'10", 1972, colour)
Me and Telephone (35 mm, 6'03", 1972, B&W)
Fair Play (35 mm?, 1973, unpreserved, collaboration: J. Łomnicki)
Niechcie (35 mm, 5'01", 1973, colour, collective film, dir. P. Kwiek)
Numbers (35 mm, 7'52", 1973, B&W)
Cine Laboratory (35 mm, 13'20", colour, collective film by many artists, coordination: P. Kwiek)
Osieki (35 mm, 15'29", 1974, colour)
Video A – A Studio Situation (video, 3'25", 1974, B&W)
Journey (35 mm, 1974, unpreserved, B&W)

37 P. Kwiek, "Model demokratycznej wymiany informacji. Plener pytań," Miastko 1978, quoted in Ł. Ronduda, *Polish Art*, p. 286–8.

Video C (video, 3'12", 1975)
Video P (video, 2'35", 1975)

PHOTOGRAPHY:
Description of A Photograph (B&W photograph, 1973)
Kwiekołom and *Łomokwiek* (photographic work which was a result and element of a joint action by P. Kwiek and J. Łomnicki during *Action Workshop*) (B&W photograph, 1973)
Untitled from the series *Photographs of Inscriptions* (B&W photograph, 1975)
Nude (B&W photograph, 1973)
Doing the Impossible Light (B&W photography, 1973)
Multiplication, Addition (B&W photographs, 1972)
From the series *Extension of an Ideal Object in Physical Reality,* (B&W photograph, 1975)
From the series *Photographs for an Exhibition of Contextual Art* (B&W photographs, 1975)
From the series *Pointing* (B&W photographs, 1975)
Untitled from the series *Touches* (B&W photographs, 1975/76)
Line A and *Line B* (B&W photographs, 1975)
Line 1 and *Line 2* (B&W photographs, 1975)
Photo-Video Drawings (B&W photographs, marker, paper, 1975)
This Is what I Want to Hold in my Hands (B&W photographs, 1975)
Anthropophotometry (B&W photographs, 1975)
I'm Standing in One Place, I'm Sitting in Another Place (B&W photographs, 1975)
Random Photograph (B&W photograph, 1975)
Chair (B&W photograph, marker, paper, 1974-76)
Pseudo-Video-Photographic Drawings (B&W photograph, marker, paper, 1976)
Light Drawings (B&W photograph, 1975)
Leaning from the Frame (B&W photograph, 1976/77)
Counting-out Rhyme (B&W photograph, 1976/77)

Antoni Mikołajczyk

(1939–2000)

Co-founder of the Workshop of the Film Form. The only member of the group who was not a graduate of the Film School in Łódź. Mikołajczyk studied in Toruń, where he was an active member of the groups Zero-61 and Zero-69, as well as a participant of the film club Pętla, among other organisations. It was then, between 1964 and 1968, that he created his films *Suite*, *Flirtation*, *Two Colts* and *Chest*. Having graduated from studies in Toruń, Mikołajczyk moved with his colleagues to Łódź, where he lectured at the State Higher School of Visual Arts (PWSSP) between 1972 and 1977. The artist did not work independently as a filmmaker within the Workshop, but collaborated with Józef Robakowski on his films *Record* and *From the Mediomagnetic Atelier of Tytus Czyżewski*.

Mikołajczyk worked primarily in the field of photography, although the artist also created video-installations that incorporated photographs.[38] For instance, *Seeming Image* from 1976 comprised an alarm clock and its photographs, as well as camera that transmitted the image of the clock onto two screens. In other works, the artist subjected video image to a variety

38 The works in question are *Colour Image* and *Black and White Image* from 1975, as well as *Object in Motion*, *Vertical Record*, *Horizontal Record*, *Seeming Image* and *Reality – Image of Reality* from 1976.

of manipulations, making use of mirror reflections, double projections or colour foil. Thus, he built complex relations between transmission, photography and reality. This approach is manifest especially in the installation *Reality – Image of Reality*, comprising two monitors with a cityscape by night. One showed a live transmission, the other – a photograph of exactly the same scene. Thus, Mikołajczyk compelled the viewer to define truth and illusion. Akin to many other works by the Workshop, it was a model whose goal was to increase the viewer's sensitivity to media manipulations, which were everyday reality, especially in television.

PHOTOGRAPHY:
Photographic Record (1973)
Anatomy (1974)

INSTALLATIONS:
Construction (1973)

VIDEO INSTALLATIONS:
Seeming Image (1976)
Reality – Image of Reality (1976)

Ryszard Lenczewski

(1948)

Studied at the Film School between 1970 and 1974. Previously active in the Łódź Photographic Society. Within the Workshop, Lenczewski collaborated as a cinematographer with other members of the group, such as Ryszard Waśko on his film *Wall* (1972). He also created his own film *Child's Room* (1974), which marked an attempt to achieve maximal objectivity by eliminating the role of the camera operator. In the eponymous room, Lenczewski arranged a scene with three actors. It was recorded on camera suspended on a hook on the ceiling; hanging on a twisted belt, the camera revolved around its own axis.

After graduating from the Film School Lenczewski began working as a director of photography. He was honoured with numerous prestigious awards in the field – among other distinctions, he received an Oscar nomination for photography to the film *Ida* (2013), alongside Łukasz Żal.

Jacek Łomnicki

(1951–2009)

Jacek Łomnicki studied at the Film School since 1970. He was an active member of the Workshop, although his did not create any films independently. In turn, Łomnicki engaged in a variety of ephemeral and performative activities in collaboration with Paweł Kwiek, with whom he established the artistic duo 'Czyży' in 1971. Their projects were difficult to grasp and define. In the memories of their witnesses, they appear as 'interventions in interventions.' In those projects, the artists often referred to their own works, for instance the film *Face*, in which Łomnicki acted and Kwiek worked as a camera operator and director. Kwiek wrote that the first version from May 1971 was 'created live – from shot to shot of the human face (facial expression) interpreted through cinematographic procedures.'[39] The artist referred to that method as 'combining the unrelated intentions of both makers in one common work. The film has a changeable function steered by form, the manner of screening (a specific way of continuous work).'[40]

That 'specific way of continuous work' was transferred to Łomnicki's and Kwiek's subsequent projects. When the only existing copy of *Face* went missing after the screening in Nowa Ruda, the artists created another film *Face II*, and the film stills from the first version were used by Paweł Kwiek during his action *Dustbin* in Zakopane.[41] In turn, within the famous *Action Workshop*, Łomnicki carried out his activity *Face*

39 R. Waśko, op. cit., p. 8.
40 Ibidem.
41 See description on p. 44.

X, in which he made a time-lapse recording of the viewers' faces.

Jacek Łomnicki was the son of the famous actor Tadeusz Łomnicki, and after the studies he also made several appearances as an actor, for instance in Andrzej Wajda's *Man of Marble*. He also worked as a cinematographer in documentary and feature films.

FILMOGRAPHY:

Face (35 mm, 6', 1971, B&W, unpreserved, collaboration: P. Kwiek)

Face X (within *Action Workshop*, time-lapse recording of viewers' faces)

Face II (16 mm, 1', 1971, B&W, collaboration: P. Kwiek)

Fair Play (35 mm, 1973 unpreserved, collaboration: P. Kwiek)

ACTIONS:

Kwiekołom and *Łomokwiek* (environment, *Action* Workshop, Muzeum Sztuki in Łódź, 1973)

Janusz Połom

(1950)

Janusz Połom became a student of the Film School in 1971. He made his first creative steps as a high school student in Olsztyn, where he was a member of the Amateur Photographic Club 'Grunwald' in Olsztyn,[42] characterised by high quality of its activities. Already at that time, Połom was in contact with the artistic avant-garde owing to Wojciech Wojczulanis, who ran classes at the club, and his older brother, Stefan (b. 1938), poet and writer, who co-created the Toruń artistic circles.

Within the Workshop, Połom created two films: *Without* (1970) and *ABC* (1974); the latter was presented at the WFF screenings. *ABC* resulted from the artist's profound reflection on the relation between sound and image in film and reality. As Ryszard Kluszczyński wrote:

> Janusz Połom carried out a number of experiments, where he confronted sounds and their respective images. As Robakowski was relieving the image from human domination (at least to a certain degree) by letting the camera work without an eye on the view-finder, and thus relieving it from the influence of cultural codes, Połom, similarly, by translating sounds into images in a direct way gave autonomy back to them and transgressed (or at least problematised) their traditional, representational character. To attain this end, he used various tools, including an oscillograph, with which he realised the film entitled *ABC* (*Alfabet*, 1974). He undertook a large number of other activities with the aim of visualising sounds.[43]

During *Action Workshop*, Połom also created *Electronic Antinomies* – probably the first work in Poland which relied on the use of computer (ODRA 1304). The artist wanted to analyse the word as a carrier of communication that loses its adequacy in the era of the development of 'electronic digital devices.' For this reason, he attempted to present all known forms of notation of words and then carry out exchanges between them. Thus, literary language, a piece of Samuel Beckett's writing, was translated into pictures language, which can be seen as an interesting anticipation of the domination of visual language in the digital age.

In the later years, Połom created numerous documentary and animated films; the artist held the position of the dean of the Direction of Photography and TV Production Department of the Film School in Łódź between 1981 and 1985.

42 Interview with Janusz Połom, May 2016 and Janusz Połom's e-mail to M. Kuźmicz, 2016.

43 R. W. Kluszczyński, op. cit., s. 26. An example of such activity is the work *Sound Images*, created by Połom in 1975 at the Remont Gallery within the event 'Two Days – Multimedia Manifestation of the Workshop.'

FILMOGRAPHY:
ABC (35 mm, 2'13'', 1974, B&W)
Text (*How it is*) (35 mm?, 1976, B&W)
PHOTOGRAPHY:
Camouflage (B&W photographs, 1972)
Towards Spring (B&W photographs, 1972)

ACTIONS, ACTIVITIES:
Electronic Antinomies (During *Action Workshop*, Muzeum Sztuki in Łódź, 1973)
Sound Pictures (performance at the Remont Gallery, Warsaw, 1975)

Józef Robakowski

(1939)

Film and cinema very early became a major part of his life. After the war, Robakowski and his family resided in Gdynia, where his mother took up a job at a kiosk in the 'Warszawa' cinema, and therefore he had an opportunity to spend many hours in film screenings, thus familiarising himself with works of world cinematography (even those reserved for adults). Robakowski was also eager to visit the projection booth, where he would sometimes receive pieces of film stock. Initially, he used them for fun – film stock was highly flammable, which beyond doubt made it attractive to play with. Yet, he soon engaged in more serious experimentation. Robakowski began to build simple projection devices consisting of a box, a light bulb and lens, as well as edit pieces of film stock and make his own slides with drawings.

The artist created his first serious films within the STKF "Pętla" in Toruń. By means of simple hand-editing and nearly household methods, Robakowski made around a dozen of experimental and documentary films on 16 mm film stock. Only one of them has been preserved, *6000000* from 1962, which was devoted to the Holocaust.

The beginning of the studies in Łódź (1966) marked an interruption of Robakowski's film practice. That paradoxical situation only confirms that the School did not provide its students with a possibility of creative work, which was one of the reasons behind the establishment of the Workshop of the Film Form in the autumn of 1970. In the meantime, Robakowski managed to create only two films, *Collage* (1969) and *After the Human Being* (1970). The next film, *Market* (1970), was already made within the Workshop and is recognised as the first work in the history of the group.

In his next film *Test I*, Robakowski returned to working directly on film stock, which he had already done during his Toruń period. He cut holes in the film stock, which let the light from the projector through and blinded the viewers, making them realise the materiality of the film stock, the role of light in cinema, as well as the phenomenon of the after-view and the properties of the human sight.[44] At the same time, it was also an eponymous 'test' of the audience's endurance, part of whom always left the hall, and therefore Robakowski started to show the film at the end of his screenings.[45] Another example of an early camera-less film by Robakowski is *Test II*. The goal of that 'test' was to investigate the relation between the sound and the visual layer of the film by juxtaposing classic organ music and colour red, which disappeared from the screen whenever the sound could be heard.

An important and characteristic group of works by Robakowski are film performances, which the artist used to explore the potential of the medium of video – a technology that was virtually inaccessible in Poland and other countries of the Eastern Bloc. Therefore, the artist tapped into different methods which offered the possibility to achieve similar results. He used production

44 Ibidem, p. 16.
45 R. Gajewski, op. cit.

trucks or operated film cameras in a similar way to video cameras. He overcame the resistance of the matter in the form of the weight of traditional equipment and the properties of classic film stock in order to anticipate the potential opened up by the simplicity and convenience of portable equipment: the possibility of individual work and pursuit of ephemeral activities. The earliest project of such type (and one of Robakowski's most well-known works) is the film *I'm Going* (1973), which is a record of climbing an old parachute tower with the camera on the artist's arm and – in the sound layer – counting the steps. The record is created in real time, without editing, which in the 1960s and 1970s was characteristic primarily of video. As a result, the film reveals the artist's growing fatigue and his relation with the camera – a mechanical device. Robakowski explored the same problem in the work *Along the Line...* (1976), in which he recorded the image whilst walking, running and jumping; and in *Exercise for Both Hands* (1976), in which he waved two active cameras about. Ryszard W. Kluszczyński remarked that the latter project allows us to observe that the relation between the equipment and the human being operates in two directions.[46] On the one hand, the camera captures and records on tape the physiological states of its operator, whereas, on the other hand, it reveals the characteristics of reality that are hidden from the operator but influence him.

Robakowski was also active in the field of photography. The artist pursued many of his cycles in this medium throughout the 1960s-1970s, and some of them until much later, a fact that marks a certain continuity of his practice. For instance, according to the artist, the cycle *Objective Records* comprises works *Jacket* (1967) and *ID* (1969), created during the Toruń period, as well as *Mechanical Photography* (1976) and *Optical Sphere* (1975), created in Łódź. the latter work bears a thematic connection with two projects from 1969, *Four Fields of Focus* and *Ten Fields of Focus*, in which Robakowski engaged with the issue of changes that occur in the field of photographic representation depending on the focus settings. Thus, he confronted the problem of our vision of photography as a medium that faithfully represents reality.

What is more, at the turn of the 1970s, Robakowski created photographic objects. The year 1969 brought the works *Kaleidoscope*, *Images for Collecting* and *Circle* (*Tautological Image*). The first two were created with the use of 'found photographs' and seem to convey a reflection on the cultural role of photographs, which expand the already quite dense iconosphere of the contemporary era. In *Kaleidoscope*, a cube whose walls were filled with photographs was hung on a constantly moving thread. The photographs could be viewed through a magnifying glass. In turn, *Images for Collecting* was somewhat of a collage – the photographs were pasted on a surface in a way that made it necessary to tear them out in order to view them. In that work, Robakowski used photographs of varied status: souvenir, family, anonymous and amateur images, thus distancing himself from the question of authorship and the category of 'work' as a museum objects meant for 'viewing.' *Images for Collecting* anticipated a characteristic motif of many projects by the Workshop: a search for various manners of engaging the viewer in the interaction with the work, or even its co-creation.

FILMOGRAPHY AND VIDEO:
Collage (35 mm, 9', 1969, B&W)
After the Human Being (35 mm, 9', 1969/70, B&W)

46 R. W. Kluszczyński, op. cit., p. 16.

Market (35 mm, 4'2", 1970, B&W, collaboration: T. Junak, R. Meissner)
Test I (35 mm, 5', 1971, B&W)
Composition (35 mm, 2', 1971, B&W)
22x (35 mm, 5'24", 1971, B&W)
Test II (35 mm, 1'58", 1971, colour)
Dynamic Rectangle (35 mm, 2'32", 1971/72, colour)
Record (35 mm, 6', 1972, B&W, collaboration: A. Mikołajczyk)
Exercise (35 mm, 6', 1972/73, B&W)
I'm going (35 mm, 2'56", 1973, B&W)
Door-Window-Chair (35 mm, 30', 1973, B&W, collaboration R. Waśko)
Metre (video, 2', 1974)
Activities (video, 1975)
My Film (35 mm, 5', 1974, B&W)
Moving Closer (video, B&W photography, 5', 1975)
Functions (video, photography, 5', 1975)
Gymnastics (video, 3', 1975)
Drama Exercise (video, 2', 1975)
Interrupted Space (35 mm, 8', 1975/76, B&W)
Instructions (video, 1976, collaboration: A. Paruzel)
Exercise for Both Hands (16 mm, 8', 1976, camera-performance, B&W)
Along the Line... (16 mm, 6', 1977, B&W, collaboration: L. Czołnowski)
Test I (video, 1976)
Test II (video, 1976)
Test III (video, 1976)
TV-Face (video-based activity, 1977)

PHOTOGRAPHY, PHOTOGRAPHIC OBJECTS:
Chair (B&W photograph, chair, 1970)
Rolls (interactive object, 1970)
Sphere (B&W photography, sphere, mirror, 1971)
Jar (B&W photography, jar, 1971)
Kaleidoscope (B&W photography, mirror, 1971)
Blowed Head (B&W photography, inflated pillow, 1971)
Comb (photography, 1971)
Air Installation (photography, 1972)
cycle *Astral Photography* (B&W photography, series made from 1972 until 2002)
cycle *Objective Photography* (B&W photography, since 1973)
cycle *My* (photography, video, 1974)
Instruction (photography, 1975)
The Optical Sphere (photography, 1975)
Three Poses (photographic action with participation of the audience, 1975)
cycle *Relations: 1 metre, 3 angles* (photography, 1975)
cycle *Energetic Angles* (various media, from 1975)
cycle *Mechanical Photography* (B&W photography, 1976)
OBJECTS
Study of the Shadow, 1971
Sound Balance Beam, 1972
A Little Car, 1972

Andrzej Różycki

(1942)

When asked about the beginning of his interest in photography, Andrzej Różycki returns to his childhood memories. The artist was born to a Polish intelligentsia family from the town of Baranowicze (in today's Belarus), where his father was an amateur photographer. When after the war the Różycki family had to abandon their home region, they left almost all their belongings behind, but took some photographs, which Różycki very often viewed as a young boy. He was fascinated by how much and, at the same time, how little they meant when not accompanied by an account or a story. Many years later, the artist used the same photographs in his own works. Viewed with hindsight and taken in as a whole collection, they came to play the role of proofs in his personal investigation pursued patiently in order to discover the rules that govern photography. That investigation, characterised by carefulness and attention to the medium, began for good between 1961 and 1966, when Różycki studied monument preservation and museum studies at the Faculty of Fine Arts of the Nicolaus Copernicus University in Toruń, and gained an additional impetus in 1969, when the artist began his studies at the Film Direction Department of the Film School in Łódź and – a year later – became a co-founder of the Workshop of the Film Form.

As opposed to the other artists from the WFF circle, Różycki devoted himself almost entirely to photography. Within the Workshop, he created several hundred photographs, most of which form several extensive and open-ended circles: *Rules of the Game*, *Analytical Photography*, *Seeming Photography*, and *Conditional Photography*. These are mostly collage compositions with a multitude of elements, which required effort-consuming processing of negatives in the darkroom and equally intensive work on the positives. The three most important and representative for the artist's oeuvre are *Seeming Identification* (1973),[47] *The Project of Launching the Photographic Image – Icarus* (1975) and *Living Projection* (1975).[48]

Różycki often returns to the fact that he preferred to work with the photographic than with the film camera, underscoring the rank of photography in the group's entire artistic activity. At the same time, it is possible to sense the artist's frustration in this regard, which may have resulted from his partial exclusion from the community. His lack of engagement in film practice by necessity excluded him from participation in the screenings of the Workshop's film sets, which, in turn, reduced the number of travels taken with the other members. *Living Projection* can be seen as a self-ironic attempt to distance himself from that situation. In a film projector Różycki located a short strip of film stock with several frames, which was set in motion by gusts of warm air emitted at times from the active film projector – thus, the artist added movement to an otherwise static image, creating a kind of paradoxical film.

Andrzej Różycki also worked in other media, but included photographs in most of his projects. For instance, in the installation *Video-Duo* from 1975, he transmitted the image of the photographic portrait of Ryszard Waśko onto one of two monitors. The other monitor also screened the image of Waśko's face, which was, however, transmitted directly from a recording camera. The viewers were unaware of the sources of the two images – they only saw the final ambiguous effect on two screens.

Różycki's photographs bring to mind the thought of Vilém Flusser (1920–91), who defined the invention of the technical image (photography) as one of two breakthrough points in the history of mankind, the other being the invention of scripture, and considered the understanding of the medium of photography as a key to understanding the contemporary world. Flusser's initial premise was that images mediate between the world and the human being – however, their mediation becomes akin to a fence. Images are supposed to function as maps, whereas they become screens: instead of presenting the world – they become the world in their own right. People forget that it was them who created images in order to use them to gain orientation in the world. They can no longer decipher

47 See description of the work on p. 41.
48 See description of the work on p. 74.

them. They consider them not as a phenomenon to be read and understood, but as windows – trusting them uncritically, and therefore enter into a 'secondary existence,' a life as a function of images created by themselves. Flusser writes:

> We observe, all around us, apparatuses of every sort in the process of programming our life through rigid automation. (...) Our thoughts, feelings, desires and actions are being robotized; 'life' is coming to mean feeding apparatuses and being fed by them.[49]

How can we liberate ourselves from the ever increasing automation and regain freedom? Flusser answers that we may try to trick the apparatus, smuggle unforeseen human intentions into its programme, force it to create unpredicted, unlikely images saturated with information or, finally, despise it and its products. In other words, liberty is a game against the apparatus, which is played by the photographer.

Różycki is exactly such a photographer figure. The artist did not know Flusser's texts, yet he undertook his challenge by applying the first three of the enumerated methods and anticipating his thought in his theoretical texts:

> The recognition of reality – whether we want it or not – takes its course in an ever stronger detachment from direct reception. It is a requirement of the time and our consent to the direction of civilisation's progress. We surround ourselves with ever more precise and complicated devices and instruments directly connected to ever more precisely delineated cognitive goals. Artists and scientists often come to use the same devices. In turn, the tools that are supposed to investigate reality [...] begin to create it themselves. Artists should constantly remember that the tools which they have come to use are 'gifts' of the mankind's technical talent. Artists are left with a creative way and method of using those tools. [...] Exploration of technology and struggle with it becomes a source of new values. The only right artistic stance can be an approach of constant humanistic revaluation of technical means used by an artist who communicates their ideas. Each attempt and barrier overcome in the humanistic recognition of the condition and technical means of mechanical record (which equals a more profound cognition of reality) is a victory of art.[50]

In this text, Różycki shows his face of an experimental photographer, who – according to Flusser's definition – understands that the image, camera, programme and information are the basic problems of art. The photographers who do not possess this awareness – as the scholar wrote – claim that they create traditional images with non-traditional methods, that they contribute to scholarly research or that they pursue a social or political engagement. Still, they are not aware of what the camera is and they thus have no idea about the revolution that it ushered in. In turn Różycki makes a conscious use of photography, declaring several years before the first edition of Flusser's *Towards a Philosophy of Photography*: 'I try to turn the camera into a

49 V. Flusser, *Towards a Philosophy of Photography*, London: Reaktion Books, 2000, pp. 79–80.

50 A. Różycki, *Analityczne rozpoznanie fotografii,* catalogue of A. Różycki's exhibition, Mała Galeria PSP ZPAF, Warsaw, March 1979, text published in R. Kluszczyński, op. cit., pp. 81–83; the catalogue is also available on the website of the Arton Foundation. http://repozytorium.fundacjaarton.pl/index.php?action=view/object&objid=3150&colid=51&catid=15&lang=pl [accessed 02-11-2016].

device that is defenceless and fully obedient to intellectual programmes and ideas.'[51]

FILMOGRAPHY:

Kowalski (35 mm, 8', B&W, 1972)
How Is It? As if It's Getting Better, (35 mm, 10', B&W)

PHOTOGRAPHY:

cycle *Conditional Photography* (since 1972, B&W photography, some coloured prints)
The Project of Launching the Photographic Image – Icarus, 1974, B&W photography
cycle *Analytical Photography* (since 1975, B&W photographs)
Rules of the Game (since 1976, B&W photography)

PERFORMATIVE ACTIONS:

Seeming Identification, 1973
Living Projection, 1975

VIDEO:

TV Seance, 1973
Video-Duo, 1975

Zbigniew Rybczyński

(1949)

Zbigniew Rybczyński studied at the Film School between 1969 and 1973. He was a co-founder of the Workshop of the Film Form, within which he created and developed his own technique throughout many years. The artist used it in his first film etude *The Square* (1972), which he described as follows:

> The work took up my whole vacation – sixteen hours a day. I analysed, through a film camera, a loop of thirty-six square black-and-white photographs representing a human being moving in a circle. What was the logic of my analysis? I decided to photograph the loop on film and repeat it 36 times. During every repetition, I divided the film window, which I made in the shape of a square, so that in every circle there was an increasing number of subdivisions; today I would say different resolutions. I put a white square of paper in the subdivisions where, in the photograph, there was a part of a figure. Where there was not, I put a black square. I had to rearrange the white and black squares at least one hundred thousand times. On the lens, I put a colour filter and then rotated it. What is the most important about this is that not being aware of computer imaging – it was the 1970s in Poland – I manufactured my own 'digital' processing on film. It's strange that I needed 26 years of work – including my work during all my next 25 vacations – to come back to *A Square* with full awareness and understanding.[52]

The film etude *Take Five* (1972) – Rybczyński's second film created within the Workshop – shows a group of dancers who build a relation between each other in the course of time. Everything happens without words, mainly through sound and colour. Thus, the artist carried out a subtle analysis of film means, such as space, acting and plot, reducing all of them to the minimum. A similar combination of a simple story and an attractive aesthetic illusion will underpin Rybczyński's further projects, including *Tango*, which was awarded with an Oscar in 1982 for the best short animated film.

51 Ibidem.

52 *1,2,3... Avant-gardes. Film/Art between Experiment and Archive*, London: Reaktion Books, 2000, pp. 79–80.

FILMOGRAPHY:

The Square (35 mm, 3'30", 1973, colour)

Ryszard Waśko

(1947)

In the second half of the 1960s, a student of the secondary technical school of construction in Nysa, who was dreaming at that time of studying architecture, joined the newly established Club of Film and Photographic Forms.[53] It was attractive mainly owing to the possibility of borrowing film and photographic equipment of relatively high quality. Waśko knew nothing about using camera, but two employees of the club gave him an instant training and asked him to film on 16 mm stock the May Day parade that was taking place the following day. Upon embarking on his task, Waśko had merely a sketch of his concept – he wanted to film the parade 'in a different way than it was done before'. He climbed roofs and trees, and even went underneath trucks parked on the route of the march. After developing the film, the Club animators advised him to apply to the Film School.

Waśko began studies in Łódź in 1970. During the summer term, he joined the Workshop of the Film Form. As he underlines, in the initial period of the group's activity, he was mainly preoccupied with the mutual relations between time and space. Therefore, the majority of his works from the WFF period are meditations on the possibilities and limits of representing space in film. Another characteristic trait of his projects are frequent references to photography. For instance, in *Record* (1972) and *Padlock* (1972), he used the camera to build static frames akin to photographs. In the latter film, he shows a house and – after a turn of the camera – a gate leading from the street into the backyard, after which he gradually moves further away from them. Introducing additional disturbances in the editing layer (which often required effort-consuming time-lapse editing), Waśko not only confronted the viewers with their habits, but also laid bare the illusory nature of the image of space in film. The artist noticed the role played in it by illusion and tapped into that knowledge to create new spatial situations, leading to the question: what is space and where are its borders?

Waśko used a similar procedure in the film *Wall* (1972), in which the camera stands still opposite the eponymous wall of a factory building. A seemingly real image of space-time is disturbed by the appearance of people, whose movement was edited with the use of randomised procedures. Their moves are fragmentary and appear without a result or cause. Introducing the distortions of the time of action, Waśko lays bare the illusion of space in film, which we take in as viewers.

With a similar purpose, in the film *Straight-Curve* (1973) Waśko imposed black geometrical figures on views of a city. Due to such a simple procedure, the film space, hitherto perceived as three-dimensional, suddenly reveals its real two-dimensionality. Thus, Waśko managed to manifest the workings of the mechanism according to which our perception automatically over-interprets flat images that unfold before our eyes.

In turn, the films *Window* (1972) and *From A to B, from B to A* (1973) mark a deconstruction of the stereotypical thinking about the space of the film frame. The former work is built of a single long shot of a street seen from the window. Thus – as Łukasz Ronduda remarked – the artist ironically referred to thinking about film in terms of a 'window on the world,' turning a static frame into a tautology of the film frame.[54] It is also

53 Interview with Ryszard Waśko, August 2016.

54 Ł. Ronduda, *Polish Art*, p. 289.

noteworthy that background sounds from beyond the frame can be heard in the film, which compel us to make guesses about an invisible plot. Thus, Waśko broadened the space of film, activating not only the viewer's attention and senses, but also imagination and creativity. A similar procedure was used in the second of the enumerated films, in which the artist went outside the frame and – using a tape recorder – 'took' the sound away with him, providing an account of the plot unfolding outside the camera's field of vision.

These in-depth studies on the question of space, which resonate with the thought of Katarzyna Kobro, were gathered in February 1974 in the text *The Theory of Space in Film and Photographic Image*. A kind of recapitulation was also provided in the film *Negation* (1973), in which the word 'no' is multiplied in the visual, textual and sound layers. It can obviously be understood as yet another analytical experiment of the WFF, yet the formal rigour combined with the directness of the message gives this work a somewhat absurd undertone, as if Waśko was distancing himself from his earlier projects and the quasi-scientific language that prevailed in the Polish avant-garde circles.

While working in the field of film, Waśko at the same time engaged with photography. His earliest works in that medium are four-part black and white photographic collages from the cycle *Cut-up Portraits* (1971). Waśko composed them of fragments of photographs of male faces. The artist combined lips, noses and ears in a way that made it impossible to identify the photographed persons. Waśko recalls that the works, despite their austere form, were criticised for their 'metaphysical character.'[55] With hindsight, we can understand them as a psychological portrait of the contemporary man, whose perception is fragmented as a result of an increased amount of stimuli. We can also presume that Waśko founded them – akin to his earlier analytical works – on his own subjectivity. For the object of his interest was not the analysis of factors and physical phenomena, but his own relation to the world in all its complexity. Insofar as Waśko made use of the 'objective' tools of analysis of such phenomena as time, movement or space, indispensable in the Workshop's practice, he also underscored his own subjective perspective through a variety of means. As opposed to Robakowski, who treated the film or photographic camera as an extension of his body, Waśko used those devices to present his own way of perceiving reality. It can be seen on the example of the work *From 0 to 180* (1971), which comprises more than a dozen of prints combined in a range that reflect the movement of the head of a man looking 'from the earth to the sky.'[56] We should not assume that this gesture is anonymous – Waśko performed it in a given place and time, whereas we can observe its traces and identify with the subject of the activity. A similar (and perhaps the most well-known) Waśko's achievement in the field of photography is the cycle *Four-Dimensional Photography*. Each of the works in this series comprises several prints. The first of them is always a static shot, whereas the next ones feature a distortion. Thus, Waśko introduced movement into still images. He not only observes and registers it, but also acts as its source and cause. Hence, the artist was able to capture being and seeing at the same time.

Waśko pursued such reflection and experiments further with the use of video – a new medium that additionally complicated the problems of the relation between time and space. In 1975, he created *Corner* – one of his most significant and characteristic video works. In the video, the topic of media representation of space led

55 Interview with Ryszard Waśko, September 2010.

56 R. W. Kluszczyński, op. cit., p. 35.

him to a radically synthetic form, where a real corner of a room is juxtaposed with its transmitted image. A similar character was adopted by the works *Measurement* (1976). The artist directed two cameras at two squares of different sizes. Their view was transmitted onto screens, on which they already had the same size due to the fact that the cameras were set at a different distance from the wall.

Video led Waśko towards performance art. A portable camera became somewhat of an extension of his body. For instance, in the work *The Fatigue of My Leg* (1976), he transmitted the view of a square drawn on the wall, holding the camera in his hand and standing on one leg. In the course of time, his fatigue built, the camera dropped lower and lower, and the image on the monitor changed. Thus, the artist re-introduced his subjectivity to seemingly purely analytical works, disturbing their neutral structure through the sheer fact of *being*.

The film *30 Sound Situations* (1975) can be understood as a recapitulation of those investigations. Waśko created sound, which resonated in different spaces, which is usually interpreted as an analysis of the relations between sound and space in film. However, I am more inclined to understand this work as a manifestation of presence – 'here and now'. Clapping with small slats attached to his hands, Waśko consciously or not approached the meditation practice *w zendo*, which consists in hitting the floor with a stick. The subsequent shots reveal the changes in the artist's surroundings (at times an empty corridor, at other times a crowded street); the sound of the hits also changes, but the subject remains unchanged. The things that happen around him do not influence the self, although they are also not ignored.

In this context, it is also worth mentioning one more work from around the same period. During the Workshop's stay in Antwerp, Waśko created the installation *Space Outside* (1976) which – akin to *30 Sound Situations* – marked an attempt to capture the presence of the subject-performer. This time, we cannot see him, but we can hear him and later follow his gaze. Remaining outside the frame, the artist outlines the space of the gallery with a felt-tip pen, determining the space in which he functions and marking his presence in a rather restrained way. He then retraces the path of the pen by means of the camera. Waśko compares the work on this installation to meditation and adds that it led him to the state 'here and now,'[57] which – with hindsight – became a synthesis of the questions that occupied him throughout the entire period of his activity in the Workshop.

FILMOGRAPHY:

Window (35 mm, 9', 1972, B&W)
Flower Pot (35 mm, 5', 1972)
Negation (35 mm, 6', 1972, B&W)
Record (35 mm, 3'5", 1972, B&W)
Padlock (35 mm, 7', 1972, B&W)
Wall (35 mm, 4'06", 1972, B&W)
Pavement (35 mm, 3', 1972, B&W)
Room (35 mm, 3'5" 1972, B&W, collaboration: L. Czołnowski)
The Journey of Wacław Antczak to the Kiosk in Główna Street (35 mm, 4'32", 1973, colour film)
Wall II (35 mm, 13', 1973, B&W)
Configuration I-VI (35, 2'20", 1973, colour film)
The Theory of Space in the Film Image (35 mm, 5', 1974, B&W)
Walk (35 mm, 3', 1974, B&W)
The Straight Curve (35 mm, 7'13", 1974, B&W)
Record II (35 mm, 2', 1974, B&W)
Inventory of Space with Numbers from

57 Ryszard Waśko, e-mail to Marika Kuźmicz, August 2016.

1 to 8 (16mm, 1976, unpreserved, B&W)

PHOTOGRAPHY:
From 0 to 180 degrees (B&W photography, 1971)
From 0 to 90 degrees (B&W photography, 1971)
cycle *Incident* (or *Accident*) (B&W photography, 1971)
cycle *Cut-up Portrait* (B&W photography, 1971)
cycle *Self-Portrait in Time* (B&W photography, 1972)
cycle *Negative-Positive* (B&W photography, 1972)
cycle *Four-Dimensional Photography* (B&W photography, 1972)
Homage to Circle and Square (B&W photography, tempera, 1973)
The Straight-Curve (B&W photography, tempera, 1973)
Getting up (B&W photography, 1974)
Self-Portrait with a Yellow, Red and Blue Line (B&W photography, chalk, 1975)
cycle *Zoom-in – Zoom-out* (B&W photography, 1976)
Inventory of Space with Numbers from 1 to 8 (B&W photography, 1976)
Hypothetic Photograph (B&W photography, pencil, paper, 1977)

VIDEO INSTALLATIONS:
A Corner of the House, 1975
Corner, 1976
The Fatigue of My Leg, 1976
Beyond Space, 1976
Measurement, 1976/77

Zespół T

In the second half of the 1970s, studies in direction of photography at the Film School were taken up by a group of artists who initially identified with the Workshop of the Film Form and later went on to develop a separate model of activity under the banner 'Zespół T' (Team T). The ephemeral collective comprised Janusz Kołodrubiec (1953), Tomasz Konart (1955), Andrzej Paruzel (1951), Małgorzata Paruzel (1953) – at the time student of the Acting Department, Janusz Szczerek and Piotr Weychert (1959). Akin to the Workshop members, they used media primarily to analyse physical and psychophysical phenomena, as well as to investigate the changing conditions of human perception. They mainly worked with video (Kołodrubiec, Paruzel, Szczerek) and photography (Konart, Weychert), and only to a lesser extent with film, although they also created works on 35 mm film stock, for instance Konart's *Film and Memory* (1978). The film comprises three parts, each with two takes, the second of which is always an attempt to repeat the first on the basis of the filmmaker's memory. The artist moves further away trying not to forget his original vision, and a moment later returns with the camera to the same place. Thus, Konart engages in a reflection on the relation between the human being and the camera – the mind and the device that record the same reality. The artist refers in an interesting way to the famous paradox of Zeno of Elea, remarking that insofar as the psychological time is perceived as linear, in film it adopts the form of point phenomena.

The group's most significant works certainly comprise Andrzej Paruzel's *Video-Photographic Situations* (1976). The artist built a space embraced by the field of vision of cameras and limited by monitors. Performing simple gestures and observing his own image on the monitors at the same time, Paruzel laid bare the installation's potential of building visual illusion. The artist wrote:

A person entering the video installation stands a chance in the process of discovering its structure to reveal the operation of one's own cognitive structures owing to the potential of manipulation and in the scope of stimuli processed by the system and in itself.[58]

In turn, *The Last Photograph* (1979) by Weychert marks a reflection on the future of photography in the face of excessive production of images in the contemporary culture, as well as a considerable amount of works that address this issue in an analytical post-conceptual convention. The work adopts the form of a triptych, whose two parts are white planes, while the third photograph shows the photographic camera directed at a white sheet of paper.

Another member of Zespół T referred to his film and video works as experiments situated at the intersection of art and science. The artist analysed cognitive processes related to the reception of film, assuming that they are based on the principle of solving perception-related problems. Owing to such an approach, nearly all films by Szczerek from that period became somewhat of riddles. For instance, in *Analysis* (1979), the audience was supposed to guess the content of a photograph which the artist – wandering around the image with his camera – showed in a large close-up on the monitor. The viewers' responses were recorded, and later provided the soundtrack of the film. The correct answer marked the end of both the action and the film.

*

Akin to the WFF, one of the reasons behind the establishment of Zespół T was the mediocrity of the curriculum of the Film School, as well as the situation of the Polish art world, which retained a seeming autonomy to the reality of the Polish People's Republic, but was in fact isolated from it. Tomasz Konart recalls that the foundation of the group was related to the realisation of the fact of 'mutual being for each other.' Standing behind that declaration was not the intention to withdraw from the world which characterised part of the avant-garde circles, but to change one's relation to reality. The goal was to cross the border between art and the everyday as well as to depart from the established scheme of functioning of artistic milieus in Poland, which consisted in organising exhibitions inaugurated with opening ceremonies, publishing catalogues or brochures, gathering audiences, and so on. The members of the group resigned from looking for audiences in favour of informal meetings and organically emerging interactions – their activities consisted in meetings and discussions in their own circle, a common search for creative solutions, and even experiments with telepathy.

Akin to the Workshop, Zespół T went beyond the field of official cinematography, criticised official institutions and operated in unobvious places, thus intentionally abandoning its place in the structure of the art world of the Polish People's Republic. Yet, in comparison to the WFF, whose intention was to transform reality, the strategy of Zespół T seemed more nihilistic, as if it originated from a more profound experience of the void of meaning inherent in all regulations as well as legal, customary and cultural norms. Such a stance can be interpreted as an anticipation of the 1980s in Poland – a decade marked by martial law, which put a definitive end to the group's activity. Piotr Weychert recalls that in 1981 the group created postcards that read 'Zespół T does not exist,' which were supposed to be sent by post to selected people and institutions. They were not dispatched because with the imposition of martial law the postal service stopped operating.

58 A. Paruzel, *Video instalacje 1976-78*, Łódź: Dom Środowisk Twórczych, 1978; quoted in M. Jankowska, p. 134.

Biogramy

Wacław Antczak

(1911-1974)

Wacław Antczak z wykształcenia był krawcem:

> Po skończeniu szkoły podstawowej wstąpiłem do terminu krawieckiego. Jednocześnie uczęszczałem do szkoły zawodowej. Po otrzymaniu dyplomu krawieckiego – mistrza – wstąpiłem na uniwersytet robotniczy w roku 1937, a w roku 1939 dnia 1 września wybuchła wojna[1].

Po jej wybuchu udał się do Warszawy „razem z innymi patriotami, w celu bronienia [stolicy] przed najazdem hitlerowskim"[2]. Walczył w batalionie robotniczym, a po jego kapitulacji wrócił do Łodzi, gdzie ukrywał się w obawie przed denuncjacją. Aresztowany w czasie ulicznej łapanki trafił do obozu w Radogoszczy, z którego udało mu się wydostać. W tym samym czasie zaczął pisać pierwsze wiersze. Po wojnie wyjechał do Gdyni, gdzie bez powodzenia próbował prowadzić zakład krawiecki. Powrócił do Łodzi, w której mieszkał do końca życia, utrzymując się z renty i pisząc poezję, od czasu do czasu statystując w filmach[3].

Antczak deklarował:

> Piszę wiersze. Chcę dać w nich to, co jest dla młodego pokolenia, które nie widziało i nie przeżywało tego co moja i starsza generacja, nie tylko polskiej narodowości, ale i tej, która nie zaznała niewoli hitlerowskiej, bezwzględnie jakich poglądów politycznych, lecz całym sercem oddana jest ludzkości, dla utrwalenia pokoju na całym świecie[4].

Antczak – charyzmatyczny reprezentant nieprofesjonalnego świata sztuki – zafascynował Warsztatowców swoją osobowością i ostatecznie stał się pełnoprawnym członkiem grupy. Brał czynny udział w interwencjach i działaniach artystycznych, między innymi w 1971 roku w Ósmym kinie. Grał główną rolę w działaniu Robakowskiego *Wyprzedaż mebli* na Rynku Czerwonym[5], w 1972 roku towarzyszył Warsztatowcom w interwencji w Zakopanem podczas V Festiwalu Filmów o Sztuce, brał udział w spektaklu *Kariera i śmierć Adolfa Hitlera* w Toruniu, w akcji *Czyszczenie sztuki* w Warszawie[6], a także w działaniu Ćwiczenia artystyczne, gry plastyczne Oskara Hansena na wzgórzu Morela w Elblągu[7]. Wykonywał własne performanse, jak ten podczas festiwalu Młode Kino w Gdańsku w lutym 1973 roku[8]. W tym samym roku Antczak uczestniczył

1 W. Antczak, *Antoś Rozpylacz – Polski Odyseusz. Najsławniejszy wojownik w walce z Niemcami hitlerowskimi. Epopeja partyzantów z czasów powstania w Warszawie*, Łódź: PWSFTviT, 2008, s. 247.

2 Ibidem.

3 Ibidem.

4 Ibidem, s. 247.

5 *Ósme kino,* druk ulotny, Łódź 1971, archiwum Galerii Wymiany, http://repozytorium.fundacjaarton.pl/index.php?action=view/object&objid=3162&colid=75&catid=18 [dostęp 2-01-2016].

6 J. Robakowski, *Żywa Galeria*, s. 67.

7 J. Denisiuk, *Mogłoby zacząć się gdziekolwiek...*, w: *Elbląg konceptualny*, red. J. Denisiuk, Elbląg: Centrum Sztuki Galeria EL, 2010, s. 49.

8 J. Robakowski, *Żywa Galeria*, s. 88.

w jednym z najważniejszych działań w historii WFF – Akcji Warsztat[9], brał też udział w zorganizowanym przez Warsztatowców w Elblągu Kinolaboratorium, podczas V Biennale Form Przestrzennych[10]. Swoistym hołdem złożonym Wacławowi Antczakowi była realizacja wykonana przez WFF na XII Biennale w São Paulo: „Przekaz osobowości Wacława Antczaka z Łodzi"[11].

Wacław Antczak zmarł w Łodzi w 1974. Po jego śmierci członkowie Warsztatu podejmowali kilkakrotnie działania mające na celu jego upamiętnienie. W 1984 miała miejsce wystawa „Hommage à Wacław Antczak", w Galerii STK w Łodzi[12].

W 2008 r. nakładem PWSFTviT ukazała się książka *Antoś Rozpylacz. Polski Odyseusz. Najsławniejszy wojownik w walce z Niemcami hitlerowskimi. Epopeja partyzantów z czasów powstania w Warszawie,* utwór literacki autorstwa Antczaka ze wstępem E. Janickiej. Maszynopis tekstu przechował w archiwum Galerii Wymiany Józef Robakowski.

9 Wydaje się, że w tym przypadku udział Wacława Antczaka był raczej bierny, Józef Robakowski nie wymienia go jako uczestnika (zob. ibidem, s. 88, ale Antczak widoczny jest na fotografiach dokumentujących działania autorstwa Z. Sowińskiego dostępnych na stronie internetowej Fundacji Arton http://repozytorium.fundacjaarton.pl/index.php?action-view/object&objid-3074&colid-75&catid-18&lang-pl [dostęp: 16-10-2016].

10 *Kronika V Biennale Form Przestrzennych Kinolaboratorium*.

11 J. Robakowski, *Żywa Galeria*, s. 91.

12 Folder towarzyszący wystawie z archiwum Galerii Wymiany dostępny na stronie internetowej Fundacji Arton http://repozytorium.fundacjaarton.pl/index.php?action-view/object&objid-3078&colid-75&catid-18&lang-pl [dostęp: 2-01-2016]; rkps scenariusza *Hommage à Wacław Antczak*, archiwum Galerii Wymiany dostępny na stronie internetowej Fundacji Arton http://repozytorium.fundacjaarton.pl/index.php?action-view/object&objid-3080&colid-75&catid-18&lang-pl [dostęp: 2-01-2016].

Andrzej Barański

(1941)

Studiował w Szkole Filmowej w latach 1969–1973. Jego *Kręte ścieżki* (1970) zostały włączone do zestawu filmów Warsztatu. Jest to obraz oscylujący między eksperymentem i fabułą, w którym dwoje bohaterów wędruje przez ulice Łodzi – ich ścieżki nie krzyżują się, a bohaterowie nie nawiązują relacji. Film, prezentujący Łódź jako miejsce raczej prowincjonalne i pogrążone w wolnym rytmie codzienności, jest jednym z przykładów zainteresowania Warsztatu łódzkim krajobrazem.

Według pomysłu Andrzeja Barańskiego powstał też film *Oda do młodości* (1974). Członkowie grupy zrealizowali go wspólnie, namawiając przypadkowych przechodniów do deklamacji jednego słowa z utworu Adama Mickiewicza i składając z ich wypowiedzi w całość poprzez montaż bardzo krótkich ujęć. *Oda* wpisuje się w szereg kolektywnych działań Warsztatu, będących próbą wyjścia poza wąski krąg profesjonalnych artystów oraz stworzenia zapisu zbiorowej świadomości.

FILMOGRAFIA:

Kręte Ścieżki (35 mm, 6'11", 1970, cz.-b.)

Kazimierz Bendkowski

(1948)

Już w okresie nauki w szkole średniej w Warszawie należał do amatorskiego klubu filmowego i z jego ramienia brał udział w licznych festiwalach, prezentując nagrania wykonane na taśmie 8 mm. Rok przed zdanymi z powodzeniem egzaminami do Filmówki otrzymał za obraz *Blask cienia* nagrodę specjalną na XVII Ogólnopolskim Konkursie Filmów Amatorskich w Nowej Hucie (23–26 października 1969).

Podobnie jak niemal wszyscy pozostali uczestnicy Warsztatu, deklarował zaintеresowanie problemem relatywności przekazu medialnego. W swoim eseju z 1975 roku pisał:

> Człowiek spotyka się z informacjami pochodzącymi ze środków masowego przekazu przede wszystkim posługujących się komunikatem wizualnym – [...] na przykład człowiekowi oglądającemu w telewizji fragmenty pustyni Gobi trudno jest ją odróżnić od Sahary. Moja praca służy wyznaczaniu granicy między obiektywnością i relatywnością komunikatów wizualnych[13].

Bendkowski prowadził swoje poszukiwania także na mało charakterystycznych dla Warsztatu polach, takich jak mistycyzm. Uważał, że sztuk jest związana ze swego rodzaju tajemnicą – ma pobudzać nie tylko zmysły widzów, ale także rozszerzać ich możliwości poznania duchowego. Oba te obszary przenikały się w jego pracach – nacechowanych jednocześnie analitycznym użyciem mediów i otwarciem na metafizykę. Jest to widoczne na przykład w serii fotografii *Złoto*, powstałej w ramach cyklu *Obraz relatywny* (który Bendkowski rozpoczął w 1970 i nad którym, jak deklaruje, pracuje nadal).

Artysta nazywa prace składające się na *Obraz relatywny* „dokamerowymi performansami". Posłużenie się autoportretem nie było więc gestem obojętnym – nie mamy tu do czynienia jedynie z analizą właściwości medium fotograficznego i jego zdolności do przekazania prawdy, ale raczej z epicką (kilka tysięcy odbitek) próbą samoidentyfikacji. W *Złocie* Bendkowski stworzył rodzaj komiksu, w którym wcielił się w rolę bohatera zmagającego się ze złotym elementem, nanoszonym wtórnie za pomocą farby. Na niektórych fotografiach przygniata go złoty trójkąt lub zalewa go złota ciecz. W prosty sposób – wprowadzając do fotografii niespodziewany i tajemniczy element – artysta uruchamiał wyobraźnię odbiorcy.

Charakterystyczne dla tego artysty elementy zaskoczenia, tajemnicy i angażowania widza odnajdziemy również w *Misteriach,* które Bendkowski organizował w Warszawie na osiedlu Rakowiec od 1971 roku[14], a także w akcji *Warsztat* z 1973 roku, w ramach której Bendkowski wykonał działanie *Dźwięk–ruch–barwa*. Wyciemniony namiot stał się w niej sceną ulotnego wizualno -dźwiękowego spektaklu. Artysta, wykorzystując pomalowaną farbą fluorescencyjną taśmę magnetofonową, stworzył ruchomą projekcję przypominającą gwiaździste niebo, której towarzyszyła nagrana na taśmie muzyka eksperymentalna. Drugą częścią instalacji była wyizolowana przestrzeń, w której zamknięto dwie osoby. Mogły być podglądane przez widzów przez niewielkie otwory zasłonięte różnymi „przetwornikami", na przykład folią barwną lub siatką[15]. Trzecim fragmentem pracy było lustro, w którym widzowie – oświetlani światłem ultrafioletowym – mogli ujrzeć się w zmienionej postaci.

W ramach działalności w Warsztacie Kazimierz Bendkowski zrealizował sześć filmów: *Koło* (1973), *Obszar* (1973), *Punkt* (1973), *Centrum* (1973), niezachowany Śmiech (1973) oraz *Soley* (1976). Pierwsze trzy są, jak pisał Łukasz Ronduda[16], interpretacjami tytułowych wielkości przestrzennych, a jednocześnie stanowią potwierdzenie deklarowanej przez artystę fascynacji wielkimi filmowymi produkcjami. Są to filmy analityczne, które nie stanowią jednak protestu przeciwko kinematografii, lecz propozycję wzbogacenia jej o dodatkowe środki. Bendkowski – w przeciwieństwie do większości

13 K. Bendkowski, *Relatywność i obiektywność komunikatów wizualnych*, w: R. W. Kluszczyński, *Warsztat Formy Filmowej*, Warszawa: Centrum Sztuki Współczesnej Zamek Ujazdowski, 2000, s. 62–64.

14 Zob. opis na s. 140.

15 Wywiad z Kazimierzem Bendkowskim, wrzesień 2016.

16 Ł. Ronduda, *Sztuka polska lat 70.*, Warszawa: Centrum Sztuki Współczesnej Zamek Ujazdowski, 2009, s. 295.

członków Warsztatu – widział możliwość podporządkowania formalnych eksperymentów warstwie narracyjnej. Na przykład w filmie *Obszar* posłużył się nimi do zbudowania surrealistycznego obrazu miasta (zniszczonej kamienicy i podwórka wraz z jej mieszkańcami). Nastrój niepokoju jest w nim oparty na częstych zmianach ostrości obrazu, ale także na dynamice ujęć, które na początku filmu są statyczne, a na końcu – bardzo ekspresyjne. Bendkowski demonstruje w ten swój szeroki zakres umiejętności operatorsko-montażowych i próbuje za ich pomocą równoważyć dyskurs poetycki i strukturalny[17]. Możemy to zaobserwować także w filmie *Centrum* (1976), jednej z najbardziej wyrafinowanych wizualnie prac powstałych w kręgu Warsztatu, w której widok rozświetlonego neonami miasta zmienia się w coraz bardziej abstrakcyjną grę świateł.

Bendkowski na przełomie 1975 i 1976 roku przebywał na stypendium w Internationaal Cultureel Centrum (ICC) w Antwerpii. Zrealizował wówczas kilka prac w trudno dostępnej w Polsce technologii wideo. W filmie *I speak image* (1976) zestawił obraz mówiącej osoby z wizualną reprezentacją jej głosu na dole ekranu (była to kontynuacja zaginionego filmu Śmiech (1972), w którym artysta zastosował podobny zabieg). Z kolei praca *I like it...* (1976), była interesującym spojrzeniem przybysza z Europy Wschodniej na zachodnie miasto – występująca w niej dziewczyna wskazywała atrakcyjne jej zdaniem elementy pejzażu miasta i mówiła: „I like it".

Kazimierz Bendkowski zakończył studia w Szkole Filmowej na etapie absolutorium, po czym rozpoczął pracę w Akademii Sztuk Pięknych w Warszawie. W 1982 roku wyemigrował do Republiki Federalnej Niemiec. Od 1984 roku do 2010 roku pracował na wydziale KomunikacjiWizualnej w Kunsthochschule w Kassel.

FILMOGRAFIA I PRACE WIDEO:
Koło (35 mm, 4', 1973, cz.-b.)
Obszar (35 mm, 6', 1973, cz.-b.)
Punkt (35 mm, 2'50", 1973, cz.-b.)
Centrum / Rondo (35 mm, 5'2", 1973, barwny)
Widok z okna (35 mm, 1974, cz.-b.)
Solei (35 mm, 1975/76, cz.-b.?, niezachowany)
Replika (35 mm, 8'3", 1975, barwny, wytwórnia SEMAFOR)
Śmiech (35 mm, 1974/75, cz.-b., niezachowany)
Lubię (wideo, 1976)
Moje (wideo, 1976)
Obraz picia (wideo, 1976)
Obraz mowy (wideo, 1976)

FOTOGRAFIA:
Obraz relatywny (cykl fotografii cz.-b. niekiedy z ingerencją autorską w odbitkę – w skład tego monumentalnego cyklu wchodzą mniejsze serie fotografii, jak na przykład Gold, powstający od początku lat siedemdziesiątych do chwili obecnej)

INNE REALIZACJE:
Misterium w ultrafiolecie, działanie w ramach Akcji Warsztat, Muzeum Sztuki w Łodzi, 1973
Różne warianty zapisu światła, realizacja w ramach wystawy „Mechaniczny zapis obrazu", Galeria Remont, Warszawa 1975.

Wojciech Bruszewski

(1947–2009)

Wojciech Bruszewski studiował na Wydziale Operatorskim Szkoły Filmowej w latach

17 Ł. Ronduda, *Warsztat Formy Filmowej. Realizacje filmowe z lat 1970–1977*, Artpapier.com, sierpień 2004, http://artpapier.com/pliki/archiwum_sierpien_04/recfilm/warsztaty%20formy.html [dostęp 7-12-2016].

1966–1970, a następnie kontynuował edukację na Wydziale Reżyserii (do 1974 r.)

Był współzałożycielem Warsztatu Formy Filmowej, wcześniej, od 1967 r. należał do Zero-61. W tym czasie zrealizował m.in. ważną pracę, serię fotogramów (1967–1969), które nosiły wspólny tytuł *xxx*. Miał on być w założeniu pozbawiony wszelkich konotacji i nie wzbudzać w widzu żadnych wspomnień czy skojarzeń. Już w tej pracy Bruszewski zakwestionował mimetyczne właściwości fotografii, zwrócił uwagę na materialność tego medium i dał wyraz swojemu przekonaniu, że najpełniejszą formą pracy twórczej jest doświadczanie przekazu[18].

W całej swojej późniejszej twórczości Bruszewski konsekwentnie rozwijał tę myśl, przyglądając się mediom, badając ich relacje z rzeczywistością (on zapewne powiedziałby: „z natury", a więc z tym, co widać i słychać), a także dekonstruując nasze przekonania na ich temat. To doprowadziło go do porzucenia sprawdzonych sposobów używania mediów[19]. Taką postawę reprezentowali w zasadzie wszyscy Warsztatowcy, ale w przypadku Bruszewskiego nabierała ona szczególnego zabarwienia. Media były dla niego narzędziem walki z podziałem na sztukę i naturę oraz wynikającym z niego mimetyzmem. Służyły mu nie do naśladowania, lecz do badania rzeczywistości – także w obszarach trudno dostępnych, wymagających kreowania eksperymentów i sytuacji paradoksalnych. Taką właśnie percepcyjną pułapką były wczesne fotogramy Bruszewskiego. Miały być „odciskiem" realnego, a nie jego zapisem. Bruszewski sprawdzał za ich pomocą, czy możliwe jest powstanie takiej fotografii, która przeniknie się z rzeczywistością nie tylko na poziomie wizualnym, ale także haptycznym, zmysłowym, materialnym. Testował, ile świata jest w stanie w sobie pomieścić to medium. Pisał:

Fotografia, jak i wszystkie pokrewne jej techniki, żyje podwójnym życiem. Jest rzeczą, papierem, folią celuloidową, ziarnami srebra, drobinami pigmentu, żelatyną, projekcją etc... a jednocześnie: reprezentacją, relacją o czymś, obrazem czegoś; czymś czym sama nie jest[20].

We wczesnym okresie działalności Warsztatu Bruszewski wychodził w przestrzeń, poza obszar fotograficznej odbitki. Przykładem mogą być prace *Ciąg dalszy – ręka* (1971) i *Ciąg dalszy – ucho* (1971), które były autonomicznymi strukturami złożonymi z fragmentów zdjęć. Bruszewski dekonstruował w nich popularne przekonanie, że fotografia jest w stanie pokazywać wyłącznie wycinek świata – w jego instalacjach kadr stawał się nie fragmentem, lecz autonomiczną nieskończonością.

Ostatnią tego typu polemiką Bruszewskiego były *Fotografie dźwięków* (1971), czyli utrwalone na papierze światłoczułym zapisy ścieżek dźwiękowych z filmów. Jednak gestem, który ostatecznie podsumował ten okres jego twórczości był *Język baletowy* (1973) – sekwencja zdjęć i rysunków przedstawiających nagiego artystę, który za pomocą swojego ciała tworzy nowy alfabet. Ta praca, będąca w gruncie rzeczy zapisem performansu, jest przejawem pogłębiającego się zainteresowania artysty problemem języka. Jednocześnie jednak przedstawiona w niej sekwencja przywodzi na myśl taniec szamana, tak jakby Bruszewski dystansował się od prób kodyfikacji jakiegokolwiek systemu znaków.

Od 1973 roku do końca lat 80. Bruszewski zgłębiał już inne medium: wideo, które – kameralne, elastyczne i otwarte na ingerencje – najpełniej pozwalało mu demaskować paradoksy rzeczywistości i realizować strategię, którą sam określał jako „zastawianie pułapek":

18 *Wojciech Bruszewski,* s. 11–12.

19 Ibidem, s. 13.

20 Wojciech Bruszewski, *Ciąg dalszy,* „Fotografia", 9, 1969, cyt. za: *Wojciech Bruszewski*, s. 39–40.

> To, co robię jest niczym innym jak zastawianiem pułapek na TO, CO ISTNIEJE. Pułapki usiłuję zastawiać w miejscu kontaktu pomiędzy „duchowym" a „materialnym", pomiędzy tym, co „wiemy i myślimy", a tym, co „jest"[21].

Bruszewski jest autorem pierwszej polskiej pracy zarejestrowanej na taśmie wideo, *Języka obrazkowego* (1973). To „widowisko telewizyjne" zostało zrealizowane w Elblągu według scenariusza przygotowanego wspólnie z Piotrem Bernackim, z pomocą realizacyjną Pawła Kwieka i z wykorzystaniem wozu transmisyjnego oraz czterech kamer wypożyczonych z zasobów Szkoły Filmowej. Twórcy zaproponowali zamianę alfabetu na kod wizualny. Na przykład literze *e* odpowiadał obraz zaoranego pola. Tym nowym kodem przekazali następnie tekst – komunikat o transporcie bagaży w liniach lotniczych LOT. Język narzucił więc sposób zaprezentowania rzeczywistości. Pracę tę można interpretować jako działanie z zakresu swoistej archeologii semantycznej, mającej na celu prześledzenie początkowych etapów procesu powstawania systemu znaków[22].

Język obrazkowy był zapowiedzią dalszych poszukiwań Bruszewskiego w obszarze metod komunikacji – innych niż mowa czy film. W kolejnej pracy wideo pod tytułem *Transmisja przestrzenna* (1974) Bruszewski poruszał się na rowerze po studiu telewizyjnym TVP w polu widzenia trzech kamer, obserwując samego siebie na monitorach podglądowych. Będąc jednocześnie uczestnikiem i obserwatorem transmisji, doprowadził do przełamania linearnej struktury medium.

Bruszewski tworzył również instalacje wideo. Były to swoiste „mentalne i wizualne paradoksy"[23], które bazowały często na określonej konfiguracji kamer, luster czy ekranów. Tak było w przypadku pracy *Kran* (1976), w której widz obserwował na ekranie wodę płynącą do góry. Z kolei w instalacji *Od x do x* (1976) odpowiednie ustawienie kamery i monitora względem rysunku sprawiało, że obraz na monitorze łączył się z rysunkiem (linii i znaku „x") widocznego na ścianie galerii, tworząc całość. Bruszewski zastosował podobny zabieg w pracy *Głośnik* (1976), którą opisał tak:

> Prawdziwy wentylator dmucha w „nieprawdziwą" flagę; obraz linii łączy się z samą linią; kartka papieru i jej odbicie w lustrze łączą się w jeden prostokątny kształt; zapytuję często sam siebie, dlaczego z tak dużą dozą sympatii akceptuję te oczywiste niedorzeczności? „Ponieważ taka jest kondycja ludzka" – odpowiada mi duch René Magritte'a. „Nonsens egzystuje wyłącznie w sferze języka" – kontynuuje mistrz – „Jeżeli coś nie pasuje, należy zgłosić pretensje do Biura Logiki. A my przecież, Pan i ja, robimy obrazy". Dopiero niedawno zauważyłem, że jedna z moich prac (*Głośnik* z serii *The Video Touch*) jest w prostej linii repliką wyżej prezentowanego obrazu [*Kondycji ludzkiej* Magritte'a] – co dzieje się na ekranie telewizora i to co ma miejsce poza nim jest jednością pod względem czasu, przestrzeni, akcji"[24]

Bruszewski w 1977 roku stał się posiadaczem własnej kamery wideo, dzięki czemu mógł powyższe prace zarejestrować na taśmie i zaprezentować je na Dokumenta 6 w Kassel pod wspólnym tytułem *Dotknięcie video* (*The Video Touch*).

21 Wojciech Bruszewski, *Co robię?*, 1976, http://repozytorium.fundacjaarton.pl/index.php?action=view/object&objid=63 [dostęp 2-1-2017].

22 Zob. M. Kuźmicz, *Magister ludi*, w: *Across Realities*, Warszawa: Fundacja Arton, 2014, s. 67.

23 *Wojciech Bruszewski*, s. 114.

24 *Ibidem*, s. 170.

To właśnie dziesięć prac składających się na ten cykl najpełniej ukazuje jego pierwotny i czujny sposób widzenia świata. Rzeczywistość była dla Bruszewskiego niejednoznacznym uniwersum znaków, których odczytanie wymaga od nas porzucenia egocentrycznego przekonania o obiektywności i obligatoryjności naszej własnej perspektywy. Dlatego Bruszewski tworzył pętle audiowizualne, odsyłające widza od jednej rzeczywistości do drugiej, nie wskazując która z nich, jeżeli którąś w ogóle, może stanowić dla nas punkt oparcia. Pisał, że zastawia pułapki na rzeczywistość. Istotnie – jego kreatywność była powściągliwa, ukierunkowana nie na generowanie nowych zjawisk, lecz na uważne obserwowanie wielkich praw świata, które codziennie przesuwają się nam przed oczami. Swoje pułapki zastawiał nieomylnie w najlepszych miejscach – tam, gdzie zachodziły sytuacje z pogranicza realności, które zdawały się być w sprzeczności z prawami natury; tam, gdzie możliwe było „złapanie" świata w kleszcze paradoksu, uchwycenie go i zamknięcie, jak w pułapce, w instalacji wideo.

FILMOGRAFIA i PRACE WIDEO:

Inwentaryzacja (35 mm, 5', 1970, cz.-b.)
Klaskacz (35 mm, 5'53', 1971, cz.-b.)
Bezdech (35 mm, 10'01', 1972, cz.-b.)
YYAA (35 mm, 2'59', 1973, cz.-b.)
Drzwi-tekst (35 mm, 1'50', 1973, cz.-b.)
Układ nowego alfabetu (35 mm, 5', 1973, cz.-b.)
Język obrazkowy (wideo, 1973, cz.-b., praca niezachowana, współpraca: P. Bernacki, P. Kwiek)
Transmisja przestrzenna (wideo, 1'08', 1974, cz.-b.)
Zapłon mózgu (35 mm, 4'5', 1974, cz.-b.)
Szesnaście sytuacji oświetleniowych (35 mm, 2'40', 1975, cz.-b.)
Krzesła (35 mm, 15', 1975, cz.-b.)
Partytura do wykonania solo i w zespole (35 mm, 3'12', 1975, cz.-b., film będący rejestracją wykonania partytur Bruszewskiego)
Głosowanie (część filmu *Żywa Galeria*, 35 mm, 4'5', 1975, kolor)
Doświadczenie audiowizualne – paczka zapałek (dwie wersje: 35 mm, wideo, 2', 1975, cz.-b.)
Doświadczenie audiowizualne – łyżeczka (dwie wersje: 35 mm, wideo, 2', 1975, cz.-b.)
Między Marcem a Czerwcem (wideo, 10', 1977)

FOTOGRAFIA:

Tekst (obiekt fotograficzny, 1970)
Ucho-ciąg dalszy (instalacja fotograficzna, fotografia cz.-b., 1971)
Ręka-ciąg dalszy (instalacja fotograficzna, fotografia cz.-b., 1971)
Fotografie dźwięków (fotografia cz.-b., 1971)

OBIEKTY:

Nowe słowa (1972)

INSTALACJE WIDEO:

Instalacja dla Galerii Labirynt (1976)
Input – Output 1 (1976)
Głośnik (1976)
Kran (1976)
Outside (1976–1977)
Struktura czasu – stoper (1977)
Moich pięć palców (1977)
Pamięć dodatnia, pamięć ujemna (1977)
Obiekt w ruchu – Obserwator w ruchu (1977)

DZIAŁANIA PERFORMAS, DZIAŁANIA AUDIOWIZUALNE:

Skrzyżowanie (w ramach Akcji Warsztat, 1973)
Tańczy Wojciech Bruszewski (zapis fotograficzny funkcjonuje jako część pracy

Język baletowy, fotografia cz.-b., ołówek, papier, 1973)
Trans-translocation (1974)
Kiedy mówię (1974)
Transmisja przestrzenna w Galerii Dziekanka (1977)
Ja liczę (wideo-performas, 1977)
Struktura czasu – Punkty (wideo-performans, 1977, później zapisany na taśmie 16 mm, 10')

Wojciech Chyła

(1950)

Ukończył liceum muzyczne w klasie fortepianu, a następnie studiował na Wydziale Reżyserii Muzycznej w Państwowej Wyższej Szkole Muzycznej w Warszawie. Jak podawał w swoim biogramie, opracowanym na potrzeby pracy dyplomowej Ryszarda Waśko:

> Nawiązał szereg kontaktów muzycznych zmierzających do zbadania możliwości ingerencji struktur fonograficznych w kody muzyczne. [...] Doświadczenia te prowadziły do otwartej techniki kompozytorskiej prowadzącej do syntezy dźwięku[25].

W ramach działalności w Warsztacie opracował warstwę dźwiękową filmów Waśki: *Ściana II*, *Układ I–IV*, *Rejestracja II* i *Chód*.

Lechosław Czołnowski

(1946)

W Szkole Filmowej studiował w latach 1973–1977. Współpracował przy realizacji niektórych prac Warsztatu, przede wszystkim filmów Waśki: *Okna, Kłódki, Chodnika* i *Podwórka* (1972). W późniejszym okresie pracował przede wszystkim jako operator filmów dokumentalnych i fabularnych, między innymi *Konstruktywizmu w Polsce* (1979) Ryszarda i Marii Waśko.

Jan Freda

(1948)

Operator dźwięku, współtwórca wielu produkcji fabularnych i dokumentalnych. Był autorem warstwy dźwiękowej niektórych filmów Warsztatu, między innymi *A-B-C-D-E-F–1-3-6* Ryszarda Waśko z 1976 roku.

Ryszard Gajewski

(1944)

Studia w Szkole Filmowej rozpoczął w 1965 roku – najwcześniej z wszystkich członków Warsztatu. Wybór uczelni był konsekwencją jego zainteresowania historią fotografii, a następnie historią filmu awangardowego, którą rozwijał w prężnie działającym Gorzowskim Towarzystwie Fotograficznym[26].

Gajewski był aktywnym członkiem Warsztatu do 1973 roku. Współpracę z grupą rozpoczął jeszcze przed jej założeniem, biorąc udział w wystawie *Szklarnia* we wrześniu 1969 roku. Swoją pierwszą eksperymentalną etiudę *Ona i on* zrealizował jednak wcześniej – w 1967 roku. Niestety nie zachowała się podobnie jak jego kolejny film *Zawodowcy* z 1969 roku, który był eksperymentalnym dokumentem opowiadającym o pobycie w Filmówce studentów z wymiany zagranicznej. Zaginął również barwny, impresyjny dokument o środowisku hippisowskim w Polsce pod tytułem *Hippie* (1970). Znamy tylko stopklatki z tej realizacji i wspomnienie autora:

> Na ćwiczenia w kolorze Szkoła dawała jeszcze mniej taśmy niż na czarno-białe. Na szczęście Orwo Color wypuścił nowy rodzaj taśmy i ja jako pierwszy

25 R. Waśko, *Warsztat Formy Filmowej*, praca magisterska, Wąd-2&lang-pl#1 [dostęp 29-12-2016], s. 5.

26 Wywiady z Ryszardem Gajewskim, styczeń i lipiec 2016.

miałem ją przetestować. Wszyscy się bali orwowskiej taśmy, bo efekty często były koszmarne. W laboratorium WFO wraz jego kierownikiem postanowiliśmy potraktować tą taśmę inaczej niż zalecali niemieccy producenci. Nie pamiętam wszystkich szczegółów, ale zwiększyliśmy czułość, zmieniliśmy czas wołania i po kilku próbach uzyskaliśmy kolory zbliżone do kodakowskich. Zrobiłem „hippisowski" film próbujący oddać odmienny stan świadomości po zażyciu narkotyków. Było to tylko moje wymyślone wyobrażenie tego stanu, bo narkotyków nigdy nie próbowałem i nie sprawdziłem czy moje wizje są prawdziwe[27].

Później, prawdopodobnie w latach 1970–1972, Gajewski pracował nad filmem *Wirówka*, włączonym do pierwszego zestawu filmów Warsztatu i pokazywanym między innymi podczas Atelier '72 w Edynburgu. Gajewski wykorzystał w nim wirowy ruch kamery oraz piosenkę *Whole Lotta Love* Led Zeppelin – kolejne ujęcia miały kojarzyć się z treścią utworu. Ostatnim filmem Gajewskiego w ramach Warsztatu był natomiast *Pierzgalski* (1971) – eksperymentalny dokument o wykładowcy Łódzkiej Filmówki, malarzu i fotografie Ireneuszu Pierzgalskim.

Po 1973 roku Gajewski zajął się całkowicie pracą w dziedzinie profesjonalnej kinematografii. Starał się przemycać do filmów niektóre rozwiązania wypracowane w ramach Warsztatu – w szczególności różnego rodzaju nowatorskie, nietypowe rozwiązania operatorskie. Niestety z uwagi na różnego rodzaju kompromisy, na które zwykle musieli pójść reżyserzy tych produkcji pomysły Gajewskiego były zazwyczaj znacznie redukowane[28].

FILMOGRAFIA:

Wirówka (35 mm, 2'50", 1970/1972, kolor)

Pierzgalski (35 mm, 8'20", 1971, kolor)

OBIEKTY FOTOGRAFICZNE:

Grzebień (zużyta taśma filmowa, 1973, praca prezentowana w ramach Akcji Warsztat)

Kiełbasa fotograficzna (zużyta taśma filmowa., 1973, praca prezentowana w ramach Akcji Warsztat)

Tadeusz Junak

(1945–2009)

W Szkole Filmowej studiował od 1970 roku. Był współzałożycielem Warsztatu. W ramach grupy zrealizował dwa filmy. *Konfrontacja* (1972) składa się z estetycznych zbliżeń wnętrza maszyny grającej, która odtwarza płytę Ewy Demarczyk. Junak starał się w ten sposób przedstawić tytułową konfrontację dwóch maszyn: jednej, która odtwarza muzykę i drugiej, która rejestruje obraz. Z kolei w *Epizodzie* (1973) Junak cofnął piętnastominutowy fragment hollywoodzkiego filmu *Słodki ptak młodości* w taki sposób, że ostatnie ujęcie pierwotnego obrazu stało się ostatnim. Tym samym Junak pokazał w bezpośredni, ale też ironiczny i przewrotny sposób stosunek Warsztatu do głównego nurtu kinematografii.

FILMOGRAFIA:

Konfrontacja (35 mm, 4'29", 1972, cz.-b.)

Epizod (35 mm, 15'27", 1973, kolor)

27 R. Gajewski, *Warsztat Form Filmowych – początki*, tekst niepublikowany, Warszawa 2014, s. 6.

28 Tak było choćby w przypadku filmu *Skorpion, panna i łucznik* w reżyserii Andrzeja Kondratiuka z 1972 roku, nad którym Ryszard Gajewski oraz Ryszard Waśko pracowali jako operatorzy.

Marek Koterski

(1942)

Marek Koterski studiował w Szkole Filmowej od 1967 roku. Dystansuje się co prawda od swojej przynależności w Warsztacie[29], ale na początku działalności grupy był jej aktywnym uczestnikiem. Brał udział w niektórych akcjach i interwencjach, a jego film *Ech* (1972) był często prezentowany w ramach pokazów WFF. *Ech* był swego rodzaju produktem ubocznym pracy Koterskiego dla instytucji publicznej, na zamówienie której miał zrealizować film o alkoholizmie. Z niewykorzystanych ujęć reżyser zmontował nowy film, który następnie został przepisany z taśmy 16 mm na 35 mm i w tej formie zaprezentowany jako film Warsztatu.

FILMOGRAFIA:
Ech (35 mm, 10'47", 1972, cz.-b.)

Paweł Kwiek

(1951)

W 1969 roku Paweł Kwiek został przyjęty na wydział operatorski w Szkole Filmowej. Z początkiem jego studiów, zbiegło się powstanie Warsztatu Formy Filmowej, w którym uczestniczył. W ten sposób rozpoczęła się dla niego niezwykle intensywna dekada lat 70.

Zawarty w pracy magisterskiej Waśki biogram Kwieka to katalog nie tylko studenckich etiud, ale także działań performerskich i parateatralnych, często podejmowanych z innym uczestnikiem grupy, Jackiem Łomnickim, a także z „grupą warszawską" tworzoną przez Jana Stanisława Wojciechowskiego oraz duet KwieKulik (czyli Zofię Kulik i Przemysława Kwieka). W związku z tym Paweł Kwiek stał się swego rodzaju „łącznikiem" między Szkołą Filmową a warszawską Akademią Sztuk Pięknych. Rezultatem tej współpracy był między innymi film *Forma otwarta* (1972), który stanowił, jak pisał Kwiek, „pierwszą na dużą skalę podjętą współpracę pomiędzy studentami w/w uczelni, polegającą na przeprowadzeniu szeregu ćwiczeń i działań z użyciem kamery filmowej"[30].

Uczestnictwo Kwieka w kilku artystycznych inicjatywach jednocześnie świadczy o jego potrzebie zrzeszania się i pracy kolektywnej. Szczególne znaczenie w procesie twórczym miała dla niego komunikacja: z kolegami z grupy, ale także odbiorcami, którzy często stawali się współautorami prac. Kwiek konsekwentnie rozwijał ideę demokratycznego myślenia o sztuce, w tym o filmie – a trzeba pamiętać, że w latach 70. film był medium elitarnym (od strony realizatorskiej) i uwikłanym w relację z władzą. Kwiek pisał:

> Film dokumentalny dąży do przekazania prawdy o człowieku. Do tej pory nie udało się jednak uniknąć deformacji tej prawdy wynikającej z wpływu realizatora na ostateczny kształt komunikatu. [...] Możemy stwierdzić, że prawdę o człowieku otrzymujemy w bezpośrednim kontakcie z nim, niezależnie od tego, co chciałby on sobą pokazać. [...] W filmie sytuacja taka może zaistnieć w momencie, gdy wszelkie decyzje realizatora podejmuje grupa lub człowiek, o której jest film. Oznacza to, że on sam będzie robić film o sobie, w tym znaczeniu, że umożliwi się mu swobodną realizację na dowolny temat[31].

Kwiek realizował tę koncepcję w praktyce przy kilku okazjach – po raz pierwszy w ramach V Biennale Form Przestrzennych Elno Laboratorium w Elblągu (1973). Powstało wtedy kilkadziesiąt jednominutowych nagrań

29 K. Krubski, M. Miller, Z.Turowska, W. Wiśniewski, *Filmówka. Powieść o łódzkiej szkole filmowej*, Warszawa: Prószyński i S-ka, 1998, s. 214.

30 R. Waśko, op.cit., s. 41.

31 P. Kwiek, *Dokument obiektywny o człowieku*, w: *Żywa Galeria*, s. 193–196.

zrealizowanych przez różnych autorów, które Kwiek złożył w jeden film pod tytułem *Kino Laboratorium*. Z kolei w ramach zainicjowanej przez Kwieka akcji *Niedziela 15 IV 73 – Dniem Sztuki w Niechcicach*, lokalna społeczność wraz z młodzieżą z tamtejszego PGR zrealizowała film *Niechcice* (1973). Złożyły się na niego sceny bójki chuligańskiej, potrącenia staruszka przez grupę młodzieży i udaremnienia samobójstwa młodej dziewczyny. Kwiek opisał też krótko niezrealizowane pomysły: ratowanie tonącego z przerębli, oczekiwanie na telefon przez małego chłopca, miłość lesbijska, kradzież kieszonkowa i lizanie muru (na którym zapisano czyjeś imię) i pokazanie do kamery pokaleczonego języka[32]. Nie finalny efekt był tu jednak najważniejszy, lecz sam proces społeczno-artystyczny. Celem artysty było „przekazanie głosu tym, którzy go do tej pory nie mieli"[33].

Paweł Kwiek najczęściej z wszystkich Warsztatowców poruszał się po granicznych obszarach filmu, tworząc – jak pisał Kluszczyński „wizję kina otwartego, nieokreślonego, negującego normy i konwencje, otwierającego się ku nieznanemu"[34]. Wykonywał między innymi formy beztaśmowe i bezkamerowe takie jak *Komentarz* (1972), który był rodzajem performansu, polegającego na opowiadaniu treści nieistniejącego filmu (Kwiek realizował ten performans wielokrotnie, m.in. podczas Atelier '72 w Edynburgu[35]), czy *Lustro* (1971), w którym artysta odbijał światło z filmowego projektora w stronę zebranej publiczności. Celem tych prac była dekonstrukcja norm postrzegania medium filmowego, a także wyzwolenie i obserwacja reakcji widzów. *Komentarz* spełniał jeszcze jedno zadanie: opowiadana przez Kwieka banalna miłosna historią miała uruchomić mentalne klisze w umysłach odbiorców i uzmysłowić im jak bardzo są nimi przesiąknięci.

W połowie lat 70. Kwiek zaczął intensywnie poszukiwać teorii opisujących ludzką inteligencję i ludzki sposób poznania świata w sposób odmienny od szkoły marksistowskiej. Taką alternatywą okazała się cybernetyczna teoria charakteru, która stanowiła istotny kontekst dla jego eksperymentów z wykorzystaniem wideo. Kwiek przejął z niej utożsamienie nowych technologii audiowizualnych ze strukturami poznawczymi ludzkiego umysłu. Pisał:

> Mamy narzędzie, które działa podobnie jak nasza wyobraźnia, jak umysł, który przegląda percypowane, zapamiętane lub właśnie wytwarzane obrazy. Odkrywanie kolejnych przybliżeń, zależności, analogii i przeciwieństw pomiędzy działaniem umysłu i działaniem środków mechanicznej rejestracji, odtwarzania i transmisji jest z jednej strony poznawaniem struktury tych środków, a z drugiej strony analogicznych struktur własnego umysłu. Rzeczywistość studia telewizyjnego była kawałkiem mózgu człowieka, który ma takie cechy jak percepcja, struktura poznawcza, pewne możliwości operacji na przedmiocie, na tym, na co patrzy, i pewne możliwości operacji na przedmiocie myślowych penetracji, czyli na samym zapisie. I kiedy dołoży się do tego strukturę żywego intelektu, który wchodzi w ten układ, w taki model rzeczywistości, jaki tworzy telewizja, to tworzy się podwójna możliwość penetracji rzeczywistości – mianowicie człowiek jest jednocześnie w rzeczywistości, która jest modelem, ale jednocześnie ten model jest rzeczywistością dla tego człowieka. [...] Modele [...] dawały możliwość obser-

32 Ibidem.
33 Wywiad z Pawłem Kwiekiem, lipiec 2014 roku.
34 R. W. Kluszczyński, op. cit., s. 33.
35 Zob. R. Waśko, op. cit., s. 129.

wacji tego, co jest poza horyzontem codzienności, co jest na krańcach poznania[36].

Ta teoria stała się punktem wyjścia późniejszych eksperymentów Kwieka, które dotyczyły wpływu mediów na ludzkie ciało i psychikę. W maju 1974 roku w studiu TVP wykonał podczas transmisji na żywo performans *Video A – Sytuacja Studia*, polegający na wydawaniu operatorom i realizatorom poleceń dotyczących kadrowania, wyboru kamery czy zmiany planu. W ten prosty sposób pokazał wielotysięcznej widowni, że każda próba relacjonowania danego wydarzenia wiąże się z selektywnością, fragmentarycznością i zniekształceniem.

W 1977 r. Paweł Kwiek zdecydował się opuścić Warsztat Formy Filmowej, kontynuując jednocześnie swoje badania nad poznawczymi zdolnościami człowieka. Stopniowo porzucał w tym procesie narzędzie, jakim były w okresie WFF nowe media, zwracając się ku doświadczeniom transcendentalnym.

FILMOGRAFIA I PRACE WIDEO:

Forma Otwarta (działanie poza Warsztatem Formy Filmowej, we współpracy z Przemysławem Kwiekiem, Zofią Kulik, Janem S. Wojciechowskim – 7-dniowa akcja dokamerowych ćwiczeń, której rezultatem był film Forma otwarta, pokazywany w ramach Zestawów Filmów Warsztatu, 35 mm, 15-17' (w zależności od wersji), 1971, kolor)
Twarz (35 mm, 6', 1971, cz.-b., współpraca J. Łomnicki)
Film fabularny (35 mm, 4', 1971, cz.-b., film niezachowany)
Lustro (film beztaśmowy, performans filmowy, pierwsze wykonanie miało miejsce w grudniu 1971 r. w Galerii Współczesnej)
Twarz II (16mm, 1', 1971, cz.-b., współpraca J. Łomnicki)
Ćwiczenie na kamerę (35 mm, 7', 1972, cz.-b., film wg pomysłu P. Kwieka z udziałem J. Robakowskiego, A. Mikołajczyka, P. Kwieka, D. Roberts, W. Bruszewskiego, T. Junaka, A. Bogusławskiego)
Komentarz (film mówiony, 1972, we współpracy z W. Bruszewskim)
Chińczyk (35 mm, 7', 1972, kolor)
Kolor (35 mm, 5', 1972, film niezachowany)
1, *2, 3...ćwiczenia operatorskie* (35 mm, 8'10", 1972, kolor)
Komentarz (film beztaśmowy, performans filmowy, pierwsze wykonanie 1972)
Ja i telefon (35 mm, 6'03", 1972, cz.-b.)
Fair play (35 mm?, 1973?, film niezachowany, współpraca P. Kwiek)
Niechcice (35 mm, 5'01", 1973, kolor, film realizowany przez wielu twórców, real. P. Kwiek)
Numerki (35 mm, 7'52", 1973, cz.-b.
Kinolaboratorium (35 mm, 13'20", 1973, kolor, film realizowany przez wielu twórców, real. P. Kwiek)
Osieki (35 mm, 15'29", 1974, kolor)
Fair play (35 mm?, 1974, cz.-b., film niezachowany, współpraca z J. Łomickim)
Video A – Sytuacja Studia (wideo, 3'25",1974, cz.-b.)
Podróż (35 mm, film niezachowany, 1974, cz.-b.)
Video C (wideo, 3'12", 1975, cz.-b.)
Video P (wideo, 2'35",1975, cz.-b.)

36 P. Kwiek, *Model demokratycznej wymiany informacji. Plener pytań,* Miastko 1978, cyt. za Ł. Ronduda, *Sztuka polska lat Sztuka polska lat 70.*, Warszawa, Centrum Sztuki Współczesnej Zamek Ujazdowski, 2009, s. 286–288.

FOTOGRAFIA:
Opis zdjęcia (fotografia cz.-b., 1973)
Kwiekołom i Łomokwiek (praca fotograficzna, która była rezultatem i elementem wspólnej akcji P. Kwieka i J. Łomnickiego w ramach Akcji Warsztat) (fotografia cz.-b., 1973)
Bez tytułu z cyklu *Fotografie napisów* (fotografia cz.-b., 1975)
Akt (fotografia cz.-b., 1973)
Zrobić niemożliwe światło (fotografia cz.-b., 1973)
Mnożenie, dodawanie (cykl fotografii) (fotografie cz.-b., 1972)
z cyklu *Przedłużenie obiektu idealnego w rzeczywistości fizycznej* (fotografie cz.-b., 1975)
z cyklu *Fotografie na wystawę sztuki kontekstualnej* (fotografie cz.-b., 1975)
z cyklu *Wskazywanie* (fotografie cz.-b., 1975)
Bez tytułu (*Dotyki*) (fotografie cz.-b., 1975/6)
Linia A i *Linia B* (fotografie cz.-b., 1975)
Linia 1 i *Linia 2* (fotografie z.-b., 1975)
Rysunki wideo-fotograficzne (fotografie cz.-b., flamaster, papier, 1975)
To, co chcę trzymać w dłoniach (fotografia cz.-b., 1975)
Antropofotometria (fotografia cz.-b., 1975)
Stoję w jedynym miejscu, siedzę w innym miejscu (fotografie cz.-b., 1975)
Fotografia przypadkowa (fotografie cz.-b., 1975)
Krzesło (fotografie cz.-b., flamaster, papier, 1974–1976)
Rysunki pseudo-wideofotograficzne (fotografie cz.-b., flamaster, papier, 1976)
Rysunki światłem (fotografie cz.-b., 1975)
Wychylanie z kadru (fotografie cz.-b., 1976/7)
Wyliczanka (fotografie cz.-b., 1976/7)

Antoni Mikołajczyk

(1939–2000)

Współzałożyciel Warsztatu. Spośród członków grupy wyróżniał go fakt, że nie był absolwentem Szkoły Filmowej w Łodzi. Studiował w Toruniu, gdzie był bardzo aktywnym członkiem Zero-61 i Zero-69, uczestnikiem m.in. klubu filmowego Pętla. To wówczas, w latach 1964–1968 stworzył swoje filmy *Suita, Flirt, Dwa kolty* i *Skrzynia.* Po ukończeniu studiów w Toruniu wraz z kolegami przeprowadził się do Łodzi, gdzie wykładał w latach 1972–1977 w Wyższej Szkole Sztuk Plastycznych. W ramach Warsztatu nie pracował samodzielnie jako filmowiec, współpracował natomiast z Józefem Robakowskim przy filmach *Zapis* i *Z mediomagnetycznego atelier Tytusa Czyżewskiego*.

Posługiwał się przede wszystkim fotografią, choć realizował także instalacje wideo z wykorzystaniem zdjęć[37]. Na przykład *Obraz pozorny* z 1976 roku składał się z budzika i jego fotografii, a także kamer, które transmitowały obraz zegara na dwa ekrany. W innych pracach artysta poddawał obraz wideo różnego rodzaju manipulacjom, wykorzystując lustrzane odbicia, podwójne projekcje bądź kolorowe folie. Prowadziło to do powstawania skomplikowanych zależności pomiędzy transmisją, fotografią a rzeczywistością. Szczególnie wyraźnie widać to w instalacji *Rzeczywistość – obraz rzeczywistości*, składającej się z dwóch monitorów, na których widać było nocny pejzaż miasta. Na jed-

37 Chodzi o prace *Obraz barwny* i *Obraz czarno-biały* z 1975 roku, a także *Obiekt w ruchu*, *Rejestracja pionowa*, *Rejestracja pozioma*, *Obraz pozorny* i *Rzeczywistość – obraz rzeczywistości* z 1976 roku.

nym była to bezpośrednia transmisja – na drugim widok fotografii, przedstawiającej dokładnie tę samą scenę. Mikołajczyk zmuszał w ten sposób odbiorcę do zdefiniowania tego, czym jest prawda, a czym złudzenie. Ta sytuacja, jak wiele innych realizacji Warsztatu, była swoistą makietą, mającą uwrażliwić odbiorcę na praktykowane na co dzień – szczególnie w telewizji – manipulacje medialne.

FOTOGRAFIA:
Zapis fotograficzny (1973)
Anatomia (1974)

INSTALACJE:
Konstrukcja (1973)

INSTALACJE WIDEO:
Obraz pozorny (1976)
Rzeczywistość – obraz rzeczywistości (1976)

Ryszard Lenczewski

(1948)

W Szkole Filmowej studiował w latach 1970–1974. Wcześniej działał w Łódzkim Towarzystwie Fotograficznym. W ramach Warsztatu współpracował jako operator z innymi uczestnikami grupy, między innymi z Ryszardem Waśko przy *Ścianie* (1972). Zrealizował także własny film *Pokój dziecinny* (1974), który był próbą uzyskania maksymalnej obiektywności obrazu poprzez wyeliminowanie udziału operatora. W tytułowym pokoju Lenczewski zaaranżował scenę aktorską z udziałem trzech osób. Rejestrowała ją kamera podwieszona do haka na suficie, która – wisząc na skręconym pasku – dokonywała wielokrotnych obrotów wokół własnej osi.

Po ukończeniu Szkoły Filmowej Lenczewski rozpoczął pracę jako operator. Otrzymał w tej dziedzinie liczne prestiżowe nagrody – był między innymi nominowany wspólnie z Łukaszem Żalem do Oscara za zdjęcia do filmu *Ida* (2013).

Jacek Łomnicki

(1951–2009)

Jacek Łomnicki studiował w Szkole Filmowej od 1970 roku. Był aktywnym uczestnikiem Warsztatu, choć nie zrealizował samodzielnie żadnego filmu. Podejmował natomiast różnego rodzaju działania efemeryczne i performatywne, zazwyczaj we współpracy z Pawłem Kwiekiem, z którym w 1971 roku utworzył dwuosobową grupę twórczą Czyżby. Ich działania były trudne do uchwycenia i nazwania. We wspomnieniach świadków jawią się jako „interwencje wobec interwencji". Artyści odnosili się w nich często do własnych prac, na przykład filmu *Twarz*, w którym Łomnicki zagrał, a którego Kwiek był operatorem i reżyserem. Kwiek pisał, że pierwsza wersja z maja 1971 roku powstawała „na żywo – od ujęcia do ujęcia twarzy ludzkiej (mimika), interpretowanej zabiegami operatorskimi"[38]. Nazwał tę metodę „połączeniem we wspólnej realizacji nie związanych ze sobą intencji obydwu autorów. Film ma zmienną funkcję sterowaną formą, sposobem pokazu (specyficzny sposób pracy ciągłej)[39].

Wspomniany przez Kwieka „sposób pracy ciągłej" przenosił się na kolejne realizacje duetu. Gdy jedyna kopia *Twarzy* zaginęła po pokazie w Nowej Rudzie, artyści zrealizowali *Twarz I*, a stopklatki z pierwszej wersji posłużyły Kwiekowi do realizacji akcji Śmietnik w Zakopanem[40]. Z kolei Łomnicki w 1973 roku w ramach akcji *Warsztat* zrealizował działanie *Twarz X*, rejestrując poklatkowo twarze widzów.

Jacek Łomnicki był synem słynnego aktora Tadeusza Łomnickiego i po studiach sam kilkakrotnie stawał przed kamerą, między innymi w filmie *Człowiek z marmuru* Andrzeja Wajdy. Pracował także jako operator filmowy przy produkcjach dokumentalnych i fabularnych.

38 R. Waśko, op. cit., s. 8.
39 Ibidem.
40 Zob. opis na s. 141.

FILMOGRAFIA:
Twarz (35 mm, 6', 1971, cz.-b., film niezachowany, współpraca P. Kwiek)
Twarz X (w ramach Akcji Warsztat poklatkowa rejestracja twarzy widzów)
Twarz II (16mm, 1', 1971, cz.-b., współpraca P. Kwiek)
Fair play (35 mm?, 1973?, film niezachowany, współpraca P. Kwiek)

AKCJE:
Kwiekołom i Łomokwiek (enviroment, Akcja Warsztat, Muzeum Sztuki w Łodzi, 1973)

Janusz Połom

(1950)

Studentem Szkoły Filmowej został w 1971 roku. Pierwsze próby twórcze podejmował jeszcze jako licealista w Olsztynie, gdzie był członkiem reprezentującego dość wysoki poziom Amatorskiego Klubu Fotograficznego Grunwald[41]. Połom już w tamtym okresie miał kontakt z awangardą artystyczną – za sprawą Wojciecha Wojczulanisa, członka grupy Zero-61, który prowadził zajęcia w klubie oraz swojego starszego brata, Stefana (ur. 1938), poety i pisarza, który współtworzył toruńskie środowisko artystyczne.

W ramach Warsztatu Połom zrealizował dwa filmy: *Bez* (1970) oraz *Alfabet* (1974), który był prezentowany w ramach pokazów WFF. *Alfabet* był rezultatem pogłębionych rozważań artysty nad relacjami dźwięku i obrazu w filmie i w rzeczywistości. Jak pisał Ryszard Kluszczyński:

> Janusz Połom prowadził liczne doświadczenia, w ramach których stawiał w bezpośredniej relacji dźwięki i odpowiadające im obrazy. Tak jak Józef Robakowski, odrywając oko od wizjera kamery uwalniał zarazem obraz (w pewnym bodaj stopniu) od dominacji ludzkiej, a tym samym od wpływu nań kodów kulturowych, tak samo Połom, dokonując bezpośrednich translacji dźwięków na obrazy, nadawał im autonomię i przekraczał (bądź przynajmniej problematyzował) ich tradycyjny, przedstawieniowy charakter. Posługiwał się w tym celu rozmaitymi urządzeniami, na przykład oscylografem, za pomocą którego zrealizował film *Alfabet* (1974). Podejmował też szereg innych działań zmierzających do uzyskania bezpośrednich wizualizacji dźwięków[42].

Podczas akcji *Warsztat* Połom zrealizował jeszcze *Elektroniczne antynomie* – prawdopodobnie pierwszą w Polsce pracę z użyciem komputera (ODRA 1304). Chciał przeanalizować w niej słowo jako nośnik komunikacji, który staje się nieadekwatny w dobie rozwoju „elektronicznych maszyn cyfrowych", dlatego podjął próbę przedstawienia wszystkich znanych form zapisu słów, a następnie zastąpienia jednych drugimi. Język literacki, a konkretnie tekst Samuela Becketta, został w ten sposób przełożony na język obrazowy, co można odczytać jako interesującą antycypację dominacji języka wizualnego w kulturze cyfrowej.

W późniejszych latach Połom zrealizował liczne filmy dokumentalne i animowane, a w latach 1981–1985 był dziekanem Wydziału Operatorskiego i Realizacji Telewizyjnej w Szkole Filmowej.

FILMOGRAFIA:
Alfabet (35 mm, 2'13", 1974, cz.-b.)
Tekst (*Jak jest*) (35 mm, 1976, cz.-b.)

41 Na podstawie relacji Janusza Połoma (rozmowa w maju 2016 roku oraz korespondencja z lipca 2016 roku).

42 R. W. Kluszczyński, op. cit., s. 26. Przykładem takiego działania była praca *Obrazy dźwiękowe* zrealizowana przez Połoma w 1975 roku w Galerii Remont w ramach wydarzenia Dwa dni – manifestacja multimedialna Warsztatu.

FOTOGRAFIA:

Kamuflaż (fotografie czarno-białe, 1972)

Ku wiośnie (fotografie czarno-białe, 1972)

AKCJE, DZIAŁANIA:

Elektroniczne antynomie (działanie w ramach Akcji Warsztat, 1973)

Obrazy dźwiękowe (działanie w Galerii Remont w Warszawie, 1975)

Józef Robakowski

(1939)

Film i kino bardzo wcześnie stały się ważną częścią jego życia. Po wojnie zamieszkał wraz z rodziną w Gdyni, gdzie jego matka podjęła pracę w kiosku mieszczącym się w kinie Warszawa – dzięki temu Robakowski mógł spędzać długie godziny, zapoznając się z przeglądem światowej kinematografii (także tej przeznaczonej dla widzów dorosłych). Robakowski odwiedzał chętnie kabinę projekcyjną, gdzie niekiedy dostawał w prezencie kawałki taśmy filmowej. Początkowo używał ich do zabawy – klisza była łatwopalna, co niewątpliwe stanowiło pewne źródło atrakcji. Szybko jednak przeszedł do bardziej poważnych eksperymentów. Zaczął budować proste aparaty projekcyjne złożone z pudełka, żarówki i soczewki, a także montować ścinki taśmy filmowej i wykonywać własne slajdy z rysunkami.

Swoje pierwsze poważne filmy zrealizował w ramach STKF „Pętla" w Toruniu. Stworzył wówczas – z użyciem ręcznego montażu, niemalże domowymi metodami – kilkanaście eksperymentalnych i dokumentalnych obrazów na taśmie 16 mm. Zachował się tylko jeden: *6000000* z 1962 roku, poruszający tematykę Holokaustu.

Początek studiów w Łodzi (1966) przyniósł Robakowskiemu przerwę w realizacji filmów. Ta paradoksalna sytuacja potwierdza tylko, że Szkoła Filmowa nie dawała wówczas studentom możliwości samodzielnej pracy twórczej, co stało się jednym z powodów zawiązania Warsztatu Formy Filmowej jesienią 1970 roku. W międzyczasie Robakowski zdołał zrealizować tylko dwa filmy: *Collage* z (1969) i *Po człowieku* (1970). Kolejny obraz *Rynek* (1970) powstał już w ramach Warsztatu i uznaje się go za pierwszą pracę w historii grupy.

W kolejnym filmie *Test I* (1971) Robakowski powrócił do praktykowanej w okresie toruńskim pracy z taśmą filmową. Wyciął w niej otwory, które sprawiały, że podczas projekcji światło z projektora raziło widzów, zawracając ich uwagę na materialność taśmy filmowej, rolę światła w kinie, a także zjawisko powidoku i właściwości zmysłu wzroku[43]. Był to jednocześnie tytułowy test na wytrzymałość widowni, której część zawsze opuszczała salę – dlatego też Robakowski zaczął z czasem umieszczać ten film na końcu pokazywanych zestawów[44]. Innym przykładem wczesnego bezkamerowego filmu Robakowskiego jest *Próba II*. Celem tytułowej próby było zbadanie relacji między warstwą audialną i wizualną, poprzez zestawienie klasycznej muzyki organowej z pojawiającą się na ekranie barwą czerwoną, która znikała w chwili, gdy rozbrzmiewał dźwięk.

Ważną i charakterystyczną dla Robakowskiego grupę prac stanowią filmowe performanse. Starał się w nich eksplorować możliwości medium wideo – techniki, która była praktycznie niedostępna w Polsce i pozostałych krajach bloku wschodniego. Sięgał w tym celu po inne metody pozwalające uzyskać podobne rezultaty. Korzystał z wozów transmisyjnych albo posługiwał się kamerami filmowymi w sposób zbliżony do kamer wideo. Pokonywał opór materii w postaci ciężaru tradycyjnego sprzętu i specyfiki klasycznej taśmy, aby antycypować możliwości, które przyniesie ze sobą prostota i wygoda przenośnego sprzętu

43 Ibidem, s. 16.

44 R. Gajewski, op. cit.

czyli możliwość samodzielnej pracy i realizacji efemerycznych działań. Najwcześniejszą realizacją tego typu (i jednym z najbardziej znanych dzieł Robakowskiego) jest film *Idę* (1973), będący zapisem wchodzenia z kamerą na ramieniu po schodach wieży spadochronowej i – w warstwie dźwiękowej – liczenia kolejnych schodów. Rejestracja jest w tu prowadzona w czasie rzeczywistym, bez montażu, co w latach 60. i 70. było charakterystyczne przede wszystkim właśnie dla wideo. W efekcie film pokazuje narastające zmęczenie artysty i jego relację z kamerą – mechanicznym urządzeniem. Robakowski eksplorował ten sam problem w pracy *Po linii...* (1976), w której rejestrował obraz chodząc, biegnąć i skacząc, a także w Ćwiczeniu *na dwie ręce* (1976), polegającym na wymachiwaniu dwoma pracującymi kamerami. Ta ostatnia realizacja pozwalała zaobserwować, jak zauważył Ryszard W. Kluszczyński, że relacja sprzęt–człowiek jest dwukierunkowa[45]. Z jednej strony kamera rejestruje i przenosi na taśmę fizjologiczne stany operatora, z drugiej ujawnia cechy rzeczywistości, które są przed nim ukryte, lecz które na niego wpływają.

Robakowski pracował również z fotografią. Wiele swoich cykli w tym medium kontynuował na przestrzeni lat 50.- 70., a niektóre znacznie dłużej, co nadaje jego twórczości wyraźną ciągłość. Na przykład do cyklu *Rejestracje obiektywne* artysta zalicza zarówno stworzone w okresie toruńskim prace *Marynarka* (1967) czy *Dowód osobisty* (1969), jak i powstałe w okresie łódzkim *Fotografię mechaniczną* (1976) czy *Strefę optyczną* (1975). Ta ostatnia praca łączy się z kolei tematycznie z dwoma realizacjami z 1969 roku: *4 polami ostrości* i *9 polami ostrości*, w których Robakowski podejmował kwestię zmian zachodzących w obszarze przedstawienia fotograficznego w zależności od ustawień ostrości, co otwiera o problem naszego przywiązania do myślenia o fotografii jako medium wiernie oddającego widzialną rzeczywistość.

Na przełomie lat 60. i 70. Robakowski realizował ponadto obiekty fotograficzne. W 1969 roku powstały prace *Kalejdoskop*, *Obrazy do pobrania* i *Koło* (*obraz tautologiczny*). Dwie pierwsze powstały z użyciem „fotografii znalezionych" i wydają się być refleksją nad kulturową rolą zdjęć, powiększających i tak już gęstą ikonosferę współczesności. W *Kalejdoskopie* kostka, której ściany wypełniały fotografie, została powieszona na nitce będącej w ciągłym ruchu. Zdjęcia można było oglądać przez lupę powiększającą. Z kolei *Obrazy do pobrania* były swoistym kolażem – fotografie zostały naklejone na płaszczyznę w taki sposób, że aby je obejrzeć, trzeba było je oderwać. Robakowski użył w tej pracy zdjęć o różnym statusie: pamiątkowych i rodzinnych, anonimowych i amatorskich, dystansując się w ten sposób od kwestii autorstwa i od kategorii „dzieła" jako muzealnego obiektu „do oglądania". *Obrazy do pobrania* zwiastowały charakterystyczny motyw wielu realizacji Warsztatu: poszukiwanie różnych sposobów angażowania odbiorcy w interakcję z dziełem, a nawet w jego współtworzenie.

FILMOGRAFIA I PRACE WIDEO:

Collage (35 mm, 9', 1969, cz.-b.)
Po człowieku (35 mm, 9', 1969/70, cz.-b.)
Rynek (35 mm, 4'20", 1970, cz.-b., współpraca T. Junak, R. Meissner,)
Test I (35 mm, 5', 1971, cz.-b.)
Kompozycja (35 mm, 2', 1971, cz.-b.)
22x (35 mm, 5'24", 1971, cz.-b.)
Próba II (35 mm, 1'58", 1971, kolor)
Prostokąt dynamiczny (35 mm, 2'32", 1971/72, kolor)
Zapis (35 mm, 6', 1972, cz.-b., współpraca A. Mikołajczyk)
Ćwiczenie (35 mm, 6', 1972/73, cz.-b.)
Idę (35 mm, 2'56", 1973, cz.-b.)

45 R. W. Kluszczyński, op. cit., s. 16.

Drzwi-okno-krzesło (35 mm, 30', 1974, cz.-b., współpraca R. Waśko)
Metr (wideo, 2', 1974)
Czynności (wideo, 1975)
Mój film (35 mm, 5', 1974, cz.-b.)
Zbliżanie (wideo, fotografia, 5', 1975)
Funkcje (wideo, fotografia, 5', 1975)
Gimnastyka (wideo, 3', 1975)
Ćwiczenie dramaturgiczne (wideo, 2', 1975)
Przestrzeń zakłócona (35 mm, 8', 1975/76, cz.-b.)
Polecenia (działanie z użyciem wideo, 1975, współpraca A. Paruzel)
Ćwiczenie na dwie ręce (16 mm, 8', 1976, działanie na dwie kamery, cz.-b.)
Po linii... (16 mm, 6', 1976, cz.-b., współpraca L. Czołnowski)
Test I (wideo, 1976)
Test II (wideo, 1976)
Test III (wideo, 1976)
Twarz telewizyjna (działanie z użyciem wideo, 1977)

FOTOGRAFIA, OBIEKTY FOTOGRAFICZNE:
Krzesło (fotografia, krzesło, 1970)
Rolki (obiekt interaktywny, 1970)
Kula (fotografia, kula, lustro, 1971)
Słój (fotografia, szklany słoik, 1971)
Kalejdoskop (fotografia, lustro, 1971)
Dmuchana głowa (fotografia, dmuchana poduszka, 1971)
Grzebień (fotografia, 1971)
Instalacja powietrza (fotografia, 1972)
cykl *Fotografia Astralna* (fotografia cz.-b., 1972, cykl realizowany do 2002 r.)
cykl *Fotografia obiektywna* (fotografia cz.-b., od 1973)
cykl *Moje* (fotografia, wideo, 1974)
Instrukcja (fotografia, 1975)
Sfera optyczna (fotografia, 1975)
Trzy pozy (akcja fotograficzna z udziałem widzów, 1975)
cykl *Relacje: 1 metr, 3 kąty* (fotografia, 1975)
cykl *Kąty energetyczne* (różne techniki, cykl realizowany od 1975 r.)
cykl *Fotografia mechaniczna* (fotografia cz.-b., 1976)

OBIEKTY:
Studium cienia, 1971

INSTALACJE:
Równoważnia dźwiękowa, 1972
Samochodzik, 1972
Instalacja powietrzna, 1972

Andrzej Różycki

(1942)

Andrzej Różycki, pytany o to, kiedy zaczął interesować się fotografią, przywołuje wspomnienie z dzieciństwa. Artysta pochodzi z inteligenckiej polskiej rodziny z miasta Baranowicze (obecnie Białoruś), gdzie jego ojciec amatorsko zajmował się fotografią. Kiedy po wojnie Różyccy musieli opuścić rodzinne strony, zostawili tam niemal cały dobytek, ale zabrali trochę fotografii, które Różycki, jako mały chłopiec, bardzo często oglądał. Fascynowało go jak wiele i jednocześnie niewiele znaczą, gdy nie towarzyszy im opis lub opowieść. Wiele lat później Różycki użył tych samych zdjęć we własnych pracach. Oglądane z pespektywy czasu i rozpatrywane jako całościowy zbiór, stały się dowodami w jego osobistym dochodzeniu, prowadzonym cierpliwie w celu poznania reguł rządzących fotografią. To śledztwo, cechujące się uważnością i wsłuchaniem się w medium, rozpoczęło się na dobre w latach 1961–1966, kiedy to Różycki studiował konserwację zabytków i muzealnictwo na Wydziale Sztuk Pięknych Uniwersytetu Mikołaja Kopernika w Toruniu, a dodatkowego impetu nabrało w 1969 roku, kiedy rozpoczął studia na Wydziale Reżyserii w Szkole Filmowej w Łodzi i – rok później – został współzałożycielem Warsztatu Formy Filmowej.

Różycki – co wyróżnia go na tle innych twórców z kręgu WFF – niemal całkowicie poświęcił się fotografii. W ramach Warsztatu stworzył kilkaset zdjęć, składających się w większości na kilka rozbudowanych i otwartych cykli: *Reguły gry*, *Fotografia analityczna*, *Fotografia pozorna* i *Fotografia warunkowa*. Były to zazwyczaj wieloelementowe, kolażowe kompozycje, wymagające pracochłonnej obróbki negatywów w ciemni i równie intensywnej pracy na pozytywach. Trzy najważniejsze i najbardziej reprezentatywne dla jego dorobku realizacje to *Identyfikacja pozorna* (1973), *Projekt uruchomienia obrazu fotograficznego – Ikar* (1975) i *Żywa projekcja* (1975).

Różycki często powraca do faktu, że wolał pracować z aparatem fotograficznym niż z kamerą, podkreślając rangę fotografii w całokształcie działalności grupy. Jednocześnie ma na tym tle wyczuwalny kompleks, który może być wynikiem częściowego wykluczenia ze wspólnoty. Brak filmów siłą rzeczy nie pozwalał mu na uczestnictwo w pokazach zestawów Warsztatu, co z kolei wiązało się z mniejszą liczbą wspólnych wyjazdów. *Żywa projekcja* może być postrzegana jako autoironiczna próba zdystansowania się do tej sytuacji. Różycki umieścił w filmowym projektorze krótki, kilkuklatkowy fragment taśmy filmowej, który był poruszany przez podmuchy ciepłego powietrza, wydobywające się momentami z włączonego projektora filmowego – tym samym uruchomił statyczny obraz, tworząc swego rodzaju paradoksalny film.

Andrzej Różycki pracował także w innych mediach, ale do większości swoich realizacji włączał zdjęcia. Na przykład w instalacji *Video-Duo* z 1975 roku transmitował obraz portretu fotograficznego Ryszarda Waśki na jeden z dwóch monitorów. Drugi również prezentował twarz Waśki, z tym, że obraz był przekazywany bezpośrednio przez rejestrującą go kamerę. Widzowi nie znali pochodzenia obu obrazów – widzieli jedynie ostateczny, dwuznaczny efekt na dwóch ekranach.

Fotografie Różyckiego prowadzą nas ku myśli Viléma Flussera (1920–1991), który wynalezienie obrazu technicznego (fotografii) nazwał jednym z dwóch, obok wynalezienia pisma, punktów zwrotnych w historii ludzkości, a zrozumienie tego medium uznał za klucz do zrozumienia współczesnego świata. Flusser wychodzi z założenia, że obrazy są mediacjami pomiędzy światem a człowiekiem – z tym, że ich pośrednictwo stało się odgrodzeniem. Obrazy powinny być mapami, a stają się ekranami: zamiast świat przedstawiać – stają się światem samym w sobie. Człowiek zapomina, że to on stworzył obrazy, aby za ich pomocą orientować się w świecie. Nie potrafi ich już odcyfrować. Postrzega je nie jako zjawisko, które należy odczytać i zrozumieć, ale jak okna – ufa im bezkrytycznie i zaczyna w związku z tym „egzystować wtórnie", żyć jako funkcja stworzonych przez siebie obrazów. Flusser pisze:

> Wszędzie wokół zauważamy, jak wszelkiego rodzaju aparaty zmierzają ku temu, aby z tępym automatyzmem zaprogramować nam życie. [...] Jak „robotyzują się" nasze myśli i działania; jak „życie" oznacza karmienie aparatów i bycia przez nie karmionym[46].

W jaki sposób możemy uwolnić się od coraz większej automatyzacji i odzyskać wolność? Flusser odpowiada, że można próbować przechytrzyć aparat, przemycić do jego programu nieprzewidziane w nim ludzkie zamiary, zmusić go do wytwarzania nieprzewidzianego, nieprawdopodobnego, nasyconego informacją obrazu lub

46 V. Flusser, *Ku filozofii fotografii*, Warszawa: Aletheia, 2015, s. 69.

wreszcie pogardzać nim i jego wytworami. Innymi słowy, wolność to gra przeciw aparatowi, którą prowadzi fotograf.

Różycki jest nikim innym, jak właśnie taką figurą fotografa. Artysta nie znał wprawdzie tekstów Flussera, ale podejmował jego wyzwanie, stosując pierwsze trzy z wymienionych przez niego metod, a także antycypując jego myśl w swoich tekstach teoretycznych:

> Rozpoznanie rzeczywistości – chcemy tego czy nie chcemy – przebiega w coraz silniejszym oderwaniu od odbioru bezpośredniego. Jest to wymóg czasu i naszej zgody na kierunek cywilizacyjnego postępu. Otaczamy się coraz bardziej precyzyjnym i skomplikowanym oprzyrządowaniem i instrumentami sprzężonymi bezpośrednio z coraz bardziej szczegółowo nakreślonymi celami poznawczymi. Niejednokrotnie tymi samymi narzędziami przychodzi posługiwać się artystom i naukowcom. Z kolei narzędzia mające badać rzeczywistość [...] same zaczynają ją tworzyć. Twórcy powinni nieustannie pamiętać, że narzędzia, którymi przyszło się im posługiwać są „darami" technicznego talentu ludzkości. Artystom pozostaje twórczy sposób i metoda użytkowania tych narzędzi. [...] Poznawanie techniki i walka z nią staje się źródłem nowych wartości. Jedynie słuszną racją artystyczną może być postawa nieustannej humanistycznej rewaloryzacji środków technicznych, którymi posługuje się twórca komunikujący swe idee. Każda próba i bariera przekroczona w humanistycznym rozpoznaniu kondycji i technicznych środków mechanicznego zapisu (co jest równoznaczne z głębszym poznaniem rzeczywistości), to zwycięstwo sztuki[47].

Różycki objawia się nam w tym tekście jako fotograf eksperymentalny, który – zgodnie z definicją Flussera – rozumie, że obraz, aparat, program i informacja to podstawowe problemy sztuki. Fotografowie nieposiadający tej świadomości twierdzą – jak pisał badacz – że tworzą tradycyjne obrazy nietradycyjnymi metodami, że wspomagają badania naukowe albo że działają społecznie bądź angażują się politycznie. Nie mają przy tym świadomości czym jest aparat i tym samym nie mają pojęcia o rewolucji, która za jego sprawą się dokonała. Różycki natomiast sięga po fotografię świadomie, deklarując na kilka lat przed pierwszym wydaniem *Ku filozofii fotografii* Flussera:

> Staram się uczynić kamerę narzędziem bezbronnym i w pełni posłusznym mym intelektualnym programom i ideom[48].

FILM:

Kowalski (35 mm, 8', 1972, cz.-b.)
Jak? Jakby lepiej (35 mm, 10', 1972, cz.-b.)

FOTOGRAFIA:

Fotografia warunkowa, od 1972, cykl czarno-białych fotografii (niektóre barwione)
Projekt uruchomienia obrazu fotograficznego – Ikar, 1975, fotografia czarno-biała
Fotografia analityczna, od 1975, cykl czarno-białych fotografii
Reguły gry, od 1976, cykl czarno-białych fotografii

47 A. Różycki, *Analityczne rozpoznanie fotografii*, kat. wyst. A. Różyckiego, Mała Galeria PSP ZPAF, Warszawa marzec 1979, tekst publikowany w R. Kluszczyński, op. cit., s. 81–83; katalog dostępny także na stronie internetowej Fundacji Arton, http://repozytorium.fundacjaarton.pl/index.php?action=view/object&objid=3150&colid=51&cat-id=15&lang=pl [dostęp 02-11-2016].

48 Ibidem.

AKCJE PERFORMATYWNE:
Identyfikacja pozorna, 1973
Żywa projekcja, 1975

WIDEO:
Seans telewizyjny, 1973
Video-Duo, 1975

Zbigniew Rybczyński

(1949)

Zbigniew Rybczyński studiował w Szkole Filmowej w latach 1969–1973. Był współzałożycielem Warsztatu Formy Filmowej, w ramach którego opracował i rozwijał przez lata swoją własną technikę. Wykorzystał ją w swojej pierwszej etiudzie *Kwadrat* (1972), o której pisał tak:

> Praca nad nią zajęła mi całe wakacje po szesnaście godzin dziennie. Przy użyciu kamery analizowałem pętlę trzydziestu sześciu kwadratowych czarnobiałych zdjęć przedstawiających człowieka poruszającego się wkoło. Jaką logiką kierowałem się przy analizie? Zdecydowałem się nagrać zapętlenie i powtórzyć trzydzieści sześć razy. Podczas każdego powtórzenia dzieliłem kwadratowy kadr tak, że przy każdym obrocie zwiększała się liczba mniejszych partii kadru. W tych częściach kadru, gdzie na zdjęciach pojawiała się figura, podkładałem białą kwadratową kartkę papieru, a tam, gdzie jej nie było – czarną. Musiałem manipulować białymi i czarnymi kwadratami przynajmniej ze sto tysięcy razy. Na soczewkę nakładałem kolorowy filtr i obracałem go. Najważniejsze, że nieświadomy technik komputerowej kreacji obrazu w Polsce lat 70., stworzyłem własną „cyfrową" produkcję filmową. Co dziwne, powrót do *Kwadratu* z pełną świadomością i zrozumieniem zabrał mi 26 lat pracy, w tym całą twórczość kolejnych 25 wakacji[49].

Etiuda *Take Five* (1972) – drugi zrealizowany w ramach Warsztatu film Rybczyńskiego – przedstawia z kolei tancerzy, którzy w miarę upływu czasu budują między sobą relację. Wszystko odbywa się bez słów, głównie poprzez dźwięk i barwę. Twórca przeprowadził w ten sposób subtelną analizę środków filmowych, takich jak przestrzeń, gra aktorska i fabuła, redukując je wszystkie do minimum. Na podobnym połączeniu prostej opowieści i pociągającej estetycznej iluzji Rybczyński będzie opierał swoje kolejne realizacje, włącznie z *Tangiem,* nagrodzonym w 1982 roku Oscarem za najlepszy animowany film krótkometrażowy.

Ryszard Waśko

(1947)

W drugiej połowie lat 60. uczeń nyskiego liceum budowlanego Ryszard Waśko, marzący wówczas o studiach architektonicznych, zapisał się do nowoutworzonego Klubu Form Filmowych i Fotograficznych[50]. Było to miejsce atrakcyjne – głównie ze względu na możliwość wypożyczenia sprzętu fotograficznego i filmowego stosunkowo dobrej jakości. Waśko nie miał żadnego pojęcia o obsłudze kamery, ale dwóch pracowników klubu błyskawicznie przeszkoliło go w tym zakresie i poleciło sfilmować na taśmie 16 mm odbywającą się następnego dnia manifestację z okazji Święta Pracy. Waśko, przystępując do zadania, miał tylko ogólny zarys koncepcji – chciał sfilmować pochód „inaczej, niż robiono to zazwyczaj". Wdrapywał się na drzewa i dachy domów, a nawet wchodził pod zaparkowane na trasie przemarszu ciężarówki.

---

49 *1,2,3 Awangarda. Film/Sztuka pomiędzy eksperymentem a archiwum*, red. Ł. Ronduda, F. Zeyfang, Warszawa: Centrum Sztuki Współczesnej Zamek Ujazdowski, 2007.

50 M. Kuźmicz, wywiad z Ryszardem Waśko, sierpień 2016.

Po wywołaniu taśmy animatorzy klubowi poradzili mu, żeby zdawał do Szkoły Filmowej.

Waśko rozpoczął studia w Łodzi w 1970 roku. W semestrze letnim dołączył do Warsztatu Formy Filmowej. Jak sam podkreśla, na początku działalności grupy zajmowała go przede wszystkim wzajemna zależność czasu i przestrzeni. W związku z tym większość jego prac z okresu WFF to rozważania dotyczące możliwości i ograniczeń w przedstawianiu przestrzeni w filmie. Inną charakterystyczną cechą jego realizacji są częste odwołania do fotografii. Na przykład w *Rejestracji* (1972) oraz *Kłódce* (1972) użył kamery do zbudowania statycznych kadrów przypominających zdjęcia. W tym drugim filmie pokazał dom oraz – po obróceniu kamery – bramę prowadzącą z ulicy na podwórko, po czym stopniowo się od nich oddalał. Wprowadzając dodatkowo zakłócenia w warstwie montażowej (często wymagające bardzo pracochłonnego montażu poklatkowego), Waśko nie tylko konfrontował widzów z ich przyzwyczajeniami, ale także obnażał iluzoryczność obrazu przestrzeni w filmie. Dostrzegł, jaką rolę odgrywa w nim złudzenie i wykorzystywał tę wiedzę do kreowania nowych sytuacji przestrzennych, prowadzących do pytania o to, czym jest przestrzeń i gdzie leżą jej granice.

Waśko posłużył się podobnym zabiegiem w filmie Ściana (1972), w którym kamera stoi nieruchomo naprzeciwko tytułowej ściany budynku fabrycznego. Pozornie realny obraz czasoprzestrzeni zostaje zaburzony pojawieniem się ludzi, których ruch został zmontowany z użyciem procedur losowych. Ich ruchy są fragmentaryczne i pojawiają się bez skutku i przyczyny. Wprowadzając zakłócenia czasu akcji, Waśko demaskuje złudzenie przestrzeni filmowej, którym karmimy się jako widzowie.

W podobnym celu w filmie *Prosto – krzywa* (1973) Waśko nałożył czarne figury geometryczne na widoki miasta. Ten prosty zabieg sprawia, że przestrzeń filmowa, którą postrzegaliśmy jako trójwymiarową, odsłania nagle swoją realną dwuwymiarowość. Waśce udało się w ten sposób ujawnić działanie mechanizmu, zgodnie z którym nasza percepcja dokonuje automatycznej nadinterpretacji płaskich obrazów przesuwających się przed naszymi oczami.

Z kolei filmy *Okno* (1972), a także *Od A do B, od B do A* (1973) stanowią dekonstrukcję stereotypowego myślenia o przestrzeni kadru filmowego. Ten pierwszy został zbudowany z jednego długiego ujęcia ulicy widzianej z okna. W ten sposób – jak zauważył Łukasz Ronduda – artysta odniósł się ironicznie do myślenia o filmie jako „oknie na świat", czyniąc ze statycznej ramy okiennej tautologię filmowego kadru[51]. Warto jeszcze dodać, że w filmie słychać pochodzące zza kadru dźwięki tła, które każą nam domyślać się jakiejś niewidocznej akcji. W ten sposób Waśko poszerzył przestrzeń filmu, aktywując nie tylko uwagę i zmysły, ale także wyobraźnię i kreatywność widza. Podobnym zabiegiem posłużył się w drugim z wymienionych filmów, w którym wyszedł z kadru i – używając magnetofonu – „zabrał" ze sobą dźwięk, relacjonując w ten sposób akcję toczącą się poza polem widzenia kamery.

Te pogłębione studia nad zagadnieniem przestrzeni, które rezonują z rozważaniami Katarzyny Kobro, Waśko uporządkował w lutym 1974 roku w tekście *Teoria przestrzeni w obrazie filmowym i fotograficznym*. Swojego rodzaju podsumowaniem był też film *Zaprzeczenie* (1973), w którym słowo „nie" zostało zwielokrotnione w warstwie wizualnej, tekstowej i dźwiękowej. Można go oczywiście odczytywać jako kolejny analityczny eksperyment WFF, ale rygoryzm formalny połączony z bezpośredniością komunikatu nadaje tej pracy nieco absurdalny wydźwięk, jak gdyby Waśko dystansował się do swoich wcześniejszych realizacji i do obowiązującego w kręgach polskiej awangardy paranaukowego języka.

51 Ł. Ronduda, *Sztuka polska lat 70.*, s. 289.

Równolegle do pracy z filmem Ryszard Waśko zajmował się fotografią. Jego najwcześniejsze prace w tym medium to czteroczęściowe, czarnobiałe kolaże fotograficzne z cyklu *Portrety pocięte* (1971). Waśko składał je z fragmentów zdjęć przedstawiających męskie twarze. Usta, nosy czy uszy łączył w sposób uniemożliwiający identyfikację sfotografowanych osób. Artysta wspomina, że prace, mimo oszczędnej formy, były krytykowane za swój „metafizyczny charakter”[52]. Z perspektywy czasu możemy je odczytać jako psychologiczny portret współczesnego człowieka, którego percepcja ulega rozbiciu w wyniku oddziaływania zwiększającej się ilości bodźców. Możemy też przypuszczać, że Waśko zbudował je – podobnie jak inne swoje wczesne, analityczne prace – na własnej podmiotowości. Obiektem jego zainteresowania była bowiem nie tyle analiza czynników i zjawisk fizycznych, co jego własna relacja ze światem, w całej jego złożoności. Waśko posługiwał się wprawdzie nieodzownymi w Warsztatowej działalności „obiektywnymi” narzędziami służącymi do analizy zjawisk takich jak czas, ruch czy przestrzeń, ale na różne sposoby podkreślał swoją podmiotową perspektywę. W odróżnieniu od Józefa Robakowskiego, który czynił z kamery lub aparatu przedłużenie swojego ciała, Waśko używał tych narzędzi do ukazania swojego sposobu odbierania rzeczywistości. Można to zauważyć na przykładz e pracy *Od 0 do 180* (1971), składającej się z kilkunastu odbitek połączonych w szereg odwzorowujący ruch głowy człowieka patrzącego „od ziemi ku niebu”[53]. Nie powinniśmy zakładać, że mamy tu do czynienia z anonimowym gestem – Waśko wykonał go w danym miejscu i czasie, a my możemy obserwować jego ślady i utożsamiać się z podmiotem tej czynności. Zbliżonym (i być możne najbardziej znanym) dokonaniem Waśki na polu fotografii jest cykl *Fotografia czterowymiarowa*. Każda z należących do niego prac składa się z kilku odbitek. Pierwsza z nich zawsze jest statycznym ujęciem, a na kolejnych widzimy zakłócenie. Waśko wprowadza w ten sposób ruch do nieruchomego obrazu. Nie tylko obserwuje go i rejestruje, jest też jego źródłem i przyczyną. W ten sposób artyście udało mu się uchwycić bycie i widzenie jednocześnie.

Waśko kontynuował te rozważania i eksperymenty z wykorzystaniem wideo – nowego medium, które dodatkowo komplikowało problematykę relacji czasu i przestrzeni. W 1975 roku zrealizował *Róg* – jedną ze swoich najważniejszych i najbardziej charakterystycznych prac wykonanych w tej technice. Temat medialnej reprezentacji przestrzeni doprowadził w niej do skrajnie syntetycznej formy, zestawiając realny róg pomieszczenia z jego transmitowanym obrazem. Podobny charakter miała praca *Pomiar* (1976). Waśko skierował w niej dwie kamery na dwa różnej wielkości kwadraty. Ich widok był transmitowany na monitory, na których – ponieważ kamery były ustawione w różnej odległości od ściany – miały już taki sam rozmiar.

Wideo skierowało Waśkę w stronę performansu. Przenośna kamera stała się swoistym przedłużeniem jego ciała. Na przykład w pracy *Zmęczenie mojej nogi* (1976) transmitował widok narysowanego na ścianie kwadratu, trzymając kamerę w ręku i stojąc na jednej nodze. Z czasem opanowywało go zmęczenie, kamera opadała coraz niżej, a obraz na monitorze ulegał zmianie. W ten sposób ponownie wprowadzał swoją podmiotowość do pozornie czysto analitycznych prac, naruszając ich neutralną strukturę poprzez sam fakt *bycia*.

Film *30 sytuacji dźwiękowych* (1975) może być odczytywany jako podsumowanie tych dociekań. Waśko wytwarzał w nim dźwięk, który rozchodził się w różnych przestrzeniach, co interpretuje się zazwyczaj jako analizę zależności

52 Wywiad z Ryszardem Waśko, wrzesień 2010.
53 R. W. Kluszczyński, op. cit., s. 35.

między dźwiękiem i przestrzenią w filmie. Ja jednak skłaniam się ku odczytaniu tego działania jako manifestacji obecności – tu i teraz. Waśko, klaskając niewielkimi deseczkami przymocowanymi do dłoni, świadomie lub nieświadomie zbliżył się do praktyki medytacji *w zendo*, polegającej na uderzaniu kijem o podłogę. W kolejnych ujęciach zmienia się otoczenie artysty (raz jest to pusty korytarz, innym razem zatłoczona ulica), zmienia się też brzmienie uderzenia, ale sam podmiot pozostaje niezmienny. To, co dzieje się wokół niego, nie wpływa na jego jestestwo, choć też nie jest przez niego ignorowane.

Warto w tym kontekście wspomnieć o jeszcze jednej pracy z tego samego mniej więcej okresu. Waśko, podczas pobytu Warsztatu w Antwerpii, wykonał instalację wideo *Przestrzeń poza* (1976), która – podobnie jak *30 sytuacji* dźwiękowych – był próbą uchwycenia obecności podmiotu-performera. Tym razem nie widzimy go, lecz słyszymy, a następnie – podążamy za jego spojrzeniem. Pozostający poza kadrem artysta obrysowuje flamastrem przestrzeń galerii, określając przestrzeń, w której funkcjonuje i zaznaczając w powściągliwy sposób swoją obecność. Następnie powtarza drogę flamastra za pomocą kamery. Waśko porównuje pracę nad tą instalacją do medytacji i dodaje, że doprowadziła go do stanu „tu i teraz"[54], który – z perspektywy czasu – stał się syntezą zagadnień, które zajmowały go przez cały czas działalności w Warsztacie.

FILMOGRAFIA:

Okno (35 mm, 9', 1972, cz.-b.)
Doniczka (35 mm, 5', 1972)
Zaprzeczenie (35 mm, 6', 1972, cz.-b.)
Rejestracja (35 mm, 3'5", 1972, cz.-b.)
Okno (35 mm, 8'28", 1972, cz.-b.)
Kłódka (35 mm, 7', 1972, cz.-b.)
Ściana (35 mm, 4'06", 1972, cz.-b.)
Chodnik (35 mm, 3', 1972, cz.-b.)
Pokój (35 mm, 3'5", 1973, kolor, współpraca L. Czołnowski)
Podróż Pana Antczaka do kiosku przy ulicy Głównej (35 mm, 4'32", 1973, kolor)
Ściana II (35 mm, 13', 1973, cz.-b., studio SE-MA-FOR)
Układ I-IV (35 mm, 2'20", 1973, kolor)
Teoria przestrzeni w obrazie filmowym (35 mm, 5', 1974, cz.-b.)
Chód (35 mm, 3', 1974, cz.-b.)
Prosto-krzywa (35 mm, 7'13", 1974, cz.-b.)
Rejestracja II (35 mm, 2', 1974, cz.-b.)
Inwentaryzacja przestrzeni za pomocą liczb od 1 do 8 (16 mm, film niezachowany?, 1976?, cz.-b.)

FOTOGAFIA:

Od 0 do 180 stopni (fotografia cz.-b., 1971)
Od 0 do 90 stopni (fotografia cz.-b., 1971)
cykl *Zdarzenie* (lub *Wypadek*) (fotografia cz.-b., 1971)
cykl *Portret pocięty* (fotografia cz.-b., 1971)
cykl *Autoportret w czasie* (fotografia cz.-b., 1972)
cykl *Negatyw/Pozytyw* (fotografia cz.-b., 1972)
cykl *Negatyw – pozytyw* (fotografia, cz.-b., 1972)
cykl *Fotografia czterowymiarowa* (fotografia cz.-b., od 1972)
Hommage dla Koła i Kwadratu (fotografia cz.-b., tempera, 1973)
Prosto-Krzywa (fotografia cz.-b., tempera, 1973)
Wstawanie (fotografia cz.-b., 1974)

54 Korespondencja z Ryszardem Waśko, sierpień 2016.

Autoportret z żółtą, czerwoną i niebieską liną (fotografia cz.-b., kreda, 1975)
cykl *Powiększanie – pomniejszanie* (fotografia cz.-b., 1976)
Inwentaryzacja przestrzeni za pomocą liczb od 1 do 8 (fotografia cz.-b., 1976)
Fotografia hipotetyczna (fotografia cz.-b., ołówek, papier, 1977)

INSTALACJE WIDEO:
Róg domu, 1975
Róg, 1976
Zmęczenie mojej nogi, 1976
Poza przestrzenią, 1976
Pomiar, 1976/77

Zespół T

W drugiej połowie lat 70. studia operatorskie w Szkole Filmowej rozpoczęła grupa twórców, która – początkowo identyfikując się z Warsztatem Formy Filmowej – z czasem wypracowała osobny model działalności pod szyldem Zespół T. W skład tego efemerycznego kolektywu weszli: Janusz Kołodrubiec (1953), Tomasz Konart (1955), Andrzej Paruzel (1951), Małgorzata Paruzel (1953) – wówczas studentka Wydziału Aktorskiego, Janusz Szczerek i Piotr Weychert (1959). Media służyły im – podobnie jak Warsztatowcom – przede wszystkim do analizy zjawisk fizycznych i psychofizycznych, a także do badania zmieniających się uwarunkowań ludzkiej percepcji. Zajmowali się głównie wideo (Kołodrubiec, Paruzel, Szczerek) oraz fotografią (Konart, Weychert), w mniejszym stopniu filmem, choć tworzyli również prace na taśmie 35 mm – by wymienić chociażby *Film i pamięć* (1978) Konarta. Obraz ten składa się z trzech części liczących po dwa ujęcia, z których drugie za każdym razem jest próbą powtórzenia pierwszego w oparciu o pamięć realizatora. Autor oddala się, starając się nie zapomnieć swojej oryginalnej wizji, a chwilę później powraca z kamerą w to samo miejsce. Konart podejmuje w ten sposób refleksję nad relacją człowieka i kamery – umysłu i urządzenia, które rejestrują tę samą rzeczywistość. Artysta w interesujący sposób nawiązuje tu do słynnego paradoksu Zenona z Elei – zauważając, że czas psychologiczny, jakkolwiek w naszym odbiorze ma charakter ciągły, w filmie przyjmuje postać zjawisk punktowych.

Do najważniejszych prac grupy zaliczają się z pewnością *Sytuacje video-fotograficzne* (1976) Andrzeja Paruzela. Artysta zbudował przestrzeń objętą polem widzenia kamer i ograniczoną monitorami. Wykonując proste gesty i jednocześnie obserwując swój obraz na monitorach, Paruzel demaskował potencjał instalacji do budowania wizualnej iluzji. Jak pisał:

> Osoba wchodząca w video instalację ma szansę w procesie poznawania jej struktury równocześnie ujawnić funkcjonowanie własnych struktur poznawczych, dzięki możliwościom manipulacji i w obrębie oddziaływań przetwarzanych przez ten system i w nim samym[55].

Z kolei *Ostatnia fotografia* (1979) Weycherta jest refleksją nad przyszłością fotografii w obliczu nadprodukcji obrazów w kulturze współczesnej, ale także dużego nagromadzenia podejmujących tę kwestię prac, utrzymanych w analitycznej, postkonceptualnej konwencji. Praca ma formę tryptyku, którego dwie części to białe płaszczyzny, a trzecie zdjęcie to obraz aparatu fotograficznego skierowanego na białą kartkę.

Inny członek Zespołu T, Janusz Szczerek, nazywał swoje realizacje filmowe i wideo eksperymentami usytuowanymi na przecięciu sztuki i nauki. Poddawał analizie procesy po-

55 A. Paruzel, *Video instalacje 1976-78*, kat. wyst., Dom Środowisk Twórczych, Łódź 1978, cyt. za M. Jankowska, *Wideo, wideo instalacja, wideo performance w Polsce w latach 1973-1994. Historia, artyści, dzieła*, Warszawa: Neriton, 2004, s. 134.

znawcze związane z odbiorem filmu, zakładając, że kierują się one zasadą rozwiązywania problemów percepcyjnych. Takie podejście sprawiło, że niemal wszystkie filmy Szczerka z tego okresu były swoistymi zagadkami. Na przykład w *Analizie* (1979) publiczność miała odgadnąć zawartość fotografii, której fragmenty artysta – błądząc po zdjęciu kamerą – pokazywał w dużym zbliżeniu na monitorze. Odpowiedzi widzów były nagrywane, aby potem stać się ścieżką dźwiękową filmu. Poprawna odpowiedź kończyła zarówno działanie, jak i film.

*

Jednym z powodów powołania Zespołu T była, podobnie jak w przypadku Warsztatu, miałkość programu edukacyjnego Szkoły Filmowej, a także sytuacja polskiego świata sztuki – pozornie autonomicznego wobec rzeczywistości PRL, a w istocie od niej odizolowanego. Tomasz Konart wspomina, że powstanie grupy było związane z uświadomieniem sobie faktu „bycia dla siebie wzajemnie". Za tą deklaracją stała intencja nie tyle wycofania się ze świata, co było symptomatyczne dla części środowisk awangardowych, lecz zmiany swojej relacji z rzeczywistością. Chodziło o przekroczenie granicy między sztuką a codziennością oraz wyjście z ustalonego schematu funkcjonowania środowisk artystycznych w Polsce, polegającego na organizowaniu wystaw rozpoczynanych wernisażami, wydawaniu katalogów lub ulotek, gromadzeniu publiczności i tak dalej. Członkowie grupy rezygnowali z poszukiwania widowni na rzecz nieformalnych spotkań i organicznie rodzących się interakcji – ich działania polegały na spotkaniach i dyskusjach we własnym gronie, wspólnym poszukiwaniu rozwiązań twórczych, a nawet eksperymentach z telepatią.

Zespół T, podobnie jak Warsztat, wychodził poza obszar oficjalnej kinematografii, krytykował oficjalne instytucje i działał w nieoczywistych miejscach, przez co intencjonalnie opuścił swoje miejsce w strukturze świata sztuki PRL. Jednak w porównaniu do WFF, którego zamiarem była zmiana rzeczywistości, strategia Zespołu T wydaje się bardziej nihilistyczna, jakby wynikała z głębszego doświadczenia pustki znaczeniowej zawartej we wszelkich regulacjach i unormowaniach prawnych, zwyczajowych i kulturowych. Można to interpretować jako antycypację lat 80. w Polsce – dekady naznaczonej stanem wojennym, który definitywnie zakończył działanie grupy. Piotr Weychert wspomina, że w 1981 roku grupa przygotowała pocztówki z napisem „Zespół T nie istnieje", które miały być wysłane pocztą do wybranych osób i instytucji. Wysłane nie zostały, ponieważ wraz z wprowadzeniem stanu wojennego przestała działać poczta.

Workshop of the Film Form / Warsztat Formy Filmowej

Publishers / Wydawcy: Fundacja Arton, Sternberg Press
Editors / Redakcja: Marika Kuźmicz, Łukasz Ronduda
Texts / Teksty: George Clark, Maeve Connolly, Marika Kuźmicz, Łukasz Ronduda, Mike Sperlinger, Jan Verwoert
Graphic design / Projekt graficzny: Artur Frankowski, Magdalena Frankowska | Fontarte (fontarte.com)
Translation / Tłumaczenia: Łukasz Mojsak, Paweł Marcinkiewicz, Marika Kuźmicz, Kaja Pawełek, Marcin Wawrzyńczak
Copyediting / Redakcja językowa: Ewa Kociszewska, Marika Kuźmicz, Jakub Zgierski
Korekta / Proofreading: Ewa Kociszewska
Druk / Print: Drukarnia Klimiuk

ISBN 978-3-95679-311-0
ISBN 978-83-938029-3-7 (PL)

Co-financed by the Ministry of Culture and National Heritage / Dofinansowano ze środków Ministra Kultury i Dziedzictwa Narodowego
This book has been supported by / Książka współfinansowana przez: Kontakt. The Art Collection of Erste Group and ERSTE Foundation

© 2017 Artists and authors, Arton Foundation, Sternberg Press
© 2017 Artyści i autorzy, Fundacja Arton, Sternberg Press

Partner merytoryczny / Merits-related Partner:

Arton Foundation / Fundacja Arton
Miedziana 11 St. / ul. Miedziana 11
Warsaw 00-835 / Warszawa 00-835
www.fundacjaarton.pl

Sternberg Press
Caroline Schneider
Karl-Marx-Allee 78
D-10243 Berlin
www.sternberg-press.com